THE CONFLICT OF GENERATIONS

THE CONFLICT OF GENERATIONS

THE CHARACTER AND SIGNIFICANCE OF STUDENT MOVEMENTS

LEWIS S. FEUER

BASIC BOOKS, INC., PUBLISHERS

NEW YORK / LONDON

Third Printing

Library of Congress Catalog Card Number: 68-54130
Manufactured in the United States of America
Designed by Vincent Torre

And Job again took up his parable, and said . . .

But now they that are younger than I have me in derision, whose fathers I would have disdained to set with the dogs of my flock. . . .

Upon my right hand rise the youth; they push away my feet, and they raise up against me the ways of their destruction. . . .

And Elihu the son of Barachel the Buzite answered and said, I am young and ye are very old; wherefore I was afraid, and durst not declare you mine opinion. . . .

But there is a spirit in man: and the inspiration of the Almighty giveth them understanding.

Great men are not always wise: neither do the aged understand judgment.

Job 30:1, 12; 32:6, 8, 9

Preface

This book is the outgrowth of an experience and observation of student movements over forty years. The first meeting which I attended as a freshman at the City College of New York in 1927 was a symposium called to protest the suspension of two radical students who had made disrespectful remarks concerning the political honesty of the faculty. I recall the excitement and enthusiasm which burgeoned with each speech of defiance toward the elder authorities. Together with my friends, I found the phenomenon new and even exhilarating. Since childhood I had listened to speeches of street-corner orators of all parties and factions, assailing, attacking, and assaulting; crowds listened to them good-naturedly though seriously. The atmosphere of the student protest meeting was altogether different; I sensed its spirit of generational revolt though I scarcely tried to analyze it. Toward the end of the meeting one speaker rose to call for a resolution of sympathy with our brethren, the Chinese students, who were sacrificing their lives in the struggle against tyranny. The Chinese world was far from New York City, yet suddenly a feeling of solidarity, transcultural and transtemporal, animated the participants, a feeling of kinship with the pure, the uncorrupted, the idealistic, with fellow-students everywhere, with whom one shared the longing to build a world which would be a fit habitation for noble youth. I recall after the meeting talking with a more involved classmate and wondering how it happened that the Chinese students seemed such a different species from us Americans, who certainly were not going to organize demonstrations and marches against the government. What made them so different? I never had an answer, but the question remained with me. It altered and expanded during the years that followed, but this book is finally my attempt to answer it.

During the thirties I observed at first hand the formation of a student movement. It was never large or really politically consequential in the United States, but its motivations and traits, insofar as it remained an independent movement, were those common to student movements everywhere. Very soon, however, the American student movement became the academic youth auxiliary of the adult Leftist parties, especially the Communist party. The movement virtually died with the outbreak of the Second World War, when the moral ambiguities of generational protest were corrupted by a self-destructive subservience to Communist discipline. Twenty years later, in 1960, I saw the first reawakenings of an American student movement in Berkeley. For a while I hoped and pondered whether it would avoid the self-destructive patterns of the thirties, but I soon began painfully to perceive that generational conflict and generational politics have their own patterns and universalities. I began in 1960 to write articles about the emerging student movement. That year too I profited from a visit to Japan during which I met often with leaders of the Zengakuren, the student organization which at that time exerted an immense moral influence on Japanese public opinion and governmental policy. I renewed these discussions two years later when that movement was in obvious decline. Then in 1963 I had the unusual experience, afforded by a sojourn of four and a half months as an Exchange Scholar at the Soviet Institute of Philosophy, of getting to know well one of the circles of student dissenters at Moscow State University which met and discussed problems raised by their aspirations toward freedom in a dictatorial political system. Here one saw students reliving, in the same buildings, the secret experiences of courageous students during Czarist times a hundred years before.

The next year, in the fall of 1964, I presented at a session of the American Sociological Association a summary of my findings and standpoint in an essay entitled "Patterns in the History of Student Movements." I described the traits of elitism, suicidalism, populism, filiarchy, and juvenocracy which one found in all student movements, and outlined the stages in the life histories of student movements; I made central the interrelation of generational conflict with the special historical circumstances making for the "de-authoritization" of the elder generation. A few days later, on my return to Berkeley, the first agitations and actions took place which grew into the events now well known as the Berkeley Student Uprising. As a social scientist, attending the "Movement's" innumerable meetings and rallies, and reading its huge literature of leaflets, I was struck by the manner in which the characteristics of previous student movements were repeating themselves in this, their latest dramatic manifestation. As a member of the university community, I did what I could to counteract the drives to irrationality which were exhibiting themselves with growing intensity. Copies of my studies circulated among student and nonstudent leaders as well as among some of the university's administrators. The Law of Generational Struggle was in full ascendancy, however, confirming my generalizations even as it rebuffed one's hopes for a higher wisdom.

This book is written nonetheless in the hope that by bringing to consciousness the irrationalities and self-destructive components in the history of student movements, it will be possible to overcome them at least in part. Student movements are the product of selfless, altruistic idealism combined with the resentment and aggression of one generation against another. It is the latter component which imparts a demonic quality to the students' emotions and actions. If social understanding can isolate and study that component, perhaps the hatreds, projections, and guilts of generational revolt may be rendered less dominant, and a higher idealism emerge. Roberto Michels once described the "iron law of oligarchy" which pervaded all social organizations, even those of the reformers, yet he hoped by his very study to help contravene that pattern of oligarchy. I have been moved by a similar hope that an honest analysis of generational conflict will contribute to making it less destructive, even more humane. No acceptance of a fateful, Oedipal determinism, as John Stuart Mill called it, underlies this book. Even as the tragedy of student movements and generational struggle unfolds itself, our working hope is that that pattern may be transcended.

LEWIS S. FEUER

Acknowledgments

Grateful acknowledgment is hereby made for permission to quote from the following:

Vladimer Dedijer, *The Road to Sarajevo*, New York, Simon & Schuster, Inc., 1966. Copyright © 1966 by Vladimer Dedijer.

A. E. Housman, "To an Athlete Dying Young," from "A Shropshire Lad," authorised edition, from *The Collected Poems of A. E. Housman*. The Society of Authors, literary representatives of A. E. Housman and Messrs. Jonathan Cape Ltd., publishers. Copyright 1939, 1940, © 1959 by Holt, Rinehart and Winston, Inc. Copyright © 1967, 1968 by Robert E. Symons. Reprinted by permission of Holt, Rinehart and Winston, Inc.

I. M. Maisky, *Before the Storm: Recollections*, tr. Gerald Shelly, London, Hutchinson, 1944.

Miguel Rotblat, "The Latin American Student Movement," *New University Thought*, Vol. I, No. 4 (1964).

Kim San and Nym Wales, *The Song of Ariran: The Life Story of a Korean Rebel*, New York, John Day, 1941. © 1941 by Nym Wales. By permission of John Day, Inc., Publishers.

Heinrich von Treitschke, *History of Germany in the Nineteenth Century*, tr. Eden and Cedar Paul, London, Hutchinson, 1917.

Tan Shih-hua, A *Chinese Testament: The Autobiography of Tan Shih-hua*, as told to S. Tretiakov, New York, Simon & Schuster, Inc., 1934. Copyright, 1934 by Simon & Schuster, Inc.

Contents

THE CONFLICT OF GENERATIONS

ONE The Sources and Traits of Student Movements

This is a book about the workings of the ethical, idealistic spirit in human history. For of all social movements, those composed of students have been characterized by the highest degree of selflessness, generosity, compassion, and readiness for self-sacrifice. And this is also a book about how the idealistic spirit has done violence to itself and to others, and has been transmuted into a destructive force in human history. Our narratives will tell of the eternal duality which pervades historical movements.

The distinctive character of student movements arises from the union in them of motives of youthful love, on the one hand, and those springing from the conflict of generations on the other. We shall thus be inquiring into the complex psychological origins of human idealism, for we cannot understand the destructive pole of student movements until we have brought to light the obscure unconscious workings of generational conflict. Then perhaps we shall know why student movements have been fated to tragedy.

The Dual Source of Student Movements

To their own consciousness, students in student movements have been the bearers of a higher ethic than the surrounding society. Certainly in their essential character student movements are historical forces which are at odds with the "social system." A society is never altogether a social system precisely because such contra-systemic "unsocialized" agencies such as student movements arise. As Walter Weyl said: "Adolescence is the true day for revolt, the day when obscure forces, as mysterious as growth, push us, trembling, out of our narrow lives into the wide throbbing life beyond self."[1] No society ever altogether succeeds in molding the various psychological types which comprise it to conform to its material, economic requirements. If there were a genuine correspondence between the material, economic base and the psychological superstructure, then societies would be static social systems, and basic social change would not take place. In every society, however, those psychological types and motivations which the society suppresses become the searching agents of social change. Thus psycho-ethical motives, which are not only independent of the socio-economic base but actually contrary to the economic ethics that the social system requires, become primary historical forces.

The Russian revolutionary student movement is the classic case of the historic workings of the ethical consciousness. When in the 1860s and 1870s several thousand student youth, inspired by feelings of guilt and responsibility for the backward people, embarked on their "back-to-the-people" movement, it was an unparalleled collective act of selfless idealism. The anarchist Prince Kropotkin conveyed its spirit in notable words:

> Thousands and thousands of Russian youth—the best part of it—were doing the same. Their watchword was "V narod" (To the people; be the people). During the years 1860–1865, in nearly every wealthy family a bitter struggle was going on between the fathers, who wanted to maintain the old traditions, and the sons and daughters. . . . Young men left the military service, the counter, the shop, and flocked to the university towns. Girls bred in the most aristocratic families rushed penniless to St. Petersburg, Moscow, and Kieff, eager to learn a profession. . . . Now they wanted to utilize it, not for their own personal enjoyment, but for carrying to the people the knowledge that had emancipated them. . . . Gradually, they came to the idea that the only way was to settle amongst the people, and to live the people's life.[2]

The students' ethical consciousness was utterly independent of class interests and class position. The largest single group among those who were arrested in the back-to-the-people movement from 1873 to 1877 were children of the nobility.[3] They could have availed themselves of the ample openings in the governmental bureaucracy. Instead, many of them chose a path of self-sacrifice and suffering. Rebuffed by the peasants, the revolutionary student youth later gave themselves to the most extreme self-immolation of individual terrorism. And when terrorism failed to produce the desired social change, circles of student intellectuals provided the first nuclei of the Social Democratic party. Lenin aptly said that the intellectuals brought a socialist consciousness to the workers, who by themselves would not have gone beyond trade union aspirations. The intellectuals Lenin referred to were indeed largely the self-sacrificing revolutionary students.

The ethic of the Russian student generations was not shaped by the institutional requirements of the society. The universal theme of generational revolt, which cuts across all societies, produced in Russia a "conflict of generations" of unparalleled intensity because of special social circumstances. The Russian students lived their external lives in a social reality which was absolutist, politically tyrannical, and culturally backward; internally, on the other hand, they lived in a milieu imbued with Western cultural values. Their philosophical and idealistic aims transcended the social system, and were out of keeping with it; the philosophical culture and the social system were at odds with each other, in "contradiction." The revolutionists, we might say, were historical transcendentalists, not historical materialists. The government opened universities to provide recruits for its bureaucracy. Some students followed the appointed path, but the universities became the centers not only for bureaucratic education but for revolutionary dedication. The idealistic student as a psychological type was recalcitrant to the specifications of the social system.

The civil rights movement in the United States has likewise owed much to students as the bearers of an ethical vocation in history. A wave of sit-ins which spread through Negro college towns began on February 1, 1960, when four freshmen from the all-Negro Agricultural and Technical College at Greensboro, North Carolina, sat down at the lunch counter of the local Woolworth dime store. The surrounding community was puzzled that it was precisely "the best educated, the most disciplined and cultured—and essentially middle class—Negro students" who took the self-sacrificing initiative. Moreover, it was recognized generally, to use one writer's words, that "for the time being it is the students who have given a lift to the established civil rights organizations rather than the other way around."[4] Then in the next years came movements which resembled even more the "back to the people" movement of the Russian studentry. The Freedom Riders of 1961, the several hundred white students in the Mississippi Summer Project of 1964 risking their lives to establish Freedom Schools among the Negroes, were descendants in spirit of the Russian students of the preceding century.

Nonetheless, the duality of motivation which has spurred student movements has always borne its duality of consequence. On the one hand, student movements during the past hundred and fifty years have been the bearers of a higher ethic for social reconstruction, of altruism, and of generous emotion. On the other hand, with all the uniformity of a sociological law, they have imposed on the political process a choice of means destructive both of self and of the goals which presumably were sought. Suicidalism and terrorism have both been invariably present in student movements. A youth-weighted rate of suicide is indeed characteristic of all countries in which large-scale revolutionary student movements are found. In what we might call a "normal" country, or one in which there is a "generational equilibrium," "suicide," as Louis Dublin said, "is much more prevalent in advanced years than during youth." But a "normal" country is one without a revolutionary student movement. Where such movements have existed, where countries are thus characterized by a severe conflict of generations, the rate of suicide has been highest precisely for the youthful group. Nihilism has tended to become the philosophy of student movements not only because it constitutes a negative critique of society; it is also a self-critique that is moved by an impulse toward self-annihilation.

Every historical era tends to have its own most significant choices. In the 1940s, for example, the yogi and commissar, as Arthur Koestler phrased it, posed a critical ethical dilemma for many people. But the double-edged choice which confronts student movements is perhaps best expressed in the title of an essay by Ivan Turgenev, "Hamlet and Don Quixote," written as the Russian student movement was being born. For Hamlet, with his negation, destructive doubt, and intellect turned against himself, was indeed the suicidal pole in the Russian student character, whereas Don Quixote, with his undoubting devotion to an ideal, his readiness to fight for the oppressed and to pit himself against all social institutions, represented the messianic, back-to-the-people component. The Russian student activist, like his later successors, oscillated between these polar impulses; rejected by the people, he would often find in terrorism a sort of synthesis, for thereby he could assail a social institution in a personalized form and hurl against it all the aggressive passions which menaced himself. Don Quixote thus became a student terrorist.[5] When his ventures in terror miscarried, his passions turned against himself; in the last act, he was Hamlet destroying himself.[6] Yet Turgenev believed that if there were no more Don Quixotes the book of history would be closed.

The student movement in Russia inscribed terrorism on its banner. Often it combined terrorism and suicide, for it became the mark of a selfless political murder to destroy oneself at the same time. The long roll of assassinations and attempted assassinations of czars, ministers of education, police chiefs, generals, grand dukes, ministers of interior, was simultaneously a roll call of student and ex-student suicides and martyrdoms. Dmitri Karakozov, Andrei Zhelyabov, Sophia Pervoskaya, Alexander Ulyanov, S. V. Balmashov, Ivan Kaliaev, P. Karpovich, and Yegor Sazonov wrote their self-sacrificial names in history beside those of Alexander II, Alexander III, Minister of Interior Sipiagin, the Grand Duke Serge Alexandrovich, commander of the Moscow military region, Minister of Public Instruction Bogolepov, and Minister of Interior von Plehve. What was true of the Russian student movement was likewise true of the German student movement of 1815 to 1819, and the Bosnian student movement as well in the years before the First World War. This predilection for an ethic in which the end justified any means whatsoever, including terrorism, the ethic of an elitist amorality, cut across all cultures, as we shall see, and was common to all student movements.

The Consequences of Student Movements for Social Evolution

In later chapters we shall undertake to show how the component of generational conflict in student movements has made for an amorality in the choice of political means. We may mention briefly, however, some salient facts in the history of student movements and the hypotheses they suggest concerning the bearing of student movements on the evolution of modern society. In so doing, we shall anticipate somewhat our later narrative. Karl Follen, the first student leader in modern history, taught his entranced followers in the Burschenschaft in 1819 that all means were sanctified by the glorious end of the "Christian German Republic." His influence proved greater than that of the professors in the German universities who tried to inculcate the ethic of the Kantian categorical imperative. One of Follen's selfless followers took his words in the most consequential sense and on March 23, 1819, stabbed to death the dramatist and political reactionary Kotzebue. All Germany was shaken by the deed. The assassin, Karl Sand, tried unsuccessfully to kill himself at the same time. Prior to the killing he had sketched a portrait of himself kneeling on the church steps and pressing a dagger into his heart. The student activists hailed Sand's deed as "a sign of that which will and must come." They came in droves to see his execution, and they purchased as sacred relics the boards on which Sand's blood was splattered. For years afterward, the members of the Heidelberg Burschenschaft would gather in a cottage built from the scaffold's timbers as guests of Sand's executioner. It was a rite for a dualistic death-wish, terrorism and suicidalism, altruism and aggression.

In Bosnia the students made a cult of Zherajitch, who in 1910 had tried to murder the governor and then killed himself. "Young Bosnia had no fixed program or stable organization," wrote a later participant, "but they had a specific ethic of their own, a very altruistic one . . . more like living saints. . . ." Zherajitch had written, "We are a new generation, we are new men in every way." The student movement took this to heart in a series of assassinations of the old men. Almost all of the attempted assassinations of Austrian officials between 1910 and 1914 were by members of the student movement. A pamphlet, "The Death of a Hero," by Vladimir Gatchinovitch, became their bible. Then followed killings and a series of attempts which culminated in the assassination of the Archduke Franz Ferdinand in June 1914 by the student Gavrilo Princip, working as a member of a three-student team, all under twenty years of age. Princip too tried to commit suicide with potassium cyanide but failed. As we shall later see, several months of psychiatric interviews with Princip as well as the testimony of his close friend show him to have been laboring under the severe strain of generational conflict—intense love for his mother which he is described as "confessing," combined with hostility toward his father. His fantasy life was filled with images of assassination. Gavrilo Princip acted out the heroic politics of his struggle with his parents on the stage of history and imposed his pattern of self-destruction on most of Europe and the rest of the world.

This brings us to what is most significant for the theory of social change—namely, the consequences of the superimposition of a student movement on a nationalistic, peasant, or labor movement. Every student movement tries to attach itself to a "carrier" movement of more major proportions—such as a peasant, labor, nationalist, racial, or anti-colonial movement. We may call the latter the "carrier" movements by way of analogy with the harmonic waves superimposed on the carrier wave in physics. But the superimposition of waves of social movements differs in one basic respect from that of physical movements.[7] The student movement gives a new qualitative character and direction to social change. It imparts to the carrier movement a quality of emotion, dualities of feeling, which would otherwise have been lacking. Emotions issuing from the students' unconscious, and deriving from the conflict of generations, impose or attach themselves to the underlying political carrier movement, and deflect it in irrational directions. Given a set of alternative paths—rational or irrational—for realizing a social goal—the influence of a student movement will be toward the use of the most irrational means to achieve the end. Student movements are thus what one would least expect—among the most irrationalist in history.

Generational revolt is not a necessary ingredient for basic social change. Indeed, revolutionary change has taken place in modern times without a concomitant involvement of a younger generation in conflict with an older generation. On the whole, for instance, as we shall see, a generational equilibrium has prevailed in American history. The advent of the Civil War was not preceded by a student abolitionist movement of any proportions in the colleges. Dartmouth, Middlebury, Harvard, were without such societies, and Harvard as a whole supported Daniel Webster in the Compromise of 1850. Harvard through its history underwent cycles of generational insurrection, but that element of the moral de-authoritization of the older generation so essential to the rise of a student movement never emerged. Student grievances did not merge with an ideological discontent and social cause to constitute a student movement. Where such a superimposition of a student movement on the processes of social change has taken place, the evidence is overwhelming that the chances for a rational evolution and achievement of social goals have been adversely affected. In Germany, the effect of Karl Follen's movement was, as Kuno Francke said, to set back for a generation the liberal aspirations of the German people.

In the case of the Russian student movement, it was the opinion of the most distinguished anarchist, Peter Kropotkin, that "the promulgation of a constitution was extremely near at hand during the last few months of the life of Alexander II." Kropotkin greatly admired the idealism of the Russian students, yet he felt their intervention had been part of an almost accidental chain of circumstances that had defeated Russia's hopes. Bernard Pares, the historian, who also witnessed the masochist-terrorist characteristics of the Russian students at first hand, wrote, "The bomb that killed Alexander II put an end to the faint beginnings of Russian constitutionalism." A half-hour before the Czar set out on his last journey on March 1, 1881, he approved the text of a decree announcing the establishment of a commission likely to lead to the writing of a constitution. "I have consented to this measure," said Alexander II, "although I do not conceal from myself the fact that this is the first step toward a constitution." Instead, the students' acts of Czar-killing and self-killing brought into Russian politics all the psychological overtones of sons destroying their fathers; their dramatic idealism projected on a national political scale the emotional pattern of "totem and taboo," the revolt and guilt of the primal sons Freud described. People turned in shock from the sick, self-destructive students; the liberals felt as if they had had the ground pulled out from under them. The Social Revolutionary party, which was most representative of the peasants, and which had the largest vote in November 1917, gave its endorsement for many years to student terrorism. Thereby the party which might have been the chief vehicle for rational evolution gave its blessing to pathological politics. As Professor Jesse D. Clarkson writes, "In retrospect, one may be convinced that the long series of assassinations of governors, ministers, and police chiefs . . . impeded, rather than aided, the attainment of the party's objectives."

No social scientist, of course, would suggest that Gavrilo Princip's deed was a sufficient condition for the outbreak of the First World War. All the familiar rivalries and hatreds among nations were involved too. Yet for two generations a tradition of peace had been taking root in Europe. Peaceful social democratic movements were gaining in influence; great figures, men of peace such as Jean Jaurès, were gaining renown and influence in Europe. It was likely indeed that Russia, if it were spared the stress of war, would continue rapidly to evolve in a liberal capitalist direction. There was hope in Europe that a rational society would emerge, a society whose prophets were Wells, Shaw, Anatole France, Norman Angell. The equilibrium of Europe was shaky, but the roots of a growing stability were there too. In Russia, the studentry was beginning to put aside the politics of generational revolt. Yet its echo in the Balkans was strong enough to upset the European balance of power and mind, and to set moving a self-destructive chain of events. Gavrilo Princip, who dreamed of killing policemen, finally achieved his place as a father-destroyer, a hero in history, even though it also meant the destruction of himself and the maiming of European civilization.[8]

What Are Student Movements? Their Definition and Character

The history of civilization bears witness to certain universal themes. They assert themselves in every era, and they issue from the deepest universals in human nature. Every age sees its class struggles and imperialistic drives, just as every age sees its ethical aspirations transcend economic interest. Every society has among its members examples of all the varieties of motivation and temperament; it has its scientists and warriors, its entrepreneurs and withdrawers. Thus, too, generational conflict, generational struggle, has been a universal theme of history.

Unlike class struggle, however, the struggle of generations has been little studied and little understood. Class conflicts are easy to document. Labor movements have a continuous and intelligible history. Student movements, by contrast, have a fitful and transient character, and even seem lacking in the substantial dignity which a subject for political sociology should have. Indeed the student status, to begin with, unlike that of the workingman, is temporary; a few brief years, and the quantum-like experience in the student movement is over. Nevertheless, the history of our contemporary world has been basically affected by student movements. Social revolutions in Russia, China, and Burma sprang from student movements, while governments in Korea, Japan, and the Sudan have fallen in recent years largely because of massive student protest. Here, then, is a recurrent phenomenon of modern times which challenges our understanding.

Generational struggle demands categories of understanding unlike those which enable us to understand the class struggle. Student movements, unlike those of workingmen, are born of vague, undefined emotions which seek for some issue, some cause, to which to attach themselves. A complex of urges—altruism, idealism, revolt, self-sacrifice and self-destruction—searches the social order for a strategic avenue of expression. Labor movements have never had to search for issues in the way in which student movements do. A trade union, for instance, calls a strike because the workingmen want higher wages, better conditions of labor, shorter hours, more safety measures, more security. A trade union is a rational organization in the sense that its conscious aims are based on grievances which are well understood and on ambitions which are clearly defined. The wage demands and the specific grievances of workingmen are born directly of their conditions of life. Their existence determines their consciousness, and in this sense the historical materialism of Karl Marx is indeed the best theoretical framework for explaining the labor movement. The conflict of generations, on the other hand, derives from deep, unconscious sources, and the outlook and philosophy of student movements are rarely materialistic. If labor seeks to better its living conditions as directly as possible, student movements sacrifice their own economic interests for the sake of a vision of a nobler life for the lowliest. If historical materialism is the ideology of the working class, then historical idealism is the ideology of student movements. If "exploitation" is the master term for defining class conflict, then "alienation" does similar service for the conflict of generations. In this book, we shall be concerned with the nature of student movements, and how their aims, methods, tactics, philosophies, achievements, and failures are related to their origin in a generational struggle which seeks to merge itself with the dominant social struggle of its time.

What is a student movement? It is not a fraternity, or a social club, or an organization of the freshman, sophomore, junior, or senior class, or an academic society, although under certain circumstances it may enlist such groups into its activities. We may define a student movement as a combination of students inspired by aims which they try to explicate in a political ideology, and moved by an emotional rebellion in which there is always present a disillusionment with and rejection of the values of the older generation; moreover, the members of a student movement have the conviction that their generation has a special historical mission to fulfill where the older generation, other elites, and other classes have failed.

Countries like Britain and the United States have virtually never (until recently) had student movements. Britain has had a strong labor movement but no student movement.[9] The United States in the thirties had weak stirrings toward a student movement. In recent years there has been a renewed striving for one and its virtual emergence. But in the sense in which Russia in the latter part of the nineteenth century, China in 1917, Burma in 1936, Korea in 1960, and Japan in 1960 had their student movements, Britain and the United States did not. Student movements are a sign of a sickness, a malady in society. They arise from conditions which have made for a breakdown in the "generational equilibrium" of the society and are reinforced by a mass apathy in which the initiative for political action devolves upon the intellectual elite.

The inner dynamic of student movements leads them to an attempt to "politicalize" all the university's activities. To "politicalize" the university means more than having all students take intelligent, informed stands on political issues. What is sought, rather, is that every activity in the university be linked with, infused by, and subordinated to the alienated ideology of the student movement. The students' work, friendships, readings, play, pleasures, the theater and concerts he attends must all be imbued somehow with the ethos of the student movement. No activity can then be regarded as neutral in the conflict of generations. In Moscow, for instance, in the early 1890s, the student activists resented the privileged existence of the Moscow student orchestra and choir, the only student activities permitted by the authorities. The nonpolitical character of these highly popular musical activities was a challenge to their ideology. By a series of maneuvers, they managed to capture administrative control of both the orchestra and choir and began using them as bases for propagandist activities.[10] The authorities thereupon dissolved these agencies of musical politics. In Berkeley, in 1966, a student writer characterized vividly what he called "the life styles of the political fraternity members": "The radical political fraternity has taken a hint from the old saw that a family that prays together stays together, and believes that a movement that screws together glues together. Or, to be specific, that Socialists who sleep together creep together."[11]

The Basic Traits of Student Movements: Juvenocracy, Filiarchy, Intellectual Elitism

A student movement thus is founded upon a coalescence of several themes and conditions. It tends to arise in societies which are gerontocratic—that is, where the older generation possesses a disproportionate amount of economic and political power and social status. Where the influences of religion, ideology, and the family are especially designed to strengthen the rule of the old, there a student movement, as an uprising of the young, will be most apt to occur. As against the gerontocracy, a student movement in protest is moved by a spirit of what we may call *juvenocracy.* If an element of patriarchy prevails in most governments, the student movement by contrast is inspired by a will to *filiarchy.* Gerontocratic societies, however, have often existed without experiencing a revolt of the younger generation. A gerontocratic order is not a sufficient condition for the rise of a student movement. Among other factors, there must also be present a feeling that the older generation has failed. We may call this experience the process of the "de-authoritization" of the old. A student movement will not arise unless there is a sense that the older generation has discredited itself and lost its moral standing. The Chinese student movement which was born in May 1919 thus issued from a tremendous disillusionment with the elder statesmen who, in the students' eyes, had capitulated with shameful unmanliness to the Japanese demands at Versailles. The Japanese student movement which arose after the Second World War was based on the emotional trauma which the young students had experienced in the defeat of their country. Traditional authority was de-authoritized as it never had been before; their fathers, elders, teachers, and rulers were revealed as having deceived and misled them. Japan in 1960 was far more technologically advanced than it had been in the twenties, and also far more democratic. Yet because in 1960 the psychological hegemony of the older generation was undermined, there arose a large student movement, whereas there had been little unrest among students in earlier and more difficult years.

A student movement, moreover, tends to arise where political apathy or a sense of helplessness prevails among the people. Especially where the people are illiterate will the feeling exist among the young that the political initiative is theirs. The educated man has an inordinate prestige in a society of illiterates. He is a master of the arts of reading and writing, and a whole world of knowledge and the powers of expression are at his command. Throughout human history, whenever people of a society have been overwhelmingly illiterate and voiceless, the intellectual elite has been the sole rival for political power with the military elite. The intellectual elite, under such conditions, constitutes a class of managerial or administrative intellectuals. Several thousand years ago an Egyptian father told his son, "Put writing in your heart that you may protect yourself from hard labor of any kind. The scribe is released from manual tasks: it is he who commands."[12] Ibn Khaldun, sociologist of the fourteenth century, meditating on his life's observations in the North African countries, was on this question as on so many others the great precursor. "When the Arabs conquered many lands, founded their empire," he noted, "the state needed many clerks." Whereas at the beginning of a dynasty, as well as its end, "the sword plays a more important part than the pen," it was otherwise when the state was flourishing. The requirements of administration brought the intellectual elite to the fore; intellectuals have always staffed the bureaucracy: "For all this it is to the pen that he [the ruler] must look for help, hence their importance increases."[13] In China, where the intellectual class ruled for two thousand years, their awareness of their community of interest as the elite most fit to govern was incorporated in the people's wisdom and sociological common sense, their proverbs:

> Without leaving his study, a Bachelor of Arts may understand the affairs of the empire.
>
> As a student—under one man; in office—over ten thousand.
>
> All scholars are brethren.[14]

Student movements are especially prone to occur in countries which have known such a tradition of intellectual elitism.

A student movement is the most mobile and tense section of the intellectual elite. It usually differs in its ethic and motivation from the mature, elder intellectuals; for within the ranks of the intellectual class itself, a sharp cleavage along generational lines usually takes place, quite apart from economic factors. In the early 1900s, for instance, Russian Social Revolutionaries declared that the chief difference between them and the new democratic liberals had nothing to do with class origins or affiliations with the bourgeoisie; they claimed indeed "that the awakening democratic liberal movement was really not tied to the bourgeoisie at all—that it represented, rather, an older generation of the intelligentsia, the members of which were related to the revolutionaries as 'fathers' to 'sons.'" It was a question, they wrote, of a liberalism which "unites only the 'fathers' of the intelligentsia, while the 'sons' constitute confirmed fighters for the revolution. . . . The 'fathers' are distinguished from us by the moderation of their tactics and demands. . . ."[15] Moreover, the fathers as established professional men and bureaucrats, as members of the Establishment, have often become realists, forsworn illusions, and made the inevitable accommodations of ideals to actualities which their existence requires. The student movement is rather an idea in its purity, a Platonic Idea seeking for a brief period an entry into time. Sometimes student movements have been called the "striking force" of the intellectual elite. A "striking force" it is because students, in the nature of things, congregate in campuses, classrooms, and academic halls. A student audience or crowd is the easiest one in the world to assemble. They are not dispersed over distances as peasants are, and their studies are rarely so demanding that they do not have time on their hands. They are not bound and exhausted by work schedules as workers are, and they usually have no families to support. Nevertheless, the student movement's relationship to the adult section of the intellectual elite is an ambiguous and shifting one. Where an oppressive military elite rules the country, where the avenues of democratic politics have been closed, the young and old of the intellectual elite will tend to make common cause. But where the elder intellectuals share power with the military elite, or where the possibilities of political compromise have opened themselves for the elders, a divergence between the generations of intellectuals makes itself felt.

A student movement, however, is not solely what is called a youth movement. It has in addition the component of intellectualism. The students are above all intellectuals, persons with ideas, ideas which they embrace with the full fervor of fresh discovery. A new idea has all the poetry, involvement, and purity of a first love. The students are pure ideologists whose consciousness determines their existence more wholly than that of any other group. They are not adult professionals, who in innumerable ways have allowed reality to determine their ideas. It was the young Joseph Djugashvili, later Stalin, who shortly after he was expelled from the Tbilisi Theological Seminary for his political activities noted how the students' condition exempted their consciousness from material determination: "Until they have plunged into the sea of life and have occupied a definite social position, the students, being young intellectuals, are more inclined than any other category to strive for ideals which call them to fight for freedom. Be that as it may, at the present time the students are coming out in the 'social' movement almost as leaders, as the vanguard."[16] In Japan in 1960, cynical politicians and functionaries would still concede that the Zengakuren activists were of "pure heart." The students, at an age when emotions are most sincerely altruistic, expressed an ethical and political idealism which compelled respect.

The Middle-Class Origin of Studentries

Student movements, like the studentries from which they arise, are almost always constituted in largest part of children of the middle classes. It is a striking sociological truth that unless the social composition of a studentry is arbitrarily determined by the political authority, it will tend, whether in capitalist or socialist countries, to be predominantly middle class. The class backgrounds of the students of the world are thus remarkably similar. In France, for instance, in 1958, 63 per cent of the students came from the middle classes (professionals, managers, government officials, craftsmen, tradesmen, farm proprietors), 19 per cent were from the upper classes (employers, owners, stockholders), while only 4 per cent were from the proletariat (industrial and farm laborers).[17]

In socialist Yugoslavia, the studentry in 1958 was likewise predominantly middle class. The percentage was 53.5 per cent, excluding peasants' sons; and if peasants were included as proprietors in the middle class, the percentage rose to 80.8 per cent. Of course, the middle class now consisted mostly of the new, bureaucratic class; only 12.4 per cent of the studentry, however, came from the working class, despite the socialistic economy. The intellectuals and state employees who composed only 13 per cent of the population provided disproportionately more than 45 per cent of the studentry; whereas the workers, who comprised 27 per cent of the population, contributed only 12.4 of the studentry. The peasantry were the majority (60 per cent) of the Yugoslav people, yet the percentage of peasants' sons among the students was only 27.30 per cent.[18]

Communist Poland had a distribution of students much like that of Yugoslavia; the majority of its studentry derived from the "new middle class."

Social Origin of Polish Studentry (1957–1958)[19]

CLASS	PERCENTAGE OF STUDENTRY
Workers	26.2
Peasants	21.7
Intelligentsia (trade, others)	52.1

The social origin of students in Sweden was much similar to the Polish; the Swedish students derived predominantly from "the families of teachers and those in government service."

Social Origin of Swedish Studentry (1956)[20]

	CLASS	PERCENTAGE OF STUDENTRY
I	Proprietors, managers, higher officials	43.2
II	Farmers, elementary school teachers, lower officials, shopkeepers	38.8
III	Workers	17.2
IV	Miscellaneous	0.8

The studentries of the backward, or industrially underdeveloped countries likewise were predominantly from the middle classes. In other words, the degree of technical development in a country no more affected the primacy of the middle class in its universities than did the type of social system. The University of Indonesia, for instance, in 1958 drew 46.4 per cent of its studentry from the children of professors, persons in free occupations, officers, entrepreneurs, and high civil servants; 41.5 per cent from the children of secondary school teachers, middle businessmen, middle civil servants, and pensioners; and 12.1 per cent from elementary school teachers, lower civil servants, noncommissioned officers, and small peasants. At least 87.9 per cent of Indonesia's studentry was drawn from its middle or upper class; the lowest classes were virtually unrepresented. This despite President Sukarno's socialism and "guided democracy."[21]

The Indonesian percentages were much like those of Turkey, 36 per cent of whose studentry in 1959 was drawn from the upper classes, 57 per cent from the middle classes, and only 7 per cent from the lower class. In India, likewise, most of the students came from the middle and higher income classes, though the average income of the middle class was low.[22] The studentry of Japan, the most industrially developed of the Asian countries, was also drawn predominantly from the middle and upper classes. Only 2.9 per cent of Japanese students were children of skilled workers, while the middle income group contributed 35.5 per cent and the upper income group 34.5 per cent of the studentry.[23]

The Danish, Swiss, and Dutch all have middle-class studentries, despite the influence in other ways of their respective social democratic and democratic philosophies. The children of academics indeed provided the largest groups in these studentries. In Denmark, as many as 34.2 per cent of the students at the time of the survey were children of professors and teachers, while only 8.2 per cent came from the working class. The Swiss studentry in 1960 was overwhelmingly middle class: 83 per cent were children of employers, managers, public officials, professionals, professors, teachers, and white collar employees; 13 per cent were children of independent tradesmen, handicraftsmen and farmers; and only 3.7 per cent were children of industrial and agricultural laborers. In the

Netherlands in 1954–1955 the higher classes provided 47 per cent of the studentry, the middle classes 46 per cent, and the lower class (workers, policemen, clerks, state office workers) only 7 per cent. The German studentry in 1955–1956 was drawn largely from families in which the parents were civil servants and lawyers (38.8 per cent), businessmen and managers (17.4 per cent), and doctors and pharmacists (6 per cent). In Britain, after almost five years under a Labour government, only 7 per cent of students at Oxford and Cambridge were the sons of manual "workers," though the percentage reached 20 per cent in the "red brick" universities. Only the Korean studentry in 1953 was predominantly (76 per cent) from the lower income group, but that only because so many of the students' families had been uprooted by the war which ended that year.[24]

Student movements arising out of such studentries have except in rare instances been composed of sons and daughters of the middle class, brought up with the culture and values of the middle class, its tensions, outlook, and hopes, and reacting to their origins with various degrees of "alienation."

The First Literary Portrayal of the Student Leader: Victor Hugo's Enjolras

Student revolutionary leaders made their debut in the world's literature in the novel *Les Misérables* by Victor Hugo (1862). The traits of the student activist, this new psychological type, were there delineated for all time. With a few changes, the characters of the Parisian student movement of the 1830s are identical with those of the Russian movement of the 1890s, the Chinese movement of 1917, the Berkeley movement of 1964. The psychological types in history are universal; in diverse eras the same cast of characters acts out eternal human drives. Thus Victor Hugo describes the student revolutionary activists in their secret circle, the Friends of the A.B.C.:

> It was a secret society, in a state of embryo, and we might almost call it a coterie, if coteries produced heroes. . . . Most of the Friends of the A.B.C. were students who maintained a cordial understanding with a few workmen. . . . These young men formed a species of family through their friendship. . . .
>
> [Their leader, Enjolras, twenty-two years old, the scion of a wealthy family] was angelically beautiful, and looked like a stern Antinous. You might have fancied that he had gone through the revolutionary apocalypse in some previous existence. He knew the traditions of it like an eye-witness. . . . He was a pontifical and warlike nature, strange in a young man; he was a churchman and a militant; from the immediate point of view a soldier of democracy, but, above the contemporary movement, a priest of the ideal. . . . He was serious,

and did not appear to know that there was on the earth a being called woman. He had only one passion, justice, and only one thought, overthrowing the obstacle. On the Mons Arentinus, he would have been Gracchus; in the Convention, he would have been Saint-Just. . . . He was severe in his pleasures, and before all that was not the Republic he chastely lowered his eyes. . . .

The varieties of student activists all appear in this first portrait of the student movement. There was the everlasting student nonstudent, prolonging his adolescence and re-enacting each semester his revolt against his elders, Balorel, a student of law, "a student in his eleventh year," who "liked nothing as much as a quarrel unless it were a riot, and nothing so much as a riot except a revolution. He was ever ready to break a pane of glass, tear up the paving-stones, and demolish a government, in order to see the effect. . . ." His motto as a law student: "Never a lawyer." There was the believer in the rule of the intellectual elite, intelligarchy (as we might call it), Combeferre, who "declared that the future is in the hand of the schoolmaster, and busied himself with educational questions." There was his more sociological fellow-student, Prouvaire: "the whole day long he studied social questions, wages, capital, credit, marriage, religion, liberty of thought, liberty of love, education, the penal code, wretchedness, partnership, property, production, and distribution, that enigma of the lower world which casts a shadow on the antheap. . . ." In all these students "the pure blood of principle flowed in their veins." Only one of them was a skeptic, and he was emotionally fixated, in a feminine, homosexual way on the student leader, Enjolras: "This skeptic, however, had a fanaticism . . . it was a man—Enjolras. . . . His mind could do without a belief, but his heart could not do without friendship. . . . His soft, yielding, dislocated, sickly, and shapeless ideas attached themselves to Enjolras as to a spinal column. . . ."[25]

Saint-Just, the *enfant terrible* of the French Revolution, was indeed, as Victor Hugo perceived, the precursor of the revolutionary student leaders. Twenty-four years old in 1793, the youngest man in the Convention, he overawed it as "an idea energized by a passion," deporting himself as one above humanity. Only a short time earlier, he had run away to Paris with his mother's silver and written an epic of pornopolitics, the *Organt,* in twenty cantos, which interspersed its critique of kings and priests with long scenes of passion, "the raping of nuns, and discourses on the right to pleasure."[26] The university students at Rheims, where he studied law, were drawn to the character and leadership of Saint-Just, and took him as their hero. He evidently had a passion for equality, the back-to-the-people spirit of the student activist, and was said to walk the roads in all weathers to bring help to needy families.[27]

Young Saint-Just had the austerity of death-seeking. "I am going to get myself killed," he said as he left Paris for the armies, and he voiced his sense of alienation: "The man who is compelled to isolate himself from his fellow-beings and even from his own thoughts, finds anchorage in time to be."[28] A skeptic at twenty, an idealist at twenty-two, an executioner at twenty-five, and himself executed the next year, the student leader Saint-Just, who declared, "*Formons la cité*" (Let us found the city), became instead the symbol for inflexible terrorist dictatorship.

The Back-to-the-People Spirit in Student Movements

From the combination of youth, intellectuality, and altruistic emotion, there arise certain further basic traits of student movements. In the first place, a student movement, unlike a labor movement, has at its inception only a vague sense of its immediate goals; indeed, its "ultimate aims" are usually equally inchoate. A trade union, as we have mentioned, comes into being because a group of workers have certain specific grievances relating to wages, hours and conditions of work, seniority rights, safety precautions. It is only with difficulty that political propagandists can get workers to think in generic terms of opposing the "system." A student movement, on the other hand, arises from a diffused feeling of opposition to things as they are. It is revolutionary in emotion to begin with, and because its driving energy stems largely from unconscious sources, it has trouble defining what it wants. It tries to go from the general to the particular, and to find a justifying bill of grievances; what moves it at the outset, however, is less an idea than an emotion, vague, restless, ill-defined, stemming from the unconscious. A Japanese student leader of many years' standing, Shigeo Shima, remarked, "One cannot understand the student movement if one tries to understand it in terms of the labor movement. The strength of the student movement lies in its energy of consciousness trying to determine existence, instead of the other way around."[29] An intellectual has been defined as a person whose consciousness determines his existence;[30] in the case of the young intellectuals of a student movement we might add further that their ideological consciousness is founded on the emotional unconscious of generational revolt.

The student movement strives further to fill the role of the conscience of society. In a gerontocracy, the older generation embodies the powers of the cultural conscience. A student movement, however, is an instrumentality of psychological revolution; in a world where the fathers have been de-authoritized, the sons step forward as the self-anointed bearers of authority. People then pay tribute to the students as the only group in society who can speak their minds honestly. We might call this process a "displacement of the superego." Toshio Kamba, whose daughter was killed when the Japanese students forced the Diet grounds in 1960, described this reverence of Japanese society towards its new student superego:

> Nobody will deny that the feeling in the students' life is the purest. It is difficult for the average man to express his pure mind. When we are mindful of our situation or of future censure, we scarcely dare to speak our opinion frankly even if we are sure that our opinion is right. The students are favored, for they can express and act on their opinions frankly. . . . The students have a natural wisdom, for they are pursuing their studies, seeking the truth. . . . So long as the student has wisdom, he knows spontaneously what he should do.[31]

The students are strategically placed for taking the initiative and acting on their beliefs. "Only students can do it, because they need not worry about their earnings at all." Organized society, moreover, is prepared to grant students liberties they would allow no other group. In Japan (as in the United States), the courts have shown an unusual reluctance to pass judgment on students involved in a variety of incidents, riots, and disturbances. The cases drag on for years, and the tribunals become the occasions for friendly interchange between the judges, prosecutors, defense lawyers, and students, as they view and review the photographic slides of the incidents. The student is perceived as society's naïve child acting on the ideas which it has been taught, and society is embarrassed by the children who quote to it its ideals; the students who only recently have been children have not yet been conditioned to act slavishly. "The students," said Toshio Kamba, "have fewer social bonds, so that they can do with free will what they think right."

A student movement thus tends to take its stand as the pure conscience of the society; it is concerned with ideal issues, not, like an economic movement, with the material, bread-and-butter ones. Every student movement, however, also has a populist ingredient. A student movement always looks for some lowly oppressed class with which it can psychologically identify itself. Whether it be to the peasantry, the proletariat, or the Negro, the students have a tremendous need to offer themselves in a self-sacrificial way, to seek out an exploited group on whose behalf their sacrifices will be made. Conceiving of themselves as deceived, exploited sons, they feel a kinship with the deceived and exploited of society as a whole. The back-to-the-people spirit is at once the most distinctive, noblest, and most self-destructive trait within student movements. The populist ingredient separates the student movement sharply from what we might call student syndicalism. The latter embraces the variety of student organizations which are primarily devoted to matters relating to student well-being, such as mutual aid, transportation, examination schedules, housing, and tuition. Student syndicates may even engage in demonstrations against the government, especially where the universities are state institutions. A student syndicate is, however, an example of studentism pure and simple; it is preoccupied with the normal interests of the student elite, and is devoid of the back-to-the-people motif. As such, it lacks an essential psychological characteristic of student movements.

As fathers and sons argued in Russia in 1860, so they have debated in other countries and times. There is no principle of cumulative historical experience; rare is the generation that is spared the mistakes of its predecessor. In Japan in 1959, Toshio Kamba argued with his activist daughter Michiko as he saw her re-enacting the back-to-the-people spirit which had swept through the Russian youth almost a hundred years before. He recalled the somber outcomes of terrorism and self-destruction. He pleaded with his daughter, "You members of Zengakuren are foolish. . . . Is there no other means . . . ? Do you say that such destructive action, the most pathetic, is also the most heroic? If you say so, I venture to reply that you are following in the footsteps of the Narodniks, and that the heroism and leadership of that intelligentsia culminated in Bolshevism." When his daughter spoke of the need for a new vanguard party, and of the historic mission of the intellectuals to guide the workers, the father replied in vain, "That is the theory, but if the students take the leadership of the political movement, it will be as it was with the intelligentsia who played the central role before Lenin's advent."[32]

The populist and elitist moods in student movements can merge into a morbid self-destructive masochism, as they did, for instance, among the Russian students. The burden of guilt which a generation in revolt takes upon itself is immense, and it issues in perverse and grotesque ways. Nevertheless, something would be lost in our understanding of student movements if we were to see in them solely a chapter of history written on an abnormal theme. For student movements, let us remember, are the most sincerely selfless and altruistic which the world has seen. A student is a person who, midway between childhood and maturity, is imbibing the highest ideals and hopes of the human cultural heritage; moreover, he lives in comradeship with his fellow-students. The comradeship of students is usually the last communal fellowship he will experience. The student feels that he will then enter into a maelstrom of competitive and bureaucratic pseudo-existence; he has a foreboding that he will become alienated from the self he now is. Articulate by education, he voices his protest. No edict in the world can control a classroom. It is everywhere the last free forum of mankind. Students meet together necessarily, think together, laugh together, and share a common animus against the authorities. The conditions of student existence remain optimal for spontaneous rebellion. When the absolutism of the Czar stifled the nascent democratic strivings in a culturally backward people, the universities stood as isolated fortresses of relatively free expression. As Lenin wrote in 1903, "The actual conditions of social life in Russia render (soon we shall have to be saying: rendered) extremely difficult any manifestation of political discontent except through the universities."[33]

The students' age, moreover, is the age of friendship and the fullness of love. And in this setting, feelings of sympathy for the deprived, the suffering, and the underdog are spontaneous and natural. The collectivity of student youth lives on long hours of talk into the night. The Zengakuren leaders Kitakoji and Kurokawa were always referring to their "heated discussions." The populist ingredient, in Japan as in America, also made "folk singing" a kind of hymnal ritual for the student movement. The Utagoe Undo (Group Singing Movement), founded in 1950, acquired great popularity among Zengakuren activists. Then, too, almost every student movement, in its filiarchical revolt, has had a commitment to struggle for "the emancipation of women," especially in the realm of sexual freedom. Michiko Kamba thus confided to her mother "that she would like to get into the emancipation movement in the future," and Zengakuren in 1954, impressed by the increasing militancy of women students' societies, adopted demands for an end to discrimination against women, and for the abolition of unreasonable restrictions on dormitory privileges.

The student movement is almost like a secret society of sons and daughters banded against the father. Here student comradeship can flourish. The secret society is like a voluntary family, a new "primary group," in which one chooses anew one's brothers and sisters. Its confidences cannot yield to those of the natural family. Student movements tend to choose a secret society form of organization not because of any political necessity but precisely because it marks the generational separation. Children have always reveled in secret groups with secret passwords precisely because these establish their mark of independence in conspiracy against the adults. A kindly and "permissive" father tells how he learned that his daughter Michiko had been a Communist: "She joined the Communist party at the end of the freshman year, I think. . . . As she had never shown the slightest sign of it to my family, we learned it for the first time at the memorial service of the Zengakuren soon after her death." Nor had the father known that shortly before her junior year Michiko had broken with the Communist party: " 'I will make my way in the direction I think right,' " she had said, "and rose up from my seat, throwing them my party badge."

Uneven Development and the Law of the Universality of Ideas

The more backward a people is with respect to its culture and intellect, the greater is the likelihood that it will have a student movement of an elitist and revolutionary character. Where the "cultural distance" between the students and the surrounding population is great, the chances for the rise of a student movement are increased. One whole class of student movements is born of "uneven development," from the unbalanced situation in which advanced ideas are combined with material backwardness. In such cases the "cultural strain," the cultural alienation, which arises between the students and the masses, is most poignant and intense, for it involves a de-authoritization of the elder generation as cultural inferiors, as persons of whom one is ashamed. The students then are in part motivated to overcome the cultural distance between their people and themselves, and in part by an acceptance of the elitist status which their cultural superiority confers. What is most important to bear in mind is that the culture of the student movements, of the intellectual elite, is the one genuinely international culture. Students at any given time throughout the world tend to read the same books. We might call this the law of the universality of ideas, or the law of universal intellectual fashions, or the maximum rate of diffusion for intellectual culture. At any rate, the Chinese students of 1917, like their counterparts in America and Britain, were reading Bertrand Russell, John Dewey, and later Lenin and Marx; earlier they had read Ibsen, Tolstoy, and Spencer. Kwame Nkrumah as a university student in America and Britain studied Marx and logical positivism, Jomo Kenyatta sank himself in the writings of Marx and Malinowski. Today in Africa the young students, like their fellows in France, the United States, and Japan, read Marx, Camus, and the existentialist writers. In the Soviet Union young university students try to find copies of Camus and Freud, and overcoming the obstacles interposed by the government against the free flow of books and ideas, succeed in maintaining a bond with the world intellectual community.

In this sphere of the intellect, historical materialism is clearly invalid, for the mode of production of the given society does not determine its mode of reading. Whatever the economic conditions, no matter how they vary from country to country, intellectuals tend to adopt the same ideas everywhere. In this sense, ideas resemble fashions; like the dress designs set in Paris, they diffuse rapidly throughout the rest of the world.[34] Thus, an international intellectual culture arises, and a worldwide community of intellectuals. There was a time when Marxists looked forward to the international unity of the working class, founded on a common perception of class interests. But a common working-class culture failed to arise; it was only among official representatives of the labor movements that a certain ritualistic acknowledgment was made of a common philosophy of the working class. In terms, however, of what they read, enjoyed, thought, and spoke, there was virtually no community among the world's workers. A workingman on an assembly line in the United States, or a skilled craftsman, shared nothing spiritually or emotionally or ideologically with coolies in Malayan tin mines or Indonesian oil workers. The world's intellectuals, however, share a common culture, and constitute a community in a far more genuine sense than that in which there ever was an international working-class community.

To the young student of a backward country whose mind is filled with the most advanced ideas, there is a heightened sense of the contradictions, the unfitness of things. Thorstein Veblen once argued that the country which was a latecomer in the process of industrialization had the advantage of being able to borrow directly the most advanced industrial techniques.[35] Certainly the intellectuals of backward countries have always been most attracted to the most advanced ideas, but the imbalance in their consciousness produces the extremes of aspiration and despair. In the stagnant world of Russia after the Decembrist defeat of 1825, wrote Alexander Herzen, "children were the first to raise their heads." Around them was a people, "frightened, weak, distracted" with its bureaucracy of "cringing officials." Not so the children. "What impressed them was the complete *contradiction* of the words they were taught with the facts of life around them. Their teachers, their books, their *university* spoke one language and that language was intelligible to heart and mind. Their father and mother, their relations and all their surroundings spoke another with which neither mind nor heart was in agreement—but with which the dominant authorities and financial interests were in accord. This *contradiction* between *education and ordinary life* nowhere reached such proportions as among the nobility of Russia."[36] The Russian studentry, no matter what their class origins, overcompensated for their society's material retardation by trying all the more to march with the intellectual avant-garde. Karl Marx in 1868 observed that his book against Proudhon (1847) as well as his *Contribution to the Critique of Political Economy* (1859) had "had a greater sale in Russia than anywhere else." "And," he added, "the first foreign nation to translate *Kapital* is the Russian." The Russian aristocratic students, educated in western European universities, he continued, "always run after the most extreme that the West can offer."[37]

This tendency of intellectuals in authoritarian and backward lands to seek the "most extreme" ideas persistently made for a psychological tension; the existing social reality was always defined in every institution as inherently the agency of frustration. A "humane" education, said Herzen, "made men of all with whom it succeeded. But a man was just what was not wanted either for the hierarchical pyramid or for the successful maintenance of the landowning regime. The young man had either to dehumanize himself—and the greater number did so—or to stop short and ask himself. . . ."[38] Japanese students, to take an Asian example, similarly brooded on the works of French and Russian novelists, on Tolstoy, Turgenev, and Dostoyevsky, in the first years of the twentieth century. The Russo-Japanese War of 1904–1905 had ended in the victory of Japan, but there was a saying in the country, "Japan defeated Russia in the war but was defeated in literature." Alienation, "the ennui in modern life," nihilism and the countervailing humanism, perturbed the Japanese intellectuals. Then Ibsen, Schnitzler, and Strindberg were read, raising questions concerning the nature of man which challenged the whole basis of Japanese social life. The aftermath of the World War set Japanese students reading the socialistic works of Bernard Shaw and Henri

Barbusse. The thirties brought Eliot, Hemingway, and Steinbeck; and after the Second World War, Camus, Sartre, Beauvoir, Arthur Miller, Norman Mailer, and Graham Greene.[39] The intellectual is what he reads, and in all societies his world of books, with its moral imperatives, has seemed more real to him than the world of men.

What Is a Generation?

A student movement is a generational movement. What then is a generation? Marx never answered at length what he meant by a class, and the concept of a generation is equally elusive. "What makes people members of one and the same age group? It is not simply the co-existence in the same period," said the political scientist, Sigmund Neumann. "Contemporaries are not merely people born in the same year. . . . What identifies them as people of one generation is decided by their common experiences, the same decisive influence, similar historical problems."[40] Generations, he believed, could be divided according to essential impressions received around the age of seventeen.

We might well distinguish between biological generations and cultural-political ones. In the biological sense, fathers and sons always succeed each other, but their modes of life and standpoints under peaceful conditions may be much the same; the generations in the biological sense do not then have a political significance. When does a "generation" become a socio-political phenemenon? A generation in the sociological sense consists of persons in a common age group who in their formative years have known the same historical experiences, shared the same hopes and disappointments, and experienced a common disillusionment with respect to the elder age groups, toward whom their sense of opposition is defined.

Often a generation's consciousness is shaped by the experience of what we might call the "generational event." To the Chinese Communist students of the early thirties, for instance, it was the "Long March" with Mao Tse-tung; that was what one writer called their "unifying event."[41] More than class origin, such an historical experience impresses itself on the consciousness of a student movement. The depression, the struggle against fascism, the ordeals of the civil rights agitation—all these were generational events; they demarcated a generation in its coming of age.

In Berkeley in 1964 the student movement said, "You can't trust anyone over thirty." They were not as exclusive as Pyotr Tkachev; expelled in 1861 from St. Petersburg at the age of seventeen, he advocated the execution of all over twenty-five. Mikhailovsky, a generation later, made the age of thirty-five the dividing line.[42] On the other hand, the Spanish student movement included all up to forty-five among the youth; but in Tunisia today, twenty-five is the year of youth's end. The length of a generation is socially determined. At Berkeley, for instance, its duration was set by the graduate student years. But the character of the historical experience was most important.

Social generations follow upon each other more rapidly in critical times than in others. In Germany, after the First World War, there was a notably rapid succession of generations. A generational system can become even more differentiated than a class system. Just as a class system can evolve with multiple levels from upper-upper to lower-lower, so *repeated historical crises within a short interval of time* can multiply the political generations which exist at any given time. Thus, the First World War differentiated generations in somewhat the following pattern. First was the prewar generation, comprised of people born before 1890, whose education was complete and whose careers had been formed before the war started. For them the war was an interruption. Second was the war-participant generation. As Neumann described it, "To them the war meant the great, formative experience. Admirable or brutal, it was in their blood. It could never leave them. This was the 'younger generation' called upon to make post-war history." It was superimposed on a prewar vanguard youth movement which had already articulated a protest against "the artificial and corrupt style of bourgeois society." What had been "a burgher's secession of a middle class youth" was "surprised and overtaken by the war." A massive political traumatic event amplified the wave of the normal generational conflict. Even as a depression accentuates the class struggle with its increased unemployment, so any world event which imposes a diversity of experience on the generations, especially one which imposes a burden of trauma on one generation and not others, tends to divide society, to intensify generational conflict, and upset the generational equilibrium: "Those who returned were cynics and skeptics. They had lost connection with their profession, with their family, with civil society. . . . They had just left school, ready to carve out lives of their own, enthusiastically open to a world to be conquered. So they joined the army, these young volunteers. War became their calling." Many were worn out by their ordeal, and later, "silent, impenetrable . . . distrusted the noisy and petty world of busy people they returned to." Others were embittered. Years later the Nazi revolution became their cause as they sought in anguish and unreason to recover a meaning for their lives. In this sense fascism, as Neumann pointed out, was "the revolution of the war generation par excellence."

The third successor generation in Germany was composed of the war's adolescent nonparticipants, many of whose fathers were away at the front. They went on with their studies, followed professions. "It sometimes seemed to their elders that they took after the grandfathers. Indeed they often locked hands with them over the heads of the preceding generation." This postwar youth was not impressed by the paramount event of the recent past—war. "They had no headaches. Economics, techniques, sport

—those interested them. . . . They did not want to reform the world. They wanted to live. The motorcycle was the embodiment of their ambitions. . . . If there was a great experience comparable to the roar which impressed this problemless generation, it was the inflation. . . ."[43] This generation was driftwood. The Nazi revolution drew them later into an alliance with the disillusioned war generation.

What keeps generational consciousness most intense is the sense of generational martyrdom, the actual experience of one's fellow-students assaulted, killed, imprisoned, by armed deputies of the elder generation. Whether in Russian, Chinese, or Latin American universities, or at Berkeley, the actual physical clash made students frenzied with indignation. The youthful adolescent resents the elders' violence especially for its assault upon his new manhood. Student movements make of their martyrs the high symbols of a common identity. The Iranian Students' Association, for example, published a leaflet in their exile to commemorate "Student Day" for three of their comrades. Its language was that of the martyrology of generational consciousness:

STUDENTS MASSACRED

On December 7th, 1953, the armed forces of the post-coup d'etat government invaded the Tehran University. Some soldiers entered a classroom and threatened to kill the professor . . . As the terrified students started to run away the soldiers opened fire with their machine guns in the hallway and wounded many students and killed three.

. . . The students were going to demonstrate against the government on December 9th, 1953, the day that Vice-President Richard M. Nixon was going to visit Iran and its "free" people. . . .

The three students, GHANDCHI, BOZORGNIA and SHARIATRAZAVI, died, but their memory and their heroic sacrifice will forever remain with us to guide the student movement of Iran. To honor their memories and to rededicate ourselves to the cause for which they gave their lives, this day will always be honored. . . .[44]

Every student movement has cherished similar memories of brothers whom their fathers destroyed.

Generational Struggle as a Universal Theme of History: Its Early Description by Plato and Aristotle

The generational struggle in politics, as a universal theme in human history, was naturally recorded by the earliest masters of political science, Plato and Aristotle, both of whom recognized its primacy as an independent factor in political change. They thus enunciated a theme which is reiterated in history through changing modes of production and social systems. To Plato, generational struggle constituted virtually the basic mechanism in political change, the always disequilibrating factor in systems of government, the prime agent in the alternation of political forms. If aristocracy gave way to timocracy, the rule of property holders, it was because the aristocrats' sons became alienated from their fathers. As Plato described it, "The character of the son begins to develop when he hears his mother complaining that her husband has no place in the government . . . that his father is only half a man. . . ." The servants tell him he must "be more of a man than his father. . . ." But then the timocrats become de-authoritized in the sons' eyes: "A time arrives when the representative of timocracy has a son: at first he begins by emulating his father and walking in his footsteps, but presently he sees him of a sudden foundering against the State as upon a sunken reef. . . ." The son, humbled by poverty, takes to "money-making," and the oligarchical form of government is the creature of the money-makers. But oligarchy gives rise to a rebellious generation which institutes a democracy. For the young son in the oligarchy is brought up "in a vulgar and miserly way"; the sons rebel against the money-making virtues; they call temperance "unmanliness," modesty "silliness," "insolence they term breeding, and anarchy liberty." "The lotus-eaters" appeal to the sons; "there is a battle and they gain the day." But democracy itself feels in turn the discord of generational strife. "The father grows accustomed to descend to the level of his sons, and to fear them, and the son is on a level with his father, he having no respect or reverence for either of his parents. . . ." In such a society, Plato continues, "the master fears and flatters his scholars, and the scholars despise their masters and tutors; young and old are all alike, and the young man is on a level with the old, and is ready to compete with him in word and deed; the old men condescend. . . ." Thus democracy founders as the sons are drawn into "a perfectly lawless life"; the son, says Plato, then dares do in reality what hitherto he has done in dream only, "he will commit the first murder." He throws aside the judgments of good and evil which he learned as a child. Democracy breaks down to be replaced by tyranny, the rule of a dictator.

Such is Plato's "model" for generational strife as the causal mechanism in political change. It underlines one fact—that to the ancients the primacy of generational struggle in history was entirely familiar and obvious.[45] Every form of government seemed to breed its own distinctive form of generational contradiction. Generational conflict seemed to them an everlasting threat to political stability. If this truth was so obvious to the ancients, why was it almost wholly lost sight of in modern times? The answer is that the Industrial Revolution brought a relative generational equilibrium to Britain and America; probably it was the first such equilibrium in world history, and it may well be that the tremendous energies unleashed in industrial development and the opening up of a new continent were energies which otherwise would have been spent in generational strife but now found more constructive channels. When discontented, rebellious sons could cross the ocean to build a new world, or become entrepreneurs in new industries, when young university men could take ship for New England, and clerks could fashion empires, the conflict of generations subsided. Thus at the same time that the revolutionary role of technology became obvious to the social scientist, the role of generational struggle receded into the background. The ancients, however, saw it in all its harsh reality, with its bitterness unrelieved by any safety valve such as a developing technology or new world.

To Aristotle, the psychological sources of generational conflict made for its universality. Generational conflict, in Aristotle's view, basically stemmed from the character of the generations. The young, he wrote, love honor and victory, "more than they love money, which indeed they love very little, not having yet learnt what it means to be without it. . . ." Thus Aristotle, in effect, was affirming that an economic interpretation does not apply to the actions of youth. Their idealism was founded on generational comradeship, on their fraternity. "They are fonder of their friends, intimates, and companions than older men are, because they like spending their days in the company of others. . . ." "They trust others readily, because they have not yet often been cheated. They are sanguine . . . and besides that, they have met as yet with few disappointments." They think of themselves as an elite which can accomplish what others have not. "They have exalted notions, because they have not yet been humbled by life or learnt its necessary limitations; moreover, their hopeful disposition makes them think themselves equal to great things—and that means having exalted notions." They think in terms of moral idealism rather than social realism, "their lives are regulated more by moral feeling than by reasoning. . . ." They overestimate their knowledge and abilities; they are dogmatists. "They think they know everything, and are always quite sure about it; this, in fact, is why they overdo everything." They are easily and naïvely moved to commiseration and social consciousness. "They are ready to pity others, because they think every one an honest man, or anyhow better than he is. . . ."[46]

By contrast the elderly men, according to Aristotle, were disillusioned, disaffected, materialistic. "They have lived for many years; they have often been taken in, and often made mistakes; and life on the whole is a bad business." They are skeptics. "They 'think,' but they never 'know'; and because of their hesitation they always add a 'possibly' or a 'perhaps.' . . . They are cynical; that is, they tend to put the worse construction on everything." Small-minded, ungenerous, money-minded, their passions slackened, they are moved not by feeling but by love of gain. Sexual desire, Aristotle noted, was the one which swayed youth most, but the old men were self-controlled because their sexual desire was gone. Aristotle, of course, placed his trust in men in their prime, who "neither trust everybody nor distrust everybody, but judge people correctly." Without excesses or defects, they combine the valuable qualities of youth and old age. The mind at the age of forty-five was Aristotle's happiest mean.

It was then, as we would say today, most free from ideology, of either the juvenocratic or gerontocratic kind.

Generational conflict, furthermore, noted Aristotle, could take an overt political form. At Cridius, for instance, the oligarchy fell apart because the generations fought each other. At cities such as Massilia, Ister, and Heraclea, wrote Aristotle, elder brothers, younger brothers, fathers, and sons, fought each other for the high places of government. Thus an oligarchy, through generational conflict, could be transformed virtually into a democracy. Such was the immense political significance of generational struggle in the Greek towns; it altered the ruling group in Heraclea from a few persons to six hundred.[47] Political revolutions, according to Aristotle, were caused not only by the conflict of rich and poor but by the struggle between fathers and sons. He documented the embittered strain between the generations as revealed in their proverbs and maxims: "Nothing is more foolish than to be the parent of children." "Never show an old man kindness."[48]

Indeed, the concept of wisdom as it was first formulated in antiquity by the Egyptian and Hebrew sages was precisely cross-generational in purpose. Wisdom was a warning against generational pride and rebellion; the son was to be his father's good pupil. Thus, history's first document on the principles of right conduct, the Maxims of Ptahhotep, was already concerned with the conflict of generations. Ptahhotep, a man of the Establishment, evidently Grand Vizier to the Pharaoh Isesi of the Fifth Dynasty in the twenty-seventh century B.C., as he set down the wisdom of a lifetime, bade youth hearken to their fathers. "A hearkener is one whom the god loves, one whom the god hates is one who hearkens not. . . . How worthy it is when a son hearkens to his father! If the son of a man receives what his father says, none of his projects will miscarry. . . . As for the fool who hearkens not there is none who has done anything for him. He regards wisdom as ignorance, and what is profitable as useless. A son who hearkens . . . reaches old age, he attains reverence. He speaks likewise to his own children, receiving the instruction of his father. . . . He speaks with his children, they speak to their children."[49] The Hebrew Proverbs echoed Ptahhotep's wisdom, yet wisdom proved feeble against the forces of generational uprising. If the fathers were forbidden to send their children into the fires of Moloch, the children sometimes seemed to seek the flames themselves in obedience to a demon within.

Generational Consciousness and Generational Struggle

Student movements are founded on *generational consciousness* in the same basic sense in which workers' movements are founded on class consciousness. Curiously, generational consciousness was not clearly recognized as a mainspring in social change in modern times until the first stirrings of the Russian student movement. It was in Russia that men became dated by their generations; one was a man of the "forties," the "sixties," the "eighties." Rudin, in Turgenev's novel of that name, for instance, as Kropotkin says, "was a man of the 'forties,' nurtured upon Hegel's philosophy, and developed under the conditions which prevailed under Nicholas I, when there was no possibility whatever for a thinking man to apply his energy, unless he chose to become an obedient functionary of an autocratic, slave-owning state."[50]

Now just as there are conditions which make for the importance of class consciousness in history, so there are conditions, as in Russia during the nineteenth century, which bring generational consciousness to the fore. At other times the consciousness of generation may be comparatively recessive. When Ortega y Gasset came to the conclusion in 1914 "that the generation was the fundamental concept in history," no one else in Europe, he says, was talking about this concept.[51] The categories of economic determinism had so shaped the perceptions of social scientists that they tended to be unaware of generational conflict. Twenty years later, however, socialist professors in Germany, experiencing the Nazi student uprising in their universities, rediscovered the concept of the generation.[52]

Generational consciousness, however, is generally not strong enough to bind students and workers of the same age. Young workers, aware that the students constitute the members of a future upper class, aware of student elitism, always remain suspicious of young redeemers. During the tense agitational years in the 1890s in St. Petersburg, for instance, although working-class and student activists were usually from the same age group, the twenties, they were separated, as Richard Pipes has noted, by deep psychological barriers. The workers, despite their years, were hardened and matured; they had been earning their bread from their early teens. They were hungry for knowledge as well, "but they resented practical advice tendered them by bookish, naïve students. The fact that, come June, the students abandoned the worker circles and left for the summer for their parental homes and country houses, while the workers had to keep on working," separated the two worlds. "Every summer, when, as the workers sarcastically used to say, 'the revolution scattered to the dachas,' there occurred a crisis in the circle movement."[53]

The psychological cleavage between workers and students of the same age has in all societies a simple basis. The young worker has generally been directing his emotional energies for several years into the struggle for existence. Whatever generational resentments he has felt, he has had to divert all his aggressive energies into the struggle for survival. He dismisses the issues of generational conflict, because he can afford no surplus energy with which to brood upon them. Moreover, he stands already as an adolescent the equal to his father, often earning as much or more. He is not irritated by a dependence relationship prolonged unnaturally into manhood. His grievances are definable and real: low wages, long hours, poor working conditions, fear of unemployment, fear of a life always at the bottom. The existence of the young worker determines his consciousness; the class struggle moves him, not generational struggle.

Generational consciousness is a phenomenon far different from class consciousness, with which, however, it can merge in great social crises. How different generational consciousness is can be seen if we try to write a Generational Manifesto on the analogue of the Communist Manifesto:

> The history of all hitherto existing society is the history of generational struggles. Old and young, fathers and sons, aged masters and young apprentices, aged employers and young laborers, old professors and young students have since the primal parricide contended with each other for the mastery of society. Every revolutionary movement has been heralded by an uprising of the young. Young Russia, Young China, Young Turkey, and even Young England. The fight continues uninterrupted, now hidden, now open; thus far it has never ended with a clear triumph of the young, for by the time they have won, they have become middle-aged. Only in recent times, with the rise of great student communities brought about by the new affluence, has it become genuinely possible for the student movement as the vanguard of the young to take decisive power.

Now such a Generational Manifesto would contain considerable truth, yet it would not be likely to win as much assent from common-sense sociology as the Communist Manifesto. For class struggles have a tangible referent; they are struggles over the distribution of income, struggles over wages, surplus value, profits, rent, over the material goods of life. Class consciousness is a response to the fact of class differences; the latter are socially grounded, the creation of society, and therefore with a certain man-madeness about them. The differences of age, on the other hand, are biological. Particular classes can be abolished, as the feudal lords were, yet society continues to exist without them. Generations, however, are part of the permanent nature of social existence. Moreover, class struggles are animated by the desire to abolish economic exploitation. Can one say that generational struggles are motivated by a desire to abolish a generational mode of exploitation?

Quite the contrary. Generational struggles often arise among students living in relative material comfort but who feel themselves driven by an ethical compulsion; the student movements give allegiance to absolute ethical conceptions of justice and right, and judge the older generation and their society in the light of these conceptions. The older generation finds itself removed as the keeper of society's conscience. In this curious way, ethical ideas become an instrument of generational struggle, the means by which the young discredit the old. If we ask for the mechanism in social change by means of which ethical ideas usually enter history, and make themselves felt, that mechanism is usually generational struggle. "Social progress," writes Otto Rank, "is essentially based upon this opposition between the two generations."[54] This is a productive duality in human history; the young, in their aggressive struggle against the old, are imbued with an altruistic devotion for the lowliest in society.

Student movements are a manifestation, furthermore, of the trauma of adolescence, which is, in large measure, a trauma of renunciation; the young man must renounce his bookish dreams and ideals and come to terms with reality. He must in other words accept an alienation of part of his self; he must give up part of himself. Not only must he give up a variety of interests to concentrate on a particular craft and job; he must also surrender the egalitarianism of the youth group, the comradeship, the friendship. The student movement is a protest against the alienation from self which the social system exacts.

Thus, generational consciousness first appears as a historical force with the romantic movement, as in France, for instance, with the "generation of 1830." No one in the sixteenth, seventeenth, or eighteenth centuries would have used such terminology, but now it became common. Generational conflict was not conceived, however, as involving primarily the activism of student movements. Ortega y Gasset, for example, emphasized the role of the "generation of '98" in the Spanish Renaissance, but assigned little importance to student movements. The basic conflict, according to Ortega, was the one between the age group of thirty to forty-five and that of forty-five to sixty; these two groups, he held, comprised "historic reality" at any given moment; the younger men had ideas, whereas the older had power. The youth under thirty, however, was described by Ortega as being in a "formidably egotistical stage of life" and as not exercising a "positive historic role." "He plays at creating things—for example, he entertains himself by publishing youth reviews—he plays at busying himself with problems of the collective type, and at times with such passion and such heroism that anyone ignorant of the secrets of human life would be led to believe that his preoccupation was genuine. But in truth, all this is a pretext for concerning himself with himself. . . ."[55] A Spanish student manifesto of 1930 entitled "The Conquest of the State" did indeed give a liberal duration to its "generation": "Those Spaniards over forty-five cannot participate actively in our works."[56]

This play of students with "collective problems," with their own political organizations and journals, has indeed its egocentricity, yet its movement alters history, overturns governments, and brings death to ministers and students alike. Moreover, one can have generational equilibrium as well as a generational struggle; we must ask, therefore, what accounts for the breakdown of generational equilibrium and the emergence of overt struggle? Age differences in and of themselves do not necessitate the outbreak of generational conflict and the heightening of generational consciousness.

There can be little doubt that the French Revolution and its Napoleonic aftermath were the prime factors in the disruption of the generational equilibrium in Europe. In their wake came not only the German movement of Karl Follen but also the Young Italy of Giuseppe Mazzini. No previous age in European history would have so honored the word "Young"; youth, with its romantic enthusiasm, displaced the old with its felt mission to rule. Secret societies of the young appeared; they brooded on death and suicide. Giuseppe Mazzini became famous throughout all Europe in the first half of the nineteenth century as its pre-eminent youth leader. Mazzini's work and his movement showed indeed all the traits which later student movements more fully exhibited. At the Royal College of Genoa which he attended, the students "were principally preoccupied with the problem of how to overthrow authority." They learned they could do so "if only they were bold enough." They organized secret societies, were thrown into the school "dungeon," and scratched odes to liberty or despair on the walls. "The great thing was to belong to a secret society," with its passwords, gestures, handshakes. A day before he was sixteen years old, in 1820, at the University of Geneva, Giuseppe helped organize a disturbance in the University Church over some trivial question of seating arrangements; he enjoyed his first arrest. The next year, in a more back-to-the-people spirit, he and his fellow-students demonstrated on behalf of the Carbonari revolt in Piedmont. They said of Mazzini that "he was born to be a Carbonaro," a member of the secret society of lumpenproletarian vagabonds and cultured aristocratic intellectuals which seized power for a few months in several Italian towns. Mazzini and his fellow-students read Byron and Rousseau; he wept at the sorrows of Goethe's suicidal hero Werther. But self-destruction was more than romantic fantasy for the young student activists. Mazzini's close friend, the student Jacopo Ruffini, killed himself in disillusionment over the betrayal of comrades in Young Italy; his eldest brother too killed himself as a student at Geneva. Young Italy drew its barrier between the generations; it excluded those over forty from its ranks and avowed that its sense of mission was not only to liberate the Italian people from foreign oppression but to liberate themselves from the old. They took to conspiracy and terrorism. Mazzini told Charles Albert of Sardinia, "Blood calls for blood, and the dagger of the conspirator is never so terrible as when sharpened upon the touchstone of a martyr." Thus the student movement was under compulsion to superimpose the irrational patterns of its generational revolt on the movement for an independent Italian nation. In 1834 Mazzini tried to found Young Europe, an international organization of youth extending on a continental scale the emotional patterns and principles of Young Italy. It failed; no students' international has ever lasted unless it was supported by the funds of guiding elderly politicians, for the student experience is too transient to provide the basis for a continuing international union.[57]

It was during the political reaction after the French Revolution that generational consciousness first became pronounced. "The young generation," writes George Brandes, "had heard in their childhood of the great events of the Revolution, had known the Empire, and were the sons of heroes or of victims." Now they saw the new order, bourgeois, timid, colorless, middle-class. An earlier youth had gone through Europe creating with its armies a new Europe and a new dream of freedom. Now the bourgeoisie ruled, with its omnipotence of economic interests, the pursuit of money. The romantic "school" emerged, and it was indeed a school, for it issued out of the feelings of protest on the part of students against the social environment. The young found themselves speaking a common language "unknown to the rest of their contemporaries." They lived with enthusiasm, and with an awe and reverence for each other, unlike their bourgeois elders. "These young Romanticists," says Brandes, "felt like brothers, like fellow-conspirators; they felt that they were the sharers in a sweet and invigorating secret. . . ." They were generation-conscious; their aim was to overturn tradition, conformity, order, formalism; they wanted passion, life, blood. Marx's famous metaphor of taking Hegel's dialectic which was standing on its head, and turning it right side up, was typical of the left Hegelian graduate students (the Doctors' Club) whom he had known at Berlin in his youth.[58] The chroniclers of the Old Testament had made use of the concept "generation," but theirs was primarily a static usage: "And so-and-so begat so-and-so. . . ." Generational consciousness, in the sense of involving an antagonism, first came into existence when the hopes of the French Revolutionary era were unfulfilled, and those of the Restoration period were de-authoritized in the eyes of the young. Thus arose "the generation of 1830."[59]

Generational consciousness, it should be emphasized, can prove more potent than any bond of ideological unity with elder radicals. The young Marxists of the Japanese Zengakuren, for instance, in 1964 felt no sense of emotional unity with the elder generation in the Socialist party. As Masatake Ono, the head of the latter's Student Policies Department, noted, "The number of students holding membership in the Japan Socialist party is so small that there is no action corps that puts into practice the policies formulated by the JSP Student Policies Department." The party itself in its twenty years' history to 1965 had never taken the initiative in the student movement. The primary reason for this separation of the party from the students was "that the party's 'grownups' hardly understand the importance of the student movement and the social influence it wields."[60] Between the generations, as Bernard Shaw said in *Misalliance*, "there's a wall ten feet thick and ten miles high."

The Stages of Student Movements

The emotional foundation of student movements, with its will to revolution and its quest for revolutionary experience, is more deep-seated than the students' particular ideological commitment. It is the state of mind and feeling which impels a person to the revolutionary experience for its own sake; he must needs feel his energies in grip with the externalized established order. Thus impelled, students turn from doctrine to doctrine, from cause to cause, ideology to ideology, examining each in series for its emotional suitability and strategic advantage. This brings us to consider the stages in the evolution of student movements.

Every student movement begins with what we may call the *circle* stage. What is a circle? It is an informal group of students who are groping for a standpoint, seeking to express the vague revolutionary feeling by which they are moved. They first engage in study, and read the world's contemporary literature of philosophy, politics, and social problems. Their culture is a literary-philosophical one.

Sometimes it has been held that student movements arise out of student welfare organizations. Actually, however, student movements usually arise altogether independently from such welfare societies or student syndicates. In Russian universities, for instance, students generally organized mutual-aid fund societies,[61] and promoted concerts, dancing parties, and refreshment bars, the proceeds of which were used for loans and help to needy students. But the political student movement did not arise out of such mutual-aid societies. Rather it had its gestation in study circles where students would debate the ultimate question, "What's to be done?"[62] Only after the study circles had made the transition from literature to activism did they then try to influence mutual-aid societies, for instance, to provide help for political prisoners, and to link themselves to the political student movement.

Every student movement before it passed into the stage of action went through a circle stage. "*Kruzhkovshchina* [circlehood]," says Allan Wildman, "was moreover an excellent political barometer—it waxed and waned with the revolutionary mood of 'society.' Thus, it flowered in the 1860s and 1870s, waned again during the reaction of the 1880s and mushroomed to life after the famine of 1891. . . ."[63] The "cult of the people" dominated these circles; the tradition of the Narodnaya Volya persisted, and youths in the circles of the late 1880s, youths such as Chernov, Lenin, and Martov, heard legends of the martyrs, and hoped to emulate them.

The circle was the organizational form of youth searching for its "cause" of conflict with the older generation, and deriving sustenance from its co-generationists. It was the secret brotherhood of the would-be revolutionists in whose intimacy they heard "the drama of daring exploits in behalf of justice, of the perils of police agents and provocateurs, of fearless courage and unshakeable adherence to one's convictions before one's accusers." Periodically student movements repeat the circle stage and in it re-enact for their members an introduction to forbidden writers as well as subjects which allegedly are denied entry into the university.

Every student movement tries to suggest to the fledgling activist that it is the keeper of secret ideas, a secret revolutionary culture, which the elder, official culture would suppress. The Russian student circles read surreptitiously the writings of Chernyshevsky, Dobrolyubov, Lavrov, and Marx. In Berkeley, the year before the Free Speech Movement, a middle-aged veteran of many student movements, Harold Draper, conducted a course for his circle, the Independent Socialist Club, which was devoted to the subject of revolutions. The young acolytes listened in a hall of the university Y.M.C.A. to tales of the Russian, German, French, American, and Chinese revolutions, learned the lore of the revolutionary masters, lived vicariously in the late evenings their triumphs and their defeats, and longed to experience their own days which would shake the world. The communistic W. E. B. DuBois Club was conducting Marxist study circles with its mentor, a veteran of the San Francisco sit-ins, who, according to the circles' announcement, would convey the message "that the nerve which had been touched in the power structure is only the beginning of a nervous breakdown."[64] In the aftermath of the Free Speech Movement, a Free University was promoted which, in effect, was a coalition of study circles, Stalinist, Maoist, pacifist, existentialist, sexualist.[65] Its leaflet-catalog announced the offering of forbidden knowledge: "We will pass beyond the permissible truth to confront the conflicts of our society and to develop concepts in place of the myths shattered by realities of Watts and Vietnam." Several such "free universities" came into existence off-campus in the United States during 1965 to 1967.[66]

An issue-searching stage follows on the philosophical quest in the study circles. It is universal in all student movements. Sometimes the passage from study to action can take place when neither the philosophy nor the issue has yet been clarified. This was pre-eminently the case with the Burmese student movement. The student leaders of Burma in the mid-thirties admired revolutionary leaders of all kinds so long as they were revolutionary. They respected Gandhi and Nehru as the spokesmen for Asian revolution, but they reserved their highest admiration for the fascists, Hitler and Mussolini. The moral degeneracy of the Nazis mattered little to them compared to the fact that they were humiliating Britain, whom the Burmese hated. Indeed, a readiness for violence and a contempt for rational democracy have tended to be universal characteristics of student movements. U Nu, later prime minister of his country, said when he was inaugurated as president of the Burmese Students' Union, "I dislike democracy, where much time is wasted in persuading the majority and in trying to get the consent of the majority. Democracy is good in name only. . . . It cannot work in the period of dictatorship of Hitler and Mussolini." As one writer says, it was part of the age's anomaly that "the idealistic youth of Burma . . . looked hopefully toward the rising star of the least idealistic of all men—Hitler—as their own hope for the future."[67] Such, however, has always been the anomaly in the idealism of student movements, the moral ambiguity in their character as generational uprisings.

When the famous Burmese students' strike began in 1936, the student leaders indeed were unable to define what they were fighting for. Confronted by newspapermen, they found themselves at a loss to explain their objectives, or generally to justify their unrest and decision to strike. In some desperation, they announced they were protagonists for modifying the University Act; but since none of them knew anything about the act, one of their number was assigned the task of studying it and finding the necessary objections to it.[68]

When an issue has been found which, given the social and political conditions, is most strategic for and expressive of generational revolt, the student movement emerges as an agency for action. This is the third stage, that of autonomous student action. The demonstration and the strike are the two foremost devices of action, especially the demonstration, which is often the university organization of students in their public manifestation. Autonomous student action then tends to evolve quickly into the fourth or back-to-the-people stage. The Russian revolutionary student movement—the classical case—was periodically returning to the people, first the peasantry, later the proletariat, beginning in the 1860s with Herzen's cry, "V *narod!* to the people!" This populist stage answers that vague emotional need for identification which is felt in advance of any political ideology. The identification with the people assuages the students' own sense of guilt. For theirs is then not simply a generational uprising, a rebellion against the fathers, but a movement on behalf of the people sanctified by the very ethic which the fathers themselves have professed but betrayed. The people, the proletariat, the peasantry, become a kind of projective alternative conscience which supersedes the fathers. Moreover, they are a source of untold physical strength still untapped, and they give to the young student intellectuals a feeling of being close to the physical sources of life. The students by themselves feel too weak to alter the structure of a society ruled by the older generation. Perhaps, in the psychoanalytical metaphor, this identification with a lower class assuages the castrational fears aroused by the students' revolt against their fathers. The Chinese student Tan Shih-hua has described most memorably the transition from the study circle through issue-searching to an identification with the proletariat. He writes:

Professor Li Tao-hsao proposed that we organize a group to study Marxism. A leaflet with a picture of Marx passed through our hands. We looked at his shaggy face and tried to pronounce his name. "Marx," heard for the first time, was difficult for a Chinese ear to catch.

Li Tao-hsao read us the Communist Manifesto. We listened, excited by the statement that revolution was inevitable. But we were a little astonished to learn that coolies, rickshaw men and boatmen were going to be the heroes of this revolution. Li Tao-hsao told us about factories and factory workers. The idea of factories had never entered my head, for Peking, as far as factories were concerned, was as empty as Sian-Shih. No smoke-stacks rose over this city.

"Workers of the World, Unite!"

That's fine, but what to do before they have united?

If only we could invent a single word—a wonderful, sincere word, and shout it across the world! Then people would repeat eagerly and take each other by the hand to march with the light step of friendship all over the globe. But how to find such a word . . . ?

There were twenty in the society. Twice a week without ever skipping a lecture, we listened to Li Tao-hsao. . . .

Soon we were not satisfied with theory alone. We wanted to put theory into practise. If the revolution was to be accomplished by coolies, how would they be able to accomplish it? Surely not by sitting endlessly near their yan-ches and playing dice. . . . They are not even able to sign their own names.

We organized a little circle for the purpose of propaganda; we called it "The Group for Popular Education." . . .

Revolution was in the air. It blew about us like a light wind—a wind like warm wine, that made people feel drunk.[69]

The back-to-the-people motif of student movements arises, in the first place, from the overflowing emotions of generosity in youth. But it always carries with it as well the vector of generational rebellion. How are these motifs of populist identification and generational rebellion, evidently so disparate, in fact allied? The acute Stendhal provides us with the answer. The life of French children in the aristocratic and middle classes during the eighteenth century, he noted, was, despite the vogue of Rousseau's teachings, not a happy one. Stendhal and his sisters, for instance, were reared with strict discipline; among other things, they were forbidden to play with "common children."[70] "My great unhappiness was at not being able to play with other children; my father . . . feared nothing so much as to see me 'going with common children,' for such was the expression of the aristocrats of that time," wrote Stendhal.[71] A wall is thus introduced very early into the social life of children; their first encounter with the distinctions of class and race comes in the form of a mandate from their elders not to play with those with whom they otherwise would but to adopt instead attitudes of suspicion and hostility. This first encounter with bigotry is traumatic for every child; his world is suddenly riven with divisions and demarcations, and he harbors unconscious resentment against the parents who have sundered his childhood world. What a student movement does in its back-to-the-people phase is to abreact and undo this original trauma. It seeks out the "common children" to whom it was denied access. Thereby it does two things: it defies the parental authority in the most direct way by choosing associations which that authority forbade; and, in the second place, it hopefully re-establishes emotional bridges to peoples of other classes and races which were once traumatically destroyed. This is the significance in generational revolt of every movement back to the people, whether they are the peasantry, the proletariat, the colored, or the backward. For a brief moment the student movement seeks to re-create the child's world.

Every student movement then goes through a series of stages which might be called its life cycle; more accurately, it should be stated that there are several alternative life cycles, for in the determination of the latter stages the specific historical circumstances in which the student movement has arisen exercise a controlling influence. What are these alternative historical circumstances and corresponding life cycles?

In the first place, the student movement may experience rejection in its back-to-the-people agitation. This took place among the young Russian students in the 1860s and 1870s. As they were rebuffed by the peasants, sometimes killed and often delivered to the police, their populist creed was confuted in a traumatic trial; the people spurned their identification. Something analogous took place in Japan beginning with the summer of 1960 when many students believed that the Japanese people had failed to respond to their revolutionary appeal. During the next months some three to six thousand Japanese students participated in a back-to-the-village movement, trying by lectures and discussions to explain to the peasants what had inspired them in June 1960—namely, their vision of a new society. It ended for most in utter discouragement.

When a back-to-the-people phase ends in frustration, there tends to ensue a loss of faith in democracy; the emphasis predominantly shifts to elitism. Russian students in the latter seventies and in "the gloomy eighties" accepted the notion that social revolution was to be effected by the small intellectual class itself, by "critical-thinking individuals." Peter Lavrov's *Historical Letters,* with its conception of the intellectual elite as the makers of history, supplanted Bakunin's notion of faith in the revolutionary peasantry.[72] With this belief in the powers of achievement of the "critical-thinking individuals" came the conviction that individual acts of terrorism could succeed in setting basic social forces into motion. The Russian student movement became a terrorist, self-sacrificial movement. Still another response to rejection by the people has been an utterly individualistic nihilism, the feeling that a nothingness pervades the historical dialectic, that man and his works are directionless; one might then as well give oneself over to sensual activities and purely personal aims. In 1961 in Japan a considerable number of recent Zengakuren activists joined themselves in an organization they called "Secto Six." Their newspaper with that name bore a gruesome black border, which framed articles on existentialism, sadism, Marxism, and nihilism. The "Secto Six" students were frankly "beto"—beatnik post-Marxists. "*Bellum omnium contra omnes*" was the slogan on one of their publications, which featured essays entitled "The Constant and Permanent Revolution," "Monologue," "Marquis de Sade," "Existentialism," "Masses and Bread, and Coup d'Etat," all adorned with stark sado-masochist pictures. They gave a nihilistic twist to Trotsky's concept of the permanent revolution; revolution for its own sake was the dominant ideology, with little attempt at a rational political content. Just as Artzibashev's *Sanine* expressed the mood of decadence in Russia during the years after 1905 when high hopes seemed crushed, so the drama and poetry of the Japanese student movement in 1961 dwelled on the theme of decadence.[73] A musical play, *Blues in Blues,* marked the beginning of a decadent phase in the Japanese student movement. Its playbill presented a diagram of the various factions and its theme song took the familiar Marxian metaphor of the locomotive of history but nihilized it:

STUDENT CHORUS: Let's get on the train without a ticket
Let's take the train without a ticket
Shu Shu Poppo Woo Woo
Oh conductor, where is the train going?
CONDUCTOR: Let me see, to a place different from this one,
To a place different from this here.
STUDENTS: What is a train without a ticket?
What is a train without a railroad track?
Let's take the train without a ticket.
The conductors are we ourselves.
What did you say?
Do you want to get off the train?
Then jump right out the window!
Shu Shu Poppo Woo Woo.

Rejection by the people is not, however, a law of history. A student movement may also meet with highly favorable historical circumstances and find itself catapulted to political power. This was the unique experience of the Burmese student movement, whose officers during the prewar years became the cabinet ministers of the postwar era; it was said that Burma after the war was ruled by the student leaders of the class of 1937 of the University of Rangoon.[74] Then again a student movement can be virtually suppressed out of existence by a ruthless regime. The overwhelming number of student political activists at Moscow University in the early twenties were enthusiastic adherents of Leon Trotsky; they were de-activated or destroyed by the police machine.[75]

A student movement can also outlive its days and decline or die. The Japanese student movement is now recessive. The zenith of the June 1960 riots, the overthrow of the Kishi government, was the culminating achievement of the student generation which could still recall the hardships of the war and postwar years. Meanwhile the academic halls have come to know a new generation which has either no recollections or only the most shadowy of the war and immediate postwar years. The new generation has not undergone the traumatic experience of the deauthoritization of the old. From childhood through adolescence it has lived through an era of phenomenal economic growth in Japan. The unemployed university graduate is today an infrequent phenomenon; posts are awaiting the young student as he secures his diploma. So the Japanese student movement languished, its work of generational protest for the nonce done. Such was the fate also of the German student movement of the first half of the nineteenth century. Until 1848, the German student societies, the Burschenschaften, were centers of democratic aspiration, and many German students were moved by radical and socialist ideas. After 1848, the German student societies became nationalistic and anti-democratic; a socialist German student became a rarity after 1871. The ruling generation in Bismarck's Germany, far from being de-authoritized, had its authority reinforced by a succession of victories, diplomatic, military, and economic. Moreover, excellent careers awaited the German student in the professions, civil service, and universities. His erstwhile spirit of rebellion was rapidly shed; the revolutionary student became the bureaucratic apprentice.[76]

Finally, there is the student movement which transforms itself into the leadership of a political party, and sustains itself through a long period of adversity and civil war until it rules the nation. This indeed was the career of the Chinese Communist party.

A democratic socialist culture, it should be observed, is not necessarily exempt from the patterns of generational struggle. When generational revolt arises within a democratic socialist society, it may develop surprising dictatorial, authoritarian tendencies. Israel, for instance, has for many years known the democratic socialist inspiration of its collective settlements, the kibbutzim, and the moderate voluntaristic socialism of the trade union federation, Histadruth. Yet, in 1963, a study of a random sample of seven hundred eighteen-year-olds showed that "a considerable majority of our 18-year-olds would accept a dictatorial regime in Israel."[77] What was striking was that the educated student sector had a disproportionately high anti-liberal, anti-democratic bias. Of the close to 58 per cent of the country's youth who pronounced themselves in favor of a dictatorial system, more than half, 53.4 per cent, were secondary and other post-elementary school graduates. Despite their education, there were "many indications that their political maturity is not correspondingly developed." Even on the kibbutzim, 45.57 per cent of the youth placed themselves on the side of dictatorship. Curiously, the youth of the poorer, more economically deprived, immigrant settlements were less dictator-minded than either the kibbutz, private farming, or urban youth. Of the eighteen-year-olds on immigrant settlements, 44.1 per cent were dictator-oriented, while in the old established moshavim the percentage was higher at 51 per cent. As many as 53 per cent of youth movement members were dictator-minded, and 55 per cent of the post-elementary school graduates. One observer noted that the dictatorial propensity seemed to hold "true not only of those who have immigrated within the last years from Islamic countries with politically unstable regimes, but also for those born in the country, including those educated in kibbutzim and youth movements." The existing political parties, despite their democratic platforms, it was said, "have no ideas or aims to offer which appeal to the growing generation."[78] The youth held, by way of justification, that "party life itself is not democratic." But if the parties of the fathers were becoming oligarchical, curiously the sons were drawn, not to democracy, but to the greater anti-democracy of dictatorship. The generation in revolt moved to the extreme in rejecting the fathers' ideology.

When leadership in student movements becomes an important avenue to political leadership and rule, the successor generation of students must search for an issue which it can use to dislodge and de-authoritize the elder generation. This makes for an inherent anti-democratic tendency in the political system. Such was the experience of U Nu, Prime Minister of Burma, who had been the leader of the Burmese students in the thirties. The student movement of twenty years later was largely responsible for discrediting his efforts at liberal democratic government and bringing the army to power.

In 1953, for instance, a student strike at the University of Rangoon disrupted the entire academic year. What were the issues? Prime Minister Nu wished to raise the standard of university education in Burma; he found there were only 118 school days in the academic year and far too many holidays, and he wanted to increase the academic days to at least 236; the country needed more trained people quickly; the people's money was being wasted in short academic years. The students, even the moderate ones, were nevertheless swept into a strike. Their leaders sensed that "they had hit upon an issue that appealed to the whole student body." When the university tried to shorten the between-terms vacation to two weeks, the move was met by a strike of almost all the several thousand students. The generational lines were sharply drawn: "The approach of an instructor would be the embarrassing signal for the students to break up and hurry away." The strike was a generational festival; picketing students "camped on the front steps, noisily singing songs, playing Burmese instruments, and dancing. Oh, it was a great lark—and clever strategy."[79]

The Student Union and strike were led by the Communist faction which had seized control of the organization through violence in contravention of its election procedures. Now they instigated violence throughout the university as well. To the Communist party all this was a godsend; having proved themselves unable to gain support among the workers and peasants, they looked to the studentry as their most available ally. Finally the army intervened and entered the university grounds. The students, barricaded in their hostels, fought off firemen and policemen; shots were fired and one heard "the frightening roars of an infuriated mob"; the students cheered the burning of a fire engine. Thus the strike ended. The Prime Minister announced that arrested students could take their case to the Supreme Court. Slowly students returned to classes "with expressions of guilt on their faces." The University of Rangoon went back to its work. It emerged even less a community of scholars and more a proving ground for generational aggression. University standards could scarcely be raised after this confrontation with the anti-intellectual syndicalism of the students. When the university tried to alter the pure examination system in order to give weight in the final grade to class work, it was compelled by student resistance to give up. In Burma, noted a visiting American professor, the "threats to a liberal education come from below. Students attempt to dictate to teachers fully as the administration may."[80] Indeed, we may affirm the generalization: wherever student movements have flourished, academic freedom has consequently declined. At the University of Rangoon, "a vogue of contempt for authority" spread and "eventually brought disrepute on the whole University body"; the leniency of the administration never seemed to appease the generational unrest. Thus the tradition of student participation in politics contributed to the undoing of Burmese democracy. The student movements became an instrumentality for a privilege-seeking elite of young intellectuals.

Proportion of Student Movements to the Studentry

When we speak of a student movement, we are almost always speaking of a relatively small elite which at critical times (especially under the provocation of a police assault) can determine the actions of the student body almost as a whole.[81] It is unlike, however, the leadership of a trade union, which is in continuous relationship with its members over many everyday issues of livelihood, and which has a continuing mandate to serve as a general staff, if necessary, for the organization of strikes and other defensive actions. The student leadership has no such mandate. At times the leaders are coextensive with the movement; at other, more critical times, the movement activates the overwhelming majority of students. The Zengakuren in Japan, for instance, was for a few short years an example of a continuous movement with a large affiliated membership, but this was made possible because at the height of its growing period an estimated one hundred students on Zengakuren's staff of "career workers" were paid salaries by the Communist party.[82] The number of Zengakuren activists, however, as the Japanese Ministry of Education in a white paper on the students published in 1952 emphasized, was remarkably small. Of course, 1952 was the period of the Red Purge, when students supporting Zengakuren were incurring especial penalties in the way of future employment. Nevertheless, the ministry's statistics had a genuine significance as a measure of the number of activists. In the Tokyo area, during all the student demonstrations from April 28 to June 17, including that of May Day, the number of participating students was relatively constant, about 2,500, who constituted 1.7 per cent of the 160,000 college and university students in the Tokyo environs; and Tokyo, it should be remembered, has generally led in the student movement. The vice-president of the youth section of the Communist party, Shunji Hirolani, gave a modest estimate of the proportions of student activism in the universities. "Roughly speaking," he said, "10 to 20 per cent of all students have the possibility of taking sides with independence, democracy and peace intentionally, another 10 to 20 per cent are satisfied with the status quo, while 60 per cent are fence-sitters. . . . We have hitherto tended to rely on only advanced elements. . . ."[83]

The activist in the student movement has been recognized as a unique type since the first recorded sociological analysis of student movements. In 1903, a revolutionary student newspaper, *Student,* which ran for three issues (a fair lifetime for an unofficial student journal), classified the studentry in terms which Lenin found apt. *Student* distinguished between four major groups among the Russian students:

1) the indifferent crowd—"persons completely indifferent to the student movement";
2) the "academics"—those who favor student movements of an exclusively academic type;
3) "opponents of student movements in general—nationalists, anti-Semites, etc.";
4) the "politically-minded"—those who believe in fighting for the overthrow of Tsarist despotism.[84]

The "indifferent students," even in the tense days of 1903, were recognized as composing the overwhelming majority, the "crowd" of the student body. The "academics" are those whom we have described as supporting student syndicalism, student welfare societies; they lack especially the populist identification and the drive to social reconstruction. The opponents of student movements are those who have not shared in the experience of the de-authoritization of the older generation; they have remained traditionalists. The "politically-minded" are the activists of the student movement. Among the student activists, there will be a spectrum of factions corresponding to the varieties of emerging revolutionary tendencies. *Student* in 1903 distinguished between "two antithetical elements—those belonging to the purely bourgeois political opposition with a revolutionary tendency and those who belong to the newly emerged socialistically-minded revolutionary intellectual proletariat." Lenin, always intent on the nascent fission of antagonisms, broke this last socialist group into two further parts, Socialist-Revolutionary and Social-Democratic students; he thus found "among the present-day students *six* political groups: reactionaries, indifferents, academics, liberals, Socialist-Revolutionaries, and Social-Democrats."

Here then was a small minority of student activists who composed the political student movement. The number of university students itself in Russia as a whole was astonishingly small relative to the total population. As late as 1880, there were only 8,193 students in all the Russian universities. The back-to-the-people movement in the early seventies was the work of between one to two thousand students.[85] It does not require a system of mass higher education to produce a student movement. Moscow University, a center of student unrest, never burgeoned in numbers during the nineteenth century. In 1825 at the end of the reign of Alexander I, it had 875 students. Under Nicholas I, the number declined to 438 in 1836, as the government pursued a policy of hostility to the intelligentsia; then it rose again in a decade to 1,251, but fell to 926 in 1848, the year of revolution. "In 1870, the middle of the reign of Alexander II, there were about 1,500 students; and at the end of the century, about 3,500."[86] A few hundred students at Moscow University, in an absolutist, backward, and largely illiterate society, became the historical spokesmen of political and economic liberation.

Similarly, on the eve of the May Fourth Movement in China, the student activists and "politically-minded" likewise constituted only about a fifth of the student body. At that time, writes Chow Tse-tsung, "college students in Peking might be classified, according to their character, into three categories: the remnant of the prodigals who still lived more or less luxurious and corrupt lives, the diligent students who devoted their attention more to study than to current affairs, and the third group who were most affected by the new ideas. This third group probably constituted only 20% of the student body, but it was the most active."[87]

Are the Student Movements the "Best Barometer" of Society?

Student movements have often been called the "best barometer" of society.[88] Are they always, however, the measure of the directional pressure of social movements? The Russian revolutionary movement during its formative era was indeed virtually a student movement. "For at least three decades" after 1861, writes Avrahm Yarmolinsky, "the revolutionary movement was to be a youth movement, manned chiefly by undergraduates."[89] After the Revolution of 1905, however, the student movement gradually declined as an indicator of the underlying direction of social unrest. Lenin's attitude toward the student movement, for instance, went through a radical change within a few years. In 1903, he characterized the students in words of tribute: "They are the most responsive section of the intelligentsia, and the intelligentsia are so called because they most consciously, most resolutely, and most accurately reflect and express the development of class interests and political groupings in society as a whole."[90] He had evidently welcomed the assassination of the Minister of Public Education in 1901 by the student Karpovich, saying that it "cleared the way for a 'new course' in the government's policy toward the universities"; the subsequent "alternating brutal repression with Judas kisses," Lenin added, "is doing its work and revolutionizing the mass of students." He called on society not to wait calmly "for the inevitable tragic events by which every student movement has been attended hitherto." He appealed with moving eloquence to the fathers not to desert their sons: "Why do we not hear the voice of the 'fathers,' when the children have unequivocally declared their intention to offer up new sacrifices on the altar of Russian freedom? . . . After all, the higher educational institutions are not attended by the proletarians' sons and brothers, and yet the workers in Kiev, Kharkov, and Ekaterinoslav have already openly declared their sympathy with the protesters. . . ."[91]

As time went on, however, Lenin came gradually to believe that a "tragic" ending was inherent in the nature of student movements, that their defeat was not due to the fathers deserting their sons but rather to the fact that the student sons were ultimately too bound to their fathers. Even when he was most enthusiastically for the student movement, Lenin objected to any analysis which placed emphasis on the "unselfishness and purity of aims" of the student consciousness; this constituted, he said, an idealistic interpretation. From the materialistic standpoint, he wrote in 1903, "the students cannot be an exception to society as a whole, however unselfish, pure, idealistic, etc., they may be. . . ."[92] Basically, moreover, Lenin felt there was an intrinsic incompatibility between the psychology of a student movement and the needs of a revolutionary party.

The great schism between the Bolsheviks and Mensheviks revolved in large part around the question of the revolutionary character of the student movement. Lenin had become disenchanted with the "circle-spirit" of the student movement, its recurrent searching into fundamental problems, its ceaseless questioning. He had made his ultimate commitment when his own student circle merged itself with the Social Democratic party; now he was tired of each student generation's renewal of the quest. He ridiculed the "loose dressing gown and slippers of the Oblomov circle domesticity." Now that he had "become a member of a party," he said, he would tolerate no longer "all the freaks and whims of the old circles." He was a Jacobin of the Social Democratic movement; it was the Girondists, the opportunists, who were concerned with "professors and high school students."[93] He recalled his own experience with typical Social Democratic student circles during the period 1894–1901, their discussions, their groping efforts to establish contact with workers, their first actions which usually ended "in immediate and complete defeat." It had been a necessary stage, but he wanted no re-enactment of it; he recalled "the short-livedness of the majority of the Russian circles (and only those who have experienced this can have any exact idea of it)."[94]

Lenin at this point wanted a disciplined party, officered by a few intellectuals but with an obedient infantry. The free-thinking and free-choosing student circles, each with its variant of political philosophy, were a stage to be surmounted. The student intellectuals had brought the socialist idea to the workers, but according to Lenin that was to be their last act as free intellectuals. From then on a discipline was to be required of which student movements were intrinsically incapable. After the split with the Mensheviks, Lenin's interest in the student movement diminished, almost to the vanishing point.

With the revolution of 1905, Lenin felt definitely that the revolutionary initiative had passed from the students to the workers. The wave of mass strikes, he said, had roused the broad masses of peasants. "The word 'striker' acquired an entirely new meaning among the peasants: it signified a rebel, a revolutionary, a term previously expressed by the word 'student.' As, however, the 'student' belonged to the middle class, to the 'learned,' to the 'gentry,' he was alien to the people. On the other hand, a 'striker' was of the people. . . ."[95] By 1908, Lenin no longer professed to see in the student movement the replica of the class struggle in the nonstudent world. The wide-spread students' strike of 1908, which erupted in St. Petersburg and spread to Moscow and Kharkov, aroused only a tepid response in Lenin. The students, in his view, were essentially linked to the liberal bourgeoisie. "Even the most active elements among the students stubbornly adhere to pure academism and are still singing the Cadet-Octobrist song. . . . Thousands and millions of threads bind the student youth to the middle and lower bourgeoisie, to the small officials, to certain groups of peasants, clergy, etc.," he said. "The mass of the youth stands closest to the democratic bourgeoisie in Russia," and the "whips" of the Black Hundred Minister of Education had not availed "to convert the present-day 'academics' into 'politicians.' "[96] The student movement, in other words, was tending to become transformed into a liberal student syndicate concerned with student welfare and such intramural questions as academic freedom.

A break between the Bolsheviks and the intellectuals was becoming manifest even in the midst of 1905 when the Teachers' Congress, for instance, excluded the Bolsheviks. The cleavage grew with the passage of years. In April 1917, recalled Krupskaya, Lenin's wife, senior high school students, unlike the working-class boys, would come in crowds to shout abuse at the Bolsheviks. Their teachers "were completely under the influence of the Socialist-Revolutionaries."[97] The students, as Trotsky recorded, were hostile to the Bolshevik revolution. They had traversed a long ideological journey since 1900: "The younger generation, the sons, the students? They were almost all hostile to the October revolution. But a majority of them too stand aside. They stood with their fathers awaiting the outcome of the battle. A number of them afterward joined the officers and junkers—already largely recruited from among the students."[98]

A reconciliation between fathers and sons was indeed taking place between 1905 and 1917. Lenin, the perpetual harsh critic of the intellectuals, seemed an alien voice. The student movement, evolving in accordance with its own motivations, was a poor barometer in 1917 for the Soviet society which would evolve over the next fifty years. By 1917 the student movement had lost its historic opportunity to promote a rational social evolution in Russia. Its idealism had for several decades been so intermixed with the apotheosis of destruction, its political consciousness had been for so long dominated by generational struggle, that it was emotionally disarmed when the Bolshevik party in October 1917 put into practice what the students so long had preached.

The import of student movements is best perceived through a study of the classical cases of their impact on modern history. Let us turn to a closer scrutiny, to begin with, of two student movements we have mentioned, the German one of 1817 and the Bosnian one of 1914. A century's span separated them, from the first years of post-Napoleonic Europe to Sarajevo and the First World War of 1914, Europe's golden century of peace. One opened the century, the other closed it. What then was the impact of the student movements on this period? How did a self-destructive drive commingle with the students' idealism to impose on historical evolution an irrational dialectic?

NOTES

1. Walter Weyl, *Tired Radicals* (New York, 1921), p. 11.

2. Peter Kropotkin, *Memoirs of a Revolutionist* (Boston, 1899), pp. 301–302.

3. V. I. Orlov, *Studencheskoe Dvizhenie Moskovskogo Universiteta v XIX Stolyetii* (The Student Movement of Moscow University during the Nineteenth Century; Moscow, 1934), p. 175.

4. Tom Kahn, *Unfinished Revolution* (New York, 1960), pp. 11–12.

5. Peter Kropotkin, *Ideals and Realities in Russian Literature* (New York, 1905), pp. 105–106.

6. Avrahm Yarmolinsky, *Turgenev: The Man, His Art, and His Age* (Collier Books edn.; New York, 1961), pp. 173–174.

7. The merging of relatively independent waves, and their consequences for economic evolution, provides a model for the study of social evolution. The economic waves which are superimposed on each other are, however, homogeneous in character. See Joseph A. Schumpeter, *Business Cycles: A Theoretical, Historical, and Statistical Analysis of the Capitalist Process* (New York, 1939), I, 161–165.

8. See Eric Hoffer, *The Temper of Our Time* (New York, 1967), p. 6: "The twentieth century in particular has seen juvenilization on an almost global scale."

9. Whether Britain's generational equilibrium will now be seriously disrupted is an open question. See Jim Daly, "Labour's Lost Students," *Socialist Commentary*, July 1963, pp. 8–10. Also, on the political moderation of Britain's students, see Ferdynand Zweig, *The Student in the Age of Anxiety: A Survey of Oxford and Manchester Students* (London, 1963), pp. 42–46, 116–119, 198–199.

10. Michael T. Florinsky, *Russia: A*

History and an Interpretation (New York, 1953), II, 1164.

11. David Kamen, "The New Left—The New Fraternity," *The Daily Californian*, August 10, 1966, p. 10.

12. V. Gordon Childe, "Social Worlds of Knowledge," *Hobhouse Memorial Lectures, 1941–1950* (London, 1952), p. 21.

13. *An Arab Philosophy of History: Selections from the Prolegomena of Ibn Khaldun*, tr. Charles Issawi (London, 1950), pp. 116–117.

14. Rev. W. Scarborough, *A Collection of Chinese Proverbs*, rev. Rev. C. Wilfred Allan (Shanghai, 1926), pp. 74–75.

15. See Leopold H. Haimson, *The Russian Marxists and the Origins of Bolshevism* (Cambridge, Mass., 1955), pp. 149–150.

16. J. V. Stalin, "The Russian Social-Democratic Party and Its Immediate Tasks" (1901), tr. from the Georgian, in J. V. Stalin, *Works* (Moscow, 1952), I, 22.

17. World University Service, *Economic Factors Affecting Access to the University* (Geneva, 1961), pp. 176–177.

18. *Ibid.*, p. 112.

19. *Ibid.*, p. 53.

20. *Ibid.*, p. 69.

21. *Ibid.*, p. 120.

22. *Ibid.*, pp. 102a, 86.

23. *Ibid.*, p. 107.

24. *Ibid.*, pp. 17, 58, 34, 36, 150, 80. A survey by the Canadian Union of Students, published in 1966, found that 48 per cent of the students gave their father's occupation as professional, managerial, or proprietory, and that Canadian students by and large "bear the characteristics of the middle and upper classes of Canadian society." See *University Affairs*, VII, No. 4 (April 1966), 10.

25. Victor Hugo, *Les Misérables*, Pt. III, Bk. IV, Ch. 1 (Boston, 1887), pp. 113–127.

26. R. R. Palmer, *Twelve Who Ruled: The Committee of Public Safety during the Terror* (Princeton, 1941), p. 10.

27. J. B. Morton, *Saint-Just* (New York, 1939), pp. 14–15.

28. *Ibid.*, p. 202.

29. See p. 201 of this book.

30. Lewis S. Feuer, *The Scientific Intellectual* (New York, 1963), p. ix.

31. Toshio Kamba, *Saigo No Bisho* (Last Smile; Tokyo, 1960). All passages quoted from this book are adapted from a manuscript translation kindly given to me by the author.

32. Kamba, *op. cit.*, p. 12.

33. V. I. Lenin, "The Tasks of Revolutionary Youth" (1903), in V. I. Lenin, *Collected Works*, VII, tr. Abraham Fineberg and Naomi Jochel (Moscow, 1961), 53.

34. See Thomas L. Hodgkin, "The Relevance of 'Western' Ideas for the New African States," in J. Roland Pennock (ed.), *Self-Government in Modernizing Nations* (Englewood Cliffs, N.J., 1964), pp. 56–57.

35. Thorstein Veblen, *Imperial Germany and the Industrial Revolution* (rev. edn.; New York, 1939), p. 86.

36. Alexander Herzen, *My Past and Thoughts: The Memoirs of Alexander Herzen*, tr. Constance Garnett (London, 1924), II, 141.

37. Karl Marx, *Letters to Dr. Kugelmann* (New York, 1934), p. 77.

38. Herzen, *op. cit.*, II, 142.

39. Saburo Ota and Rikutaro Fukuda (of Japan P.E.N. Club), *Footprints of Foreign Literature in Japan* (Tokyo, 1957), pp. 7–8. Also see Futabatei Shimei, *Ukigumo: Japan's First Modern Novel*, tr. M. G. Ryan (New York, 1967), pp. 99–102, 143–144.

40. Sigmund Neumann, "The Conflict of Generations in Contemporary Europe," *Vital Speeches of the Day*, V (1939), 623–628.

41. Donald W. Klein, "The 'Next Generation' of Chinese Communist Leaders," *China Quarterly*, No. 12 (October–December 1962), p. 73.

42. On Pyotr Tkachev, see Michael Karpovich, "A Forerunner of Lenin: P. N. Tkachev," *The Review of Politics*, VI (1944), 336–350; Dinko Tomasic, *The Impact of Russian Culture on Soviet Communism* (Glencoe, Ill., 1953), p. 267; Avrahm Yarmolinsky, *Road to Revolution: A Century of Russian Radicalism* (New York, 1959), p. 146; Max Nomad, *Apostles of Revolution* (New York, 1961), p. 218. Albert L. Weeks, *The First Bolshevik: A Political Biography of Peter Tkachev* (New York, 1968), p. 64. Mikhailovsky's statement is cited in V. I. Lenin, *What Is to be Done?* (New York, 1932), p. 166.

43. Neumann, *op. cit.*, p. 625.

44. Leaflet, the Iranian Students' Association of Northern California, December 1963.

45. Also see *Plato's Epistles,* tr. Glenn R. Morrow (Indianapolis, 1962), p. 220; *Plato's Laws,* XI, 929c.
46. Aristotle, *Rhetoric,* tr. W. Rhys Roberts (New York, 1954), pp. 123–124.
47. Aristotle, *A Treatise on Government,* tr. William Ellis (New York, 1928), p. 154.
48. Aristotle, *Rhetoric,* pp. 85, 139.
49. James Henry Breasted, *The Dawn of Conscience* (New York, 1933), pp. 129–130.
50. Kropotkin, *Ideals and Realities in Russian Literature,* p. 97.
51. José Ortega y Gasset, *Man and Crisis,* tr. Mildred Adams (New York, 1958), p. 51.
52. Karl Mannheim, "The Problem of Generations," in *Essays on the Sociology of Knowledge* (London, 1952), pp. 276–320.
53. Richard Pipes, *Social Democracy and the St. Petersburg Labor Movement, 1885–1897* (Cambridge, Mass., 1963), p. 11.
54. Otto Rank, *The Myth of the Birth of the Hero and Other Writings,* tr. F. Robbins and Smith Ely Jelliffe, ed. Philip Freund (New York, 1964), p. 68.
55. Ortega y Gasset, *Man and Crisis,* pp. 51, 56–57. See also his *The Modern Theme,* tr. James Cleugh (New York, 1933), pp. 14–17; Helene Weyl, "José Ortega y Gasset," *University of Toronto Quarterly* (July 1937), p. 470.
56. The Federación Universitaria Española, from its inception in January 1927, contrasted the pessimists of '98 with the new spirit of youth. A student strike in Madrid, on behalf of their expelled leader Sbert, was a principal factor in the overthrow of the dictatorship of Primo de Rivera in 1930. See David Jato, *Rebelión de los Estudiantes* (Madrid, 1953), Ch. 1.
57. See E. E. Y. Hales, *Mazzini and the Secret Societies: The Making of a Myth* (London, 1956), pp. 29, 40, 42, 84, 64, 62.
58. Karl Marx, *Capital: A Critique of Political Economy,* tr. S. Moore and E. Aveling (Chicago, 1906), p. 25.
59. George Brandes, *Main Currents in Nineteenth Century Literature,* V, *The Romantic School in France* (New York, 1906), 2–15.
60. Mitsuo Nakamura, "Renovationist Parties and the Student Movement," *Keizai Hyoron,* December 1964, tr. in *Summaries of Selected Japanese Magazines* (American Embassy, Tokyo, March 15, 1965), p. 15.
61. See, for instance, A. Terpigorev, *Reminiscences of a Mining Engineer,* tr. W. Chumak (Moscow, 1959), p. 32.
62. See Allan K. Wildman, "The Russian Intelligentsia of the 1890s," *American Slavic and East European Review,* XIX (1960), 158.
63. *Ibid.,* p. 158.
64. Leaflet, W. E. B. DuBois Clubs of America, Berkeley Branch, September 27, 1964.
65. Leaflet, Free University of Berkeley, First Session, 1966.
66. Ralph Keyes, "The Free Universities," *The Nation,* CCV (October 2, 1967), 294–299. The same phenomenon has appeared in West Germany at Berlin where a "critical university" was founded by students who hoped it would become a "counter-university," "a school for practical revolution," "a cadre school for social revolutionaries." See "Berlin Leftists Set Up a School," *The New York Times,* November 2, 1967.
67. Richard Butwell, *U Nu of Burma* (Stanford, Calif., 1963), p. 19; U Nu, *The People Win Through* (New York, 1957), pp. 18–19.
68. Butwell, *op. cit.,* p. 22.
69. Tan Shih-hua, *A Chinese Testament: The Autobiography of Tan Shih-hua,* as told to S. Tretiakov (New York, 1934), pp. 251–254.
70. Matthew Josephson, *Stendhal: or The Pursuit of Happiness* (New York, 1946), p. 12.
71. Stendhal (Henri Beyle), *The Life of Henri Brulard,* tr. C. A. Phillips (New York, 1955), p. 73.
72. See Paul Milyoukov, *Russia and Its Crisis* (Chicago, 1905), pp. 398 ff.
73. Herbert Passin, "The Sources of Protest in Japan," *American Political Science Review,* LVI (1962), 400–401. A Western observer in 1963 noted, "Many former Zengakuren students have retreated into a Japanese version of 'Beatnikism.' . . ." See Philip Altbach, "Japanese Students and Japanese Politics," *United Asia,* XV (1963), 486.
74. Virginia Thompson and Richard Adloff, *The Left Wing in Southeast Asia* (New York, 1950), pp. 81, 241–262; Albert Ravenholt, "Burma's New Deal from the Army—Is It a Pattern for Asia?" *American Universities Field Staff Reports*

Service, Southeast Asia Series, VII, No. 12, 10–11.

75. In 1923, "of twenty-five university Communist cells, only one had a non-Trotskyist secretary." See Raphael R. Abramovitch, *The Soviet Revolution 1917–1939* (New York, 1962), p. 285; Edward Hallett Carr, *A History of Soviet Russia: The Interregnum, 1923–1924* (New York, 1954), pp. 325–327.

76. An astute observer wrote, "The universities ceased to be political centres and became once more, what they always should have been, mere seats of learning. When I came to Germany for the first time, in 1861, the change had been substantially effected. . . . The manners and character of the students have, beyond all question, undergone a marked change. The student of the present day is not the student of 1830 or 1840 or even 1850. . . . He feels more and more that he is but one and not the most important link in the great political nexus. He is soberer, toned down, disposed to look upon his university membership as a means of social and intellectual enjoyment rather than a stronghold for offense and defense. . . . I was impressed with the metamorphosis on revisiting Germany in 1872–1873. . . . I never had occasion to note any political demonstrations on the part of students. . . . The only topic of general interest was the relations of Germany to the rest of Europe, and here national pride and the flush of success made them as one man." James Morgan Hart, *German Universities: A Narrative of Personal Experience* (New York, 1878), pp. 165–167. Also see Granville Stanley Hall, *Aspects of German Culture* (Boston, 1881), pp. 116–117; Edward Yarnell Hartshorne, *The German Universities and National Socialism* (Cambridge, 1937), pp. 42–46, 54–55. "The freedom-loving spirit remained alive up to the era of Bismarck. Only then occurred the change which made the majority of German professors servile and willing tools of an imperialistic policy, whereas most of the students became uncritical jingoes bent only upon their own careers." W. Sternfeld, "German Students and their Professors," in Hans J. Redfisch (ed.), *In Tyrannos: Four Centuries of Struggle Against Tyranny in Germany* (London, 1944), p. 161.

77. "Israeli Youth and Dictatorship," *New Outlook: Middle East Monthly*, VII, No. 1 (January 1964), 58.

78. *Ibid.*, p. 59. The research on the Israeli youth was done by the Department of Political Science of the Hebrew University.

79. George Mannello, Jr., "Student Strike at an Asian University: A Case History," *AAUP Bulletin*, XLIII, No. 2 (1957), 255–256.

80. *Ibid.*, pp. 249–251.

81. Thus, at the University of Padua until the end of 1847, two types of students were in bitter antagonism, the "Pedrocchini," the intellectuals at the cafes, as against the "gradassi," the ruder, more masculine students. "But in January 1848, all these feuds were laid aside by universal consent" when Italian students of Pavia were slain by the Austrian soldiery. See George Macaulay Trevelyan, *Manin and the Venetian Revolution of 1848* (London, 1923), pp. 22, 24, 63, 73, 147–148.

82. Lawrence H. Battistini, *The Postwar Student Struggle in Japan* (Tokyo, 1956), p. 33.

83. Scott C. Flanagan, *Zengakuren and the Postwar Japanese Student Movement*, M.A. Thesis, Berkeley Library Archives, 1963, p. 130; Nakamura, *op. cit.*, p. 14.

84. V. I. Lenin, "The Tasks of Revolutionary Youth," *Collected Works*, VII, 44.

85. Avrahm Yarmolinsky, *Road to Revolution*, p. 105; Milyoukov, *op. cit.*, p. 407. A report by the Russian Ministry of the Interior published in 1890 on 1,083 revolutionists shows that there were more than six times as many students as workers involved, and more than fifty times as many as peasants. See Ivan Avakumovic, "A Statistical Approach to the Revolutionary Movement in Russia, 1878–1887," *American Slavic and East European Review*, XVIII (1959), 182–186.

86. Cyril Bryner, "Moscow University 1755–1955," *Russian Review*, XIV (1955), 210.

87. Chow Tse-tsung, *The May Fourth Movement: Intellectual Revolution in Modern China* (Cambridge, Mass., 1960), pp. 96–97.

88. The origin of the expression has been traced to N. I. Pirogov. See J. M. Meijer, *Knowledge and Revolution: The Russian Colony in Zuerich, 1870–1873* (Assen, the Netherlands, 1955), pp. 16, 170; also Nicholas Hans, *The Russian*

Tradition in Education (London, 1963), p. 60.

89. Yarmolinsky, *Road to Revolution*, p. 105.

90. Lenin, "The Tasks of Revolutionary Youth," *Collected Works*, VII, 45.

91. Lenin, "Signs of Bankruptcy," *Iskra*, February 15, 1902, in *Collected Works*, VI, ed. Clemens Dutt and Julius Katzer (Moscow, 1961), 79–81.

92. Lenin, "The Tasks of Revolutionary Youth," *Collected Works*, VII, 53.

93. Lenin, *One Step Forward, Two Steps Back*, 1904 (Moscow, 1947), pp. 92, 93, 81.

94. Lenin, *What Is to be Done?* pp. 95, 36.

95. Lenin, "Lecture on the 1905 Revolution," January 22, 1917, in Lenin, *The Revolution of 1905* (New York, 1934), p. 48.

96. Lenin, "The Student Movement and the Present Political Situation," October 1908, reprinted in Lenin, *The Young Generation* (New York, 1940), pp. 14, 19, 20.

97. N. K. Krupskaya, *Reminiscences of Lenin*, tr. Bernard Isaacs (Moscow, 1959), pp. 352, 151; Oliver H. Radkey, *The Agrarian Foes of Bolshevism* (New York, 1958), p. 61.

98. Leon Trotsky, *The History of the Russian Revolution*, tr. Max Eastman (New York, 1933), III, 191.

TWO Terrorism and Suicidalism in the German Student Movement

The student movement came into being in Germany during the years after the War of Liberation against Napoleon. It was born out of a crisis of de-authoritization and disenchantment with the older. As Heinrich von Treitschke wrote, "The young men felt as if they had been betrayed and sold to the enemy when the prose of the quiet labors of peace resumed its sway. How were they to understand the nature of the economic cares which tortured the minds of their elders?"[1] The War of Liberation had been marked by an outburst of enthusiasm in the universities. Frederick William III, king of Prussia, aroused the students with the promise that a liberated Prussia would know the just reward of a responsible, representative government. The philosopher Fichte delivered his eloquent "Addresses to the German Nation" at the Academy of Berlin in the winter of 1807–1808.[2] Heard by only small audiences in the occupied city, the lectures were recognized later as having caught the spirit of a student generation soon to emerge. Then, in the aftermath of the war, the promise of representative government which Frederick III had made was violated. The students' unrest grew. Under the absolutist conditions which prevailed, they took the political initiative. As Carl Schurz later wrote, the students were "among the first in line to raise the cry for the fulfillment of the pledge given by the princes."[3] The German studentry demonstrated their generational solidarity, their unity as an intellectual elite, and their mission to reform the nation at a great festival on the Wartburg on October 9, 1817. This was the first major conclave of students in modern history.

The Wartburg Festival was a demonstration of the newly organized

Burschenschaft of the German students. Every student movement seeks to found a new organizational form which will express its new revolutionary emotions. Such students' protest organizations customarily do not outlast more than the three or four years of a student generation; they do not have the longevity of trade unions. If they do last longer, they are invariably transformed from protest into social organizations. Thus, at Jena on June 12, 1815, a new Burschenschaft had been founded which sought "to unite all the students in a single association" and to supersede divisive territorial, tradition-bound, aristocratic students' corps. Its whole aim was totalitarian, for it wished to impose its disciplne upon all students and to abolish all other students' associations. The new Burschenschaft regarded the old students' corps and their dueling antics in much the same way as American activists in the Berkeley Student Movement regarded the social doings of the aristocratic playboy fraternities on the hill. The seed from Jena spread to fourteen other universities, where Burschenschaften on the Jena model were founded. Finally, in October 1818, on the first anniversary of the memorable Wartburg Festival, delegates convened to organize the Allgemeine Deutsche Burschenschaft ("Universal German Students' Association").

The Burschenschaft incorporated a variety of motifs common to all students, plus a few which reflected the peculiar outlook of a German elite. Like all student movements, it had a strong latent aim for political power, for ruling the nation. It combined the themes of juvenocracy and intelligarchy into the notion of its own historic mission. As Treitschke wrote:

> The conceit of the Burschen now became intolerable. With important mien, the executive and the members of the committee strode every afternoon up and down the market place [in Jena], deliberating in measured conversation the weal of the fatherland and of the universities; they regarded themselves as lords of this small academic realm, all the more because most of the professors exhibited for these youthful tyrants a quite immoderate veneration, compounded of fear and benevolence; even now, the leaders of the Burschenschaft looked forward to the time when their organization would rule all Germany.

The students were a political elite who bore the mantle of leadership because the masses were apathetic. "Among the Germans," acknowledges Treitschke, "it was the students who took the first step, and nothing can show more plainly the inertia of political life in those days." Among politicians, princes, and the people alike, "the student acquired an incredible prestige, being here honored as a born tribune, there regarded with suspicion as a professional conspirator. . . ." The French ambassador wrote to his friend Niebuhr, "I am sorry for your statesmen, they wage war with students!"[4]

Furthermore, a curious cult of gymnastics characterized the German student movement. It had its origins in the exertions of Turnvater (Father of Gymnastics) Friedrich Jahn—Father Jahn—a hero of the war and a blustering, uncouth enthusiast who set himself to regenerate the German youth physically and to redeem it from "effeminate" French influences.[5] Jahn was thus the father of modern gymnastics, which in its origin subserved a psycho-ideological function. There was an element of homosexuality in this new cult of the body. The students lined up in jackets of unbleached linen, with bare necks and long hair, hopped, ape-leaped, frog-leaped, and somersaulted on the trapeze and parallel bars. They went on long cross-country hikes, and they sang:

> Close rooms, sitting round the stove
> Make weaklings Frenchified.
>
> When for the people's old and sacred rights
> Bravely the Turnermeister, Friedrich Jahn,
> Strode to the field where man for freedom fights,
> A warlike generation followed on.

They took an aggressive pride in their chastity, and "made it a point of honor to render themselves odious to women."[6]

This was an era, it should be observed, in which the largest group of German students were in theological faculties. Twelve years later, the theological faculties were still the primary ones in German universities. In 1830, 26.8 per cent of German students were studying with evangelical faculties, 11.4 per cent were occupied with Catholic theology, 28.3 per cent were with the law faculties, 15.8 per cent in medicine, and 17.7 per cent in the philosophical faculty. In numbers, Protestant theology had 4,267; Catholic theology 1,809; law 4,502; medicine 2,355; and the philosophical faculty 2,937 out of a total of 15,870 students.[7] Given the primacy of theology at this time, it was natural that the German student movement should cast its revolutionary ideology in theological terms with its demand for a "Christian German republic." The later Russian student movement was to express similar aspirations of self-sacrifice, amorality of means, the will to martyrdom, and intellectual hegemony, but in a scientific-Marxist idiom. By contrast, the "Great Song" which Karl Follen, the German student leader, had composed at least in part, told of Christ, their Brother, the ideal Republican, the highest type of man, and ended, with a Hymn to Revolution, in a "Chorus of Free Christians":

> *Ein Herz, Ein Arm, Ein Blut sind wir geworden*
> *Der ew'gen Freiheit heil'ger Märt'rerorden.*[8]
>
> We now are one; one heart, one arm, one blood;
> The martyr order of eternal freedom.[9]

The student activists were historicists, terrorists, totalitarians, and anti-Semites, as well as Christian republicans. "Our judgment has the weight of history itself, it annihilates," they said. The voice of the students was the voice of history; they were its heirs and executioners. They had "an ineradicable hatred for the Jews." Germany's intellectual leaders, from Luther to Fichte (with the solitary exception of Lessing), had been anti-Semites, and the German studentry followed in their footsteps. They accused the Jewish cosmopolitans of having been friendly to Napoleon and the French during the War of Liberation, and of having avoided military service in the Prussian army. Jewish writers in reply ridiculed the "Germanomania" of the younger generation and emphasized the Jewish contribution to the war, despite a law of 1812 which had denied them officers' rank. This "arrogance" outraged the German student activists even more. "The students regarded themselves as a neo-Christian knighthood, displaying their hatred of the Jews with a crude intolerance which strongly recalled the days of the crusades," wrote Treitschke, himself an anti-Semite. The Burschenschaft in fact proposed to drive Jewish students out of the universities altogether. Thus, on October 19, 1817, at the Wartburg Festival, the German student activists, while burning two dozen books on the bonfire, shouted, "Woe unto the Jews!" As one speaker said, the world "can know what is to be expected from us in the future."[10] Adolf Hitler was the executor of the students' will.

The Wartburg Festival, celebrated in the annals of student movements, was a great collective generational rite. About fifteen hundred Burschen took part, half of them coming from Jena, whence they were accompanied by four professors. It was the Jena Burschenschaft which had taken the initiative in proposing a great fraternal festival, ostensibly to celebrate jointly Luther's Reformation and the triumph at Leipzig over Napoleon. Generational solidarity fused with republican aspirations. As the different university groups arrived, "they were greeted at the gate with loud hurrahs." The next morning there was a colorful procession through the forest "two by two, among them a number of heroic German figures, many of them bearded (which to the timid already sufficed to arouse suspicion of treasonable designs). Delight shone from every eye, for all were inspired by the happy self-forgetfulness of youth. . . ."[11] This was the first manifestation in which the beard became a revolutionary symbol.

An observer, one of the Jena professors, Lorenz Oken, described the atmosphere:

When general silence was obtained a student delivered a speech on very much the following lines: he spoke of the aim of this assembly of educated young men from all circles and all races of the German Fatherland; of the thwarted life of the past; of the rebound, and the ideal that now possessed the German people; of hopes that had failed and been deceived; of the vocation of the student and the legitimate expectations which the Fatherland founded upon it; of the destitution and even persecution to which a youth devoting himself to science had to submit; finally, how they must themselves take thought to introduce among them order, rule, and custom, in a word, student-form . . . and encouraging, of grown-up people who unfortunately could attain to nothing more themselves. . . . The audience, and we men among them, were moved to tears, tears of shame that we had not so acted . . . of joy too for that we had so brought up our sons that they should one day win the victory where we in our folly had failed.

Then another speech exhorted the students: "You must not let this moment of emotion and exaltation pass in smoke." "Are we members of a greater society? Does each of us only represent the Students' Unions of his individual university, or do we together form branches of a universal German Students' Union?" "All students are one." "He speaks no more the speech of his village . . . he is a universal man!"

Thereupon some six hundred students proceeded to the city church to listen with deep feeling to a sermon. They performed gymnastic exercises in the market place, then marched, each with a torch in hand, to the hilltop, where beside a triumphal bonfire they sang songs. Next day, from all localities, they "threw themselves into each other's arms and made friends." This was the "sacred moment of freedom," in which the students would show the courts and senates, with their laws and periwigs, how they would not yield to "their policy of intimidation (there is a more expressive word, emasculation)."[12] The students refused to be "emasculated." When the evening's festivities were done, the young men bade each other farewell "with streaming eyes," and "for most of them there remained a life-long memory, scintillating like a May-day in youth. . . ."[13] They were truly brethren now, and the unity of their fatherland seemed at hand.

All Europe took notice of the Wartburg Festival; it evoked a controversial literature, "raising this outburst of students' revelry to the level of a European event." A half century later Europe witnessed the formation of the International Workingmen's Association; earlier in the June days of 1848 they witnessed the first independent action of the Parisian working class. But in 1817, the German student movement made its first mass demonstration, and it was the first overt, self-conscious assertion of the intellectual elite as a political force in modern history. The liberal press hailed it as an awakening: "this silvery sheen in our history, this blossoming of our epoch."[14] Like all awakenings, however, it had a potential of evil as well as good.

The German student movement, it should be observed, unlike the later Russian, Chinese, or Japanese student movements, flourished not in an urban center such as Berlin but rather in the small "provincial" universities. Thuringia, not Prussia, was the cradle of the Burschenschaft. At the Wartburg Festival, of the fifteen hundred Burschen, about half, according to Treitschke, were from Jena and only thirty from Berlin; the rest came from Giessen, Marburg, Erlangen, Heidelberg, and other universities of the smaller states. There were so few Burschen in the Prussian universities that only Berlin had accepted the invitation. Jena was in the forefront of the student movement simply because it had a tradition of freedom. "There was no other university town in which the dominance of the students was so complete."[15] In the 1790s, for instance, following a dispute with the town's authorities, they had marched out en masse to Erfurt, and returned only when the townsmen abjectly surrendered. "And in Jene live we bene" went the old students' song. Despite their provincial situation, the Wartburg Festival probably attracted close to 10 per cent of the total German studentry. And in the case of such small universities as Jena and Giessen, the percentage of participants was much higher; in Jena the overwhelming majority seems to have been involved.[16]

The student activists, filled with love for each other, with idealism abetted by a touch of homosexuality, drank to their blood-brotherhood. It was indeed a brotherhood; there were no women students. They regarded their Burschenschaft as a "youth's federal state," and they were feared because "here for the first time in the forcibly disintegrated nation was constituted a corporation embracing the whole of Germany." They were indeed, we might say, the only political party in Germany, and as the movement spread in 1818 through fourteen universities, it seemed a formidable force. Their numbers were not large, but they were filled with fanaticism "to the pitch of terrorism";[17] and in Karl Follen they found a leader who expressed the whole spirit of the uprising of the student elite against the corrupt older generation, and who advocated the redemption of the nation by a direct act of will.

Karl Follen was the first student leader of modern times; in his bearing, ideology, and character he was the prototype for all the student leaders of the next century and a half. As a child, Karl Follen had experienced in sharp form all those conflicts with the father which have so characterized student leaders even to the distant places and times of U Nu and Mao Tse-tung. The teasing of his father and elder brother tormented him almost beyond endurance. In the words of his wife:

> He was too proud to confess how much he suffered, and he knew there was no intention to hurt him; but it was painful for him to remember the violent fits of anger and grief that he endured in consequence of these trials. He has told me, that he often wished himself dead, from his desire to escape this suffering; and it was only by great and constant effort, that he at last acquired that perfect self-control, which was a distinguishing trait of his character.[18]

In later years he still remembered with "the most serious feelings of disappointment" his father's severity and lack of response to his own desire for love; he recalled how he had grieved when his father rebuffed him as a "foolish boy." He hated "to speak of his early life, so many painful thoughts did it recall, but occasionally he would relate his contests with some of the petty tyrants of his university, who were in almost daily opposition to him. They were in the habit of domineering, in a very tyrannical manner, over those whom some unfortunate circumstances had placed in their power." Follen is said to have befriended the weak, and to have fought duels with the "bullies." Without asserting his manhood, "he could not even have remained in the university." He grew up humorless, and remarked "that it was not till he was a man, that he could learn to relish a jest." His childhood had been one in which he did not "fully sympathize with boys, and had not a true relish for the common pleasures of mankind." His burst into manhood came when, as a university student, he served, together with two brothers, as a volunteer in a student corps of riflemen in the War of National Liberation. Answering the call to arms, the students felt the burgeoning of a selfless idealism. When the campaign ended in 1814, Follen returned to the study of jurisprudence and theology at Giessen. A political vision, however, was upon him. "The great idea of a Christian brotherhood, to be first formed in the universities, and afterwards to be spread over all Germany, fired the hopeful and aspiring soul of Charles Follen."[19] All tyranny whatsoever, he felt, was sinful, for man was and of right ought to be free. Karl Follen undertook to propagandize for the moral and political regeneration of Germany. At first he organized literary clubs for the promotion of patriotism and science, clubs not unlike the later Russian students' circles. Here was to be found a more earnest and Christian philosophy than that which prevailed among the rowdying, dueling Landsmannschaften. For the aim of life, Follen insisted, was a Christlike perfection, and the students were apostles of the universal brotherhood taught by Christ. From Fichte's philosophy they drew a language of vocation and freedom in which they could express their aspiration as a revolutionary intellectual elite. Soon, like all student movements, they were fashioning their own distinctive garb; theirs was the old German model, long hair, black velvet coat, and dagger. Karl Follen himself described the genesis of their ideology:

> When local divisions and an oppressive system of rank were wasting, by angry collisions, the free powers of individuals and of the whole student body, there arose among the students of Giessen the idea of a Christian-German Republic in which the officers should be on a complete level with all the others, where the will of the whole, obtained by a free, general discussion in all assemblies, open to all, should rule in the concerns of their students; and where in a close union of all their youthful powers, in their manners and conduct, and in their public sentiment an earnest, patriotic effort, a striving after learning, physical culture, and freedom as citizens should be unfolded. Many students who were spiritually united by the same striving after Christian and rational progress went steadily onward to the attainment of the object in friendly union, held together only by a true inward indissoluble bond of conviction.[20]

Despite his Christian ends, Karl Follen with his ideology of total regeneration was soon advocating the principle that all means were justified in the students' struggle. As Kuno Francke said: "He [Follen] openly embraced the Jesuit principle that for the attainment of ends which to the moral consciousness appeared as necessary there was an absolute indifference of means."[21] He became all the more fanatical as he found himself and his movement rejected and hated by the majority of students, and persecuted by the government and university. The student body denounced his followers as Jacobins, black bandits, traitors to the state, revolutionary plotters against the sovereigns. The Academic Senate at Giessen decreed in 1817 that the Burschenschaft was henceforth a forbidden association. Follen responded to such rejection by becoming even more extremist. He declared:

It is cowardice to speak of legitimate means for the obtaining of liberty. Nobody has a right to keep liberty from us; and every means is justified against those who presume to do this. Rebellion, murder of tyrants, and all acts which in ordinary life are designated as crime, are legitimate means for the conquest of freedom. There are no other means. Against legal acts they know how to protect themselves; therefore they must tremble before our daggers. He who resorts to these measures, knowing that he is sacrificing his own life and all that is dear to him for the sake of his country, is morally all the nobler, the harder it is for him to overcome his natural aversion to such an action.

When Follen was asked whether he would not halt before destroying good and just men, he replied calmly, "No. If matters come to the worst all who are wavering in their opinions must be sacrificed; this is not a matter of feeling, but of necessity."[22] His defense of an amorality of means to achieve the students' end took on an absolutist character—the hallmark of the fanatic:

There are few men who in ordinary life would not, under certain circumstances, resort to a little lying; but from lying roundly and boldly for a great principle they are kept back by a certain awe which after all is nothing but cowardice. They would not hesitate to defend themselves against a highway robber by shooting him down, but to draw the dagger against the great robbers and murderers of popular freedom they do not dare. What then is more precious? Their own miserable life and property, or the welfare of a whole nation?

A fellow-student who listened to Karl Follen's discourses recorded the conflicts they provoked within him:

We sometimes felt in listening to his speeches, as though we were standing on the brink of a fathomless abyss, and were commanded to risk the plunge into its depths. To evade his consequences as soon as you had granted his premises was impossible; and yet the innermost feeling of these young men who had set themselves such high moral ideals, revolted against it.

Karl Follen had the curious intensity which characterizes student leaders, an ideological single-mindedness in which self and cause are fused so that one is as sacrosanct as the other. He could be kindly and confiding in manner, recorded Robert Wesselhoft, another leader of the Jena Burschenschaft, welcoming the newcomer like an old friend, with the familiar *du,* "but there was in his whole appearance and bearing, in the tone of his voice, in his gestures and glances, something so noble . . . such determination and almost proud earnestness—a something peculiar to himself, which imperceptibly inspired all who came in contact with him with a deep feeling of respect." With his broad forehead, rosy complexion, "deep, soulful eyes, and blonde hair hanging around his neck in wavy locks, in his blue German student's coat," he aroused the emotional warmth of his followers. "We have nowhere met his equal nor anybody who could be compared with him for purity and chastity of manners and morals. He seemed to concentrate all his energies upon one great aim—the revolution."[23]

A death-wish was strong in Karl Follen; he fashioned a society of students who lived in death-aimed dedication. They were called the "Unconditionals," for they had joined themselves in a holy, "indissoluble covenant of death-brethren," pledged to a martyrdom of freedom. These Unconditionals accepted what Follen called his "Maxim," namely, that in the struggle for freedom, "daggers and oath" (murder and perjury) were justifed; others of the original Burschenschaft, the so-called "Moderates," rejected the Maxim. The Unconditionals recited the "Great Song" of which Karl Follen was a composer:

Arise, ye princes! ye people, arise!
Freedom and vengeance in full career,
God's tempests in blood are approaching!
  Up, that when the world is blazing
  You may not be then found sleeping!
Rise from thy slumbers, lazy worm, rise,
To the heavens look up; 'midst glorious storms
In splendor thy death-star has risen!

They sang the "*Stimmen aus dem Volke*" (Voices from the People):

O freedom, first smile of my lips,
My ideal, my earliest prayer,
Which still in my heart ever glows,
Yet in thy might shall the German youth rise,
To the starry height of their ancient truth. . . .
The crown of thorns shall I seize with joy. . . .
And Freedom! Freedom, shall be my Amen, my Amen!
  But the young,
  They still sung
Fresh, merry and free,
Worthy sons of the gymnasium,
Eyes are sparkling, swords are flashing. . . .[24]

These songs of the communion of death-brethren transmuted the meaning of "freedom" into collective death.

For a brief while, Karl Follen, having taken his doctorate in law, lectured at Jena and agitated its Burschenschaft. He and his brother nurtured the project of another monster meeting of German students from all universities which would then proclaim the abolition of royalty, summon a parliament to adopt a constitution for "one free German Republic," and compel the governments of thirty-three German states to submit to the students' will. Events, however, took a far different turn. There were students who were thoroughly resolved to live by Follen's "principle," that one must realize unconditionally and with any means the goal of the righteous society, and "that anything was permissible for the sake of popular freedom—lying, murder, or any other crime. . . ."[25] The Unconditionals, in control of the central committee of the Burschenschaft, began to discuss daily who should be "corpsed" for the sake of freedom. Who should be assassinated? Metternich was not at hand, none of the German princes was an especial symbol, while the Czar Alexander omitted Jena on his itinerary in 1818.[26] A dramatist and Russophile, Kotzebue, however, a "flippant old rascal," "seemed the prototype of all the sins of the elder generation."[27] On March 23, 1819, Karl Sand, member of the Jena Burschenschaft, murdered Kotzebue.

The student Sand had a typical activist's ideology. "He looked upon the whole world as divided into two great camps: on the one side the pure, free, and chaste students, and on the other the corrupt minions of tyranny." It was a world in which the pure younger generation aimed to destroy the evil old. Kotzebue was a shadowy figure to his assassin, the vague object of popular polemics. The young Sand's mind, however, was suffused with the imagery of suicide and self-sacrificial death. He wrote to a friend in 1818, "Our life is a hero's course; speedy victory; early death! Nothing else matters if only we are real heroes." Kotzebue's murder, he said, would be justified "because he wishes to suppress the divine in me, my conviction." As he pondered the assassination, Sand "sketched a portrait of himself kneeling on the steps of a church and pressing a dagger into his own heart," while on the church door, pinned with another dagger, was Kotzebue's death-sentence.[28] Each day the student Sand absorbed Karl Follen's words until he drew the final conclusion and stabbed old Kotzebue in the throat. Then he tried to stab himself to death in the breast, "as it were to make an atonement to the son," as he said, a small boy who had rushed to his father's aid. Sand was subsequently tried and condemned to death. Karl Follen managed to extricate himself from direct complicity in the crime, though his moral involvement was quite clear.[29] Follen tried to persuade the students to march on the town of Mannheim and liberate the prisoner, but they refused. Sand was beheaded on May 20, 1820. Though the majority of the studentry stood aloof from his ideas and character, the student activists (as we have previously told) hailed Sand's deed as "a sign of that which will and must come." They came in multitudes to witness the execution, and they treasured as sacred objects the wood on which Sand's blood was spilled. For years members of the Heidelberg Burschenschaft would assemble in a cottage built from the platform's timbers as guests of Sand's executioner, a gruesome ritual of the death-wish, terrorism, and heroism of the first student movement.[30]

After Sand's deed one other plot and attempt at assassination was made by Unconditionals. In this case, in July 1819, the assassin's blow miscarried and the designated victim, President Ibell of Wiesbaden, survived. The would-be assassin, a young man named Löning, in order to protect his comrades, killed himself in prison by swallowing pieces of glass.

What did the tactics of the German student movement accomplish? What political advances can be traced to their melange of terrorism, suicide, elitism, juvenocracy, and idealism? What did their ideology of generational struggle achieve? Kuno Francke writes that the effect of Follen's activity and influence was to "put an end, not only to the unhampered development of Jena student life, but also for the time at least—to the liberal aspirations of the German people."[31] The veteran chancellor, the reforming liberal Hardenberg, who had co-signed in 1815 with King Frederick William III the promise of a constitution, said when he heard of the murder, "Now a constitution is impossible!"[32] The murder of Kotzebue was the occasion for the passage of the Carlsbad Resolutions, which remained in force for almost thirty years, from 1819 until the revolution of 1848.

That the student movement was largely responsible for the defeat of German constitutionalism has been the judgment of the most recent historical scholarship. Professor Walter Simon writes:

> The development in southern Germany that held the most significance for Prussia and her constitution was the assassination of Kotzebue in Mannheim. Those who believed in the existence of a widespread seditious conspiracy found powerful confirmation in this event. Here, they asserted, was evidence that the time was far from propitious for giving the people a chance to participate in government by granting a representative constitution; on the contrary, measures must be taken to suppress popular unrest which was giving rise, not merely to acts of disrespect toward the monarchy and the established order like those on the Wartburg, but now to bloodshed as well.[33]

As Hardenberg's influence declined, that of Metternich rose. Liberal democracy thrives when the rational spirit in people grows; it is enfeebled correspondingly by the infiltration of unreason.

The larger German states, under Metternich's leadership, joined in a series of measures directed against political and intellectual freedom in the universities. Governmental agents kept an eye on the instructors to see if they showed the proper spirit in their public lectures and regular courses; the governments pledged themselves to dismiss all teachers who deviated from their duty or who propagated "doctrines hostile to public order or subversive of existing governmental institutions"; teachers dismissed in one state were denied appointment in another; students expelled in one university were not admitted to another; and the Universal Students' Union (the Allgemeine Burschenschaft) was dissolved; persons remaining as secret members were debarred from public office. Moreover, not only was a strict censorship of the press inaugurated, but an extraordinary investigating commission was authorized to inquire into "the origin and manifold ramifications of the revolutionary plots and demagogical associations directed against the existing constitution" of the several states.[34] Even many young men with the most moderate liberal views were arrested and imprisoned. During the next decades in which the Carlsbad Resolutions remained in force, writes Frederic Lilge, "students and professors were persecuted, imprisoned, and a number of them fled abroad."[35] The universities were haunted by police spies, as professors and students lived under surveillance. Thus, the upshot of the Wartburg Festival and Kotzebue's assassination was, as Engelbrecht wrote, a "white Reign of Terror."[36] Liberalism went underground, as the Bundesrat investigating committee pursued its work of rooting out allegedly dangerous persons. The temper of the country became apprehensive and repressive.

To be sure, there were isolated incidents of student unrest after 1819. In the winter of 1830–1831, for instance, the students of Hanover led a democratic insurrection, disarmed the town guards, and held the town for several weeks with their own sentinels and patrols, until they were subdued by an army corps.[37] In 1832, a group of about fifty students and graduates of Heidelberg and Göttingen tried to storm the Frankfurt guardhouse, seize the treasury chest, and abolish the Federal Diet. Their efforts came to naught. The police remained vigilant. In 1836 a hundred and ninety-two students were convicted of belonging to illegal societies; some were even sentenced to death, though these sentences were then commuted to long terms of imprisonment. In April 1843, they raided the home of the philosopher Ludwig Feuerbach. In his words, "They searched this home of a hermit, scholar and thinker for letters . . . from students and information regarding Students' Unions."[38]

A liberal spirit, in order to thrive, must be carefully nurtured. It involves the growth of habits of tolerance, fair play, and discussion. It presupposes a common humanity among all adversaries and a common ethical standpoint, even when differences are most severely argued. It presupposes that one's sense of identity with others is greater than one's differences. Liberalism always remained weak in Germany. It failed subsequently in 1848 as it did later when confronted by the Nazis. One of the reasons was that the German student movement in its formative years took the way of terrorism and amorality, and contributed to a violent polarizing of the community. The initiative oscillated between extremes, first to the reactionaries and then once again to the revolutionists of 1848. Reason was the principal casualty. The student movement had indeed contributed to the rise of irrationalism. This was what Karl Follen in later years preferred not to remember.

And what of Karl Follen? His fate was a strange one. Deprived of his lectureship at Jena in 1819, he contemplated for a while founding with his comrades a German state in the United States. Threatened with another arrest, he fled to France in 1820, but was then expelled and went to Switzerland. The Holy Alliance made his tenure at the University of Basel impossible. With his arrest ordered once again, Follen escaped to Le Havre on November 1, 1821, and embarked for America. In the course of time, with the help of Lafayette and George Ticknor, he became in 1825 an instructor of German at Harvard College, and in 1830, the first Professor of German Literature at that institution. The memory of his youthful years as a student leader was something which he later wished to repress. He found in America a climate which dispelled ideology. He wrote to his father in 1826:

There is in this country, where law alone governs, no more quiet citizen than I. . . . I would remark, that, since I became a citizen here, I have publicly renounced, under oath, all further connexion with foreign governments. Therefore I am, as to Europe, politically dead. . . . The hatred against the governments on the other side, which I brought on board ship, has changed into entire indifference; and I only wish that my persecutors would allow me the blessing of their forgetfulness.

In 1829 he wrote to his family, "I probably produce more realities here than poems—probably, because my boldest European poems are here realities."[39] He glowed with joy when he received his full American citizenship in 1830. "For a long time he had felt unwilling to be called a foreigner." Then, when his child was born, he said, "Now I shall have no more home-sickness." Karl Follen became a Unitarian preacher and the friend of William Henry Channing, with whom he found much in common. J. Elliott Cabot, pondering on the Karl Follen he knew, wrote that for those who knew this "apostolic man," it was harder than one could imagine "to bring together the image of this fiery and not too scrupulous reformer-destroyer, with the recollection of that patient, tolerant, much-enduring (for he was still too radical for the conservatives and too liberal for the radicals) yet always sunny and cheerful face." Follen, however, did become an ardent abolitionist. His enrollment in the American Anti-Slavery Society in 1833 may have been the reason why Harvard failed to renew his professorship. Follen lost his life on a steamship which caught fire on the Long Island Sound as he was traveling from New York to Lexington to dedicate a new church. John Greenleaf Whittier addressed his dead friend:

Friend of my soul! as with moist eye
I look upon this page of thine,
Is it a dream that thou art nigh,
Thy mild face gazing into mine?

There are those who have argued that many of Karl Follen's "rabid utterances" as a student leader were for the most part "harmless braggadocio." Such was the opinion indeed of the author in 1824 of the first psychological study of a student political action, C. E. Jarcke. Although acknowledging that Follen advocated the use of assassination, Jarcke and Follen's American friends absolved him of involvement with Kotzebue's murder. "He could hardly have passed through life as a teacher of Christlike perfection without betraying at some time in some way his duplicity." The German student movement, according to Jarcke, was not "a momentary aberration of a few eccentric young people" but a phenomenon of historical necessity in which "many of the best heads and noblest hearts in the German universities were drawn into the magic circle of the revolutionary movement."[40] Subsequently they became "the noblest and best men."

Student movements, however, have tended finally to help destroy the goals to which they were dedicated. The amalgam of generational uprising with political protest produces its distinctive set of extreme means and attitudes. Political action becomes irrational when it is made the vehicle for generational revolt. Terrorism and the assassination of symbolic figures of the older generation have become tactics for student movements not because they are politically wise or helpful or conducive to the goals one is seeking on the manifest level; rather they have been adopted because they satisfy the needs of generational hatred on the latent, unconscious level. Suicidal tendencies and self-destructive imagery were traits of the student consciousness because the student activists were punishing themselves; since they were incompletely liberated from their fathers, their unconscious demanded that their symbolic murder of the father be atoned for by self-inflicted death. The most violent and fanatical student leaders like Karl Follen could later become noble individuals because the generational hatred declined with the years, and especially so if they were transplanted into an environment such as the American one in which generational conflict was virtually absent.

The greater number of the first generation of Burschenschaft activists were in later years ultraconservatives; a few became liberal leaders.[41] The later generations of students till 1848 refrained from overt political activities, though they still wore the forbidden black-red-gold ribbon under their coats. In 1848 they provided the revolution with its outstanding leaders.[42] The German student movement, however, was probably more elitist than any other, and was relatively lacking in the back-to-the-people spirit. Its liberalism was conceived in terms of the hegemony of an intellectual elite. For this reason, when after 1848 its elitist aims were satisfied, the German student movement rapidly became a thing of the past.

The heritage of the German student movement of 1817 was transmitted to the Nazis. It was Heinrich Heine, mocking, sardonic, but always penetrating unflinchingly to the irrational, destructive ingredient in student idealism, who wrote the best characterization of the significance of the German student movement:

Upon the Wartburg, the Past croaked its raven ditty, and follies were enacted worthy of the silliest days of the Middle Ages. There it was that Teutonism made an exhibition of itself. Ostensibly it whined for charity and faith; but its charity was nothing but hatred of the stranger, and its faith consisted of an irrationalism, which, in its ignorance, could find no expression other than the burning of books. . . . In my University days at Göttingen (1824), as I was sitting in the beer-cellar, I had once an opportunity of admiring the minute care with which my Primitive-German friends prepared the proscription lists against the day they should come into power. Any German descended, if only in the seventh degree, from a Frenchman, a Jew, or a Slav, was condemned to banishment. Any one who penned even a few lines against Father John and the Primitive-German absurdities had to expect death, and death by the axe, not by the guillotine. . . . Have these impenetrable fools disappeared from the scene of history? No! . . .

As the judicious Max Beer, historian of socialism and sage wrote, "Those were the grandfathers of the Nazis."[43]

The Viennese Students of 1848: The Academic Legion in Power and Defeat

When the Revolution of 1848 erupted in Central Europe, the student movement was at once a source of its idealism and in large part a source of its defeat. Only recently has the generational aspect of the revolution been studied; but in 1848, a contemporary observer, the American consul in Vienna, William H. Stiles, noted the predilection of the student revolutionaries for the symbolism of death. It was the motif of suicidalism. "The students established among themselves a legion known as the Death's Head Legion, and bearing on their caps, as emblematic ornaments, a skull and cross-bones." Their dedication to the cause of liberty was total; they "expressed their determination neither to yield nor accept pardon in the struggle for it." The usual back-to-the-people theme was in evidence as the Viennese students, according to the American consul, "began now to cultivate a most cordial intimacy with the lowest classes of the population. Declaring war against the nobility, clergy, military and court . . . they became the flatterers of the mob, talked to the *proletaria* of their sacred rights. . . ." Soon, however, the messianic elitism and the drive of generational revolt began to assert themselves, causing a rift in the generations which contributed to the subsequent undoing of the revolution. The students, wrote the puzzled American consul who knew none such in the United States, "became perfectly intoxicated by the glory which they had acquired." Nonstudents, political propagandists, came from all over Europe to "base their operations" on the students. The American observer wrote with naïve indignation of the nonstudents of 1848: "So artfully did they flatter the vanity and minister to the pride of the inexperienced youths, that they found it but an easy task to convince them of their fitness to perform the first parts in the drama before them, and to utter the leading voice in the reorganization of the state. . . ."

The Viennese students were in the forefront of the March Revolution of 1848. At Vienna, there were all told 4,491 students, from whose ranks the revolutionary activists were drawn; a few professors joined them. On March 12, the students resolved to present a petition for political freedom (written by a professor) to the university; their words "exhibited a degree of boldness and energy which struck great terror to the hearts of their more prudent and timid instructors." The next morning they marched on the Landhaus. Evidently the activist demonstrators constituted a minority of the studentry, for according to the American observer, "a large number of the students, fearing that their names would be inscribed in the 'black book,' refused to join the procession, which was mainly composed of the more reckless portions. . . ." Student leaders spoke from the shoulders of their fellows or from the fountain in the court: they were soon carried away by their own eloquence and generational élan; "pale with terror at their own daring," they addressed the crowd. A deputation of students entered the building to present their petition. Excitement was in the air. Somehow some of the petitioners got the idea they were entrapped; generational fears and projections evidently were vivid, for they "raised the windows and cried out to their comrades in the yard below that they had been entrapped in a snare."[44] With a furious cry, their fellow-students surged forward to their rescue. Generational solidarity was high in the March Days.

The students fought nobly. As Frederick Engels observed, the working classes "and the students had borne the brunt of the fight, as far as fight there had been; and the students, about 4,000 strong, well armed, and far better disciplined than the national guard, formed the nucleus, the real strength of the revolutionary force. . . ."[45] When the Viennese Revolution of 1848 foundered, however, it was nonetheless largely because generational struggle divided the revolutionary ranks.

As Rolland Ray Lutz, Jr., wrote in his informative study "Fathers and Sons in the Vienna Revolution of 1848": "There were two groups of revolutionaries involved in the Vienna Revolution, an older group consisting largely of persons in their middle and later years, and a younger group consisting, for the most part, of persons who were of college or near college age. It was the younger of these groups which touched off the insurrection leading to the Vienna Revolution of 1848 . . ."

The younger generation had imbibed its ideology in the student secret societies, the nine Burschenschaften organized in Vienna during the forties on the German model. The older generation desired reforms which would transform the Austrian Empire into a liberal constitutional monarchy. The younger generation wished union in a Greater Germany, together with universal suffrage. The fathers sought gradual change with limited objectives; the sons aimed at radical basic change. The revolution could have succeeded if the unity of the generations had been preserved; as it was, the absolutist monarchy survived because the violence of the young caused the elder generation of liberals to draw back. On March 13, 1848, the day of the Student March, two or three thousand students and alumni were drawn into solidarity as they were attacked by imperial troops. Henceforth Vienna's student movement "emerged full-blown with its own group spirit and its own sense of direction. Henceforth it defied all attempts by adult liberals to bring it under their control." On the part of the older generation, "by September the movement led by the fathers had virtually ceased to be a liberal phenomenon and had become an anti-radical alliance which included some elements which could be labeled counter-revolutionary. . . ." Thus the impact of the student movement was to polarize the generations. "Beneath the liberal-radical split of revolutionary Vienna was a conflict of generations, which played a dynamic role in the course of events. This conflict was involved in the outbreak of the revolution. It played a part in the violence and excesses of the revolution and in the failure of the liberals to capture control. Finally, it was involved in the destruction of the revolution itself. From beginning to end, the phenomenon of the generations was an integral part of the Vienna Revolution of 1848."[46]

For a few months, Vienna was in effect governed by a dictatorship of the student leaders (the so-called Aula group) and the suburban guard; they administered the public works program, directed the labor force, supervised weights, measures, and the purity of foods, and controlled the militia and police forces. Debacle, however, was soon at hand to terminate the Student Commune.

The largest single group of students came from bourgeois families, in which the fathers were medium and small businessmen; they included 409 students or about 22 per cent. But the sons of handicraftsmen were right behind with 21 per cent, or 399 students. The activists, insofar as they emanated from the secret societies, the Burschenschaften, probably came from the middle classes.

Some economic hardship was perhaps present in the background of Viennese students. Of the 1,899 students who matriculated in the academic years 1845–1846 and 1847–1848, 743 or about 39 per cent were excused from tuition because they were classified as "poor."

As Engels observed, the defeat of the Viennese Revolution "was as decisive for Germany as the proletarian struggle had been for France."[47] The Academic Legion, "the stronghold of the movement party, the centre of continuous agitation," in Engels' words, became "obnoxious to the more moderate burghers of Vienna." Taking advantage of this division between the generations, the imperial party pressed forward to provoke a struggle between the bourgeoisie and the working class. "The unity and strength of the revolutionary force was broken." Engels observed sadly the lack of judgment in the revolutionary student movement: "The Academic Legion, full of zeal for the struggle against Imperial despotism, were entirely incapable of understanding the nature of the estrangement of the two classes, or of otherwise comprehending the necessities of the situation." The Academic Legion, the student movement in arms, was filled with zeal, was "brave and enthusiastic," and "militarily speaking," Engels acknowledged, "the only force which was in a state to do its work successfully." Its failure arose from the inherent compulsions of student movements generally; it waged a dual struggle, one against the imperial despotism, the other against the fathers, the elder generation of liberals. A rational politics would have bade the generations to maintain their community of purpose and to wield their conjoined strength against the imperial regime. The Viennese Revolution would then, in all likelihood, have had an altogether different outcome—a liberal democratic constitution. As Engels noted, German leaders realized in 1848 that "here [in Vienna] the great battle of the German Revolution was to be fought." It was the element of generational conflict which made it impossible for Robert Blum, the leader of the "Moderate Democracy," to mount sufficient forces to withstand the reactionary attack on Vienna. Elsewhere in Germany in 1849, when the workingmen took up arms on behalf of a reluctant National Assembly, the student movement was no such cohesive force as it had been in Vienna. "The students particularly, the 'representatives of intellect,' as they liked to call themselves," wrote Engels, "were the first to quit their standards, unless they were retained by the bestowal of officers' rank, for which they, of course, had very seldom any qualifications."[48] The Viennese Academic Legion superimposed the patterns of generational revolt on the patterns of political evolution; in Germany proper, students were more simply elitists associating themselves for upward political mobility with the working class cause. Thus the Revolution of 1848 failed in part because of the irrational drive of generational politics. A pall of pessimism then settled once more over Europe; in the despair of defeated hopes, Schopenhauer's philosophy came into vogue, with its doctrine of the futility of political efforts.[49] The euphoria of generational uprising was followed by the dysphoria of generational defeat.

The Viennese student revolution of 1848 was also noteworthy as the first which saw Jewish student leaders coming to the forefront. Among them were August Silberstein, secretary in 1848 of the Academic Legion; Adolf Buchheim, an editor of the *Studentenkurier* and grandson of the Rabbi of Austerlitz; Moritz Habrofsky, president in 1848 of the Student's Committee; and Joseph Unger, a leader in that body. Several young doctors and journalists emerged to student leadership: Ignaz Kuranda, editor of the *Grenzboten,* an exile from Prague; Dr. Joseph Goldmark, who headed the student committee for safety on March 15, the day the Emperor granted a Constitution; and Ludwig Frankl, secretary of the

Jewish Community and editor of the *Sonntagsblätter*; Frankl wrote the most successful poem of student revolt of all time, *Die Universität*, which sold a half-million copies and was set to music by twenty-seven composers; it was the first publication to greet the abrogation of the censorship in 1848. Above all, among the student leaders was Dr. Adolf Fischhof, a man of singular nobility of character who embodied all that was best in the student revolt and tried always to guide it into constructive channels.

Adolf Fischhof, assistant physician at the General Hospital, could remember many things. Born in 1816, he had attended a gymnasium in Budapest where in every class he had had to sit on the special "Jew-bench." In March 1848, he stood among the spectators at the students' assemblage in front of the *Landhaus* where the Estates were in session. And then, "it was as though all his subconscious brooding had come into the foreground; seething emotions against the prevailing injustice suddenly broke the bounds. . . ." The words rushed from him. "The aimless crowd came to life. . . . It was a moment of immeasurable importance in universal history," wrote a historian of the Viennese Jews.[50] The students raised Fischhof to their shoulders; he called for freedom of the press, the conscience, the academy, and for popular representation and ministerial responsibility. Then Dr. Goldmark spoke: "We have had enough monologues. Let us try to begin a dialogue with the representatives of the Estates of the Land." Again Fischhof acted decisively. He said: "If the Estates will not come to us, let us go to the Estates." The students marched on to Parliament House. Thus began the Viennese Revolution of 1848. Two days later, with the granting of the constitution, Ludwig Frankl said: "Out of a morning and evening the third day came. God saw, and we saw with Him, that it was good."

Late in May 1848, Adolf Fischhof became chairman of the student-citizen Committee of Security, and as such, the virtual ruler of Vienna, and indeed, Austria. He always wore the uniform of the Academic Legion in which he held the rank of Commander of the Medical Corps. When the Constitutional Reichstag was convened in July, he felt the Committee's work was done. But reaction was soon triumphant. The middle class was alienated from the democratic cause, especially by the lynching in October of the Minister of War. The Imperial troops subdued Vienna and executed revolutionary leaders. The Reichstag was prorogued. Adolf Fischhof refused to flee and was imprisoned. Both he and Goldmark were charged with high treason and conspiracy for the murder of the Minister of War. After more than a year the case against Fischhof was dropped. A military dictatorship ruled; at the end of 1852, the Emperor abrogated many of the freedoms he had granted during the revolution.

The casualties among the Jewish student activists and leaders were high. A Jewish student, Heinrich Spitzer, killed by the Imperial troops, was the first victim of the Revolution in March 1848. When the collective funeral of the fifteen dead took place, the Jewish Rabbi was accorded the honor of speaking first. He spoke of the two Jewish dead: "With their life and blood, they won a victory for their Fatherland which world history will immortalize in its books. They showed themselves descendants of the heroic race of Samson, Gideon, David and Jonathan." Ludwig Frankl was wounded when he fought as a member of the Students' Legion in the uprising of October 6, 1848 against the government. Hermann Jellinek, age twenty-six, was executed in a savage reprisal of the governmental forces on November 23, 1848. August Silberstein was imprisoned for two years. Adolf Buchheim fled to London and became Professor of German Literature at the Royal College. Joseph Unger, member of the Central Committee in 1848, was baptized, and in 1881 became President of the Imperial Court of Law. And what was the fate of Adolf Fischhof, the courageous Commander of the Academic Legion? Released from prison, he worked as a doctor in private practice, but after a few years, was compelled by nervous illness to retire. In 1882, his last public meeting was disrupted by National Germans. Political anti-Semitism became a portentous movement in Austria after 1848. Soon the Viennese students were anti-Semites and "Nazis long before Hitler," in the words of Martin Freud.[51]

In the annals of student movements, the song which the Jewish non-student activist, Ludwig Frankl, wrote remains as a memorial to their enthusiasm of 1848. Frankl wrote it while serving on sentry duty with the Academic Legion on the night of March 14. It celebrated the themes of idealism, self-sacrifice, comradeship and the redemption of society by the student youth.

THE UNIVERSITY

Lo, who be these so proud in bearing?
  The bayonets flash, the flags fly free,
They come with silver trumpets blaring,
  The University!

The daylight hour at last is breaking
  Our hopes and prayers have yearned to see;
'Tis your young hearts to light awakening.
  The University!

When Kaiser Joseph came in thunder
  To bind the tongue's sweet liberty,
Who dared to burst the bonds asunder?
  The University!

Our tongues wake with the lark to singing;
  O hear their dithyrambic glee!
Heart calls, and heart sends answer ringing,
  The University!

Where spirits of the dead are beckoning,
The dead who died for freedom, see—
With the first victim paid her reckoning
The University!

And when our sons in reverence finger
Each glorious page in history,
On thy name, writ in gold, they'll linger,
Our University!"[52]

NOTES

1. Heinrich von Treitschke, *History of Germany in the Nineteenth Century*, tr. Eden and Cedar Paul (New York, 1917), III, 3. This section of von Treitschke's work is favorably evaluated in G. P. Gooch, *History and Historians of the Nineteenth Century* (2nd edn.; New York, 1913), p. 151.

2. H. C. Engelbrecht, *Johann Gottlieb Fichte: A Study of His Political Writings with Special Reference to His Nationalism* (New York, 1933), pp. 128–132, 176; Robert Adamson, *Fichte* (Edinburgh, 1892), p. 84.

3. Carl Schurz, *The Reminiscences of Carl Schurz*, I (New York, 1913), 109.

4. Treitschke, *op. cit.*, pp. 52, 53, 67.

5. The most illuminating study of Father Jahn as "the first storm trooper" is in Peter Viereck, *Metapolitics: The Roots of the Nazi Mind* (rev. edn.; New York, 1961), pp. 63 ff.

6. Treitschke, *op. cit.*, p. 10.

7. W. Lexis, *Die Deutschen Universitäten*, Erster Band (Berlin, 1883), p. 126; also his *A General View of the History and Organization of Public Education in the German Empire*, tr. G. J. Tamson (Berlin, 1904), p. 50.

8. George Washington Spindler, *Karl Follen: A Biographical Study* (Chicago, 1916), p. 55.

9. Charles Follen, *The Works of Charles Follen* (Boston, 1842), I, 600. Note: After moving to the U.S.A., Karl Follen called himself Charles Follen. For consistency, I shall use "Karl" in text but will follow the style of the original references in my notes.

10. Treitschke, *op. cit.*, pp. 44, 50, 56–57.

11. *Ibid.*, p. 55.

12. Translated and quoted in J. G. Legge, *Rhyme and Revolution in Germany* (London, 1918), pp. 22–24.

13. Treitschke, *op. cit.*, p. 58.

14. *Ibid.*, pp. 54, 38.

15. *Ibid.*, p. 58.

16. The total enrollment in German universities was 15,870 in 1830 and 11,567 in 1840. We may infer an enrollment on this order for 1817. See R. H. Samuel and R. Hinton Thomas, *Education and Society in Modern Germany* (London, 1949), p. 112. In 1831, the universities of Jena, Giessen, and Berlin had enrollments of 501, 355, and 1,821 students, respectively. See Lexis, *Die Deutschen Universitäten*, pp. 118–119.

17. Treitschke, *op. cit.*, pp. 52, 67–68.

18. Eliza Cabot Follen, *Life of Charles Follen*, in Charles Follen, *op. cit.*, I, 8–9, 25–26, 7.

19. Charles Follen, *op. cit.*, I, p. 27.

20. Charles Follen, *op. cit.*, I, 30; see also Spindler, *op. cit.* (Chicago, 1916), p. 20.

21. Kuno Francke, "Karl Follen and the German Liberal Movement," *Papers of the American Historical Association*, V (New York, 1891), 71–72; also Spindler, *op. cit.*, p. 40.

22. See Spindler, *op. cit.*, p. 41.

23. *Ibid.*, p. 45. Francke, *op. cit.*, pp. 70–72.

24. Charles Follen, *op. cit.*, I, 593–595.

25. Treitschke, *op. cit.*, pp. 70–71.

26. Spindler, *op. cit.*, pp. 72–75; Treitschke, *op. cit.*, p. 174.

27. Treitschke, *op. cit.*, p. 170.

28. *Ibid.*, pp. 169, 170.

29. Spindler, *op. cit.*, p. 62.
30. Treitschke, *op. cit.*, p. 178.
31. Francke, *op. cit.*, p. 79.
32. J. G. Legge, *Rhyme and Revolution in Germany* (London, 1918), pp. 54–55; see also Frederic Lilge, *The Abuse of Learning: The Failure of the German University* (New York, 1948), pp. 23–24.
33. Walter M. Simon, *The Failure of the Prussian Reform Movement, 1807–1819* (Ithaca, N.Y., 1955), pp. 207–208.
34. See James Harvey Robinson and Charles A. Beard, *Readings in Modern European History*, II (New York, 1909), 20–22.
35. Lilge, *op. cit.*, p. 24.
36. Engelbrecht, *op. cit.*, pp. 160–161.
37. James Morgan Hart, *German Universities: A Narrative of Personal Experience* (New York, 1878), p. 163.
38. Legge, *op. cit.*, p. 174. H. P. Adams, *Karl Marx in his Earlier Writings* (London, 1940), p. 18.
39. Charles Follen, *op. cit.*, I, 264, 267, 169.
40. Spindler, *op. cit.*, pp. 67, 75, 228. Francke, *op. cit.*, p. 81.
41. Treitschke, *op. cit.*, p. 52.
42. Carl Schurz, *op. cit.*, I, 110.
43. Max Beer, *Fifty Years of International Socialism* (London, 1937), pp. 213–214. The passage is translated from Heinrich Heine, *Ludwig Börne* (1840), in *Heinrich Heines Sämtliche Werke*, Siebenter Band, her. Ernst Elster (Leipzig, 1890), p. 95.
44. William H. Stiles, *Austria in 1848–49* (New York, 1852), I, 143, 122, 117; II, 357.
45. Frederick Engels, *Germany: Revolution and Counter-Revolution* (New York, 1933), p. 41.
46. Rolland Ray Lutz, Jr., "Fathers and Sons in the Vienna Revolution of 1848," *Journal of Central European Affairs*, XXII, No. 2 (July 1962), 161–173. See also Veit Valentin, *1848: Chapters of German History*, tr. E. T. Scheffauer (London, 1940), p. 190. Priscilla Robertson, *Revolutions of 1848: A Social History* (Princeton, 1952), Ch. 11.
47. Engels, *op. cit.*, p. 65.
48. Engels, *op. cit.*, pp. 67, 68, 70, 72, 78, 103.
49. James Sully, *Pessimism: A History and a Criticism* (London, 1877), pp. 449–450; William Wallace, *Life of Arthur Schopenhauer* (London, 1890), pp. 190–194.
50. Max Grunwald, *History of Jews in Vienna*, tr. Solomon Grayzel (Philadelphia, 1936), pp. 273, 285, 515. *The Jewish Encyclopedia* (New York, 1902), II, 333. *Ibid.* (New York, 1903), V, p. 495.
51. Martin Freud, "Who was Freud?," in Joseph Fraenkel (ed.), *The Jews of Austria: Essays on Their Life, History and Destruction* (London, 1967). P. G. J. Pulzer, "The Development of Political Antisemitism in Austria," *ibid.*, p. 430.
52. Ludwig August Frankl, *Gesammelte Poetische Werke*, Erster Band (Leipzig), pp. 228–229. Translated in Legge, *op. cit.*, pp. 271–272.

THREE

Gavrilo Princip: The Bosnian Student Movement Blindly Provokes the First World War

The impact of generational struggle and a student movement on an unstable European political world was in large part immediately responsible for the outbreak of the First World War. We all know in a shadowy way that a Bosnian student, Gavrilo Princip, assassinated the Archduke Franz Ferdinand of Austria on July 28, 1914. What is less well known is the extent to which this incident was the outcome of generational conflict and of the superimposing of the psychological traits of the student movement on the processes of political change.

A new Bosnian student class came into being at the turn of the twentieth century. It was the product of scholarships and assistance from the Serbian government and from welfare societies. The sons of Bosnian peasants went to the universities of Belgrade, Zagreb, and Vienna. They drank deeply of the new literature of revolt: Bakunin, Ibsen, Kropotkin; they hated their fathers for their peasant parochialism and for their submission to the Austro-Hungarians, and they hated the Austro-Hungarians for oppressing their fathers.[1]

In 1914, in Bosnia, the conflict of generations was especially acute. It arose against the background of the strong nationalist resentment which, for more than half a century, the Slavic Bosnians had borne against the rule of the Austro-Hungarian empire. In 1913, however, the Austrian government introduced a more liberal policy; the Bosnian Landtag was reopened, and much freedom was extended to the press. The restive youth, however, were contemptuous of the middle-aged parliamentary approach. To them the existing Bosnian parties, representative of the bourgeoisie, and committed to legality, reflected an acquiescent "older generation." The "new generation," known as "Mlada Bosna" (Young Bosnia), which came into being in the first years of the twentieth century, was impatient with all politicians and legal forms of opposition. Largely composed of students, its members, wrote Sidney B. Fay, fed

> upon Russian revolutionary and anarchistic literature, especially the writings of Herzen and Kropotkin. They were fired with the success of violence in the Russian revolution of 1905. They developed the "cult of the individual deed," that is, they believed that terrorist acts of assassination were the best means of putting a speedy end to the temporizing methods of Bosnian politicians and of throwing off all Austrian control to prepare the way for a new "Jugoslav nationalism."[2]

It was a "student trio," in Fay's words, which conspired at Belgrade to go to Sarajevo to murder the Austrian archduke. One of them, Trifko Grabezh, had been expelled in 1912 from high school for slapping a teacher, but then transferred to Belgrade to complete his studies. The capital of Serbia was the center for the organization of revolutionary student groups. "Nearly all of the attempted assassinations of Austrian officials between 1910 and 1914 were made by youths who had just come from spending some months in Belgrade."[3]

Vladimir Gatchinovitch was the principal student leader; it was he who inspired the Bosnian students to carry out the attempt on the archduke. The son of a priest, he had refused to follow his father's calling, seeking his own in revolutionary Russian literature instead; he established contact with "direct action" circles. Curiously, several years later in 1914, after the outbreak of the First World War, Gatchinovitch became friendly in Paris with Leon Trotsky, who published an introduction to the Serbian's articles. As Trotsky described the student terrorist, "Despite the very strange crowd, one's eyes must rest upon him even against one's will. He is one of those types which are born to provoke a feeling of uneasiness among orderly people."[4] Gatchinovitch attended the University of Vienna, spending more time, however, organizing Slavic students' revolutionary circles than attending classes. He wrote a pamphlet, "The Death of a Hero," in praise of political assassins, which "circulated widely among young students upon whom it had a profound and decisive effect." It especially exalted the student Bogdan Zherajitch, who tried in 1910 to murder the Austrian governor, General Varesanin, in Sarajevo, and then committed suicide as one fore-ordained to be "a national offering." The pamphlet rendered homage to the students' forebears, the Russian terrorists and the unsuccessful would-be assassin of Napoleon III, Orsini. It criticized the Serbian people for not appreciating "those who are coming" who would "kindle revolution in the minds and thoughts of young Serbs." Elitist and juvenocratic, it was also both terroristic and masochistic in its glorification of the figure of the political assassin, the "man of action, of strength, of life and virtue, a type such as opens an epoch, proclaims ideas and enlivens suffering and spellbound hearts." The pamphlet went on to announce:

> The Serb revolutionary, if he wants to win, must be an artist and a conspirator, must have talent for strength and suffering, must be a martyr and a plotter, a man of Western manners and a *hajduk* [bandit mountaineer], who will shout and wage war for the unfortunate and downtrodden.[5]

Bogdan Zherajitch, with his doubts and despair and will to self-destruction, was indeed the pure type of young Bosnia. A student of law at Zagreb in 1908, he had drunk deeply from the pages of Kropotkin; he had returned in 1908 to his native Herzegovinian village saying that "Kropotkin has the soul of that handsome pure Jesus who for us comes from Russia."[6] When Bosnia and Herzegovina were annexed to Austria-Hungary in 1908, Zherajitch, in typical student activist fashion, fled to Serbia to join the guerrilla volunteers known as the *komite*. Later he spent most of his time in Zagreb cafés arguing politics. For a while he advocated Thomas Masaryk's ethical back-to-the-people program for working in the villages to raise the cultural level. By 1910, however, he was convinced that Bosnia "for its awakening needed the smell of blood more than the 'three R's.'" He wrote Gatchinovitch with a despair which indicated how he was approaching a self-destructive choice of political means: "I am suffering from tremendous emotional torments, my feelings are extremely gloomy. . . . I do not trust in anything any more, I only believe that I have bad luck. . . . The individual spirit is chained by the shackles of the general will."

Then Zherajitch borrowed a revolver from a Bosnian student of engineering. He had decided on an act of political assassination. For (in Gatchinovitch's words) he believed in the mission of the student youth: "We, the youngest, have to make a new history. Into our frozen society we have to bring sunshine, we have to awaken the dead and cheer up the resigned. We must wage a deadly war against pessimism, against fear and low spirits, we the messengers of new generations and new people. Having a belief stronger than life and a love which is capable of lifting people out of the grave, we shall win." At first Zherajitch planned to assassinate the Emperor Franz Joseph on the latter's visit to Sarajevo in May 1910. He could not bring himself to make the attempt and sank into an even greater alternation of despair and exaltation. As a fellow-student described him, "We were in a kind of ecstasy. Zherajitch, trembling with his beautiful, deep burning black eyes."[7] In such an exalted mood Zherajitch shortly afterward tried to murder General Varesanin and then killed himself. Zherajitch's grave became a shrine for pilgrimages of the Bosnian studentry, as Karl Sand's had been a century earlier for the German students. In 1912, Gavrilo Princip swore beside it to avenge his death.

Gatchinovitch called on the young to be the redeemers of Bosnia: "These young people, not yet awakened, will be our apostles, the creators and cross-bearers of new religions and new hearts. They will awaken our dead gods, revive our fairies who had withered away because of sadness and love, they will bring a new empire of liberty and man, and save the Serbian soul from vice and decay." Through the length and breadth of little Bosnia Gatchinovitch traveled, organizing the radical youth into secret revolutionary circles known as *Kruzhoci*. "It is certain," writes Fay, "that they existed in all the towns with secondary schools—Banja Luka, Tuzla, Mostar, Trebinje, and especially in Sarajevo."[8] The fruits were soon in coming. "Early in 1912 there was bloodshed in front of the University of Zagreb"; the first joint demonstration of students of all three major religious groups, Orthodox, Catholic, and Moslem, took place in Sarajevo on February 21, and one young Moslem was killed when the police fired on the crowd.

The mantle of student self-immolation now passed to Luka Jukitch, Bosnian law student, political poet, and an ardent advocate of political assassinations. Like all student activists, he was preoccupied by his place in history. "History will remember Jukitch," he told a friend when he deserted from the Austrian army. In 1912, he led in organizing a demonstration in Sarajevo at which the students burned a Hungarian flag; one of them was wounded by a rifle bullet, seventeen were arrested. Among the student leaders was Gavrilo Princip, who was wounded by a police saber stroke. The next day the students proclaimed a general strike in all the Bosnian schools. "Princip went from class to class, threatening with his knuckle-duster all the boys who wavered in coming to the new demonstration," recorded one student in his diary.[9] The demonstration was dispersed by army units. One thousand students, however, clashed with the police. One of them noted the generational cleavage within the Left: "Among the Serbs only the Old Radicals refused to take part in the demonstrations." Jukitch found the pace of the Young Bosnians and Zagreb University students too slow. When Count Cuvaj, Governor of Croatia, suspended the Croat constitution and started to rule by decree, Jukitch told them, "This schoolboys' movement is not enough. It is too innocent. Other means must be applied, and Cuvaj should be removed at all costs and I am prepared to do it." He proposed to use poison or bombs and revolvers. Then Jukitch on June 8, 1912, made an unsuccessful attempt to kill the governor but killed instead the chief of the Education Department and a policeman. Jukitch stood trial in August 1912, together with eleven other students ranging in age from fifteen to eighteen years; Jukitch himself, the nonstudent student leader, was twenty-five. Jukitch alone was sentenced to death, though the sentence was commuted. The government also suppressed most of the student papers and magazines, and arrested many more students; during the first four months of 1913, two hundred trials for high treason took place. Terrorism, by this time, was embedded deeply in the students' consciousness. At the end of October 1912, another attempt on the life of Count Cuvaj took place; the would-be assassin, Ivan Planinscak, a law student, shot at him but missed; then he killed himself.[10] It was all part of the Student Mission of Making History.

Throughout this period there were the usual police assaults on meetings of university students. The students of the University of Zagreb on January 31, 1912, for instance, barricading themselves in the University Hall, hoisted the black flag and held off police saber attacks for thirty-six hours. Thus the generations fought, provoked by political absolutism into meaningless battle.[11] A pamphlet entitled "Schoolboys' Movement," circulated among the Croat students, had a preface by Jukitch: "The youngest generation of the Croat-Serb people has already been carefully watching for some time what goes on in Croatia. . . . The struggle is in the hands of the youngest fighters for liberty." In March 1912, the government was obliged to close all Croat-Serb schools indefinitely.

The scattered student groups meanwhile were organized into a "Serbo-Croat Nationalist-Radical Youth"; new student journals of protest began to appear in various towns: *Val* in Zagreb, *Prepored* in Ljubljana, *Novi Srbin* at Sombor, *Srpska Omladina* in Sarajevo, *Ujedinjenje* at Split. Terrorist ideas spread, and plans of action sometimes followed. In August 1913, a Croat student, Dojichich, came back from America to try to kill Baron Skerlecz, but only wounded him severely. "By this time not merely the University students but the middle school youth in most Jugoslav towns of Austria-Hungary, were thoroughly infected by revolutionary ideas."[12] Street demonstrations, followed by expulsions, followed by sympathetic strikes, were the order of the day. "Young agitators from the Universities," writes Seton-Watson, "went secretly from town to town and encouraged the formation of student societies or clubs." Gatchinovitch, the student leader, who had moved meanwhile to Lausanne University, ostensibly to study sociology, at this time, according to a close associate, "held the half of revolutionary Bosnia in his hands." "He had hypnotised the younger generation," and his morality evolved with a typical generational dialectic "to the same strangely immoral conclusions as the writings of Savinkov, the famed Russian terrorist."[13] The generational conflict took familiar forms. At the gymnasia of Mostar and

Tuzla, for instance, older pupils publicly insulted professors and assaulted one of them. Mostar was closed down in June 1913 for a whole year.

The young Bosnian students were in a state of total alienation from their society. "They rebelled against all of Bosnian society, its taboos, its primitivism, and its inequalities," says Vladimir Dedijer. They gave increasing heed to the romantic words of Gatchinovitch: "Never has Serbian life so much longed for a hero as today, when there is so much emptiness, so many vices, so much pain, when all this has penetrated into our veins and entered our hearts. . . . But new souls are on the horizon. . . ." The cult of Zherajitch provided a student martyrology. In all Bosnia, schoolboys rehearsed the details of the attempted assassination of the governor as if they were the lines of a Balkan medieval epic—how the hero had awaited the tyrant, fired five shots, then killed himself with the sixth, shouting, "I leave my revenge to the Serbian cause," how the Austrian general kicked the student's body and ordered it buried among common criminals. As the Bosnian student activists placed wreaths upon his grave in the night, they rehearsed Zherajitch's last testament to his generation as he bade the last farewell to Gatchinovitch: "He embraced me with such force we parted as if he was seeing me for the last time. He did not say a word. Only when the bell announced the departure of the train, he whispered: 'our generation has to be ready for sacrifices. Please tell everyone.' "[14]

This was Zherajitch's generational testament, the epitome of amorphous emotion seeking to realize itself. "Young Bosnia had no fixed program or stable organization," writes Dedijer, "but they had a specific ethic of their own, a very altruistic one . . . more like living saints, the last puritans of our civilization, than people who cared about their own lives." Young Bosnian students could read and reread the letters of Zherajitch:

> Down in Bosnia the whole of our life is inclined towards slavery. . . . Our land and our schools gave us some kind of fear, indecisiveness. We, the youngest, have to make a new history. We have to fight against pessimism, against despair. We are a new generation, we are new men in every way.[15]

Gavrilo Princip especially enshrined in his consciousness the memory of Zherajitch, the students' martyr.

The Bosnian student activists, moreover, were in thoroughgoing revolt against their fathers' ways. Gatchinovitch wrote to Trotsky that they had "a rule of obligatory abstinence from love-making and drinking. . . ." Chastity was the strict rule among the Young Bosnians, and their asceticism, notes Dedijer, was "a personal reaction against the stark realities of Bosnia and Herzegovina, a wish to be different from their fathers." Neither Zherajitch nor Gavrilo Princip ever had sexual intercourse in their lives.[16]

The assassination of the Archduke Franz Ferdinand was the culminating achievement of the Yugoslav student movement. It was no isolated occurrence involving a single demented lad, but the final consequence of the emotions and ideas which the student movement had actively promoted.

In January 1913, the student leader, Gatchinovitch, tried to persuade some Young Bosnians to assassinate the governor of Bosnia, General Potiorek. He provided them with equipment, instructed them how to commit suicide after the deed, but the young conspirators, either recovering their rationality or taking fright, threw their weapons away at the border. Early in 1914, the indefatigable Gatchinovitch was helping to organize the attempt on the archduke's life. Gavrilo Princip became his chosen instrument.

What manner of person was Gavrilo Princip, student, whose act tipped the historical scales to bring about the First World War? We have, it so happens, first-hand notes of a psychological report on Gavrilo by his psychiatrist, Dr. Martin Pappenheim, professor at the University of Vienna; their conversations took place in the fortress-prison of Theresienstadt between the months of February and June 1916.[17] Young Princip was the son of a quiet, enterprising peasant, who was quite uninterested in politics. Gavrilo, however, was soon participating in nationalistic demonstrations. "Was in the first lines of the students. Was badly treated by the professors." Generational grievance and revolt were in full evidence. Gavrilo brooded. "Was not much with other schoolboys, always alone." When his father and brother would not send him more money, he "promised to be a good student." Thus, he remained at Belgrade. He fell in love; it was "ideal love"; he never wrote to or kissed the girl. "In this connection will reveal no more of himself." His motives, he said, were "revenge and love." He wanted "to revenge the people"; he was a "mass of ideals."

Two years after his deed, Princip told how much he had admired terrorists and how he had longed for his own death:

> There already had been attempts at assassinations before. The perpetrators were like heroes to our young people. He had no thought of becoming a hero. He merely wanted to die for his idea. Before the assassination he had read an article of Kropotkin about what we can do in case of a world-wide revolution . . . The older generation wanted to secure liberty from Austria in a legal way; we do not believe in such a liberty.

Loyal to the tradition of student terrorism, he had tried to commit suicide. After shooting the archduke, he took potassium cyanide "but was weak and vomited." His fantasy life for several months before the attempt was filled with murderous imagery: "In Serajevo used to dream every night he was a political murderer, struggling with gendarmes and policemen. Read much about the Russian revolution, about the fightings. This idea had taken hold of him. Admits that the earlier constraints had vanished." He thought of himself as one of the intellectual elite who aimed to guide the masses:

> He considered that if he prepared the atmosphere the idea of revolution and liberation would spread first among men of intelligence and then later in the

masses. Thought that thereby attention of the *intelligentsia* would be directed upon it.

He could not face the question of the consequences of what he had done. He struggled to hold on to the notion that his deed had not been in vain, though doubt obtruded: "Cannot believe that the World War was a consequence of the assassination; cannot feel himself responsible for the catastrophe; therefore cannot say if it was a service. But fears he did it in vain." He was a man of books: "Books for me signify life." But the books he read so much of his life were primarily the literature of revolt. "Read many anarchistic, socialistic, nationalistic pamphlets, *belles lettres* and everything." He bought these books, brooded on them, "did not speak about these things."

What was, indeed, the emotional source of Gavrilo Princip's strange combination of traits—his terrorism and suicidalism? The quest to understand Gavrilo and his comrades of Bosnia will, indeed, take us to the unconscious of the Bosnian student movement. Most helpful facts are given to us by the gifted and authoritative Yugoslav writer, Vladimir Dedijer, the official biographer of Marshal Tito and the lone defender as well of the frank-speaking critic, Milovan Djilas. Dedijer's uncle Konstantin was the close friend and comrade of Gavrilo Princip in Young Bosnia. Dedijer recalled their emotions toward their mothers and fathers:

Konstantin was a member of a secret organization in the school that belonged to the Young Bosnia movement. Under the influence of Chernyshevsky, Konstantin became interested in the problems of the social relations between men and women in the country. This intellectual interest had its emotional side: He adored his mother, Nana, and his sisters. As a boy he had had a severe shock one night, when he saw his father, Risto, returning from a drinking-party in the local cafe. He was flat on the floor, vomiting pure rum, and Nana was standing above him beating herself with her fists in despair.

Princip had much the same attitude towards his own mother, an energetic peasant woman from a village in West Bosnia. She was the real protector of the family. . . .

Konstantin's notebooks are full of citations from Serbian folksongs on the role of mothers in the life of the Serbian people, and Gavrilo confessed to Konstantin his devotion to his own mother. Konstantin's ideal was Jevrosima, the mother of Prince Marko.[18]

The curious terminology in Dedijer's account of Gavrilo Princip will, of course, not fail to strike the reader. Gavrilo "confessed" to his love for his mother. In normal situations, a son would not feel that a statement that he loved his mother was a "confession," for a "confession" involves the notion that one feels guilty concerning the confessed behavior. Yet here we have the two activists of the Bosnian student movement confessing to each other of their inordinate attachment to their mothers. And the traumatic event in Konstantin's boyhood was the memory of the humiliation of his mother by a drunken father. Intense, unresolved Oedipal feelings, a tremendous attachment to their mothers, and a violent hostility to their fathers, were evidently salient traits of the student activists of Young Bosnia. In traditional societies, the latent, unconscious conflict of generations is strong but is kept in leash by powerful socially repressive forces and sanctions. A political dislocation, however, can introduce the factor of the de-authoritization of the fathers; into this breach in the defensive structure of the older generation's authority surge forward all the accumulated energies stemming from the resentment of the young. The Bosnian student movement, as Dedijer indicates, had such an emotional mainspring in generational conflict:

The conflict of generations in Bosnian society occurred also in our family. My mother's brother, Uncle Konstantin, at the age of fourteen, became a member of "Young Bosnia," the organization of rebels against every form of Bosnian traditionalism, of which his own grandfather, Jovan Babic, was an outstanding representative. For Jovan Babic, woman was nothing but an object of man's lust; for Konstantin and his generation, even the expression of love for a woman was an encroachment upon her personality. Konstantin consciously gave his life at the age of nineteen for the achievement of his ideal, in the same way as did his friend, Gavrilo Princip, the Bosnian schoolboy who assassinated Franz Ferdinand.

The fathers and grandfathers who humiliated the mothers were those who allowed the Serbian motherland as well to be humiliated. Repressed mother-love was so strong that it entered into all relations with women; sexual asceticism was a defensive mechanism against sexuality, which was always diffused with Oedipal feeling and its attendant guilt.

The "student trio," assassins of the archduke, all less than twenty years of age, were too young to be given the death penalty. All three died before the war's end of the disease of so many student revolutionists—tuberculosis. Gavrilo Princip, filled with dreams of killing policemen, had finally killed an imperial father figure. He avoided confronting his fantasy life with reality, and preferred to dwell in the dream world of his pamphlets: "What he now thinks the right thing he would not say. Has no desire to speak on the matter. It makes him unquiet to speak about it. When he thinks by himself, then everything is clear, but when he speaks with anybody, then he becomes uncertain." Thus, Gavrilo Princip enacted his heroic politics of generational struggle and unknowingly imposed its pattern of self-destruction on all Europe and most of the world. Millions of men moved to their death, and over civilization drifted a nightmare which has not yet lifted.

A death consciousness prevailed in the ranks of the Bosnian student activists. When Leonid Andreyev's *The Seven Who Were Hanged* was translated into Serbian in 1910, it made the deepest impression on the Young Bosnians. On the eve of the assassination of the Archduke Franz Ferdinand in 1914, Danilo Ilitch, co-conspirator of Gavrilo Princip, wrote that Andreyev in this work "has tried to solve the problem of the conquest of death, of its subjugation in the name of a higher goal. . . ." Death mysticism was the answer to the guilt which gnawed in the unconscious of the student activists. In the portrait of the death of Russian student terrorists, they found their own compulsive drives to self-destruction assuaged. The politics of generational revolt was a politics of death worship, not of life.[19]

It would be erroneous, of course, to say that Gavrilo Princip's deed was *the* cause of the First World War. The familiar rivalries and hatreds among nations have had their libraries of documentation. Yet for two generations a tradition of peace had been taking root in Europe. Peaceful social democratic movements were gaining influence: great figures, such as Jean Jaurès, were growing in stature and in their European significance. It was likely indeed that Russia, if it had been spared the stress of war, would have continued to evolve in a liberal capitalist direction. Lenin, before the war, as he observed the development of the Russion agrarian structure in a bourgeois direction, was giving up hope of seeing the revolution; after it had taken place, he said its "main" cause had been the war, for what propelled the revolution was the overwhelming desire of the peasant-in-uniform for peace.[20] There was hope in Europe that a rational society would emerge, the society whose prophets were Wells, Shaw, Anatole France, Norman Angell. The equilibrium of Europe was unstable, but the roots of potential stability were there as well as the possibilities of disruption. In Russia, the studentry was gradually turning away from the politics of generational revolt. Its echo in the Balkans was strong enough, however, to upset the European balance of power and mind, and to set moving the self-destructive chain of events. Gavrilo Princip had killed his policeman and achieved his place as a hero, a father destroyer, in history.

Thirty years later the same emotions of conflict with the older generation which nurtured Gavrilo Princip and his terrorist friends issued in the heroism of the Yugoslav Partisans.

It seems to me that it was precisely the repressed dark moods, this psychologizing, that provided the base for a political and social discontent which was all the more profound because it was moot and unconscious—out of the very fabric of the soul, out of every pore of one's inner life. Later, in Belgrade, when I became acquainted with my fellow students at the university, I noticed that they, too, each in his own way, to be sure, had traveled the same path—the same literature à la Dostoyevsky and Krleza, the same inner crises and somber moods, dark discontent and bitterness over cruelty, and injustice among men and in society generally.

Russian literature, pre-eminently the artistic document of generational conflict, once again exerted the greatest influence on students' ideas:

It was classical and humanistic literature that drew me to Communism. . . . The only thing that could exert any influence, and indeed did, was great literature, particularly the Russian classics. . . . Awakening noble thoughts, it confronted the reader with the cruelties and injustices of the existing order.[21]

The ceaseless familial strife in the Montenegrin hills where "everything is at war with everything else," even parents against children, the blood feuds of families in which one's father lost honor when he failed to avenge his father's murder, unending bloodshed and cruelty, the fear when one's friendship transgressed the blood feud, the shame with the utter filth and backwardness of one's family, all these made students such as Djilas into generational revolutionists long before they were political ones. The revolt against the political order, the political dictatorship, was surrogate for a revolt against the emotional dictatorship of the familial order.

Vladimir Dedijer has recently argued in his monumental *The Road to Sarajevo* that the student terrorists cannot be fully understood without reference to the South Slav tradition of tyrannicide; especially influential, he says, was the legend and folklore which surrounded the murder of the Ottoman Sultan Murad by the Serbian nobleman Milos Obilic at Kosovo in 1389.[22] The peasant masses fed on this folklore with its idealization of the heroic Violent Type. And yet the fact remains that the Bosnian student movement was in revolt against the fathers' culture, and was ashamed of its tradition.

The terrorist propensity of the Bosnian student movement was a compulsive pattern which issued from the intensity of its generational revolt. The specific peculiarities of Bosnian tradition and folklore were not the primary causal factor. The Bosnian students were immersed in the writings of Kropotkin and Ibsen; from Kropotkin especially they drew the inspirational message of the intellectual's vocation to make history. They were immersed in the modern literature of revolt, and drew from it the sanction of modernity for their individual actions. If the traditional Serbian folklore had been the source of the terrorist compulsion, one would have expected Bosnian peasants to have figured largely among the assassins. But almost all the terrorists were students, not peasants—students whose emotions were shaped by the advanced, modern, revolutionary literary culture of the student environment. The hugely disproportionate role of students among the terrorists testifies in itself that not tradition but causal influences peculiar to students were the controlling factors in their actions. To be sure, generational revolt tended to be strong among peasants' sons in the measure that the fathers' culture in its backwardness and primitiveness was de-authoritized in the sons' eyes. The folklore that moved the students was that of the Russian revolutionary movement with its self-sacrificing intellectual elitism—Chernyshevsky, Bakunin, Kropotkin; the revolutionary students of the world have their own generational pantheon, whatever culture and tradition they have issued from.[23]

The necessary and sufficient condition for the rise of a student movement, whatever the cultural background and whatever the varying circumstances of economic development, is this "alienation" from the elder generation, and the de-authoritization of its status. This was noted by Milovan Djilas in an essay he wrote in 1937 on Gatchinovitch in which he compared the movements of Bosnia with those of nineteenth-century Russia:

It would be a mistake to identify the situation in Bosnia and Hercegovina with the Russia of the 1880's, when the Russian Populists and other dissatisfied elements organized conspiracies and secret societies. In the Russia of that period (especially in Great Russia) there was no national problem; besides, the Russian capitalism of that period was on a lower level than that of Austria at the time of the annexation of Bosnia and Hercegovina. . . . A similarity existed between the two intelligentsia: both were isolated from society, that is all.[24]

The Russian student movement was the admired prototype of Young Bosnia and the Serbian student movement, as it has been for most student movements in the modern era. It therefore warrants next our closest attention.

NOTES

1. Vladimir Dedijer, *The Road to Sarajevo* (New York, 1966), p. 176.
2. Sidney Bradshaw Fay, *The Origins of the World War*, Vol. II, *After Sarajevo: Immediate Causes of the War* (New York, 1929), p. 95.
3. *Loc. cit.*
4. Dedijer, *op. cit.*, pp. 182–183.
5. Fay, *op. cit.*, p. 98. See also R. W. Seton-Watson, *Sarajevo: A Study in the Origins of the Great War* (London, 1926), p. 70; Dedijer, *op. cit.*, p. 213.
6. Dedijer, *op. cit.*, p. 237.
7. *Ibid.*, p. 237.
8. Fay, *op. cit.*, p. 100.
9. Dedijer, *op. cit.*, p. 272.
10. *Ibid.*, p. 272.
11. *Ibid.*, p. 262.
12. Seton-Watson, *op. cit.*, p. 72.
13. *Ibid.*, p. 73.
14. Vladimir Dedijer, *The Beloved Land* (New York, 1961), p. 84.
15. *Ibid.*, p. 83.
16. Dedijer, *The Road to Sarajevo*, pp. 208–209.
17. Hamilton Fish Armstrong, "Confessions of the Assassin Whose Deed Led to the World War," *Current History*, XXVI (1927), 701 ff.; Dedijer, *The Road to Sarajevo*, p. 357.
18. Dedijer, *The Beloved Land*, pp. 85–86.
19. Dedijer, *The Road to Sarajevo*, p. 308.
20. See Bertram D. Wolfe, *Three Who Made a Revolution* (New York, 1948; Boston, 1962), p. 361; *Strange Communists I Have Known* (New York, 1965), p. 18. Also see Joachim Remak, "Sarajevo—Design and Accident," *Journal of Central European Affairs*, XXI (July 1961), 165–175.
21. Milovan Djilas, *Land without Justice* (New York, 1958), pp. 352–354.
22. Dedijer, *The Road to Sarajevo*, pp. 250–251, 236.
23. " 'Chernishevsky's *What Is to be Done* was passed from hand to hand. Whole pages from it were copied and learned by heart. Besides Chernishevsky, the most esteemed writers were Bakunin, Herzen, Dostoyevsky (especially *Crime and Punishment*) and Maxim Gorky. . . . Special study was devoted to the Italian and German liberation movements.' Mazzini was 'the real and great man.' " See Dedijer, *The Road to Sarajevo*, pp. 177–178, 227, 232–233, 185.
24. Dedijer, *The Road to Sarajevo*, p. 227.

FOUR

The Russian Student Movement: The Heroic Will to Martyrdom

STUDENT

by Nikolai Platonovich Ogarev

He was born to an unhappy lot
He studied in a miserable school
But endured his young years' torment
For the living labor of science.
With year to year of life
His devotion to the people strengthened.
His thirst for the common liberation grew warmer
His thirst for a better common lot.

And, persecuted by Czarist vengeance
And Boyars' fears,
He set out to wander,
For the peoples' call,
To cry out the cry to all the peasants
From the East to West
"Assemble in friendly column
Stand bravely, brother behind brother,
To conquer for all the people
Their land and freedom."

He ended his life in this world
In the snowy Siberian camps.

No hypocrite, but all his life
Remained faithful to the struggle
Up to his last breath
He was telling in the midst of exile
Fight for all the people
For their own land and freedom.

1868
(Dedicated, on Bakunin's urging,
to "My young friend Nechayev")

No student movement underwent the extremes of passion and exaltation as much as the Russian. Its tragedy and achievement, its hope and despair, have been the theme of some of the world's greatest literature. Yet it remains uncomprehended, a phenomenon with an unfathomed source, moving across history with an ill-understood message of youthful martyrdom. What we have to say may be regarded as a series of footnotes to Ivan Turgenev's immortal *Fathers and Sons;* we can only try to transcribe into sociological prose what his novelist's genius perceived at the very beginning of the movement.

For several decades the Russian student movement was in a contest for power with the Czarist government. In the course of this struggle, terrorism, suicidalism, and elitism became the movement's dominant traits. When the Fighting Organization of the Social Revolutionary party undertook, for instance, to assassinate the Minister of Interior, von Plehve, in 1904, it was natural that almost all those chosen for the deed were students who had been expelled from the universities for their political activities during the years immediately preceding. The Czarist government, with its ceaseless repression of the students, had raised successive generations of bitter adversaries. "During the revolutionary epoch of 1905," noted Boris Nicolaievsky, "the leaders of all the revolutionary organizations, Social Revolutionary as well as Social Democratic, were almost entirely recruited from the former participants in the student movements."[1] Moreover, as Eva Broido wrote, "almost the whole of the student body" was at the end of the nineteenth century, in sympathy with the revolutionary ideas and hostile to the government.

What was it that moved the Russian student movement? What made it the most consequential in the history of the world, as it shaped in basic ways the course of Russian political evolution?

The Russian student movement, classical exemplar of all modern student movements, concentrated in an almost pure state the characteristics of emotional, generational revolt which have inspired all student movements. Ceasing to respect their elders, the students looked elsewhere for guidance among the most advanced contemporary philosophical prophets. Stirred by an amalgam of emotions—with all the ingredients of self-sacrifice and self-destruction, the desire to identify with the lowliest, along with the contrary desire to rule as the highest—the student movement tragically combined a high idealism with a violent irrationality destructive of its own ideal. The Russian student movement was the historical integument in which the anxieties of children externalized themselves in political form.

Contemporary Americans found it hard to understand the unrest among the Russian students. The great anarchist, Peter Kropotkin, as he completed a journey through the United States, tried to explain it to American readers in 1901:

> The last student disturbances in Russia were quite different from all the disturbances which have taken place in the Russian universities for the last forty years. They began, as all student movements begin, with an insignificant incident, which concerned the students alone; but, owing to a series of circumstances quite peculiar to Russia, they took all of a sudden, a political complexion. . . .

Kropotkin had, of course, seen nothing like it among the happy American students: "During my stay last month, at Cambridge," he wrote, "the Harvard students held a noisy meeting to protest again the 'mutton monotony' of their food at Memorial Hall." At the same time Russian students at Kiev had been agitated by the arrest of one of their fellows for misconduct in the streets. Harvard and Kiev, however, were located in two different political universes. "At Harvard, the meeting ended in fun; but at Kiev the dean of the university excluded a number of students from the university for one year. . . ." The Czar's troops were called upon to disperse the students' meeting. It did not start with anything political, said Kropotkin, "and there lies the cue to all the students' disturbance of the last forty years."[2]

The Russian studentry indeed inhabited a psychological universe wholly outside the ken of the Americans. When Count Sergius Witte visited Columbia University in 1905, he inquired "whether student riots and disturbances, such as are customary in Russia, were possible in the American universities. The idea apparently never occurred to the professors. Should any student attempt, they said, to devote himself at the university to other activities than study, he would be immediately cast out of the school by his own comrades."[3] What, then, was the character of the psychological world which the Russian studentry inhabited?

The Psychological Source of the Student Movement: The Student Unconscious and the Spirit of Generational Revolt

Again and again, Russian revolutionists testified to the strange, undefined feeling of revolt which would come over them during their student days. It seemed to arise from somewhere deep in themselves, they knew not how; the revolutionary unconscious was in existence long before the revolutionary consciousness. It set them looking for a cause to which they could give themselves; it set them in search of a community with the economically discontent, but it itself usually had no origin in a personal sense of economic grievance. Julius Martov, the closest personal friend of Lenin's youth, and later the most distinguished of the Menshevik leaders, described this revolutionary unconscious:

> Vague feelings disturbed me and upon my conscience I could not determine just what stirred my soul. . . . The striving for pure science, for cognition of the world, was remarkably interwoven with just as intensive a striving for comradeship with those who protested against reality and were incensed by it, and whom I expected to meet in the student milieu.

There was an incipient comradeship of the sons in a revolt against the "reality" which their fathers represented:

> By the same sort of threads then yet unclear, comradeship in the task of pursuing scientific truth was combined in my imagination with a militant fraternity of youth, hostile to the "social order," although I could not as yet concretely picture the form of my future "rebellious" activity. A romantic sensation that I had entered upon the threshold of exploits and dangers was not foreign to me.[4]

The longing for universal fraternity took on the aspect of a sociological mysticism for the young students. Freedom was where revolt was brewing. Thus Peter Struve, early co-worker of Lenin, and author of the first platform of the Russian Social Democratic Labor party, wrote that at the age of fifteen a "passion for freedom" was born within him "with something like an elemental force." He gave himself with his fellow-students to the new socialistic asceticism as a way of life; they spurned parties and jollity, holding austerely to their "strictly ascetic tea-drinking, with serious talks on social and personal morality."[5] The renunciatory, ascetic ethic, this self-punishment, was a sign by which the students demonstrated to their own consciences that theirs was a selfless revolt. It was the way in which they tried to assuage at least partially the guilt which every revolt against the fathers entails.

A few years later, the student Ivan Maisky, later Soviet Ambassador to Britain, was experiencing similar Byronic yearnings, discontents which emanated from some unknown core of his existence and pervaded his consciousness; he had no clear sense of what the student movement stood for, but when he heard of it he knew instinctively this was his home:

> In spite of the fact that my moods in the winter of 1899–1900 were melancholy and set in a master key, my search for the lights of life continued. And it was a very intensive search, only it inevitably bore the stamp of these moods. I read a good deal, but I was now mostly attracted to melancholy, demonic, soul-stirring literature. At this period Byron made an irresistible impression on me. I was enthusiastic about him to the point of self-forgetfulness . . . most of all I was carried away by *Manfred* and *Cain*.

In this self-destructive and other-destructive romanticism, Maisky recounts:

I hated Tsarism and played with the idea of destroying the autocratic system. I sympathized with the students' movement and read "political economy" zealously . . . but in reality I had no clear sense of what I wanted, where I was going or in what concrete forms I would satisfy my "struggle for freedom." Indeed, what ought I to do when I got to St. Petersburg? Study at the university? Write articles in *Russkoye Bogatstvo*? Organize students' strikes? Study history and "political economy"? Compose passionate hymns in honor of the struggle for freedom? Grieve over the bitter lot of the peasant and the worker? What was that "liberating army" which I liked to talk about so much?

Then he remembered the "exiled students" and their strange message, which now reached him like the mysterious answer to his quest. He would follow the path opened by the modern Manfreds, the Cains of his time, proud in their defiance of the mighty ones:

Then I remembered that when I was still at Omsk I had occasionally heard something from the "exiled students" about the strikes and unrest in our factories. They usually talked about this in a whisper and with a mysterious air as though it were a great secret, although I was always left with the impression that they themselves had only a vague idea of such matters.[6]

Russian students were moved by powerful unconscious forces to sunder their ties with the prevailing, parental culture. In 1889, Gleb Krzhyzhanovsky, later head of the State Planning Commission and Lenin's friend (and together with Martov one of the two men whom Lenin ever addressed with the familiar *ty*), became a student at the St. Petersburg Technological Institute. The following year he joined the student Left Wing:

I remember that I and my new friends were at first full of some undefined but strong desire to "burn our boats"—to break with that philistinism that had nurtured us, who had come together under one roof from every corner of the country. Threads linking us with recollections of the struggle of the hero-revolutionaries. . . .[7]

Many generations of students shared the feeling of young Alexander Kerensky as he arrived at the University of St. Petersburg: "We newcomers experienced an exhilarating sense of freedom. Most of us had been living at home and were now for the first time at liberty to do as we liked." They took an especial pleasure in boycotting and snubbing politically unpopular professors. "I remember," recalls Kerensky, "that we particularly enjoyed making things unpleasant for Professor Erwin Grimm. . . . As soon as the object of our scorn appeared in the corridor we would break into jeers and follow him into the lecture hall, where his words would be drowned in pandemonium. . . . The campaign was carried on until the fun began to wear off, and then peace was restored." Such were the joys of generational revolt. It could become fixated in revolutionary commitments, or it might be a transient phase. But its unconscious motive power was undeniable. Kerensky, for instance, at the end of his second year, found himself at a students' meeting on the main staircase of the university. Suddenly he made his way through the crowd to the top of the stairs "and launched into an impassioned speech." "I still do not know what prompted me to speak," he writes, but he urged the students with deep feeling to help the nation in its struggle for liberation.[8]

The revolutionary student activist was, indeed, an invariant, unchanging psychological type from his first appearance in the 1860s to the early 1900s. The tragic Sophia Perovskaya, for example, heroine of the Narodnaya Volya, had all the character traits in their purity of the student revolutionist. At the age of twenty-six the chief woman conspirator in the assassination of Czar Alexander II, Sophia was molded politically in the Chaikovsky Circle, a movement principally active among students during the seventies and filled with the back-to-the-people spirit. She was driven by the compulsions of generational revolt. Sophia came from a noble family; her father was governor-general of St. Petersburg at the time when Dmitry Karakozov tried to kill the Czar in 1866. The father was a "typical petty tyrant, harsh, powerful, dull-witted," tyrannical especially to his family.[9] Little Sophia watched her mother being humiliated. The father, wrote Vera Figner, "was a despot of despots, who not only insulted the mother of his children, but forced his little son to insult and abuse his mother. . . ." A staunch advocate of serfdom, the father brought its violence into his own home. Sophia "came to hate her father; this hatred became the decisive psychological factor in her development."[10] She extended her hatred to "any animal-like manifestation of crude masculine power," indeed to all masculine power whatsoever.[11] She linked the noisy aristocratic worldly life which she knew with that of "the image of her father-tormentor."[12] When her father forbade her to receive her friends in her house, Sophia decided to leave her father's house. She was sixteen years old. Evidently she never saw her father again; when she wished to see her mother, she used the back stairs. She studied to become a schoolteacher, and the Chaikovsky Circle became her family. She became the most cold and austere of revolutionists; the idea of personal happiness so long as others were suffering repelled her. She evidently inspired the remark one revolutionist made to another: "Have you noticed that our women are more cruel than our men?"[13] Such were the ultimate nuclei in the unconscious from which the energies for the student movement were liberated.

The adolescent years were thus often the crucial ones in the life of the student activist. His experience of revolt became fixated in him as a permanent way of life. The young Lenin was almost the ideal-typical case, according to his wife, Krupskaya, of a student revolutionist conceived in the experience of generational revolt. His break with religion at the age of fourteen or fifteen was at the same time an intense symbolic rejection of his father. Young Vladimir's father once complained that his children were poor church attenders; a teacher friend advised using the rod. "Upon hearing this Ilyich, burning with indignation, decided to break with religion;

he rushed into the garden, took off the cross that he wore around his neck, and threw it away."[14] He sought a different way of life in the writings of the nihilist, Pisarev. When his elder brother, Alexander, was executed for participating in the student plot to murder the Czar in 1887, the young Lenin felt it was "a good thing" that the father had died earlier, for he would have been against the son.

That year Lenin became a student at Kazan University, and shortly afterward, according to his sister, was transformed by "student issues" into an activist. The workers and peasants in 1887, she recalled, were in a lull and political depression; "only among the students did unrest flare up sporadically instead of lying dormant as was the case with the rest of the population." The "student issues" were the customary ones:

> . . . the compulsory wearing of uniform, the system of informers, close surveillance and spying in the University, prohibition of all organizations, even of such innocuous ones as societies of students originating from the same rural areas, expulsion and sending home of all who were to any extent compromised in the eyes of the authorities—all this electrified the atmosphere in the universities. . . .

To a large extent, all this irrationality was itself the regime's anxiety-haunted response to the students' plot to assassinate the Czar. A vicious spiral mutually heightening irrationality was characteristic of the relations of the student movement to the absolutist government. Shortly afterward the young Lenin was said to have been "in the front ranks in a state of great excitement, practically threatening the inspector with his fists."[15] Arrested together with thirty-nine other students, he was banished from Kazan. He had burned his bridges behind him.

The emotion of a son's revolt against his father always remained dominant in Lenin's character. When he wrote his basic tract, *What Is to be Done?*, he characteristically chose the title of the most sympathetic of the novels of generational revolt, Chernyshevsky's novel of that name. One would have thought that in exile he would have appreciated the Swiss democracy in which the wife of the highest official did her own cleaning every day. But no, it was a world of "Philistinism" and "petty-bourgeois dullness"—in short, his father's way of life. The petty-bourgeois life lacked the death-motif which made a play like Tolstoy's *The Living Corpse* so significant for Lenin.[16] He was always uncomfortably aware that his revolutionary ideology emanated from an irrational, emotional source which he never dared examine. That was probably why when, in his early twenties, fresh from the university, he read Chekhov's story, "Ward No. 6," with its probing of the delicate balance between sanity and insanity, the young Lenin "felt positively afraid." "I just could not remain in my room," he said, "but had to get up and go out. I had the feeling that I, too, was locked up in Ward No. 6."[17] Samara, his father's town, had become for him, says his sister, "a sort of 'Ward No. 6' "; his revolt against his father seemed, indeed, linked to a struggle to preserve his sanity.

The leaders of all the Russian revolutionary parties and factions were spawned in the shoals of student rebellion. Not only the Bolshevik Lenin and the Menshevik Martov but also the Social Revolutionary leader, Victor Chernov, later the first and only president of the Constitutional Assembly, were products of the student movement. Victor's first arrest came when, after a student strike at Moscow in 1894, he was convicted of association with a student populist group, and exiled for three years to his native province.[18]

Lenin all his life venerated the memory of the student terrorists, Zhelyabov and Kaliaev. From the "ladders and scaffolding" of a centralized party of professional revolutions, he wrote in 1902, "there would soon ascend Social-Democratic Zhelyabovs. . . . That is what we ought to be dreaming about!"[19] Sixteen years later, when the Bolsheviks in 1918 were struggling to hold power, Lenin defended his policies as in the tradition of the student terrorist, Kaliaev, assassin in 1905 of the Grand Duke Sergei, the Czar's uncle. The Bolshevik ethic was the ethic of the Russian student movement fulfilled. Lenin wrote:

> Let us suppose Kalyayev, in order to kill a tyrant and monster, acquires a revolver from an absolute villain, a scoundrel and robber, by promising him bread, money and vodka for the service rendered.
>
> Can one condemn Kalyayev for his "deal with a robber" for the sake of obtaining a deadly weapon? Every sensible person will answer "no." If there is nowhere else for Kalyayev to get a revolver, and if his intention is really an honorable one (the killing of a tyrant, not killing for plunder), then he should not be reproached but commended for acquiring a revolver in this way.[20]

The rebellious theological student, Joseph Stalin, similarly found his calling as a "professional revolutionist": "I joined the revolutionary movement when fifteen years old," he said, "when I became connected with underground groups of Russian Marxists then living in Transcaucasia. These groups exerted a great influence on me and instilled in me a taste for underground Marxist literature."[21] Sons in revolt against their elders have always tended to be drawn to a secret society of kindred. A few years later in 1898, Stalin, then nineteen years old, became a student at the Tbilisi Theological Seminary, the alma mater to a whole generation of student leaders who attended the seminary because there was no university in Georgia. The young Stalin (Djugashvili) was soon attracted to a circle led by a student leader, Lado Ketskhoveli, who had been expelled together with more than eighty comrades from the seminary in 1894. These theological students were in revolt against their surrogate fathers and their theology. "In protest against the outrageous regime and the jesuitical methods prevalent at the seminary, I was ready to become, and actually did become, a revolutionary, a believer in Marxism," said Stalin. There was virtually no working class in Tbilisi, and its people still had the outlook, according to D. M. Lang, of the Oriental bazaar world.[22] But the young student revolutionist, in rising up against the seminary, sought to project his inner revolt on the political world, and began to seek out circles of artisans, tobacco workers, masons, and shoemakers, to whom to evangelize about socialism. At the theological seminary, said Stalin, what outraged him most as a student was the prying and spying of his teachers:

Their principal method is spying, prying, worming their way into people's souls and outraging their feelings. What good can there be in that? For instance, the spying in the hostel. At nine o'clock the bell rings for morning tea, we go to the dining room, and when we return to our rooms we find that meantime a search has been made and all our chests have been ransacked. . . . What good point can there be in that?[23]

Thus Stalin in middle age recalled his formation as a student activist in the Tbilisi Theological Seminary; he later outdid his fathers by prying and spying upon them tenfold.

From the first, among all the student revolutionaries there was an awesome preoccupation with the problem of guilt and responsibility. It became central in students' minds toward the end of the sixties; they continued thenceforth to brood over their guilt toward the people, and how their lives could be truly ones of repentance.[24] Thus, the founder of Russian Marxism, George Plekhanov, as a student in 1874, a "conventional, industrious, self-disciplined youth" as Leopold Haimson writes, "became suddenly at seventeen the victim of an aroused and insistent sense of guilt." There was an "unpaid debt" (in his words) which hovered in his consciousness. It made him feel guilty before every ordinary workingman: "When I met Mitrofanov for the first time and learned that he was a worker, i.e., one of the representatives of the people, a mixed feeling of smallness and discomfort stirred in my soul, as if I had been guilty of something before him."[25] To overcome the loneliness, estrangement, and alienation from the world which this guilt imposed, one had to seek a "fusion with the people," as the anarchist followers of Bakunin described it. The conflict of fathers and sons, as in Plekhanov's own case, generated emotions of guilt which colored all one's social perceptions. One looked at social realities with an existential a priori, and every social fact was categorized, as through a prism, in terms of one's personal guilt. The sense of personal guilt which centuries earlier would have sent young men to monasteries now directed them into a new self-immolation, in which they submerged their individual identities among the people. One's sense of self, with its burden of guilt, was something of which one longed to be rid.

The Longing for Fusion with the People: The Back-to-the-People Motif

Every student movement seeks to identify itself with the lowliest in society, with a vicarious source of massive strength. That is what we might call the populist ingredient in student movements. It has several psychological sources. The sons are emotionally ready to identify themselves with those whom their fathers oppress. Mao Tse-tung, for instance, recalls how he made common cause as a boy with those peasants whom his harsh father exploited. Then again, the students as intellectuals feel that they lack the physical support, in numbers and sheer force, to effect social change.[26] A numerically small student movement especially searches the social environment for potential allies with whom it can unite. It may go through a process of trial and error in this quest for a mass ally; and when spurned by the masses, will turn to tactics based on the direct assertion of the students' will, whether in terrorism or other modes of direct action. There has thus been a typical "dialectic" in student movements: first, their restlessness and search for an issue; then their quest for a class ally among the lowly masses whose allegiance is forecast by the attractive power of the defined issue; then often the students' experience of rejection by the masses, and finally the turn to terrorism and direct action. Thus, the Russian student movement sought out the peasantry, suffered rebuffs, then hurled itself into a heroic terrorism based on its own resources. Thus, later student movements sought out the proletariat or, as in America during the fifties and sixties, turned from a socially complacent working class to link up with the Negro in his movement for civil rights. All finally experienced rejection.

Every student movement tends to assume a distinctive garb. What this garb proclaims is generally an identification with the lower classes. The girls will be unkempt, unwashed, and wear the plainest and drabbest of clothes. The men will wear the clothes of lumpenproletarians, and be as unshaven and ungroomed as the derelict of Skid Row. Student movements have always adhered to a voluntary asceticism. The Russian studentry at the turn of the century, as Berdyaev noted, was imbued with this "revolutionary asceticism."[27] In the United States, students in a populist enthusiasm would fancy themselves white Negroes, cultivate a speech and gait modeled on the Negro, walk on picket lines clapping their hands and prancing in a way which seemed to them to fulfill this identification. In Russia they would don workingmen's and peasants' clothes as part of an experience of transfiguration akin to that of the wearer of priestly vestments. Under ordinary circumstances, fashions diffuse downward from the upper to the lower classes. In the emotional climate of student movements, on the other hand, fashions are borrowed from the lower classes and diffuse to the upper. The law of fashion thus diverges in student movements from its customary workings.

Thus, the cycle of the students' movement entered its back-to-the-people phase. It began with an exaltation of the people and of the students' own mission, with all the fervor of selfless dedication. As Kropotkin recorded:

In every town of Russia . . . small groups were formed for self-improvement and self-education. . . . The aim of all that reading and discussion was to solve the great question which rose before them. In what way could they be useful to the masses? Gradually, they came to the idea that the only way was to settle amongst the people, and to live the people's life.[28]

Alexander Herzen in 1862 sounded the keynote of this new era:

But where are you young people to go who have been forbidden learning? Shall we tell you where?

Listen, for darkness does not prevent listening: from all regions of our vast, vast country, from Don and Ural, from Volga and Dnieper the sigh grows, the protest rises; it is the first roar of the tidal wave which rises, big with storms, after an ominously long silence. In to the people! To the people!—there is your place, exiles of science, show these Bistroms they will not make church servants out of you, but fighters, and no hirelings without a country, but fighters of the Russian people! Hail to you! You are starting a new epoch, you have understood that the time of whispering, of distant allusions, of forbidden books is coming to an end. You still print in secret at home, but openly you protest. Hail to you, younger brothers, and our blessing for the future! Oh, if you knew how our heart beat, how the tears sprang into our eyes when we read of the students' disorders in St. Petersburg![29]

The anarchist Bakunin similarly addressed an appeal to the students of Russian universities in apocalyptic grandeur. "My young friends, abandon as soon as possible this doomed world, these universities and schools, from which they are expelling you now and in which they have always endeavored to separate you from its people. Go to the people! There you will find your field, your life, your knowledge."[30] The movement reached its height in 1873. As one activist, Sergei Kravchinski (later known as Stepniak), described it:

They went out as bearers of a revelation rather than political propagandists. It was as if a voice resounded throughout the Empire, calling on those whose souls were not yet dead to serve the cause of the people and of humanity. They heard the call, felt the shame of their past, abandoned homes, riches, honors and family. They threw themselves into the movement with a passionate enthusiasm, with an ardent faith that knew no obstacle and counted no sacrifice . . .[31]

The Middle Ages had seen its Children's Crusade against the Moslems. The Revolutionary Era began with a Students' Crusade against Despotism. As Stepniak wrote:

Yet it was not a *political* movement. It rather resembled a *religious* movement. . . . With the spring of 1874 all discussion ceased among the circles of the revolutionary youth. The time for talking was over; actual "work" was in contemplation. The working-people's gear—boots, shirts, etc.—were hurriedly being prepared. Short greetings and laconic answers were heard: "Whither?"—"To the Urals," "To the Volga," "To the South," "To the river of Don," and so on. . . . There were warm wishes for success, and robust squeezings of hands. . . . And so, like an electric spark, that cry "to the people" ran through the youth; sure of themselves, daring and wide-awake, though unarmed and unorganized, they dashed in full sight of the enemy, into the storm.[32]

To give oneself to the movement meant to give oneself fully to the people; it was an act of social expiation. Pavel Axelrod, moving spirit among the students at the University of Kiev, stated the creed of the generation of 1874, with its mixture of messianic elitism and masochistic self-denial typical of the political redeemer, who calls upon his followers to abandon kith and kin:

He who wishes to work for the people must abandon the university, forswear his privileged condition, his family, and turn his back even upon science and art. All connections linking him with the upper classes of society must be severed, all of his ships burned behind him; in a word, he must voluntarily cut himself off from any possible retreat. The propagandist must, so to speak, transform his whole inner essence, so as to feel one with the lowest strata of the people, not only ideologically, but also in everyday manner of life.[33]

A literal mania spread among the Russian student activists for the "burning of one's ships," a recurrent metaphor for the symbolic act of severing the umbilical cord, the son's declaration of independence. And indeed, this quest for independence from the older generation ran through the whole student movement. Careers and professions were sacrificed, studies were abandoned, as students offered their lives to a strange collective abstraction, "the people," which for its part seemed indifferent, apathetic, sometimes hostile. A novel vocation, that of the professional revolutionist, was born with the student movement. It was something new in history, this notion of a full-time calling in which one would re-enact all one's life the inner psychological drama of personal revolt. In 1875, for instance, the young George Plekhanov was a conscientious student at the St. Petersburg Mining Institute. When the agitator Axelrod met the young scientist, he reproached him: "If you take so long to perfect yourself in chemistry, when will you begin to work for the revolution?" Deeply impressed by Axelrod's "supreme loyalty to the revolution," Plekhanov devoted himself more and more to revolutionary activity, less and less to his studies. He had won a stipend at the end of his first year for his excellent work; at the end of the second, he was expelled for failure to attend classes. George's mother was distressed by her son's deepening involvement in the "back-to-the-people" movement. "But you will perish," she murmured. He replied, "And what would happen if everyone reasoned that way?"[34] Thus, the student revolutionary has always felt himself in the role of society's conscience, enunciating its categorical imperatives, seeking to be its categorical *imperator*, to replace the father.

The back-to-the-people phase recurred with each alternating wave of the student movement. Successive generations of students re-experienced its idealistic vocation and longing for identification. Twenty years after the movement of the early seventies, a secret student congress at Kiev adopted a program which could have been written by their Narodnik fathers. The students were called on to go to the help of the starving, to teach them how to take health measures against epidemics, to enter into the Sunday schools and teach workers how to read, in short, to strengthen their ties with the workers so as to prepare them for political revolution.[35]

Still a generation later, young Pitirim Alexandrovich Sorokin, later professor of sociology at Harvard but at this time the anonymous "Comrade Ivan," itinerant missionary of the revolution, who spoke to clandestine cells of villagers and factory workers, and circulated mimeographed leaflets, was filled with similar emotions along with his comrades:

> Their life was similar to that of the first missionaries of a new unorganized religious denomination regarded as "subversive" and persecuted by the well-established spiritual and secular powers. Continuously hunted by the police, now and then having no shelter or food or other necessities, risking being fired upon at meetings they addressed, they lived a life as full of danger, hardship and martyrdom as that of the first apostles of Christianity. . . .[36]

The students' emotion sought appropriate scientific expression. For this was an age of social science, not religion, though the underlying emotions were isotopic. In a state of intense emotional excitement they would read Marx, and something akin to a conversion experience would seize them. An apocalyptic vision overwhelmed them, a historical mysticism, in which they experienced an Intellectual Love of the Historical Process not unlike Spinoza's intellectual love of God. "*Amor intellectualis historiae*" was the ideological projection of this new experience. Marx's phrases would resound like formulae for world-historical equations. Krupskaya, Lenin's wife, tells of her own experience of this sort as a student in St. Petersburg in the Higher Course for Women at the age of twenty in 1889:

> Early one evening I was sitting on the porch, reading the lines, "The knell of capitalist private property sounds. The expropriators are expropriated." I could hear my heart go thumpety-thump . . . It never occurred to me then that I would live to see "the expropriators expropriated." That question did not interest me then.[37]

The need for self-dedication to a noble cause, a will to self-donation, compelled belief; the sociological phrases about social development were vehicles for emotional identification. This all had begun, Krupskaya narrates, when "one day I happened to attend a students' political circle—and that opened my eyes." She stopped going to her courses and began to read. She came to believe that "to be useful, one had to dedicate oneself completely to the workers' cause."[38] The will for a self-offering sought an object. She went to circle meetings for three years, but wanted to do something, not just to know. But ties between workers and students were virtually nonexistent. To unite herself with workers, she became a teacher at a Sunday evening school. "To the proletariat!" had replaced "To the people!"

The populist, back-to-the-people spirit alternated with the most terroristic moods. Despair with the passivity of the people would be followed by the most extreme and self-destructive acts of individual terror. The student activist reacted like a rejected lover destroying both his victorious rival and himself. These violent fluctuations of mood among the Russian intellectuals and students were analyzed by their Marxist critic, George Plekhanov:

> The Russian Socialist Populists did not always appeal only to themselves, they did not always place their hopes on the "intelligentsia" only. There was a time when they tried to rouse the "people," they naturally meant the peasants, the bearers of the village community ideals and the representatives of community solidarity. But as was to be expected, the peasants remained deaf to their revolutionary calls and they were obliged against their will to try to carry out the revolution with their own forces. Well, and what could they do with those forces? . . . there was no other course for them but what we call terror . . . individual rebellion.[39]

Terrorism, furthermore, went hand in hand with suicidalism. The student activists lived under an obsession not only to murder czars, ministers, and generals but also to attain heroic self-immolation; the act of self-destruction was reality experienced in its most intense form. Meaning in life could be found only in the supreme moment when it was shattered into meaninglessness.[40]

Suicidalism and Terrorism: The Students' Impulse to Self-Destruction

The student movement made a dual cult of self-destruction and terrorism. The Moscow student circle in 1865–1866, which nurtured Dmitry Karakozov, the would-be assassin of the Czar, was a prototype of the union of the themes of generational politics—parricide, regicide, and suicide. Its bold spirits planned to form a terroristic band which they called Hell. As Avrahm Yarmolinsky writes:

> Each member of this secrecy-shrouded body was to be a dedicated and doomed man. He had to give up his friends, his family, his personal life, his very name. To disarm suspicion, the one chosen by lot to act was to abandon himself to dissipation, even play the informer. The deed done, the terrorist

must destroy himself by squeezing a pellet of fulminate of mercury between his teeth, so as to make his features unrecognizable.[41]

To secure money one member of the organization was to poison his father. Another was to steal from the mail, while another was to rob a merchant. One rational student, Nikolai Nozhin, a brilliant young scientist, tried to dissuade the circle from violence; he was found murdered in his room the night before Karakozov, "an enemy of his," made his attempt on the Czar.[42]

The bitter theme of suicide was always in the consciousness of the Russian student movement. A leaflet of the Kiev Student Union in 1899 complained of a "whole series of suicides, poisonings, caused by the wild Bacchanalia of the authorities" and told of "the shocking treatment in prison which had led the Moscow comrade Liven to burn himself."[43] The students of St. Petersburg demonstrated in 1897 on Kazan Square in memory of Maria Fedoseyevna Vetrova, a student in the Higher Course for Women, who had killed herself with kerosene and fire. The reactionaries said the cause of her death was a secret between herself and God, but the students insisted that she had been driven to suicide as the only means of protesting outrages committed in prison. Then the name of S. S. Kostromin was much in students' minds in 1899. A mechanical engineer, he was arrested in St. Petersburg in March 1898 and cut his throat the next month with broken dishes.[44] Soon afterward, in 1900, a wave of student suicides spread through the universities. When 183 Kiev students and 27 St. Petersburg students were drafted punitively into the army as privates, several of them committed suicide in the barracks.[45] A tremendous resentment swept the Russian studentry, and in retaliation the twice-expelled student, Karpovich, assassinated the Minister of Public Instruction, Bogolepov. The students hailed Karpovich as the "Brave Falcon." Self-destruction alternated with the destruction of others. During the 1880s, for instance, the muted decade which followed the assassination of Alexander II, many students turned to drink "in the shame of their helplessness." The frustrated terrorist turned his death-longing upon himself. "Pistol shots resounded in the gloomy silence over Russia; suicide had become the last resort of intellectuals driven into a blind alley."[46]

Suicidalism became a theory of the truth of ideas. A man's ideas were not tested against the facts; rather they were tested by the degree to which he was prepared to sacrifice himself for them. At the time of the strikes of 1899, for instance, a student said to the young Englishman, Bernard Pares, then studying at Moscow, "You must take our side, because we sacrifice everything."[47] A masochistic variant of pragmatism became the student movement's theory of truth. It judged the truth of propositions neither by their cash value nor by their status value; that it left to its elders. Rather it judged the worth of a doctrine by its self-destructive consequences.

Suicide was the ultimate test of one's sincerity; it was also one's self-punishment for violating the revolutionary code. In 1895, for instance, a student, Rizenkampf, committed suicide; he had broken down under police questioning and divulged the activities of his circle. His confession had led to the imprisonment of his comrade, Yuri Zederbaum, later known as the Menshevik leader, Martov. Excommunicated by the students' revolutionary circle, Rizenkampf shot himself. Life outside the fraternal circle was devoid of meaning, and within it one lived in the proximity of death.[48]

The suicidal propensity was strong among the Russian youth. A youth-weighted rate of suicide, we have observed, is indeed characteristic of all countries in which large-scale revolutionary student movements are found. In what we have called a "normal" country, the relative frequency of suicide increases with advancing age.[49] But a "normal" country is one without a revolutionary student movement. Where such a movement exists—in other words, in an abnormal country, one characterized by a severe conflict of generations—the rate of suicide is highest precisely for the older adolescents. The statistical facts concerning suicide in such countries as Switzerland and Sweden as compared with Russia and Japan will exemplify this truth. There were no Swiss or Swedish revolutionary student movements, and they accordingly had a "normal" distribution of suicide rates. In Switzerland, for instance, during the years from 1901 to 1920, the suicide rates among single men for the age groups twenty to twenty-nine, thirty to thirty-nine, forty to forty-nine, fifty to fifty-nine, sixty to sixty-nine, and seventy to seventy-nine were respectively for every one hundred thousand persons, 36.4, 76.1, 104.1, 116.9, 133.8, and 135.1. Thus, the youthful persons had the lowest frequency of suicide. In Sweden likewise, for the years from 1911 to 1920, the rates of suicide for single men rose for the age groups twenty to twenty-four, twenty-five to twenty-nine, thirty to thirty-nine, forty to forty-nine, fifty to fifty-nine, sixty to sixty-nine, seventy to seventy-nine as follows: 12.1, 18.7, 34.0, 44.6, 64.8, 61.3, 75.8.[50] The contrast between the suicidal phenomenon in these countries and in Russia during the revolutionary era is striking. Among the Russian youth in Moscow during the years 1908 and 1909, the frequency of suicide far exceeded that of the older people. Of every one thousand Muscovite suicides during those years 381 were of an age between fifteen and twenty, 179 of an age between twenty-one and twenty-five, 134 of an age between twenty-six and thirty, 117 were between thirty-one and forty, and 73 between forty-one and fifty.

A student of Odessa, twenty years old, wrote in his farewell letter of his motive for suicide. He spoke for many like himself who refused to accept life on the terms offered by social reality. What lay behind their declarations of self-destruction?

> To live as I would, is impossible now, and live as it is possible I cannot. . . . I cannot witness atrocities and suffering, cannot bear the complaints and the sobs of the oppressed, and at the same time feel my impotence to solace, however little, this horror that is life. And I am going out of life for there is nothing to live for.

The advent of revolution brought hope, and a lowering of the frequency of suicides. In 1904, there were 427 suicides in St. Petersburg; but in 1905, the year of revolutionary action and temporary success, the number went down to 354. When defeat came in 1906, however, the number of suicides rose again to 532. Odessa, likewise, had 256 suicides in 1905 and 642 in 1908.[51]

The malaise of the Russian studentry became a subject for national discussion. The frequency of students' suicides elicited a report by the Ministry of Public Instruction in 1909. Nadezhda Krupskaya, Lenin's wife and a devoted educationalist, in 1911 wrote an article on the subject entitled, "Suicide among Students and the Free Labor School." What makes the cup overflow for the students and children, she asked, so "that nothing binds them to life, that they are terribly lonely although they are surrounded by parents, teachers, and comrades . . . and the child itself unable to get close to anybody retreats into himself, wanders shyly, 'homeless and orphaned, feels unneeded, superfluous, and alien to everybody'?" Some people blamed "the dissoluteness of the students," she noted; others said the schools were not responsible but rather "the oppressive Russian reality." But, complained Krupskaya, "the school does not fight against this oppression but acts in the same direction on the children, killing every joy of life. . . ." She pleaded for warmer relations between people, for entering their skin, for an end to formalism in the relations between teachers and students: "Is it common for a student to talk with a teacher about his sincere thoughts, his doubts? Does he look for moral support from his teacher? In the worst case the student and teacher are two enemy camps."[52]

Self-destruction, moreover, could show itself in compulsive forms of self-denial and self-immolation other than actual suicide. There were students, for instance, who "gathered from Dostoyevsky's writings that it would be noble for them to redeem someone, and, not stopping to study their own qualifications as redeemers, they married women off the streets."[53] Thus, one sought to forget one's pain by sharing the greater pain of others. There was a suicidal ingredient in the back-to-the-people movement. But it was only an ingredient. At times when the young redeemer found himself rejected by the people, the last hope seemed gone; the sociological path of redemption having proved a failure, one killed oneself. In Avenarius' novel, *The Plague*, for instance, a young woman student dedicates herself to founding a reading room for common people; when it fails, she and her friend, another nihilist associated with "progressive students," go to the Neva River to drown themselves.[54] Nihilism, as a philosophy of student movements, was not only a negative critique of society; it was a self-critique joined to an impulse toward self-annihilation.

To the young, growing adolescent, there was a wonderful aura of mystery about the terrorist, self-destroying students. The Soviet novelist Ilya Ehrenburg recalls that as a youngster he would hear that the students were marching. "The gates would be locked tight and sentries would be posted. I would creep out into the street and wait for the mysterious student. . . ." They "were supposed to throw Cossacks off their horses, and then the Tsar off his throne." The boy's father, a liberal, urged his son that a revolution wasn't necessary. "The chief thing is tolerance," he said. But as Ehrenburg remembers, "It is hard to make tolerance attractive to a fifteen-year-old with a bristly shock of hair and a long-standing desire to pick up heavy, immobile stones and throw them about. 'All or nothing.' " The choice of ideology was dictated as the emotional a priori of generational revolt. "Everything, but precisely everything must be turned upside down." Ilya was fascinated by his mother's horror over a visiting student terrorist who "used to show me and my friends how to handle a revolver." Later he rejoiced in the atmosphere of violence which filled the university in 1905. "We were organized in groups of ten . . . if the enemy broke through, we would stop them by hurling stones. Camp-fires were lit. We ate sausage sandwiches and sang till morning: 'Boldly, friends, boldly, never lose courage in the unequal fight!' I wasn't yet fifteen so it is easy to understand that I didn't 'lose courage.' " Life seemed most wonderful under the banner of rebellion. "I must find an underground organization," thought young Ilya. The death-allure enveloped the young political activists with its death-mysticism. Self-destruction was a sacred rite in the student revolutionary religion. Take, for instance, the case of Nadya whom Ilya loved. "At fifteen Nadya became an underground worker, at sixteen she was arrested, at nineteen she began to write poetry, at twenty-two she realized: 'I'm only a poetess'—and shot herself." Death followed the revolutionary act; for the utmost of emotion having been experienced in the revolutionary act, the possibilities of life were exhausted.

Student terrorists debated "whether a terrorist who killed a political enemy ought to try to escape or pay for the assassination with his own blood. . . . For such people terrorism was not a weapon of political struggle but the world in which they lived." It was in short a world in which the drama of parricide was perpetually re-enacted. The students quoted a poet's lines: "Who, in the excess of feeling, when the blood boils and freezes, has not known your temptations—Suicide and Love?" The student activists, if they did not destroy themselves, practiced an extirpation of their feelings; they tried to excise the responses of "ordinary human kindness" as a weakness, to toughen themselves. Self-aggression was concomitant with the guilt of generational rebellion; in its wake came "weariness, disillusion, emptiness." When Ehrenburg came to Paris in 1909, Lenin questioned him closely about "the general mood of the student movement." By that time, however, Lenin in his own self-extirpation of his intellectual questioning and spontaneous feeling had turned impatiently from the student movement and its historical idealism.[55]

The Russian student movement tended from its beginnings to impose its self-destructive pattern on political action. Its annals, therefore, read like a series of case studies of a death-wish in political enactment. Joy in death became the creed of the young activist. As Leopold Haimson describes it:

A cult of heroism became prevalent among the members of the intelligentsia: punishment at the hands of the authorities came to be viewed as the price of admission to the society of the elect, and death as the apotheosis of the intelligent's life. In this code of heroic martyrdom, little value could be assigned to the humdrum of maturity and middle age. The student youth, many of whose members could, and did live out the heroic code, laid an incontestable claim to the spiritual leadership of the intelligentsia—a claim that their elders could not dispute since their survival was in itself indicative of their inadequacy. The student youth became veritable objects of worship for the intelligentsia.[56]

The intellectuals, as a whole, tended to suffer from a fixation on youthful martyrdom. As Berdyaev observed in 1909, Russia had "so few orderly, stable, understanding people" because "in his world view, the *intelligent* remains all his life a student youth." Successive generations of students graduated into emotional bankruptcy, from heroism to "wines and cards, if not worse."[57]

The self-sacrificial, masochistic demonstration of one's purity of motive became the mark of the student in politics. Suicidalism disguised as a will to martyrdom spoke in a thousand student utterances and writings. A young girl student, a Social Democrat, told how she and her fellow-students looked forward with joy to imminent death as they went to join the demonstration of December 11, 1904, in St. Petersburg:

I went with a pure, unburdened heart, all joy; and I was not the only one. We all—all my friends and I—came out expecting death, and we did not hope ever to come back to our homes. We took leave of each other, and we were shining with joy. No clouded face, no word of sorrow. At noon we were on the Nevsky.

As the students marched in fraternal unison singing the "Marseillaise," they were attacked by cavalry with drawn swords. Then came the moment of supreme self-immolation: "I can forget everything, all the joys and sorrows of my life, but I shall never forget *that*, especially the horrible moment when, with my body writhing, I lay down and saw my friends struck and wounded, and heard their cries and groans."[58]

The politics of the death-longing mingled terrorism with self-destruction. In 1906, Maria Spiridonova, twenty-one years old, student of nursing at Tambov, killed the military commandant. Then she cried, "Shoot me!" and pointed the revolver to her temples. The Cossacks beat and raped her. Maria, a person of fortitude, became in later years leader of the Left Social Revolutionary party which participated with the Bolsheviks in the first Soviet government. The longing for death was stark in her young student deeds, writing, and speech. Soon after her death sentence had been passed she wrote:

Comrades, sometimes I lie awake all night. But in spite of that I feel very cheerful. I dream about myself being hanged. My wish to die has become very strong, and I should not know what to do if I were pardoned. I want no favors from them. . . . My death appears to me to be so worth-while from the point of view of society that I should regard any favor from the State as a revenge, a fresh insult.[59]

The delight in death was similarly strong in Ivan Platonovich Kaliayev on the eve of his assassination of the governor-general of Moscow, the Grand Duke Sergei. His student days barely over, Kaliayev looked forward to ending it all by committing hara-kiri in the Japanese style. His murder done, Kaliayev (whom, as we saw, Lenin admired) wrote to his friends:

I often think of the last moment; I should like to die on the spot. It is an enviable fate. But there is a still greater happiness—death on the scaffold. Between the act and the scaffold there lies a whole eternity. It is perhaps the supreme happiness of man. Only then does one know and feel the whole strength and beauty of the Idea. To commit the deed and later to die on the scaffold—it is like sacrificing one's life twice.[60]

To his mother, Kaliayev wrote, "From my early boyhood, I felt I was doomed."[61]

Thus the Russian students proved to their consciences that their deeds of assassination were selfless, and not done in pursuit of personal profit, power, or prestige; this was a joint offering to History, a common sacrifice of both oppressor and liberator. As Isaac Steinberg, Left Social Revolutionary and subsequently first Minister of Justice in the Soviet government, wrote, "The Russian revolutionary terrorists always tried to expiate their deeds by sacrificing their own life." It was part of the students' political neurosis that they immolated themselves to prove to some high surrogate conscience that they were selfless and guiltless in destroying their fathers and their fathers' society. The later premier Alexander Kerensky was, as a youth of twenty-four, much involved with students' organizations in 1905. So much did he share of what he called their "revolutionary romanticism" that he tried to join a plot to assassinate the Czar. He had come to the conclusion, he writes, "that individual terrorism was inevitable. I was quite willing, if need be, to take upon myself the moral sin of killing the incumbent of supreme power."[62]

The morbid appeal of terrorism became a defining characteristic of the Russian student movement. The *Narodnaya Volya* (the People's Will) took to terroristic acts in the late seventies and early eighties with a fetishistic awe. Twenty years later, terrorism was still the most revered form of "political behavior" within the student movement. A terroristic act became something of a puberty or initiation rite for the revolutionary student generation:

Young boys and girls with no high moral qualifications either made attempts on government officials singlehanded, or they joined the organization of terrorists, sometimes from mere motives of imitation, sometimes under moral pressure of their party colleagues, who thought participation in terrorist attempts the highest manifestation of voluntary spirit. The number of terrorists grew, their quality went down.[63]

Student circles at the universities idolized the assassins of Czarist officials. In 1901, for instance, university students rendered homage to the killers of the Ministers of Public Instruction and the Interior: "Postcards with the pictures of the terrorists hung in students' rooms along with those of Leo Tolstoy and Maxim Gorky."[64] Kerensky recalled that when the twice-expelled student, Peter Karpovich, assassinated the Minister of Public Instruction, Bogolepov, "his deed made an indelible impression on many people, including myself: We looked upon this willingness to die in the name of justice as an act of great moral heroism." The Minister of Public Instruction was assassinated for having threatened to conscript rioting students into the army; the Minister of Interior was killed because he had persecuted national minorities and allowed the maltreatment of peasants and political prisoners. The terroristic act struck at the various grades of evil-doers.

The students resented any aspersion on the moral purity of the terrorists. In 1891, their ire was aroused by the religious philosopher, Vladimir Solovyev, who had declared that the famine that year was God's punishment for those who "stirred up violence" in Russia. The young student leader, Peter Struve, succeeded in mobilizing all the students' circles to sign a protest against the philosopher. The students took it for granted that Solovyev was maligning the sacred memory of the People's Will terrorists.[65] But when the students' deputation marched on Solovyev, he told them to their chagrin that he had been referring to the violence of the anti-Jewish pogroms. Such was the "comic" episode, as Martov characterized it. Yet in a strange way, as the student revolutionaries perhaps realized, all these forms of violence were akin to each other, interrelated in one political psychology and ethic. The People's Will terrorists had welcomed the pogroms because they felt the peasants and proletarians would become attuned to violence, and go on to practice it more successfully against the regime itself.[66]

An inner moral corruption began early to develop in the Russian student movement with its terrorist ethics. No one described it better than the revered veteran terrorist, Vera Figner. Struggle through terror, she wrote,

> arouses ferocity, develops brutal instincts, awakens evil impulses, and prompts acts of disloyalty. Humanity and magnanimity are incompatible with it. . . . On the one hand, the party declared that all methods were fair in the war with the antagonist, that here the end justified the means. At the same time, it created a cult of dynamite and the revolver, and crowned the terrorist with a halo; murder and the scaffold acquired a magnetic charm for the youth of the land, and the weaker their nervous system, and the more oppressive the life

around them, the greater was their exaltation at the thought of revolutionary terror.

Every revolutionist likes to see concrete results in his lifetime; a terroristic act seemed indeed something done. And side by side with this killing of authority figures—indeed, as a consequence of it—grew the feeling of brotherhood among the student terrorists. The sons shared the common bond of a killing of the fathers. As Vera Figner said, "But the gloomy side of revolutionary activity was brightened by the concord and brotherhood which existed among the revolutionists themselves"; terrorism "redeemed itself through renunciation of material benefits, through the fact that the revolutionist was not satisfied with personal well-being." The government retaliated with more violence, and society became accustomed to the degradation of human dignity. "Retaliation, an eye for an eye and a tooth for a tooth, became the watchword of all." The corruption spread into the movement itself. With all sense of right and wrong extirpated by terrorist casuistry, comrades began to betray each other. "This was the greatest moral blow dealt to us revolutionists, a blow which shook our faith in mankind." The revolutionaries became vulnerable to the spread of "a veritable moral pestilence," as dark suspicion spread in "the midst of our revolutionary brotherhood. . . . We might soon have reached a stage where our hands would have been crimsoned by blood perhaps as innocent as the blood of Ivanov, which Nechaev had shed."[67] The student exaltation of terrorism induced a deterioration of the moral spirit, "the terrorist organization became a sort of aristocratic division of the Socialist-Revolutionary party, its members looking upon themselves as revolutionary supermen and permitting themselves liberties condemned in ordinary life."[68]

The novelist Maxim Gorki, observing the student terrorists and the assassinations they perpetrated, which were becoming as frequent as common-law crimes, was repelled by their amoral smugness. He recalled, as if in a "nightmare," one student who had killed a governor:

> "He" is a boy of twenty-three to twenty-five years. . . . Standing near a window, he watches with condescension the people who hastily tread the liquid mud of Petersburg. . . . His hands in his pockets, he chews the end of his burnt-out cigarette. His person gives forth the strong and suffocating odor of an imbecile. . . . That ass feels himself satisfied as if he had accomplished something which everybody in the world would recognize as important and useful.

The elders fawned on the young assassins. One of the latter, his deed completed, was giving his report and had to go to the toilet. One of the chiefs, an aged man, followed him, knocking at the door to offer him toilet paper. Gorki was repelled by the elder's adulation and loss of self-respect in the presence of the assassin. It was symbolic of how the sick young corrupted the weak old.[69]

The Literature of the Death-Longing

The poignant dedication to the death-longing and its masochistic theory of truth was indeed the principal theme in the most reportorial of the novels of terrorism, *What Never Happened;* its author, Boris Savinkov, himself a chief of terrorists, portrayed his student associates of 1905. The death-seeker and death-bringer, in its pages, argue for a knowledge that no others have. "Then where is the law? In the Party program? In Karl Marx? In Engels? In Kant? But that's nonsense," he whispered in agitation. "Neither Marx, nor Engels, nor Kant ever killed people. You hear? never nobody. Then they cannot know what I know, what you or Volodya know."[70] The young terrorist student, David Cohn, the night after an assassination, flings off his student's cap and goes with his revolver toward the Kremlin to certain capture and death.[71] A new recruit, Ruvin Epstein, "a notorious St. Petersburg student, who had been expelled from the university for participating in the revolution," repeats endlessly his schoolboy speech of no mercy to the "contemptible bourgeois"; he lacerates his Jewish self with the new notion that for the great goal of free anarchist communes "all means were permissible."[72] Ippolit, former student in a military academy, who "had donated everything his father had left him to the cause of terrorism," is "frail, girlish, shy, unpretentious"; in joyous self-abnegation, submission, and blind faith in the Party, he carries out its order of terrorism and martyrdom.[73] A terrorist's young student brother is overjoyed by the fact that his brother is a revolutionist, and a sister is awed by his dual role, "a martyr and a murderer," for that is the definition of a revolutionist. She recalls the summons in Luke: "If any man come to me, and hate not his father, and mother . . . and his own life also, he cannot be my disciple."[74] And the young brother too resolves to give his life not only for the People but for the Party and the mysterious committee.[75] Many a young student took a perverse delight in becoming a nameless soldier, and in finding in a self-sacrificing struggle in the Socialist party "the eternal truth, the immutable commandments of Christ."[76] This was St. Petersburg in 1905, where one witnessed the students' uprising: "A young student from the Technological Institute, with coat unbuttoned, was haranguing the crowd in a thin, timid voice. Comrade! . . . Manifesto! . . . Liberty!"[77] All told themselves that a "higher unknown force" had willed them to commit murder.[78] Was this but an agnostic recognition of all the emotions of generational unrest, the anguish in the revolt and guilt of the younger generation?

This death-longing echoed through the literature of the student revolutionaries. In the novel *The Career of a Nihilist,* the terrorist Chieftain Stepniak tells the dream of his hero, Andrey:

A terrible vision rose suddenly before his memory.

It is night. A dimly lighted cell in one of the southern prisons. Its inmate—a young student—is stretched upon the straw mattress. His hands and feet are tightly bound with ropes. His head and body are covered with bruises. He has just been shamefully beaten by the gaolers, because he did not show himself sufficiently submissive. Smarting under the brutal insult, he is meditating the only revenge left him—that of a frightful suicide. Fire shall be his instrument. In the dead of the night he rises with effort from his bed. He takes off with his mouth the hot lamp glass, which scorches his lips; he unscrews with his teeth the burner, and upsets the oil over his mattress. When it has saturated the straw, he drops upon the mattress the burning wick, and stretches himself once more upon this bed of fire. There he lies, without a groan, whilst the fire licks and burns his flesh. When the gaolers, attracted by the smoke, rush into the cell, they find him half charred and dying.

This was no nightmare. It was a frightful reality. For months the harrowing vision had persecuted Andrey, and now it rose before him as if he had seen it but yesterday.

Such was the torment of the death-wish in the revolutionary unconscious—Andrey was looking for a suicidal revenge upon jailers who had "shamefully" beaten him, like a child plotting suicide to make its father feel sorry, for certainly the hardened jailers would not. The revolutionist wondered whether his zeal was "but an ebullition of youth and of love of strong sensations"; meanwhile, he was prodded to self-immolation by "the pangs of self-condemnation."[79]

The student revolutionist in Turgenev's classic novel of the back-to-the-people movement, *Virgin Soil,* was similarly dominated by a longing for death; consciousness of death was a cardinal characteristic of the student consciousness. In Turgenev's novel Nejdanov, student at St. Petersburg, felt "utterly lonely in spite of the untiring devotion of his friends." "He was haunted by sad and gloomy reflections about the inevitable end, death." He contemplated taking up the hatchet. "But against whom, with whom, and what for? It would only be a complicated form of suicide! It would be better to make an end of yourself—you would at any rate know when and how, and choose the spot to aim at." He thought of joining some people's war, "not so as to free others but to make an end of myself." And finally, rejected by the peasants, he still felt "some dark, underground hand" clutching at the very root of his being, and not letting go. A generous love offered to him was of no avail. He shot himself, and it seemed to his closest friends "that they had foreseen it all along." These revolutionary students often regarded themselves as Hamlets, and like Nejdanov complained they were born out of joint. The comparison to Hamlet, experiencing all the drives and guilt of Oedipal feelings, went deeper, however, than they surmised. "O Hamlet! Hamlet! thou Prince of Denmark! How escape from the shadow of thy spirit? How cease to imitate thee in everything, even to reveling shamelessly in one's own self-depreciation?" cried Nejdanov. When he realized he didn't believe in the cause itself—that is, that the cause had been the vehicle for personal feelings quite unrelated to the peasants' conditions, that political action had been the projected field for nonpolitical personal emotions which he had never understood, he felt he had no alternative but self-destruction. Revolutionary politics was thus the sublimative form of a self-destructive impulse. "He wanted to die, he knew he would soon die. . . ." And in all the portraits of the revolutionary students, there recurs the theme of their uprising against their own fathers. Nejdanov, literally in Russian the "unexpected one," resentful of his father, the prince, who stamped him with the mark of illegitimate birth, is angered by his father's efforts to emasculate him by forcing him to study "aesthetics," rather than politics and social questions. "Bold and timid at the same time," "like a repentant sinner ashamed of his sins," "ashamed alike of his timidity and his purity," scoffing at all idealism in order to appear hard, manly, to himself, Nejdanov was ashamed and "furious" with his father, who on his side "had a violent hatred for nihilists." Thus, a generational tension of unparalleled magnitude cut its swathe across Russian history. The older generation indeed regarded the younger—as its unexpected offspring, as the prince regarded Nejdanov.

The Social Composition of the Student Movement

The Russian student movement cannot be understood in terms of its participants' social origins and class interests. It involved students from all classes linked in a common generational solidarity. The students' experience as students tended to liberate them from the forces of economic determination, and to make the student movement the unique example of ethical-generational politics.

The young Stalin, fresh from his own student days at the theological seminary, wrote in 1901 most clearly of the relative independence of the student movement from economic determination: "Until they have plunged into the sea of life and have occupied a definite social position, the students, being young intellectuals, are more inclined than any other category to strive for ideals which call them to fight for freedom."[80]

The conditions of student life, for a brief while, place the student in an enclave whence he looks upon social struggles from a purely ethical standpoint. The student experience has a way of detaching students from their class origins: while it lasts, a generational solidarity, guarded by pure idealism, can supersede social loyalties. The student from a noble or wealthy family in revolt against his social background, his father's society, may be stirred by deep feelings of sympathy for the oppressed, and feel guilty for his father's deeds. The son of the civil servant will thrill to the accents of a doctrine which speaks of human brotherhood rather than estrangement, and feel shame at the callous indifference of his bourgeois father. The son who is born of poor parents, tense with an ambition they share that he should rise out of his class, will feel his own self-seeking tempered by a selfless love for the people of his childhood; indeed, he may revolt against that very ambition which his poor parents have thrust upon him. The student society is as near as one can find to a classless society, binding those who have not yet been riven by competition and who, learning together, hoping together, sharing the common knowledge which they prize, and prizing too the universal values of scientific truth and human well-being, feel themselves, spontaneously and without benefit of party, comrades.

Throughout all its variations in social composition, the Russian studentry in the nineteenth and early twentieth centuries tended to respond to crises and to the social environment with the same degree of revolutionary emotion. This revolutionary character was perhaps most pronounced when the studentry was drawn predominantly from the middle and upper classes.

At first almost wholly aristocratic in origin, the Russian studentry later became preponderantly middle class, and finally had a pronounced lower-class leavening. As these changes took place, its revolutionary emotion remained strong, though there was some decline as the children of the poor entered the universities. During the years immediately before 1914, when the lower-class proportion was at its highest, there was actually a slackening in the revolutionary student movement. But, on the whole, the revolutionary emotion of the Russian student movement was relatively independent of the changing class character of the Russian students. The same kinds of student disorders occurred, with about the same frequency, and the same back-to-the-people aspiration recurred throughout the history of the Russian studentry, despite its variations in social composition.

The universities in the mid-nineteenth century were overwhelmingly composed of students drawn from the aristocracy. In 1853, for instance, at St. Petersburg University, 299 of the 422 students (or 73 per cent) came from the nobility.[81] At Moscow University in 1861 and 1863, about one half the students were sons of the noblemen; the fathers of two thirds of them were either noblemen or officials.[82] One fifth of the studentry, however, came from the "declassed" nobility; that is, their fathers were among the so-called "third element," the broad stratum of civil servants and intellectuals, village doctors, teachers, statisticians, who served the Zemstva, the organs of local administration founded after the abolition of serfdom.[83]

A class revolution began in Russian higher education at the outset of the reign of Alexander II, when the doors of the universities were opened to all persons, regardless of social class. In 1855, the total number of students in all the six Russian universities was 3,659. Then, as young men flocked to the halls of learning, the number of students doubled at Moscow and increased fourfold at St. Petersburg. A growing number came from families which could not support them. The students

had left home, some of them travelling long distances on foot, in the hope of making their way by tutoring and odd jobs. But there were not enough of these or of government scholarships either. In 1859 only 360 out of the 1,019 students of the University of Petersburg paid the tuition fee; in 1863 half of the students of the University of Moscow needed financial aid. Some of the young people lived on the edge of starvation. Typhus and tuberculosis decimated the student body. All this exacerbated the unrest natural to youth.[84]

According to the distingished historian Franco Venturi:

The most revealing figure we have is that in St. Petersburg three hundred and seventy out of about a thousand students were unable to pay the admission tax which was then about twenty-five roubles . . . they slept two in a cupboard, and, in summer, in the public gardens if allowed to by the police.[85]

Student poverty, however, was *sui generis* and not the cause of unrest. Sons of the nobility, gentry, middle classes, priests, and peasants would, as students, share much the same life. The poorer ones would engage in tutoring and secure scholarships. The activists came from all classes; a serf's son, like Zhelyabov, could consort in the movement with a nobleman's daughter, like Sophia Perovskaya, child of the governor-general of Moscow.

The Russian students always lived on the edge of poverty. "Of all European students, the Russian students were certainly the most impecunious," wrote Paul Novgorotsev; "poverty was something quite normal in the life of the Russian student."[86] The poverty which the students endured in 1859 was of the same order as that which they still knew fifty-five years later, in 1914. Student poverty remained a virtually constant factor in the universities from 1860 to 1914. The proportion of impecunious students in Russian universities in the years preceding the war was estimated at about 53 per cent. At the University of Yuriev it reached 83 per cent, while at St. Petersburg 72 per cent of the men students were classified as impecunious and as many as 82 per cent of the women.

By the end of the nineteenth century, the bulk of the students were children of lower and middle-class parents. For them the university diploma was to be an instrument for social mobility. They were *raznochinsty*—persons from all social classes detached by education from their parents' class. The percentage of the needy continued to grow until the century's end.

FACULTY	NUMBER OF STUDENTS	NUMBER OF NEEDY STUDENTS	PERCENTAGE OF NEEDY STUDENTS	NUMBER OF THOSE RECEIVING AID
Philological	273	170	62.27%	160
Mathematical	468	235	50.21	225
Natural Sciences	604	300	49.52	280
Law	1,523	734	48.19	654
Medical	1,149	697	60.73	638
TOTAL	4,017	2,136		1,957

This professorial questionnaire at Moscow in 1901, aiming to discover the causes of the students' unrest, thus presented evidence that the majority of the students lived in penury.[88] According to another survey, the percentage of needy students at Moscow increased from 14 per cent in 1876 to 33 per cent in 1896. The Society for Aid to Needy Students was contributing help to 9 per cent in 1874 and 16 per cent in 1894.[87]

Yet the students never alleged their poverty to be a cause of their militancy. They wrote on the questionnaires that its causes were the "Regulations," the police assaults, the humiliation of the police inspection, the suppression of free student organization; the one reference to an economic factor was the complaint that aids and fellowships were unfairly distributed. More than 91 per cent of the "needy" students were receiving financial aid at a time when the student movement was at a high point of militancy.

The "needy" students, furthermore, were overwhelmingly children of the middle classes; they were not proletarian. The 52.7 per cent of the Moscow studentry in 1904–1905 who were classified as needy were constituted of the following social groups:[89]

Children of	petty and medium officials	1,126	20.6
	petty bourgeoisie	1,027	18.8
	peasants	312	5.7
	clergy	268	4.9
	petty and medium officers	94	1.7
	public school teachers	22	0.4
	doctors' assistants	20	0.4
	former nobility	9	0.2
		2,878	52.7

The student activists themselves, however, came predominantly from relatively comfortable social strata. At their movement's height, they were mostly children of the middle-middle classes. In 1902, the largest single group of activists came from the "third element," which included the professional personnel of the Zemstva, the doctors, teachers, and statisticians. The student activists constituted the following proportions of their social peers:[90]

Percentage of Activists in the Social Strata at Moscow University, 1902

SOCIAL STRATUM	PERCENTAGE
Third Element	32.4
Officials	3.7
Peasantry	15.7
Petty Bourgeois	15.1
Merchants	12.8
Clergy	10.7

Children of the petty bourgeoisie and the well-to-do merchants were nearly as well represented among the activists as they were among the studentry at large. Children of well-to-do merchants were 16.9 per cent of the Moscow studentry in 1904; they constituted 12.8 per cent of the activists in 1902. Petty bourgeois children were correspondingly 18.8 per cent of the studentry, and 15.1 per cent of the activists. By contrast, children of professional persons like those of the clergy were heavily overrepresented among the activists. The Third Element as a whole provided almost a third of the activists, while the clergy's sons were more than a tenth, disproportionately more than twice their percentage in the studentry.

Most notable was the change in the social composition of the Russian studentry which took place from 1880 to 1914. Just as earlier in the century bourgeois sons had joined the sons of the nobility in the university's classrooms, workmen's and peasants' sons in turn became their classmates. The following table tells this story of social change:[91]

Social Origins of Students in Russian Institutions of Higher Learning (1880–1914)

SOCIAL ORIGIN	7 UNIVERSITIES IN 1880 %	9 UNIVERSITIES IN 1914 %	5 HIGHER TECHNICAL STATE INSTITUTIONS IN 1914 %
Gentry and Officials	46.6	36.1	24.5
Clergy	23.4	10.3	2.4
Merchants and Citizens	14.3	14.8	19.1
Workers and Craftsmen	12.4	24.3	31.6
Peasants	3.3	14.5	22.4

The majority indeed of the Russian students in the immediate prewar years were able to pursue their studies at the universities only if they had outside jobs, scholarships or allowances from the government, or help from societies or charitable groups. In 1913, the situation was so bad that the Society for the Relief of the Impecunious Students of Moscow University contributed to the tuitions of 1,460 students, and provided 130,000 free meals. Hundreds of regional mutual aid societies proliferated at the universities especially after 1905 and there were a variety of cooperative consumers' and relief associations.[92] Curiously, as student economic associations grew, their political activities seemed to decline. Or rather, it would be more accurate to say: as students withdrew their energies from revolutionary political action which had reached its zenith in 1905, they re-allocated their organizational creativity and emotion toward more direct and practical measures for their own welfare. Poverty by itself has never been a sufficient condition for a student movement. Only where there is a strong ingredient of generational resentment and de-authoritization of the old does a student movement arise.

The "proletarianization" of the studentry thus, rather than stimulating the growth of the student movement, tended to reduce its militancy. "After 1905," writes Novgorotsev, "a radical change took place in the minds of the students, whose thoughts were now turned to the practical application of knowledge."[93] An ever-increasing number of students turned to the newly founded technical and engineering institutes rather than the literary-philosophical universities. The children of the working classes were the single largest group in the higher technical institutes in 1914, numbering 31.6 per cent of the students. The social composition of the technical institutes, notes Nicholas Hans, was "considerably more democratic than in the Universities."

Technical education indeed grew apace. The Kiev Polytechnic Institute, founded in 1898, rose from 598 students to 2,500 in 1912; the Kharkov Technological Institute, founded in 1885, grew from 812 in 1899 to 1,400 students in 1912; the St. Petersburg Electrotechnical Institute, established in 1886, grew from 143 in 1899 to 750 students in 1912. The Tomsk Technological Institute, founded in 1900, had 1,171 students by 1912 and the Polytechnic Institute Sosnovka in St. Petersburg, founded two years later, had as many as 5,215 students in 1912.[94] But the Russian technological and engineering students, like their group generally in the history of student movements, were less inclined to revolutionary ideology than their humanistic contemporaries. They were often nonpolitical, wholly vocational in their attitude to their studies. At the St. Petersburg Technological Institute in 1907, one fifth of the studentry declared itself "non-party"; another fifth were moderate liberals. At the Polytechnic Institute that same year, as many as 28.2 per cent were non-party, and 15.5 per cent liberal.[95]

The technicization of higher education, together with its democratization, in Russia coincided with a partial de-politicization of its studentry.[96] The Russian studentry by 1914 was no longer overwhelmingly leftist in spirit. With the "differentiation" of students, moderate, rightist, and nonpolitical elements gained ground among the studentry.[97] During the revolution of 1917, the studentry was a relative bastion of patriotism and order against the Bolshevik trend. The Moscow Soviet of Students' Deputies rejected a demand for the cessation of the war.[98] Moderate students were predominant in their Moscow Soviet, and they looked to the Constituent Assembly and political democracy to solve their country's problems.

Poverty was the virtual law of student life, and since it was a constant in the social existence, it cannot explain the decline which took place in the students' revolutionary militancy. For such a decline did ensue with the admission in great number of sons of workingmen and peasants into higher education. The working-class boy, engaged in technical studies and struggling to master technological science, was far less apt to become a revolutionary militant and to spend his time at student movement meetings than the middle-class son engaged in studying philosophy and literature. The working-class son could sublimate his generational resentments in objective study and struggle with the physical environment.[99] The middle-class son, on the other hand, found his generational tensions aggravated by "advanced ideas" and the literature of revolt.

Generational solidarity in a crisis was always the strongest motive power for students' strikes and demonstrations. When called on to vote for a direct strike action, the studentry as a whole were generally reluctant to do so. The student activists could, however, initiate student strikes with mass participation by appeals in "crisis" situations to generational solidarity. A vote taken by the studentry itself would invariably, however, show a preference for peaceful negotiation rather than strikes. At the height of the February 1899 disturbance, for instance, the St. Petersburg movement sent a delegate to Moscow asking the Moscow students to strike in solidarity. An Executive Committee was formed, consisting of former members of the Union Council of Zemlyachestva. A strike call failed to close the university, for only the radicals struck. Thereupon they threatened to use force to prevent the "careerists" from attending classes. "Their motives are egotistical, while ours are high," said a bulletin of the Moscow Executive Committee.[100] Finally the university was closed. But when a students' meeting took place on March 3, a majority, by a vote of 800 to 724, opposed the continuation of the disorders. On March 5, the vote was even more decisive—1,130 to 622. The radical students were bitter about this decision, which a later Bolshevik historian characterized as a "shameful surrender" due to the vacillations of the petty bourgeois students.[101] In March 1899, with resentment running high against the university's violation of a promise to reinstate arrested students, a student meeting voted, nevertheless, by 1,366 to 679, against a strike which the radicals actually called.[102] In the atmosphere of a crisis mass meeting in the university courtyard, the revolutionary activists could dominate the decisions and make their most effective emotional appeal to generational solidarity.

The leftist groups which were the core of the Russian student movement often protested against what they called the "economism" of the student aid societies; that is, their concern with issues purely of material welfare, of shelter, clothing, and bread.[103] "Economism," they noted, went hand-in-hand with a bourgeois or apolitical standpoint. The leftist organ, *Moskovskoe Studencheskoe Delo* (The Students' Cause), called on all students' organizations to regard themselves "as part of a general students' movement" aspiring "to great and important ends, instead of confining itself to paltry calculations." Lenin in *What Is to be Done?* declared that the workers by themselves were able to develop only a trade-union consciousness, that a socialist consciousness had to be brought to them from without by the intellectuals. Similarly, the student movement conceived of itself as bringing a socialist consciousness, "great and important ends," to the students' organizations; the studentry itself, instead of being inspired by noble self-sacrifice and great goals, might too easily be content with "economism." Nothing is so alien to the student revolutionary unconscious as an economic interpretation of history.

The Russian student activists, however, though their own actions could not be subsumed under historical materialism, were much drawn emotionally to the doctrine, imagery, and summons of Marxism. The Russian studentry was almost the only one in all Europe which, in the 1870s, began to find in Marxism an ideology of protest. Marx was virtually unknown to Western European students when he died in 1883. Not so, however, to the students of the Moscow Petrovsky Academy who asked to place a wreath on "the coffin of the unforgettable author of *Capital* . . . the defender of the rights of the workers in theory and of their realization in practice," and they were joined by students of Odessa, the St. Petersburg Technological Institute, and Russian women students. As Peter Lavrov said, "The students of the Russian universities were the first to whose lot it fell to hear a sympathetic exposition of the theories of the mighty thinker. . . ."[104] To be sure, Marx himself, as a historical materialist, was embarrassed by the Russians' interest in his work. He mistrusted an intellectual movement which sprang, not from the materialistic conditions of existence, not from the economic workings of history, but from the idealistic aspirations of aristocratic youth. To his good friend, Dr. Kugelmann, Marx confided, as we have seen, that not only had his early books "had a greater sale in Russia than anywhere else" but that also "the first foreign nation to translate *Kapital* is the Russian." He also added, "But not too much should be made of all this. The Russian aristocracy is, in its youth, educated at German universities and in Paris. They always ran after the most extreme that the West can offer."[105] It was, indeed, a case of the idealism of the student generation feeding itself, especially in backward countries, on the most advanced ideas. Marx said mockingly that it was "pure gourmandise," a typical aristocratic indulgence, which did "not prevent the same Russians, once they enter State service, from becoming rascals." Nonetheless, such student movements, recalcitrant to the categories of the Marxian historical understanding, put their impress on modern history. Marx, despite himself, became for the Russian students a spokesman for generational protest.

The Student Movement: Uncertain Ally of the Working-Class Movement

The student movement brought to the political struggles its own distinctive tactics and emphases—the demonstration and the assassination. But for all its self-sacrificial ardor, it was usually in a relationship of tension with the workers' movement. The middle-class fathers may have regarded their sons as the "conscience of society" and "the best barometer of society," but there was much skepticism on this score among the workers.

A rift arose very early between the working class and the student movement. In 1896, the Moscow Workers' Union invited the Student Union Council to stop engaging in disorders and to join them instead in organizing a Workers' party.[106] The students replied that they were all fighting under one flag and defended their disorders:

Thus we help the working class; and the disorders aren't "created" by a certain faction, but by life itself. Although we know that the disorders result only in repressive measures, we are still in favor of them as one form of protest. The more frequent, the better. And the victims of the disorders particularly will continue the struggle.

The students claimed they were adding to the number of socialists and thus helping the working class. The Moscow Workers' Union was, however, not convinced. Again they answered that the students' disorders were senseless. Only a small minority, "a little over 15% of the Moscow studentry of 4,000, were for the disorders," they said. "The others either are indifferent or consider them senseless." They noted cogently that of the 1,200 students who had taken part in the voting for the Union Council, only 612, a bare majority of 51 per cent, had supported the disorders, while 31 per cent had been opposed. The activist group could therefore not claim the support of the majority of 4,000 Moscow students. And as for the 1,000 who participated in the disorders, said the Moscow Workers' Union, "they were without social ideals, but had only solidarity; nor did they analyze the reasons for their defeat."[107]

The Moscow Workers' Union, indeed, believed that the self-sacrificing of the student movement was tainted with elitist pretensions. The workers and students, it felt, did not share common economic interests. As for student action, all this, it said, was "action which does not take real life into consideration." The workers felt the student consciousness was largely affected with fantasy.

An estrangement thus developed between the workers and the students to a point where the Social Democratic Labor party three years later was basically uninterested in the student movement. Social Democrats, both the leaders and rank and file, felt that the student movement was a wasteful expression of revolutionary energies and that the students were not a genuine social force. "The Social Democrats," Nicolai Berdyaev recalled, "did not regard the student movement as their business, and their attitude towards it was somewhat patronizing."[108] The students were regarded as a stratum removed from contact with the workers, and as a group whose grievances were of small moment compared with the grim sufferings of the workers. Such was the attitude of the majority of the social democratic organizations in St. Petersburg.[109] The students' meetings during the February strike of 1899, reported a coldly objective socialist observer, "were, in spite of all the heightened emotions, very lively and gay." Workers' meetings, by contrast, were somber and serious, never lively and gay. The boss and foreman were no rectors to be whistled at. A workers' vote to strike was no occasion for a holiday; it meant one's family had even less food. Every worker's decision was laden with consequences for his family's survival in its struggle for mere existence. To the workers, the students had the best of the two worlds; young members of the elite, indulged in for their youth, valued for their future place, they could still revel in revolutionary gestures. A students' strike was half a lark, an all-night party prolonged awhile. The students' solidarity could scarcely be merged with the workers' class consciousness.

The intellectual leaders of the Social Democratic party naturally tried to overcome the estrangement between the studentry and the working class, though with little success except for the brief period of 1905. *Iskra,* the party organ, reproached the party committee for failing to call on the workers to support the student demonstration of February 19, which failed for lack of popular support. Pavel Axelrod paid tribute to the student movement for having provided the stimulus for the first explosions of political discontent on the part of the masses.[110] The Social Democrats felt it important, however, to convert the studentry from idealism to materialism, from Berdyaev to Karl Marx—that is, to proletarianize their mode of thought. The St. Petersburg Committee of the Social Democratic Labor party published on February 8, 1903, a remarkable "Open Letter to the Studentry." The studentry, it said, hesitated and vacillated for lack of a revolutionary world-view and understanding.

> Our youth went away from scientific socialism, and took refuge in ethics, religion, aesthetics, and metaphysics. Our gospel is Marx's *Capital*. . . . If the students and people had had a good theoretical preparation, they would have known that no revolution is possible without the broad participation of the people. . . . Now the peasants, workers, and liberals are active, but the Russian studentry, the "barometer of Russian life," is silent. Marx is in the background, and *The Problems of Idealism* holds the center of attention. . . . Wake up, prepare for life, you are called on to work.[111]

The Problems of Idealism, a symposium published in 1903, contained Nikolai Berdyaev's article, "The Ethical Problem in the Light of Philosophical Idealism."[112] Its personalist standpoint led the Marxists to assail Berdyaev as an apostate; the lines from Pushkin with which it began voiced the student elitist temperament forthrightly:

> A king thou art—live on alone!
> Go thy free way, thy proud mind leading on.

Shortly afterward, a Social Democratic university group, at a meeting attended by six hundred, resolved to work for the unity of students with the proletariat, along the lines indicated by Ferdinand Lassalle.[113] Lassalle's name, however, was a symbol of intellectual elitism because of his eloquent advocacy of the intellectuals' vocation to guide and rule the workers' movement.

The Revolutionary Unity of Students and Workers in 1905: The Students' Seizure of Power in the Universities

At the turn of the century, a change began to take place in the student movement; it moved from an academic to a radical stage.[114] Beginning in 1900, there was renewed criticism of the purely student-minded orientation of the movement. One bulletin at St. Petersburg University called for a student movement which would go beyond the masochism of protest and arrest: "The disorders are safety-valves in which the accumulated energy escapes. . . . Our excitement is not a protest but a self-castigation useful only to the police. . . . We have to protest not with weak outbursts of wrath but by battle with the political structure of Russia."[115] The cause of the student disorders, said the Students' Mutual Insurance Fund in February 1901,

> . . . lies obviously somewhere deeper, in the ethical dissatisfaction of the studentry, which is a result of the contradictory conditions in which the institutions of higher learning are placed by the pressing demands which life itself poses to learning, its priests and temples. The government . . . does not undertake to eliminate the basic causes of the movements. . . .[116]

A debate commenced between two different factions in the student movement, one seeking to establish contacts with the working class and to join together with it for social revolution, the other devoted to such academic goals as university autonomy and liberties and engaging in political action to secure such goals. The student leaders themselves often tended to be far more radical than their rank and file, arguing that the achievement of academic goals was impossible without a radical change in the social structure. The leaders pressed in April 1901, for instance, against any resumption of classes until dismissed students were reinstated.[117] But the majority did not share their militant viewpoint.

Gradually the radicals, the politicals, gained influence. The so-called "Fund of the Radicals," a newly formed organization which combined mutual aid with revolutionary activity, zealously conceived the student movement as the vanguard, the "ferment of disintegration of the existing absolutist bureaucratic structure." The students, it said, would be followed by the "great army of labor, which will effectuate the decisive blows."[118] And indeed in 1901 this theory was a correct description of the relations between the student movement and the nascent labor movement. The radicals put their faith in the potency of demonstrations as the means for the political education and direction of society as a whole. The first All-Russian Student Congress which took place at the end of March 1902, with forty delegates present, declared in its manifesto that demonstrations would be the first means of social struggle; they would call society's attention to the abnormal state of things.[119] By 1904, as Woytinsky recalled, "The revolutionary spirit prevailed in the University." The scene at the University of St. Petersburg was much like the exceptional scene at the University of California sixty years later: "In the entrance hall of the students' mess, the Social Democrats and Socialist Revolutionaries had desks for the collection of money and distribution of illegal literature printed abroad. There was also a desk of the 'liberal' non-Socialist party, but Socialist groups predominated among the students."[120]

The outbreak of the Russo-Japanese War politicized the student movement to an extent beyond anything the radicals had expected. Student meetings protested against the Czarist foreign policy. "We, the students of the Forestry Institute," resolved one of them, "declare our protest against the adventurous policy of our government, the policy of Czardom, the main hindrance to Russian cultural development." "Patriotism means serving the people, not a bunch of exploiters," said the students of the Mining Institute.[121] Then came the fall of Port Arthur, followed a few days later by a strike of the workers in the Putilov munitions plant in St. Petersburg, then a general strike, followed by the massacre of several hundreds on Bloody Sunday, January 9, before the Winter Palace. The universities soon became the political centers of the country, the meeting place for revolutionists of all classes. W. S. Woytinsky recalled those days:

> A general meeting of students had been called to take a stand on the massacre of January 9. It was held in the main hall of the University, which could accommodate three thousand persons standing and was packed to capacity. A young man opened the meeting in the name of the coalition committee of revolutionary organizations of the University and invited the audience to elect a chairman. When he himself was elected unanimously, he announced the agenda.
>
> All the speakers urged the students to strike as the only effective protest against the infamous crime of the government. This course had been determined, in advance, after consultation among revolutionary groups. They called for strikes in all Russian universities, institutes, and colleges without a time limit. Their arguments were moral and political. We cannot study when the soil under our feet is soaked with blood. We cannot accept education from the hands of a government of murderers. We must show the workers and peasants that the students are on their side.
>
> The response was unanimous: to close the University indefinitely and call on other students in Russia to do the same. This was by no means the first strike of Russian students, but it was the first universal and purely political strike. . . .
>
> The meeting ended in solemn silence, interrupted by a loud call from the rear of the crowd: "Do not break up, comrades!"

The Revolution of 1905 thus saw the brief merging of the students' and workers' movements, in a way exceptional in the history of the student movement. Students were thrust into places of leadership, and university halls became the chambers for workers' soviets. G. S. Khrustalev-Nosar, with his reputation as the Social Democratic leader among the St. Petersburg studentry, became president of the Workers' Soviet in 1905. The university became the forum of revolution. The great students' strike of January 1905, which followed the massacre of Bloody Sunday, brought drastic changes to the academic world. A Students' Soviet virtually administered the University of St. Petersburg. "Throngs of workers found their way to the University to see and hear what was going on. . . . To satisfy them it was decided to hold meetings in the University twice a day; in the morning, on academic issues; in the evening, on political questions."[122] The university in the evenings came to belong to the revolutionary workers.[123]

In Odessa, for instance, a Menshevik student, Shavdiya, was elected chairman of the Soviet: "He was known to a great many working-men and women, for he often presided at meetings in the university."[124] Students' meetings metamorphosed into mass meetings of socialist parties. In October 1905, armed detachments were organized in the Odessa University lecture hall to combat the government's pogrom; the university itself finally became a beleaguered fortress, which the army prepared to storm.[125] In some cities, demonstrations of students and workers were attacked by armed bands directed by police agents. In Tomsk, a meeting place of intellectuals was set on fire, and three hundred persons were burned alive or clubbed to death as they sought to escape. At St. Petersburg, on October 11, recalled W. S. Woytinsky, "some thirty thousand workers came to the University. The main hall was assigned to railroad employees. After the report of the convention's delegates, the meeting unanimously decided to join the all-Russian railroad strike." This was only the climax of many such meetings; the workers on October 7, wishing to know what was happening in the Moscow railroad stoppage, had overflowed into the university's courtyard; on October 8 they had argued the question of a general strike at the Military Medical Academy. Then, on October 13, a handful of delegates from factories and mills met in a classroom of the Polytechnic Institute. Out of this meeting was born the St. Petersburg Soviet of Workers, meeting on October 15, with 226 delegates from nearly a hundred plants. The Executive Committee of the Soviet was in session at the Women's College on October 17; a crowd demanded that it lead them in procession to liberate the political prisoners, but a trio of leaders, including young Trotsky, persuaded them to disperse. Such were typical events of 1905, when the Soviets, then under Menshevik, not Bolshevik, leadership, had a working alliance with the students. Russia was indeed in those heroic days brought close to the permanent achievement of a democratic constitution. Probably, however, it was the rift which developed between the left and the liberals which presaged the failure of Russian constitutionalism. Woytinsky noted:

They [the liberals] continued to distrust the government but some of them distrusted the revolutionary parties even more. Some would have accepted the goal of a freely and democratically elected Constituent Assembly if it had not been associated with the ideas of armed revolt and a future struggle for socialism.[126]

Where the student movement fell down was precisely in its failure to bring liberalism to the workers, to join liberal values with the workers' quest for equality. The students failed, indeed, to provide the guidance of the intellect; they responded to the stir and animation of events rather with the instincts of generational uprising.

The student movement had a one-sided idea of academic freedom; it wished to impose its own orthodoxy on the professors. At St. Petersburg, the Students' Council, dominated by a Social Democratic majority, tried to shape the university to its own authoritarian notion. While demanding the reinstatement of dismissed liberal professors, "it also decided to apply an 'active boycott' against ten professors considered to be reactionaries." A kind of mass meeting acted as the jury which voted on the "proscribed list" of unwanted professors. There were charges against each of them; one of them, indeed, was alleged to have denounced his colleagues to the secret police thirteen times. "With a roar of indignation the meeting voted for his proscription." No notion of due process of law seems to have disturbed the student activists.

When the students' committee met with a committee of professors, they were told, "What you have done, gentlemen, is a trial by the mob, a moral lynching. You have condemned people without giving them an opportunity to defend themselves." The students thereupon asked the accuser, a radical assistant professor, to present his evidence against the chief accused professor. The radical assistant professor declined with embarrassment. The student committee, angered, had to report that the charges were a slander. Their audience of students jeered at them with loud catcalls; but the committee, chastened by its experience, held its own, and the matter was ultimately shelved. Meanwhile, "the University remained in the hands of revolutionary students until the showdown that marked the climax and turning point in the revolution."[127]

In October 1905 came the great general strike throughout Russia, in response to which the Czar had recourse to military repression. The student activists, mindful of the new role of the universities as sanctuaries for the revolution, refused to have the universities closed. Almost unanimously they resolved, "The University, opened in the interest of the revolution, will stay open whatever may come." The faculty followed the student leadership.

The students began to organize an Academic Legion; all they had, however, was armbands but no arms. The workers evacuated the halls, and the Cossacks moved against the university. Gradually the first Soviet Revolution was suppressed. The elected Duma came to the fore as the stage for constitutional hopes. By January 1906, the Students' Council of St. Petersburg had terminated its brief venture into revolutionary leadership and was preoccupied with the more prosaic task of organizing a cooperative canteen.[128] A social revolution in 1905, had it taken place, might well have been led by a student elite. During the next decade, however, the professional revolutionists of the socialist parties came to dominate the revolutionary movement completely. The student activists, with their personal heroism, initiative, and idealism, came to be regarded as unreliable elements by the professional revolutionaries and party organization men. Lenin, as we have seen, developed grave doubts about the student movement as a reliable revolutionary force. He evidently surmised that the dynamic of generational revolt ran a course different from that of working class discontent. A brief chronicle of the Russian student movement will, indeed, exhibit the distinctive forms and patterns of generational struggle in their coalescence of idealism and irrationality.

Chronicle of the Russian Student Movement

LAW OF THE GENERATIONAL CYCLE

A compelling and discernible pattern runs through the repeated events of Russian student protest. A typical student action might begin with a small political group, advocating some particular political or social reform. At first the majority of the students would be quite indifferent. Then some episode of repression would take place; the authorities and police would deny the students the right of free association or use sheer physical violence against them. Thereupon, indignation against the elders would sweep the studentry. The minority political movement would become transformed into a majority generational uprising. Generational solidarity of the most primitive kind would then manifest itself; demands for students' rights, manifestoes of generational independence would come to the fore.

Remarkably also, a strange generational cycle seems to have been at work within the Russian student movement. The cycle was of about eighteen to twenty years' duration; about every twenty years the intensity of student unrest would reach some new crest, a new maximal level. Thus, the year 1861 was one of maximal intensity in the student movement, then the year 1881, and finally 1899–1900. Before the First World War intervened, 1911 was also a year of high student activity. The salient numerical facts concerning Russian student unrest thus exhibit what may be called a "law of the generational cycle."

The Russian studentry for three quarters of a century experienced a persistent crisis of the spirit such as no other studentry in the world has had to endure. The German student movement of 1817, by contrast, was a transitory phenomenon of two or three years, and even the Chinese student movement of 1919 knew nothing of the prolonged agony which wrought its turmoil year after year in the Russian student consciousness.

YEAR	PERCENTAGE OF STUDENTRY PENALIZED
1861	43% imprisoned at St. Petersburg
1873–1877	2½% arrested every year
1881	12% dismissed at Moscow for demonstration against the assassinated Czar
1887–1893	2½% dismissed at Moscow every year
1894–1899	6% dismissed at Moscow every year
1896	10% arrested at Moscow in the Khodynka Memorial Demonstration
1899	81% of Russian studentry on strike
1900	10% arrested at Kiev, and 5% punitively drafted
1902	7½% dismissed at Moscow
1905	General strike in Russian society
1911	15% of Russian studentry dismissed.

Let us narrate briefly in chronicle form the external facts of the Russian student unrest.

THE EARLY SIXTIES: CLOSING OF THE UNIVERSITY OF ST. PETERSBURG

Student "disorders" became in the early sixties a permanent characteristic of Russian higher education. The year after the Crimean War, in September 1857, a student protest took place in Moscow against police cruelty and surveillance. It began trivially when students at a birthday party refused to admit the police; soldiers then were summoned, and the students were arrested and beaten. The next day there was agitation at the university for judicial action against the police, two of whom were eventually punished. Then in 1858 at Kharkov a students' strike, perhaps the first, took place. Again the trouble began when several students were beaten by the police. Thereupon 280 of their classmates, approximately 54 per cent of the studentry, asked to be dismissed from the university. Collective self-sacrifice, as an expression of generational solidarity, was always to be a trait of the students.

The year 1861 saw large-scale student protests at St. Petersburg and Moscow. The "causes" which provoked them were unimportant, say a Communist historian.[129] But all student movements, as generational uprisings, tend to be activated by some symbolic incident of the elders' oppression. The ferment over the abolition of serfdom was in the air as well as the promulgation of new university rules. On February 8, the students were excited at the denial to a professor of the right to give a speech. Then on February 21, two days after the emancipation of the serfs, a students' meeting became disorderly and was attacked by a Cossack detachment. The Czar, Alexander II, a few months later decreed new harsh rules which deprived students of the right to hold meetings, raised their university fees, and drastically reduced the number of scholarships. When the students returned to the university after their vacations, they were met with a leaflet calling on them to act. Was this the first leaflet in the history of the student movement?[130]

The St. Petersburg students responded by forming a committee of action; then on September 25 they broke into a closed auditorium to hold a protest meeting against the new rules and the rector. The next day the university locked its doors. Thereupon the students, joined by many nonstudent allies (who numbered about one fourth of the demonstrators), marched across the city to the rector's house to protest. French shopkeepers on the Nevsky Prospect shouted apprehensively, "Revolution! Revolution!" There were many arrests during the next days. When the university was reopened on October 11, the government ordered those students who would not accept the new rules to leave the capital. About three hundred of the one thousand students refused to capitulate. At the university gate, where they tried to persuade the nonsigners to their cause, they were surrounded by the police, arrested, and taken to the fortress at Kronstadt. Again some were beaten by the police and the military. "The tedium of captivity was relieved by the singing of forbidden songs, political discussions, concerts, and private theatricals. One prisoner remembered those days as among the happiest of his life." Many girls came bearing gifts to the imprisoned students; and blue, their favorite color, the color of heaven, became the fashion.[131]

The students were imprisoned for two months; 132 of them were expelled from the university, five were banished from the city, and thirty-two were exiled to their provinces. Five liberal professors were ousted. The university itself remained closed for two years; not until the fall of 1863 did students enter its halls again. When they did, they were a fraction of their former numbers. There were 1,442 students at St. Petersburg University in 1861; in 1863, there were 265.[132]

Meanwhile, the disturbance spread like a wave to Moscow, where the students were, on the whole, less restive than those of St. Petersburg and the professors entirely indifferent. The St. Petersburg students called on their Muscovite comrades for help. Some four hundred students of the two thousand at Moscow took part in a demonstration in front of the governor's house. As usual, many were beaten and arrested; twenty-seven were expelled. Factional differences now made their first appearance. On the one hand, there were the "reds," the "furious" ones, and on the other the moderates, who numbered the majority and who said "we ask for" instead of "we demand." The student leader, P. G. Zaichnevsky, wrote in a language which was to become typical of student movements in all times and places: "We finally wanted to tell that truth which some people feared and others couldn't say and others didn't want to say. People falsified, lied, and awaited good from above, it was so sickening, so vile, that if we hadn't done so then others would have done the same after us."[133]

Events the following month took a tragic turn. Five hundred moderate students in October 1861 signed petitions for the redress of grievances and brought them to the curator for transmittal to the Minister of Public Instruction. When the curator refused to receive them, insults were exchanged, the police were summoned, and in a subsequent clash several students were killed. Three hundred and forty students were arrested, and thirty-nine received prison sentences. The Czar finally consented to receive three student deputies and their petition, but found them thoughtless and illegal.

Meanwhile, at Kazan too a dispute between a professor and a student, in the tense atmosphere, rapidly "escalated" into a student uprising; the university was closed for about a month, and about sixty students were expelled. At Kharkov, a protest meeting against new rules was held.

To allay the discontent in the universities, the Czar's government enacted the statute of June 30, 1863, restoring to them the traditional "autonomy" which they had enjoyed from 1804 to 1861. But self-government in the universities did not extend to the students, whose organizations remained illegal. Moreover, the statute took a strong stand against the burgeoning unrest among women students. Women were simply forbidden to attend lectures at the universities. Thereupon began the first migration of Russian women students to foreign centers, especially Zurich, where the growing socialist, revolutionary culture rapidly infiltrated the students' consciousness.[134]

DMITRI KARAKOZOV'S ATTEMPT ON CZAR ALEXANDER II (1866)

The terroristic ingredient in the student movement intervened disastrously in 1866 in the form of an attempt to assassinate Czar Alexander II. Dmitri Karakozov, expelled in 1861 from the University of Kazan, dropped in 1865 from the Moscow rolls for not paying his tuition fee, was a typical "nonstudent" participant in the student movement and a member in good standing of a secret socialistic circle, principally composed of students, some of whom reveled in a fantasy world of assassination plots. In the winter of 1865–1866, he spent two months in the infirmary of the University of Moscow. There he feared that "he would die without having done anything for the cause." Karakozov wavered between suicide and regicide, and decided upon the latter. His attempt of April 4 on the Czar's life misfired. It brought deleterious consequences, including a governmental decree imposing a strict supervision over students' private lives.[135] A self-destructive circle of repression, retaliation, and repression became characteristic of the relations between the Russian government and the studentry.

THE SEVENTIES: CLASHES AND COMMITTEES OF INQUIRY

Student disorders erupted in St. Petersburg in 1869 and 1874 but did not reach major proportions, for these were the years in which the student activists turned from the university to the people. The back-to-the-people spirit, with its tremendous hope of raising the cultural and political consciousness of the peasantry, of serving the people as their teachers, doctors, and nurses, moved the most idealistic of the students. During the years, therefore, from 1869 to 1878, there were no large episodes within the universities themselves.[136]

The most infamous of nonstudent student leaders, Sergei Nechayev, organized a circle of some four hundred members at St. Petersburg. Meanwhile, disturbances continued. Nechayev's oft-told story illumines through extremes some underlying motifs of student movements. His bizarre activities especially contributed to making Karl Marx suspicious of student activism. Nechayev, a servant's son, entered St. Petersburg University in 1868 and became prominent there as a student agitator. He liked to represent himself as a grand chieftain of grandiose secret societies and liked to lie about his alleged imprisonment in the Fortress of Peter and Paul. His nature was an adolescent's run wild, and he was obsessed with fantasied exploits against the older generation. But then he proceeded to use and manipulate the older Russian revolutionaries who were similarly obsessed. Nechayev went abroad to Switzerland in 1869 and captivated the anarchist leader, Bakunin, who wrote rhapsodically, "They are admirable, these young fanatics—believers without God and heroes without phrases!" The old revolutionist and the young one formed a sickly "quite intimate super-secret society."[137] Bakunin wrote the *Revolutionary Catechism,* which Nechayev had printed. It announced, "There is only one science for the revolutionary, the science of destruction," and therefore "the end justifies the means"; lying, terrorism, the infliction of suffering were all justified if they drove people to revolt. Nechayev returned to Russia to found a society on (what we might call) these "unprinciples"; he demanded the unquestioning obedience of his followers to the super-secret revolutionary committee. One student, Ivanov, expressed disbelief in the committee's existence; Nechayev and several associates murdered him in November 1869. Then Nechayev escaped abroad and proceeded to try to blackmail Bakunin and otherwise deceive and betray his friends. The "Nechaevtsy," however, were tried; of approximately 150 accused, about one third were students or former students; 13 per cent were sons of priests and theological students; a little more than a fourth came from the bureaucratic and military classes, and one fifth from the nobility. Their median age was twenty-two years; only one artisan and five peasants were numbered among the conspirators.[138]

In 1872, the Swiss government turned Nechayev over to the Russians as a common criminal; Nechayev died in 1882 in the Fortress of Peter and Paul. In the annals of student movements, he looms almost as a caricature of the leaders of student movements, and his relationship with Bakunin stands as a bizarre parody of the enthusiasm with which the aged who are alienated seek to revivify themselves in a worshipful symbiosis with the young. E. H. Carr best summed up Nechayev's significance in the history of student movements: "Before Nechayev . . . none of these young men had been bold enough to press negation to its logical and ultimate conclusion. In practice, nobody had dared to reject and defy moral as well as political obligation. Nechayev took the final step. He raised revolution to the status of an absolute good; and he recognized no other kind of moral obligation."[139] He was a prototype for the nihilism in the Russian student movement as Karl Follen was for the German.

Meanwhile disturbances continued. One in 1869, directed against an unpopular lecturer, resulted in the expulsion of several students. Still another took place in 1874. Indeed, during these years, unpopular professors became the scapegoats for all the repressed generational resentment of students. An incident of this kind provided the later regicide, Andrei Ivanovich Zhelyabov, with his political debut. On October 16, 1871, an Austro-Czech, Professor Bogishich, who expected a certain minimal decorum from his students, was lecturing at the University of Odessa. He scolded a student who was lounging on his seat with the words, "Do you think you are in a drink shop?" and "hustled" him out of the room. The next day the students hissed the professor. There were negotiations for an apology, a mass meeting; and the following week, Andrei Zhelyabov, student representative, was on the rostrum "declaring amid tumultuous applause that it was a matter of principle for the whole body of undergraduates that satisfaction be obtained from Bogishich."[140] During the next weeks the Minister of Public Instruction became involved; Zhelyabov and two other students were suspended for a year and banished from Odessa.

A Committee of Inquiry, the first of many such, was appointed in 1874 by the government to examine the whole problem of the universities. With Karakozov's attempt on the Czar's life still unforgotten, a reactionary mood pervaded the committee's proposals. Disturbances continued unabated and in 1878 spread to all the universities.[141]

Meanwhile, however, a merging of generational with political issues was truly in process. Karakozov, in 1866, on the eve of his attempt, had indited a statement "To Worker Friends" which said he had decided "to destroy the wicked Czar and die for my beloved people," so that "all will be equal and the Russian people will live happily and honestly." In the intervening years the back-to-the-people mood had become an integral part of the student unrest. Then, in the spring of 1875, a funeral took place in St. Petersburg of a student activist who was said to have been tortured to death by his jailers; it naturally became the occasion for a student demonstration. A year and a half later, on December 6, 1876, a crowd of several hundred, again composed mostly of students, gathered on Kazan Square in St. Petersburg to protest once more the imprisonment and torture of students involved in the back-to-the-people movement. The impassioned young speaker was George Plekhanov, then in his twenty-first year and a second-year student at the St. Petersburg Mining Institute. He waved a cap, cried, "Comrades," and spoke of the hundreds of imprisoned youth whose cause was that of the peasants. A red flag was unfurled, and police stormed the assemblage.[142]

All authorities were becoming discredited in the students' eyes, and were perceived as enemies to be overthrown; students then began to use physical violence against professors and rectors. At Kiev in 1878 the rector was slapped and fainted. One hundred and twenty students were expelled and fifteen of them exiled. It all happened because the police intervened against overenthusiastic students who were calling at a theatrical performance for more than three curtain calls.

The student unrest weighed deeply on the minds and consciences of the university authorities and the government. The professors saw the causes of the unrest in a far different light than did the government. The Council of St. Petersburg University in a report on December 29, 1878, placed the chief responsibility on the governmental repression of the studentry: "The prejudiced and suspicious attitude of the Government, which regarded the students as a disloyal element," the "undue police restriction of the private life of the students," and the "indiscriminate arrests and banishment of students by police, which entirely wrecked their careers."[143] The government, on the other hand, looking upon the students as conceived in evil, spoke of their "frivolity of disposition," the disorienting impact of the social reforms of the sixties, the ferment of ideas which led to exaggerated notions, their status as the "offspring of the generation in whose veins glowed the fever of the reform period," the defects of their religious and moral training, and the effect of "Buckle's writings" as well as Russian literature which produced in "eager and critical minds an exalted notion of their own mission as the saviors of society."

The reports of both the professors and the officials were curiously truthful; each perceived the conflict of generations from a different vantage point. But the government failed to realize that its repressive measures would only exacerbate the generational struggle. The government was not only a political and economic absolutism, it was a generational absolutism.

Academic issues in the tense Russian atmosphere tended to be translated directly into political ones. A defense of a doctoral dissertation on Adam Smith at Moscow University in 1881 became the occasion for a student demonstration. When a socialist student who challenged the nonsocialist doctoral candidate was forbidden to speak, students demonstrated and the police were summoned. Two hundred and two students suffered various degrees of expulsion and suspension.[144] The university's anniversary day on February 8, 1881, was marked by a student leader's slapping the Minister of Public Instruction. These were protests (though supported by a minority) against the new harsh rules of 1879, which gave government inspectors virtually complete jurisdiction over the students.

THE GLOOMY EIGHTIES: THE AFTERMATH OF THE ASSASSINATION OF ALEXANDER II

The murder of Alexander II in 1881 terminated the few tentative efforts which were being made for a more liberal policy toward the students. Such lost hopes had included, for instance, recognizing the right of students to organize their own cooperative restaurants, libraries, and mutual aid societies. The student movement generally welcomed the Czar's assassination. The efforts of a few students at Moscow to try to collect money for a wreath for the Czar's coffin were met with such violent opposition that clashes ensued which led to the dismissal of more than three hundred students. At Kazan, hundreds of students attended a meeting on the campus at which the dead Czar was denounced. Students were regarded as so closely involved with the assassins that for a while they prudently avoided wearing their uniforms in public, while young women let their hair grow out of fear of popular indignation.[145] The repressive Statute of 1863 was restored, and a new period of reaction began with the appointment of Delyanov as Minister of Public Instruction. All the universities experienced disturbances in the period after the Czar's assassination; they persisted in 1882 at St. Petersburg, Kharkov, and Kazan. Delyanov responded with the Statute of 1884 which decreed a virtual governmental dictatorship in all universities; the faculties' elective powers were abolished; regional curators, appointed by the government, became the ruling supervisors of the professors and their students; inspectors, appointed by the ministry, were authorized to assist the curators by watching the students both inside and outside the universities. During the next years, furthermore, a *numerus clausus* of 10 per cent was imposed on Jewish students in the universities. Students' uniforms, which the authorities had once disliked, were now made compulsory so as to facilitate police surveillance. The number of students from the lower classes was even more reduced, and prohibitions of student activity became even more stringent.

Thus, the repressive cycle took a new turn. Student demonstrations multiplied in protest against the new harsh measures. "From 1873 to 1877, 532 students and 297 school boys were arrested for revolutionary propaganda. But during the reign of Alexander III, arrested students were counted by the thousands."[146] Since the total number of students in 1875 was 5,151, we can say that after 1873 2.5 per cent of the studentry were arrested every year; the percentage was augmented several times in the reign of Alexander III.

The students always searched for some weakness in the enemies' moral armor. In 1882, the administration of St. Petersburg wrote a letter of thanks to a rich man thanking him for a large contribution for a student dormitory. Thereupon the students demonstrated in protest, alleging that the rich man was seeking governmental contracts for his factories. Kiev and

Kazan both saw street demonstrations by students in 1884 and 1886 respectively. At St. Petersburg in 1886, the students demonstrated illegally to commemorate the twenty-fifth anniversary of the emancipation of the serfs. Later that year, on the twenty-fifth anniversary of Dobrolyubov's death, they demonstrated again. When they came with a wreath to the cemetery where the distinguished writer was buried, they were surrounded by Cossacks. The students published a leaflet in which they said they would oppose spiritual force to the government's brute force.[147]

The slapping of authorities, however, was resumed in 1887. That year the inspector of Moscow University, Bryzgalov, was called to account by a student. The inspector, said to have been organizing the student orchestra and chorus into a reactionary "Black Hundred" Society, was slapped at a concert by a student, Sinyaev.[148] The students, at protest demonstrations, argued that Sinyaev's slap had been delivered for all of them, that it was no personal slap; in other words, it had been a generational slap. Professors tried in vain to mollify them. The police clashed with the students at an outdoor meeting on Good Friday ("Holy Slaughter," it was called in a pun), the university was temporarily closed, and Sinyaev was sent into a disciplinary battalion for three years. Two hundred and twenty-two students were punished for taking part in these events; of these, ninety-seven were banished from Moscow. Sympathetic demonstrations took place at Kharkov, Kazan, Odessa, St. Petersburg, and Kiev, and the universities at the first two were partially closed. At Kazan, indeed, a student, Alexeev, slapped the rector, Polapov, with the approbation of a whole crowd; and when an inspector later tried to apprehend him, he beat the inspector. Alexeev subsequently was sentenced to three years in a disciplinary battalion and is said to have shown remorse for his violence. As usual, the causal chain of circumstances was confused. The students at the time of a doctoral defense had brought a petition to the rector which he refused to read. Disorders followed. A student dismissed for having an underground press led a demonstration in a lecture hall. Meanwhile, the Muscovite students were asking for a sympathetic demonstration. The Kazan students themselves sought the usual university autonomy, rights of assembly, petition, their own libraries, mutual funds, and restaurants, and the reinstatement of expelled students. But they added two distinctive demands: the students themselves should have the right to distribute fellowships and aids according to their own criteria, and class restrictions for entrance to the university should be abolished. Altogether ninety students were dismissed as a consequence of the Kazan episode.[149] It was at Kazan that Vladimir Ilyich Ulyanov, later known as V. I. Lenin, in 1887 became actively involved in the student movement.

Once again, in 1887, an assassination effort intervened, this time upon the life of Alexander III. Organized at the University of St. Petersburg, the terrorist circle was led by Pyotr Shevyrov, author of the leaflet of protest against police violence in 1886 on Dobrolyubov Day.[150] Pyotr Shevyrov was obsessed with the idea of assassinating the Czar. With ten other students, including Alexander Ulyanov, he set out to do so. One student had transferred from Kazan to St. Petersburg because he hoped to kill the Czar. The would-be regicides were arrested; five were executed, among them Ulyanov, the gold medallist in zoology who said at the trial that there would always be those who would "not consider it a sacrifice to lay down their lives for the cause."[151] Five universities were closed because of student tensions provoked by these events. At Kazan, Ulyanov's brother, the young Lenin, was shortly arrested with thirty-nine other students, jailed, and then expelled from the university.

THE REVIVAL OF THE NINETIES

The decade of the nineties saw a recrudescence of student demonstrations which now became a continuous rather than fluctuational characteristic of student life. In the fourteen years after 1887, there were only five years in the universities that were relatively quiet.[152] The decade of the nineties began with unrest in seven universities. Memorial services for Russian writers became the occasion for demonstrations.[153] The death of N. G. Chernyshevsky, the famous radical critic, late in 1889, was followed by a demonstration at Moscow University; and a similar manifestation in 1891 followed the death of the writer, Shelgunov.[154] One thousand two hundred students were dismissed from the University of Moscow in the six years between 1894 and 1899. Every year, on the average, 6 per cent of the studentry was dismissed.[155] The number of dismissals in this period was twice that of the preceding seven years, 1887 through 1893, during which it had averaged annually about 2.5 per cent of the student body. In the year 1890–1891, as many as 595 students were dismissed from Moscow University, probably the majority of the radical studentry. Of these, 127 were arrested and exiled.[156] The famine of 1891 added to the disorganizing effects of the growing industrialization, the total de-authoritization of the older generation, and the spread of Marxist ideas.

During the decade of the nineties the classrooms and lecture halls themselves became the fields for generational conflict. Professors unpopular for their political views found their academic careers made uncertain by students' uprisings. The student movement had no more regard for academic freedom than did the Czar's government; it was determined to enforce its will as far as it could against critics, conservatives, and reactionaries alike. A series of incidents led to great bitterness between the professors and the studentry. In 1894, for instance, a Professor Yanzhul tried to lecture on February 19, a day usually celebrated as the anniversary of the abolition of serfdom. One hundred students came to whistle and hoot; then most of them left. Then there was an attempt on the students' part to oust a professor of criminal law, L. E. Vladimirov, whom they deemed a reactionary. A professor of medicine was forced to transfer elsewhere. The students' territorial associations, the Union of Zemlyachestva, through reports and evaluations of their professors, which their "legal commission" published, became a potent weapon against the professors.[157] Then in November 1894, a noisy students' demonstration took place in the lecture hall of the famous historian, V. O. Klyuchevsky. It was the occasion of his return to the university after having tutored a son of Alexander III for a year, and Klyuchevsky gave a speech in praise of the late Czar which incensed the students; ten students were arrested at Klyuchevsky's lecture and three were later exiled. When three hundred students assembled to protest these verdicts, the police were called and the university closed; forty-nine more students were arrested and exiled. The following year the student activists complained of a Profesor Zakharin, who was forced to retire; and in 1896, the Union of Zemlyachestva voted by one thousand to ninety to start disorders against his successor, Professor Popov. The majority of students who were outside the union felt the reasons assigned were much too petty for such an action. Nevertheless, the students on November 6 created a disturbance during Professor Popov's lecture and he left.[158]

Generational warfare became endemic in the universities. Solidarity with one's injured fellow-students led to two major incidents in 1891. When the students of St. Petersburg were prohibited from celebrating their annual holiday, the Moscow students demonstrated sympathetically and were attacked by Cossacks. Four hundred students were subsequently imprisoned, of whom 150 were later exiled and twenty-six expelled. In November 1896, the Moscow Joint Soviet of Students called a demonstration in memory of the many persons who died in the Khodynka stampede which marred the new Czar's coronation. The inevitable clash with the police took place; more than seven hundred students were arrested, and 660 of them dismissed.[159]

The suicide of Maria Fedoseyevna Vetrova in 1897 in the Fortress of Peter and Paul led three thousand students to a massive demonstration at her funeral. Vetrova, arrested because of suspected participation in an underground press, set herself on fire (as we have seen) with kerosene. It was widely believed that she had been humiliated in prison. At Kiev, a demonstration in her memory led to the arrest of two hundred students, and there was a memorial meeting likewise at Kharkov. Thus, the generational solidarity of the studentry united itself around its martyrs.

Academic life, in the ordinary sense, was gradually undermined in the Russian universities. The public defenses of doctoral dissertations in Russian universities became the occasion for ideological clashes. Reactionaries and revolutionaries alike vied with each other to make scientific objectivity impracticable. In 1898, for instance, a thesis at Moscow by a protégé of the Minister of Public Instruction evoked a hostile demonstration by the Student Union Council. It was the universities' age of ideology, and it proved incompatible with science.

THE STUDENTS' GENERAL STRIKE OF 1899

In 1899, a demonstration by St. Petersburg students against an unpopular rector brought the intervention of Cossacks' knouts and evolved into a major uprising of the Russian studentry. It began when the students were asked by the rector of St. Petersburg to behave themselves in a dignified fashion at the celebration of the anniversary of February 8. The students found the rector's manner "sarcastic" and hooted him down instead. A detachment of Cossacks was greeted with a volley of snowballs from the thousand or so students. The Cossacks rode in on the students, whipped one woman and trampled another student. According to Kerensky, "it was this event that laid the foundation of a *political* student movement."[160] The next day two thousand students met and voted to strike against the university as their only means of protest against the police cruelty.[161] Again the Cossacks appeared in force, surrounding the university. The students' strike began on February 12. The students declared they would not attend classes until a guarantee of personal inviolability from the police was given to all the university students of Russia.

The generational revolt swept the children of leading officials into its vortex. The son of the governor-general of St. Petersburg was involved. Witte, the leading minister in the Czar's government, was furious with the rector for having allowed things to get out of hand. He should not have threatened the students, said the Finance Minister, but appealed to their sense of honor. "The majority of youth," he declared, "find themselves in a transitional age when the person fears to lose his sense of dignity," and their sense of honor is "pathological." It had indeed become "pathological" in Russia at this time.[162] Though the goals of the 1899 strike were liberal ones, as the Bolshevik historian V. I. Orlov concedes, its leaders, on the other hand, were revolutionary socialists of all kinds.

Within a week, other higher institutions in St. Petersburg had joined the movement, which then quickly spread to every university in Russia. The struggle between the students and authorities lasted for three whole months, and ended only at vacation time.[163] Three successive committees of student leaders were expelled, forty-three in number. At Moscow, the police banished 222 students. Kiev, Odessa, Kharkov, Kazan, Tomsk, Riga, Dorpat, Warsaw, and Novo Alexandria were all united in the general strike. In all, about thirteen thousand students were on strike throughout the empire. All the universities were declared closed by the government when summer came, and all students summarily dismissed. They could be readmitted only after a study of their individual applications. Three to four thousand students were not allowed to return to the universities. That is why the enrollment for 1899 was 1,359 less than that for 1898 in spite of several thousand new students. Moscow alone lost 1,089 students, and 244 fourth-year Kiev students were ousted.

The eminent historian, Bernard Pares, then a student in Moscow, witnessed the events of 1899 and recorded the atmosphere of the student movement, its excitability, vehemence, irrationality, generational anger, and will to martyrdom:

Letters, travellers, rumors brought the news to Moscow. A number of the Moscow students met and declared for a strike; but the hall was full of disguised policemen, who suddenly closed the doors and took the names of all present. That night the student leaders were expelled from Moscow. Next day the great staircase of the University was thronged with angry groups of talkers. Hardly any professors got an audience for their lectures. As my professor entered his classroom, the men stood up and refused him a hearing. He was far more likely than most of them to make real sacrifices when the right time came, as was abundantly proved afterwards, but cries of "Place-hunter" were hurled at him. Not in the least disturbed by the constant interruptions, he made them an admirable little speech. He would not enter into political questions; they well knew that there would be no result of their action except broken careers; he was here to read his lecture; politics had nothing to do with the continuance of their studies; those who wished to go out might do so. One bearded student (with a Little Russian accent) called out, "Thoroughly right, Professor." A heated discussion was held by the men, of whom about one-half left the room. . . . Some of these returned quietly during the lecture. On the next day, during the interval, a poll was taken in each class-room on the question of the strike. This was done with remarkable boldness and celerity: a student rushed in, stated the question and the figures already registered for and against, took the votes, and disappeared in a twinkling. There followed further arrests, and finally the University was closed for the term.[164]

At Kiev University, the students' strike had its tragicomic aspect. As a contemporary report tells:

In one of the halls Professor Samofonov was lecturing. He was approached with the request that he stop lecturing, and when he did not agree to it, one of the obstructionists began to read aloud from some book. After that a noise started, and the old professor broke out sobbing. The students explained to him that they didn't have anything personal against him.

The temple of science [they said] had become a temple of violence.[165]

The consequences, however, were unmitigatedly tragic for many students. Two hundred and fifty-five of them were dismissed, including for no evident reason, one hundred and sixty Jewish students. Elsewhere, at Tomsk, forty-five students were sent away; and at Kharkov the whole student body was dismissed.

Recriminations now began among the studentries of the several universities. The Kiev students reproached their comrades of Moscow and St. Petersburg as being laggard in pressing their demands, whereupon the Muscovites renewed a campaign for the reinstatement of the arrested students. The new rector, a liberal, not only granted this demand but also allowed political meetings. The studentry was returning to normal life when the rector took sick; the vice-rector at once violated the university's promises. Bitter at this betrayal, the student activists struck again, though in the vote which was taken a majority opposed the strike by 1,366 to 679. The university responded with a lockout of the students for five days. The Students' Executive Committee was arrested on March 22; a new committee was formed but was in turn arrested on March 26; then its successor encountered arrests on April 21. The usual toll of expelled students followed. Eight hundred and fifteen students were dismissed, and of these 603 were banished and twenty-one imprisoned. When the spring was past, the student bodies of St. Petersburg, Moscow, and Kiev were each of them smaller by several hundreds. The universities were scarcely now communities of scholars. An effort, however, to disrupt the examinations at Moscow failed when the studentry failed to heed the radical pickets. A last demonstration on April 10 brought out only two hundred tired students. It was a protest over the suicide of an arrested student, E. Liven. Again, eighteen students were arrested.[166]

The students' general strike of 1899 was without organization or clear program. It was moved by an accumulated resentment against the universities' police methods in their dealings with students. The university mirrored the repressive aspects of the Czarist absolutist state. The Administrative Councils in the universities, which tried students accused of serious offenses, were dominated by government-appointed inspectors. The inspectors were assisted by hirelings without academic background, the so-called *pedelia* (beadles), who kept a surveillance on the activities of individual students, their associations, their meetings, their attendance at classes. These *pedelia* were too often degraded men, corrupt, dishonest, stupid, and anti-intellectual. The degradation of these police spies in the universities was sometimes almost beyond belief: E. J. Dillon writes:

> Loth to give credit to the sensational stories afloat, which, if true, would amply bear out this severe judgment, one of the professors (an intimate friend of mine) sent for the beadles and interrogated them. Unabashed, they avowed everything. Turning to one of these Russian Catos, he asked: "What was your profession last year, before you were appointed beadle?" "I was a waiter in the T. Dancing tavern, where abandoned women of the town come in of a night to earn a little money by immoral conduct." "And you?" he inquired, nodding to the other. "I was a checker-out in a brothel. I also had an interest in the concern myself, but it burst up and I had nothing to live on, so I got this position of university beadle, God be praised."

When these stories and worse were told a few days later to the curator of the university, the appointee of the Minister of Public Instruction, he roared with laughter and, as big tears rolled down his venerable cheeks, said, "Just the kind of fellows to drill the scoundrelly students and teach the blackguards the way they should go."[167]

Such were the accusers, and against their accusations the students were often denied the chance to defend themselves. Moreover, the police had the arbitrary power to banish students "administratively" from the university town; such police intervention, indeed, could be made in disregard of the university's jurisdiction.[168] The Russian university was thus subordinated to a police system which furthermore operated without guarantees of due process of law. It was an academic system which had ceased to be an academic community; for both academic autonomy and individual rights had been abrogated. The professors, the older generation in such universities, were indeed a de-authoritized generation. In the eyes of the young studentry, to earn one's livelihood in this system was necessarily to have submitted to it.

The students' general strike of 1899 prompted the government once more to appoint a Commission of Inquiry. The Minister of Public Instruction, Bogolepov, refused to recognize the idealistic basis of the student movement; the sheer material misery of student life, he felt, was the chief cause for their discontent. Therefore, he reasoned, if he could alleviate the students' material conditions, he would undermine the student political movement. To this end, he proposed to establish cheap hostels for poor students, where they could eat cheaply and be supervised cheaply. At the same time, he reinforced the ban on students' organizations, increased the number of inspectors, and decreed that students could attend only the university in their district. Finally, Bogolepov invoked the notorious Provisional Regulations of July 22, 1899, which provided that expelled students would be drafted punitively into the army and, moreover, that their military status would be the same as that of peasant privates.[169]

Early in 1900, several liberal professors were ousted from the university as part of Bogolepov's program. Disorders spread among the students in protest on February 8, and the cry, "Oust Bogolepov," was sounded.[170] The student movement as a whole acted against the government. A secret congress of student representatives from all universities convened in Odessa in June 1900. All the representatives were subsequently arrested, but the organization continued to function.

THE ERA OF TURMOIL: 1900–1905

The students' general strike of 1899 was the harbinger of an era of turmoil. The famous Kiev University demonstrations of 1900, which excited Lenin, followed shortly in typical escalatory fashion. A students' meeting protested against an outrage upon a young girl by some wealthy ne'er-do-wells. Two student leaders, sentenced to four days' solitary confinement, proved so disobedient that they were expelled. Thereupon, students demonstrated at the railway station and then convened at the University Hall, refusing to disperse until the sentence was reversed. Troops were summoned and surrounded the university's main hall; all the students were arrested.

They demanded that solitary confinement be abolished and the expelled students reinstated. Instead, 183 of them were drafted punitively into the army. Bogolepov, the Minister of Public Instruction, threatened 202 others that their next offense could bring a similar punishment. This judgment of December 31, 1900, soon brought fatal consequences for the minister.

Kiev was tense with incidents. A student demand for the dismissal of a professor met with resistance and the students demonstrated.[171] At Moscow, Kharkov, and St. Petersburg in 1900 and 1901, the students were embattled with Cossacks, and "in every case the Cossacks attacked the protesting students and flogged them mercilessly." In Moscow, the performance of an anti-Semitic play, *The Smugglers*, on November 23, 1900, at the Mali Theatre provoked a demonstration. Thirty students were expelled from the university, and again their fellow-students demonstrated on their behalf.[172]

The generational conflict now nearly reached the proportions of a generational civil war. In 1901, at St. Petersburg, a students' meeting in front of the Kazan cathedral was attacked by gendarmes and Cossacks. The church proved no sanctuary, as students were flogged both inside and outside it. Seven of them were killed, among them a woman student. Many were wounded. One month later, on February 14, 1901, a twice-expelled student, Karpovich, assassinated N. P. Bogolepov, Minister of Public Instruction since 1898.[173] Student disturbances followed in all the universities. Professor Florinsky writes, "This bloody deed was extolled by speeches at student demonstrations held in St. Petersburg, Moscow, and other University cities."[174] At Moscow, the student uprising met with unprecedented success. A spontaneous strike held its own against Cossack detachments. Students climbed on the tops of streetcars to address the crowds; streets were blocked. A student general assembly, illegally convened, was held prisoner at the riding academy as the crowds milled around outside. The government finally yielded and ordered the Minister of Public Instruction to treat the students with "cordial solicitude." The students seemed briefly to have won the right to meet freely; the hated *pedelia* and inspectors vanished overnight.

Students' general strikes now became a regular feature of the Russian student movement. The first strike in 1899 was followed by others in 1901, 1902, and 1904. A nation-wide, organized student movement was founded on a network of secret committees in every university. The bases for these committees were the so-called Zemlyachestva, the regional mutual-aid societies of students, which, although prohibited by law, were present in every university. At first without political aims, they were persuaded by the propaganda of the revolutionary circles and the persecution of the government to take a political direction. Every society elected one representative to a "coalition committee, a Joint Council which was granted dictatorial powers to declare a strike without a previous vote among students."[175]

Thus, there emerged at this time what we might call "student sovietism"

—that is, a dominance of the studentry by student activists with dictatorial powers and revolutionary aims. The unions of Zemlyachestva in every university acted under the direction of a Joint Council (Soiuznyi Soviet); in turn, the Joint Councils of the various universities acted together for common purposes.[176] The word "soviet" had long been used as a name for governmental and professional councils. One wonders, however, if the idea of a "soviet" as an organizational form for the revolutionary workers' movement was imported from the student movement in 1905.

Deeply affected by the assassination of Bogolepov, the Council of Moscow University undertook once more on February 28, 1901, to inquire into the causes of student unrest. Its report stressed that prohibiting all student societies only contributed to the founding of illegal organizations. The new Minister of Public Instruction, Vannovsky, did promulgate more liberal rules in December 1901, granting students the right to organize their own dining clubs, libraries, and mutual-aid societies, and to elect their "elders" who were to be responsible for allocating scholarship funds among the poorest students and for negotiating on such questions as examinations with the professors; student meetings were to be allowed under supervision. The government's concessions, however, failed to quell the student unrest.

Nineteen hundred and one indeed was a year in which the student movement at Moscow took on a nervous, irrational aspect. There was the incident, for instance, concerning an aged professor, Guerrier, an author of the liberal Moscow report. A kind of hysterical outcry against Guerrier arose among the political activists. "Let's catcall Guerrier!" was the slogan. The old professor was a scholarly historian, well known as a defender of the right of women to a university education. The activists, however, alleged that Guerrier, as director of the Women's College, had treated women "like an Oriental despot." Their charges, which are said to have been an "absurd and malicious slander," caused a bitter division between the ultra-activist "politicians" and the "academics," who felt the student movement was becoming the agency of mob rule. The Moscow student movement at its emotional peak was indeed prone to becoming embattled on behalf of its women members. A students' "parliament," for instance, was called that year to consider an "insult" to a woman student printed in an article in a reactionary paper, *Grazdanin* (The Citizen). Its author, Prince V. P. Meschevsky, was actually a notoriously immoral man who exercised a great political influence on Czar Nicholas II. Subsequently the students appended a demand for the abolition of the admissions quota for Jewish students. In the running controversy between the "academics" and the "politicals," the former proposed to confine themselves to the achievement of a free university, organized a League for Academic Freedom, and advanced the slogan, "Down with the board of inspectors"; the "politicals," on the other hand, sounded the battle cry "Down with autocracy!" The factional dispute was resolved externally though temporarily when both factions were arrested as they met illegally toward the end of the year to organize against the new Provisional Regulations.

The list of the thousands of expelled students, their careers ruined, seemed always to grow. November 1901 saw the ouster of all the first-year students in the Kharkov Veterinary Institute and fifty-two at Kharkov University. Three months later, in February 1902, the Moscow students were once more striking for freedom of speech and assembly and the reinstatement of expelled students. As usual, episodes of police cruelty aroused the students' anger.[177] Once again, about four hundred students were expelled from Moscow University and banished. Strikes followed in Kiev, Kharkov, Kazan, Odessa. Banishments were carried out "administratively" by the Minister of Interior, D. S. Sipiagin, against whom feeling ran high. Again a student assassination intervened. In April 1902, a Kiev student, S. V. Balmashov, twenty years old, veteran of a term of correction in the army, disguising himself as an aide-de-camp to the Czar, gained entry into the governmental building and killed the Minister of Interior.[178] The assassin was executed. Thereupon, another students' general strike took place which led to Siberian exile for another 115 students from Moscow and St. Petersburg. Among those barred from attending either Moscow or St. Petersburg was a close personal friend of Balmashov, Alexis I. Rykov. He therefore matriculated at the University of Kazan, where he joined the Social Democratic Labor party. Twenty years or so later Rykov became Lenin's successor as premier of the Soviet Union; he subsequently perished in one of Stalin's purges.[179]

The new Minister of Interior, von Plehve, hoped to suppress the revolutionary students; but, mindful of world public opinion, he sent his chief of gendarmes to Siberia to negotiate with the students and to get their promise to abstain from further striking. Only about half the students agreed to see him, and even these refused to promise anything.[180] In Plehve's time, as Pares tells, "black reaction reigned everywhere. A group of students were not allowed to walk down the street together. Espionage raged everywhere in the universities and the schools." Even the Women's Medical Institute was shut down in March 1903 when the students insisted on meeting to demand changes in the order of their examinations.[181]

In July 1904, with the advent of the Russo-Japanese War, a young student, Yegor Sergeyevitch Sazonov, an expellee from Moscow University, and son of a wealthy conservative merchant, killed the Minister of Interior, von Plehve.[182] Soon afterward, in February 1905, a young man, Ivan Kaliaev, veteran of the Organization Committee of the student movement at Kiev, but later expelled, killed with a bomb the Grand Duke Sergei Alexandrovitch, commander of the Moscow military region and the Czar's uncle and brother-in-law.[183]

There was very little studying in Russian universities during the latter part of 1904 and all of 1905. On Sunday, January 9, 1905, Father Gapon led a great procession of workers in St. Petersburg with petitions for the Czar. It ended as "Bloody Sunday," as the troops fired on the peaceful petitioners, killing and wounding several hundreds. Excitement ran so high at the universities that after the Christmas holiday the faculties petitioned for the postponement of the new term. The general students' strike (which we have described) spread in January throughout all the universities, and the government closed the academic halls. On April 16, the Czar decreed that students would have to repeat that year's work, and closed all students' boarding houses and dining clubs. He threatened to expel all students and professors involved in any repetition of disorders. The government, however, was compelled during the revolutionary year, in August 1905, to retreat and restore university autonomy. That autumn it still proved impossible to resume normal academic work. The leftist student groups succeeded in turning the halls of the universities into meeting places for workers and political parties; the university became a "revolutionary tribune." For another year it ceased to be an academic community; no studying was done.[184] A political recession followed, a torpor came over Russian society, and the Russian student movement itself subsided.

DECLINE AND DEFEAT OF THE STUDENT MOVEMENT, 1906-1914

After 1906, the leftist student movement in Russia no longer had the undisputed hegemony it had held prior to 1905. The percentage of liberals, moderates, and nonparty students, as we have seen, tended to grow.[185] The moderates were not intent on challenging the faculty, and instead of advocating political demonstrations, wished the students' organizations to devote their energies to such enterprises as relief funds and canteens. The leftist students, the so-called "democratic students," on the other hand, regarded their principal mission as revolutionary demonstrations. Like all revolutionary student movements, the leftists also appended a demand (which proved illusory after the Bolshevik Revolution) for the participation of students in the administration of universities, and the revision of curricula on the basis of the "free cooperation of students and professors."[186]

Incidents of student protest continued to occur after 1906, though less frequently. At Kiev, in the autumn of 1907, eighty students were expelled, and at Odessa twenty elected student representatives were tried by the criminal courts as political offenders. In June 1907, the rules for students' societies were liberalized; they were now allowed to form any kind of society which did not contravene the law.[187]

Again, however, the appointment of a reactionary Minister of Public Instruction, A. N. Schwarz, terminated a brief liberal interlude. On July 14, 1908, the students were forbidden to elect their "elders." Women were once again denied entry into the universities, and the *numerus clausus* for Jewish students was reinstated. Soon Schwarz was superseded by an even more reactionary minister, L. A. Casso, under whom the saying arose, "Casso has made a whole cassation." It was during the administration of this illiberal man that the last great wave of student demonstrations took place in Russia. On November 7, 1910, the revered novelist, Leo Tolstoy, died. The whole country mourned, and students, everywhere deeply moved, organized memorial meetings and planned to make his funeral into a great demonstration against capital punishment. In Moscow, St. Petersburg, Kharkov, Kiev, and Odessa, the students went on strike and marched with flags and placards bearing the slogan, "Away with capital punishment!"[188] The government undertook to stop them with special formations of armed reactionary students. Violence broke out at Odessa University; one pro-Tolstoy student was killed and several others wounded. Casso thereupon, on December 10, ordered the expulsion and banishment of all leaders of the student pro-Tolstoy demonstrations. At Odessa about two hundred students were thus punished "administratively." The police invaded the universities. Students answered by proclaiming a general strike which lasted all through the semester.

Nineteen eleven thus became a year in which the rights of students were under continuous assault by the government. The Minister of Public Instruction met the Tolstoyan protests by destroying the few that remained of the liberal rules of 1907; student societies and meetings were forbidden. Everywhere students demonstrated and protested. The roll of the punished grew: for the month of January, 375 were arrested and banished at Tomsk Technological Institute, 392 at St. Petersburg University; for February, seventy-five expelled at Moscow, fourteen at Kharkov, sixty-six at Odessa, twenty-eight at Kiev; then a later day of February brought 370 more expulsions at Moscow. The rector and several professors at Moscow were dismissed. A students' general strike developed again in a violent direction. Casso intensified his repressive measures, sending detectives disguised as students into the lecture halls and filling the seats with policemen and armed reactionaries. The students replied with chemical warfare in the form of noxious gases. The lecture halls were rendered unfit for use. The roll of expelled students rose to six thousand, which constituted more than 15 per cent of the studentry. Later there were still other "cassations." A special summer session announced by the minister in St. Petersburg was resisted by the students. Thereupon, he dismissed almost the entire body of students, 1,338 of them, who happened to be in the city. A more moderate policy came only after the Prime Minister Stolypin was assassinated on September 1, 1911. The last demonstrations in the universities before the war were provoked by changes in the Statute of the Military Medical Academy and by the shooting of workingmen in the Lena gold mines in 1912.

The war years brought a liberal swansong. Women were readmitted, the quota against Jews was relaxed, and the autonomy of the universities recognized. But war brought about a social collapse in Russia which destroyed the chances for a liberal social evolution.

Natural Science: The Ideological Subject

A field of study becomes an ideological one for students when, under the given circumstances of time and place, it provides a fulcrum for the rejection of the elder generation's standpoint. The actual content of the subject may be quite devoid intrinsically—that is, logically—of any ideological consequence. Nevertheless, the emotions of those who study it will attach such consequence to its propositions.

Throughout the history of the Russian student movement, students of the natural sciences were the most involved group. When serious disorders erupted at the University of Kazan toward the end of 1887, for instance, the natural science students were the most active.[189] In 1895, the students of natural science and medicine were the most active in the student disorders; while the next year, 1896, the natural science students at Moscow similarly, according to Klyuchevsky, participated in the greatest numbers.[190] The prestige of the natural sciences was so high that even so philosphical-religious a character as young Berdyaev felt himself impelled to enroll as a student in that department when he came to Kiev in the late nineties.[191] Russian students long regarded chemistry as the most ideological science and expected from it the solution of the social question.[192] In the high schools, a battle raged on behalf of science as against the classics, and generational conflict took a curricular turn. "Down with the Classics! Up with Science!" shouted the students. "Thousands of people throughout the length and breadth of Russia were coming to the same conclusions," recalls Ivan Maisky.[193] High school boys revolted against their Latin masters and won the sympathy of many townsfolk, soldiers, and bureaucrats for their stand.

Indeed the students of medicine and natural science, reported an official investigator, were the most hardened criminals among the five hundred students or so who, between 1873 and 1876, were being watched, tried, or deported.

The sciences at this time enjoyed a high emotive-ideological status. Young students took to heart the earlier injunction of Pisarev and Herzen that science was the way to freedom and the betterment of the human lot. The nihilist Bazarov in Turgenev's *Fathers and Sons* had spent his spare time dissecting frogs; it was like a ritual of the new religion, for Dmitri Pisarev, the ideologist of nihilism, evangelized "dissecting frogs."[194] Books of popular materialism, such as Büchner's *Stoff und Kraft*, had a great vogue. The Czarist government, too, came to believe that the study of natural science had a radicalizing effect and therefore decided to ban its teaching as well as that of history and geography from the gymnasia; the curricula were refashioned almost exclusively for the study of Latin and Greek—with the emphasis on grammar. The enforced formalistic study of the classics ranked in the students' consciousness among the great social problems of Russia;

it was all part and parcel of the vicious social order to which the elder generation was committed. "Half of Russia is dying of hunger!" cries Nejdanov in Turgenev's *Virgin Soil.* "They want to introduce classicism, the students' benefit clubs have been closed, spies everywhere, lies, betrayals, deceit!" Dmitri Pisarev, indeed, led an assault on aesthetics. "No man of our generation," he wrote, "is likely to waste his life in piercing sensitive hearts with deadly iambs and anapests."[195] Scientism was an essential component of Russian student ideology in 1868, and it continued to be so until the Bolshevik Revolution.

The study of science also served as a protest against the romantic, futile, effete older generation. Bazarov, in *Fathers and Sons,* looks upon the fathers as ineffectual: "The so-called advanced people were good for nothing, talking about art . . . when it was really a question of daily bread." The kindly father, Nikolai Petrovitch Kirsanov, pleads that he has established his peasants on their land, "so that I am even regarded as a Red all over the province; I read, study, I do everything I can to keep abreast of contemporary requirements—but they say my song is sung." But he is a romantic, plays the cello, and has not read Büchner's *Stoff und Kraft.* These students in rebellion worshiped science; but if there was ever a group that took their science joylessly, in an ascetic spirit, it was the young nihilists. Science was studied not for the joy of knowing, but because it provided an anti-elder-generation ideology. There was a sado-masochistic reduction of romantic feelings: love—"These mysterious relations between man and woman? We physiologists know what those relations are." "A decent chemist is twenty times more useful than any poet," says Bazarov. The nihilist seeks to extirpate the romantic emotion in himself—"love in the ideal sense . . . the romantic sense, he called nonsense, an unforgivable stupidity"—and yet he recognized that its feelings were deep within him. Even to his death, the nihilist was moved by an impulse to self-destruction. Bazarov, the medical student, volunteering to do an autopsy on a typhoid case with unsterile lancets, was seeking his own death. "The study of individual personalities is not worth the labor," said Bazarov. Yet his effort at self-obliteration was finally a failure. He apotheosized the "rejection" of art, poetry, all that concerns the feelings. Some mode of self-laceration is characteristic of all student movements, all student unrest. "Rejection" was not a scientific outlook; it was a generational stance, an emotive a priori, not a logical one. No doubt, if science had been loved for its own sake, student strikes would not have abounded in Russia. In 1891 the great chemist, Mendeleev, admonished the St. Petersburg students that one could be useful to the people without making a revolution.[196] The ideological students, however, were far more moved to revolution than science. Nevertheless, "science" was inscribed on their banner; and whatever their underlying emotional drives, they were to be projected in scientific language.

Few scientists emerged out of the student movement; for its ideological scientism, the outcome of a generational fervor, had little in common with the genuine scientific spirit. The outstanding exception was Vladimir Haffkine, the Jewish student at the Imperial Novorossisk University in Odessa who became the celebrated conqueror of cholera in India. Haffkine, at the age of twenty-one, was among three students expelled in 1881 for organizing a demonstration against a reactionary dean. He was also the favorite pupil of the great Metchnikoff, who reproached "his boys" for forsaking scientific seminars for illegal conspiracies, and for reading prohibited pamphlets instead of their textbooks. But Metchnikoff himself, finding the oppressive atmosphere insupportable, soon resigned in 1882 and several years later left for Paris; Haffkine followed shortly. He turned completely from the self-destructivism of the Narodnaya Volya party to the fruitful labor of science; "nothing was farther away from his thoughts than taking his own life."[197] The way of science, with its patience and objectivity, was far removed from the emotions of the student movement.

Under the impact of generational politics, science itself in the Russian universities became "politicized" and "ideologized." An American observer of 1906 and 1907 reported, "The student about to choose a university knows that most of the faculty of the University of Moscow are Revolutionary Socialists. The trend in Petersburg is towards Social Democracy. Kharkov—the blind university of the Empire—leans to the Constitutional Democratic Party. And the student chooses according as his temperament inclines him to one group of ideas or another."[198] A professor of biology reviewing a book on Darwinism would irrelevantly digress that the hope of Russia was in the proletariat. A professor of literature reviewing a book on Shelley would interpolate that disagreement with the Social Revolutionaries was a sign of lack of culture. The line between science and ideology became indistinct; it was typically part of the irrationality of the times.

The Causal Factors in Student Protests

What, then, may we conclude from our brief chronicle of the Russian student movement? The records available to us are often fragmentary, and the circumstances surrounding the student protests are obscure. The anonymous acts of student groups have a youthful transience which baffles historiography. Nevertheless, from our narrative and tabulation of upwards of eighty-three strikes, demonstrations, disturbances, and disorders among the Russian studentry during the years from 1857 to 1914, certain conclusions can be drawn. Economic self-interest was a relatively minor motive. In only three actions were such issues as those of university fees, scholarships, and living conditions central in the minds of the student activists. Most powerful in the students' consciousness were their resentment against rules restricting their freedom of speech and assembly, resentment against police surveillance and cruelty, and the overriding bond of generational solidarity with their maltreated fellows. In at least thirty-eight incidents, student actions were undertaken in protest against the denial of the right to hold meetings and organize societies. In at least thirty-nine cases, the students were moved to protest the harsh actions of the police. It is perhaps hard for us to comprehend the near hysteria into which the Russian students would be driven by the repressions of police, secret agents, and troops. These constituted an assault upon their elemental human dignity, on their claim to manhood as they emerged from adolescence. The sheer physical outrage, the Cossacks' knouts, the soldiers' rifles and bayonets, aroused the students to a heat of generational resentment and militant comradeship. The exiled students of St. Petersburg, who had been beaten by the hundreds at the demonstration in February 1899, sang in bitterness:

> O little knout, O little knout,
> My little knout so merry!
> Do you remember, little knout,
> The eighth of February?[199]

Generational solidarity with injured, humiliated, imprisoned, arrested, or expelled fellow-students was almost a universal emotional mainspring of the student demonstrations.

Moreover, there were twelve cases in which student disturbances were directed against particular professors, lecturers, or doctoral candidates. One has the impression that many more such episodes occurred than have been recorded, and that they became especially frequent during the time immediately before a major student outbreak. Between 1894 and 1896 at Moscow, there was thus a cluster of five such incidents.

What is noteworthy is that the actions of the student movement were independent and almost completely separate from actions of the workers' and peasants' movement. The general strike of 1905, of course, was the outstanding case in which students acted in concert with the community as a whole after the massacre of "Bloody Sunday." The Tolstoyan demonstrations of 1910 likewise had a populist aspect. But there was only one demonstration explicitly on behalf of a group of workers, that in support of the Lena gold miners, and another as a memorial for the people killed at the Khodynka coronation stampede. These four instances, with one of major magnitude, were, nonetheless, exceptional in the history of the Russian student movement. An ingredient of insult to their own generation, of direct provocation to themselves, generally had to be present to call forth a major incident of student protest. Given the conditions of Russian society, the government's suppression of free thought, the role of the universities as agencies of the Czarist bureaucracy, and the activities of the police and inspectors, student demonstrations in the majority of cases tended to take on an anti-governmental aspect. In at least fifty-three cases out of those we have enumerated, events indicate that the identities of the university and government had coalesced to become the common object of student protest. Probably the number was much higher.

Peripheral issues arose from time to time. The Tolstoyan demand in 1910 for the abolition of capital punishment was probably symbolic for all manner of grievances against the government—against all the punishment, torture, and humiliations of the police. But this was an issue raised explicitly only once. Similarly there were five demonstrations which were moved in part by sympathy for women who had endured maltreatment and suffering at the hands of jailers, reactionary students, or a despotic professor. Lastly, in only one recorded case did a demonstration arise in protest against anti-Semitic behavior.

The recurrent themes of student disturbances and demonstrations were generational resentment and generational solidarity. A struggle for the "autonomy" of the university against the governmental authorities always elicited the maximum of support. We have seen the typical pattern of "escalation" of incidents in student disturbances. Something would occur which would call forth the protest of a small group of students; then the university authorities would call upon the police to intervene; whereupon large groups of sudents would join in protest on behalf of students injured or arrested by the police; a spontaneous rally would take place against the force used against the younger generation; the original causative incident soon was lost sight of in the intensity of the generational uprising.

Freedom for students to form their political organizations and freedom from political surveillance were the most persistent issues for conflict with the absolutist government. When they were dramatized and personalized by police cruelty they evoked the maximum of generational solidarity. A variety of other issues, ranging from protest against the free sexual activities of rectors to the abolition of capital punishment, rode like intermittent waves, with the more basic carrier wave of generational resentment.

Generational Disequilibrium in Russian Society

During more than half a century, student unrest was a constant in Russian society. Every few years commissions, committees, and conferences were convened (as in 1866, 1869, and 1883) to study the problem. Always the "alienation" of the students showed through the documents and reports.

The Advisory Commission of Moscow University in 1901, for instance, summarized the students' condition in terms which astonish one because they are so like those used to characterize the California students in 1964.[200] The same words appear—"isolation," "alienation"—the same plaint of the impersonality of the university, the lack of personal contact with the professors, and the dehumanizing rules and infringements on freedom of speech and assembly. The university, said the students, was not truly an alma mater; it was devoid of the warmth of a family. Isolation (*razobshchennost'*) was the student lot.[201] Rules which forbade clubs and associations made fruitful informal contacts with professors difficult. There was no students' court for judgment by the professors of disciplinary cases. Government inspectors were both accusers and judges, and hireling spies spread their mistrust. Serious students were depressed in such a university setting. They experienced "alienation" from the university (*otchuzhdenie ot universiteta*).[202] The students and the administration became two enemy camps. Frustrated, the students turned to illegal organizations and mass demonstrations. Yet, most of the students denied that the majority of the demonstrators were moved by specific political aims.

The professors, on the contrary, tended to regard the student unrest as a reflection of the political mood in society as a whole. Some thought that political agitators were the root of evil, that revolutionary political organizations, outside the university, encouraged student adherents to foment disorders for the purposes of propaganda. Still others blamed the sheer crowdedness of the university. Some thought the high schools (gymnasia) were to blame for their lack of discipline. Other professors said that the formalism and specialization in the university were at fault, and that the students consequently turned to radical publications for guidance, feeling under a moral concern to protest. Liberal professors asked whether their students should be made to suffer for their youthful sensitivity, idealism, their conviction in the necessity of moral protest, their readiness for self-sacrifice.

The students' actual program for the university was much like the professors'. They added, however, some proposals of their own. They wanted students to be able to audit lectures at will in other faculties, the examination system to be reformed, and the percentage of Jews in the university to be increased. But by the early 1900s the "politicals" in the university were making it clear that their quarrel was with society at large, and that for them the university was simply the bastion for class struggle, the place where battle first was joined.

The list of so-called student grievances does not take us to the deepest, underlying cause of the Russian student movement. Nor, indeed, do we find the explanation simply in a law of generational conflict, for such conflicts are a universal theme in human history. What we must explain is the unusual intensity of generational conflict in Russian society.

The generational equilibrium in Russia, indeed, virtually collapsed for fifty years. An English observer in 1882 wrote, "Parental authority, which a few years ago was such a marked feature in domestic life in Russia, has become a thing of the past as far as regards the majority of the students, and university and government officials are equally condemned."[203] The traditional notions of sexual morality were especially under assault: "The ideas of family ties and of the obligations of married life which prevail in the home of students are probably lax enough, but even these are cast to the winds by the young men and women who adopt a code of morals of their own in the Bohemian society of which they have become members." The conflict of fathers and sons impinged on the consciousness of young intellectuals even more than the conflict of classes. "In the autumn of 1899," Ivan Maisky recalls, "the war of 'Fathers and Sons' was at its height. I fought the war stubbornly and energetically, but still it was depressing and, to some extent, it disturbed my peace of mind. . . . We were playing in our house another variation on the theme of 'Fathers and Sons,' which is as old as the hills."[204] What produced such an unparalleled conflict of generations, what made suicidalism and terrorism into natural expressions of the Russian student consciousness?

We would be tempted to correlate the traits of student movements, their intense "revolt against the father," with the existence of a strict family structure. Certainly, where a sternly patriarchal family exists, it may well prepare the psychological soil for a revolutionary student movement. But such was not the case in Russia. From all the evidence we have, the Russian family was an extremely permissive one, especially as concerned the relations between fathers and sons. Turgenev's *Fathers and Sons* depicts Bazarov and Arkady on terms of almost idyllic affection for their fathers. Yet, the generational resentment was there with an unseen fierceness. It was born not of the social structure of the Russian family, but of the crushing "de-authoritization" of each generation by the next. Each generation of elders was regarded as having been a moral failure, as having betrayed its ideals, as having proved itself unmanly, as having allowed itself to become emasculated. The family might be generous and permissive, but the sons loathed the notion that they would become amiable liberals like their fathers. All the generations were nourished on an advanced philosophical culture; and by the criterion of these ideas, each preceding generation had allowed itself to live a life which was a grotesque caricature of what it believed. If American Negro students felt ashamed of their predecessor Uncle Toms, every Russian son looked upon his father as another Nikolai Petrovitch Kirsanov.

It was not the strength of fathers which made their sons react by becoming revolutionary activists. Rather it was their weakness, their failure, their femininity.

Each generation looked back on its youthful years with disillusionment and even bitterness. The student experience, where it had been enjoyed, receded into a kind of meaninglessness. Each generation in its post-student years mocked its student hopes, and in turn their sons looked upon them as persons who had made the Great Betrayal and surrendered their ideals to the Bureaucratic System. Each generation was in turn "de-authoritized" in the eyes of its young. The student movement, because of its own high exaltation and exhilaration, prepared the mental and spiritual collapse of its own generation.

The Bureaucratic System usually succeeded in extirpating the philosophical longings of student activists. As Bernard Pares recorded in 1907 (italics mine):

On no account should it be forgotten that the bureaucrat is very often an ex-student. In Russia nearly everyone is directly or indirectly an official. . . . But it is easy for there to be a conflict between Government employment and personal ideals in a country which has had the history of Russia, and in a class which has suffered as the Russian Intelligents. To accept a frankly official post may seem to some almost like a recantation. . . . The man who settles down into official life may in some measure have to break his connection with the past. But unfortunately, this sudden sacrifice of what a man counts to be best in himself is often demanded at the moment when the student finds it necessary to earn a living; he has hardly any choice except either to take a great many things as he finds them or to set himself against the whole system of society. Naturally it is very few who have the moral courage to choose this second lot; and even they will hardly find in their ideals or in their training sufficient strength to guarantee them a safe conduct through so great a struggle. *The evidence of all my informants goes to show that those students who have shouted loudest against the Government become the most submissive and self-seeking officials.* I remember, in particular, an official who told me his own story. The students of Kharkoff rose to remedy several very real grievances; they demanded that spies should be excluded from the University, and that the rigorous control of the police should be replaced by a university court of honor. As one of the ringleaders, he was sent to serve as a private soldier in the Army. . . . Of his former ideals no trace was to be seen except the bitterness which they had left behind them. "Once," he said, "I had to touch my hat to them," pointing to the railway conductor who passed through the compartment; "now they must touch their hats to me." . . . He seemed to find pleasure in his personal escape from tribulation.[205]

Moissaye J. Olgin, participant in the Kiev demonstrations of 1900 and later the leading Jewish Communist editor in the United States, gave a similar life history for the typical student revolutionary:

This was the ordinary biography of a Russian intellectual, at twenty, an ardent revolutionist (in theory) repudiating compromises (in discussions with his friends), cherishing the most novel social ideals; at twenty-five, a county physician, or a teacher, or an agriculturist, or a public-service officer, trying to be progressive and human, and being handicapped at every step by the bureaucratic machinery and the indolence of so-called "society"; at thirty, a "tired" man, exhausted by the unequal struggle, disgusted by his failures, gradually yielding to the habits of his surroundings, drinking whisky and playing cards every evening out of sheer boresomeness; at thirty-five, a moral wreck, assimilated by his environment beyond recognition. . . .[206]

All the intellectuals, young and old, subscribed to a common, advanced philosophical culture. All shared the same high ideals of liberation and equality. And precisely by this common standard, each generation was quickly de-authoritized in the eyes of its successor. Each generation was cast on its own without moorings. Every generation had to reconstruct anew its self-respect and sense of manhood, for it derived no psychological support from its fathers. Ashamed of them for their effeminacy, it feared to recapitulate their fate and strove to fend off surrender and emasculation by parricide, regicide, and suicide.

The de-authoritization of generations in Russia was cumulative. The great-grandfathers failed in the 1820s and 1830s, the grandfathers failed in the fifties, and the fathers failed in the seventies. Each generation found itself unable to honor its father, each generation refused to be morally castrated as its fathers had been.

It was this de-authoritization of the older generation (this dethronement of the superego) which was the root cause of the Russian student movement. The inventory of grievances, usually adduced, the restrictions on student political action, the formality of the university, were all secondary. Angelica Balabanoff, as a student revolutionary, was dismayed, for instance, by the absence of a German student movement when by all her Russian criteria there should have been a most militant one:

> The atmosphere at the German universities was that of a well-disciplined army post over which ruled the faculty as the general staff. The chasm between teachers and pupils was symbolized in the curt and arrogant nods with which the former acknowledged the military salutes and heel-clicking of the latter. The incredible formality and authoritarianism of academic life appalled me, but even more incredible was the complacency with which the students accepted the regime. One looked in vain for some hint of rebellion, of irreverence, of good-natured mockery. If there were any radicals among the Leipzig students, I did not discover them—and this in one of the most revolutionary centers of all Germany.[207]

But the basic fact was that the German elder generations enjoyed a series of political successes in the Bismarckian era which gave them pride and prestige in the students' eyes.

The Russian Jewish Students: Twofold Revolt and Twofold Guilt

Lenin observed that Czarism hated particularly the Jews because "the Jews furnished a particularly high percentage of leaders of the revolutionary movement" and also because "to the credit of the Jews, they furnish a relatively high percentage of internationalists."[208] The participation of Jewish students in the Russian student movement deserves special consideration. Involved in an intense generational conflict with their own fathers, rejecting their own roots, they found themselves rejected in turn by the Russian culture. Their oscillations between terrorism and suicidalism became all the more violent.

Jewish students were first admitted to the Russian gymnasia and universities in 1856, during the reign of Alexander II with his comparatively liberal policies. By 1872, there were three hundred Jewish students in the universities and 2,362 in the gymnasia. Fourteen years later, in 1886, the number of Jewish university students had grown to approximately 1,700, out of a total studentry of about 11,600.[209] In the secondary schools, the percentage of Jews rose from 1.25 per cent in 1853 to 13.2 per cent twenty years later.[210] They came predominantly from the middle and upper groups of the Jewish communities.

The Jewish students, enraptured with the new culture and ideology, thought themselves comrades in spirit and deed of Chernyshevsky, Herzen, Pisarev, Dobrolyubov. Thus commenced what A. L. Patkin described as "an explosion of revolutionary emotion among Jewish Student Youth," which was channelized almost entirely into Russian revolutionary socialist channels.[211]

Jewish students were strongly drawn to revolutionary student movements, for the Jewish family was riven by a searing cultural conflict of the generations. Virtually every Jewish father was de-authoritized in the eyes of his son. The young student, Pavel Axelrod, pioneer in revolution, was moved in the 1860s not only by memories of poverty but by "memories of fear and anger when his parents scraped and bowed before the passing *pans* or trembled at the sight of officialdom."[212] Virtually every Jewish father was emasculated in the eyes of his son by his submission to anti-Semitism and contemptuous abuse. Every Jewish father in the eyes of his son was in an elemental sense something less than a man, and the religion of the "chosen people" seemed a shroud for one's humanity. Then the Jewish student stepped from his home, in which an ancient, prefeudal religion and culture prevailed, with its alien rites and languages, and its orthodox ritual, into a university where he breathed the most advanced scientific ideas.

Ashamed of his parents, who often could scarcely speak any Russian at all, without moorings at home, rebellious with a fury which he could never fully voice at home to a father already persecuted by society, the Jewish son veered to the extreme revolutionary course. When the Jewish student joined the student movement, he was usually rejecting his own people. "For a Jewish Narodnik the motto—'Go to the people'—meant go to the Russian people."[213] Jewish students from rabbinical institutes, writes S. M. Dubnow, "also began to 'go to the people'—the Russian people, to be sure, not the Jewish."[214] Generational revolt reached into the rabbinical seminary of Vilna even as it was penetrating the theological seminary of Tiflis, Georgia; in 1872, Jacob Finkelstein, a student at the rabbinical seminary, organized an illegal library, where one could obtain the writings of the latter-day prophets, Chernyshevsky, Pisarev, Dobrolyubov, Lavrov. The first Vilna revolutionary circle consisted mostly of students from the rabbinical seminary.[215] By 1875, Vilna had become a center of socialist propaganda, as students and ex-students of the rabbinate took the initiative in agitation.[216] Of these the most famous in revolutionary annals was Aaron Sundelevitch, organizer in 1872 of the first Vilna group, and prototype for the character David in Stepniak's novel, *The Career of a Nihilist*. Sundelevitch became a member of the executive committee of Narodnaya Volya, and was celebrated for his courage and daring in the execution of terrorist acts. He spent twenty-six years of his life as a convict in Siberian mines.[217] Yet Sundelevitch could never share the enthusiasm of Russian students for their people. For there was an ambiguity in the life of the revolutionary Jewish student. When Lev Deich went among the peasants, he was asked, "Are you not a Jew?" He remained silent.[218] Most of the Jewish Narodniks were stunned by the anti-Semitism they encountered, not only among the peasants but among the comrades.[219]

The *numerus clausus* alienated the Jewish students doubly, from the Russian culture and from their own fathers. First introduced in 1887, it established quotas for Jewish students ranging from 10 per cent in the Pale to 3 per cent in St. Petersburg and Moscow. Subsequently the quotas were lowered. Meanwhile they were evaded in part by bribery.[220] But bribes could be paid only by those who could afford it, and inevitably it lowered the father, noble though his purpose was, in the son's esteem. The son unconsciously cursed his father for his ignominy. He was shaken emotionally, however, by the pogroms which began in Odessa in 1881. At that time a change came over many Jewish students. In 1880, a Jewish student seeking among his fellow Jewish students for contributions for a Jewish trade school could get no response.

> Some refused to contribute on principle, asserting they would give nothing to specifically Jewish causes, and those who did gave reluctantly. However, when the pogrom occurred the students were the first to organize a self-defense group, and the number of those interested in the plight of their people steadily grew.[221]

Students from the University of St. Petersburg came in large numbers in uniform for the first time to the synagogue and addressed the congregation in Yiddish and Russian. It came as a shock to many Jewish students that even the revered Tolstoy and Turgenev would fail to raise their voices against the pogroms, that only Saltykov-Shchedrin was moved to speak his horror. One Jewish Narodnik, lost among the pogromists in Kiev, witnessed their attack on the Jewish poor; then he had a nervous breakdown.[222] Above all, Jewish students were appalled by the fact that Narodnik leaders welcomed the pogroms as an expression of the revolutionary instincts of the people. In 1881, the executive committee of Narodnaya Volya in the Ukraine actually published a proclamation encouraging the people to commit violence against the Jews, as the alleged greatest exploiters of the peasants.[223]

There thus began among Jewish students what Shmarya Levin called "the backward flow—the return of the penitents."[224] Of these the best known and most unusual was Vladimir Medem. He grew up in a thoroughly assimilated family; his father was an army doctor who had Vladimir baptized into the Orthodox church. Medem entered the University of Kiev, became a leader in a student strike, and was expelled. He began to inquire into

Jewish culture and to work with a group of Jewish Bundists (as the members of the Jewish Social Democratic organization were called). He learned Yiddish, which he had not known at all, and became the Jewish Bund's most noted orator and writer.[225] He could never recollect clearly how he had made his back-to-the-people journey to the Jews. It was evidently hard for him to bring to consciousness all the workings of guilt, shame, disillusionment, identification, and self-sacrifice. Other Jewish students took the Zionist direction, going back to the people in a religion of labor, which bade them return to the soil in Palestine as farmers. Twenty years later Zionist students and Bundist students argued and polemicized with each other. At Berne University in Switzerland, a three-evening debate took place in 1902 before the Russian Jewish student colony; there the young Chaim Weizmann debated with the even younger Vladimir Medem.

The early Zionist movement was a student movement:

> Among the student youth, groups were founded whose purpose was to foster the Zionist ideal. Jewish students formed the first group of Zionist pioneers known as Bilu, for the Hebrew words Beth Yakob le-khu be-nelkha, "Oh House of Israel, come ye, and let us go" (Isaiah 2:5). The first Bilu group founded at Kharkov in 1882 was composed of twenty-five students.[226]

Many of them were rejected by the Jewish masses as the Russian students were by their people; the experience was disillusioning. Then lastly there were some Jewish students who responded as Leon Trotsky did to their problem of twofold alienation. When challenged by Medem in 1903 to identify himself either as a Russian or a Jew, young Trotsky replied, "No you are wrong! I am a social-democrat, and that's all."[227]

The Jewish student activists often had a twofold guilt, a twofold suicidalism, a twofold messianic elitism, a twofold populism, as well as a twofold readiness for daring violence. For their conflict was with their own Jewish people as well as with the Russian social environment. They tried, never altogether successfully, to convince themselves that the persecution of the Jews was an incident in the persecution of the Russian peasantry or proletariat. "Why should I love your peasants, who hate and ill-treat my people with blind barbarity?" asks the young Jewish terrorist in Stepniak's novel, *The Career of a Nihilist*. With this strange combination of guilt-experience, it was natural that "the Jewish Socialists distinguished themselves by their eagerness to undertake the most desperate and most dangerous enterprises."[228] The Social Revolutionary party had an even higher proportion of Jews among its leadership than the Bolsheviks and it had young Gregory Gershuni as its guide in terror.[229] The percentage of Jews among the political prisoners rose steadily and disproportionately right through the eighties. "While in 1873–77 Jews constituted only 6 per cent of all political prisoners, the percentage jumped to 14 in 1884–90, 579 out of the total number of 4,307."[230]

The Jewish students in the seventies and eighties cast themselves with ardor into the revolutionary and terrorist movements. Mark Natanson, founder of the Society of Land and Liberty, received his political baptism in 1869 as a student in St. Petersburg where he led a series of students' riots. He also had himself baptized into Greek Orthodoxy in order to make his approach to the Russian peasants more convincing. The first Russian Marxist, and indeed the Russian representative on the general council of the International Workingmen's Association, Nicolas Utin, was a veteran of the revolutionary student movement whose activities had obliged him to flee the university; he too was baptized into Greek Orthodoxy. Vladimir Jochelson, activist in many terrorist ventures of Narodnaya Volya, began his career in the student movement at the Vilna Rabbinical Seminary. Gregory Goldenberg stood as a terrorist shadow over the relatively liberal minister, Count Loris-Melnikov, in 1880. The count escaped assassination that year at the hands of another Jewish convert to Christianity, Meir Molodetsky. Goldenberg meanwhile, to avenge the flogging of students in the Kharkov prison, carried out the assassination of the governor-general, Prince Kropotkin. Imprisoned himself, however, Goldenberg broke down under cross-examination in doubts about the wisdom of terrorism, and then killed himself.[231]

The families of Jewish intellectuals were strained in poignant conflict. The fathers in the sixties and seventies were often enlightened men, *Maskilim*, who believed a formula could be found which would reconcile their Jewish religion and their Russian allegiance: "Be a Jew at home and a man outside." The sons, however, as Patkin says, "who tasted a great deal more the fullness of European and Russian culture than their fathers, revolted against this 'ostrich' philosophy of 'neither here nor there.' "[232] They essayed a complete rejection of their fathers' people and culture. They borrowed from the Russian writers and peasants a conception of their own fathers and of Jews generally as a class of parasites. The fathers, on the other hand, after cajoling and bribing officials to evade the *numerus clausus*, came home (as in Shalom Aleichem's story "Gymnasie") to find their student sons on strike, united in a resolve not to return to school; such was the new freedom.[233]

Suicidalism, hitherto almost unknown among Jews, made its appearance among Russian Jewish students. Throughout their history, notwithstanding the intensity of persecutions, suicide had never been the Jewish response to suffering. Now, however, as the agonies of generational conflict arose among them in the Russian setting, suicide intruded into the Jewish family. The famed Shalom Aleichem delineated the havoc to which the new student culture gave rise. In "A Daughter's Grave," a bereaved father cannot comprehend what has taken place.

> Maybe you think it was one of today's tragedies? Black smocks, red flags, Siberia? Heaven forbid! That much, at least, God has spared me. I saw to that! After all, I had reason to. An only daughter. Such a gifted girl. So beautiful and clever. And a high school graduate!

It was all the fault of the strange books. She and a friend, the cantor's daughter, and a male student ("the Angel of Death") took to reading (as the father called it) *Sanni*, a novel by Archie Bashe's (*Sanine*, by Artzibashev). The cantor's daughter fell in love with a Gentile army officer, all in the midst of a pogrom. The older generation was beside itself. Finally the two girls both killed themselves with poison. The daughter wrote:

My dear, faithful parents. . . . Forgive me. We promised each other that we'd do it—Haika and I . . . I know, dear parents, that I am committing a great wrong. I fought with myself for a long time, but it had to be. . . .[234]

A hopeless void divided the passive older generation, with its traditional religious culture, from the student activists, with their scientific, secular, socialist consciousness. The rabbi of Minsk in 1902 warned the children in Jeremiah-like terms against the example of a poor Jewish shoemaker who had tried to assassinate the governor:

How do we Jews, who are likened to a little worm—the worm of Jacob—come to get messed up in such matters? . . . how do we Jews dare to climb up to such high places and meddle in politics? Oh, beware, Jewish children! . . . Our people always were proud of one thing—that they never had any rebels among them; and now you desire to wipe out this virtue too.[235]

It was just such a philosophy, however, which de-authoritized the older generation and sent the children into the revolutionary student movement. And the same children were smitten with a double guilt when they beheld the sordid character of the Russian people for whose sake they were abandoning their own fathers. A document of 1881 stated their tragic double alienation:

The "enlightened" Jews had repudiated their history, forgotten their traditions, and come to despise everything that made them conscious of belonging to an eternal race. . . . How pathetic is the position of those who advocated fusion with the Russian people through national self-abnegation. . . . Either one openly declares oneself a renegade or one decides to share the sufferings of his people.[236]

The revolutionary student movement seemed to many young Jews a third alternative, a chance to reject both traditional cultures, Jewish and Russian, to form a group of all the sons united against all the fathers, and to atone for one's revolt against one's father by an even higher degree of selfless suffering. Through self-sacrifice in the student movement, one proved to one's conscience that suffering was not only the father's Jewish badge.

What did the revolutionary student movement among the Jews accomplish? Did it contribute to a rational solution of their problems? Of their matchless courage and selfless idealism there can again be no question. Those especially who went to the Jewish masses, "the poorest of the poor, proletarians among proletarians," brought the message of a new political vision, which gave meaning to impoverished lives.[237] And yet, one cannot help but feel that much of this selfless idealism, tinged as it was with the will to self-destruction, had the effect of deflecting political choices in an irrational way. The idealistic "meaning" could hide a compulsive will to meaninglessness, to self-annihilation.

A Jewish student or worker had a basic choice to make—to remain in Russia or to emigrate. There were young Jewish students engaged in revolutionary activities who decided wisely that they could never lead humane lives in Russia. Abraham Cahan, born in 1860, made such a decision and came to the United States, where he made a great contribution as editor of a Yiddish newspaper, the *Jewish Daily Forward*.[238] Sidney Hillman, rabbinical student in Kovno in 1902, began at the age of fifteen to attend secret meetings of the Bund. Less than two years later he was at the head of a May Day parade of a hundred workingmen. He was arrested, imprisoned, and beaten by the police in the usual manner. But he did not turn informer; as with others, his mark of pride was in enduring the beating of the police without flinching. Finally, in 1906, his mother persuaded him to emigrate. He found his way to America, and a few years later was president of the Amalgamated Clothing Workers.[239] The American philosopher, Morris R. Cohen, was a twelve-year-old in Minsk in 1892. Had his family remained in Russia, no doubt he would have found his way into the revolutionary student movement. Forty years later, Harold Laski talked with Cohen's parents, who were still unable to speak English. The woman's eyes "became twin fires as she said: 'I am poor and ill, but when I think of my son I bless America for making me the richest woman in the world.' "[240] America was more than a promised land to Russian Jews; it was a land with neither Canaanites nor Philistines, where freedom and opportunity beckoned from the soil and cities. An "emigration fever," says Louis Greenberg, spread among the Russian Jews; their enthusiasm was "religious," recalled Abraham Cahan. In 1882, in the city of Kovno, almost the entire Jewish youth, including high school students, prepared to emigrate. "In their eagerness to leave the country Jews disposed of their belongings for practically nothing."[241] Clearly this was the rational choice—to leave Russia, with its Czarism, pogroms, *numerus clausus*, anti-Semitic peasants, and an intellectual class which often condoned the perpetrators of the pogroms. By contrast, the United States Congress in 1882 had adopted a resolution recording the sympathy of the American people over the miseries which had been inflicted on the Jews in such pogroms as those of Kiev and Odessa. There were many young students and ex-students who chose emigration. Sometimes emigration was combined with socialist hopes; a student of Odessa University, Hirsch Leib Sabsovitch, for instance, was a leader in the Am Olam (Eternal People) movement, which aimed to set up agricultural cooperatives in the United States.[242] Abraham Cahan, too, was for a time a member of this movement. The expulsion of the Jews from Moscow in 1891 set in motion an exodus which was non-ideological; emigrants moved along six main routes to quit Russia.

The Smolensk railway station in Moscow saw mass farewells and new beginnings.

This was the way of reason: not to curse one's being, not to try to prove one's manhood to the Russians by undertaking the most daring terroristic acts, not to destroy onself to demonstrate one's idealism and absence of self-seeking, not to merge oneself with the religion and culture of the pogromists or to ape their ways, not to inflict on oneself a burden of guilt which belonged rather on Russian shoulders. In short, the revolutionary Jewish student movement was for all its heroism and courage the most masochistic of all.[243] To the extent that it persuaded students to its ideals, it led them to a path of self-destruction. As Chaim Weizmann, later the first president of Israel, said, "The mass of Russian-Jewish students in Switzerland had been bullied into an artificial denial of their own personality."[244] The rational ones did not allow their persecutors to master their unconscious; they took the train and ship, choosing reason and freedom in the simplest way.

Was the Russian Student Movement Worthwhile?

We come to the overall vexed question: Was the Russian student movement worthwhile? Did it impede or advance the cause of Russian reform? Were its measures and tactics such as to promote the happiness of the Russian people? Of the generous ardor and self-sacrificing spirit of the students there can be no doubt. Yet there is a fatal flaw in the politics of generational struggle. The generation in revolt tends to work out its inner conflict on the outer political world; it projects its own emotional guilt and will to self-destruction on the larger political canvas. And as one reviews the gloomy story of the Russian student movement, its predisposition to regicide and suicide, one has the feeling that it may have corrupted and sickened even further the already corrupt and sick Russian society.

The politics of regicide and suicide tended to uproot the occasional shoots of liberalism in Russia which would have required the most careful nurturing. Peter Kropotkin, the noblest and most distinguished of the Russian anarchists, and a great admirer of the idealism of the Russian student movement, acknowledged, as we have seen, that "the promulgation of a Constitution was extremely near at hand during the last few months of the life of Alexander II."[245] Chance intervened against these hopes: "It is a fact that it was only owing to a chain of circumstances, almost accidental in character, that Russia did not get a Constitution during these five or six weeks."[246] Bernard Pares, the noted historian of Russia, as we have already noted, gives a similar opinion: "The bomb that killed Alexander put an end to the faint beginnings of Russian constitutionalism."[247] A half-hour before the Czar set out on his last journey on March 1, 1881, he had approved the text of a manifesto announcing the establishment of a commission which was likely to lead to the writing of a constitution. "I have consented to this measure," said Alexander II, "although I do not conceal from myself the fact that this is the first step toward a constitution."[248] Instead, the acts of Czar-killing and self-killing (as we have already written) brought into the domain of Russian politics the psychology of sons destroying their fathers, re-enacting on a national political scale the dramatic emotions portrayed by Freud in *Totem and Taboo,* the revolt and guilt of the primal sons. The people turned from the sick self-destructive students; the liberals felt as if they had had the ground pulled out from under them.

The Social Revolutionary party, which in time became the favorite of the Russian students and was overwhelmingly supported by the peasantry, gave its endorsement to student terrorism.[249] Thereby the party, which might have been the chief agency for rational evolution, entered the domain of pathological politics. This was the party which at the election for the Constituent Assembly held in November 1917, even after the Bolshevik seizure of power, still received the largest number of votes. Its endorsement and practice of terrorism had not helped cultivate a liberal democratic soil. We may reiterate the conclusion of Professor Jesse D. Clarkson:

> In retrospect, one may be convinced that the long series of assassinations of governors, ministers, and police chiefs . . . impeded, rather than aided, the attainment of the Party's objectives. Certainly, however, the government regarded these activities as more seriously dangerous than those of any other variety of socialists.

The proverb became current among Russian chess players: "The position is worse than that of a governor." Terrorist activity "played into the hands of the government by lending it an appearance of righteousness in vigorously repressing manifestations of revolutionary sentiment."[250] From its inception the student movement was, as Marx and Engels wrote, inclined to the sickness of secret societies and terrorist action. It was attracted strongly to Bakunin's creed of destruction, secrecy, and authoritarianism. The new Russian studentry, Marx and Engels believed, was made up "in great majority of the sons of peasants and other poor people," who "dreamed of putting [socialist ideas] into immediate application." They tended therefore, Marx and Engels felt, to be irrational and irresponsible. Aware of all the conditions which had called forth the demonstrations at the University of St. Petersburg, Marx and Engels nonetheless respected, not the activists in the political secret societies but "the more serious" who met the repression by organizing mutual-aid societies. The many students who joined secret societies, said Marx and Engels, often ended as useless exiles in Siberia. The serious mutual aiders, on the other hand, while constructively lending a helping hand to their poorer classmates, gave the government no pretext for suppressing them. The bizarre terrorist Nechayev had achieved a vogue in Russia as "the ideal type of the student." With his mixture of brilliance, fraud, deceit, masochism, sadism, Jesuitism, and amorality, he could electrify Russian student circles, but for Marx and Engels he was an aberration of political psychopathology. The adolescents and the youth, however, were drawn by the "fictions—lies on the extent and power of the secret society, prophecies on the imminence of the revolution prepared by it," and they were indeed ready to compromise morally and exploit financially the most advanced people. This Russian activist studentry felt itself privileged to act without regard to political ethics, and fancied itself beyond good and evil.[251]

To Marx and Engels, the political primacy of the Russian student movement was an index of the psychological disintegration of the Russian society, and their activities seemed pointless. "The foolish antics of the Russian students," wrote Marx in 1877, "are only a symptom and valueless in themselves, but they are a symptom. All sections of Russian society are economically, morally and intellectually in a state of disintegration."[252] Eight years previously, in 1869, their great antagonist, Bakunin, had looked with eager anticipation to the redemptive role of the Russian student leadership: "I believe exclusively in the peasant community and in the educated community of irreconcilable youths for whom there is neither place nor occupation in Russia. A phalanx forty thousand strong, these youths, whether they know it or not, belong to the revolution."[253] Engels, however, felt this prospect of forty thousand revolutionary students (exaggerated though it was) an appalling one for the socialist movement:

> How awful for the world . . . that there are 40,000 revolutionary students in Russia, without a proletariat or even a Russian peasantry behind them and with no career before them except the dilemma: Siberia or abroad—to Western Europe. If there is anything which might ruin the Western European movement, then it would have been this import of 40,000 more or less educated, ambitious, hungry Russian nihilists: all of them officer candidates without an army.[254]

For all their idealism, there was an evident sickness in the student movements; they were ready to be misled by dominance-craving personalities eager to exploit naïve and guilty adolescents. The student circle as a secret society easily became an alternative primary group against father and family, a union of brothers in common revolt against their fathers; but, as a substitute primary group, it tended to look for a new power, a new father, to rule over itself.

The student movement, as we have seen, glorified the assassins and would-be assassins of Czars, Czarist ministers and officials.[255] "Educated Russian Society," wrote Paul Milyoukov, "in its public gatherings and assemblies, paid silent homage to its martyr-executioners."[256]

It is a question, however, whether the student martyrs were more concerned with martyrdom than with the professed advancement of freedoms. For the martyr in double death with his father-surrogate killed the latter whom he hated and at the same time destroyed himself, whose anxieties of guilt he could not alleviate. Certainly almost every assassination or attempt at assassination brought a setback for students' liberties and rights. Karakozov's attempt on the life of Czar Alexander II in 1866 brought as its consequence an unparalleled surveillance of students' private lives. The killing of Alexander II in 1881 intensified the deep-seated suspicion of students, and was followed by renewed repressive measures against them. The eleven students who plotted to assassinate Alexander III added to the depressive gloom which enveloped Russian society like a shroud, giving it the aspect of a society permeated with a death-wish. The suppression of the students increased as did the government's rigidity. The years 1901 and 1902, which saw the murders of a Minister of Public Instruction and a Minister of the Interior, also were a time in which the student movement became the vehicle for absurdities, almost like a generation running amok. The murder of Sipiagin in 1902 was followed by a tremendous strengthening of the secret police and an increase in espionage.[257] As one calls the roll of the student terrorists, Dmitri Karakozov, Andrei Zhelyabov, Sophia Perovskaya, Alexander Ulyanov, Stepan V. Balmashov, Ivan Kaliayev, P. Karpovich, we become aware that the political circle had become a pathological one, and that political tactics had become primarily a vehicle for the unconscious; political means became irrational, in the sense that they were not chosen as the best ways for realizing the conscious political end but as ways for satisfying hatreds festering in the unconscious.

Without doubt, "the initiative belonged to the students," wrote M. N. Pokrovsky, the eminent Bolshevik historian.[258] It was an initiative, however, which superimposed strange patterns on the Russian aspiration for democracy, and perhaps made the achievement of a liberal society all the harder. The students did set the workers in motion. The young Stalin, in one of his earliest articles, rendered tribute to the students, who, by their noble example, had taught the workers how to demonstrate. In 1901 Stalin wrote:

> At the present time the students are coming out in the "social" movement almost as leaders, as the vanguard. The discontented sections of different social classes are now rallying around them. At first the students tried to fight with a weapon borrowed from the workers—the strike. But when the government retaliated to their strikes by passing the brutal law ("Provisional Regulations") under which students who went on strike were drafted into the army, the students had only one weapon left—to demand assistance from the Russian public and to pass from strikes to *street demonstrations*. And that is what the students did. . . . We must be grateful to the students for the lesson they have taught us: they showed how enormously important political demonstrations are in the revolutionary struggle.[259]

Demonstrations were so much the tactic of the student activists that the First All-Russian Student Congress in March 1902 declared in its manifesto that they constituted the primary means for calling society's attention to an abnormal state of affairs; new forms of protest would then follow.[260]

The psyche of the student movement, with its ethic of collective self-immolation, carried, however, a strange new overtone, which had relevance for the rising people's movement. The student demonstration, as Stalin observed, was a weapon of unusual psychological potency. It attracted "curious onlookers" and transformed bystanders from spectators into activists. "The backward and timid section," wrote Stalin, were swept by a sudden emotion into the demonstration; "they cannot help yielding" to its attraction as they see the "courageous fighters," "hear free voices" and "stirring songs denouncing the existing system and exposing our social evils." The magnetic power of the demonstration was "why so many people offer their backs to the lash of the Cossacks' whips. . . . Thereby, the whip lash is rendering us a great service, for it is hastening the revolutionization of the 'curious onlookers.' "[261]

Was incitement to offering one's back to the whiplash, however, the way to build the modes of emotion and thought which a liberal democracy requires? There is a remarkable continuity in the sado-masochistic tradition of student generational politics from its inception, from the students' first submission to the Cossack knout to the submission of the intellectuals to the Stalinist terror—the self-immolation to History. The American student movement in the sixties contrived the tactic of "going limp," its analogue to the Russian's offering his back to the lash.

Perhaps the deepest failure of the Russian student movement was that characteristic of almost all student movements—it failed to develop a devotion to liberal values and liberal democracy. The immense forces of idealism which it released were combined with all the marks of generational politics—arrogance, the conviction that the generational perspective alone grasped the truth, physical rejection of the elders, impatience, the propensity for violence. A student population arose which tended to regard its degree of manhood as proportional to its degree of revolutionism. At the elections at Moscow University in 1906, it was made abundantly clear that fifty years of student unrest and generational warfare had produced a student body the majority of whom were revolutionist in sympathies, not liberal. That year 5,450 students, about 63 per cent of the total student body, voted in the elections for the central university organ. The Leftist parties received about 70 per cent of the votes:[262]

Social Democratic	2,044
Social Revolutionary	1,259
Freedom of the People	122
Others	157

The moderate liberals, the Constitutional Democrats, obtained 1,463 votes, while the Rightist Independents received 213. Only about 26.5 per cent of the Moscow students were thus liberals; the Left had a clear hegemony, and it was a Left furthermore imbued with the most fanatical varieties of Marxist or terrorist doctrines. The virtues of liberal judgment were out of keeping with the collective passions of student crusades.

When the Bolshevik Revolution, however, finally took place, the students stood back perturbed and bewildered. They seemed at the last to realize that the contempt for rational liberal values brought with it inevitable consequences—contempt for individual rights, a party and personal dictatorship, mass terrorism, anti-intellectualism. The next Russian student movement born in a Soviet world would have to grope for its return to liberalism.

NOTES

1. Boris Nicolaievsky, *Aseff: The Russian Judas*, tr. George Reavey (London, 1934), pp. 74–75. During the years from 1885 to 1897, St. Petersburg Social Democracy "was for all practical purposes a movement of intellectuals, mostly students from the university and the Technological Institute." See Richard Pipes, *Social Democracy and the St. Petersburg Labor Movement, 1885–1897* (Cambridge, Mass., 1963), pp. 119–120. As late as 1899, according to Eva Broido, there were strictly speaking "no revolutionary parties in St. Petersburg. There had been groups, above all, students' groups." See Eva Broido, *Memoirs of a Revolutionary*, tr. Vera Broido (London, 1967), pp. 18–19.

2. Peter Kropotkin, "The Crisis in Russia," *North American Review*, CLXXII (1901), 711.

3. Count Sergius Witte, *The Memoirs of Count Witte*, tr. Abraham Yarmolinsky (New York, 1921), p. 171.

4. Translated from Julius Martov, *Zapiski Sotsial demokrata* (Berlin, 1922), by Allan K. Wildman, in "The Russian Intelligentsia of the 1890's," *American Slavic and East European Review*, XIX (1960), 160.

5. Peter Struve, "My Contacts and Conflicts with Lenin," *Slavonic and East European Review*, XII (1934), 575, 576, 585; Richard Kindersley, *The First Russian Revisionists: A Study of "Legal Marxism" in Russia* (Oxford, 1962), p. 35.

6. I. M. Maisky, *Before the Storm: Recollections*, tr. Gerard Shelley (London, 1944), pp. 127, 172–174.

7. G. M. Krzhyzhanovsky, "Vladimir Ilyich," *Recollections of Lenin* (Moscow, 1956), p. 11. Also see Louis Fischer, *The Life of Lenin* (New York, 1964), p. 56; Bertram D. Wolfe, *Strange Communists I Have Known* (Bantam edn., New York, 1967), pp. 112–113.

8. Alexander Kerensky, *Russia and History's Turning Point* (New York, 1965), pp. 21, 26.

9. N. P. Asheshov, *Sophia Perovskaya* (St. Petersburg, 1920), p. 9.

10. Vera Figner, *Memoirs of a Revolutionist*, tr. C. C. Daniels (New York, 1927), p. 109; David Footman, *Red Prelude: The Life of the Russian Terrorist Zhelyabov* (New Haven, 1945), p. 41.

11. Asheshov, *op. cit.*, p. 9.

12. Asheshov, *op. cit.*, p. 11.

13. Avrahm Yarmolinsky, *Road to Revolution: A Century of Russian Radicalism* (New York, 1959), p. 238.

14. N. K. Krupskaya, *On Education*, tr. G. P. Ivanov-Mumjiev (Moscow, 1957), pp. 37, 41.

15. Anna Ulyanova-Yelizarova, *Reminiscences of Lenin* (Moscow, 1956), pp. 25–26.

16. N. K. Krupskaya, *Reminiscences of Lenin*, tr. Bernard Isaacs (Moscow, 1959), p. 311.

17. Ulyanova-Yelizarova, *op. cit.*, p. 43.

18. Francis B. Randall, *The Major Prophets of Russian Peasant Socialism: A Study in the Social Thought of N. K. Mikhailovskii and V. M. Chernov* (New York, 1961; University Microfilms, Ann Arbor, 1961), p. 9.

19. V. I. Lenin, *What Is to be Done?* (New York, 1929), p. 158.

20. Lenin, "The Itch," *Pravda*, February 22, 1918, reprinted in *The Revolutionary Phrase* (Moscow, 1965), p. 31.

21. J. Stalin, *Talk with the German Author Emil Ludwig*, December 13, 1931, Moscow, pamphlet, p. 15.

22. David Marshall Lang, *A Modern History of Georgia* (London, 1962), p. 124.

23. Stalin, *op. cit.*, p. 16.

24. J. M. Meijer, *Knowledge and Revolution: The Russian Colony in Zurich, 1870–1873* (Assen, The Netherlands, 1955), p. 3.

25. Leopold H. Haimson, *The Russian Marxists and the Origins of Bolshevism* (Cambridge, Mass., 1955), p. 32.

26. The young intellectual often suffers from a sense of physical impotence; he is regarded as a "sissy." Perhaps in his unconscious he is especially affected by a "castration complex" or its residual effects. The populist motivation would then derive from an attempt to counteract this threat to his manhood.

27. Nicolas Berdyaev, *Dream and Reality: An Essay in Autobiography*, tr. Katherine Lampert (New York, 1962), p. 116. On the exceptional role of the women students' circle at Zurich, "from which emerged the most famous Russian women revolutionaries" in the seventies, see Theodore Dan, *The Origins of Bolshevism*, tr. Joel Carmichael (London, 1964), p. 67.

28. Peter Kropotkin, *Memoirs of a Revolutionist* (Boston, 1899), pp. 301–302.

29. Meijer, *op. cit.*, p. 17.

30. Max Nomad, *Apostles of Revolution* (New York, rev. ed., 1961), p. 228; E. H. Carr, *Michael Bakunin* (New York, reprinted 1961), p. 394.

31. Cited in Footman, *op. cit.*, p. 43.

32. Quoted in Paul Milyoukov, *Russia and Its Crisis* (Chicago, 1905), pp. 405–406. Also see Dan, *op. cit.*, p. 100, on the peaceful, nonviolent character of the movement. On the role of Peter Lavrov as an ideologist of student elitism, "the critically thinking individual" as the maker of history, see Julius F. Hecker, *Russian Sociology: A Contribution to the History of Sociological Thought and Theory* (New York, 1915), pp. 87 ff.

33. Samuel H. Baron, *Plekhanov: The Father of Russian Marxism* (Stanford, Calif., 1963), p. 15.

34. *Ibid.*, p. 17. Axelrod exerted the same arguments and pressure in 1872 on Andrei Zhelyabov, the future regicide, who was then still contemplating a professional career. See Haimson, *op. cit.*, p. 29.

35. Wildman, *op. cit.*, p. 165.

36. Pitirim A. Sorokin, *A Long Journey* (New Haven, 1963), pp. 48–49.

37. Krupskaya, *On Education*, p. 16.

38. *Ibid.*, pp. 16–18.

39. G. Plekhanov, "A New Champion of Autocracy" (1889), in *Selected Philosophical Works*, tr. R. Doxon (Moscow, n.d.), p. 423.

40. Felix Dzerzhinsky, the Polish revolutionist who later became the fanatical first chief of the Soviet secret police (the Cheka), wrote revealingly on the generational tension among the intelligentsia which oscillated from extreme populism to nihilism: "The moment a conflict sets in between the level of material life and the level of spiritual life, the requirements of the former predominate, with the result that man becomes nihilistic, a cynic, drunkard or hypocrite. And this inner conflict is never resolved. . . . It is only among the oppressed that one finds no disharmony between the older and younger generations." Dzerzhinsky wanted his own son to become "not a crippled intellectual but a real man. . . . As to the intellectual, he regards his crippled state as a sign of his superiority, with the result that it is incurable." See Dzerzhinsky, *Prison Diary and Letters*, tr. John Gibbons (Moscow, 1959), pp. 239–241.

41. Yarmolinsky, *Road to Revolution*, p. 137.

42. Randall, *op. cit.*, p. 6.

43. V. T. Chertkoff, *Studencheskoe Dvizhenie 1899 goda* (The Student Movement of the Year 1899; Essex, England, 1900), p. 46. On the suicide of a Kharkov student, see G. Engel and V. Gorohov, *Iz Istorii Studencheskago Dvizheniya 1899–1906* (From the History of the Student Movement 1889–1906; St. Petersburg, 1906), p. 16; V. I. Orlov, *Studencheskoe Dvizhenie Moskovskogo Universiteta v XIX Stolyetii* (The Student Movement of Moscow in the Nineteenth Century; Moscow, 1934), p. 308.

44. A. Terpigorev, *Reminiscences of a Mining Engineer*, tr. W. Chumak (Mos-

cow, 1959), p. 32; Leon Trotsky, *My Life* (New York, 1930), p. 104.

45. Figner, *op. cit.*, pp. 272–273.

46. Mark Popovsky, *The Story of Dr. Haffkine*, tr. V. Vezey (Moscow, 1965), p. 33.

47. Bernard Pares, *Russia and Reform* (London, 1907), p. 217.

48. Haimson, *op. cit.*, p. 68; also Martov, *op. cit.*, pp. 109–128. Israel Getzler, *Martov* (Melbourne, 1967), pp. 14, 38.

49. Louis I. Dublin and Bessie Bunzel, *To Be or not to Be: A Study of Suicide* (New York, 1933), p. 23.

50. *Ibid.*, pp. 408–410.

51. Alexander Kornilov, *Modern Russian History* (New York, 1917), p. 332. Since the absolute numbers in the various age-groups are not known, it is not possible to calculate their relative percentages of suicide in Moscow. The preponderance of youth was nonetheless clear to observers at the time.

52. N. K. Krupskaya, *On Education*, I, 139.

53. Bernard Pares, *op. cit.*, p. 324.

54. Charles A. Moser, *Antinihilism in the Russian Novel of the 1860's* (The Hague, 1964), p. 195.

55. Ilya Ehrenburg, *People and Life: 1891–1921*, tr. Anna Bostock and Yvonne Kapp (New York, 1962), pp. 36, 29, 37, 38, 41, 46, 68, 192–193.

56. Haimson, *op. cit.*, p. 216.

57. Cited in Haimson, *loc. cit.*

58. Paul Milyoukov, *op. cit.*, pp. 505–506. Plekhanov in 1905 wrote that "the intelligentsia believed in terror as in a god." See Dan, *op. cit.*, p. 175.

59. I. Steinberg, *Spiridonova: Revolutionary Terrorist*, tr. Gwenda David and Eric Mosbacher (London, 1935), pp. 32–33.

60. *Ibid.*, p. 33; Boris Savinkov (Ropshin), *Memoirs of a Terrorist*, tr. Joseph Shaplen (New York, 1931), pp. 83, 97.

61. Moissaye J. Olgin, *The Soul of the Russian Revolution* (New York, 1917), p. 343.

62. Kerensky, *op. cit.*, p. 62.

63. Olgin, *op. cit.*, p. 336.

64. W. S. Woytinsky, *Stormy Passage: A Personal History through Two Russian Revolutions to Democracy and Freedom: 1905–1960* (New York, 1961), p. 6; Kerensky, *op. cit.*, p. 25.

65. Wildman, *op. cit.*, p. 164; Martov, *op. cit.*, p. 78.

66. See Louis Greenberg, *The Jews in Russia*, II (New Haven, 1951), 162–163; Edmund Silberner, "Two Studies on Modern Anti-Semitism," *Historia Judaica*, XIV (1952), 104–106; Yarmolinsky, *Road to Revolution*, pp. 308–309.

67. Figner, *op. cit.*, pp. 120–122.

68. Olgin, *op. cit.*, p. 336.

69. Maxim Gorki, "Assassins," from *Extrait de Mon Journal*, reprinted in *Europe*, XVI (1928), 12–13, tr. Dumesnil de Gramont.

70. Boris Savinkov (Ropshin), *What Never Happened: A Novel of the Revolution*, tr. Thomas Seltzer (New York, 1917), p. 126.

71. *Ibid.*, pp. 108, 35–36.

72. *Ibid.*, p. 189.

73. *Ibid.*, pp. 244–246.

74. *Ibid.*, p. 55.

75. *Ibid.*, p. 56.

76. *Ibid.*, p. 251.

77. *Ibid.*, p. 70.

78. *Ibid.*, p. 320.

79. Stepniak (Sergyei Mikhailovich Kravchinski), *The Career of a Nihilist* (New York, 1889), pp. 20–21.

80. J. V. Stalin, "The Russian Social-Democratic Party and Its Immediate Tasks" (1901), tr. from the Georgian, in J. V. Stalin, *Works* (Moscow, 1952), I, 22.

81. William H. E. Johnson, *Russia's Educational Heritage* (Pittsburgh, 1950), pp. 139, 277.

82. Orlov, *op. cit.*, p. 216.

83. Dan, *op. cit.*, p. 62; Orlov, *op. cit.*, pp. 36–37.

84. Yarmolinsky, *Road to Revolution*, p. 103.

85. Franco Venturi, *Roots of Revolution: A History of the Populist and Socialist Movements in Nineteenth Century Russia*, tr. Francis Haskell (London, 1960), p. 222.

86. Paul J. Novgorotsev, "Universities and Higher Technical Schools," in *Russian Schools and Universities in the World War* (New Haven, 1929), pp. 141–144.

87. See Rafail Vydrin, *Osnovnye momenty studencheskogo dvizheniya v Rossi* (Basic Movements of the Russian Student Movement; Moscow, 1908), pp. 31–32. At the beginning of the 1870s, 72 per cent at Kazan required fellowships or financial aid. At Kiev, from 60 to 70 per cent were in this penurious situation, and at Odessa as many as 80 per cent. According to Miliukov, the number of

students requiring financial help rose from 49 per cent in 1866 to 78 per cent in 1874. At Moscow in 1876, as many as 59 per cent of the students were excused from payment of tuition.

88. *Ibid.*, p. 49.

89. *Ibid.*, p. 77.

90. Orlov, *op. cit.*, p. 9.

91. Nicholas Hans, *History of Russian Educational Policy, 1701–1917* (London, 1931), pp. 239–240.

92. Novgorotsev, *op. cit.*, pp. 141–142, 105.

93. *Ibid.*, p. 145.

94. Johnson, *op. cit.*, pp. 288–289.

95. Novgorotsev, *op. cit.*, pp. 138–139.

96. "After 1905 the revolutionary groups lost their ascendancy in the universities, and new currents appeared, hostile not only to the old political bias, but to political tendencies in general." *Ibid.*, pp. 147, 140, 142.

97. *Ibid.*, p. 152.

98. *Ibid.*, pp. 221–222.

99. The worker's son, Strelnikov, writes Pasternak in his novel *Dr. Zhivago*, "did not participate in the revolutionary movement in those years [1905] . . . at the university because young men who come from a poor background value higher education more and work harder than the children of the rich. The ferment among other students left him uninvolved." Boris Pasternak, *Dr. Zhivago*, tr. Max Hayward and Manya Harari (New York, 1960), p. 210.

100. Orlov, *op. cit.*, p. 341.

101. *Ibid.*, p. 345.

102. *Ibid.*, p. 350.

103. Novgorotsev, *op. cit.*, p. 139.

104. Peter Lavrov, *Reminiscences of Marx and Engels* (Moscow, 1962), pp. 350, 354–355. See also Engels' letter to V. I. Zasulich, April 23, 1885, in Karl Marx and Frederick Engels, *Selected Correspondence* (Moscow, 1953), p. 460.

105. Karl Marx, *Letters to Dr. Kugelmann* (New York, 1934), pp. 77–78.

106. That same year, 1896, there was a similar conflict in Vilno among the Lithuanian Social Democratic party between the workers and the intellectuals, especially the students, who were taking the leadership. See Dzerzhinsky, *op. cit.*, pp. 13–14.

107. Orlov, *op. cit.*, pp. 302–305.

108. Berdyaev, *op. cit.*, p. 121.

109. Orlov, *op. cit.*, pp. 333–334.

110. Engel and Gorohov, *op. cit.*, pp. 112–113.

111. *Ibid.*, pp. 117–118.

112. Donald A. Lowrie, *Rebellious Prophet: A Life of Nicolai Berdyaev* (New York, 1960), p. 64; Berdyaev, *op. cit.*, p. 13.

113. Engel and Gorohov, *op. cit.*, p. 121.

114. *Ibid.*, pp. 3–4.

115. *Ibid.*, p. 22.

116. *Ibid.*, p. 29.

117. *Ibid.*, p. 39.

118. *Ibid.*, pp. 54–55.

119. *Ibid.*, p. 73. V. I. Orlov tells, however, of an earlier "first" congress in 1900 at Odessa, and still earlier congresses in 1889, 1891, 1892, and 1896; see Orlov, *op. cit.*, pp. 231–236.

120. Woytinsky, *op. cit.*, pp. 10–11.

121. Engel and Gorohov, *op. cit.*, p. 99.

122. Woytinsky, *op. cit.*, pp. 13–14. Also see Paul Studenski, "Scholar and Man of Action," in *So Much Alive: The Life and Work of Vladimir S. Woytinsky*, ed. Emma S. Woytinsky (New York, 1962), pp. 31–34; Alexander Kerensky, *op. cit.*, The idea of the autonomy of the university was advanced by *Iskra* "not, however, so much in order to resume academic pursuits as to open university auditoriums for popular meetings and mass-meetings. The *Iskra* slogan was taken up by an immense majority of the students. . . . The Petersburg, Moscow and other universities and institutes of higher learning became in the pre-October and October days, genuine centers of mass agitation for all revolutionary parties. A torrent of people passed through their auditoriums from morning to night." (Dan, *op. cit.*, p. 350.)

123. The students, wrote Trotsky in 1908, joined the proletarian masses in 1905 as supporters of the St. Petersburg Soviet. Thousands of students recognized the political leadership of the Soviet and ardently supported it in its decisions. See Leon Trotsky, "The Soviet and the Revolution (Fifty Days)," reprinted in *1905: Before and After* (Colombo, 1953), p. 18.

124. Osip A. Piatnitsky, *Memoirs of a Bolshevik* (London, 1933), p. 92.

125. *Ibid.*, pp. 80, 86–87.

126. See Woytinsky, *op. cit.*, pp. 31, 13–14, 18, 27, 37, 44, 45. The central figure of the St. Petersburg Soviet of Workers, the student leader Khrustalev,

had been expelled and exiled several times, and had helped organize the students' congress of 1897 and the students' strike of 1898. Nosar was his real name but he adopted that of a workingman who gave him his credentials to the Soviet. See William English Walling, *Russia's Message* (New York, 1909), pp. 364–365.

127. Woytinsky, *op. cit.*, p. 29.

128. *Ibid.*, p. 95.

129. Orlov, *op. cit.*, p. 146.

130. Peter Tkachev was the most unusual of the revolutionists who had their baptism in the St. Petersburg disturbances of 1861. He later became famed as "more Blanquist" than Blanqui himself, and carried on an extensive polemic with Engels. Tkachev exemplified the spirit of pure activism by an intellectual elite. He believed in action *now* by an elite, and thought the initiative of the peasantry was a "myth." Revolution should be attempted, he said, "not in a remote future, not *some* time, but *now*, at the present juncture." See Michael Karpovich, "A Forerunner of Lenin: P. N. Tkachev." *Review of Politics*, VI (1944), 341.

131. Orlov, *op. cit.*, pp. 146–148; Yarmolinsky, *Road to Revolution*, p. 104; Nicholas Hans, *The Russian Tradition in Education* (London, 1963), p. 59; Bernard Pares, *A History of Russia* (def. edn.; New York, 1956), p. 376.

132. Meijer, *op. cit.*, pp. 26, 14–15.

133. Orlov, *op. cit.*, p. 162.

134. Meijer, *op. cit.*, p. 23; Hans, *History*, pp. 107–109.

135. Yarmolinsky, *Road to Revolution*, pp. 136–141. Hans, *History*, p. 142.

136. Orlov, *op. cit.*, p. 173.

137. Boris Nicolaievsky and Otto Maenchen-Helfen, *Karl Marx: Man and Fighter*, tr. G. David and E. Mosbacher (Philadelphia, 1936), p. 347; Carr, *op. cit.*, pp. 394, 398. Michael Prawdin, *The Unmentionable Nechaev: A Key to Bolshevism* (London, 1961); Nomad, *op. cit.*, pp. 214–256.

138. See Dinko Tomasic, *The Impact of Russian Culture on Soviet Communism* (Glencoe, 1953), III, p. 137.

139. Carr, *op. cit.*, p. 391.

140. Footman, *op. cit.*, p. 32.

141. Hans, *History*, p. 142.

142. Baron, *op. cit.*, pp. 18–19.

143. Hans, *History*, pp. 142–143.

144. Orlov, *op. cit.*, p 181.

145. Yarmolinsky, *Road to Revolution*, pp. 290–291.

146. Hans, *History*, p. 146; Johnson, *op. cit.*, p. 287.

147. Yarmolinsky, *Road to Revolution*, p. 330; Orlov, *op. cit.*, p. 189.

148. Orlov, *op. cit.*, p. 192.

149. Aleksandr Ivanovich Georgievsky, *Materialy po Istorii Studencheskago Dvizheniya v Rossi* (Materials for a History of the Student Movement in Russia), II (London and St. Petersburg, 1906), 106–117.

150. Yarmolinsky, *Road to Revolution*, p. 330.

151. *Ibid.*, pp. 330–332. See especially *Comet in the Night: The Story of Alexander Ulyanov's Heroic Life and Tragic Death as Told by His Contemporaries*, compiled A. I. Ivansky, tr. Taras Kapustin (Moscow, 1968), pp. 167–169.

152. Orlov, *op. cit.*, p. 201.

153. Hans, *History*, p. 146; George Fischer, *Russian Liberalism: From Gentry to Intelligentsia* (Cambridge, Mass., 1958), p. 53.

154. Orlov, *op. cit.*, pp. 201, 215.

155. This calculation is based on the figures for enrollment in Moscow University in Johnson, *op. cit.*, p. 286.

156. Orlov, *op. cit.*, p. 253.

157. *Ibid.*, pp. 256, 260.

158. *Ibid.*, pp. 270–272, 285–287, 289.

159. Michael T. Florinsky, *Russia: A History and an Interpretation* (New York, 1953), II, 1165.

160. Kerensky, *op. cit.*, p. 25.

161. Chertkoff, *op. cit.*, pp. 5–8.

162. *Ibid.*, pp. 5–8; Orlov, *op. cit.*, p. 332.

163. Thomas Darlington, *Education in Russia*, in Board of Education, *Special Reports on Educational Subjects*, XXIII (London, 1909), 448.

164. Pares, *op. cit.*, pp. 217–218.

165. Chertkoff, *op. cit.*, p. 40.

166. Orlov, *op. cit.*, pp. 356–357.

167. E. B. Lanin (pseud. for E. J. Dillon), *Russian Characteristics* (London, 1892), pp. 40–41.

168. Darlington, *op. cit.*, pp. 448–449.

169. V. I. Lenin, "The Drafting of 183 Students into the Army," in Lenin, *Collected Works*, Vol. IV, Bk. 1, tr. J. Fineberg (New York, 1929), p. 70.

170. Orlov, *op. cit.*, p. 361.

171. Lenin, *Collected Works*, Vol. IV, Bk. 1, p. 70; Hans, *History*, pp. 171–172.

172. Engel and Gorohov, *op. cit.*, p. 19.

173. Kornilov, *op. cit.*, p. 292; Johnson, *op. cit.*, p. 178.

174. Florinsky, *op. cit.*, p. 1166.
175. Hans, *History*, p. 168.
176. Darlington, *op. cit.*, p. 447.
177. Engel and Gorohov, *op. cit.*, p. 65.
178. Olgin, *op. cit.*, p. 89.
179. Paxton Hibben, "Alexis I. Rykov, Soviet Russia's New Premier," *Current History*, XX (1924), 25. Lev B. Kamevev, another close co-worker of Lenin's, and for a brief period one of the triumvirate together with Stalin which ruled the Soviet Union, was also imprisoned as a Moscow student in 1901. When he left Russia in 1902, he wrote articles on the student movement for the Social Democratic organ *Iskra*. Kamevev was executed in Stalin's purge of Old Bolsheviks in 1936. See Leon Trotsky, *Stalin*, tr. Charles Malamuth (London, 1947), p. 46.
180. Hans, *History*, p. 174.
181. Engel and Gorohov, *op. cit.*, p. 83.
182. Savinkov, *Memoirs of a Terrorist*, pp. 20, 62; Florinsky, *op. cit.*, II, 1164.
183. Engel and Gorohov, *op. cit.*, p. 15; Florinsky, *op. cit.*, II, 1172.
184. Hans, *History*, pp. 196–197.
185. See above, p. 117.
186. Novgorotsev, *op. cit.*, p. 139.
187. Hans, *History*, p. 199.
188. Olgin, *op. cit.*, pp. 381–382; Novgorotsev, *op. cit.*, pp. 149 ff; Hans, *History*, pp. 201–203.
189. A. Georgievsky, *op. cit.*, I (London and St. Petersburg, 1906), 22.
190. Orlov, *op. cit.*, pp. 296–297; Georgievsky, *op. cit.*, II, 11.
191. Lowrie, *op. cit.*, p. 33.
192. Thomas Garrigue Masaryk, *The Spirit of Russia: Studies in History, Literature, and Philosophy*, tr. Eden and Cedar Paul (London, 1919), II, p. 71.
193. Maisky, *op. cit.*, p. 108.
194. Meijer, *op. cit.*, p. 13.
195. Avrahm Yarmolinsky, *Turgenev: The Man, His Art, and His Age* (Collier Books edn.; New York, 1961), p. 185.
196. Orlov, *op. cit.*, p. 214.
197. Popovsky, *op. cit.*, p. 34; Semyon Zalkind, *Ilya Mechnikov: His Life and Work*, tr. X. Danko (Moscow, 1959), pp. 13–14, 180–187 (note: Ilya Mechnikov changed the spelling of his name to "Elie Metchnikoff," as in text above, after emigrating to France).
198. Albert Edwards, "The Spirit of the Russian Student," *Intercollegiate Socialist*, II, No. 1 (October-November 1913), pp. 19, 25.
199. Maisky, *op. cit.*, p. 115.
200. A. Georgievsky, *op. cit.*, II, 19 ff.
201. *Ibid.*, pp. 19, 23.
202. *Ibid.*, p. 24.
203. E. F. G. Law, "The Present Condition of Russia," *Fortnightly Review*, XXXI (1882), 466.
204. Maisky, *op. cit.*, p. 122.
205. Pares, *Russia and Reform*, pp. 326–327.
206. Olgin, *op. cit.*, p. 319.
207. Angelica Balabanoff, *My Life as a Rebel* (New York, 1938), p. 21.
208. V. I. Lenin, "Lecture on the 1905 Revolution" (1917), in *The Beginning of the Revolution in Russia* (Moscow, n.d.), p. 113.
209. A. L. Patkin, *The Origins of the Russian-Jewish Labour Movement* (Melbourne, 1947), pp. 65–66.
210. Salo W. Baron, *The Russian Jew under Tsars and Soviets* (New York, 1964), p. 48.
211. Patkin, *op. cit.*, p. 91.
212. Haimson, *op. cit.*, p. 27.
213. Greenberg, *op. cit.*, I, 146–148.
214. S. M. Dubnow, *History of the Jews in Russia and Poland*, tr. I. Friedlaender, II (Philadelphia, 1918), 222, 200.
215. Patkin, *op. cit.*, pp. 104–105.
216. Koppel S. Pinson, "Arkady Kramer, Vladimir Medem, and the Ideology of the Jewish 'Bund,'" *Jewish Social Studies*, VII (1945), 247.
217. Patkin, *op. cit.*, pp. 105–106.
218. Greenberg, *op. cit.*, II, 150, 153.
219. *Ibid.*, II, 163.
220. *Ibid.*, II, 85; Salo W. Baron, *op. cit.*, p. 57; *Russian Jewry*, Jacob Frumkin, Gregor Aronson, Alexis Goldenweiser (eds.), tr. M. Ginsburg (New York, 1966), pp. 412–413.
221. Greenberg, *op. cit.*, II, 160.
222. *Ibid.*, II, 58, 161.
223. Abraham Ascher, "Pavel Axelrod: A Conflict between Jewish Loyalty and Revolutionary Dedication," *Russian Review*, XXIV (1965), 251–252.
224. Shmarya Levin, *Youth in Revolt*, tr. Maurice Samuel (New York, 1930), p. 143.
225. *Ibid.*, p. 157; Pinson, *op. cit.*, p. 247.
226. Greenberg, *op. cit.*, II, 169; Patkin, *op. cit.*, p. 144.
227. Pinson, *op. cit.*, p. 250; Greenberg, *op. cit.*, II, 158.
228. Levin, *op. cit.*, p. 143.

229. Bertram D. Wolfe, *Three Who Made a Revolution* (New York, 1948), p. 185.

230. Greenberg, *op. cit.*, II, 105.

231. Salo W. Baron, *op. cit.*, pp. 54–55; Patkin, *op. cit.*, pp. 77, 80, 83, 92; Yarmolinsky, *Road to Revolution*, pp. 210, 264–268; Footman, *op. cit.*, p. 90.

232. Patkin, *op. cit.*, pp. 76–77, 83.

233. See Shalom Aleichem, *Yiddish Tales*, tr. Helena Frank (Philadelphia, 1912), p. 178.

234. Shalom Aleichem, *The Old Country*, tr. Julius and Frances Butwin (New York, 1946), pp. 402–411.

235. Pinson, *op. cit.*, pp. 234–235.

236. Greenberg, *op. cit.*, II, 56.

237. Patkin, *op. cit.*, p. 264.

238. J. C. Rich, "60 Years of the Jewish Daily Forward," *New Leader*, June 3, 1957.

239. Matthew Josephson, *Sidney Hillman: Statesman of American Labor* (New York, 1952), pp. 28–35.

240. Oliver Wendell Holmes and Harold J. Laski, *Holmes-Laski Letters*, ed. Mark De Wolfe Howe (Cambridge, Mass., 1953), II, 1311.

241. Greenberg, *op. cit.*, II, 72–73.

242. Mark Wischnitzer, *To Dwell in Safety: The Story of Jewish Migration since 1800* (New York, 1948), pp. 60 ff.

243. According to Joshua Kunitz, the play by E. Chirikov, *The Jews*, was the most adequate portrayal of the conflict of generations within the Pale. In the setting of a ghetto town in 1903 at the time of the Kishinev pogrom, the play depicts the children of a watchmaker becoming involved in revolutionary activities at the university, and the daughter's suicide as her Gentile student lover dies at the hands of the mob. See Joshua Kunitz, *Russian Literature and the Jew: A Sociological Inquiry into the Nature and Origin of Literary Patterns* (New York, 1929), p. 156.

244. Chaim Weizmann, *Trial and Error: The Autobiography of Chaim Weizmann* (New York, 1949), p. 50. Also see Ahad Ha'am (Asher Ginzberg) *Selected Essays*, tr. Leon Simon (Philadelphia, 1912), p. 193.

245. Kropotkin, "The Crisis in Russia," p. 721.

246. *Ibid.*, p. 722.

247. Pares, *A History of Russia*, p. 403.

248. Yarmolinsky, *Road to Revolution*, p. 293.

249. The Social Revolutionaries, unlike the Bolsheviks, concentrated primarily on recruiting students. See Oliver H. Radkey, *The Agrarian Foes of Bolshevism* (New York, 1958), p. 129; also I. N. Steinberg, *In the Workshop of the Revolution* (New York, 1953), p. 118; Milyoukov, *op. cit.*, p. 511.

250. Jesse D. Clarkson, *A History of Russia* (New York, 1961), pp. 369–370.

251. E. Dupont, F. Engels, Leo Frankel, C. Le Moussu, Karl Marx, Aug. Serrailler, *L'Alliance de la Democratie Socialiste et L'Association Internationale des Travailleurs* (London, 1878), pp. 60, 74. The circumstances of the composition of the "Alliance pamphlet" are set forth in Franz Mehring, *Karl Marx: The Story of His Life*, tr. Edward Fitzgerald (New York, 1935), p. 521; also Gustav Mayer, *Friedrich Engels*, tr. G. and H. Highet (New York, 1936), p. 226.

252. Mehring, *op. cit.*, p. 541.

253. G. M. Stekloff, *History of the First International*, tr. Eden and Cedar Paul (London, 1928), p. 166.

254. Engels' letter to Marx is cited in Nomad, *op. cit.*, p. 133; Shlomo Avineri, "Feuer on Marx and the Intellectuals," *Survey*, No. 62 (January 1967), p. 154.

255. Woytinsky, *op. cit.*, p. 6.

256. Milyoukov, *op. cit.*, p. 538.

257. Milyoukov, *op. cit.*, p. 375.

258. M. N. Pokrovsky, *Brief History of Russia from the Earliest Times* (London, 1933), II, 74.

259. J. V. Stalin, "The Russian Social-Democratic Party," p. 22.

260. Engel and Gorohov, *op. cit.*, p. 73.

261. Stalin, "The Russian Social-Democratic Party," p. 26.

262. Vydrin, *op. cit.*, pp. 64–65; Orlov, *op. cit.*, p. 33.

FIVE — The Revolt against Gerontocracy in Traditional Societies

Student Elites in Traditional Societies

Student movements have been the most dramatic force in the making of history during the last half century in the so-called "underdeveloped" societies. There has been a tendency, therefore, to regard these movements as an episode in "modernization," in the development of a modern technology and economy; a whole series of restless manifestations in Asia, Latin America, and Africa have been interpreted as symptomatic of social organisms which are achieving industrialization. Yet Japan, which is a well-industrialized and highly literate society, has had its militant student movement too. Evidently what is basic to the rise of a student movement is a crisis in the de-authoritization of the elder generation. This can take place in an industrial society as well as in a proto-industrial or pre-industrial one. But it is especially likely to take place in a so-called traditional society which finds itself challenged by forces emanating from advanced societies. For in such a situation, the generational equilibrium of the traditional society is shattered. The young are ashamed of the old and want to avoid the emasculation which the traditional society inflicts on its members.[1]

A traditional society always houses within itself deep antagonisms between the generations. Traditional society is probably best described in psychological terms; it is "repressive." And all traditional societies have been characterized by the rule of the old; they are gerontocracies.[2] The aged grandfather, or father, ruled with almost absolute powers in the

Chinese family; the Confucian ethic inculcated filial piety. Ecclesiastes spoke for the traditional society of the Near East in warning, "Woe to thee, O land, when thy king is a child, and thy princes eat in the morning" (10:10). A fatalistic spirit hangs heavy on traditional societies; it is a fatalism common to all peasant societies, whether Egyptian, Mexican, or Indonesian, which have seen an eternal sameness in things, with the defeat of every rising generation predestined. The Egyptian fellahin's proverbs of social resignation and self-denial typify the attitude of peasants in all traditional societies: "Patience is beautiful." "To everyone the fate God gives him." "Greed is a humiliation, but satisfaction with one's lot is a full purse." "Such is the fellah's resignation," says a discerning observer of Egypt, "carried to the extent of servility and degradation. . . ." The fellah living always under fear, his entire social life controlled by endemic fear, despising his work and his life, rooted to the ground, is typical of the human foundation of traditional society.[3]

Then, too, the traditional society usually is one permeated both in its social structure and mentality by the notion of hierarchy. The Egyptian fellah lives in fear of his master. Similarly, "For the Latin American," writes John P. Gillin, "the universe, including human society, has traditionally been arranged in a series of strata, and the culture is still strongly influenced by the values which he attaches to hierarchy."[4] Traditional society is thus pervaded with political and cultural masochism; such is the universal testimony of its observers and analysts. According to the philosophical sociologist, Samuel Ramos, for instance, "The Mexican psyche is the result of reactions that strive to conceal an inferiority complex."[5] At the bottom of society, the large Indian segment remains brooding with "resentment against a dominating race which mistreated and humiliated them." Again and again, Latin American writers have blamed themselves for their accursed backwardness. The famed Sarmiento believed that the relative failure of colonization in Latin America was due to the inferiority of the Spanish race. "The evil is within us!" said the great Argentine. As for the mestizo, the man of mixed blood, he "carried on his brow the mark of degradation and infamy," writes Leopoldo Zea, "his birth condemned him to the misfortune of being the pariah of society."[6] When these masses, disinherited and trampled, rose in anger, they sought a "dictatorship of vengeance"; the political masochists turned sadists, and found in the brutality of military dictators, the *caudillos*, a satisfaction for their anger.

The cultural masochism which traditional society instills in the masses of its population tends to go hand in hand with a cultural sadism, or cult of masculinity, in the political elite. The Latin Americans have thus made much of what they call *machismo*, the cult of virility. The ethic of bushido of the Japanese samurai has left a similar imprint on the Japanese character. The Mexican man, notes Ramos, will react to a threat by shouting, "I am a *macho*," projecting his male organs and imputing femininity to his enemy.[7] Intransigence is the primary trait of the *macho*; his way is the right way. "Any kind of moderation in action," writes a Latin American, "will be censured as being feminine." There are no middle grounds; life is governed by all-or-none principles, by violence and submission. Under such conditions, political life tends to be authoritarian and dictatorial; the political elitist must be a "charismatic" personality if he would rule—that is, he must dominate as an omnipotent father, and transcend all criticism.

The student movements which arise in such traditional societies mirror in basic respects the society which they presumably aim to democratize. The student movements too tend to be authoritarian, intransigent, violent, and are susceptible to charismatic dominance. The student movements too have their *machismo*, their cult of virility; the students would show themselves more men than their fathers were; for the older generation in every traditional society is regarded by the younger as having capitulated, as having submitted to internal hierarchy or external suppressor. In this sense, the cult of *machismo* is always an expression of generational resentment. In the student movements of Latin America, it finds a more direct political expression than the customary male struttings.

"The Reform Movement is the great rupture with the Mother," wrote Octavio Paz, and in this sense student movements shared a collective preoccupation with an assertion of masculinity. "The *macho* represents the masculine pole of life. The phrase 'I am your father' has no paternal flavor and is not said in order to protect or guide another, but rather to impose one's superiority, that is, to humiliate." *Macho* power "almost always reveals itself as a capacity for wounding, humiliating, annihilating." The search for masculinity had deep historical origins. When the Aztecs were conquered, they forsook their warrior-gods and returned to feminine deities. It was, says Paz, a return to the maternal womb, and made popular the cult of the Virgin. The Son was venerated as a bleeding and humiliated Christ. In colloquial language, the Chingada is the violated mother, and the Mexican shout reveals the inner wound: "*Viva Mexico, hijos de la chingada!*"[8] The young student, observing his father, notes "how nothing really rids him of his sense of inadequacy, of which everyone is conscious, and how he tries to conceal his inadequacy under swagger and vulgarity and boastfulness."[9]

In traditional societies, there have customarily been two elites, the military and the intellectuals. In the highly civilized Chinese society, the intellectual elite held the paramount role of scholar-gentry. In the backward Latin American society, the church held a subordinate ideological role to that of the landed militarists. In all these traditional societies, the new intellectuals, the modern intellectuals, the revolutionary intellectuals, and above all, the students inherited the prestige of the bygone traditional intellectual elite. And to it they added the prestige of the new sciences, the commanding status of scientific enlightenment and knowledge. The Chinese Marxist student inherited the mantle from the Confucian scholar:

the Latin American Leninist had all the authority that the nineteenth- and eighteenth-century *pensadores* had wrested from the churchmen.

In the African Sudan, for instance, where new intellectual and military elites were so emerging, and where the rivalry between scholar and soldier familiar in Moslem countries was a natural one, a conflict between the two erupted in 1964 with the student intellectuals in the forefront. In October of that year, the Students' Union of the University of Khartoum led in overthrowing the Military Council which had ruled for six years, and re-established civilian rule. The story was the familiar one: the military dictatorship suppressed political discussion; the police broke up a students' meeting and arrested its leaders; the studentry as a whole demonstrated in protest; the police opened fire, killing one student and wounding six others; a great funeral procession brought a response of martial law; then a nation-wide general strike brought everything "grinding to a halt"; and a few days later the Military Council surrendered power to the National Front.[10] The young, idealistic Khartoum students led their people.

Thus, too, the Revolution of 1910 in Mexico was the outcome of a merging of the generational struggle with that of the peasantry and middle classes. As Octavio Paz wrote, "A new generation had risen, a restless generation that desired a change. The quarrel of the generations became a part of the general social discord. The Diaz regime was not only a government of the privileged but also of elderly men who could not resign themselves to giving up power. The nonconformity of the young expressed itself as an anxiety to see the principles of liberalism realized at last."[11] And the most vigorous intellectual circle, led by two young men, Antonio Caso and José Vasconcelos, was known aptly as the Ateneo de la Juventud (Atheneum of the Young).[12]

The revolt against traditional society is felt most directly by the sons as a conflict with their fathers. For traditional society is the one to which the fathers acquiesced, and that very acquiescence is a constant reminder of the fathers' failure. Everywhere, then, in traditional societies, the students try to supersede the fathers, to dethrone the traditional superego, and to install themselves as a higher conscience, justified by the law of history. A study of Middle Eastern students, carried out at the American University of Beirut in Lebanon, has the appropriate title, "The Dethronement of the Father." The author reported that 80 per cent of a large sample of students believed that the older generation did not understand their problems. Moreover, the sheer gap in the levels of education between the two generations made their rift more intense; the elder generation was often illiterate or poorly educated. "The parents of these subjects may be living in the medieval age while their children are in the 20th century." The sons had very little of the attitude of "submission to fate" which characterized their elders. All this, the study concluded, "undoubtedly contributed to conflicts between the two generations."[13] Indeed, the intensity of the conflict varied with the extent of the educational gap between the generations. Furthermore, Middle Eastern students, as compared to Americans, "tended to be significantly more authoritarian." An authoritarian student in the Middle East differed, however, from an authoritarian student in the United States in one important respect. American authoritarians tend to idealize their parents; in the Middle East, on the other hand, they do not hold them as models. Also, the Middle Eastern authoritarians favored socialistic programs, unlike the chief group of American authoritarians hitherto.[14] Thus, generational conflict expressed itself in the psychology of Arab students.

Everywhere in traditional societies, whether in China, Africa, or the Middle East, the student activist found himself an alienated man, alienated by his Western education from his own culture and history, yet also estranged from the Western world which humiliated his people and made them conscious of their inferiority. In the Middle East, noted one observer in 1951, "young men and women from the humblest villages and hamlets . . . have learned about the Renaissance and the Reformation, read Shakespeare in their literature classes, can quote Rousseau and Voltaire, have discussed atomic fission in their physics lectures, and are deeply conscious of the role of power politics and the expansion of Europe in their own countries."[15] The sensitive student found himself rejecting his father and his culture; the son educated in a higher culture de-authoritized the father and his lowly culture. Yet the son also hated those who had humbled his father. Thus the Middle Eastern student became an "anti-Westerner" in exactly the same degree to which he rejected his own elders: "He lives uncomfortably on the margin of two worlds. Falling prey to various emotional complexes, he either withdraws into an ivory tower of his own, or, hurt and frustrated, he turns round and joins the other extreme as an embittered and violent 'anti-Westerner.' Standing at this other extreme is the most disturbed and disturbing group: the 'anti-Westerners.' They are in a state of mental and spiritual rebellion against any authority, whether ecclesiastical or political, that is imposed on them by force." This was a rebellion which had fermented for many years. The French consul-general in Beirut in 1888 had noted that "our Colleges are to a certain extent the cause of this revolution." It gathered more recruits as the student bodies grew in number; the total number of students at all levels, for instance, in Syria and Lebanon jumped during the twenty-two years from 1924 to 1946 from 123,576 to nearly 350,000, while the three universities reached an enrollment of five thousand. This was a studentry which read both Machiavelli and Turgenev's *Fathers and Sons,* for they felt the pangs of generational bitterness, yet longed for power to strike at some externalized or surrogate embodiment of its cause. They nourished the legends of student revolutionary tradition, of how the Arab national movement had begun when "five young men who had been educated at the Syrian Protestant College in Beirut formed a secret society."[16]

The young men of intellect in all the Arab-speaking countries, as in all traditional societies, saw themselves as the elite anointed and appointed by history to guide their backward peoples. They saw themselves as the voices of their voiceless peoples, as its political class, as its benevolent rulers. The first political party in Morocco emerged from a small student circle at Rabat and one at Qarawiyn University.[17] In several instances, the intellectual elite merged with the military elite, and the revolutionary student movement was at the same time a movement of military cadets. In Turkey, for instance, at the end of the nineteenth century, an adequate education was available only in the military schools, which thus became the Achilles heel of the ruler who wanted only to be protected. (The University of Constantinople was not founded until 1900, and was then the only university in Turkey.) To them flowed the young intelligentsia of the Ottoman Empire. Thus, it was at the Imperial Military Medical School in Constantinople in 1889 that the revolutionary student movement emerged with a plot to overthrow Abdul Hamid II; the preceding year the whole student body had been involved in a strike against the administration. The movement, patterned on the secret Italian Carbonari, spread to the other government schools—the military academy, the veterinary school, the civil college, the naval academy, the artillery and engineering school. By contrast, the students in the theological school became supporters of counterrevolution. In defeat, the revolutionary students went to Paris; they read science and philosophy, and became known as Young Turks, "*un groupe d'adolescents rusés et naifs.*" Their message about the students' mission was heard: Mustafa Kemal, the later dictator of Turkey, became a revolutionary as a student and was arrested the day he was commissioned.[18] In later years, he reminisced about his formative student experiences: "New ideas emerged among some of my companions and myself. We began to discover that there were evils in the administration and politics of the country, and we felt the urge to communicate this discovery to the thousands of students of the College. We founded a handwritten newspaper for them to read. We had a small organization in the class. I was in the committee, and I used to write most of what appeared in the paper."[19]

This curious alliance between the student movement and the military elite has indeed continued to be an underlying theme in Turkish history. The student movement in 1960 initiated the series of events which led to the overthrow of the Menderes government. The army, however, provided the final force; and when it had taken power, it called on the faculties of the Ankara and Istanbul universities to furnish the trained persons to carry out the governmental functions. The ill-fated Menderes government, by contrast, had committed the cardinal sin of estranging the intellectual elite; in 1953 it enacted a law which required professors to confine themselves to scientific, educational work and to avoid involvement in active partisan politics. The consequence was that the universities became centers of opposition to the government. Then in April 1960, the government opened an investigation of the opposition and suspended its political activity; thereupon, the students took to the streets and the revolutionary events began. The students later regarded themselves as the "heroes in the 1960 Revolution"; this elitism proved to have an exhilarating and yet detrimental effect for the Turkish studentry and universities.[20]

The sense of themselves as the historical elite, the makers of history, characterizes students in action more spontaneously than it does labor, peasant, or bourgeois movements. Marx tried hard to inculcate in the working class a sense of historic mission; Lassalle tried similarly to impart to workers a sense of their vocation. Fundamentally, however, this kind of self-image arises easily only among intellectuals, especially the student sector. As the young, the pure in conscience, the uncorrupted, the disinterested, and above all as the custodians of intellect, they feel themselves to be anointed. A newspaper put out by and for Iranian students living temporarily in the United States spoke naturally in such terms: "The core of each nation's strength depends on her 'armies' of intellectuals—without whose dynamism Iran's progress would remain a passing memory. . . . A unity of goals between our educated minority (here called 'intellectuals') and the people of Iran would be the essential nucleus necessary for progress and improvement."[21] The students of Teheran University, "a beehive of political ferment," could, according to qualified observers, bring down the government at any time, yet according to the correspondent for *The New York Times* "the Government and the police will not—and probably cannot utilize real force against the students and professors." " 'Should we turn machine guns on them?' asked an officer whose mission was the defense of the state. 'We cannot do that. After all they are our children.' "[22] Here was the source of the remarkable privileged status of student movements serving as combat forces for the intellectual elite. They were the children, after all, the sons, only recently emerged from boyhood and in the throes of adolescence, holding the loving admiration of their elders. And society, acting for the gerontocracy, felt its hand stayed; in active generational struggle, the older generation is handicapped by affection in a way the young are not. The young are feeling their strength, sensing the rising power of their aggressive energies, and their moral condemnation is a weapon of psychological warfare which unnerves the older generation.

Thus, student movements have emerged as the makers of social change in traditional societies, but there is a fatality about the patterns which generational struggle imposes on such societies. Their origin in a psychology of alienation, their moving powers of intellectual elitism and messianism, have in a very short run turned them into mechanisms for fashioning authoritarian regimes. The student intellectual, self-ordained as his people's liberator, acting selflessly, heroically to the point of martyrdom, becomes his people's dictator, ruling selfishly on behalf of a bureaucratic elite, and making martyrs of others. The rise of rational, liberal democracy is more closely linked to the rise of economically inspired movements of the bourgeoisie and workingmen. The money-seeking of the scorned middle class, their "economic calculation," has been in the long run the chief force for rationality and liberal values. The idealism of the student movements in Asia, Africa, and Latin America has almost invariably been transmuted into irrationality and repression.

The Chinese Student Movement: From May Fourth to Maoism

Behind the revolutionary energy of the Chinese student movement, with its momentous consequences, was the same restless searching, the will to break with the past, the revolt against the de-authoritized father. The conflict of generations once again merged with the struggle of classes and made the latter its instrumentality. The number of Chinese students, inheritors of all the prestige of the Chinese intellectual class, which had ruled for almost two thousand years, multiplied during the first quarter of the twentieth century. Students poured into the new schools for modern learning. "From over one hundred thousand students in modern schools in 1905, the number leaped to two million in 1911. In 1922 there were over six million. At the same time thousands of students who had been studying abroad became their teachers, indirectly influencing them to take revolutionary measures."[23]

Students were from the beginning the first revolutionary cadres. As early as December 1903, the Hua Hsing Hui (Society for the Revival of China), the first revolutionary organization founded in Hunan, consisted almost exclusively of students returned from or preparing to go to Japan. Sun Yat-sen in 1905 turned to the Chinese student groups in Tokyo and European centers to provide his revolutionary nuclei. The twenty thousand Chinese students in Japan in 1905 and 1906 were the group to which Sun especially looked for support—a young, militant, restless intelligentsia. And this early Chinese student movement reflected all the classical patterns of self-destruction and other-destruction, of suicidalism and terrorism. Late in 1905, several thousand Chinese students went on strike to protest the new restrictions placed on them by the Japanese Ministry of Education. One student, Ch'en T'ien-hua, went further; he committed suicide by drowning himself off a Tokyo beach. In his last testament to his fellow-students, he said he hoped his deed would open their eyes to the "ugly realities of their existence." Meanwhile, fellow students of his had organized themselves into the T'ung Meng Hui (United League of China), taking an oath to work for the expulsion of the Manchus and the founding of a republic. The organization proved to be very enthusiastic about making bombs, and its leader, Wang Ching-wei, urged the assassination of officials as a political tactic.[24]

As Russian students several generations earlier had read and brooded over the advanced Western philosophers, so the Chinese students harkened to the unseen revered Western masters whose new wisdom opened up vistas toward a liberated future. Mill, Huxley, Darwin, Kropotkin, Marx became prophets of Young China. When John Dewey and Bertrand Russell came in person to China in 1919, it was as if all the noblest in philosophy had come to help guide the younger generation. Scientific method was the philosophy of the Chinese renaissance, for science was the Promethean force, the liberator of enslaved man. "Under such influences of Western Europe through the leaders of the Chinese renaissance, young China broke loose from tradition and authority."[25] Dewey, Russell, Ibsen, Bergson, Nietzsche supplanted Confucius and Lao-tze. The law of the universality of ideas, transcending the uneven material levels of diverse societies, asserted itself. The young Chinese intellectuals, confronted by the explosive mixture of advanced ideas and backward societies, tried to leap many social stages in a few short years. To liberated youth, with energies released from gerontocratic repression, all seemed possible. The career of Chen Tu-hsiu, editor of *La Jeunesse*, was to be a guiding model for the sociological actions of his disciples, the young student intellectuals. *La Jeunesse* was "the greatest single influence that brought about the New Culture Movement." In its first issue of September 15, 1915, Chen began with an article called "My Solemn Appeal to Youth." As Alexander Herzen had called upon Russian youth to regenerate their country, so Chen called upon the Chinese students to take up the struggle. The old people, he said, were hopeless, and should well be eliminated through nature's workers. Youth, not the old, possessed the wisdom and the strength to create the future. The British and Americans wanted the old to stay young, but the Chinese wanted the young to act old. The freedom to be young was for Chen the first of the freedoms. Five years later, Chen Tu-hsiu founded the Chinese Communist party.[26]

Mao Tse-tung, later Chairman of the Chinese People's Republic, was molded in his politics by the student movement, participating in all the stages from circle to party to government. His political ideas took shape at the Hunan Provincial First Normal School, where he organized (in his words) "a group of students around myself, and the nucleus was formed of what later was to become a society that was to have a widespread influence on the affairs and destiny of China. It was a serious minded little group of men and they had no time to discuss trivialities. . . . They had no time for love or 'romance' and considered the times too critical and the need for knowledge too urgent to discuss women or personal matters." After the May Fourth Movement, he continues, he devoted most of his time to student political activities: "I was editor of the *Hsiang Chiang Review*, the Hunan students' paper, which had a great influence in South China." Mao's childhood and adolescence had been years marked by perpetual conflict with his father, a rice merchant and "severe taskmaster," who frequently beat Mao and his brothers, exploited him as well as his laborers, and gave him the most meager food. Mao was drawn to his mother, who gave food to the poor during famines. Mao narrated this family rift, so psychologically suggestive, in stylized Marxist language:

> There were two "parties" in the family. One was my father, the Ruling Power. The Opposition was made up of myself, my mother, my brother and sometimes even the laborer. In the "United Front" of the Opposition, however, there was a difference of opinion. My mother advocated a policy of indirect attack. She criticized any overt display of emotion and attempts at open rebellion against the Ruling Powers. She said it was not the Chinese Way.[27]

The family civil war was the prototype for the political civil war of later years, even to the maternal lessons in guerrilla tactics. "The dialectical struggle in our family was constantly developing," wrote Mao. Once, "my father denounced me before the whole group, calling me lazy and useless. This infuriated me. I cursed him and left the house. My father insisted that I apologize and k'ou-t'ou as a sign of submission." When poor villagers seized one of the rice consignments of his father, "I did not sympathize with him," writes the son. The sons everywhere were beginning too to rebel against the marriages arranged by their parents. "My parents had married me when I was fourteen to a girl of twenty," says Mao, "but I had never lived with her, and never subsequently did." Into this atmosphere, tense with generational conflict, came the news of the new student activism: "Many students were now joining the army. A student army had been organized. . . . I decided to join the regular army instead, and help complete the revolution." The word "socialism" was beginning to appear in the new revolutionary journals, and to it students' emotions attached themselves.[28] There were the typical students' enthusiasms—for "radical" educational methods, for the new natural sciences, for physical culture, and indeed, an anarchist phase as well. They knew by an emotional a priori that they were socialists long before they knew what socialism was. "At that time" (in 1920), said Liu Shao-ch'i, later to become President of Communist China and its chief party ideologist, "I only knew that Socialism was good . . . but I was not clear what Socialism was or how it could be realised."[29] It was all part of the youthful restlessness which was seeking an aim to give direction to its energies.

A poem that Mao wrote in later years, "Changsha," recalled the mood of his student days:

> I have been here in days past with a throng of companions;
> During those crowded months and years of endeavour,
> All of us students together and all of us young,
> Our bearing was proud, our bodies strong,
> Our ideals true to a scholar's spirit;

Just and upright, fearless and frank,
We pointed the finger at our land,
We praised and condemned through our writings,
And those in high positions we counted no more than dust.[30]

Mao's conflict with his father and its primacy as a motivation for his political ideas were typical of the Chinese students who emerged with him as leaders in the Communist movement. Of the seven autobiographies of Chinese teachers and students which Nym Wales recorded, three spontaneously dwelled on the struggle of the generations, three others were sketchy in their accounts, while only one seemed definitely without such a spur to action.

Wu Liang P'ing, propaganda chief, said, "My father was severe and beat me at times if I did not come up to his approval . . . I feared my father." When his father wanted a pretty concubine, Wu hurried by steamer to tell his mother. "She rushed to Ningpo and threatened to kill herself, so Father dared not carry out his plan." Later, "a big conflict with my family over the marriage question took place, and we fought back and forth a whole year." Meanwhile, to strike against the president of his college was becoming a more agreeable and fruitful variety of struggle.[31]

Hsü Meng-Ch'iu, historian of the Long March, was moved to leave his family, not only because he wanted new knowledge, but because "in 1920 my family ordered me to marry a girl who was old-fashioned and ignorant and I was determined not to have that kind of wife."[32]

Wang Shou-tao, political commissar, narrated likewise that when he was fourteen, his father wanted him to marry. "I refused. I had acted in a play as the girl victim of an arranged marriage and felt strongly on the subject." Wang subsequently went through the various stages in the evolution of student activism—a brotherhood of students formed under the influence of the May Fourth Movement, a back-to-the-people phase in which he organized a village night school, an attack on the school authorities, and finally expulsion. As always, the revolutionary emotion preceded the search for a class which would provide the "mass base" for actualizing the revolution. Wang and other student leaders converted to Marxism and sought out the peasants as their historically appointed allies.[33]

Hsiao K'e, the "military scholar" and "youngest general," was utterly clear as to the power of generational conflict as a source of revolutionary emotion among students:

One of the main reasons for my revolutionary tendency was my resentment against the old Chinese family system, which I experienced in its most disintegrating phase. As a child I received a bad impression of family life and I was glad to escape from it. Since I left it, I have never written a letter to my home. . . . Even as I talk I feel bitter toward my feudal family. . . . I hate intensely the feudal concept of the family. My father was very authoritarian and dominated his family. It was under an absolute dictatorship, and so was I. I obeyed my father without hesitation on every point . . . he tried to destroy my spirit with a conservative education. I was not a rebellious child at home, but when I was released from the family yoke for a little while, I was always carefree and daring. . . . I remember too how I loved the village theater where there was noise and freedom. What a relief it was from the stern teachings of my father and his dull rules from Confucius and Mencius. It was natural that I should want to run away from home.[34]

"Most of the Communists who had been to school at all seemed to have been leaders of the student body," observed Cheng Tzu-hua, leader of the Tayeh uprising. He had revolted against his family, which wished to apprentice him to a merchant: "I did not want to be treated as a servant," he said. At the normal school, whose master was Chao Tai-wan, the struggle of generations was unremitting: "One of Chao's sons was a leftist; his father put him in jail, where he died. Another student was in Yenching University when the student movement began. His father warned him that he would send a squad to arrest him for being a Communist. . . . The progressive students in Chao's school were dismissed if they expressed any liberal ideas." When the uprising of the students took place in 1925, "the student body rose up and drove all the department heads from the school, about thirty altogether. We began by destroying furniture in the house of Yen's secretary; then, unsatisfied, we held a meeting and considered eliminating all the department heads." In the disorder of approaching embattled armies, the students wrested control of the government and administration of the school.[35]

As we have seen, a struggle of generations, in and of itself, however, will not give rise to a massive student movement. What is always required, in addition, is some signal event in which the de-authoritization of the older generation, as a collective whole, is vividly dramatized. The May Fourth Movement, the turning point in modern Chinese history, arose from such a conjunction of generational conflict with the de-authoritization of the elders.

The immediate incidents which ignited the May Fourth Movement brought about a crisis in the relations of the generations. It was at the end of April 1919 that the news reached Peking of the humiliation of the Chinese government at the Paris Conference. The elders had submitted abjectly to the Japanese; they had acquiesced in the surrender of Shantung to Japan. A group of student study circles resolved to call a mass demonstration on May 7, National Humiliation Day, the fourth anniversary of Japan's so-called Twenty-One Demands. These student circles were small; the influential New Tide Society, for instance, had only thirty-seven members, all of them students at Peking University. They became leaders, however, in the May Fourth Movement. Then the official student bodies of the colleges and universities in Peking voted to join the demonstration—25,000 in all, according to their own claims, probably exaggerated. Disquieting news concerning the Chinese "traitors," the diplomats and ministers, brought a mass protest meeting on May 4. Three thousand students from thirteen colleges and universities gathered in the afternoon at the Square of Heavenly Peace. The students marched through the Peking streets bearing a pair of funeral scrolls which berated the names of the "traitors" of the older generation: "The names of Ts'ao Ju-lin, Lu Tsung-yü and Chang Tsung-hsiang will stink a thousand years. The students of Peking mourn for them with tears." There followed the inevitable clashes with the police and troops as the students tried to force the legation quarter. In accordance with the pattern of student movements, the Chinese students were suddenly possessed by violence. As a participant said, "Upon hearing that force was employed to threaten us, our middle group pushed forward like madmen . . . our minds were instantly inflamed to a hitherto unknown degree." They then stormed the house of the vice-foreign minister, set it on fire, and mauled several officials. As the participant described it, they got hold of the "arch traitor," the Chinese minister to Japan. "Once he was thrown down, we beat him, kicked him, and stamped on him. Soon his face and body were covered with blood, and his clothes were nearly stripped off him. When we felt sure he was dead, we took to our heels."[36] One student died, thirty-two students were arrested; twenty of them were from Peking University.[37]

The students' demonstration of May 4, 1919, thus began a new era in Chinese history. The students' protest moved the nation as no recent political events had. The students had acted as the nation's conscience and vanguard. The United States Ambassador, Paul S. Reinsch, perceived at once the significance of the incident as an uprising against the elders; the students, he wrote, were "anxious and stirred because of the reported action of the old men at Paris."[38] John Dewey, America's distinguished philosopher, arrived in China in time to witness May Fourth at first hand. "It is hard to estimate the significance of the fact," he wrote, "that the new movement was initiated by the student body. . . . Yet this is the first time that students have taken any organized part in politics." The Student Union of Peking came into existence as China's first permanent united student organization. Then, on May 19, the first general students' strike of Peking took place as all the students in eighteen colleges and universities joined in a refusal to attend classes. The strike spread to Tientsin, Shanghai, Nanking; fifteen thousand students answered the call of the Student Union of Tientsin, twenty thousand in Shanghai. During this period "the students alone played the major role in protest against the government," writes Chow Tse-tsung; merchants, industrialists, and workers followed their lead.[39] When Sun Yat-sen, the Father of the Chinese Republic, met the student leaders, he is said to have bowed three times and to have congratulated them, saying, "I started three revolutions and could not overthrow the corrupt oligarchy of Peking, but you by a single stroke killed them all."[40] John Dewey was deeply stirred as he observed the student movement entering upon its back-to-the-people phase: "And as the vacation period comes on these students are dispersing all over China peddling goods and speaking, speaking, speaking."[41]

The back-to-the-people movement thrived vigorously for a few months after May 1919. Students worked with enthusiasm to found unions among the workers. In 1918 there had been only twenty-five strikes in China; the number rose in 1919 to sixty-six. The education of the masses was pursued with an apostolic zeal. In January 1920, the Student Union of Peking University founded a Night School for the Plain People; it marked a rupture with the traditional self-monopoly of Chinese scholars. Sixteen free schools were established for poor children in Shanghai; students went to the countryside to lecture to the peasants. A tremendous hope arose in the possibility of quickly educating the people and thereby liberating them from their age-old apathy. But the Chinese students were soon encountering obstacles. The forces of cultural inertia did not yield readily to students' appeals. The number of strikes declined in 1920 to forty-six. Older liberals such as Hu Shih and leading industrialists withdrew their support from the student movement. They expressed the opinion in May 1920 "that student demonstrations and strikes should cease and that the duty of students was to study." As was the case with the Russian student movement, the experience of rejection caused the Chinese student movement to veer toward elitism and violence. In May 1920, a group composed mostly of students from the University of Peking founded the Chinese Communist party; students likewise predominated at its congress in July 1921.[42] Student activists welcomed the declarations by Sun Yat-sen that China could be saved only by a party of professional revolutionists, that it was impossible to secure the necessary reforms by education in the setting of a corrupt military-bureaucratic system. A Student Union of All China had been founded on June 16, shortly after the May Fourth incident. "Later on," according to a leading Chinese political historian, Li Chien-nung, "the Chinese Communist party and the Kuomintang relied mainly upon the student unions in provinces under the control of warlords as headquarters for propagating their doctrines and securing young members." The student movement of 1919 entered a new phase in its life cycle, that of transformation into a political party with the consequent struggle for power.

The classical traits of student movements came to the fore in the great Chinese awakening of 1919. Not only was there the elitism, the juvenocracy, and the propensity to violence; there was also the self-destruction, the suicidalism of the young activist driven by strange, unconscious demons within himself. Suicidalism was a recurrent phenomenon among the Chinese students. When early in the century the Boxer Rebellion had failed, "a number of students committed suicide because of the hopeless situation."[43] The humiliating aftermath of the First World War created a similar despair among student activists.

An American professor in China during the students' strike of 1919 met two students weeping bitterly; they were both members of the university football team. He told the story:

"What's the matter?" I asked in alarm.

"We are weeping," they replied, "at the disgrace of our country."

It is hard for westerners to appreciate the dramatic value of such a spectacle. We are tempted to laugh when we hear of the patriotic student in Tientsin who tried to kill himself by butting his head against a stone pillar in the Chamber of Commerce. But to the Chinese he was visible rhetoric. There, into the sanctuary of trade, where the sleek and satisfied merchants refuse to risk their profits in a boycott of Japanese goods, comes the student patriot willing to give something more precious than profits, if by so doing he can shame the selfish into sacrifice. It is something the people do not easily forget. So also the student of Wuchang, who drowned himself last June in the Yangtse River as a protest against the lethargy of his compatriots in the face of a possible partition of China, is celebrated as a national martyr.[44]

The student movement likewise reinforced the family revolution. As Chu Teh, later the military commander of Chinese Communism, recalled, "Men brought [to parties] their wives and sisters who, for the first time, learned to discuss ideas with men who were not members of their immediate families. . . . The emancipation of women was one of the many aspects of the May Fourth Movement." The movement set the students looking for the mighty class ally which would put its physical force at the service of the students' intellect and idealism. As intellectuals, proud inheritors of the scholars' mantle, the students felt the vocation to rule; as young idealists, they experienced a social mysticism, a need to merge their identities with the humble people; this dualism of intellectual elitism and populist mysticism was typical of student movements. The Marxist message of the historical role of the proletariat was hard to grasp; it so patently violated the realities of intellectual elitism and the virtual absence of an industrial working class. As Chu Teh said, "Our study club in Luchow could not conceive of the proletariat guiding a revolution . . . we thought of the proletariat as servants, coolies, and salt workers who could not read and write. It was confusing because Communist writers who preached Marxism were themselves high professors, students and other intellectuals and not workers."[45]

Thus, the politics of generational and class struggle began to converge, with generational struggle, however, the dynamic, awakening, bestirring component. In China, as elsewhere, the students were immersed in a literary culture which nurtured feelings altogether at variance with the material environment. The youth read Kropotkin and Marx; they even became Ibsenites, and acted often in *The Doll's House*, with young men students having to play the part of Nora. There was the eternal hope of youth: "The youth of China would prevent a repetition of history."[46]

The magnificent heroism of the Chinese student movement makes it difficult for one to evaluate it dispassionately. Did it fulfill its high promise or was it a primary agency for the rise of totalitarian, elitist rule? There were observers who had their doubts about the Chinese student movement from its very inception. Hu Shih, Dewey's disciple and the inspirer of the literary renaissance, did not share his master's enthusiasm for the May Fourth Movement. Despite the involvement of his own students, he felt it the "most unwelcome interruption" of the renaissance.[47] It is clear that the Chinese student movement, in its unrestrained enthusiasm for the abolition of discipline, controls, examinations, and all authority, created a situation which only increased the social chaos. Paul Monroe, who knew China intimately, and under whom the large majority of visiting Chinese teachers studied in the United States, wrote in 1927:

That the untrained and undisciplined student should now rule and control teachers in the land where, above all others, age and scholarship had so long been revered, constitutes an aspect of the present revolution that brings despair to the Chinese educator. That in the land where formal examination for fitness of office had so long and so completely prevailed, students should now successfully—and all but universally—rebel against any examination, any test of fitness for any office, and should hold any grading of students on the basis of attainment, any awarding of aid on the basis of ability, to be an infringement of liberty and of the principles of the Revolution is indeed in itself so complete a revolution as to be startling in its consequences.[48]

Thus, once again, the pattern of generational revolt, with all its irrationalities, imposed itself on the political process, adding to it a feverish force, destructive and directionless. In the 1920s, as Monroe indicated, the students, as the activists of the intellectual elite, were the one alternative political force to that of the dictatorial militarists and the confused, mixed groupings in the Nationalist party. But the students failed as an agency for creating a sense of democratic discipline. Their minds filled with Utopian literature, their feelings dominated by rebelliousness against all elders, all authority, their message one of "creative chaos," they paved the way for a reaction to dictatorship, whether militarist or Communist. Curiously, both the militarist and Communist elites were largely composed of previous generations of student leaders who had completed their journey from anarchic activism to authoritarian elitism.[49]

The Utopian motif, at first, pervaded the minds of the student activists. Hsü Meng-ch'iu, the official historian of the Long March, recalled, "We wanted to experiment in the Hsin Ch'eng [New Village] Movement, and our ideas were of Utopian socialism like Fourierism or Owenism." In 1923, his friends "still wanted to build the new society according to the Utopian 'New Village' idea."[50] Frustrated Utopians, bitter at the slowness of people to heed their message, have often turned into dictatorial authoritarians, demanding all power to fit people to the Utopian blueprint. The student movement, with its total vision, total demands, and total methods, was prone to take this authoritarian path.

Alternately, the students engaged in forays against deans, presidents, and professors, humbling them in perpetual generational civil war, and in self-sacrificing missions of propaganda among peasantry and coolies, urging them to class struggle. The notion of building a liberal democratic society was simply a casualty in the perpetual generational civil war. Hsü Meng Ch'iu tells how as a student leader in 1921 he first organized a strike at his commercial school to drive away "the incompetent and dishonest principal," then in 1922 at a tuition-free agricultural school he was again organizing a struggle against "the corrupt school authorities" and opposing the senior students "because they worked with the authorities." Then in 1923 "we had an uprising in the school and our group fought physically with another group. About ten students were dismissed, including myself, for I was the leader." Such is the story which monotonously repeats itself among student leaders and later Communist personages. Terrorist tactics to dominate the school and physical violence scarcely made the schools into proving grounds for democracy, despite John Dewey's enthusiasm for the students. Hsü finally went to the newly founded Shanghai University, where "all except the president were Communists"; there, presumably, there was no nonsense about bourgeois liberal tolerance for diverse views. Wu Liang-p'eng tells how he and his comrades organized a week-long strike in an unsuccessful effort to oust the president of Amoy University; "it was a democratic move against the tyranny of the president."[51] Liao Ch'eng-chih, later a member of the Central Committee of the Communist party, tells how he organized a strike at the Canton Christian College, which failed, he said, because "the reactionary students of the college lost their patriotic fervor."[52] And Mao Tse-tung, as editor of the Hunan students' paper, tried to give the students' strike a higher significance by directing it against the local *tuchun* (warlord), demanding his removal.[53]

That many of the students' grievances were well founded cannot be gainsaid. The teachers, paid by the lecture hour, were often indifferent both to their subjects and to their students; the administrators were often without the spirit of education. The students lived in overcrowded barracks and had little opportunity for recreation and athletics; young and impressionable when they left home, often only thirteen to fifteen years of age, and living in great congregated numbers, twenty to thirty thousand of them in the packed dormitories, they composed an explosive mixture of adolescent emotions. But the destructive impact of the student movement was scarcely a rational response to these problems. By 1926 and 1927, its demands were so "absolutely disruptive of school organization," wrote Paul Monroe, that few schools were in session; the just demands for student self-government and representation in university decisions were debased into a situation where, "contrary to all accepted Chinese standards," responsible authorities were flouted and respect for teachers became a sin against one's own generation.[54] Moreover, the Communist influence over the students was invariably used against all authority, whether in government, private or mission schools.

At the height of its influence, there were students who were troubled by their movement's readiness for violence. One student, mindful of all the movement had done to reawaken the Chinese people, observed that "when thousands of people with a sense of being wronged gather together, even the educated can hardly refrain from committing violence on the slightest provocation." He noted that strikes were being used indiscriminately, and that when school work ceased the students were finally the losers, "a wanton squandering of time." The strike was such a readily available weapon and so apparently without consequences for the students that they were constantly tempted to use it against whoever displeased them. As one student wrote: "Strike, primarily adopted as a measure against the government, seems to have shifted its target to the school authority. If one cares to read the records of the numerous student strikes of the past eight months (September 1919 to April 1920), one would find as many strikes declared against the school authority as against the government . . . Where complaint of wrong is refused thoughtful consideration and denied redress, the only way that remains is strike. But it would be diabolical for one to think that strike is almighty!"[55] Evidently the strike became the device by which a Younger Generational Utopia was sought. Thus, the students in the seven or eight leading Peking institutions sought by direct action to abolish the system of regular examinations on the ground that many European and American educators decried the examination system. Their strike led to the resignation of several presidents and principals but scarcely contributed to furthering education in China. Here in a nutshell was the oft-repeated story of youthful idealism mixed with sheer generational aggression. The student movement presented society with a wonderful vision, even as every day it contributed to society's disorganization. The students behaved with nobility as they went to the people. "On every street corner," reported Paul Monroe, "in all the larger cities youths are addressing small groups or crowds at all hours of the day or evening." Usually the meetings were small, but sometimes they were attended by huge masses, occasionally by as many as one hundred thousand.[56] The students became the dominant molders of public opinion, the consciences of coolies and merchants alike. Yet the example they set was inevitably the example of their own actions, authoritarian, lawless, coercive. André Malraux caught the mood of the student leaders in *Man's Fate,* their death-consciousness, the sense of desperation and alienation which hovered about their deeds. In this sense, the student movement was the sick conscience of the Chinese society, not a guide to its recovery. Even the back-to-the-people spirit was infected with self-hatred and anti-intellectualism. Mao Tse-tung describes this phenomenon: "I began as a student . . . the intellectuals were the only clean persons . . . the workers and peasants seemed rather dirty." His soldier years, he said, terminated his intellectual pride. "It was then and only then that a fundamental change occurred in the bourgeois and petty-bourgeois feelings implanted in me." It was the intellectuals who were unclean, he said, and needed remolding. "The workers and peasants are after all the cleanest persons."[57] Such an attitude always works finally in an anti-liberal and anti-democratic direction; the intellectual values of rational deliberation, recognition of the many-sidedness of problems, and open-mindedness are rejected. The intellectual is asked instead to assume the worst traits of the most ignorant peasant rather than having the peasant acquire intellectual values. In this sense, the students' participation in a back-to-the-people movement can be a partial manifestation of a self-destructive impulse.

The high points of Chinese student activity coincided with high moments in the de-authoritization of the older generation. These occurred in 1919, in 1925, 1931, and 1935, and always had to do with the abject submission of the government to foreign powers. The de-authoritization of the elder generation, we have emphasized, is a phenomenon which involves the conjoining of both the universal pattern of generational conflict and the particular historical circumstances of the time. An elder generation in moral defeat and moral betrayal in the eyes of the young, an elder generation which has lost its moral authority, has to deal with unprecedented bitterness on the part of the young. The conflict of generations is a universal theme of history; the de-authoritization of the old depends on particular historical circumstances and experiences. The movement of 1919 was ignited by the surrender of Shantung to the Japanese; then "from 1920 to 1923 there was no student movement in China."[58] That of 1925 began when Japanese textile owners in Shanghai wanted to reduce wages and lengthen the hours of work; but as the Movement of May Thirtieth developed, its slogans broadened to "Down with British Imperialism!" "Cancel the Unequal Treaties!" "Drive Away the Military Forces of the Imperialist Powers in China!" "Get Back Control of the Customs!" "Oppose Extraterritoriality." The student movement was the heart of the anti-imperialist movement, and Shanghai University led the way. "The May Thirtieth Incident was the beginning of the Great Revolution of 1925–1927, though we did not suspect what we were starting," wrote an officer of the Shanghai Student Union. "After May 30, many students joined the Communist Youth as I did, though my family did not know about it then."[59] The later movements of 1931 and 1935 arose when the Chinese government responded weakly to Japan's aggressions in Manchuria and North China. During the sixteen years from 1919 to 1935, then, the advent of a massive student movement meant that the nation, and especially the elder generation, was undergoing political humiliation by a foreign power.[60] "The students are the most sensitive fighters, and the foremost sentries in the struggle for liberation of semi-colonial nations," said the noted Chinese writer, Lu Hsun. When war actually broke out in July 1937 the student movement as such vanished; for the foreign humiliator became the direct object for national attack, and generational resentments were absorbed in this larger task.

The student movement was a basic, essential force in the Communist rise to power in China.[61] Yet when Communism was achieved, it was as if all that the student movement had striven for was in vain. Mao Tse-tung came to regard the intellectuals with suspicion. The so-called "Hundred Flowers Movement" of 1956, in which a Hundred Schools (as the phrase went) were called on to "contend with and emulate each other," quickly passed within a year. Students of Peking University were now suspected of planning a demonstration for liberal ideals.[62]

The waves of generational struggle have their own immanence, their relative autonomy, and a Communist system may not dampen them. Communist leaders became concerned over the enmity "between old and new cadres," over their mutual enmity and distrust; Liu Shao-ch'i, their principal theoretician, said that this mutual distrust made for a new form of sectarianism, another form of "mountain-topism"; where one's loyalties had been spatially circumscribed, they were also now temporally bounded.[63] As early as 1940, the Party had been troubled by a "deviation" which they called "Youthism."[64] Mao Tse-tung in his old age wondered whether the next generations, shaped by the Communist economy, would nonetheless be moved to a new, unpredictable revolt. Mao acknowledged that a generational uprising against the Communist order might take place. The journalist Edgar Snow put the question to him: "You have fundamentally changed the environment in China. Many wonder what the younger generation bred under easier conditions will do. What do you think about it?" In reply:

> Mao said he also could not know. He doubted that anyone could be sure. There were however two possibilities: There could be a continued development of the revolution toward communism, or the youth could negate it and make peace with imperialism, bring the remnants of the Chiang Kai-shek clique back to the mainland. . . . He did not hope for counter-revolution but future events would be decided only by future generations. The youth of today and those after them would assess the work of the revolution in accordance with their own values. Man's condition was changing with ever increasing rapidity. A thousand years from now all of them, even Marx, Engels and Lenin, would possibly appear rather ridiculous.[65]

Thus, according to Mao, the values of the next generation might well contravene the socialist economic foundation. Youth might be moved to "negate" the development toward Communism. The will of the younger generation to "negate" the older thus appeared as a relatively independent variable in the workings of history. "Negation of negation" was not merely a phrase for describing a dialectical succession of economic stages; it was perhaps even more basically the dialectical metaphor of generational struggles and their historical outcomes. In 1966, Mao took steps to coalesce the forces of generational struggle with those of the struggle against "imperialism" and "revisionism" as he conceived it.

The "Great Proletarian Cultural Revolution": A Student Movement Incited for Generational Struggle

In June 1966, an unprecedented event took place in the history of student movements; it was the beginning of the so-called "Great Proletarian Cultural Revolution" in China. Mao Tse-tung, the septuagenarian Chairman of the Chinese Communist party, once again assumed his role of fifty years before—that of student leader. To maintain his own hegemony and the supremacy of his own uncompromising stand, Mao enlisted all the potential energies for generational struggle in Chinese society. In order to fight the "old," the "revisionists," the moderates, the "bourgeois intellectuals," to fight the apparatus of the Chinese Communist party itself, Mao unleashed all the generational hatreds for the Chinese gerontocracy. He hoped the new studentry and new youth could recapture the old spirit and relive the experience of the May Fourth Movement and the Long March of 1934–1935. They would re-experience the sense of the student movement and youth as the country's elite, re-experience the back-to-the-people movement, re-experience attacks on their bourgeois professors and bourgeois education. The middle schools and universities were depleted of students and virtually closed for a year. It was a student strike in a new form. The first battalion of Red Guards was organized on May 22, 1966, at the secondary school attached to the Tsinghua University of Technology in Peking. "Their first act was to 'reduce' the school's principal and eight other 'reactionary' teachers to the status of school servants; forcing them to do such chores as sweeping floors and growing vegetables!"[66] At least twenty-two million young Red Guards marched on the cities of China. "We must establish a period of red terror and big disorder," proclaimed a Red Guard directive at Szechuan University, "because only in this way is it possible to create a new world of Mao Tse-tung's ideas." The party's organ, *Jenmin Jih Pao,* on January 14, 1967, said it was the mission of the Red Guard to "crush the old world into pieces and create a new world in the debris." Twelve million Red Guards reached Peking and were reviewed in batches of a million by Mao and his associates. It was a great National Sit-in and Mao March. "Peking was swamped with Guards roving the streets, sleeping in school buildings, eating in huge mess halls or from handouts of householders." Meetings were staged at which the old were attacked—especially the "four old ones"—old ideas, old habits, old culture, and old customs. As in May 1919, old officials were publicly humiliated and sometimes "their harsh treatment caused some deaths." The graves of the old, their art collections, family altars, family furniture, old books, and historical monuments—in short, all symbolic objects of the traditional culture—were destroyed by the Red Guards.[67] According to Radio Peking, "in the afternoon of August 24. a revolutionary fire was ignited in the Central Institute of Fine Arts to destroy the sculpture of emperors." In many places, peasants and workingmen fought the militants of the young generation.

Mao sought to reawaken the Yenan spirit, of the days when comrades dwelled with each other in austere self-sacrifice, comrades in guerrilla warfare. It was the spirit of the young Marx to whom he appealed; intellectuals would be manual workers, and manual workers would be intellectuals—community would overcome alienation.[68] Mao said of the Long March, "It is a manifesto, a propaganda force, a seeding-machine." The "Little Long Marchers" (as they were called) recited his poems, brandished his quotations; detachments walked a thousand kilometers to Peking, telling people on their way that "the education they received at school was basically of a bourgeois character and was utterly divorced from reality."[69] The "Little Long Marchers" had "get-togethers with old workers, old poor peasants, veterans of the Eighth Route Army and revolutionary students; they listened, they said, to old poor peasants telling of their undying hatred for the old order; they pledged to heed Chairman Mao's admonition to learn from the masses."[70] They said the peasants called them the "red descendants of the old Red Army." Their populism merged with anti-intellectualism. With the Party they called for repudiating the "scholar-tyrants," "the bourgeois scholar-tyrants," the "so-called academic authorities."[71] Hundreds of thousands of "revolutionary students" pledged themselves before Mao "to be a generation of pathbreakers." And Mao responded with a dramatic gesture. "The world is yours," he had long told them, "you young people . . . like the sun at eight or nine in the morning. All hopes are placed on you."[72]

Great student congresses were called to affirm the mission of the young Red Guards. Ten thousand Red Guards of Peking's middle schools, according to the *Peking Review*, gathered on March 25, 1967, to found the Congress of Red Guards of the Middle Schools of Peking. Their declaration affirmed the teachings of Mao, the new Red Guard Marxism: "In the last analysis, all the truths of Marxism can be summed up in one sentence: 'To rebel is justified.' "[73] Mao's wife, Chiang Ching, greeted them, saying, "The Red Guard movement was born in Peking's middle schools." Both she and Chou En-lai, the Foreign Minister, praised them for the warfare they were waging against the "four olds," against "the reactionary idea of 'family lineage.' " The Congress of Red Guards of Universities and Colleges in Peking had had a similar session the preceding month.[74] All over the country the "revolutionary students" called for "smashing the old educational system." They quoted Mao's words: the period of schooling should be shortened, the domination of the bourgeois intellectuals should be ended.[75] Grades and examinations, a traditional bugaboo for all student movements, were denounced as devices of Soviet revisionism; the Russians were excoriated for placing "marks above everything." A new man, an ideological man, was sought, not one moved by "economism," by materialistic motives, but one moved by the idealism of which the student movement was the pre-eminent representative.[76] In this way Mao hoped to see the psychology of student movements projected on a nation-wide scale.

Thus generational struggle emerged in the Chinese Communist society. It threatened that society's stability; it threatened the peace of the world, with the posturing of its elitist mission and ability to destroy all opponents; it endorsed Mao's words about the creative mission of destruction. The Soviet Marxists took heed and said the phenomenon reminded them of German fascist youth. In the meantime, the emotions and ferocity of generational struggle were more intense than those which class struggles had elicited.

A Note on the Korean Student Awakening

The Korean student movement, a sister to the Chinese, exhibited the same uniformities of terrorism, suicidalism, elitism, populism, and de-authoritization. As May Fourth was a turning point in the Chinese student movement, so March 1, 1919, prepared the dividing line for the Korean students. As one of the leaders, Kim San, recalled, on that morning his teacher told the class that Korea was independent and that President Wilson at the Peace Conference would defend its independence. Then came bitter disillusionment: "The shock of the betrayal from Versailles that came a few weeks later was so great that I felt as though the heart had been torn out of me. What pathetic, naïve creatures we Koreans were then, believing in words!" Soon student demonstrators were being arrested by the Japanese police and beaten.

> Before March First I had attended church regularly. . . . After this debacle my faith was broken. I thought there was certainly no God and that the teachings of Christ had little application for the world of struggle into which I had been born. . . . I was dissatisfied with all the teachings of my youth. A torment entered my soul and mind. March First was the beginning of my political career. All over Korea, young men felt the same. The desperate terrorist movement followed logically from the tragedy.[77]*

In the background was the generational tension accumulated in the Korean patriarchal family. Kim San was at war with his father even as Mao Tse-tung had been. "At the age of eleven I got into a fight with one of my rivals at school and broke his nose. Father was furious. I defied him and decided to run away from home forever. I have never gone back except for brief visits." His elder brother too ran away from home, stealing some money from the father. "Father would never have anything to do with this truant son after he ran away. He was a stern master of his house, like others of the Confucian patriarchal tradition, and never forgave an offense against filial piety. But Mother came to see my brother and me secretly. . . . Father

* Reprinted from Kim San and Nym Wales, *The Song of Ariran* (New York: John Day, 1941). © 1941 by Nym Wales. By permission of John Day, Inc., Publishers.

was always heavily in debt, so life was constantly difficult for the family." The father was a poor, independent farmer, yet a Korean family was always being humiliated. At the age of seven, Kim witnessed two Japanese policemen slapping his mother's face till she bled. When he wished to strike back, he was told, "Hush, hush. You must never strike back." Thus, the fathers were de-authoritized.

The Korean student movement which emerged veered from self-sacrificial Tolstoyism to terrorism. Underlying the Tolstoyan-terrorist syndrome was the tremendous drive of guilt and the will to destroy the self or others. The students admired Kim Yak-san, "the classical type of terrorist." "He almost never spoke and laughed but spent his time reading in the library. He loved Turgenev's story, *Fathers and Sons,* and read all of Tolstoy. He did not like girls. . . . Many Korean Tolstoyans became terrorists. This is because Tolstoy's philosophy is full of contradictions which are never resolved, hence the necessity for direct action and struggle in a blind attempt at resolution." The Tolstoyan phase, which in Kim's case lasted from middle school to 1922, was one which characterized the formative stage of most Asian student movements:

> Tolstoy has had the greatest total influence in the Far East of any individual, I think, for he has had a broad popularity and following in China, Japan, Korea, India, and elsewhere, as well as Russia. . . . He paved the way for Leninism. . . . There is hardly a modern thinker and writer in the Far East who has not been a Tolstoyan at one time or another.

"From Tolstoy," wrote Kim San, "I learned the philosophy of sacrifice, not only of life, but of desire." The young Tolstoyan renounced love and women. "Man is historical; woman is not. Woman is immediate," he said. Tolstoy's picture of Russia seemed "equally true of Oriental countries in their first period of change"; the motifs of saving the peasants, distributing the land, and giving oneself to the peasantry were there. For the Korean students, like other Asians, it was a journey from Tolstoy through terrorism to Marx.

The Koreans were a "gentle folk, peaceful and quiet and religious." Exasperated, however, by their fathers' passive acquiescence in suffering, the youth turned to terrorism—by means of the bomb, the gun, or the knife. Gentle sons were transformed, wrote Kim, into "fiery individual heroes, seeking immolation in sacrifice. This is a dialectical process." Terrorism became an "integral phase" of the Korean struggle against the Japanese. When Kim San became a medical student, he thought, "There were few doctors in our ranks, and I could aid the wounded terrorists and secure their admittance to hospitals." The principal terrorist group which emerged in 1919 was the Yi Nul Tan, the "Practice Justice Bravely Society." From 1919 to 1924, it carried out three hundred acts of terrorism against the Japanese in Korea. The price the members paid was fearful. "By 1924 nearly 300 of the best and most courageous members of Yi Nul Tan had been killed by the Japanese, and the society was demoralized by the sacrifices which showed so little result. The majority of the remaining Yi Nul Tan joined the Communists and wanted to enter the mass political work. Nearly all remaining former Yi Nul Tan members were killed from 1925 to 1927, fighting for the Chinese Revolution."

And what were these young student terrorists like? Much like their Russian forebears, studying books, practicing sharpshooting, living "like a special cult." "Death was always before them, so they lived life to the full while it lasted. They were a strikingly handsome lot. . . . They were very fond of taking photographs—thinking them always to be their last."

The Korean Communist movement was born out of the ranks of the student movement. "In 1924, the party was created in Korea proper. The first party members in Korea were all ex-Nationalist students. There were no workers among them and no merchants—all intelligentsia." Students were the mainstay of the Communist party during its height from 1926 to 1928, before it was suppressed. "It was easy to see who was a Communist in those days. They were all Bohemians—with long hair and red neckties. They wore old shoes and carefully kept them unpolished in order to appear proletarian, and carried a modern-style thick walking stick. They considered it bourgeois to shave and were all studio Bolsheviks in appearance."

The Korean students first learned their ideology in Japan. "Tokyo then was the Mecca for students all over the Far East and a refuge for revolutionaries of many kinds." Before 1919, there were one to two thousand Korean students in Japan, and in the next years about three thousand or more. One third called themselves "lumpen-intelligentsia." They worked their way through the universities, "usually by pulling jenrickshas." One could live for a whole day on the fare from a single ride. The Japanese-trained students were Tolstoyans in theory and practice, whereas those educated in America mostly became democratic Nationalist leaders; they were "gentlemen." "The Communists are nearly all Japanese-returned students," noted Kim San. The Japanese pogrom of Koreans in the earthquake of September 1923, however, led Korean students to go to China instead for their education. Meanwhile, unemployment confronted the Korean students.

At Peking, the Nationalists and Marxists engaged in ideological debate. The three hundred students in the twenties split into two rival groups, the Nationalist-led faction remaining pro-terrorist while the other, the Communist-led Korean Student Union, renounced terrorism. Seven journals edited by students appeared. Kim San moved from terrorism to Marxism: "Very soon (in 1921) I realized the importance of scientific mass struggle and the futility of *coups d'état* and terrorist acts. I still admired the heroic sacrifices of the terrorists and liked the free spirit of comradeship among my Anarchist friends. But I felt clearly that doom was upon them." He joined the Communist Youth in 1923. Kim Chung-chiang, a Red Buddhist monk, made a Communist of him. They met at a student meeting in the Korean Y.M.C.A. The two Kims and eight others founded a bi-monthly student magazine, *Revolution*, in 1923. The young monk had carried on propaganda in the villages and studied Hegel and Marx. He wrote out the whole magazine of thirty-two pages in his own calligraphy. Asceticism, populism, suicidalism all joined together.

Looking back over his life, Kim San tried to hold on to his faith that the way of self-immolation had been well chosen. "My whole life has been a series of failures. . . . I have had only one victory—over myself." But what was he trying to conquer in himself? He never seemed to know or inquire. "Who shall know the will of history? Only the oppressed who must overthrow force in order to live. . . . Millions of men must die, and tens of millions must suffer before humanity can be born again. I accept this objective fact." Thus, suicidalism merged with death-rationalization.

"I have learned that there is only one important thing—to keep one's close relation with the mass, for the will of the mass is the will of history. This is not easy, for the mass is deep and dark. . . . You must listen for whispers and the eloquence of silence." Thus, a populist mysticism supplanted a religious mysticism. And the self-immolation? "Death is not good or bad. It is either futile or necessary. To be killed fighting voluntarily for a purpose in which you believe is to die happy." "The revolutionaries died happy in their sacrifice; they did not know it was futile. One man's happiness is another man's sorrow. I claim no right to it."

In 1960, a Korean student movement achieved world-wide renown when, apart from the army, it was the leading force in compelling the resignation of the President of Korea, the eighty-five-year-old Syngman Rhee. The usual patterns of de-authoritization of the old and a precipitating incident of police violence against the young welded the students together. Most students a year later gave the "corruption in government" as their primary motivating factor. According to two Korean political scientists, there was "something uniquely Korean about this movement—Korean to the extent that the strongest motivational force of the revolution was the Korean concept of what was 'right' and what was 'wrong.' To this extent, what Aristotle and Mencius (particularly Mencius) said about the causes of a revolution better fits into the Korean pattern." But the ethical conception, the moral condemnation of the elders, has always been a trait of student movements, and though Mencius was closer to the Asian outlook than Aristotle, their moral sense was much the same.[78] At any rate, the students were indignant over the widespread fraud in the "rigged" election of the vice-president, Lee Ki-poong. A demonstration took place, and citizens were killed by the police.

> Then, on April 11, a fisherman in Masan picked up the mutilated body of a high school boy with part of a police tear-gas grenade driven into his skull. There followed a chain-reaction throughout the country, an explosion of the pent-up feelings of hatred and dissatisfaction caused by a variety of factors. . . . Students, particularly college and university students, the carriers of modernization in a repressive traditional oligarchical society of Korea, became the center of the reaction. College and university professors joined in the march. In Seoul, more than one hundred persons died.[79]

The army swung to the students' side. Syngman Rhee resigned, and the unfortunate Lee Ki-poong, together with his entire family, committed suicide. Students and soldiers rejoiced together; a military government, however, came to the fore. The student activists were drawn mostly from the younger and day students; the older and evening students were working, and most had families to support.

The Korean student movement was a typically Asian one, characterized by the revolt against gerontocracy, by its own intellectual elitism, its juvenocracy, its appeal to a higher ethic, and subsequently its conflict with the military elite. It remained to be seen whether it would ally itself in the long run with liberal democratic values.[80]

The De-authoritization of the Elders: The Zengakuren of Japan

A gerontocratic traditional society, as we have said, is not a sufficient condition for the rise of a student movement. There must be above all a feeling that the older generation has discredited itself and lost its moral standing. While such de-authoritization has taken place most often in pre-industrialized countries it can affect so-called "advanced" or industrial societies as well. The Japan of the 1920s was less technologically developed than the Japan of 1960; its government, furthermore, was at that time highly authoritarian, whereas in 1960 it was democratic. Nonetheless, no real student movement arose in the twenties, whereas there was a powerful one in 1960. To be sure, a number of small societies came into existence in 1918 and 1919, largely under the influence of the Bolshevik Revolution. Small in numbers, they bravely raised issues which were to repeat themselves in their sons' minds thirty-five years later; campaigns against war, conscription, and the thought control of the Peace Preservation Law were on their agenda. The Japan Social Science League, the Gakuren, was founded in 1925 with 1,600 members, but it lasted only until 1929; it could not withstand the powerful governmental machine.[81] The prestige of the gerontocracy and military was high during the decade of the thirties. The traditional leadership was evidently taking the Japanese people from one military victory to another; and when their nation stood alone in solitary defiance of the League of Nations, there was a splendor in that gesture which appealed to youthful feelings. This was not an era for a student movement to burgeon. Professor Toshio Kamba, whose daughter Michiko, a Zengakuren militant, died tragically on June 15, 1960, when the students forced the Diet grounds, recalls the contrast between the students of the twenties and those of 1960:

> The student life that I experienced was very different. . . . The student movement at that time could hardly be seen even if we wished to see it. Nevertheless at that time the first sacrifice of the student movement was made. . . .

Indeed, such movement [*sic*] existed, though taken as a whole, they were tiny and slight. Thus in my schooldays I did not know at all there was a student movement.[82]

The Japanese student movement in the mid-twenties had so ephemeral a sociological reality that it escaped the view even of such a qualified observer as Toshio Kamba.

What brought the student movement of Japan into momentous actuality was the tremendous emotional trauma that young students experienced with the defeat of Japan in the Second World War. Traditional authority was undermined as never before. The psychological hegemony of the old was shaken. During four months in Japan in 1960 and 1962, I spent much time with the leaders of Zengakuren in discussion. They generously agreed to reply to many items of an autobiographical questionnaire.[83] In every interview which I had what stood out most sharply was the heightened sense of the conflict of generations on the part of the Zengakuren leaders. Transposed before my eyes was a poignant re-enactment of the drama of Turgenev's *Fathers and Sons*. There follows a sample of autobiographical recollections of Zengakuren leaders.

1. Kenichi Koyama, chairman of Zengakuren, 1956–1958. Kenichi's family had lived in Manchukuo during the war; during the post-war period his father, a chemical engineer, was "drafted" (held prisoner) by the Chinese for work. Koyama describes his experience at the high school in Japan when his family returned:

Especially our teacher in English was bad, and taught us a lot of mistakes. I led a boycott against him by telling all the students of my class to turn in a blank paper on the examination, which we did. The teacher in social studies was no better. Formerly he had taught the national history of Japan according to the ultra-nationalist fashion. I embarrassed him by questioning the validity of the existence of Emperor Jimmu, supposedly the founder of the Japanese Empire. He told us not to smoke, not to wear our hair long. So I talked back to him that he should not smoke or wear his hair long either. The home-room was introduced around this time for the democratization of the everyday life of the students at school.

When the Korean War started, the whereabouts of Kenichi's father were still unknown. Kenichi "began to work by peddling kimonos, wooden clops, and sweets with my younger brother." He began to feel a kinship with the poor. "Getting thus to know people living at the bottom of society, my eyes were opened to the existing social discrepancies." This awakened perception was deepened by a conflict with his uncle, a surrogate father figure. "My uncle, who was a druggist, was a dilettante philosopher. He preached the philosophy of love, while he acted, at least to my eyes, contrary to what he said. In order to refute him, I read Tolstoy and Kitaro Nishida's philosophy. All these experiences contributed to my inclination toward socialism."

2. Akio Takei, first chairman of Zengakuren, 1948–1952:

There were two factors that made me a Communist. The first was out of humanism. The second was the mistrust of the teachers at my senior high school (the Metropolitan Senior High), who converted from militarism to "democracy" overnight in the post-defeat Japan. When I was at the senior high, the members of the Marxian Reading Circle of Tokyo University came to our school to lead us in the movement to expel war criminals among our teachers. I was the chairman of the dormitory "autonomy" of our school during the war. In the spring of 1945, the school authorities abolished the system of "autonomy," and instead installed military officers. . . . The teachers who had abolished the dormitory "autonomy" system now turned into democrats after the war. The movement to expel such teachers was motivated, not by Marxian ideas, but from a revulsion against such turnabouts among the teachers with respect to their beliefs.

3. Yoshinobu Shiokawa, chairman of Zengakuren, 1959, said, "I was happy when I was told that the war was over. After the war I returned to my former school in Tokyo. The teachers who had gone off to the war with such brave words now returned with severe criticism of the military life. This confused me and made me feel that I could not trust their words."

4. Satoshi Kitakoji, chairman of Zengakuren, 1961–1962:

I believed in Japan's victory, and was upset when I heard the news of the mass suicide of the soldiers on the Pacific Islands. I was evacuated to a village during the air raids. Four years after the end of the war, I came back to my city home, and was exposed to the "new education." I thought democracy was a fine thing, since that helped us to protest against the tyranny of the upperclassmen. I organized Red Cross Boys. I joined the staff of the school newspaper, and had to confront the autocratic school principal.

Kitakoji's case is unusual because his father was a Communist. The senior Kitakoji, a high school teacher in Kyoto, lost his position during the ousters of Communist teachers which followed in the aftermath of the Korean War. He then worked in the secretariat of the Japan Teachers' Union. The son Satoshi was deeply affected by his father's expulsion. Nevertheless, a sharp ideological conflict developed between them as the son revolted against the official Communist party in 1959. "My father accused me strong. My father's opinion is moody, not theoretical," the son said to me.[84]

5. Shigeo Shima, secretary-general of Kyosan Shugisha Domei (Communist League), also called the Bund, 1958–1961; also for three years previously, member of the Tokyo Metropolitan Committee of the Japan Communist party; member, Central Executive Committee of Zengakuren, 1956–1958:

My former teacher came back from China, and started a training camp on a farm in Tokyo. He was a rightist, and believed that the true war was to come after defeat in the present war. . . . Immediately after the war, in my high school, a Communist students' cell was organized under the leadership of Takei, the first chairman of Zengakuren. Distrust of teachers was implanted in my mind when I was at the farm training camp. I saw them blackmarketing food. After the war, the teachers, who had been rightists during the war, changed to democracy. I disliked both rightists and leftists. I was opposed to the Red purge, since my father was on the side of the purger. I became interested in Communism. At the time I entered the university, the Korean War started. There was a general feeling of emergency. I felt an inferiority complex toward the Communist party, mingled with the sentiment of rebellion against my parents. Unless one entered the Communist party, it was almost impossible then to be active in the student movement.

6. Mitsuo Nakamura, president, Socialist Student League, 1956–1958: member, Central Executive Committee, Zengakuren, 1956–1957.

Nakamura was unusual in that he wished to denigrate the significance of generational conflict as a cause of student movements: "I don't think the main reason is the conflict of generations, because the conflict itself is caused by the social transformation. It is especially sharp in the peasant families, where peasant beliefs have influenced the older generation. In modern cities, however, the middle class still retains these beliefs."

Nakamura, a student of anthropology, wished to probe the social sources of generational conflict. His own autobiographical remarks, however, sketched an intense drama of bitterness between the generations, the tragedy of the de-authoritization of the fathers in the postwar years.

Mitsuo's father had been an industrialist in Manchuria. He was held prisoner by the Soviet army for nine years after the war. Then he became a Protestant minister. When asked what events or experiences in his own life had contributed to his turning to Communist ideas, Mitsuo replied, "My father's detention in the Soviet Union left within me a tremendous impression. And I think it was out of the sense of atonement for what my father did that I entered the Young Communist League." Probably because of his Christian upbringing Mitsuo tended to use the language of "atonement." He was in the second year of high school when he returned to Japan from Manchuria. "I belonged to the Youth for Christ, and participated in missionary activities on the street." Then he read Kropotkin's *Appeal to the Youth* and the *Communist Manifesto* and joined the Young Communist League, hoping "to make Christianity and Communism compatible." Nakamura felt that his guilt-experience was exceptional among Zengakuren activists:

In my generation, it is almost an exception to enter the political movement out of a sense of collective guilt-conscience. When I was in Manchuria, our family belonged to the upper social stratum, the class enemy of the Chinese people. But when we came back to Japan, our style of life degenerated in such a way as to be at the bottom. The sense of atonement is derived from what my father did when we were in Manchuria. There is a terrific process of dissolution going on within the family among the upper social strata in Japan now. The fathers in their fifties cannot communicate with their sons in their twenties, who rebel against their fathers, feel alienated, and possessed by a sense of ennui and of their being black sheep.

Here then is the alienation of the generations which is the primary cause of student movements; in Nakamura's honest description, it stands out in such phrases as "sense of atonement" for "what my father did," phrases which he reiterated.

Because student movements are founded on generational protest, they do not reach their full momentum on purely economic issues. During the first three or four years after the Second World War, Japanese students were ill-fed, ill-clothed, ill-housed. Malnutrition and tuberculosis were wreaking their toll. Nevertheless, the very first demands which were drawn up by a general meeting of students at the Tokyo University of Commerce on December 5, 1945, were concerned less with such practical matters than with the political struggle of the generations. The students demanded: (1) the dismissal of the president of the university, whom they regarded as fascistic, (2) the abolition of the section for student thought control, (3) the replacement of the university's administrators, (4) the dismissal of reactionary and incapable professors, (5) the participation of the students in the reform of the school system, (6) the establishment of student study societies and autonomous activities.[85]

According to Lawrence Battistini, the underlying stimulus, however, for the unification of Japanese student societies into the Zengakuren was "the over-all agitation of the students against tuition increases that were being put into effect at this time." Nevertheless, it is a remarkable fact that economic demands raised in isolation were not strong matters for agitation. When such issues as the increase in tuition fees were posed without any conjoined demand of generational protest, the militancy engendered was far less than when an outright political, generational issue was the focus of conflict.

The first great student strike in Japan exemplified the primacy of generational revolt over the economic factor. June 1948 was a time of severe postwar economic hardship. That month, however, the Kokugakuren (the Federation of Government University Self-Governing Societies) ascertained that more than half the students at the 180 government schools were opposed to a boycott of increased tuition charges. To assure the militancy required for a nation-wide student strike, the Kokugakuren decided, therefore, to merge its campaign against higher tuition fees with one for the "rehabilitation of education," that is, a greater freedom for student political activity and control of the universities. The general student strike began on June 22, 1948, and continued for five days until June 26; it involved two hundred thousand students and 133 governmental schools. Nonetheless, the higher tuition fees went into effect and, moreover, were accepted by the students, though provisions for scholarships and part-time jobs were increased.

A second general student strike was called by Zengakuren for June 3, 1949. Here the issue was clearly one of generational protest—in this case, opposition to the pending University Administration Bill. Zengakuren proposed that it should be represented in the central administrations of the universities; it wanted an end to all repressive measures on student life. Such strikes over generational issues invariably tended to provoke violence, sometimes violence of a crude sort. At Kyoto, for instance, two hundred students staged a sit-down strike and held the university president prisoner in his office. Three hundred policemen liberated him. The strike itself lasted a month and a half. Anti-Americanism soon provided a new vent for generational protest. In 1950, an American speaker, Dr. Walter Eells, embarked on a lecture tour of Japanese universities to call for the ouster of Communist professors. In the minds of Zengakuren activists, he was promoting a restoration of the discredited persons of the old order. The Americans were abetting the counterrevolution of the fathers. Dr. Eells became a national issue as students disrupted his lectures. Soon stones were being thrown at American soldiers in Tokyo. With the outbreak of the Korean War, the police raided more than fifty Zengakuren offices but wisely forebore dissolving the organization. A proliferation of incidents now ensued. The so-called emperor incident at Kyoto University in November 1950 saw a thousand students picketing with placards, "No More Deification of the Emperor," "No More Wars." On May Day 1952, a demonstration of ten thousand, principally students, zigzagged their way into the Imperial Plaza and set fire to fourteen American cars; one student was killed, many injured, and ninety-seven were arrested.[86]

As Zengakuren became increasingly the vehicle of generational protest, and predominantly concerned with the political issues of peace and a new society, as it relegated to the background economic issues of student welfare, the numbers of its membership grew proportionately:[87]

1952	80,000
1953	151,000
1955	180,000
1956	233,000
1957	264,000
1958	280,000

Efforts to found a competing national student organization which would stress student welfare and economic issues came to grief. In 1952, for instance, a General Federation of Student Associations (Gakusei-Sokyo) undertook to capture the self-governing associations from Zengakuren. The newcomer emphasized such items as opposition to increased tuition fees and advocacy of a student health insurance plan. But Zengakuren's anti-rearmament and peace demands had a far more potent appeal.[88] Indeed, when in June 1955 Zengakuren briefly undertook to transform itself into a student welfare organization, devoted to cultural and sports activities and the questions of campus life, the attempt miscarried. That interlude was the product of the new line for the Communist party which stemmed from Nikita Khrushchev's policy of liberalization. Zengakuren for the first time in its history held a ball for its members. Membership declined as the Communist party urged students to return to their studies. The student movement seemed in the doldrums. But the energies of generational revolt could not dance themselves away or be confined to petty campus politics. Militant Zengakuren leaders, previously expelled from the Communist party, soon ousted the Party from its positions of control. A third general student strike took place in May 1956 as a twofold demonstration: first, against the testing of hydrogen bombs by the United States; and second, against the Japanese government, which was accused of trying to return to prewar practices for the suppression of free thought and speech.[89] For a while Zengakuren activists in the so-called Renovationist group had a bold plan to seize control of the Communist party; indeed, for a brief period they controlled a majority of the Tokyo Communist Metropolitan Committee.[90] Soon, however, the Zengakuren activists, expelled in droves from the Communist party, were leading their organization in a dual generational revolt: first, against the tired old Communist bureaucrats; and second, against the governmental bureaucrats. The "bureaucracy" against which they always inveighed coincided curiously with the old men, the gerontocracy. No established Communist party, we might note, has ever been comfortable with a student movement, for generational revolt can strike against a deauthoritized Communist elder generation as well as any other.

PORTRAIT OF A JAPANESE STUDENT LEADER

The word "Zengakuren" entered the international political vocabulary in June 1960, when zigzagging lines of thousands of students jogged up and down around the Diet buildings in Tokyo to the chant of their ancient folk ritual, "*Wassho! Wassho!*" Zengakuren, the National Federation of Student Self-Government Associations, had at that time more than three hundred thousand members, and their initiative brought forth the largest movement of mass democratic protest which Japan has ever experienced. The Japanese students played a major part in overthrowing the cabinet and reversing their government's decision to welcome a President of the United States.[91] The United States State Department denounced them as Communists; the Japanese Communist party denounced them as Trotskyites.

When, that winter, I asked Japanese socialists, Communists, and liberals about the Zengakuren leaders, I found the elders knew little about their sons. I received the most diverse answers: they were Communists, they were existentialists, they were Trotskyites, they began to read Trotsky after they were called Trotskyites, they were Maoists, they were rich boys indulging themselves in a political pastime, they were poor university students who resented the social system, they were the vanguard of a new political movement, they were inarticulate nationalists, they were sexually repressed young men, they were sexually free young men who had lost the discipline of family, they were naïve young men who were misled by underpaid radical professors, they were bold young men who had swept timid professors for the first time into political participation, they were revolting against the Japanese cultural superego, they were creating a new social consciousness in a Japanese world dominated by corruption, indifference, and moral callousness. When I interviewed the leaders of Zengakuren, I found myself transported back to the setting of the Russian student movement at the end of the nineteenth century. Kenichi Koyama, president of the Zengakuren from 1956 to 1958 and its general secretary from 1955 to 1956, might well have changed places with Peter Struve, Julius Martov, or Vladimir Ulyanov.

Koyama I found living with his parents and two brothers in a modest, pleasant house in the Mitakashi district in the outskirts of Tokyo. He was not the untroubled campus politician but an earnest young man, deeply concerned with the philosophical basis of life, and seeking with his friends a way for his people to surmount the legacy of an anxiety-haunted culture. Koyama was twenty-seven years old, a graduate student in economics at Tokyo University. His horn-rimmed glasses and his zippered sweater seemed a natural part of the room lined with books, and for a moment I found it hard to identify him as the agitator who, in the turmoil of the previous spring's riots, had climbed a gate to address the police. He spoke English hesitantly but, as our talks continued, with growing self-confidence, and finally we conversed without an interpreter.

I observed that Koyama had on his bookshelves the works of Marx, Lenin, and Trotsky. Yes, he replied, his basic work as a graduate student was in Marxian economics and the theory of imperialism. He showed no interest in the theory of economic planning or its Soviet practice; his theoretical concerns were very much like those of Marxist graduate students in America in 1935. He had old German editions of such works of Trotsky as *Literature and Revolution* and the Japanese copies of *The Revolution Betrayed* and *My Life*.

I asked Koyama, who was himself "purged" by the Communists in June 1958, to explain the differences between the "mainstream" of the Zengakuren and the Japanese Communist party. He told a story of generational conflict. There had been discord between the Communists and the Zengakuren as soon as the student group was formed. At the outset, in 1948, the Communists disliked the idea of a mass student organization; they preferred an elite organization which they would be able to control more easily. But the student self-governing associations proliferated after the Second World War; the returning veterans were very radical. The struggle against higher tuition was the original economic basis for Zengakuren's nation-wide organizing drive. Its first leaders were Communists, and their slogan was: *Heiwa, Minshushugi, Yoriyoi Gakuseiseikatsu* ("Peace, Democracy and the Betterment of Student Life"). It was not long, however, before ideological issues superseded economic ones. The Zengakuren undertook to drive from the academic halls those professors who had been apologists for militarism during the war. They organized boycotts, petitions, rallies, and in many cases achieved their aims.

The differences with the Communists became especially acute in 1956, Koyama said. The students took Khrushchev's speech on Stalin's crimes far more seriously than did the Communist party. The Communist bureaucrats tried to pass it all off, but the students continued to ask why the Communist movement had been perverted from its original aims and ideals. They began to collect and study old documents and the history of the Comintern. They read attentively the dramatic pages of Trotsky's *History of the Russian Revolution.* The Communist elder generation, we might say, became de-authoritized in the mind of the young. Generational differences then took on an ideological form.

The Communists maintained that Japan had become a colony of the United States, and the struggle against imperialism was one of the Japanese nation against the American empire. To the Zengakuren, on the other hand, the fight was essentially one between the Japanese working class and Japanese imperialists. The Communist party maintained that the security treaty with the United States was a device for promoting the colonization of Japan. The Zengakuren objected to the treaty on the grounds that it might help revive Japanese imperialism. Koyama admitted that many demonstrators had crudely identified anti-imperialism with anti-Americanism, but he denied that this had ever been the standpoint of the "mainstream" of the Zengakuren.

I remarked to Koyama that it was hard to believe that there was any real possibility for a revival of Japanese imperialism; it was quite shorn of aggressive military power, I said, and incapable of exploiting other areas by political control. I found the Zengakuren's definition of its enemy unreal and as unconvincing as the Communists' claim that American "imperialism" threatened the world. Koyama replied that they no longer understood "imperialism" in Lenin's prewar sense, but rather as referring to the continuing dominance of Japanese state power by economic monopolies, which were beginning to look to Southeast Asia and Africa for new markets to exploit.

During the early postwar years, Koyama went on, the Zengakuren respected the Communists as the only political group which had consistently fought the militarists and fascists during the war and prewar years; they were the sole bearers of the revolutionary creed. But, as the years went on, the revolutionary heroes congealed into the tired, obsolescent bureaucrats of Yoyogi (the popular nickname for the Communist party, referring to the location of its headquarters). They oscillated fitfully from "Right opportunist" to "Left opportunist" policies. During 1950 to 1952, under the pressure of the Cominform, the Communists decreed the "fire bottle" policy, urging their members to throw home-made bombs at police boxes. They even tried to emulate the Chinese Communists of Yenan in 1930 by setting up a kind of imitation soviet in the mountain area of Ogochi and organizing a nuclear self-defense corps there. Several years later, however, they forsook violent tactics and announced their intention to become the people's "beloved party."

In 1958, Koyama said, the party's relations with the Zengakuren disintegrated. The student leaders were expelled from the party, and the Zengakuren Communist faction retaliated with a resolution calling for the expulsion of the entire Central Committee of the Communist party. The Communist apparatus, in turn, responded by expelling one thousand students from the party's ranks. When Koyama was expelled, the Communist organ, *The Red Flag,* labeled him, together with many others, as a "traitor to the working class" and an "agent of American imperialism."

At the height of the June 1960 demonstrations, the Communist newspaper devoted more space to denouncing the "Trotskyist provocateurs" of the Zengakuren than to supporting the aims of the demonstrations. The Communists accused the student federation of responsibility for the death of Michiko Kamba, the young woman student of Tokyo University who was one of the leaders of the demonstration, and refused to attend her funeral. The Communists, according to Koyama, feared that the Zengakuren might become the basis for a new independent Left movement. The middle-aged, chair-bound bureaucrats of Yoyogi were panic-stricken by the fact that in the first genuine mass movement in Japanese history the Communist party had exercised no leadership.

It was with Koyama's help that I met and talked with almost all the other leaders of Zengakuren. Most of them were the sons of middle-class families. Koyama's father is a chemist; the father of Shugo Nukaya, chairman of the United Front Committee, was a retail merchant; Hiroyoshi Hayashi, of the Executive Committee, was the son of a high school principal; Yoshihisa Fujiwara, secretary of the Socialist Student League, was a doctor's son; Shimizu, the head of the International Affairs Committee, was the son of a music teacher in an elementary school; Nobuo Aruga, chairman of the Tokyo University Autonomous Society, was the son of a municipal civil servant. The one Zengakuren officer who came from a wealthy family was Yoshimobu Shiokawa, president of the organization for six months in 1959.

In any case, the unrest which Zengakuren has channeled could not be explained on grounds of economic determinism. The opportunities for employment for university graduates in Japan had never been as good as they were in 1960.[92] Almost every graduate was finding a position in business, government, teaching, or journalism. The political ferment among Japanese students was not based on the kind of unemployment which oppressed the intellectuals in India. To some extent, the Zengakuren did express the feelings of a new generation of university students who came from social classes which previously had had less of an opportunity for higher education. Almost all of them experienced in their childhood the searing dislocation of war—their homes in flames, evacuations from the city, bewildered parents, the atomic bomb. Above all, the Japanese family, with its father so often de-authoritized by war's defeat, became the locus for an intense conflict of generations.

Occasionally one met a Zengakuren leader whose personal experience of poverty had been a determining fact. One evening Manabu Tanaka, a member of the Tokyo Executive Committee, told me his story. His father was a small farmer in Hiroshima; poverty was the family's daily lot. "Then," he said, "when I entered Tokyo University, I read Marx." For almost all the Zengakuren leaders, reading Marx was an experience which illuminated the darkness of their everyday lives. Many Japanese students, living on sparse diets, survive by working at all sorts of jobs outside of school. The *arbeit-student,* as he is called, is a familiar phenomenon on Tokyo campuses. The working student, however, is not apt to be a Zengakuren activist. Economic opportunity and self-interest in the future expanding economy beckon to Japanese students.

The Zengakuren leaders devoted long hours to their political activities. Puritan revolutionists, they had little leisure time for theater, games, or romance. They worked in a dilapidated, ramshackle store which had been converted into a national headquarters; the seats were skeletons which had long ago lost their backs, and the floors, table, and walls were littered with dusty batches of incendiary handbills and leaflets. Koyama slept on these floors during the June 1960 demonstrations, and the long nights left him with tuberculous lungs, an affliction common among Japanese intellectuals.

What deeply concerned Koyama and his friends was the appearance of "Blanquist" tendencies among the new, inexperienced leaders of the Zengakuren. It had been many years since I had heard the term "Blanquism" used in any serious political discussion, but in Japan it represented a very live potential in the student movement. When I asked the new Zengakuren leaders what work they wished to pursue when they were older, they replied without exception, "Professional revolutionary." These students were regarded as so extreme that they could not expect to obtain jobs in any of the large trade unions. Moreover, their messianic and elitist tactics estranged them from the Japanese working class. In the summer of 1960 a group of new Zengakuren leaders decided to intervene in the Miike miners' strike, which had been going on for several months under conditions of hardship and bitterness. The student activists summoned the miners to follow them on more adventurous paths. The miners would have nothing to do with them and finally ordered them "out of town."[93] Both socialists and Communists strongly condemned the students, who reacted by becoming more doggedly Blanquist, convinced that the "opportunism" of the existing Leftist parties had led to the miners' defeat.

The Japanese student movement in 1960 was one of the most "alienated" in the world. I asked the Zengakuren leaders whom they admired among contemporary statesmen. They admired no one, they replied, not Nikita Khrushchev, not Tito, not Mao Tse-tung. They respected Mao's way of life but criticized his ideology as too conservative. The Tokyo University chairman, for instance, thought that Mao was still laboring under the illusion that "coexistence" was possible. Among the men of the past, only Marx and Lenin were regarded as truly great. When I asked the Zengakuren leaders whether there was anyone in all Japanese history whom they admired and whose work and achievement might guide their own, they said there was no one. They were the most traditionless of revolutionaries in a society where tradition is most powerful. "To deny completely is to create," one of them said to me.

Despite its nihilism, the Zengakuren had somehow remained in the Communist-controlled International Union of Students (IUS), which had its headquarters in Prague. They took their membership in the IUS seriously, despatched delegates to its annual conferences and received from it large batches of propaganda material. Koyama, who was a delegate to Prague in 1955, told me that even prior to the Hungarian revolt, differences of opinion were being sharply debated in the IUS. The West European students constituted the Right wing; the Chinese, Japanese, and Arabs were the Left wing; and the Soviet students were the Center. The Zengakuren pressed for a strong anti-imperialist line; the Soviet students wanted a program for peace and friendship. When the Soviet representatives advised Koyama to read Lenin's *Left-Wing Communism: An Infantile Disorder*, he responded by telling them to read *What Is to be Done?* The battle of the pamphlets was temporarily resolved in a compromise resolution.

Lenin's elitist tract *What Is to be Done?* has an unusual authority among the Japanese student leaders. Once I said that the vocation of a "professional revolutionary" might have made sense in Tsarist Russia, where the people were denied channels of democratic expression, but that in Japan today it would isolate one from the realities of contemporary life. The former general secretary of Zengakuren, Takeo Shimizu, told me I was wrong. Lenin's *What Is to be Done?*, he said, with its concept of a party of professional revolutionaries, applied fully to Japan in its present circumstances. A rigid bureaucracy dominated Japanese life, he continued, and it embraced all political parties. "Bureaucracy" was the favorite denunciatory word of the Japanese student leaders; it had the same overtones as their American counterparts' use of "Establishment."

Latent in their Blanquism was the tendency towards advocacy of dictatorial rule by a self-constituted elite of intellectuals. This tendency clothed itself in the Marxist-Leninist language which most Japanese intellectuals speak. I had a long meeting with three young graduate students in political science who had been leading activists in the June demonstrations. One of them, who had been badly beaten by the police, confidently affirmed—despite his Marxist training and affiliations—that the bearers of the world-historical mission today were the intellectual class.

The Tokyo University students, a Communist party secretary told me, had a special sense of belonging to an elite. Before the war, he said, Tokyo graduates had the brightest future, and there were Tokyo cliques in business and government. He believed that this elitism has now been transferred back into the ideological field. On the whole, it was true that the ablest students were generally taking the revolutionary initiative. Tokyo University, whose student body was the most militant and politically involved, had the most difficult entrance requirements and was the haven for brilliant students from poor families; its tuition requirements, as a government university, were the lowest. On the other hand, the studentry of Nippon University, a large private institution with low entrance requirements, was the least politically involved.

The Japanese student movement was beset by intolerant factionalisms. The Communist party withdrew its members from the Zengakuren Executive Committee. The character of personal leadership generally determined whether the studentries took a Communist or non-Communist (mainstream) direction. The non-Communist mainstream was in the ascendancy at Tokyo, Meiji, Chuo, Waseda, and Tama Fine Arts; but at Hosei, Ochanomizu, the evening session of Chuo, and the literature department at Waseda, the Communist faction was dominant.

The largest group of Zengakuren leaders were students of economics. They pored over the volumes of Marx's *Capital*, and argued the validity of the law of the declining rate of profit with a subtlety which evolved from the logical to the theological. The most gifted of them had got beyond Volume III, which was the Marxian barrier to the erudite American activist of the 1930s; on the Tokyo campus, one saw them with the German edition of Volume IV, the recondite *Theories of Surplus Value*. It seemed a strange scholasticism, particularly when one met Marxist professors who were elaborating combinations of the Marxist dialectric with Zen nothingness; but when one talked with textile workers, miners, and teachers, it came home with force that Japan is, in many ways, the most classically capitalistic country in the world today. It would have taken an Engels to write, as he did for Manchester in 1844, a *Condition of the Working Classes in Japan in 1960*.

The student leaders were young romantics seeking to lift their people out of submissive attitudes and abnegation before authority; they had a faith in the sheer force of their own will. They would quote long passages from Wordsworth's nature poetry and Heine's love songs; they read Pushkin, Chekhov, and Turgenev. They seemed poised between a politics of revolutionary romanticism and a Bakuninist blend of self-destructiveness together with the sheerest aggressive adventures. They lived in a world peopled in large part by unrealities born of their own real frustrations. They reveled in words of revolt and were susceptible to an "anti-American" fever.

One sensed a deep striving within the Japanese student movement for a new ethic and way of life. I watched the students one night during the great demonstrations at Hibiya Park when they were protesting the murder of Inejiro Asanuma, the socialist leader. They spoke of Asanuma as a rare intellectual who had lived his philosophy; they told how Asanuma had gone directly from his graduation at Waseda to work in one labor union after another, how he had lived all his life in a small apartment in a working-class neighborhood. The students' associations and labor unions were grouped under hundreds of banners and lanterns which punctuated the darkness with their light. In moments between speeches and parades, they clasped each other's arms and waists and, swaying to and fro, sang new songs: "The Song of Happiness," "Let us link the world with a garland of flowers." They told me that this sort of singing had begun only after the war, and that they preferred these new songs to the old, more ponderous revolutionary anthems. This young generation had undertaken to undermine a two-thousand-year tradition of masochistic self-denial, and one could but wish them well. Yet one wondered whether they too would founder in the irrational politics of generational revolt.

Nineteen-sixty saw the zenith of Zengakuren's power. Shortly thereafter came disillusionment, factionalism, nihilism. A new generation shortly entered the universities, a generation which had no memories of the war years, none of the experience of de-authoritization of the fathers.[94] Japan's prosperity and economic growth were unparalleled. The Japanese student movement receded into a perhaps cyclical phase of decline.

The Japanese student movement then fell apart, among other reasons, precisely because of the propensity of student movements to violence. The various factions showed a mutual intolerance which kept turning meetings into brawls. Idealism was a bedfellow of contempt for others' freedom of speech; self-sacrifice joined with the will to suppress others. In 1962, for instance, a meeting held to commemorate Michiko Kamba, the girl student martyred two years before, degenerated into a bedlam of violence and intolerance. Though the meeting was organized by Zengakuren, students of the mainstream itself (the Federation of Marxist Students) massed in the front ten rows, heckled the speakers, and disrupted the session. The socialist representative "was greeted with catcalls, boos and cries of 'Go home, Asukata!' repeated in a chanting chorus." A Leftist woman speaker dared to reproach the students. According to the newspaper account, "Pandemonium broke out when Miss Matsuoka suggested to the students, 'You should listen to opinions even when you don't agree with them.' Anything she might have said after that was not recorded. Amid the shrieks and catcalls, not a word she said could be heard." When the chairman of Zengakuren, Jin Nemoto, got up to speak, a barrage of heckling and hooting opened up from another part of the auditorium. Another faction, the anti-mainstream Federation of Socialist Students, took its turn to be disruptive. Then when its leader rose to speak, "all hell broke loose for the third time." When the speaker was hit with a flagpole, "a free-for-all ensued. . . . Blows were exchanged between members of the rival factions on the stage. Savage brawls broke out in the body of the hall." Then commenced the showing of a film dealing with the events of June 15 two years before. "Suddenly, in the middle of the film, someone set off smoke bombs on the stage." Firemen rushed to the fore, and things came to a halt again. A new speaker chanced to use the word "actuality." "Immediately, there was a shout from the hall, 'What the hell, we can't understand high-falutin' words like that!' " Once more there were catcalls, boos, and jeers. Professor Ikutaro Shimizu, once a spiritual leader of the students, tried to speak, but "was drowned out in a chorus of boos and shouts."

The mother of Michiko Kamba subsequently wrote "An Open Letter to Mr. Kitakoji, a Leader of the Student Movement," a moving document in its inquiry into how idealism and self-sacrifice could evolve into gangsterism and intolerance:

> "For pity's sake, stop using my daughter's name for your dirty ends!" . . . I trembled uncontrollably with rage and sorrow. It was then that I realized that I would get hurt if I fought against the Zengakuren mainstreamers. . . . Michiko used to tell me: "We must be pure in heart; we might get hurt, but we shouldn't be afraid of that." I too am no longer afraid of getting hurt. My daughter Michiko was pure in heart, just as you would expect a young girl at school to be. Since Michiko was pure in heart I supposed the student movement to which she belonged was an association of young people who were decent and honest. I was totally betrayed. The Zengakuren students are no different from political racketeers, hoodlums and gangsters![95]

The Japanese student movement thus for all its heroism and self-sacrifice failed to instill in its adherents a dedication to the values of liberal democracy. During the last years its annals have recorded a series of forays into violence; it has become enamored of demonstrations. When demonstrations, instead of marking an unusual situation, become the normal political tactic of protest, they inevitably suggest that the procedures of liberal democracy have been rejected. The fixation on demonstrations always forebodes an attack on democratic institutions. The internecine warfare between the student sects has never flagged; if anything, it has tended to become more violent. "Hired thugs, wooden swords, and bare bayonets" were so much used in 1962 by contending factions that the Japanese press referred to the struggle "as the mainstream 'Zengakuren West Side Story' after the popular American play and film about gangs and hooligans on the streets of New York."[96] The new "Fourth Generation" of Japanese society, however, has grown up without having experienced the trauma of the de-authoritization of the elders. As George R. Packard writes:

> Born in the years of defeat, today's 20-year-old cannot remember the Emperor's surrender message, General MacArthur, the black markets, the rubble, and the hunger. He began first grade the year Japan regained its independence and finished ninth grade in 1960, too young to participate in the riots over the security treaty that year. From earliest memory, the economic miracle of Japan's recovery, not Japan's defeat, has been the natural order of things, a basic fact of life, and today, with per capita national income standing at $565 and rising fast, his is the first generation of Asians that can look forward to enjoying life in a relatively affluent society.[97]

Competition for jobs remains keen among Japanese college graduates. Moreover, Japanese universities grow ever more impersonal as they expand to accommodate a studentry which in 1963 included 15.7 per cent of the total youth of that age bracket; indeed, the Japanese percentage of youths in the universities was higher than that of Britain, France, or West Germany.[98] The "exam hell" is still taking its toll of the Japanese studentry, and probably contributes to the fact that the suicide rate for the age group fifteen to nineteen is the highest in the world.[99] Nevertheless, Zengakuren, with its nine factions and subfactions, has been in visible decline; "especially in the last four years," noted an observer in 1964, "the total number of Japanese students who take part in the programs organized by all or any one of these Zengakurens has been steadily going down."[100]

Zengakuren's failure was the consequence, in large part, of its inability to abide by democratic processes. And as the new "Fourth Generation" came to maturity with an ethos in which generational struggle had lost its intensity, the factions of Zengakuren appeared more bizarre and pathological to the average student and no longer expressive of his unconscious. When some incidents of unusual armed violence occurred at Waseda University in 1964 between two Zengakuren factions, the student newspaper the *Waseda Guardian* characterized them as "too active, nervous, and emotional."[101] An era of relative generational equilibrium seemed possible.

And what happened to the Japanese student leaders of 1960 in their later lives? Seven years later a majority of them were young university teachers, junior corporation executives, lawyers, or public school teachers. Of the three chairmen in the period of 1960, Kenichi Koyama was a lecturer in economics at Gakushuin University, and mastering computer science; Yoshinobu Shiokawa was a tutor at Tokyo; Kentaro Karoji was running a "Let's Go Sailing Club." Another leader was involved with gangsters in anti-union activities. Takeo Shimizu, an exception, was working for a small non-Communist leftist publishing firm.[102] Critics derided the tranformations as capitulations to a corrupt society. The deeper truth, however, was that political action founded on obscure emotions of generational rebellion tends to terminate with the end of that generational phase.

The Indonesian Students Run Amok: The Massacre of October 1965

In the revolutionary and post-revolutionary years after 1945, Indonesian youth was in revolt against the traditional society of the villages which located final responsibility in the hands of the village elders. Many, indeed, felt their estrangement so much they drifted into banditry. "Encouraging many youths in their drift away from society was the dimly sensed feeling that the caliber of their individual contributions and sacrifices should have culminated in something more than the dubious advantages of settling down into a village life."[103] The post-revolutionary youth, alienated from traditional society, responded to Sukarno's "guided democracy" and the appeal of the Communist party. But as Jeanne Mintz wrote in 1965, "For Communists as other politicians, there comes a day of reckoning. Promises must one day be redeemed. That day is not yet upon the PKI (Indonesian Communist Party), but it has had to contend with dissatisfied and increasingly restless elements among its supporters."[104]

The Indonesian studentry had from its inception a tradition of elitism; students from aristocratic families, finding their avenues to power and place blocked by the Dutch colonial regime, founded the first nationalist movement.[105] To the new student youth of 1965, the revolutionaries of '45 seemed to have betrayed the promises of independence. They were consequently reduced in the students' eyes to a collection of de-authoritized elders fit for removal.

The Indonesian student movement in 1965 joined forces with the military to take measures against the Communist party. In October of that year the Indonesian Communist party, or some part of it, was involved in an insurrectionary attempt which began with the murder of six generals. It was widely believed that President Sukarno, who had led the country to independence twenty years earlier in 1945–1946, and had transformed his regime in the name of "guided democracy" into a personal dictatorship, was privy to the Communist plot. The reprisals against the Communists took on the character of a nation running amok, a national lynching party, which the students often led. Under the leadership of the Action Command, the students mounted demonstrations demanding an end to the Communist party; their actions soon went far beyond demonstrations, into terrorism and murder.[106] "My students went right out with the army," said one teacher in a village near Jogjakarta. "They pointed out P.K.I. members. The army shot them on the spot." In Bandung a student leader said that his group had turned in at least five hundred Communists to the army. In Solo, a town in Central Java, a member of the student group which joined with the army in its operation claimed that they had accounted for 1,290 Communists.[107] Another correspondent reported, "University students were armed and trained before being turned loose to round up the Communist and Youth Corps cadres who had dominated the city (Solo) and the outlying areas. According to a participant, the students slew 2,000, usually by bullets in the neck, before the Army called off the slaughter." The university students began the killing of Communists directly after the army had recaptured the town from a dissident battalion which had supported a "people's government" for about twenty days.[108]

By the spring of 1966, the students were recognized as "one of the country's most powerful political forces." The correspondent for *The New York Times* wrote, "Indonesia's students went into the streets of Jakarta again and every politician and Cabinet minister stopped to watch what they were doing." Within the previous month, they had, "with deadly efficiency, sacked Government Ministries, made a rush at Mr. Sukarno's palace and generally brought life in Jakarta to a standstill." There was now "a question in the minds of many Indonesians whether the armed forces were leading the students, or the students, through their courage, energy and organization, were forcing army leaders to stand up to Mr. Sukarno and make him oust the palace group surrounding him."

The students had listened for years to Sukarno's speeches; now they were disillusioned. They listened instead to their own leaders, to Zamrony behind the microphone, "a short, chunky student leader with a voice and platform manner that caused even a stranger who did not understand Indonesian to listen."[109] Their organization, capacity for mobilization and expression, and sense of confidence made the estimated two hundred thousand university students of Indonesia its one genuine civilian political force. It was a force that had all the power which comes from the readiness to act and self-sacrifice. And at this juncture, with all their propensity to violence, they avowed liberal goals—a free press, free expression, as well as cheaper food and clothing.

Underlying the outburst of student atrocities was the bitter resentment against a whole generation whose leaders had failed to fulfill the hopes raised by independence. The Indonesian student faced a dismal prospect—either unemployment or miserable subsistence in a swollen, parasitic bureaucracy. Unemployed university graduates in law and the social sciences abounded; over thirty thousand would-be teachers found themselves, as early as 1958, jobless because of lags in the construction of schools.[110] The bureaucracy grew from 280,000 in 1940 to nearly two million in 1958; it was inefficient, lazy, apathetic, defeatist.[111] Indonesian students still turned in largest numbers to law and political science rather than to technology. This had been the trend under Dutch colonial rule but it still prevailed after independence. In the year 1953–1954, of the 14,622 students in the two biggest state universities, the University of Indonesia and Gadjah Mahda University, the largest group, or 37 per cent (5,530 students), were attending the faculties of law, social science, and political science, while engineering drew only 23.8 per cent (3,467 students), and agriculture only 5 per cent (736 students). As the anthropologist Clifford Geertz wrote, the bureaucracy and the educational system were locked in a "self-perpetuating circle of distension" in which the second produced more and more diplomaed graduates which the first was forced to absorb.[112] The students, moreover, lived under a perpetual anxiety: would they succeed in finding their niche in the bureaucratic elite, already swollen with the smug members of previous generations? Dishonesty and violence became rampant: "Public pressure on teachers and examining boards has ranged from instances of parental attempts at bribery, to kidnapping and seizure of teachers as hostages by students wishing to pass examinations. Refusal to be intimidated has brought cries of alleged 'colonialist.'" The cult of titles and diplomas blended with the aversion of the traditional hereditary nobility to whatever smacked of labor and technology.[113] Political activity, with its promise of an elitist role of leadership, remained in contemporary Indonesia, as it had been under the Dutch, "the indicated path for those who, with varying degrees of schooling, were unable to satisfy their status ambitions."[114] A politics of destroying the defeated elder generation was the most primitive means for opening the bureaucracy to the students.

The "guided democracy" of Sukarno, conceived unconsciously in generational terms, had had within it the seeds of generational conflict. "The Generation of '45" was recognized as the dominant functional group in the national council comprised of labor, youth, peasants, intellectuals, and entrepreneurs.[115] When students at the University of Indonesia in 1959 protested the hegemony of "the Generation of '45" and the Communists, and complained about the defacing of their buildings with the slogans of guided democracy, a Communist gang replied with warning fire from a Sten gun.[116] Though the Generation was not a party in the ordinary political sense, it was recognized as a political entity, and given cabinet posts. The Communists, at first restive about recognizing a generational group, accepted the arrangement.[117] For both sought to appeal to the new bureaucrats, offering to "the middle classes, constituting barely 10 per cent of Indonesian society, a place in the new order, promising them the prestige and security of the straw boss and bureaucrat."[118]

The generational resentment that the Indonesian students held against the entrenched older, de-authoritized bureaucrats was well founded. But if historical experience is any guide, one may also believe that participation by the Indonesian student movement in the massacre of 1965 will not in the long run have proved to be a contribution to liberal democracy. Once more it imposed on the historical process bitter hatred and irrationality—the dark emotional projections of the unconscious of the sons in traditional society.

The Relative Absence of an Indian Student Movement

The Indian studentry lives under conditions of hardship and impoverishment. A survey in Calcutta in 1954 found:

Of nearly 70,000 students enrolled at the University and its affiliated colleges, 23,000 live with their families with an average total floor space of barely 24 square feet. Possibilities for studying at home are, therefore, virtually non-existent. Many a student does his work by the light of a street lamp or on a railway platform. The poverty of the students is reflected in the fact that 13,000 come from families whose *per capita* monthly income is less than

SF 27, and another 14,000 are from families whose *per capita* income is between SF 27 and SF 45. About 43 per cent of the students suffer from malnutrition.[119]

India, however, is notable among Asian countries in having no massive student movement. This difference is not due to an absence of generational conflict. On the contrary, incidents of such conflict in the universities are numerous and significant. What has inhibited the rise of a student movement has been that a political de-authoritization of the elder generation has not taken place. Above all, national independence was achieved successfully by nonviolent means and constitutional processes. If the student movement before the Second World War had had its way, it would have chosen violence. Mahatma Gandhi, Pandit Nehru, and the Congress party, however, kept the people's allegiance and succeeded in their policy. During the years of independence, the government has pursued, despite numerous difficulties, its policies of industrialization, community development, and birth control. Communist China's military incursions into Tibet and Northern India, moreover, embarrassed the Communist movement in the students' eyes. The government meanwhile has systematically discouraged student political activity. On the whole, student demonstrations and other activities have been directed toward amelioration of their material conditions as students.

By 1938, before the Second World War, student unions were to be found in almost every important educational center in India. In 1936, the All-India Students Federation was organized, with a program which included fighting for students' rights and for national freedom.[120] The prospects of unemployment and frustrated ambitions for upward mobility loomed gloomily before the students. The publications of the Indian students (like the Russian students' literature of the 1890s) told of student suicides and autocratic university authorities. One student committed suicide after he had been flogged for attending a public meeting; another student who had been caned committed suicide. The elders were denounced; the students spoke of the strains of the "matric [matriculation] massacre," the terrible significance of failure in the "ruin of career." University officials were described as "the Neroes of the university," who flunked sixty thousand students, and made profits while doing so. There were strikes in various colleges, and yet the activists recognized sadly that the studentry at large was more interested in sports and movies than in politics. The studentries were called upon to emulate their fellows in the Egyptian and Chinese student movements.[121] In the early thirties, when Gandhi's efforts seemed at a dead end, student activists began to question the efficacy of nonviolence. When Bhagat Singh shot a British police official, thousands of students gathered outside the Jail Court shouting revolutionary slogans. "Every student had a photograph of Bhagat Singh in his room."[122] Nevertheless, a student movement, with its independent standpoint and action, failed to emerge; as in Bengal, "only very rarely, students directed the movement on their own lines, chalking out a distinctive course of action. . . ."[123] The Congress movement was well organized and led by men immensely respected, whom the violence-minded students could scarcely challenge; Gandhi and Nehru held the reverence of the peasant and urban masses in a way in which no Russian leader before 1917 did. When Civil Disobedience failed in 1932, the new militant leadership of Nehru kept students loyal to the Congress party. Student strikes in the thirties were moved by resentment against authoritarianism and their own impoverished lot; economic anxiety was pervasive. "The problem of the educated unemployed is the burning topic of the day in India," wrote Prabodh Chandra; nonetheless, the student strikes generally had "little political tinge."[124] In the Pakistani universities, according to R. C. Wright, student agitation in the pre-partition days was directed against either the British or the Hindus. Strikes were called against the British one week and the Indian Congress the next. "It is now apparent that students were used by Moslem League leaders, that they were often uninformed as to the underlying reasons for certain movements and that they were prey to emotional, religious, or nationalistic appeals."[125]

When independence was achieved, Congress leaders aimed to depoliticize the students; they argued that there was no longer any need for a national student political movement. The Student Congress did indeed dissolve itself.[126] Nonetheless, generational conflict is rampant in Indian universities. Student indiscipline is a problem in India as nowhere else. As Margaret L. Cormack writes, "Examiners are threatened on dark streets, effigies are burnt, vice-chancellors' home are invaded, staff members are physically assaulted, university gates are locked and speakers hooted off platforms. Indiscipline seems to be the order of the day." The social fabric as a whole is said to be permeated "with discontent, distrust and unrest. . . . Our youth has come to know that 'rewards' await those who defy authority." "One hears almost daily of strikes in schools and colleges, of assaults on teachers by students, of examinations postponed on account of disturbed conditions, or worse still of examinations conducted under police guard. But most appalling of all is the well-known and undisciplined bribery among examiners in some universities, where marks are sold according to an established schedule."[127] During the eight months from August 1961 to March 1962, more than thirty-four colleges and five high schools were involved in strikes, which lasted anywhere from one morning to five months and involved anywhere from two hundred to six thousand students.[128]

The tension and strain of securing a place in India's professional classes weighed on the Indian students. Traditional society was changing rapidly; the task, therefore, was to secure access to the privileged places of the new middle and upper classes, the bureaucracy and the professions. There was a singular absence of social idealism in the students' organizations; political demonstrations were the exception rather than the rule.

In Calcutta students "rioted over difficult examinations and walked out in refusal to take them; hundreds of students in Mysore demonstrated in unruly fashion their right to attend the World Youth Festival; two students of Doab College went on a hunger strike in protest against the 'rustication' of the president of the Students' Union on a charge of indiscipline." At the Benares Hindu University students' demonstrations against its policies and appointments resulted in its closure for three months and the resignation of its vice-chancellor. Students protested the alleged corruption of the vice-chancellor at Aligarh University. Four hundred students forced their way into the Patna Commerce College and assaulted the principal and four professors. At Allahabad University, a student who had failed his entrance test undertook to fast to death unless the university admitted him; his hunger strike won him the support of the student union. At Lucknow University, the student union demanded the dean's ouster on the ground that he was a "womanizer" and had made a girl student pregnant; the police were summoned and the university was closed. In May 1965, thirteen students at Aligarh University were charged with "murderous assault" on the vice-chancellor. Only the medical and engineering students remained immune to indiscipline. "They tend to be highly selected students, are secure in their job prospects, are busy with their studies every day, and they are studying what makes sense to them in terms of the life to follow."[129] It was in 1949 that students struck for the first time to protest an examination; the government yielded to their demands and the students received promotions without examination. The pattern for subsequent skirmishes and revolts was set.

In India, generational revolt is directed not against the sons' fathers but against university authorities. The resentment against authority is strong, but "because the family is so sacred . . . the feeling will be concentrated on school and university authorities."[130] As Aileen D. Ross writes, "The college authorities are the only ones against whom they can safely and successfully rebel. The family is still too strong to challenge individually."[131] But the political consciousness of Indian students seems to have declined since 1947.[132]

Such acute observers as Aileen Ross find in the sexual frustration of the Indian student a basic cause of his indiscipline. Girl students are teased mercilessly: "They will surround the girls, calling them names and ridiculing them," shouting out rude remarks, or forcing girls on the way to class to run a gantlet between two lines of men. The young men students are confronted by a system in which young Indian women "are still carefully guarded by their parents and wardens."[133]

But the attribution of a major causal role in student movements to sexual frustration must be seriously questioned. There have been periods in America, for example, when students who were equally ascetic in their sexual behavior nonetheless lived in generational equilibrium; students in the Middle East, on the other hand, for all their more frequent relations with prostitutes, have been politically turbulent.[134] Certainly, sexual frustration would be a condition making for potential student unrest. In the causation of political student movements, however, generational conflict, whatever may be the factors which heighten it, is the crucial factor; and such conflict, all-recurrent as it is, will not give rise to a political student movement unless some critical historical occurrences de-authoritize the elder generation. In this sense, India has yet been spared a massive student movement. The National Council of University Students of India is concerned with such issues as securing better conditions of housing, cooperative cafeterias, and "book banks."[135] The revolt against the gerontocracy has hitherto taken a primarily academic rather than a political form. But if it does take a political form, the student movement will probably not make a liberal democratic contribution. The Indian students' sado-masochistic tactics, ranging from physical assaults on chancellors to starving themselves to death, have not prepared them for leadership toward a liberal democratic society.[136]

The Student Elite in Primitive Societies: The Dual Alienation of African Students

Perhaps nowhere was the significance of (what we might call) a "dual alienation" more clearly exemplified than in that small handful of African student leaders who guided their people to independence. The African student leaders were a creation of Western education, usually Roman Catholic missionary schools; they were so-called "mission boys." "It was inevitable that the new educated African elite should use political agitation as a successor to the old initiation rites and as a proving ground in the Western world," writes George Delf, "but it was a pity that the Government proved incapable of governing successfully that small but vital number of 'mission boys.' "[137] The typical pattern was for the "mission boy" to secure scholarships which enabled him to study in the United States, Britain, or France. As a student in America or Europe, the young African would become more estranged from the culture of his own people; he would admire the white civilization and yet hate the whites, too, for their humiliation of his people. The African students were doubly alienated, from their fathers and from their fathers' oppressors. The student movement aimed to uproot them both; the revolutionary student leaders aimed to succeed where a previous generation of tamed, domesticated bureaucrats had failed. Kwame Nkrumah, Prime Minister of Ghana, Jomo Kenyatta, Prime Minister of Kenya, Julius Nyerere, Prime Minister of

Tanganyika, were all graduates of mission schools who followed the student path to leadership. Other "mission boys" who rose to leadership were B. N. Azikiwe, Governor General of Nigeria, Chief Awolowo, leader of the Action group in the Nigerian Parliament, Joseph Kasavubu, President of the Congo Republic, Moise Tshombe, President of Katanga, Antoine Gizenga, Deputy Premier of the Congo Republic, Kenneth Kaunda, President of Northern Rhodesia, Dr. Hastings Banda of Nyasaland, and Patrice Lumumba, the first Prime Minister of the Congo. The political elite of the Congo consisted mainly of alumni in the Association des Anciens Elèves des Pères de Scheut (Association of Former Pupils of the Scheut Fathers).[138]

Kwame Nkrumah, a prototype of the African intellectual and student leader, educated for eight years at Roman Catholic mission schools, subsequently made his way in 1935 to the United States where he studied sociology and economics at Lincoln University. In his wanderings he encountered his "first experience of racialism below the Mason-Dixon line."[139] From association with an American Trotskyist group, he writes, "I learned how an underground movement worked." He continued graduate studies in philosophy, first at the University of Pennsylvania, then studying logical positivism at the University of London under A. J. Ayer. In America he had served as president of the African Students Organization; in 1945, in Britain, he came into contact with the unusual London group associated in the West African Students' Union. Founded in 1925 by a dozen law students, this organization had grown, with the help of financial grants from the paternalistic British Colonial Office, until its membership was nearly a thousand. The Colonial Office later regarded it as "nothing more than a training ground for political agitators. They could point out that practically every leading member of the Union had become a politician on his return to West Africa."[140] Here the African student imbibed the most advanced political and economic ideas, became still more estranged from his tribal culture, learned Fabianism and more especially Marxism, and how to regard the British hosts as exploiters whom the historical dialectic would inevitably supplant. The young Africans saw themselves as their people's elite; they "took their role as intellectual leaders of West Africa greatly to heart."[141] They responded to Marxism because it offered a practical approach to immediate achievement by direct, violent action; they even responded with sympathy to Adolf Hitler when he came to power because, as their magazine said, "the answer to oppression is not servility, but self-assertion, courage, and determination to win for one's people the same opportunities which the others enjoy."[142] Nkrumah became vice-president of the West African Students' Union.

There he encountered an older African student, Jomo Kenyatta, who in 1936 had taken a doctorate in anthropology under Bronislaw Malinowski at the London School of Economics; his thesis, *Facing Mount Kenya,* had been a study of his own native Kikuyu culture and the blows it had sustained under the impact of European civilization. Both Nkrumah and Kenyatta had to come to terms with the tribalism from which they were alienated. Nkrumah, the positivist-Marxist, began to dabble in blood ritual; he organized a secret society called "the Circle," and "proposed," recalls the black South African novelist, Peter Abrahams, "that each of us spill a few drops of our blood into a bowl and so take a blood oath of secrecy and dedication to the emancipation of Africa."[143] Such was the secret society of student activists, and when shortly afterward in 1947 Nkrumah became the leader of the Convention People's Party in the Gold Coast, all the authoritarianism of the student circle was imposed on the party. Its members swore a similar oath of loyalty: "I pledge with all my life my support to the Convention People's Party, and to my leader, Kwame Nkrumah; I swear to follow my Leader's guidance, to execute faithfully his commands, to resist with all my power all imperialist attempts to disrupt our ranks, to strive with all my heart to rebuild our lost nation, Ghana, so help me God!"[144] Nkrumah found his most devoted followers among students. When he was imprisoned, a number of them went on strike and were expelled. To provide for them, Nkrumah improvised a school which became the Ghana National College. At its founding, he stated the elitist creed of the student intelligentsia: "As soon as an awakened intelligentsia emerges among so-called subject peoples, it becomes the vanguard of the struggle against alien rule."[145]

The poignancy of alienation set Jomo Kenyatta too on a political journey from Communism to tribal terrorism and to an uncertain conclusion. Born a Kikuyu, he was one of that small group of "mission boys" in Nairobi who "tended to stick together and thought of themselves as a 'top-class' among the Africans, most of whom were employed as laborers and house servants."[146] In a thatch-roofed house ringed by a bamboo stockade, Kenyatta read Wells, Galsworthy, Nietzsche, Schopenhauer. In Britain in the early thirties he joined the Communist party, and with the help of a scholarship studied at the London School of Economics and later at Moscow University. To a parliamentary group in 1930 he pleaded for a tolerant understanding of female circumcision among the Kikuyu; let it die a natural death under the impact of education. But the depth of his alienation he revealed to his roommate, Peter Abrahams:

> For me, Kenyatta became that night a man who in his own life personified the terrible tragedy of Africa and the terrible secret war that rages in it. He was the victim both of tribalism and of westernism gone sick. His heart and mind and body were the battlefield of the ugly violence known as the Mau Mau revolt long before it broke out in that beautiful land.
>
> And then Kenyatta began to speak in a low, bitter voice of his frustration and of the isolated position in which he found himself. There was no one in the tribe who could give him the intellectual companionship that had become so important to him in his years in Europe. The things that were important to him—consequential conversation, the drink that represented a social activity

rather than the intention to get drunk, the concept of individualism, the inviolability of privacy—all these were alien to the tribesmen in whose midst he lived. So Kenyatta, the western man, was driven in on himself and was forced to assert himself in tribal terms. Only thus would the tribesmen follow him and so give him his position of power and importance as a leader.

To live without roots is to live in hell, and no man chooses to voluntarily live in hell. The people who could answer his needs as a western man had erected a barrier of color against him . . . they had forced him back into the tribalism from which he had so painfully freed himself over the years.[147]

So Kenyatta returned in part to tribal ways which he despised. To be a tribal man was to live under the rule of the ancestors, the fathers, the dead; it meant not to be an individual. "If there is a drought, if there is a famine, it is a sign that the ancestors are angry because someone has broken a rule of the tribe." Kenyatta, rejecting the tribal culture of his fathers, seeking to reconstruct the mores of his tribesmen, contemptuous of their unreason and barbarity, could never be a natural democratic leader; he could tell the tribesmen the scientific truth and enforce it as a new chief with the old sanctions. A "psychological retreat," says Kenyatta's biographer, led him to channel the energies of the embittered young men in Nairobi to the terrorist tactics and the oath mystique of Mau Mau.[148] Yet student movements have always tended toward secret societies and oath mysticism; tribalism and student intellectualism strangely coincided in part, for primitive emotions are involved in the genesis of student movements. As an alienated man, Kenyatta regarded his people as savages, and could therefore emotionally rule them only as savage subjects should be ruled. The dictator-intellectual is always a student who became alienated from his people; dictatorship for the intellectual is his revenge against those from whom he was estranged in childhood and youth. The intellectual's dictatorship is in its furthest causal source a delayed response of generational revolt—the son finally subduing the surrogate fathers and their culture.

The American Negro novelist Richard Wright vividly described the alienation of the African intellectuals from their own peoples: "The Africans I met knew that I knew something in general of the conditions of their lives, the disorder, the polygamy, the strange burial customs, etc.; these were the things in which they most deeply believed, yet they were ashamed of them before the world. How could one believe in something that one was ashamed of? . . . Western civilization had made them want to hide their traditional lives and yet that civilization had given them no other way to live." The African personality was afflicted with "a numbed defensiveness, a chronic lack of self-confidence." Wright recorded his own shame as he watched African men and women urinating publicly so continually and unashamedly.[149] This was a race that was not toilet-trained, and to mitigate such primitivism the shamed intellectuals invented a compensatory ideology of the African personality.

The alienated intellectuals, arrived in power, tended to be authoritarian and dictatorial precisely because they were alienated from those they ruled. They regarded their peoples with a basic contempt, looked on them as barbarians even when they cajoled them for votes. Democratic societies thrive when the governors feel essentially akin culturally and morally to the governed; alienated intellectuals feel no such kinship. Therefore, for all its use of the rhetoric of democracy, a student movement come to power tends to assume the posture of a dictatorship; the intellectual takes naturally to a principle of hierarchy which enthrones him.

The African student movement, insofar as it was moved by generational struggle, tended to develop an irrational attachment to authoritarianism and violence, trying vainly to conquer the generational ghost within its unconscious. African students regarded their intellectual predecessors, whom the colonial system had absorbed, in much the same way as Russian students in the nineteenth century had regarded their forebears whom the bureaucratic system had broken and tamed. Indeed, as Thomas Hodgkin points out, African students were aware of their kinship with the Russian populist youth. The tamed older intellectuals were a "prefabricated" elite, whereas the revolutionary young were a "committed" elite:

> To the prefabricated category belong those African students who are manufactured to a colonial design . . . capable of serving Europeans as reliable NCOs. They represent, intellectually at any rate, an earlier generation, persuaded . . . that the only way forward lay through "showing the White man that one was just like him: hence the parliamentary comedy, the religion of diplomas; the myth of the lucrative job." The elite of this generation must live differently. They must not be ashamed to develop their own proper virtues—"optimism, the taste for life, enjoyment of other people. . . ." They must put behind them the "temptation of the West" for to be "committed" means to be committed to Africa. With perhaps a conscious look over their shoulders at the students of nineteenth-century Russia, these students take seriously their obligation to the peasantry, from whom they have sprung. . . . "Le paternalisme, voilà l'ennemi" is the conclusion. What is meant by paternalism? Partly to assume the superiority of European culture. . . . But above all "paternalism" is meant to refer to the entire furniture of the European mind when confronted with Africans—the jungle; the witch-doctor. . . .[150]

The revolt against "paternalism" was, however, a dual one. If it was directed, on the one hand, against the European, it was even more basically against the passivity, submissiveness, and backwardness of one's own fathers. Moreover, the tactics chosen to oppose the Europeans were tactics which the fathers rejected. Thus, the anti-imperialist movement was in itself also an anti-older-generation movement.

The achievement of national independence constituted a generational revolution for the small group of African student activists. In the Belgian Congo, at the time when independence was proclaimed, 80 per cent of the students in the seminary where the sociologist Father Houtart taught "ran away in order to occupy a new position in the new government."[151] In the Cameroun Republic in 1961, young men who had just completed their studies and who had been home less than a year held the following posts: Director of Public Health, Adjunct Director of Public Health, Director of Agriculture, Director of the Budget, Director of Primary Education, Director of Economic Affairs, Vice-President of the Court of Appeal, Director of the Bank of Development, Inspector General of Administrative Affairs, Director of Aeronautics, Director of Public Functions, Director of Social Security.[152]

The legislative assemblies of the new republics which were carved out in French West Africa were constituted of secondary school activists rather than the necessarily scarce university ones: 22 per cent of the legislators in 1957 were teachers, 27 per cent were civil servants, 20 per cent were from the liberal professions. Only 14 per cent were drawn from commerce and industry. The great majority of those with a secondary education had received it at the École Normale William Ponty at Dakar, "the main educational source of the elite that initially organized and led the post-war parties."[153] The next generational conflict, we might say, would be between the teachers and their pupils, or between the graduates of the University of Dakar and those of the École Normale William Ponty.

During the brief period following the political consummation of independence, however, generational conflict usually subsided as opportunities for constructive action multiplied.

The educated Guinean, for instance, was "actively caught up in a project [which, it was said] he regards as historically momentous—the creation of a modern socialist but completely African state." Neither lineage, nor seniority, nor wealth were keys to authority as much as intellectual status. "The fact that the vast majority of the newly educated will most certainly be absorbed into the governmental apparatus itself as teachers, doctors, administrators, or technicians intensifies their commitment to the political system."[154]

A generational equilibrium was more probable when the intellectual elite was predominantly a technological rather than a humanistic one. Of 794 Guinean students studying abroad in 1960, as many as 560 were in technical training, 48 in medicine and pharmacy, 33 in natural science, while only 47 were in economics or political science, 34 in liberal arts, and 72 studying to be teachers. The Ministry of Education itself was promoting this distribution of studies, which certainly would diminish the potential for a new political student movement. But the Guinean situation was scarcely typical of most of the African republics, where a new violent generational conflict was developing.

To the inquiries of French anthropologists among African students in the new republics came universal testimony of an alienation from the fathers:

"The destiny of our fathers," wrote a Malagasy student, "was to obey and to execute, that of the young is to take in hand and to direct."

"The generation of the fathers," said another, "is the generation of resignation, that of the sons is one of desires without limits."

"The old generation," said a Nigerian, "regards its situation as having been not so bad; it keeps insisting that happiness depends on how you think of it. It therefore judges very severely the impatience of the young."[155]

The generation of fathers was made up of men who were thirty years or older in 1945. They had grown up in the prewar era, when the colonial power was strong and unchallenged; they accepted generally the superiority of the white. The new generation grew to maturity in the postwar era. Many more of them went to school and to the university.[156] "It's the colonial schools which destroyed colonialism," said one writer.[157] At the same time the new universities were creating a conflict of generations between the first governing intellectual elite and their student successors.

A political elite born of a student movement is confronted with an anomaly, perhaps a "contradiction." It is compelled often to constrain the new, emerging generations of students, especially if it fails to fulfill the high promises of a new society without alienation which it made in the days when it was agitating for power. The generations of students succeed each other rapidly, and the young have a short political memory. Very quickly a new conflict of generations breaks out. As the political and economic situation of Ghana, for instance, deteriorated, and as Nkrumah ("Osagyefo," the self-styled Redeemer) concentrated within himself a dictatorial monopoly of political power, the students, particularly at the University of Ghana, became a center of opposition.[158] For seventeen days the university was closed in order to deactivate the students during Nkrumah's referendum in 1964 for approval of his one-party state and subservient judiciary. The trade unions were mobilized for demonstrations against the university. The president of the National Union of Ghanaian Students, a young law student, A. K. P. Kludze, was imprisoned without trial; for the Students' Union had dared to pass two resolutions which offended Nkrumah—one which deplored racial discrimination against African students in Soviet and Communist universities, another which criticized the arbitrary dismissal of Ghana's Chief Justice for his acquittal of three high officials charged with treason.[159]

The new generation of university students, moreover, felt itself to be a far more highly qualified intellectual elite than the host of semi-intellectuals who had moved into bureaucratic power with Nkrumah. The "Veranda Boys," so-called in colonial days, because they never got beyond the veranda when they asked for good jobs, comprised the thousands who had not received a higher education; they always felt resentful toward the "Lounge Boys" with their university degrees, European manners, and diplomaed status. Nkrumah's Convention People's Party had provided the avenue for the "upward mobility" of the semi-intellectuals. But now the university students wanted the places in which semi-intellectuals were entrenched; they demanded their recognition as an intellectual and ultimately political elite, and Nkrumah feared their challenge. The alienation of generations was such that an American Negro observer reported, "I never met a single student who expressed any commitment to, or interest in the government's vast program to improve the lives of the common people of Ghana."[160]

In Senegal, a similar development was taking place as students reached for places of power in the governmental elite. Though most of the Senegalese educated persons were finding jobs in the civil service, opposition to the government was centered mainly in the younger generation at the University of Dakar. The students there generally maintained that " 'traditional' and 'French-oriented' elements in the government were stifling the development of Senegal's true African personality and the rise of younger politicians." This newer generation of rebellious students pointed to Sekou Touré's Guinea as their hopeful model. Most of the Senegalese students at Dakar were pursuing humanistic rather than technological studies; of the 434 Senegalese in Dakar's enrollment of 1,398 in 1960, 239 were in law, as compared with 81 in science, 49 in medicine, and 65 in letters. Law remained the chief avenue for a would-be political class.[161]

Nigerian students at the University College, Ibadan (UCI), were similarly becoming disaffected with democracy and politicians, and claiming that the African personality was not being realized. "The African personality, which is the key and foundation of our humanism, aspires," wrote Alioun Diop, "to being freed from the Western grip. It requires that our people should speak through us."[162] Nigerian students shared this conviction. The older generation, which had achieved national independence, was still regarded as too subservient to the European white world, as not manly enough, as not African. The ideology of the African personality thus became an ideology for generational criticism and conflict. It also went hand in hand with the desire of the student intellectuals to supersede the older ones as the holders of political power. As W. J. Hanna wrote, "One of the more important reasons for the students' attitudes toward politicians is that the latter had the power that the students coveted. The students, using their higher education as a base value, desired and were moving toward power. The conflict was thus between a contemporary elite and a challenging group."[163]

Then too there was the anxiety of "the growing body of the young and underemployed intelligentsia," which cast its shadow on the students.[164] The students were indeed apprentices for the new bureaucratic class. Seventy-five per cent of Nigerian graduates in 1959 went directly into government service; only 18 per cent chose teaching, and as few as 8 per cent joined commercial firms and corporations.[165]

The student movement in Nigeria, with its predilection for demonstrations, was a poor model for the people of the workings of representative democracy. Within the Nigerian political parties, the students' role and power was quite limited, but their demonstrations exerted an influence throughout the country. In November 1960, for instance, several hundred students of University College, Ibadan, stormed Parliament in order to protest the defense pact between Nigeria and the United States. Despite the tear gas, the students forced their way into the reception hall of the legislative chambers; the country took notice. When the students protested a pension bill, it was withdrawn, and the governor-general Azikiwe ("Zik") said they were right. From January 1959 to June 1960, the students engaged in five major demonstrations, one against Prime Minister MacMillan for Britain's passivity toward apartheid in South Africa, another against South Africa for the Sharpeville shootings, another against the French for testing atomic weapons in the Sahara, and two against pension and housing bills. As W. J. Hanna wrote, "The student demonstration or protest had considerable influence for the same reasons that students in general played an important political role in Nigeria: the dearth of non-governmental intellectuals and the resulting lack of 'an effectively critical evaluation' of government policies."[166] The Nigerian students sought to act as the people's conscience; for instance, seven hundred of them protested an inordinate housing allowance paid to Chief Awolowo, Premier of Western Nigeria; their memorandum alluded to the "fantastic salaries" that were being paid to the emerging class of professional politicians in Nigeria. Awolowo's supporters naturally retaliated by denouncing the student movement. Two generations of student activists, of the past and present, fought each other. The Lagos *Daily Service* observed: "Nigeria is not the first country to have the experience of undergraduates who seek to run Governments of their respective countries from their University campus." Nigerian students, it continued, were "in their enthusiasm and ignorance" trying to apply to public affairs "data copied from text books" even as students traditionally had done. "There is not enough thinking at the University College" was the title of the editorial; reading social science did not confer on one a practical social sense.[167]

What was most ominous to an American observer in Nigeria as early as 1962, however, was the pervasive "negativism" (or nihilism) of the students toward politics, a negativism which was directed toward politicians and political processes generally. "The students' political negativism," wrote W. J. Hanna, was also "an outlet for adolescent and young adult revolt, which is intensified in a transitional society where conflict between tradition and modernity fuses with the ambivalence of youth toward authority."[168] The students, as it were, were making a last futile protest before surrendering to careers in the Nigerian Civil Service, where, as one student said, they would be "governmentalized" and restricted in their political activities.

The psychology of generational rebellion, however, did not contribute to a strengthening of either the students' or the people's allegiance to liberal democratic values. Most of the Nigerian students rejected parliamentary democracy and preferred a dynamic, charismatic dictator whose fortunes would be linked with their own. The Prime Minister of Nigeria, Sir Abubakar Balewa, soon to be assassinated, said that "democracy is essentially government by discussion." The Nigerian students in practice, however, spurned freedom of discussion. A student newspaper said in 1959, "Go to any meeting and try to express an opinion not acceptable to the majority and you are at once shouted down . . . it is a disgrace to us."[169] Such was the situation at the University College, Ibadan, Nigeria, where the students were highly involved in politics, and where "almost all indicators"—political discussion, membership in organizations, attendance at meetings, participation in demonstrations, protests, and campaigns—showed the students to be more politically involved and activist than the students of Britain and the United States. The actions and attitudes of the African students confirm the generalization: to the degree that a studentry tends to be politically involved and to develop a student movement, to that degree it rejects the values and procedures of liberal democracy.

What was true of sub-Sahara Africa was also true of the more advanced North African countries. In Algeria and Morocco, the student movements were closely linked to the Communist parties; only in Tunisia was the student movement not committed to policies of violence and revolution. The president of the National Union of Moroccan Students, Hamid Berrada, was in 1964 actually sentenced to death in absentia for incitement to revolt; he went into exile. His successor, Mohammed Haloui, was imprisoned several months without trial. The Moroccan student movement in 1965 was incensed against the government, primarily because the latter wanted to direct more secondary school students into technical education. The students in universities and secondary schools demonstrated at Fez on March 25, 1965; sixty of them were injured in clashes with the police, and twenty-five persons were reported killed and 724 jailed.[170] Communist governments, of course, usually impose the primacy of technical education as a matter of course, but the same policy advocated by a non-Communist government results in outbreaks by students. In Algeria, the Communist-dominated leadership of the National Union of Algerian Students opposed the government of Colonel Boumedienne, who seized power from President Ben Bella on June 19, 1965. The student leaders either were jailed or went abroad or into underground activities. Only one fourth of the Executive Committee declared its allegiance to the government. The Minister of Education, a former student leader himself, tried to win the students' support by assuring them that they would still get as many scholarships as before, and that the price of board and room would stay the same; he described how he had been physically tortured by former

President Ben Bella.[171] Despite the student leadership's disapproval of the 1965 coup, there was little evidence on their part of a devotion to liberal democratic values; the movement remained that of an apprentice intellectual elite, seeking special privileges and prerogatives. Most students, however, repelled by the factionalism, dissension, and authoritarianism of the student movement, meanwhile withdrew into "apoliticism"; they were tired of all the wrangling about the definition of "Algerian socialism."

By contrast, the Tunisian government under President Habib Bourguiba pursued a vigorous policy intended to foster a generational equilibrium. To the congress of the ruling Neo-Destour party in October 1964, Bourguiba said, "We must fight against the monopoly (of authority) exercised by the old militants and open the door to youth." The congress voted to "mobilize" the Tunisian youth through a new Civic Service Corps to assist the ten-year development plan. It appealed to the youth's elitism by adopting a motion calling on them to "raise themselves to the level of the historic mission that has been passed onto them by the national Party." This theme appealed to the General Union of Tunisian Students, which at its congress in August 1964 emphasized "the training of cadres to strengthen national independence"; the path chosen was Destourien (constitutional) socialism. The studentry at the University of Tunis, more moderate than the radical Tunisian students living in France, emerged as the dominant force. It congratulated the government on achieving the departure of all foreign troops and the nationalization of lands held by foreigners. The national elections in November 1964 reinforced the trend toward a younger ruling elite; Bourguiba's son, thirty-seven years old, became Foreign Secretary.[172] Nonetheless, despite Bourguiba's juvenocratic policy, serious student outbreaks took place in 1967 at the University of Tunis; policemen fought with hundreds of rebellious students. The generations were becoming the shortest in history. "What are your chances in government," asked one young man, "if you are 25 and your minister is 28?" President Bourguiba announced that 1967 would be the "year of the students." But it seemed as if a new conflict of generations, that among the age-classes of the juvenocrats themselves, was in the offing, a struggle between the young who had fought for independence as against the very young who wanted to savor the revolutionary experience themselves.[173]

Student Elitism in Latin America: Student Syndicalism, Conflict with the Military Elite, and Guerilla Warfare

The Latin American student movement, in ferment for two generations, has been a curious amalgam of rhetoric, student syndicalism, terrorism, elitism, and self-sacrificing struggle against military dictatorship. Born of the celebrated Córdoba Manifesto of 1918, the student movement aimed to modernize the university curriculum, extending the middle-class revolution from the sphere of politics to that of education and opening the way to revitalizing an apathetic people. The "autonomy" of the university and its "co-government" by students jointly with faculty were not ends in themselves; they were envisaged as the organizational form which would make it possible for the students to bring the universities out of the Middle Ages to Modern Times.

The student movement had a second task; it was the "striking force" of the intellectual elite in its conflict with the military elite. The history of Latin America, in the setting of a nondemocratic society with a largely illiterate population, has largely consisted in the conflict of rival elites: the military, the church, the lay secular intellectuals.[174] The students were the intellectuals' mobile battalions; heroic, idealistic, inspiring, they were the force most readily available to challenge and withstand the regiments of the military dictators. With the masses for the most part illiterate, ignorant, and indifferent, the students often stood as their people's sole protest against pretorianism.

Within a short time the bright hopes and prospects of the Latin American student movement were largely twisted and distorted. The slogans of "autonomy" and "co-government" became the tools of a growing student anti-intellectualism used to advance the selfish, narrow aims of a student elite. Generational conflict was conducted on the plane of economic interests. The overriding fact became the students' anxiety to secure for themselves posts in the governmental bureaucracy and professions. The Latin American student unions became student syndicates whose aims often were to see to it that examinations remained easy and academic requirements low so that the students would find open the doors to social status and position. The Russian students and the Chinese students were moved by great visions of social reconstruction. By contrast, the Latin American student unions were more often agencies of student syndicalism, concerned with securing preferential treatment for students with respect to bus fares, financial grants, and legal privileges. It was an economic version of generational struggle. They indulged in populist rhetoric about raising the cultural and material standards of the peasants and Indians, but nothing took place that was on the scale of the Russian back-to-the-people movement. The Latin American student movement was usually a trade union of apprentices to the bureaucracy and professions. In their status, however, as activists of the bureaucratic and professional middle classes, they found themselves in a developing contest with the military elite. The intellectuals and soldiers vied with each other for hegemony. And in the course of this contest, a new blend of elitism and populism began to appear. Student leaders looked for new class allies in their struggle with the military, as well as for new leader-models to inspire them. At times the elder generation was de-authoritized in the eyes of the young by some presumed capitulation to the political and economic power of the United States. In such instances the ideology of anti-

Americanism would become virulent; it was an emotion directed by the students against both the Americans and their own Latin American fathers who were being unmanned, emasculated, humiliated by their passive submission. The cult of *machismo*, masculinity, so prevalent in Latin America, was itself a defensive measure against an anxiety about social effeminization. And where anti-Americanism as an ideology of generational protest became most intense, the student movement veered toward admiration and adulation of its new heroes, Fidel Castro and Mao Tse-tung.

As compared to the Russian and Chinese student movements, the Latin American has not had the overwhelming traumatic experience of a deauthoritized elder generation. It is noteworthy that in the whole body of Latin American literature one does not come across any novel which deals with the conflict of generations.[175] There is no Latin American *Fathers and Sons* or even *Virgin Soil*. The underlying emotion of generational revolt has been present, but in attenuated form. Consequently, the Latin American student movements have not exhibited as markedly two characteristics of student movements which spring from strong experiences of guilt—back-to-the-people longings and suicidalism. In recent years, however, the movements have evinced a sharp increase in the emotions of generational revolt, and traits of populism and terrorism have become more evident. A sense of guilt has also manifested itself in the contrast of the students' comfort and the masses' poverty. "A natural guilt, like being white in the United States, is the result." It associates itself with generational revolt: "All are searching for moral issues," reported one observer, "with which to challenge the world, and finding them in the neglect of their elders."[176]

The Latin American student is first and foremost fighting against economic odds for a place in the intellectual elite. As such, he will share in the solidarity which binds the intellectual elite against the military. His solidarity is more elitist than generational. The Latin American student is a secular intellectual, but he retains as a direct inheritance the pretensions to political rule which characterized the Catholic Jesuit intellectuals. The secular intellectuals came to prominence very early in the course of their countries' independence. In Brazil, the reign of Pedro II (1841 to 1889), for instance, was called, in Gilberto Freyre's words, "the reign of the college graduates."[177] In Mexico, Comtist positivism superseded Catholic theology, but the Comtist *científicos*, during the many years of the presidency of Porfirio Díaz (1876–1880, 1880–1911), were just as elitist and authoritarian in their attitudes as their churchly forebears. This sense of themselves as an intellectual elite, demanding the status of an administrative middle class, and wishing to come abreast of the culture of the intellectuals in the advanced Western countries, was from its beginnings the ideological basis of the Latin American student movement.

The famous Córdoba Manifesto of 1918 is fittingly taken as the birth date of the Latin American student movement. The movement began at a time of relative economic prosperity. Argentina had profited from its neutrality during the First World War. "From 1916 to 1919 the Argentine peso was quoted above every other major currency in the world."[178] It was a period, however, when the liberal elder generation of the middle class, which had for the first time come to political power, was disappointing the idealistic hopes of the young. In 1916, the Argentine people for the first time chose their president in a free election. Hipólito Irigoyen, the new President, a civilian leader who had built the Radical party, was idolized by the middle and lower classes. He had succeeded by peaceful means where the university graduates in the Union Cívica de la Juventud using force had failed. But Irigoyen in power was confused and without a clear program. When workers in Buenos Aires finally tried, in January 1919, to hasten matters, there was much bloodshed. Irigoyen then undertook to rule autocratically. It was in this atmosphere of growing disillusionment with the slowness and lack of initiative in the "radical" older generation that the Córdoba student movement took shape.

The Córdoba students sounded the call for a generational seizure of power in the universities; only thus could they quickly lift the university from medieval to modern times. They appealed to generational solidarity, missionism, and elitism, in a vocabulary which a Student Soviet might well have used that same year in Moscow. Their words were to be often repeated in all the Latin American universities.

We, members of the free republic, have just broken the last chain which, in the twentieth century, still attached us to the old monarchical and monastic domination. We have resolved to call everything by its proper name. Córdoba has redeemed itself. From today on we can count in our country one shame fewer and one liberty more. The miseries which remain are the liberties we lack. We do not think we are deceiving ourselves—the resoundings of the heart tell us so; we are making a revolution, we are living a vital American hour. . . .

They assailed the senile professors, their torpid teaching, the hired apologetic:

Up to now the universities have been the secular refuge of mediocrity, the salary of ignorance, the safe hospital for all intellectual invalids, and—what is more—the place where all forms of tyranny and insensibility found the chair where they could be taught. The universities have thus become faithful mirrors of those decadent societies which offer the sad sight of a senile immobility. That is why science, facing these closed and shuttered houses, remains silent or mutilated and grotesque, merely serves bureaucracy. When, in a fleeting period of liberalism, the university opened its doors to the higher spirits, it very soon repented and made the existence of those spirits within its walls impossible. That is why the natural forces under such regimes carry education towards mediocrity, and that is why the vital development of the university bodies is never the fruit of an organic process, but only the breath of revolutionary periodicity.

In the name of their generational revolution, the Córdoba students demanded the rule of the students in the universities:

Our university regime—even the most recent one—is anachronistic. It is based on a sort of divine right—that of the university staff. It is created by itself. . . . It maintains an Olympian indifference. The Córdoba University Students Association rises up in arms to struggle against this regime, and understands that this struggle may cost its own existence. It demands a strictly democratic government and affirms that the university demos, its sovereignty, its right to choose its own government depends mainly on the students themselves. The authority of a rector or a teacher in a student center can never be based on the power of rules of conduct, which are foreign to the very substance of study. In a student center, authority cannot be implemented through demands, but through suggestion and love, i.e., through teaching.[179]

Only the word "alienation" was lacking in the Córdoba Manifesto. Otherwise its themes were the familiar ones of the revolution of student youth, proclaiming a community of love to replace the cruel indifference of the old. The "mutilated," castrated science of the immobile bureaucracy was to be superseded by the wholeness of living science and scholarship.

The Córdoba movement united in curious fashion the ideologies of both bourgeois liberalism and the medieval university. The "autonomy" of the university became the slogan word of the Latin American student ideology. For in countries where political pluralism has been absent, "university autonomy" signifies a protest against monopolistic control over cultural activities by the state, army, or church. In the United States, by contrast, most colleges began as autonomous institutions, with charters as voluntary associations, and with boards of trustees independent of state or clerical authorities. The Dartmouth College case of 1818, celebrated in the history of constitutional law, was (one might say) a victory for the principle of autonomy. The Latin American countries, however, from colonial time onward lived under political and theological absolutism; their universities too acted as agencies of absolutism in their curriculums and administrations; every professor was an ideologist of the ruling order. "Autonomy" was the natural slogan of student movements in countries which had not gone through a bourgeois cultural and political evolution; it was the wedge for the entry of liberal and scientific ideas. In medieval society, students organized as "nations" had fought for their autonomous rights against clerics and townfolk. Now students proposed to use "autonomy" to bring a liberal scientific content into the universities, and to secure the universities' independence of military and clerical elites. Thus, the students' struggle merged with that of the bourgeois intellectual elite for political hegemony against the traditional elites. This indeed was the essence of the university reform movement.[180]

The students were the militants of bourgeois liberalism, seeking new books, new ideas, new professors, rebelling against the dominance of theology in the curriculum. It was more than an academic movement. "University Reform," wrote Julio V. González, "demonstrates the resurgence of a new generation . . . bringing forth a new sensibility, ideals, and a mission to be accomplished. . . . It would be absurdly erroneous to consider reform as a problem of classrooms. . . ." It was "a consequence of the crisis created by the war." Basic to the whole movement as it developed was the crisis of the middle class, to which the majority of the students belonged. "University reform," wrote Mariano Hurtado de Mendoza, "is a consequence of the general phenomenon of the proletarianization of the middle class."[181] The Latin American middle class was largely an administrative and professional class—of teachers, lawyers, doctors, journalists, civil servants. There was only a relatively weak commercial, industrial, and entrepreneurial middle class. And in such countries the student struggle to insure their entry into the middle class becomes especially severe; the student movement tended to become an agency to guarantee the students' chances for a middle-class existence. Therefore, unlike most other student movements, the Latin American always had the aspect of a trade union, a syndicate. To enhance their life chances, the students struggle to prevent the military elite from cutting the university budgets. In a "normal" country, such as Britain, the evolution and growth of the middle class proceeded hand in hand with the development of industry and the displacement of the aristocratic military elite; Herbert Spencer's law of the evolution from military to industrial societies was amply exemplified in Britain's case. The Latin American students, however, found themselves the vicarious representatives of an industrial culture in societies dominated by military elites. If an intellectual elite is to win permanent hegemony over a military elite, it can do so only if it can bring an industrial society into existence; otherwise it will continue to be a group of lawyers, doctors, teachers, and bureaucratic civil servants, the professional aides to a military elite. An intelligentsia can assure rule for itself only if it becomes a technocracy. Such a perception was in the consciousness of the nascent Latin American student movement. Thus, the very pursuit of its syndicalist, trade union aims tended under the conditions of military rule to attach political aims to the student movement.

The syndicalist rather than political component tended for more than forty years to prevail in the university reform movement. "The present Reform Movement," wrote Kalman H. Silvert in 1961, "as backed by the majority of university people, now stands for, among other things, no tuition payments, academic freedom largely in the limited sense of freedom of speech in the classroom, no permanent tenure for professors, cheap lunches, dormitories, and a voice and vote for students and alumni in running the universities."[182] At its outset in 1919, the movement, however, had been touched with juvenocratic messianism and something of the contagious millennial zeal of the Russian Revolution. "The movement is closely connected with the post-war atmosphere," wrote Mariátegui. "The messianic hopes, the revolutionary feelings, the mystical passions characteristic of the post-war period greatly influenced Latin American student youth." Yet the generational revolt inherent in the Córdoba movement tended to taper off into an attack on an elder generation of incompetent teachers. The pragmatic significance of student participation in university government was primarily "a moral control over teachers' performances," thereby providing "the only impulse for life, the only element of progress in the university."[183] The students resented the unqualified teacher, the slovenly one, the indifferent one, who was often either physically or spiritually absent from the classroom. And they wanted a curriculum that befitted the twentieth century. "University reform is proposed, in the last analysis," wrote Luis Alberto Sánchez, historian and former rector of the University of San Marcos, "only to adapt the classical university to the requirements of modern social life."[184]

For a brief period after 1919 it seemed, however, that a deep generational revolt might arise in the Latin American universities, merging itself with more basic aims for social reconstruction. The movement reached its highest point in Peru; in 1920, a national student congress convened in Cuzco, following a strike by the Federación de Estudiantes del Perú, which won representation on the University Council. Victor Raúl Haya de la Torre emerged as *el primer estudiante de América Latina,* the president of the National Council of University Students, during the students' revolution. He spoke the language of generational struggle:

A vast intellectual renaissance has manifested itself among the students of Latin America, which shows a profound divergence between the thought of the rising generation and of the generation that preceded it. These students are championing new principles and adopting new attitudes, not only toward intellectual life, but also toward political and social policies, which are capable of being converted later into more precise forms of action. Thus a conflict has arisen between the younger and the older generation. The young are following no master, for they have denied all.[185]

This conflict was compounded of three elements. First, a partial deauthoritization of the elder generation took place during the twenties. The students accused "the old politicians of complicity in imperialism."[186] The old had submitted to the emasculating Yankee yoke. Second, the young, in a populist spirit, declared they were turning toward the poor, the mass of whom were of another race, Indians. "In Peru, in Chile, in Cuba, in Guatemala, in Mexico, and in other countries," wrote Haya de la Torre, "the students have founded popular universities, centres of education for the workers and peasants. This closer contact between workers and students has formed in each republic of Latin America a strong vanguard of youth that includes both manual and intellectual workers."[187] Such was the back-to-the-people mood of the Latin American students in this brief phase. Third, the Latin American studentry was militantly anticlerical. Aiming to effect the leap from the medieval university to the modern university, it felt that education by priests and a theological curriculum had emasculated their fathers. The students rejected such a fate. Thus, when the university revolution reached the University of Lima in Peru in 1919, the students proclaimed a general strike and demanded not only the dismissal of sixteen professors "completely dominated by an antiquated spirit," but also the abolition of the courses in canon law. This was the oldest university in America, having been founded in 1551, and it was still spiritually in the Middle Ages. The University of Córdoba itself, where the movement began, had remained a citadel of medieval-mindedness ever since it was founded in 1614 by a Spanish friar.

The Peruvian student movement was the first of the Latin American movements to evolve into a full-fledged party of socialist revolution, the so-called Aprista party, which made of anticlericalism a central tenet.[188]

A memorable battle ensued in 1923 between the Peruvian students and the government over the issue of anticlericalism. That year the President of Peru, Augusto B. Leguia, in an endeavor to conciliate the Church, proposed a curious ceremony, a dedication of Peru to the "Sacred Heart of Jesus." Led by Haya de la Torre, the students and workers organized a demonstration on May 23, 1923, against the government. "The government attacked the demonstration; the university buildings became a battle scene as the demonstrators resisted. In the fighting, one student and one worker were killed. The union of the Lima students and workers was thus sealed in blood." The government was forced to suspend the dedication to Jesus, but it also closed the university, and many of the students were imprisoned and exiled from the country. Haya de la Torre, also imprisoned, went on a hunger strike. Finally, in October 1923, he was deported from the country.[189]

Indeed the Church in Latin American countries constituted a society of surrogate fathers which was a natural target for the first outbreaks of generational uprising. In part, anticlericalism probably formed a channel for energies and resentments which otherwise might have gone into a more direct generational revolt.

The Church, by dominating and constricting the education, character, and psychology of students, had a pre-eminent role in determining the direction and motivation of the student movement. "Tradition, the interests of the dynasty of the 'learned,' Catholic influence as changeless as a Spanish relic, all set their faces against the students' proposals. The masters of the Latin American universities exercised a truly implacable dictatorship," wrote Haya de la Torre.[190] The desire for a scientific culture expressed the younger generation's desire for a new life, its protest against a culture which was unmanning. The "restless discontent," as Haya called it, among the Latin American students, thus has an ingredient of anticlericalism distinct from the dominant syndicalist motivation.

As the student movement developed, however, the generational themes of populism, anticlericalism, and the de-authoritization of the old receded; the movement emerged in its dual role as antagonist to the military elite and spokesman for student syndicalist interests. "University reform" became a catch phrase for all these roles and themes; whether it was a question of troops entering the university grounds or of difficult examinations being given, "autonomy" and "co-government" of the university were invoked. Student movements had a primary part in the ouster of the dictator Jorge Ubíco in Guatemala in 1944, in the overthrow of the dictator Rojas Pinilla in Colombia in 1957, in the overthrow of the dictator Pérez Jiménez in Venezuela in 1958, in the civil war against the dictator Batista in Cuba, and in the removal of José Lemus in El Salvador in 1960.[191]

This was the tradition of the Latin American student movement at its noblest—the resistance of the young intellectual elite to the military elite. It could trace its lineage to the memorable days of 1928 when the Venezuelan student activists had tried to overturn the dictatorship of General Juan Vicente Gómez. But its links with the people, despite the students' intermittent populist enthusiasm, remained tenuous from the beginning. Romulo Betancourt, then a second-year law student and a leader in the Federación de Estudinates de Venezuela, and later President of Venezuela, recalled during his exile the gulf between the studentry and the people:

> The student movement had initially been wrapped within the cloak of university pride. We students considered ourselves . . . the ones to transform the country. Then the people suddenly made known their presence; and without leaders, without labor and political organizations, without action committees or strike funds, the people organized a massive demonstration in Caracas.[192]

The student movements were always in the forefront in the struggle against the military dictators. Although dissident army officers led the revolution which overthrew the dictator Pérez Jiménez, and the final blow was that of a general strike, "the public looked upon the students as having been the earliest and hardest workers toward the desired goal."[193] Then again, the students were foremost in saving the democratic republic when it was evidently threatened in July 1958 by a group of army officers.

> Early on the morning of July 22, the Central University announced the suspension of the final examinations that were going on and called upon the faculty and students to defend their country from impending danger. At a meeting that morning an emissary of the government solicited the aid of the students and promised that they would be issued arms if necessary. The President of the Federation of Student Centers gave instructions as to how the students should distribute themselves in strategic locations to defend the city if the army should make a move. Having been told how to make "Molotov cocktails" out of soft drink bottles and gasoline . . . (they) then took up their stations at the indicated strong points, where the poorer classes rallied behind the student leadership. . . .[194]

Later that day the student leaders organized a great demonstration before the Presidential Palace; that evening the Provisional President went to the University City to thank the students for having helped save the republic. The army never revolted, and the Minister of Defense and alleged coconspirators were exiled.

The university students were similarly the bravest and most persistent fighters in the Dominican Republic against the tyranny of General Rafael Trujillo. The dictator suppressed the student organizations and placed a military guard in control of the University of Santo Domingo. The students tried to organize a strike of sugar workers against the dictator, and finally in 1959–1960 took part in a plot to assassinate him. The death toll of students was a terrible one. "It was estimated that in the last years of the dictatorship 30 to 40 students were arrested a day; many of these were hanged or shot or simply vanished."[195] After Trujillo's assassination on May 30, 1961, a Trujillist group tried to maintain military rule. The students responded by organizing the first national student union in thirty years and demanding the university's autonomy. When the military regime sought to impose a henchman as rector of the university and to organize a regime-controlled student organization, street riots took place and students were killed by the police. A year later, when on September 25, Juan Bosch, the civilian President, was overthrown by a military junta, the students alone resisted. The largest student organization, the Bloque Revolucionario Universitario Cristiano, which had a social Christian ideology, denounced the coup d'état and held two protest meetings at the university. Many of their leaders were arrested. Then, under the leadership of the Federación de Estudiantes Dominicanos, two thousand assembled on October 7 at the university to march peacefully on the National Palace. Thereupon, they were surrounded by the police; a violent encounter took place, and the military regime proclaimed a state of siege. The students, entrenched in the university, retaliated in vain with a hunger strike.[196]

In Colombia, the Federación Universitaria Nacional waged a strike for a hundred days when the army occupied the Industrial University of Santander. There were demonstrations in Bogotá and a serious altercation in June 1963, when the students burned buses and barricaded the streets in the University City.[197] The following month, a military junta in Ecuador ousted the President, Dr. Carlos J. Arosemena; resistance was offered only by the Quito chapter of the Federation of University Students of Ecuador, whose leader, Washington Bonilla, organized street meetings of protest. The people at large, however, approved of the military's taking power as the national student monthly, *Voz Universitaria*, recognized. A few months later, in October 1963, the Federation of Honduran University Students protested in vain against a military coup which ousted the President. It published a vigorous statement in defense of constitutional government, called for agrarian reform and an amnesty for political prisoners, "especially our university comrades."

Yet the elitism of the Latin American student movement which could issue in such signal heroism was also a source of its perversion into anti-democratic and anti-liberal channels. In one country after another, student movements, instead of undertaking to strengthen democratic governments, have added their measures of violence against them.

In Bolivia, for instance, in June 1961, the Leftist chiefs of the Student

Federation of San Andres University took a leading part in provoking the unrest and violence which led to the fall of the legally elected democratic government of President Paz Estenssoro. Struggling to raise Bolivia's economic standards, the government was harassed by an active Castroist-Communist group, to which the Confederación Universitaria Boliviana gave support. A military regime came to power, with which the students, self-described as "the conscience of society," were naturally at loggerheads. When a civil war broke out anew between the Communist-led miners and the government, student leaders came forward to negotiate a truce; the workers' leaders meanwhile had taken sanctuary in the University of San Andres. The head of the university section of the Bolivian Communist Youth was a principal negotiator. The next month, to the students' dismay, the military regime began to disarm the miners and to arm the peasants, "whose inadequate political development," the students complained, was "easily exploited by those in power."[198] Violent conflict with the military elite became the customary pattern; the students had rejected democratic government, only to reap a military authoritarianism.

Latin American student movements indeed were moved by a compulsion to discredit liberal democracy and the United States. The arrival of Adlai Stevenson in Peru as a United States Ambassador on June 7, 1961, led the student activists at the ancient University of San Marcos to riot in the streets of downtown Lima. The president of the San Marcos Student Federation, a Communist, denounced Stevenson as "an undesirable person" and a representative of "American commercial interests." The Communist students demanded as well the resignation of the rector, Dr. Luis Alberto Sánchez, a member of the Apra party, saying that he had failed to get more money for the university from Peru's legislature.[199] Whatever the state of Peruvian economy, the students insisted in elitist fashion that 3 per cent of its national income should be allotted to the universities.

Distinct generational lines among the students, moreover, began to separate those who favored Maoist communism from the pro-Soviet adherents. Just as pro-Soviet communism had once signified a generational break with Apra, so now Maoism began to signify a generational break with the middle-aged, pro-Soviet party. Among themselves, the factions of the Peruvian student movement behaved with typical intolerance and authoritarianism, devouring each other before a revolution. The tenth National Student Congress in Peru, held in Cuzco in November 1964, was virtually torn apart by factional hatreds. Called by the Student Federation of Peru, it became the field for bitter violence. When the congress concluded on the night of November 24, its president, Gustavo Espinoza, pro-Soviet in orientation, was attacked and almost killed in the Plaza de Armas; Maoist students were believed to have made the assault. The animosities between the factions in the Credentials Committee were such that the congress could not continue. The Maoist faction, with its untrammeled commitment to violence and dictatorship, emerged as dominant.[200]

A similar enmity developed in the Colombian student movement between pro-Chinese and pro-Russian factions among the nonstudent leaders of the Federación Universitaria Nacional.[201]

The majority of the Communist youth proved to be "renegades," Maoists; when they were expelled from the Communist ranks, they formed their own Young Vanguard, which denounced the Muscovites as a "closed circle" confining itself to the student sector while ignoring the workers and peasants. In Bogotá, pro-Muscovites in 1964 drove Maoists from the classrooms with stones.[202] A student leader, recently returned from a visit to Communist China, assumed the headship of the Maoist faction.

The pro-Peking faction in the Colombian student movement, triumphing over the Muscovites, regarded the orthodox Colombian Communist party as too "tame" and dominated by "old men." With the country's political system in equilibrium, and the presidency alternating between the conservatives and liberals, the Maoists held that "only violent revolution can solve the country's problems," and called for increased strikes and riots. The new Maoist militancy soon provoked a nation-wide strike of more than thirty thousand students in May 1965. An academic controversy at the University of Antioquia was "escalated" by the Maoists into a national stoppage; "contradictions" were presumably being raised to a higher level.

The provocative incident and subsequent events at Antioquia followed a typical pattern. Student demonstrators in the streets clashed with the police; no permission had been secured for the demonstration. The police pursued the students onto the university grounds, allegedly at the rector's request. Thereupon the latter was charged with violating university "autonomy." Within a few days, students were rioting throughout the country in "sympathy" for the Antioquia students. As many as nine thousand students at the National University in Bogotá answered a strike call from their student council. In the eleven days of rioting which followed, more than one hundred were wounded and one student was killed. The President of the Republic proclaimed a state of siege. To appease the students, he asked for the resignation of the rector at Antioquia, Dr. Ignacio Vélez Escobar. The students agreed to terminate the strike on that condition. As happened in other student strikes throughout the world, the symbolic destruction of one father figure brought the strike movement to a close.[203]

To the extent that a commercial and industrial middle class developed, with an orderly parliamentary life, to that extent the studentries themselves became more disciplined and their political action more rational. In Chile, for instance, the radicalism of students was found, when studied, to be "rational and principled rather than pathological"; student political action was reported not to be a significant avenue "for working out emotional problems stemming from psychological maladjustment."[204] Indeed, there is comparatively little involvement of Chilean students in politics. The vast majority of students are indifferent even to the affairs of the Student Federation of Chile. Although between 55 to 60 per cent of those eligible voted in the 1956 and 1957 student elections, no more than fifty to sixty persons were involved in the federation's everyday operations, and of these many were only marginally involved. Moreover, the Social Christians and Conservatives in 1957 constituted the largest single group. The distribution of votes that year was significant:

Social Christian-Conservative	2,970
University Radical	2,210
Communist-Socialist	1,800

The largest group, Social Christian-Conservative, felt that political intrigue should be eliminated from the Student Federation and that student energies should be concentrated on student welfare. Their political philosophy, influenced by Catholic allegiance, emphasized the traditional values of family and marriage, and proposed workers' profit sharing. Pragmatism was dominant in the Chilean student movement; even the socialists and Communists were not much concerned with theory but "thought of themselves as practical politicians."[205] The pragmatism, however, of the Chilean studentry and student movement was atypical of the prevailing trend among their fellows on the continent.

Co-gobierno (co-government), for example, throughout almost all Latin American student movements has turned into an instrument primarily for venting generational resentment against professors and examinations. Once conceived as a device for raising university standards, it has become the means whereby mediocre and inferior students keep standards low. *Co-gobierno* serves as the collective defense for a studentry dragged down to its lowest common denominator. It sacrifices the interests of education and science to the narrowest elitist motives of the students in their quest for diplomas and status. The high hopes entertained for *co-gobierno* overlooked the duality in student movements, their penchant for class elitism as well as idealism, their readiness to fight professors with high standards as well as those with low. *Co-gobierno* thus became the administrative device for the "mediocritization" of universities.

The medical faculty at the University of San Marcos, Peru, seeking to raise the level of its staff, proposed to end *co-gobierno*; at its request, the Peruvian Congress rescinded the requirement that students have one-third representation on its governing council. The medical faculty felt its work was so technical and professional that student meddling was uncalled for; it threatened otherwise to resign as a body. The medical students, however, were recalcitrant, and a protracted strike took place which involved more than ten thousand students in all the country's universities. Even the Catholic University was involved. Generational solidarity carried the day, but medical education was hardly advanced.[206]

The National University of Mexico and the Central University in Venezuela both undertook to eliminate the plague of "fossilism." A "fossil" is a man of mature years who keeps failing his examinations indefinitely and who makes a profession of student life. He avails himself of a right to fail and fail and take the subjects over again. Often he takes over the role of student political leader and at the age of thirty-five is still re-enacting in demonstrations his unresolved adolescent conflicts. At Venezuela, the passage in 1964 of a rule requiring that a student be expelled after a certain number of failures provoked a students' strike which paralyzed the university for a month. In Mexico, in 1961, Dr. Ignacio Chávez, a distinguished cardiologist, on becoming rector of the university, resolutely expelled students for not maintaining an adequate scholastic average. He also denied admission to persons who failed the entrance examination, and refused to allow the university treasurer to contribute to a student strike fund. Thereupon bullets were fired into Dr. Chávez' home. Five years later, a group of rebellious law students, threatening him with death, compelled Dr. Chávez to resign. Thirty of his staff resigned with him. The law students led the storming of the administration building and erected "barricades of stolen buses manned by bicycle-chain wielding students and coeds." Six weeks before, they had set up a barbed-wire barricade around the faculty buildings.[207]

Similarly in 1962 a strike broke out at the medical school of the Caracas Central University. The school tried to introduce a new rule requiring entrance examinations. Student activists provoked disturbances during the two days of tests; one student was almost kicked to death. Faculty members helped the applicants to crawl through tunnels and to climb rear windows ino the examination hall. "Others took students in their cars to secret examination sites." The student strike finally disintegrated.[208]

Would-be full-time political activists, generally Communists, felt they were directly threatened by entrance examinations. In Honduras in 1962, the new requirement for entrance examinations in law, medicine, and other specialties did result in a shift in the balance of political power in the Federación de Estudiantes Universitarios de Honduras. Would-be political activists were unable to pass through the examination "filter" and their proportion in the studentry fell sufficiently so that the democratic student group defeated the Communist by several hundred votes.[209]

What did university *co-gobierno* thus signify? As S. Walter Washington wrote,

> If the students didn't like a test, for instance, they would walk out in a body, or they would decide they were going on their holidays. If a professor tried to penalize them, he generally failed. After the fall of Pérez Jiménez, the students reasserted themselves and exercised more administrative power over the university than ever before. In most cases they were the deciding voice in dropping professors alleged to have been partisans of the recent dictator.[210]

Kalman H. Silvert has justly appraised the workings of *co-gobierno*:

> So they wish to "democratize" the university, a process which involves student participation in university policy making but also seems to mean that students

may feel absolutely free to make and break professors, judge what research is apt and what is unimportant . . . take the university into activist politics whenever they feel it fitting. There are innumerable cases of students ousting individual professors by strike or simple hectoring. . . .[211]

The Latin American student syndicates, under the sway of generational rebellion and narrow elitist interest, thus tended to become agencies of anti-intellectualism and anti-progress. At the University of Buenos Aires, for instance, Dr. Bernardo A. Houssay, Nobel Laureate in medicine, began a movement to introduce entrance examinations. At once the student activists denounced this as "black reaction," as "a plan borrowed from Yanqui Capitalist universities," and directed against children of the working class.[212] It would have been one thing for the student movement to advocate special assistance and courses for working-class children, but it was demagoguery to invoke this just concern in order to keep the university a backward institution.

The notion of *co-gobierno* simply tended to destroy the vocation of a student and to reinforce the pattern of conflict, strikes, and demonstrations. A typical academic year in Brazil began with a strike in September over a constitutional crisis, and went on to a November strike against cramming for examinations, an April strike against the appointment on the local campus of a certain professor, and a national strike in June to secure a one-third student participation on governing boards. Perpetual disorders made the studentries themselves long for a "strong government"; the endless generational conflicts led to a contempt for liberal democracy, and a longing for a new paternalism, a new father. At Buenos Aires, 70 per cent of the youth indicated on a poll that they wanted a "strong government that can put everybody in his place"; in Brazil likewise, as an American student observer reported, the students believed in paternalistic government with a strong central authority. The student movement's mixture of elitism and populism, the students' insistence on their own special privileges at the same time as they were organizing peasants' leagues, culminated in an advocacy of dictatorship.[213]

Generational revolt infused the slogans "autonomy of the university" and "co-government" with an irrational content. Generational revolt imposed on them its own psychological dialectic. University autonomy had originally signified freedom for the intellectual elite to carry on in its own work, and freedom from interference by the army or the church.[214] It was a concept born of the feudal society, in which each person was bound by his estate; in such a society the towns growing up in the interstices had fought for their autonomy from feudal lords; the church had fought for its autonomy from the temporal, military, feudal rulers. Similarly, the universities had early fought for their prerogatives and status and had to define their place in a feudal world. The clerks, the clerisy, were precursors of an intellectual class. Thus, "autonomy" is a word laden with traditional significance in Latin

America; it almost suggests academic freedom, an enclave for research and free discussion. In fact, however, it has come to mean the denial of academic freedom; and, above all, it has even come to signify an enclave for the organization of guerrilla warfare against society. "Autonomy" has been corrupted to mean the freedom to establish a university base for guerrilla operations and violence. Far from being a liberal democratic concept, it has become one for an intellectual elite which claims immunity from democratic law.

Take the case of Venezuela in 1960. President Romulo Betancourt was striving energetically to strengthen the democratic government and procedures, to achieve social reforms within a constitutional setting. Then, armed high school students intervened in a strike of telephone company workers, setting fire to buses and automobiles. The company accepted arbitration; but high school and university students, shouting Castroite slogans, tried to storm police and radio stations. Two hundred armed university students fortified themselves in the Central University, calling their area "Stalingrad," and fired on troops. Finally the University Council secured their evacuation. The major trade unions supported the government, but the radical student movement, linked to the revolutionary Left and to the Communists, fought a brief civil war against the government, with "university autonomy" as the slogan for a privileged student sanctuary for terrorist activity.[215]

The "autonomy" of the universities was thus carried to the absurd extreme of justifying the creation of an anti-state within a state. When subsequently the Communists were using terror and violence against the democratically elected President Betancourt, Hector Mujica, a Communist leader, and nonstudent, was permanently ensconced on the university's grounds. "The free territory of America" it was called, because the police could not enter. As a terrorist, Mujica would have been arrested if he went downtown; the university was like a medieval church sanctuary against the laity, except that the church in this case was a terrorist intellectual one. "When his visitors come he shows them his towels and bedding, which he keeps in his file cabinet, and offers them fruit his family brings him," reported *The New York Times* correspondent.[216] Thus student elitism claimed privileges outside the law.

In the late fifties Fidel Castro became the symbol of the student movement in arms, at its most successful synthesis of elitism and populism. "The Cuban Revolution radicalized Latin American student politics and changed the nature of radical student political activity," wrote David Spencer. Before 1959, student organizations, predominantly functioning as syndicates for student interests, would make sporadic forays, as "undefined Leftists," into violence. Now, however, there was the Cuban model to emulate; "organized and systematized rather than merely sporadic violence was used, either through direct action within the university, or by demonstration, riots, student guerrilla warfare and urban terrorism outside the university."[217]

If terrorism was the glorified expressive tactic of the students of the nineteenth century, and terrorists the admired figures, then "guerrilla warfare" became the admired means of students of the twentieth century.

The Latin American student movement traversed the road from the Córdoba Manifesto, with its stirring liberal declaration for university reform, to Fidel Castro's guerilla warfare. Violence was held to be justified on the ground "that university reform could not be achieved before a general social revolution took place. . . . Therefore, the role of the student was to struggle actively against 'national and international forces of oppression.' "

Student guerilla warfare, inspired by the Fidelista example, became a reality in a series of countries—Venezuela, Guatemala, Honduras, Nicaragua, Colombia, Ecuador, Peru, Haiti, the Dominican Republic. There were "direct confrontations" with the government, often under Fidelista auspices, in El Salvador, Nicaragua, the Dominican Republic, Venezuela, Ecuador, Guatemala, and Panama.[218]

The notion of waging "guerilla warfare" on society excited student activists. The high point of Fidelista appeal came in 1963 in Peru when a Fidelista candidate of the Peruvian FLN (Frente de Liberación Nacional), Mario Castillo, was elected president of the student Federación Universitaria de San Marcos. The retiring president of the student federation, Juan Campos Lama, said he would go from the university to the mountains to give the peasants "a political conscience and a more revolutionary outlook." Soon afterward, seven students were captured who had abandoned their studies to practice the precepts of Che Guevara's manual *Guerrilla Warfare.* The group, which included several former student leaders, clashed with Civil Guards after crossing the Bolivian border; they evidently were returnees from Cuban guerrilla training. One guardsman was killed, and four students were wounded and one killed. The young student guerrillas had evidently planned on a rendezvous with a peasant leader, Hugo Blanco, with whom one of them had attended the Colegio Nacional de Ciencias. "The would-be guerrillas were also linked with a plot to kidnap the Papal Nuncio in Lima and hold him until the rest of the political prisoners jailed since January were released." Shortly afterward, on May 30, Hugo Blanco, the "Fidel Castro of the Andes," was arrested in a peasant hut. The government, a military junta, was meanwhile retaliating against terrorist outbreaks with repressive legislation which exceeded its constitutional powers.[219]

Throughout Latin America, student activists were moved by Che Guevara's call to the intellectuals to take the lead as guerrillas. The vocation of guerrilla leadership was a proven road to power that satisfied both elitist and populist impulses. "The directors of guerrilla warfare," wrote Guevara, "are not men who have bent their backs day after day over the furrow. They are men who understand the necessity for changes in the social treatment accorded to peasants, without having suffered in the usual case this bitter treatment in their own persons."[220] The communist *World Student News* had an article titled "Student Guerrillas," on its Venezuelan comrades, about whom it spoke with evident pride: "The members of the Anzoategui group are for the most part students: José Romula Nino, political mentor of the undertaking, is a B.A. in philosophy and letters and a student of economics. He is 26 years old. . . . Máximo Canales is 21, chief of the Rudos Menzones detachment and an economics student. Juan Montilha is 29 and studies law. Jesús María Hernandez, 21, is an engineering major, Carlos Hidalgo, 22, is the same. . . . Antonio López, 21, studies economics, while José María Paláez, also 21, attends an evening school." The Anzoategui group consisted of nine Venezuelans who seized the ship of that name and, defying the Venezuelan and United States navies, raised the banner of "National Liberation" from the elected government of Betancourt and then sailed into Brazilian waters. "It is up to us, the young people, to liberate our country. We have more fighting spirit. We are less tied down by life." It was the typical messianic activist speaking. "You are all only children!" the Communist correspondent could not help observing.[221]

The cleavage of the generations became more acute in Latin American society as student activists felt the attraction of "guerrilla warfare." The most symbolic case was that of the student José Manuel Saher and his father, Pablo Saher Perez, governor of the state of Falcon in Venezuela. The father, a supporter of the democratic President Romulo Betancourt, was working efficiently to eradicate the guerrilla bands. His son, José, a student of economics at the Central University, became a disciple of Castro. Joining an underground Armed Forces of National Liberation, he assumed a new identity as "Commandate Chema," leader of a guerrilla band. Father and son exchanged bitter letters in 1962. "Dear Father," wrote the son, "I cannot live under the same roof with a man who is responsible for the assassination . . ." The father could not understand how his son, with his Roman Catholic upbringing, had chosen rebellion. Later the son was captured, but after two years' imprisonment was pardoned by the President. He was sent to study in London, but returned clandestinely to lead another guerrilla band in the mountains. In March 1967 he was killed during a surprise attack on an army patrol. The soldiers brought the son's body back to the father.[222]

In Fidel Castro, the Latin American student movement saw a model technician for its takeover of political power. Here was a movement led and officered by students, proceeding without benefit of support by the labor movement, creating its own generational version of Marxism. The old Marxist-Communists were middle-aged bureaucrats; the Apristas, born of the student movement of the thirties, were tired and stodgy. Fidelismo, as an ideology on the other hand, reflected the activist mood of the new student elite. When it ruled Havana University, it ended academic freedom permanently.[223]

In his speech, "I am a Marxist-Leninist," on December 2, 1961, Castro gave explicit recognition to the fact that the July 26th Movement had been led by students. The Directorio Revolucionario, he said, represented "fundamentally the student sector."[224] This, then, was a movement and ideology which lent itself admirably to the purposes of student leaders ambitious for political power. It was adapted to countries where the masses as a whole were sunk in political apathy. For the Cuban peasantry had contributed only a small minority of Castro's revolutionary force. As for the proletariat, it too had stood aloof from the movement in its civil war days. Castroism was an ideology of bourgeois intellectuals; forging claims to leadership without benefit of peasant or proletarian class support, the Castroites claimed nonetheless to be acting on behalf of the oppressed classes.

Students who had achieved political power expounded the new ideology of the crucial role of the student elite in the model Cuban revolution to C. Wright Mills, an admiring sociological reporter:

> Our revolution is not a revolution made by labor unions or wage workers in the city, or by labor parties, or by anything like that. It is far from any revolution you ever heard of before. First of all, as we've already told you, its leaders have been young intellectuals and students from the University of Havana. They were the ones who made the first moves. They made a lot of first moves for a long time before some of their moves began to pay off. Then, as they moved, the movement they were building picked up the power of the Cuban peasants, of the *campesinos*. Our revolution really began—and the fate of Batista was sealed—when a handful of these young intellectuals really got together with the peasants. . . .
>
> So far as the different classes of Cuba are concerned, the revolution looks like this: Throughout it has been, and it is, led by this young intelligentsia . . .
>
> It is not an "economically determined" revolution, either—in its origins or in its course . . .[225]

And if it was not an economically determined revolution, then what was it? It sprang from the generational revolt of students, that product of selfless idealism, elitist power-seeking, literary culture, and rebellion against the elders:

> The revolution was incubated at the university. Now, you have to realize that universities in Latin America are just not like North American universities. In Cuba, even in the old order, Havana University was a curious island of thwarted freedom in the sea of Batista stupidity and tyranny. The professors who ran it took orders neither from the politicians nor the police. You might think this strange, but it really isn't. The students in the old order were mainly sons and daughters and friends of the ruling groups, and their radicalism was seen as "a passing phase," something they were just going through. Also, these students, after they grew up, were going to be the government officials and politicians, as well as the doctors and lawyers.

Of course, even so, students were beaten up by the Batista police, and shot at. And during the last year of the tyranny, the university was just closed down. But before all that the university was the cradle of the revolutionary ideas. And it was only at the university that any more or less free "politics" went on. . . . The students were politicos, noisy and angry. They made speeches and put out manifestos, and they took to the streets. And it was in this place, this half-free island in the middle of the Cuban misery, that, beginning in 1945, Fidel Castro—son of a rich man and a student of law—found his gift as an orator.[226]

Generational revolt, indeed, as it grew in Cuba, finally found its ideology in Castroism. "The tragedy of the Cuban middle class," wrote the Cuban writer, Linos Novas Calvo, was a kind of "schizophrenia," which resulted in large part from the discontinuity and estrangement of fathers and sons.[227] "The sons and daughters of the bourgeoisie," as Theodore Draper said in July 1960, "dedicate themselves to the destruction of their own class in the name of nationalism and socialism."[228] The old middle class, businessmen, shopkeepers, small factory and farm operators, sent their children to the University of Havana. There men were trained for the bureaucracy and liberal professions in numbers which outran the economy's absorptive capacity. Students arose who were more ready to agitate than to study. Fidel Castro, son of a poor Spanish immigrant grown rich in sugar and lumber, went to the University of Havana Law School, where, as he said, he belonged to those who "never went to class, never opened a book other than on the eve of examinations." Indeed, he once cried, "How many times have I deplored the fact that I was not forced to study something else."[229] Talking to students, he repeatedly blamed others, that is, his father, for his own entry into legal study, and this repetitive theme suggests some of the roots of Castro's own generational conflict and indirectly of his anti-Americanism.

In his blaming of others for having misled him, the United States became a surrogate father to be blamed. Jean Paul Sartre wrote, "If the United States didn't exist, the Cuban revolution would perhaps invent it."[230]

Castro, the charismatic student leader, exerted an appeal that crossed class lines; his was a common denominator of appeal to the youth among peasants, workingmen, and bourgeois. Theodore Draper writes, "We are accustomed to 'class analyses,' but we have yet to devote enough thought to a 'generational' struggle that cuts across classes and even wins converts from the younger generation of the class marked out for destruction."[231]

From the drives of the generational unconscious arose not only the propensity to terrorism but also the associated trait of suicidalism, even among the Latin American students in a Roman Catholic culture. A young Argentine writer, Haroldo Pedro Conti, has depicted the self-destructive mood in his story "The Cause": "Marcelo had suffered a real triumph in the final Y.C.L. [Young Communist League] meeting. Not only had the cops beaten them up, they had forced them to chew their handbills and rub the slogans off their walls with their fingers. Someone even got killed. A student as usual. So that between the funeral, the silent protest march, the demonstrations, and the memorial masses, Marcelo collected a really impressive set of bruises. Especially the scar over his left eyebrow, which looked so good to him." Marcelo was simply characterized: "Marcelo: chronic student and chairman of the F.S.U. supported the Reform. Had fought the cops at a Y.S.L. [Young Socialist League] meeting That gave him a special aura. . . . When the Reform finally triumphed, he'd have to scrounge around for something else."[232]

The suicide rate in Latin American countries which had militant student movements exhibited something of the youth-weighted pattern typical of countries which suffer from generational conflict. In 1962, for instance, a year of militancy for the Venezuelan and Dominican student movements, the number of suicides in absolute terms was highest for the young twenty-year-olds.

Number of Male Suicides in Venezuela and Dominican Republic by Age-Groups in 1962[233]

AGE-GROUP	VENEZUELA (WITHOUT INDIAN TRIBES)	DOMINICAN REPUBLIC
10–14	—	1
15–19	20	3
20–24	48	14
25–29	33	4
30–34	39	6
35–39	24	3
40–44	20	4
45–49	25	4
50–54	19	7
55–59	17	1
60–64	8	—
65–69	13	—
70–74	10	2
75–79	1	—
All ages	282	50

In terms of percentages of every one hundred thousand male population, the suicide rate in Venezuela for the early twenties exceeded that of other groups up to the age of forty-five.[234] The pattern was midway between that of "normal" countries like Canada, the United States, and France and those most abnormal, such as Russia in the 1900s.

The Soviet Communist world, however, remains suspicious of the Latin American student movement, precisely because the psychology of generational revolt stands outside the Marxist philosophy; the Soviet Communists pay tribute to its idealism, but regard it as an uncertain ally. They feel uncomfortable with movements not grounded in class realities but rather in idealism. "Most Latin American students come from families belonging to the urban middle classes," notes the *World Marxist Review*, the international organ of the Communist parties. "Students are impelled to the revolutionary movement," it observes, "by such intrinsic elements of their way of life and psychology as the *traditions* of democratic struggle, which in the course of the past century have become a material force. . . ." Of course, it contravened the historical materialist standpoint to regard a psychological and idealistic determinant as a "material force."[235] To explain the sources of student radicalism, the *World Marxist Review* found itself obliged to think in non-Marxist categories: "the traditional student nonconformism, their indifference to conventions and defiance of bans, their spirit of rebellion and gravitation towards the new." Suddenly the Marxist analysis found itself begetting a non-Marxist antithesis, a law of generational struggle, as invariant as and perhaps more basic to history than the law of class struggle.

The historical initiative in traditional societies, the *World Marxist Review* recognized, is taken by the student:

> It is natural that the student youth and the intelligentsia and the "intellectual elite" of Latin American society should be the first to realize the need for change and to see the kind of change the people need. This is the rule in all countries on the threshold of revolutionary changes, especially those at the stage of historical development now reached in Latin America. . . . It is not fortuitous that the Latin American youth have written some of the finest pages in their history precisely in the struggle against dictators (Machado, Pérez Jiménez, Ubico, Martínez, Trujillo, and the present military junta in Ecuador) and against naked U.S. intervention (Panama and the Dominican Republic).[236]

Marxist analysis is baffled by the surd motivation, from its standpoint, in the student movement—the students in their youthful years are prone to "revolutionary romanticism, and faith in their own powers (not to speak of the predominance of emotion over reason)." Here then is a movement in which emotion is primary, not one's interest, not one's rational calculations, but romance, irrational yearning; here is a movement made up of noneconomic men, bourgeois youth whose consciousness has not yet been shaped by class existence. If all persons were like students, historical materialism would be false. "Alas, youth and student years are transient. Usually it is taken for granted that after graduation young people often forget the revolutionary principles they once upheld, frequently at the risk of their lives, and settle down to a measured life within the framework of the existing order." In short, when they become historical materialists, the students cease being revolutionists.[237]

Where emotion predominates over reason, furthermore, where generational rebelliousness resists Communist party discipline itself, the student movement becomes an untrustworthy ally. The student youth, complains *World Marxist Review*, upset the progressive front by opposing the Peronist regime in Argentina and the revolution in Bolivia; they have failed, it says, to help unconditionally anti-imperialist (i.e., anti-American) regimes. In Guatemala, "successive generations of students" fought against the dictatorship, but says *World Marxist Review*, when it affected their property interests, the students became reactionary.[238] There was indeed a curious unpredictability in the Guatemalan student movement as in the Latin American generally which defied Marxist categories.[239]

NOTES

1. See Joseph Fischer, "The University Student in South and South-East Asia," *Minerva*, II (Autumn 1963), 38, 45.

2. The term "gerontocracy" was invented by Sir James G. Frazer. In discussing the Australian aborigines, he wrote that the political constitution of their tribe, insofar as they could be said to have one, was "an oligarchy of old and influential men, who meet in council and decide on all measures of importance, to the practical exclusion of the younger men. Their deliberative assembly answers to the senate of later times: if we had to coin a word for such a government of elders we might call it a *gerontocracy*." See Sir James G. Frazer, *Lectures on the Early History of the Kingship* (London, 1905), p. 107. Also see W. H. R. Rivers, *The History of Melanesian Society*, II (Cambridge, Eng., 1914), 68, 105.

3. Henry Habib Ayrout, S. J., *The Egyptian Peasant*, tr. J. A. Williams (Boston, 1963), pp. 145–152.

4. Richard N. Adams *et al.*, *Social Change in Latin America Today* (New York, 1960), p. 34.

5. Samuel Ramos, *Profile of Man and Culture in Mexico* (Austin, Tex., 1962), pp. 9, 37, 56–58, 64. See also Gilberto Freyre, *The Mansions and the Shanties: The Making of Modern Brazil*, tr. Harriet de Onís (New York, 1963), p. 58.

6. Leopoldo Zea, *The Latin-American Mind*, tr. James H. Abbott and Lowell Dunham (Norman, Okla., 1963), pp. 54–58, 73, 83.

7. Evelyn P. Stevens, "Mexican Machismo: Politics and Value Orientations," *Western Political Quarterly*, XVIII, No. 4 (1965), 848–857; Octavio Paz, *The Labyrinth of Solitude: Life and Thought in Mexico*, tr. Lysander Kemp (New York, 1962). Also see Richard S. Weinert, "Violence in Pre-Modern Societies: Rival Colombia," *American Political Science Review*, LX (1966), 341.

8. Paz, *op. cit.*, pp. 88, 81–85. "The inferiority complex thus becomes contagious, and so we get the unique case of Spanish America, in which the college and university man feels unfit for command." See José Vasconcelos: *A Mexican Ulysses: An Autobiography*, tr. W. Rex Crawford (Bloomington, Indiana, 1963), pp. 137–138.

9. Keith Botsford, "Latin America: Masses and Messiahs," *New Leader*, XLVI (December 23, 1963), 10.

10. George W. Shepherd, Jr., "Seven Days that Shook the Sudan," *Africa Today*, XI, No. 10 (December 1964), 10–13.

11. Paz., *op. cit.*, p. 137.

12. *Ibid.*, p. 139. At college, writes Vasconcelos, the director was a Porfirista colonel who "never allowed us to congregate in the patios or around the college. . . . The fear that tyranny has of public assembly was very keen, even if we got together for nothing more than to read poetry." See Vasconcelos, *op. cit.*, pp. 37, 35. When Vasconcelos became Minister of Education, he became in turn the target for student uprisings; see his pp. 168, 176–177, and his allusion to "the farce of university autonomy." Also

see John H. Haddox, *Vasconcelos of Mexico: Philosopher and Prophet* (Austin, 1967), p. 5.

13. Levon Melikian, "The Dethronement of the Father," *Middle East Forum* (January 1960), pp. 23–25. Dr. Melikian, chairman of the Department of Psychology at Beirut, studied 2,250 college and secondary students in Egypt, Lebanon, Jordan, Syria, and Iraq. Also see Guthrie Moir, "Student Frustration in Iraq," *Contemporary Review*, December 1957, pp. 328–330. This author regards sexual frustration as the primary factor in "the explosive emotions of these armies of youngsters" in the coffee shops; he notes that girls have virtually no social life outside their families, and that sports are sadly lacking.

14. Levon H. Melikian, "Some Correlates of Authoritarianism in Two Cultural Groups," *Journal of Psychology*, XLII (1956), 237–248. See also Morroe Berger, *The Arab World Today* (New York, 1962), p. 377.

15. Z.N.Z., "Youth and Politics in the Near East," *World Today*, (March 1951), p. 103.

16. George Antonius, *The Arab Awakening: the Story of the Arab National Movement* (London, 1938), pp. 106–107.

17. Douglas E. Ashford, *Political Change in Morocco* (Princeton, 1961), p. 34.

18. Ernest Edmondson Rasmaur, Jr., *The Young Turks: Prelude to the Revolution of 1908* (Princeton, 1957), pp. 14–19, 21, 63, 85, 95. Actually, an earlier Turkish student movement had been responsible for the ouster of the Sultan Abdul-Aziz in 1876. "The forces used to carry out the coup which had unseated Sultan Abdul-Aziz had been provided by the cadets of the Ottoman Military Academy. . . . The participation of the students was an early indication of the extent to which libertarian concepts would find echoes among military students. Some of the more current Western political conceptions had in fact been introduced by Suleiman Pasha into the school, thinly disguised as a reader in world literature." See Serif A. Mardin, "Libertarian Movements in the Ottoman Empire 1878–1895," *Middle East Journal*, XVI (Spring 1962), 178.

19. Bernard Lewis, *The Emergence of Modern Turkey* (New York, 1961), p. 238.

20. Walter F. Weiker, "Academic Freedom and Problems of Higher Education in Turkey," *Middle East Journal*, XVI (Summer 1962), 281–283.

21. Parviz Takerpour, "Portrait of a Nation," *Iran Nameh*, III, No. 16 (March-April 1962), 1.

22. Frank Howard, "U.S. Press and Iran," *Iran Nameh*, III, No. 16 (March-April 1962), 3; Harrison Salisbury in *The New York Times*, December 4, 1961.

23. T. C. Wang, *The Youth Movement in China* (New York, 1927), pp. 91–92.

24. Chün-tu Hsüeh, *Huang Hsing and the Chinese Revolution* (Stanford, Calif., 1961), pp. 35–39, 42–43, 59, 73–76, 199. Also see Robert A. Scalapino and George T. Yu, *The Chinese Anarchist Movement* (Berkeley, Calif., 1961), pp. 1–2, 34, 59–60.

25. Wen-Han Kiang, *The Chinese Student Movement* (New York, 1948), pp. 22, 24, 134–135.

26. Edgar Snow, *Red Star over China* (New York, 1938), pp. 153–154; Wen-Han Kiang, *op. cit.*, p. 76.

27. Snow, *op. cit.*, pp. 125–126.

28. *Ibid.*, pp. 130, 138. Also see Siao-Yu, *Mao Tse-Tung and I Were Beggars*, tr. Phyllis Ling-cho (Syracuse, 1959), pp. 61, 67–69.

29. Howard L. Boorman, "Liu Shao-ch'i: A Political Profile," *China Quarterly*, No. 10 (April-June 1962).

30. Mao Tse-tung, *Nineteen Poems*, tr. Andrew Boyd (Peking, 1958), p. 9.

31. *Red Dust: Autobiographies of Chinese Communists*, as told to Nym Wales (Stanford, Calif., 1952), pp. 49, 51, 54.

32. *Ibid.*, p. 58.

33. *Ibid.*, p. 77.

34. *Ibid.*, pp. 134–135.

35. *Ibid.*, pp. 143–144.

36. C. C. Yu, "A Student in the Students' Movement," *Chinese Students' Monthly*, XV, No. 5 (March 1920), 31–32. The verbatim account is that of C. K. Chuang.

37. Chow Tse-tsung, *The May Fourth Movement: Intellectual Revolution in China* (Cambridge, Mass., 1960), p. 108.

38. *Ibid.*, p. 99.

39. *Ibid.*, p. 144.

40. "The Significance of the Student Strike," *Chinese Students' Monthly*, XV, No. 2 (December 1919), 9–10.

41. John Dewey, "The Student Revolt in China," *New Republic*, XX (1919), 16–18.

42. Chow Tse-tsung, *op. cit.*, pp. 164, 247–248; Snow, *op. cit.*, p. 157; Tsi Chang Wang, *The Youth Movement in China* (New York, 1927), p. 110; Wen-Han Kiang, *op. cit.*, p. 76; Benjamin I. Schwartz, *Chinese Communism and the Rise of Mao* (Cambridge, Mass., 1952), pp. 10–11; Harold R. Isaacs, *The Tragedy of the Chinese Revolution* (rev. edn.; Stanford, Calif., 1951), pp. 53–54.

43. Tsi Chang Wang, *op. cit.*, p. 60.

44. James Arthur Muller, "The New East I. The Student Movement in China," *The Nation*, CIX (1919), 833.

45. Agnes Smedley, *The Great Road: The Life and Times of Chu Teh* (New York, 1956), pp. 120, 123–124; Lu Hsun, "Regret for the Past," in *Chosen Pages* (New York, 1959?), pp. 19, 205, 219.

46. Chu Teh, in Smedley, *op. cit.*, p. 120.

47. Vincent Y. C. Shih, "A Talk with Hu Shih," *China Quarterly*, No. 10 (April-June 1962), p. 163. Also see Harley Farnsworth MacNair, *China in Revolution: An Analysis of Politics and Militarism under the Republic* (Chicago, 1931), pp. 66–67; Jerome B. Grieder, "Hu Shih: An Appreciation," *China Quarterly*, No. 12 (October-December 1962), p. 98.

48. Paul Monroe, *China: A Nation in Evolution* (New York, 1928), p. 272. Also see John Pierrepont Rice, "China and the Chinese," *Chinese Students' Monthly*, XVI (1921), 571.

49. Nym Wales, *op. cit.*, pp. 60, 143.

50. *Ibid.*, pp. 59–60.

51. *Ibid.*, p. 51.

52. *Ibid.*, p. 29.

53. Snow, *op. cit.*, p. 153.

54. Monroe, *op. cit.*, p. 288.

55. See Min-Ch'ien T. Z. Tyau, *China Awakened* (New York, 1922), pp. 154–155.

56. Monroe, *op. cit.*, pp. 294–295.

57. Mao Tse-tung, "Talks at the Yenan Forum on Art and Literature," May 2, 1942, in *Selected Works of Mao Tse-tung* (London, 1956), p. 67.

58. Nym Wales, *op. cit.*, p. 51.

59. *Ibid.*, p. 54; also see Wen-Han Kiang, *op. cit.*, p. 95.

60. Hubert Freyn, *Chinese Education in the War* (Shanghai, 1940), pp. 7–8, 81; Wen-Han Kiang, *op. cit.*, p. 117.

61. "In the north they joined the Communists, while in central China they became Kuomintang officers. The students who succeeded them were a mixed crew. By law any student at a high school or university was exempt from the draft. . . . Enrollment boomed." See Theodore H. White and Annalee Jacoby, *Thunder out of China* (New York, 1946), p. 109.

62. Mu Fu-Sheng, *The Wilting of the Hundred Flowers: The Chinese Intelligentsia under Mao* (New York, 1962), p. 168; *The Storm: Student Unrest in China, China Viewpoints* (Hong Kong, 1958); Michael Harrington, "Chinese Students Take Lead in Bold Fight for Democracy," *Labor Action*, April 21, 1958, p. 5.

63. Liu Shao-ch'i, *On the Party* (Peking, 1954), pp. 111–116.

64. Klaus H. Pringsheim, "The Functions of the Chinese Communist Youth Leagues (1920–1949)," *China Quarterly*, No. 12 (October-December 1962), p. 86.

65. Edgar Snow, "Mao Tse-tung: A Worried Man at 72?" *China Report*, I, No. 4 (June 1965), 1–3; see also "Peking Reshaping Higher Education," *The New York Times*, June 25, 1966, pp. 1, 3.

66. "Youth in Mao's China," *Youth and Freedom*, VIII, No. 4 (1966), 2.

67. "Red Guards' Influence in Maoist Cultural Revolution Found to be Wanting," *The New York Times*, March 5, 1967. A Soviet correspondent reported, " 'Red Guards' from Peking University ran riot in the cemetery in the western part of Peking where rest the mortal remains of the famous Chinese painter Chi Pai-shih. They toppled many gravestones to the ground . . ." See "Inside China: Eyewitnesses," and "Literature, the Arts, and Education," *Survey*, No. 63 (April 1967), pp. 47, 74; also "Youth in Mao's China," *Youth and Freedom*, VIII, No. 4 (1966), p. 2.

68. See the quotations from *People's Daily* in *China Report*, VI (October-November 1966), 3.

69. "Revolutionary Young Fighters Going on Long Marches," *Peking Review*, No. 48 (November 25, 1966), pp. 9–10.

70. "The Long March Detachment of Red Guards Walks 1,000 Kilometres to Peking to Exchange Revolutionary Experience," *Peking Review*, No. 44 (October 28, 1966), pp. 17–19.

71. "Circular of Central Committee of Chinese Communist Party (May 16, 1966)," *Peking Review*, No. 20 (May 19, 1967), pp. 8–9.

72. "Chairman Mao Once More Receives a Million Young Revolutionary

Fighters," *Peking Review*, No. 39 (September 23, 1966), pp. 5–6.

73. "Congress of Red Guards of Peking Middle Schools Established," *Peking Review*, No. 14 (March 31, 1967), p. 13.

74. "Congress of Red Guards of Universities and Colleges in Peking Formed," *Peking Review*, No. 11 (March 10, 1967), pp. 5 ff.

75. "Chinese People Resolved to Make Every Undertaking a Great School of Mao Tse-tung's Thought," *Peking Review*, No. 36 (September 2, 1966), pp. 20, 23; see also "Comrade Lin Pao's Speech," *Peking Review*, No. 37 (September 9, 1966), p. 10.

76. "Oppose Economism and Smash the Latest Counter-Attack by the Bourgeois Reactionary Line," *Peking Review*, No. 4 (January 20, 1967), pp. 12 ff; "Soviet Revisionist Leading Clique Restores Capitalism," *Peking Review*, No. 48 (November 25, 1966), p. 28. "Many young people are led not to study for the revolution but to immerse themselves in books for the university entrance examination and to pay no heed to politics." The examination system, it was urged, should be abolished; instead, students "should first of all get 'ideological diplomas' from the working class and the poor and lower-middle peasants." See "Peking Students Write to Party Central Committee and Chairman Mao Strongly Urging Abolition of Old College Entrance Examination System," *Peking Review*, No. 26 (June 24, 1966), pp. 18–19.

77. Kim San and Nym Wales, *Song of Ariran: The Life Story of a Korean Rebel* (New York, 1941), pp. 22, 27.

78. Master Meng said, however, "Anything can be a matter of duty, and duty towards parents is the root of them all." See E. R. Hughes (ed.), *Chinese Philosophy in Classical Times* (London, 1950), p. 100.

79. C. I. Eugene Kim and Ke-soo Kim, "The April 1960 Korean Student Movement," *Western Political Quarterly*, XVII (March 1964), 84, 94. This was a study based on a survey of 231 students in the Department of Political Science of Konkuk University in Seoul in April 1961.

80. "Students' Rioting Renewed in Seoul," *The New York Times*, July 4, 1967. Once again, fifteen thousand students from fourteen colleges and universities demonstrated against corruption and the re-election of the government of the President, the former general, Chung Hee Park.

81. Lawrence H. Battistini, *The Postwar Student Struggle in Japan* (Tokyo, 1956), pp. 115–116; Michiya Shimbori, "Comparison between Pre- and Post-War Student Movements in Japan," *Sociology and Education*, XXXVII (1963), 65–66.

82. Toshio Kamba, *Saigo No Bisho* (Last Smile; Tokyo, 1960). All passages cited from this book are adapted from a manuscript translation provided by its author.

83. I am grateful to the Zengakuren activists who joined with my assistants in working out the details of the questionnaire. A grant from the Center of Japanese Studies at the University of California made possible the employment of two assistants and interpreters.

84. Interview of August 3, 1962.

85. Battistini, *op. cit.*, pp. 20–21.

86. Scott C. Flanagan, *Zengakuren and the Postwar Japanese Student Movement*, unpublished master's thesis, University of California, Berkeley, 1963, pp. 69–81; Battistini, *op. cit.*, pp. 68–71.

87. Flanagan, *op. cit.*, pp. 184, 191, 214; Battistini, *op. cit.*, 40, 89, 101.

88. Flanagan, *op. cit.*, p. 141.

89. *Ibid.*, pp. 171–175.

90. *Ibid.*, pp. 197–200.

91. See Matsumoto Shigeharu, "What Happened in Japan: A Symposium," *Japan Quarterly*, VII, No. 4 (1960), 407; Kanichi Fukuda, "The May-June Incident," *Far Eastern Survey*, XXIX (October 1960), 149–150; Herbert Passin, "The Sources of Protest in Japan," *American Political Science Review*, LVI (1962), 393.

92. The Japanese studentry is in 1968 even more of an elite than it was before the war. In 1936, one applicant out of every 1.64 was admitted to the universities; in 1959, on the other hand, only one out of every 5.11 applicants was admitted. This decline in the ratio of admitted students to applicants had taken place despite an expansion of the overall number of students admitted from 7,549 in 1936 to 45,817 in 1959. The elite selection in the public universities was more arduous in the public colleges than in the private; in 1959, one out of every 77 applicants was admitted to the former, and one out of every 3.91 to the latter. See "Education Booming in Japan," *Japan Times*, November 2, 1960, p. 7.

93. Benjamin Martin, "Japanese Mining Labor: the Miike Strike," *Far Eastern Survey*, XXX, No. 2 (February 1961), 29.

94. See George R. Packard, "They Were Born When the Bomb Was Dropped," *The New York Times Magazine*, August 29, 1965, pp. 28 ff.

95. *The Yomiuri*, July 20, 1962, p. 3.

96. *Youth and Freedom*, VI, No. 3 (1964), 13. Also see *Youth and Freedom*, VI, No. 6 (1964), 13.

97. Packard, *op. cit.*, p. 92.

98. "Education in Japan," *Youth and Freedom*, VII, No. 1 (1965), 4.

99. Packard, *op. cit.*, p. 92.

100. "But in Japan—Violence among Some Students," *Youth and Nation*, VI, No. 6 (1964) 26.

101. *Loc. cit.* A poll of Japanese high school students in Tokyo and Hyoto, published in February 1967 in the magazine *Shukan Asahi*, showed that more than 70 per cent of them condemned the practices of the Chinese Red Guards. See "Japan's Students Score Red Guards," *The New York Times*, February 19, 1967.

102. "Zengakuren: Where Are They Now?" *The Japan Times*, November 16, 1967. I owe this item to Professor Basil Rauch of Columbia University.

103. Jeanne S. Mintz, *Mohammed, Marx, and Marhaen: The Roots of Indonesian Socialism* (New York, 1965), pp. 102, 145, 13.

104. *Ibid.*, p. 206. The name *Perserikatan Kommunist di India* adopted in 1920 means in Malayan "Communist Party of the Indies."

105. *Ibid.*, p. 17.

106. "Gibes at Sukarno Divert Jakarta," *The New York Times*, May 13, 1966.

107. Seth S. King, "The Great Purge in Indonesia," *The New York Times Magazine*, May 8, 1966, pp. 25, 89.

108. Richard S. Elegant, "Indonesia's Slaughtered Reds," *San Francisco Chronicle*, May 5, 1966, p. 2E.

109. Seth S. King, "Students Emerge as Jakarta Force," *The New York Times*, April 2, 1966.

110. Justus M. Van der Kroef, "The Educated Unemployed in Southeast Asia," *Journal of Higher Education*, XXXI (April 1960), 177–178; Jeanne S. Mintz, *Mohammed, op. cit.*, p. 206.

111. Justus M. Van der Kroef, "The Cult of the Doctor in Indonesia," *Journal of Educational Sociology*, XXXII (1959), 388.

112. Cited in Van der Kroef, "The Cult of the Doctor," pp. 387–388; from Clifford Geertz, *The Development of the Javanese Economy: A Socio-Cultural Approach* (mimeographed; Cambridge, Mass., April 1956), p. 72.

113. Van der Kroef, "The Cult of the Doctor," p. 385.

114. *Ibid.*, p. 387.

115. Arnold C. Brackman, *Indonesian Communism: A History* (New York, 1963), p. 233.

116. *Ibid.*, p. 235.

117. *Ibid.*, p. 236.

118. *Ibid.*, p. xiv. See Mochtar Lubis, "The Indonesian Communist Movement," *Far Eastern Survey*, November 1954.

119. World Univcrsity Service, *Annual Report: 1954–1955* (Geneva), p. 39.

120. Prabodh Chandra, *Student Movement in India* (Lahore, 1938), pp. 48, 51, 54.

121. *Students' Call*, Journal of the Bombay Presidency Students' Federation, April 1937, pp. 3, 4, 6, 11, 12, 25, 26, 30, 31; "Strike Wave in Punjab," October 1937, p. 27, June 1937, p. 3; June 1937, pp. 10, 11; July 1937, pp. 3, 11.

122. Prabodh Chandra, *op. cit.*, p. 69.

123. *Ibid.*, p. 85.

124. *Ibid.*, pp. 119, 135, 150.

125. Ruth Caldwell Wright, "Students in West Pakistan," *Far Eastern Survey* (February 22, 1950), pp. 38–41.

126. Myron Weiner, *The Politics of Scarcity* (Chicago, 1962), p. 165.

127. Margaret L. Cormack, *She Who Rides a Peacock: Indian Students and Social Change* (New York, 1961), p. 174.

128. Aileen D. Ross, "Student Indiscipline in a Developing Country" (mimeographed), American Sociological Society, 1962, pp. 4–5. Also see Gene D. Overstreet and Marshall Windmiller, *Communism in India* (Berkeley, Calif., 1959), pp. 395–399.

129. Cormack, *op. cit.*, pp. 180, 182, 186–187; "India Acts to End University Riots," *The New York Times*, May 23, 1965.

130. Cormack, *op. cit.*, p. 207.

131. Ross, *op. cit.*, pp. 19, 6.

132. *Ibid.*, p. 7.

133. *Ibid.*, pp. 10–11.

134. Berger, *op. cit.*, p. 122; Levon Melikian and E. Terry Prothro, "Sexual Behavior of University Students in Arab Near East," *Journal of Abnormal Psychology*, LCXIX (1954), 59.

135. "News Items," *Youth and Freedom*, VI, No. 3 (1964), 14.

136. In 1966 and 1967 student protests and riots were occurring, and several students were killed in clashes with the police. The *Times* correspondent found no clear statement of the grievances but inferred a "vague discontent with the conditions of Indian life in general." See "India Acts to Bar Student Protest," *The New York Times*, November 18, 1966. "Nine Killed in India as Policemen Fire on Student Rioters," *The New York Times*, January 6, 1967.

137. George Delf, *Jomo Kenyatta* (New York, 1961), pp. 60–61.

138. Ronald Segal, *African Profiles* (Baltimore, 1962), pp. 198–211, 154, 160, 170, 94, 89; Colin Legum, *Congo Disaster* (Baltimore, 1961), pp. 49, 95.

139. Kwame Nkrumah, *Ghana: The Autobiography of Kwame Nkrumah* (New York, 1957), p. 43.

140. A. T. Carey, *Colonial Students: A Study of the Social Adaptation of Colonial Students in London* (London, 1956), pp. 84 ff; Philip Garigue, "The West African Students' Union: A Study in Culture Contact," *Journal of the International African Institute*, XXIII (1953), 64–65.

141. Philip Garigue, *op. cit.*, p. 58.

142. *Ibid.*, p. 61.

143. Peter Abrahams, "The Blacks," *Holiday* (April 1959), p. 112; reprinted in Langston Hughes (ed.), *An African Treasury* (New York, 1961), p. 55.

144. Richard Wright, *Black Power* (New York, 1954), p. 60.

145. Nkrumah, *op. cit.*, pp. 89–91.

146. Delf, *op. cit.*, p. 45.

147. Abrahams, *op. cit.*, p. 119; also see Thomas Hodgkin, *African Political Parties* (Harmondsworth, 1961), p. 134.

148. Delf, *op. cit.*, p. 187.

149. Richard Wright, *op. cit.*, pp. 104–107.

150. Thomas Hodgkin, "Black Students Speak," *Spectator*, No. 6624 (July 15, 1955), 88–89.

151. Henri Desroche, "Conference Report," *Sociology and Religion: Proceedings of the Hazen International Conference on the Sociology of Religion* (Washington, D.C., 1962), p. 31.

152. Jean Darcet (ed.), *Les Conflits des Générations* (Paris, 1963), p. 39.

153. Thomas Hodgkin, *African Political Parties* (Harmondsworth, 1961), pp. 29–30. Teachers likewise were the single largest group in the Gold Coast House of Assembly elected in 1954.

154. Helen Kitchen (ed.), *The Educated African* (New York, 1962), pp. 540–541.

155. Darcet, *op. cit.*, p. 33. Also see Joseph Ki-Zerbo, "African Personality and the New African Society," in *Independent Black Africa: The Politics of Freedom* (Chicago, 1964), p. 57.

156. For recent enrollments in African universities, see "Africa's Educational Revolution," *Youth and Freedom*, V, Nos. 1–2 (1962) 6.

157. Darcet, *op. cit.*, pp. 42–43.

158. Hodgkin, *African Political Parties*, p. 138.

159. Lloyd Garrison, "Portrait of Nkrumah as Dictator," *New York Times Magazine*, May 3, 1964, pp. 108–109; "Critic of Ghana: Conor Cruise O'Brien," *The New York Times*, March 29, 1965; Conor Cruise O'Brien, "An African University," Lecture at University of California, Berkeley, May 3, 1965.

160. Julian Mayfield, "Ghanaian Sketches," in Roger Klein (ed.), *Young Americans Abroad* (New York, 1963), p. 191; see also K. A. Busia, "The Present Situation and Aspirations of Elites in the Gold Coast," *International Social Science Bulletin*, VIII, No. 3 (1956), 428–429.

161. Helen Kitchen, *op. cit.*, pp. 450–452. The communist International Union of Students observed that for eleven territories "not a single university was established by the French colonialists until 1956, when they founded the University of Dakar . . . This at a time when French companies amass billions of francs from African riches." See the International Union of Students, *Africa and Its Students* (Prague, n.d.), pp. 4–5.

162. Colin Legum, *Pan-Africanism* (New York, 1963), p. 118.

163. William John Hanna, "Students," in James S. Coleman and Carl G. Rosberg, Jr. (eds.), *Political Parties and National Integration in Tropical Africa* (Berkeley, Calif., 1964), p. 437; James S. Coleman, "The Politics of Sub-Saharan Africa," in Gabriel A. Almond and James S. Coleman (eds.), *The Politics of the Developing Areas* (Princeton, 1960), pp. 344–345.

164. "Africa, A Country-by-Country Situation Report," *African Report*, November 1963, p. 3; "Nigeria, Too Many

Graduates?" *Youth and Freedom,* VII, Nos. 4–5 (1965), 19.

165. World University Service, *Economic Factors Affecting Access to the University* (mimeographed; Geneva, 1961), p. 84.

166. Hanna, *op. cit.,* pp. 429–430.

167. *Ibid.,* p. 431.

168. *Ibid.,* p. 436.

169. Hanna, *op. cit.,* p. 440; quoted from an editorial in *The Bug,* February 21, 1959, p. 2.

170. *Youth and Freedom,* VII, Nos. 4–5 (1965), 16–17.

171. *Ibid.,* pp. 15–16.

172. "Bourguiba Meets Youth Half Way," *Youth and Freedom,* VII, No. 2 (1965), p. 9.

173. "Student Disturbances Puzzle a Stable Tunisia," *The New York Times,* January 21, 1967.

174. Alvaro Mendoza Diez, "Los Doctores y la Revolución en America Latina," *Revista Mexicana de Sociologia,* XII (1960), 747–779.

175. Arturo Torres-Rioseco, *The Epic of Latin American Literature* (New York, 1946), p. 189. In later years, young social novelists took up the theme of the miseries of Indian slavery.

176. Keith Botsford, "Latin America: Masses and Messiahs," *New Leader,* XLVI (December 23, 1963), 8–9.

177. Freyre, *op. cit.,* p. 356.

178. George Pendle, *Argentina* (2nd edn.; London, 1961), p. 70.

179. Miguel Rotblat, "The Latin American Student Movement," *New University Thought,* I, No. 4 (1964), 30.

180. Manuel Durán, "The Reform Movement," in *University Reform in Latin America: Analyses and Documents* (International Student Conference, 1959), p. 55; Francis Donahue, "Students in Latin-American Politics," *Antioch Review,* XXVI (1966), 96–98.

181. See José Carlos Mariátegui, "Ensayos de Interpretación de la Realidad Peruana," in *University Reform in Latin America,* pp. 74–75.

182. Kalman H. Silvert, *The Conflict Society: Reaction and Revolution in Latin America* (New Orleans, 1961), p. 164.

183. Mariátegui, *op. cit.,* pp. 72, 78.

184. Luis Alberto Sánchez, "The University and Democracy," in *University Reform in Latin America,* p. 66.

185. Victor Raúl Haya de la Torre, "Latin America's Student Revolution," *Living Age,* CCCXXXI (October 15, 1926), 103.

186. *Ibid.,* p. 106.

187. *Ibid.,* p. 105; see also Beate Salz, "Indianismo," *Social Research,* II (1944), 441–469.

188. Harry Kanter, *The Ideology and Program of the Peruvian Aprista Movement* (Berkeley, Calif., 1953), p. 9.

189. *Ibid.,* p. 10.

190. Haya de la Torre, *op. cit.,* p. 104.

191. Daniel Goldrich, *Radical Nationalism: the Political Orientation of Panamanian Law Students* (East Lansing, Mich., 1962), p. 42; Kalman H. Silvert, "The University Student," in John J. Johnson (ed.), *Continuity and Change in Latin America* (Stanford, Calif., 1964), p. 210.

192. Quoted in John D. Martz, "Venezuela's 'Generation of '28'; The Genesis of Political Democracy," *Journal of Inter-American Studies,* VI (1964), 20.

193. S. Walter Washington, "Student Politics in Latin America: The Venezuelan Example," *Foreign Affairs,* XXXVII (April 1959), 468.

194. *Ibid.,* p. 470.

195. *Youth and Freedom,* VI, Nos. 1–2 (1963), 32.

196. *Ibid.,* VI, Nos. 1–2 (1963), 35.

197. *Ibid.,* VI, No. 6 (1964), 17.

198. *Youth and Freedom,* IV, No. 2 (1961), 14; VII, No. 3 (1965), 23.

199. *Ibid.,* IV, No. 2 (1961), 17.

200. *Ibid.,* VII, No. 1 (1965), 18–19.

201. *Ibid.,* VI, No. 6 (1964), 17.

202. *Ibid.,* VI, No. 4 (1964), 21.

203. *Ibid.,* VII, No. 3 (1965), 24–25.

204. Frank Bonilla, "Student Politics in Latin America," *Political Research: Organization and Design Prod.,* III, No. 3 (November 1959), 12–15.

205. Frank Bonilla, "The Student Federation of Chile: 50 Years of Political Action," *Journal of Inter-American Studies,* II (July 1960), 311–334.

206. Clark C. Gill, "Strikes in South American Universities," *Schools and Society* (March 10, 1962), p. 119.

207. "Mexican Students Seize University," *The New York Times,* April 28, 1966; "50,000 to Enroll at University of Mexico," *The New York Times* (western edn.), January 15, 1963; M. D. Rosenberg, "Collegian Real Power in Politics of Latins," *Washington Post,* July 2, 1962.

208. "Setback for Venezuela's Leftists," *The New York Times,* October 25, 1962.

209. *Youth and Freedom,* VI, No. 3 (1964), 24.

210. Washington, *op. cit.,* p. 467.

211. Silvert, *The Conflict Society,* p. 166.

212. Samuel Shapiro, "The Argentine University," *AAUP Bulletin,* XLVI (December 1960), 376; also see the rejoinder by Mario Bunge, "The Argentine University: A Defense," *AAUP Bulletin,* XLVII (March 1961), 53–55.

213. Shepard L. Forman (Brazil), "Up from the Parrot's Perch," James W. Rowe (Argentina), "What Ever Happened to the Happy Lands?" in Klein, *op. cit.,* pp. 223–233, 263–264; Donahue, *op. cit.,* pp. 99–102.

214. See Antonio M. Grompone, *Universidad Oficial y Universidad Viva* (Mexico, 1953), pp. 161 ff., 306; Roberto Mac-Lean y Estenos, *La Crisis Universitaria en Hispano-America* (Mexico, 1956), pp. 19 ff.

215. *Youth and Freedom,* III, Nos. 5–6 (1961), 25; Donahue, *op. cit.,* p. 99.

216. Richard Eder, "Setback for Venezuela's Leftists," *The New York Times,* October 25, 1962.

217. David Spencer, "The Impact of the Cuban Revolution on Latin American Student Politics," in David Spencer (ed.), *Student Politics in Latin America* (United States National Student Association, 1965), p. 91.

218. *Ibid.,* p. 101. The leader of the leftist guerrilla group in Guatemala, the so-called Rebel Armed Forces, was Luis Turcios; with the help of "a majority of student supporters," Turcios had seceded from the Thirteenth of November Movement to organize his own. Subsequently he was recognized as "the over-all guerrilla leader." Turcios died at the age of twenty-four. He had the support of Fidel Castro and had moved to Marxism, he said, by reading Lenin and Mao. See *The New York Times,* October 4, 1966.

219. *Hispanic American Report,* XVI, No. 5 (July 1963), 485–487.

220. Che Guevara, *Guerrilla Warfare* (New York, 1961), pp. 45, 49, 126.

221. Raimundo Nonato, "What the student guerrillas of the Anzoategui have to say," *World Student News,* XVII, No. 16 (1963), 1–2.

222. "Venezuelans Kill Son of Governor," *The New York Times,* March 26, 1967.

223. "Havana University Gets its First Party Cell," *The New York Times,* June 15, 1965.

224. Theodore Draper, *Castroism: Theory and Practice* (New York, 1965), p. 131.

225. C. Wright Mills, *Listen, Yankee: The Revolution in Cuba* (New York, 1960), p. 46.

226. *Ibid.,* pp. 39–40.

227. Quoted in Draper, *op. cit.,* p. 113, from "La Tragedia de la Clase Media Cubana," *Bohemia Libre* (New York), January 1, 1961, pp. 28–29, 76–77.

228. *Ibid.,* p. 112.

229. Draper, *op. cit.,* p. 114.

230. *Ibid.,* p. 123.

231. *Ibid.,* p. 128.

232. *Prize Stories from Latin America: Winners of the Life en Español Literary Contest* (New York, 1963), pp. 265–283.

233. World Health Organization, *World Health Statistics Annual, 1962,* I (Geneva, 1965), 66–67, 106–107.

234. *Ibid.,* p. 474.

235. Roque Dalton, "Student Youth and the Latin-American Revolution," *World Marxist Review,* North American edn. of *Problems of Peace and Socialism* (Prague), IX, No. 3 (March 1966), p. 54.

236. *Ibid.,* p. 55.

237. *Loc. cit.*

238. "After the democratic victory in 1944, 80 per cent of the National Congress consisted of students and leaders of the student movement, but a few years later only 10 per cent remained supporters of the revolution. The majority of the students supported the counter-revolution throughout the entire period of the Arbenz administration. This seriously retarded the consolidation of the revolution and hastened its defeat in 1954." See Dalton, *op. cit.,* pp. 54–56. According to a study of Guatemalan students published in 1960, more than 65 per cent felt that foreign investments were needed, half said they would oppose a Communist government, and 63 per cent felt that democracy had good possibilities for stocking roots in Spanish America. Solomon Lipp, "Attitudes and Opinions of Guatemalan University Students," *Sociology and Social Research,* XLIV (May 1960), pp. 335–338.

239. A few years later, in 1962, the activists of the Asociación de Estudiantes Universitarios were heroically leading the opposition to the government of President

Ydigoras Fuentes, which rested on the support of an oligarchy of large landowners. The students demonstrated against congressional elections, which they said were a sham, their demonstrations were broken up by force, the students erected barricades, six of them were killed and fifty wounded; fighting continued with students using Molotov cocktails, while the police engaged in terrorism against the students. The labor unions were moved to side with the students. See Joe Love, "Special Report on Guatemalan Student Situation," in Robert Aragon and Joseph Love (eds.), *Background Paper: Latin American Student Affairs* (Philadelphia, n.d.).

SIX The Student Elite of Europe: Generational Unrest in Capitalist and Socialist Societies

The Capitulation of the European Intellectuals to Fascism

No European student movement rose in the 1930s to do battle with the Nazis and Fascists. The failure of the students was more profound than that of the European working class. The workers, to the end, voted for their Social Democratic and Communist parties and remained sullen and resentful toward the Nazis and Fascists. The students, on the other hand, were ready to flock to Nazi banners. The junior intellectuals were the first traitors to intellect among the intellectual class, a phenomenon which Harold J. Laski, Marxist and professor of political science at the London School of Economics, summed up in memorable words: "It was the failure of the Italian intellectuals . . . that allowed Mussolini to steal into power. It was the failure of the German intellectuals which permitted Hitler to establish his ugly empire. It was the failure of the French intellectuals after 1919 which created the conditions out of which France was overthrown in 1940."[1] The students' capitulation to the Fascists was a willing one, and there were almost no islands of resistance such as those which marked the defeat of the working class. In the ominous year of 1936, the executive secretary of the American Student Union reported dolefully from the European scene on the failure of the left-wing student activists and the triumph of the fascist spirit among the studentry:

The European Socialist and Communist student acted on the theory that it was hopeless to organize a large section of the student population which was bourgeois around a progressive program. At most only a small handful of enlightened and emancipated souls might become interested in the labor movement. Thus the European left wing student movement has been little more than a glorified Marxist study circle. Meanwhile the fascists were more sensitive to the distress, insecurity and malaise of the student population. As a solution, however, they posed an attack upon parliamentary government and democracy in general, whose indecisiveness, they declared, was preventing an end to the crises. As a catalyst to winning student loyalties, they called them into action on the boulevards and campuses.[2]

The student movements of western Europe, in their prevalent form, have often been more truly student syndicates, or student trade unions, devoted to the advancement of the material welfare of students in their status as apprentices to the intellectual elite. Where, however, a military elite has come to political power with consequences of deprivation for the intellectual elite—as in Spain—the students have come forth as the striking force of the intellectuals and the cause of freedom. Above all, in the Communist societies of eastern Europe, the dissident student, whose traditions of activism and self-sacrifice reach back a century, remains an unknown, unpredictable variable; when, where, how, and why he may act in the future are questions which intrude upon the apparent stability of Communist orders. Generational conflict is a haunting problem for Soviet society, with its impersonal bureaucracy and Marxian categories.

The European student movements thus constitute a diffraction spectrum of the constituent factors of stability and instability in their respective societies. Let us briefly review their variety.

France: The Activists of the Left Bank

France, the country of the Great Revolution, burgeoned in the first half of the nineteenth century with an idealistic student movement. Yet very quickly the movement's idealism was dominated by a species of revolutionary elitism known as Blanquism. This was the self-conscious ideology of a revolutionary intellectual elite, predominantly composed of students, which was determined as a vanguard to seize political power through its own insurrection. The French student movement early became a school for conspiratorial action and dictatorship, not for liberal democracy. When an indigenous workers' movement arose in the latter part of the century, the French students were by and large aloof and indifferent. When a movement seemed able to dispense with an intellectual elite, the studentry lost interest in social action. A reactionary student movement then arose far more influential than the Leftist.

THE SOCIALIST STUDENT MOVEMENT

"The Paris students," writes John Plamenatz, "were the first organized republicans in nineteenth-century France, and they were also revolutionaries."[3] Students in Paris had, in September 1818, formed the first republican association, "The Friends of Truth," under the protective cover of Freemasonry. Less than two years later, they were plotting an insurrection of six hundred armed students, but the police got wind of it and it came to naught. The student leader, Bazard, shortly evolved into an ardent Saint-Simonian, proselytizing especially among the engineering students at the Ecole Polytechnique on the need for organizing society under a "hierarchy of the able." By 1829, Bazard was formally installed as a "father" of the "family" in the hierarchy of the Saint-Simonian sect.[4] Meanwhile, another student plot to seize power, the so-called Charbonnerie, had failed in 1821, and students began to look for allies and physical power among the workers. The revolution of 1830 indeed took place under student initiative. A student organization, formed in January 1830, took to the barricades on July 27, 1830; the workers followed.[5] By the next evening all the eastern part of Paris was in revolt, and the following day the Bourbons fled. An American observer reported that when the barricades were going up in July 1830, the commanding officers were students: "Nor were subordinate leaders now wanting. . . . The ardent young students of the Schools of Law and Medicine, and the beardless boys of the Polytechnic School. . . . Today they came forth in a body, particularly the young men of the Polytechnic School; and instantly gaining the confidence of the people. . . ."[6]

The regime of Louis Philippe scarcely satisfied the revolutionary hopes of either students or workers. Student revolutionary clubs proliferated in the 1830s: a student, Sambuc, organized the "Society of Order and Progress"; every member was to provide himself with a musket and cartridges, and "the society, wholly composed of students, intended to direct the state according to the ideas of the Latin quarter. . . ."[7] The student activists, of course, composed only a minority of the student body. As the police agent La Hodde observed:

> The majority of the students . . . are occupied in the study of law, of medicine, or some other science, and not in reforming the government at the point of the bayonet; hence, in speaking of the youth of the schools, we mean only those of whom the anarchical journals take it on themselves to be the interested flatterers—those who parade at the clubs, political meetings, and other rude places. . . . When an order of the day is given, they hasten to all the estaminets in the Latin quarter of the town. . . .[8]

The Friends of the People and the Rights of Man were thus overwhelmingly student groups composed, as La Hodde reported, of "the ambitious and turbulent youth of the middle classes." They could not always reckon on the support of the studentry at large. During one crisis, for instance, the activists tried to take command of a meeting attended by fifteen hundred students; but the students, instead of manning barricades, marched to the Palais Royal to pay their respects to the king.[9] In July 1839, however, wrote Louis Blanc, "I saw with my own eyes, 3,000 students arrive at the Place Vendôme, bare-headed, with crape on their arms," to demand pardon for a condemned Blanquist leader; they did secure the commuting of the sentence.[10] A student journal, *La Lanterne du Quartier Latin,* founded in 1847, helped organize the students in opposition to the government of Louis Philippe.[11] Finally, in February 1848, the students led a demonstration against the minister Guizot; their chiefs were the editors of *Advance Guard,* a small student journal, and "a pretended student, M. Bocquet."[12] "It was once again the students who started a revolution," remarks Plamenatz.[13] As they marched on the Palais Bourbon, two hundred strong, on a route through the workers' districts, the crowd grew and the barricades rose. When most of the troops proved friendly to their cause, the fall of the government was assured. Within a few weeks, former students of the Ecole Centrale des Arts et Manufactures were serving as the officials of the socialistic National Workshops and learning painfully the extent of the gap between words and deeds.

The student leader who became the director of the National Workshops, the ill-fated first state socialistic experiment in Europe's history, was Emile Thomas, a young man of twenty-six, who had attended the Ecole Centrale des Arts et Manufactures. His residence was the headquarters for the students who already were serving as administrators of the workshops and who brought him their complaints of the system's inefficiency. Thomas drew up a scheme for reorganizing the National Workshops along military lines, which was enthusiastically accepted by the Minister of Public Works; that is how the student leader became director of the National Workshops. His penchant for dictatorial methods was typical. In a sense, he was one of the ancestors of the concept of the "dictatorship of the proletariat"; for when the workshops declined into an anarchic state, Emile Thomas proposed "*une sorte de dictature*" to ensure unity of control from above. Shortly thereafter he was arrested and exiled; his arrest contributed to the workers' unrest which led to the sanguinary outbreaks of the June Days, the first independent proletarian insurrection in history. Meanwhile, however, Thomas had tried to rule the National Workshops through the "moral influence" of students of the Ecole Centrale, who occupied the command positions in the militarily styled organization. The students were the "officers," while the "workers" were organized in "brigade and company units." The students became "captains" and "lieutenants" of socialism; and in fact, all the officers were students, recent graduates, or former students of the Ecole Centrale, especially of the second- and third-year classes. Thus, the Parisian students of the Ecole Centrale were the first "new class," the first managerial elite in modern history.

The new student managerial elite encountered grave problems. Curiously one of them arose from the long-standing hostility and rivalry between two schools, the Ecole Centrale and the Ecole Polytechnique. The government career engineers were graduates of the Polytechnique; Polytechnicians indeed had been in the forefront of the February Revolution, but they looked askance at the indiscipline and inefficiency of the National Workshops. The Ecole Centrale students, on the other hand, found in the workshops an outlet for their longings for prestige and for their social patriotism. The rivalry of schools was one, in other words, between revolutionary, alienated bureaucrats as against Establishment bureaucrats. Emile Thomas himself was evidently a Bonapartist, seeing in Louis Napoleon's socialistic schemes a prospect for the rule of an intellectual elite. The National Workshops foundered, but the brief weeks of their existence were a notable episode in the history of student elitism.[14]

During this era Louis Auguste Blanqui emerged as the ideologist of intellectual elitism and dictatorship, and the inspirer of several generations of student activists.[15] Blanqui, perhaps the first "professional revolutionist," made his debut on the Paris barricades while still a student, in July 1827. Students played a large part in the Society of Families which he organized in 1835, though Blanqui always suspected one of them of betraying him to the police. A Blanquist uprising in May 1839 failed when the students of the Ecole Polytechnique refused to join. In the latter years of the Second Empire, the indefatigable Blanqui undertook to organize a revolutionary political party; its rank and file was working class, but its leaders were mostly students, including Paul Lafargue, Marx's future son-in-law. Medical students especially were active in the movement, which was organized on the basis of secret groups of ten. By 1870, it numbered about 2,500 adherents. Blanquist students were active in 1865 in the French delegation to the International Students' Congress at Liége. They carried black flags of mourning in place of the tricolor, and told the congress they came from a country which had lost its liberty. When the students returned to France, they were expelled from their schools.

Blanquism, in effect, became the creed of the French student movement.[16] It had its historic opportunity in the Paris Commune of 1871;[17] the Blanquists, as Friedrich Engels observed, were in the majority and were responsible for the Commune's political decisions:

> Brought up in the school of conspiracy, and held together by the strict discipline which went with it, they started out from the viewpoint that a relatively small number of resolute, well-organized men would be able, at a given favorable moment, not only to seize the helm of state, but also by a display of great, ruthless energy, to maintain power until they succeeded in sweeping the mass of people into the revolution. . . . This involved, above all, the strictest dictatorial centralization. . . .[18]

Such a leader of the Commune as Raoul Rigault was a product of the Blanquist student circles, and the author of many essays in praise of revolutionary terrorism in the ephemeral student magazines of the Latin Quarter.[19]

The Paris Commune is an imperishable legend in the annals of revolutionary movements. Behind the myth, however, and the reality as well of its courage and heroism was the sober fact that it followed a self-destructive policy, that it sought heroic death rather than less dramatic achievement.[20] Karl Marx did more than any man to build for the Communards a sanctified place in the Socialist Pantheon, yet when he evaluated the Commune without benefit of rhetoric he wrote, "With a modicum of common sense, however, it could have reached a compromise with Versailles useful to the whole mass of the people—the only thing that could be reached at the time." Instead, the Commune's leaders issued apocalyptic appeals to the provinces to form a free federation of Communes. The Blanquists in exile remained fixated at the level of emotion of student revolutionists; typical nonstudents, they re-enacted in fantasy the uprisings of their student days. Engels described them in London in 1874: "They prepare the next 'outbreak' by drawing up lists of proscriptions for the future, in order that the line of men, who took part in the Commune, may be purified. For this reason they are called 'The Pure' by the other fugitives. . . . Their meetings are secret . . . although this does not prevent the whole French quarter from ringing with them next morning." Engels was repelled by their Messianic elitism, arrogance, and abrogation of ethics:

> But what a lack of judgment it requires to declare the Commune sacred, to proclaim it infallible, to claim that every burnt house, every executed hostage, received their just dues to the dot over the i! . . . Does not that repeat the saying about the first French Revolution: Every beheaded victim received justice, first those beheaded by order of Robespierre and then Robespierre himself?

In prescient terms, Engels characterized the inner dialectic of the Blanquist ideology: it led inevitably to the personal dictatorship of an elite.

> From Blanqui's assumption, that any revolution may be made by the outbreak of a small revolutionary minority, follows of itself the necessity of a dictatorship after the success of the venture. This is, of course, a dictatorship, not of the entire revolutionary class, the proletariat, but of the small minority that made the revolution, and who are themselves previously organized under the dictatorship of one or several individuals.

The attraction of Parisian students to Blanquism was but a special case of the general pattern of student movements—their propensity to elitist, anti-democratic ideas, emotions, and actions.[21] From the engineering students at the Ecole Polytechnique, drawn during the Restoration to Saint-Simon's authoritarian technocratic ideas, a species of scientific fascism, to the Blanquist medical students of the Second Empire, there was the continuous strain of intellectual elitism.[22]

For the next three-quarters of a century, after the Paris Commune, no significant French socialist student movement existed. Though "the humiliating memory of the Franco-Prussian war" (in Alvan Sanborn's words) was always present as well as what they regarded as the failures of the Third Republic, the students did not generally affirm themselves as Leftists. The student revolutionists seemed to have discredited themselves by their Blanquist extremism; the workers' syndicalist movement found leaders from their own ranks, while careers for university graduates multiplied in the bureaucracy, professions, and industry as the French economy expanded. After the amnesty of the Communards, such socialist leaders as Guesde, Vaillant, and Lafargue went to live in the Latin Quarter to proselytize among the students. "We became acquainted with hundreds of young men," reported Lafargue. "Our ideas attracted them one day, but the next day the wind blew from another quarter and turned their heads."[23] On the eve of the First World War, Jean Longuet, Marx's grandson, observed sadly, "Socialism has never been in French universities the dominating power it has been for many years in darkest Russia, where nearly all the intellectual fighters for political liberty are at the same time convinced adherents of the economic freedom of the masses."[24] A small student socialist group, associated with Jules Guesde, existed briefly in Paris from 1878 to 1880. Then in 1891, as parliamentary socialism developed, a move to create a significant student circle arose; students in law, medicine, and at the old Sorbonne organized the "Groupe des Etudiants Socialistes Révolutionnaires Internationalistes de Paris." Soon, however, it was dominated by deviant and anarchist elements, and it vanished by 1893. A few more normal seceders founded that same year the "Groupe des Etudiants Collectivistes de Paris," which affiliated with the Marxist section of the French socialists, led by Guesde. The Collectivist Students numbered, however, only twenty-five to forty members, though lectures they presented would attract more than a thousand persons. They insisted on their Marxist orthodoxy, and it was therefore a great occasion when in 1894 they expelled one of their founders.

Warned, however, that students "should not expect to enter the movement as leaders, for the working class had to lead itself," the French student movement was deprived of the elitist *élan*.[25] The Dreyfus case, however, posed a genuine moral issue to the nation, and stirred the liberal students' altruistic sympathies. "In those years, 1898 and 1899, clashes were frequent in the Sorbonne corridors. . . . A voice shouted: 'Durkheim is being attacked, Seignobos invaded!'—'Rally!' said Péguy, who had a liking for military terms. . . . They all seized their sticks and raced after him to the Sorbonne. *Ça va, ça va,* Péguy went humming—he knew no other song. . . ."[26] The membership of the Collectivist Students' Club rose to as many as two hundred. With the vindication of Captain Dreyfus, however, the moral vocation of the movement declined. The liberal bourgeoisie, moreover, which with the socialists' help had defeated the military and clerical elites, was strengthened in its sense of authority, and "in the Latin

Quarter the students' movement reached its lowest level." "From 1905 to 1908," reported Longuet, "we find little activity in the Latin Quarter, and a sleepy little club"; a revived club, however, in 1908 recruited a hundred members.[27] On the other hand, a general disaffection with the *status quo* existed. As an acute American observer wrote in 1905, "There is no possible doubt of the students' growing disgust with the corruption and hypocrisy of the present republic—this nominal democracy that is really a plutocracy. . . ."[28]

During this era, the mentor of the ablest socialist students was a librarian at the Ecole Normale, Lucien Herr, who imparted to them by the nobility of his character a sense of socialist idealism. Herr himself felt a kinship with the Russian revolutionary students, and was intimately associated indeed with Peter Lavrov, the spokesman of Russian intellectual elitism, and his circle; Herr, in fact, was the guardian of Lavrov's archives. He was, however, no archivist in the emotional intensity of his sympathies. He was always ready to help Russian terrorists in hiding and in distress, and when the student Sazonov assassinated Minister von Plehve, he wrote articles of warm approbation. But Herr fathered no effective French student movement. The proportions among students of "*la révolte des parents*" were too meager to sustain a movement.[29] French students, however, were moved to a warm sympathy with the persecuted Russian students. It is said that the fear of "student displeasure" kept the Czar from entering Paris on his visit to France.[30]

What was the final contribution of the Leftist student movement to the nation's political life? The radicalism of the students generally ended with their student days; it was, in other words, a brief episode coeval with the time of their generational revolt and idealism. Only about one fourth of student socialists remained socialists, Longuet estimated, after graduation; a much larger percentage, on the other hand—70 to 80 per cent—of the small activist corps, the Collectivist Students, remained socialist militants in later years. Ten former student activists were sitting as one-seventh of the socialist members in the Chamber of Deputies; and they were now professional men, including lawyers, two professors, a chemist, and a physician. The general manager of *L'Humanité*, the socialist newspaper, and four members of the Party Executive Committee were likewise graduates of the French student movement. In short, a disproportionate number of student activists found careers in the socialist movement, for these were genuinely careers with the emoluments of parliamentary seats. As such, the socialist student movement became an extracurricular academy for parliamentary life, merging with the phenomenon in French politics of "*la république des professeurs*." An intellectual elite came to be the rulers of France, and this fact was probably the cardinal factor in explaining the absence of any socialist student protest, especially during the years of the Third Republic. The rise of the intellectual elite was already marked before 1871; the historians Guizot and Thiers filled the highest posts of state, while the poet Lamartine was a foremost political leader in the Revolution of 1848. But the phenomenon became a landslide after 1871. The list of prime ministers was a roll call of illustrious French intellectuals: Georges Clemenceau, journalist and writer; Paul Painlevé, mathematician; Edouard Herriot, professor of rhetoric; Edouard Daladier, professor of history; Léon Blum, literary and dramatic critic, author of a bold book, *Du Mariage;* Georges Bidault, professor of history. Jean Jaurès, professor of philosophy, was the most powerful personality on the Left during the years before the First World War. Edouard Herriot, the patriarch of the Radical Socialists, helped found in his youth a literary review to which Proust contributed; a staunch Cartesian, he listened to Anatole France speak (under the protection of the infantry) at the dedication of a statue to the heretical Ernest Renan. He recalled the cry of the churchmen in 1898, "The enemy is intellectualism," and he felt himself an involved and committed intellectual. Herriot's book, *Philon le Juif*, was crowned by the Académie Française in 1897.[31] To rise through the *agrégation* at the Ecole Normale, then to a post in a secondary school or university, was a recognized prelude to a political career. Even under the presidency of General Charles de Gaulle in the Fifth Republic, it was the intellectual elite, not any military group, which held the hegemony, with such leading personages in varying circumstances as the social anthropologist Jacques Soustelle and the novelist-adventurer André Malraux. The general himself became an assimilated intellectual, a man of letters, admired for the pure cadences of his style.

Generational struggle among the French studentry during this era was directed against the liberal democratic Third Republic itself, against the generation shaped by the Dreyfusard movement. The socialist movement itself declined steadily until the Second World War in its attraction for young students. It did not fulfill the promise of careers open to talent, which it had seemed to offer at its inception, while the workers' syndicates evolved their own leaders and needed no help from an intellectual elite. It was an instance of the general phenomenon observed by Leon Trotsky in 1910:

> At the beginning of the social-democratic movement, every intellectual who joined, even though not above the average, won for himself a place in the working-class movement. Today every newcomer finds, in the Western European countries, the colossal structure of working-class democracy already existing. . . . Only a man of exceptional talent would in these circumstances be able to hope to win a leading position for himself—but such a man, instead of leaping across the abyss into a camp alien to him, will naturally follow the line of least resistance into the realm of industry or state service.[32]

THE REACTIONARY STUDENT MOVEMENT

The French student movement, indeed, from the beginning of the twentieth century to the Second World War was predominantly right-wing.

"By tradition," writes Samuel Osgood, "French students have been both politically minded and *chahuteurs*" (rowdies). Their dominant movement was always anti-liberal, anti-democratic, elitist, and authoritarian. In 1920, for instance, the Left Bank was dominated by the student activists of the reactionary Action Française; the secretary of the Etudiants d'Action Française reported that year that his was the leading student group in Paris, the strongest and most active. Royalist students were presidents of the General Students Association and foremost in its committees. Well into the late thirties they dominated the studentry at the Sorbonne, challenged only by the socialists. In 1920 they began publishing their own monthly review, *L'Etudiant français*, which nurtured several generations of French right-wing intellectuals.

The pattern of student generational revolt in France thus on the face of it was altogether unusual. Sons in revolt against republican fathers became royalists. "Young men are royalists in 1933, as their grandfathers were republicans under the Second Empire," wrote an observer in the *Gazette de Lausanne*. Indeed, the first leaders of the Action Française were mostly in revolt against a republican family heritage; they included grandsons of Jacobins, children of Communards, and the great-nephew of Danton. If the regnant ideology of the student movement shifted in accordance with the law of generational revolt, the pattern of its tactics, the pattern of the politics of generational rebellion, was invariant.

As Bernard de Vésins, an Action leader, said of the students, "*Ils constituent l'élément le plus actif, celui qui fournit les meilleures Commissaires. . . .*" The principal activity of the student activists was to disrupt the lectures of liberal professors at the Sorbonne and to demonstrate against Republican governments in the streets with the hope of overthrowing them.

In 1908, the students demonstrated against Charles Andler, a professor of German and a disciple of the socialist Jean Jaurès. Andler had organized a students' tour of Germany during the Easter holiday, with the aim of promoting international good will. This angered the Action Française students; there was fighting in the lecture halls and courts of the Sorbonne, and in the streets. Andler's lectures continued, but only because many disrupters were arrested. The angered activists then undertook to demonstrate against the President of the Republic during the ceremonies for the ashes of Emile Zola at the Pantheon.

In 1909, the student activists (with the Etudiants de l'Action Française and Camelots du Roi taking the initiative) disrupted the courses of a professor, François Thalamas, who though a conservative had referred to Joan of Arc as a witch who deserved her punishment.[33] The professor was beaten up in the amphitheater of the Sorbonne. He was jeered at and deluged with a barrage of rotten eggs. A student leader slapped him. Thalamas required a heavy military guard in order to give his lectures, and even then his voice was overwhelmed by the uproar of thousands. Jewish lecturers as well as the dean of the faculty, Lyon-Caen, were then assaulted. One Left Bank nonstudent leader seized the lecturer's podium and gave a lecture on the Action Française. The greater number of those arrested, however, were less than twenty years old. "Some were students only by virtue of being habitués of Left Bank cafés." The nonstudent leader Maurice Pujo defended these tactics of direct action in terms familiar today: "The only really effective means of making ourselves heard will be by attacking the façade of public order. . . ." Students presumably could "communicate" only through disruption. The police fired on two students, whereupon the Action Française threatened retaliation against the Minister of the Interior and "the Jews of whom he was the agent." The dean was chased from the amphitheater when he tried to lecture; finally he resigned. As Osgood writes, "The very weakness and lack of fervor of the republican student groups which came to the defense of its victims showed that the Movement of Integral Nationalism was becoming the dominant political force in the Latin Quarter."

In 1921, the student activists launched an anti-Sorbonne campaign, organizing numerous *chahuts* (rowdy disturbances) to disrupt lectures at the university; several lectures could not be continued. Special effort was directed against Professor Victor Basch, a distinguished teacher of aesthetics and a leader of the League for the Rights of Man, who had spoken up in favor of imprisoned Communists. The police were summoned to clear the professor's lecture hall. (Twenty years later Victor Basch was killed by the Nazis.)

In 1925, the student activists of the Action Française organized riots to prevent Professor Georges Scelle from lecturing at the Paris Faculty of Law; evidently political favoritism had played a part in his appointment, which was characterized as an instance of democratic and Masonic corruption. The police were called upon to intervene every time the professor tried to lecture. By the end of the month, the disturbances reached frenzied proportions. A hundred demonstrators and eleven policemen were injured. Thereupon the Faculty of Law was closed by order of the Minister of Education. The Chamber of Deputies debated the nature of the student movement. A rightist deputy, Jean Ybarnégaray, defended their protest as that of a professional corporative movement (that is, the intellectuals' fascism). Premier Edouard Herriot, the Radical Socialist leader, defined their menace to liberal democracy: "If we do not resist a movement of this sort, we shall find ourselves helpless in the future against the insolent pressures of this group."

But the cabinet of Edouard Herriot was not to survive the crisis. The day after the debate, the General Association of Paris Students, dominated by the Action group, ordered a strike in sympathy with the law students. The students of medicine, pharmacy, and letters responded, and the strike spread to the provinces. The problems of the Herriot government, already beset by a financial crisis, were complicated. The cabinet fell a few days later. Professor Scelle resigned the day after Herriot's resignation; the royalist newspaper announced "Student Victory." Among the factors thus accounting for the fall of this liberal democratic government, "some credit" must be given, says Eugen Weber, "to the forceful action of the Action Française student groups, whose initiative and persistence largely determined the disturbances in the Latin Quarter."

Edouard Herriot, the heir to all that was valid in the Jacobin tradition, and the outstanding liberal democratic statesman in France between the two World Wars, was the special object of hatred of the right-wing student activists. He was the father figure of the Republican France which they detested. In 1925, they shouted him down and insulted him when he addressed the ceremonies for the award of prizes at the Lycée Louis le Grand. In December 1932, it was the student activists of the Action Française who began the riots on the Left Bank which continued for two days until a crowd of thirty thousand surrounded the Chamber and six thousand police and Republican Guards were summoned. That night the government of Premier Herriot was overthrown, and Léon Daudet, the prophet of the student activists, exulted in "the Action Française's new victory."

As the crisis of the thirties deepened, the student activists ranged themselves against liberal democracy. They demonstrated wildly in February 1932 against the fall of Pierre Laval's right-wing cabinet, especially against the Senate which had defeated him, chanting, "*Les sénateurs sont des cochons*." The troops were summoned, the Senate was placed under guard and the Left Bank in a state of siege. Senator Henri Chéron, kicked and pummeled by the student activists, addressed the Senate on the danger to democracy posed by the student movement: "I fear for democracy: I fear the forces of money and of violence. I do not understand why gilded youth should be allowed to make itself master of the streets, apprentice itself to Revolution, outrage Parliament." A few months later the students were burning Chéron in effigy, for the Senator was now taking part as Finance Minister in a left-wing majority government led by Paul-Boncour. A taxpayers' revolt against the government began, and the Action Française, using its student activists, "did its best to spread the anarchy throughout France." Once more the law faculty, "a stronghold of integral nationalism, was in something like a state of siege."

The appeal of Fascism was powerful for the student activists; many agreed with the Paris deputy who declared that the Fascist way was their way of achieving socialism, for it combined straightforwardly elitist authoritarianism with a revolt against the liberal bourgeois. When Mussolini invaded Ethiopia, the French student activists intervened on behalf of Fascism. They organized strikes and riots against the professor of the School of Law, Gaston Jèze, who was serving as Ethiopia's legal representative in the League of Nations; they alleged he had thereby disqualified himself from teaching law to French students. In November 1935, Professor Jèze was forced by student demonstrations to suspend his courses. When he attempted to lecture again in January 1936, the violent demonstrations led to the suspension of the whole law faculty's work. There were wounded among the students, faculty, and police, as students at other schools and provinces joined in the movement. Professor Jèze's courses were then transferred to the Musée Pédagogique; but when one lecture was terminated by a stink-bomb, a rightist journal rejoiced in the smell for old France. Professor Jèze curiously was a conservative, but he had offended the student activists by daring to stand against Mussolini's imperialism.

The Etudiants d'Action Française, after an existence of thirty-one years, was brought to an abrupt end in February 1936. On February 13, Léon Blum, the socialist leader, and soon to be Premier of the Popular Front government, was physically attacked by right-wing student activists. The incident took place on the Left Bank as Blum's car tried to pass through the funeral cortege of the anti-Semitic writer Jacques Bainville. Blum was wounded and bled profusely, though he was not severely injured.[34] Herriot expressed the majority view that "a situation intolerable for the honor of the Republic" had to be ended. A few hours later the cabinet decreed the dissolution not only of the Action Française and the Camelots du Roi but of the organization of student activists, the Etudiants d'Action Française. The student activists, however, continued to struggle actively against the Popular Front. Léon Blum, a Jew and socialist, was their primary target, and anti-Semitism became more than ever the cardinal tenet of the French student movement; to be anti-Marxist, said *L'Etudiant Français* on April 10, 1937, meant to be an anti-Semite. That was the student generation's political philosophy simply stated, and thus the French student movement helped prepare its people for capitulation to Hitler. What there was left of a student movement in 1941 supported the Vichy regime of Marshal Pétain.

It was not for naught that Léon Daudet, the leader of the Action Française, looked to the student movement as the source of leverage for dictatorship. When they overthrew Herriot's Cartel des Gauches in 1925, he was almost persuaded that their time had come. How large was this student activist group which contributed to destroying French democracy? At its height in 1925 the Etudiants d'Action Française claimed 2,200 members in Paris, distributed in twenty-six student groups, besides twenty-eight student groups in lycées. Sixteen years earlier, in 1909, the Action Française had been able to count on only sixty student activists to participate in its riots. Evidently its tactic of violent demonstration designed to provoke police intervention achieved recruitment through generational solidarity. Though the activists came to dominate French student political life in the twenties, their 2,200 members were clearly a minority in the universities and lycées of Paris. From time to time, liberal students organized and combatted the activists. In February 1926 a student, Pierre Mendès-France, was chairman of a meeting organized for Professor Scelle; the meeting was attacked and broken up by an Action group. Pierre was injured. The "bright upper-class students and dilettantes" who found their ideological guide in the Action

Française saw themselves, however, as the intellectual elite of a future France. Suspected and mistrusted by the syndicalist-minded French working class for their elitist aims, and themselves rejecting the bourgeois republic of their fathers, from which high idealism seemed to be gone, the *jeunesse dorée* enacted its unique politics of generational revolt. If France has remained democratic, it has not been thanks to its gilded youth.[35]

One asks what were the psychological sources of the reactionary character of the French student movement. Why did idealism take this perverse direction? A crisis of de-authoritization of the elder generation provided the occasion for the founding of the Action Française; above all, as Eugen Weber tells us, there were "the circumstances of the Dreyfus Affair." The army, the Church, the national tradition, national justice were discredited, and for some years, the Republican politicians themselves. Ordinarily, such injustice might have led the youth to feel a warm sympathy with the oppressed. Back-to-the-people movements, after all, have moved idealistic youth to sympathy and identification with the lowliest. The trouble, however, was that the Jews, in the students' eyes, were not of the lowliest. They competed for the highest places in the universities, in literature, law, medicine, and finance. Idealistic youth felt its own traditions and status menaced by a redoubtable competitor. Student loyalties and populist identifications veered to the ancient institutions which were under indictment. François Coppée, in a letter to Léon Daudet, expressed this mood in 1906 when he wrote of his despair; the Jew was rising, and their France which they loved, its faith, patriotism, honor, were perishing; perhaps the young would see the awakening.[36] Thus generational idealists were transmuted into ideological gangsters of anti-Semitism.

The symbolism of the French student movement casts an important light on its unconscious sources. The right-wing activists made a veritable cult of Joan of Arc. For instance, as we have seen, their disruption of the lectures of Professor Thalamas at the Sorbonne in November 1908 was the direct outcome of his denigration of Joan. The cult of Joan was a deep one. At a protest meeting against the sacrilegious professor, one speaker said, "Thus, when a professor charged with teaching history to high-school students pronounced some ignoble words against her, the national conscience experienced a sensation of rape and outrage, and every day for a week now the magnanimous youth of the schools has not ceased to protest energetically in the streets and in front of Joan's statue. . . ." Joan was contrasted with Marianne, the slut, *La Gueuse*, who personified the Republic, and the students often said they would "hang the slut." The cult of Joan also provided the basis for a cult of physical violence. The students regarded themselves as "privileged" to employ any means for achieving their end. For when Joan's honor was sullied, they were ready to rush to use chivalrous violence against university professors, Republican politicians, and socialists.

As always, there was a cult of the heroic among the students. The Republican fathers scarcely seemed like heroes. Ernest Psichari, grandson of Renan, grew up among Dreyfusards; but when he went to the Sorbonne, he was attracted to the Action Française and became a worshipper of force; the military way of life seemed to him superior to the "decadent" bourgeois culture.

Indeed, the bifurcation of Joan and Marianne in the students' minds was the most significant expression of their deepest conflict. Sons who are in revolt against their fathers are horrified by the thought of the sexual relations to which their mothers have had perforce to submit. Marianne, the "slut" of the Republic, was indeed their mother prostituted to their bourgeois fathers; she had been rendered impure, a creature for sale to the series of monetary bidders. The Maid of Orleans, on the other hand, virgin, untainted by bourgeois fathers—here was the mother rendered pure and noble. The intensity of devotion to Joan was proportionate to the intensity of rejection of the bourgeois fathers. If the French working class had not already achieved its independence, and regarded the intellectuals askance, the student activists might have assumed a more proletarian identity; if the French peasantry had not rested secure in their ownership of their parcels of land, the students might have sought them out as allies. But in the France of the bourgeois Republic, where the fathers were engulfed in the pursuit of gain, the law of generational conflict produced strange vectors—a generation of right-wing activists who sought a restoration of Virginity to their Mothers from the Rape by their fathers.[37]

SYNDICALISM AND IDEALISM IN THE POSTWAR ERA

The aftermath of the Second World War brought a certain reawakening of student idealism which reached its highest point in 1960 with the crisis of conscience over the Algerian War. By and large, however, the French student movement evolved into a student syndicate with the elitist aims of a narrow interest group. Above all, it made central such an issue as that of the demand for pre-salaries for students, for outright grants rather than loans—a demand which was clearly undemocratic since it asked that the people at large should finance the higher education of the future economic upper class. But the French student syndicate was little troubled by the undemocratic, elitist aspect of its program.

During the Second World War some students engaged in resistance activities, though they are said to have been "isolated," and there was no massive student action or fighting against the Germans as such.[38] The Union Nationale des Etudiants de France (UNEF), for several decades "the spokesman and bargaining agent for French students, particularly the great mass of students living in Paris," prudently abstained from involvement in the Resistance.[39] With the war's end, student activists who had participated in the Resistance tried to impart its ideology to French student syndicalism. Nonetheless, "apoliticism" remained dominant among the

French studentry. One student newspaper, *L'Observateur Etudiant*, the organ of the law students, the Corporation des Etudiants en Droit de Paris, expounded the virtues of apoliticism; the science students were pragmatically apolitical. There were said to be two sorts of French youth: on the one hand, the two and a half million who were unorganized, interested in sports, and content; and on the other, the little world of the Latin Quarter, "organized for disorder, sucking at the breasts of the Communist Party."[40]

The Algerian crisis, however, evoked a massive student protest and even a de-authoritization of the old. As Pierre Gaudez, the president of UNEF, wrote, "The war voted by the old has to be fought by the young, that is the scandal."[41] In May 1958, about fifty religious and secular student groups opposed to the war coalesced to form a "Groupe d'Etudes et de Rencontres des Organisations de Jeunesse et d'Education."

In April 1960, the annual congress of the National Union of French Students, by a vote of almost three-fourths, expressed its advocacy of negotiations with the National Liberation Front. It proceeded to its own direct negotiations, and in June met at Lausanne with representatives of the General Union of Muslim Students of Algeria. It was as if the Students' International was intervening directly to end the war, though all they did was issue a joint communiqué denouncing the "anachronistic" war as "absurd and cruel," and as "cruelly opposing the two youths. . . ." It was a noble, idealistic gesture, however. Less than ten days later, the Minister of National Education, Louis Joxe, announced that the government was canceling its annual subsidy to UNEF (80,000 francs, less than one third of the Union's budget) on the ground that it had "overstepped the bounds of normal student activities." In the debates in the National Assembly, the student leaders of UNEF were denounced for "fraternizing with the enemy."[42]

The UNEF again took the initiative in October 1960 by organizing resistance to the Algerian War. After several months of protracted negotiations, it secured the cooperation of the three national trade union movements as well as the Federation of National Education to form "a national manifestation for a negotiated peace in Algeria." The Communist party, fearing the undisciplined energies of the younger generation, discouraged this united front of students and workers but was unable to prevent its own unions in the Confédération Générale du Travail from participating.[43] The government tried at first to prohibit the demonstration, but then yielded. The demonstration was "a great success." "In Paris, the Palais de la Mutualité was filled to capacity (4,000) and some 10,000 demonstrators filled the surrounding streets." Many workers struck for one symbolic hour. A majority of the French studentry evidently supported the efforts of UNEF for a negotiated peace, yet even at this time the slates of political candidates in students' elections were defeating the apolitical ones by only a narrow majority. At the Institute of Political Studies in Paris, for instance, when nearly 1,500 students voted in November 1960 for their Executive Committee, the pro-UNEF slate received 740 votes, while the apoliticals garnered 717.

The political student movement, however, rapidly receded after the Algerian question was settled. The major issue which had stirred the generational anger of the French students was gone: De Gaulle emerged as a re-authoritized figure. The student movement began to devote itself primarily to the economic welfare of the studentry as a social stratum, and to expend the residual energies of generational conflict in making demands for democratizing the university and for eradicating bureaucratic methods of education. Student demonstrations and strikes occurred primarily as a protest against what the students regarded as the government's inadequate support of education. Placards with the slogan "Classrooms, not cannons" made their appearance, while the Communists maintained that these elitists and interest-group demonstrations showed that "the student movement is a part of the French workers' struggle against the arms race policy."[44] Dominant at the annual Congress of UNEF at Toulouse in April 1964 (attended by eight hundred delegates, representing some eighty thousand students) were the issues of modernizing the university and democratizing education. By 1965, however, economics was in the ascendancy. The UNEF national bureau decided to give priority to the demand for governmental allocation of study grants; it shelved the vague issues having to do with democratizing the university. The margin of the vote was small, 407 to 354, but the trend toward depoliticization and student syndicalism was clear. The general secretary, Marc Kravetz, a member of the Union of Communist Students, felt obliged to resign. The students refused to follow his proposal for linking university reform with a campaign against the De Gaulle government. The resigning secretary complained that student apathy was a "natural consequence of the present state of French society." His complaint was really against the return of a generational equilibrium in French society, which would constitute an unfavorable milieu for a political student movement.[45] "Fewer young people join the Party; in the universities the number of Communist students has shrunk to a fraction of what it was a decade ago," wrote Charles Micaud.[46] The Communist party apparatus alienated the students by dissolving the student Communist newspaper *Clarté* and expelling a whole faction.[47]

Insofar as political generational conflict persisted in France, it was rather within the Communist ranks themselves. The Communist student movement found itself warring with the established elder leadership in the French Communist party. At the Seventh Congress of the Union of Communist Students at Paris in March 1964, the majority of the delegates, led by the Union's political bureau, called for greater student independence from the French Communist party. This majority itself was composed of two antagonistic groups, liberal ultra-Khruschevites and extremist Maoists; both, however, shared a common generational revolt against the "dogmatic" reigning Stalinist bureaucrats of the party. The students demanded the right to participate in making the party's policy and to "contradict the Party, if necessary."[48] Even on the question of student grievances, the Communist students shared the views of their student generation rather than their party. The party, when it approached the problem of the allocation of financial grants, tried to apply the classical Marxist formula: "To each according to his needs." The Communist students, on the other hand, joined with UNEF in thinking of themselves as a class apart and demanding an overall "pre-salary" regardless of class origin or economic need. The generational bond was stronger than the party card.

Thus it happened that the student movement which had campaigned so vigorously against the Algerian War was a few years later preoccupied with such trivial and dubious issues as "the free distribution of cyclostyled copies of lecturers' notes."[49] The student disaffection which vaguely persisted arose, not over any great individual moral issue, but reflected dissatisfaction with the student's lot—the heightened competition in examinations for entrance, for survival, and place in the intellectual elite. The studentry, which had numbered seventy thousand before the war, was now over 230,000, and of these more than a third were concentrated at the University of Paris. In the 1960s children of the lower middle class were competing in large numbers for the academic avenue of upward mobility. Many of the students were now married. A syndicalist spirit waxed strong among the students. If they were no longer stirred by a back-to-the-people spirit, they wanted more of the world's goods and ease of mind for themselves—freedom from want and freedom from examination worries. They became political narcissists rather than altruists; hence their demands for student allowances and a greater role in determining the conduct of university classes and examinations.[50]

Yet when the record of the French student movement for a century and a half is evaluated without sentimentality, one cannot say that it has been a significant force for liberal democratic values. If in its first generations, it tied itself to Blanquist revolutionary elitism, it has latterly espoused syndicalist elitism. Its recent demand for an "*allocation d'études,*" of a study salary of eighty dollars a month, is hardly democratic. One can acknowledge that every person has a right to realize his full potentialities, and provide assistance for all those who lack the material means to complete their education. But the notion that those who are preparing for entry into an economic upper class must have all their educational costs paid for en route by the citizenry in general contravenes the meaning of democracy. The students, however, with their readiness to riot, were prepared to bypass all democratic processes. "We would rather count on mass movements than discussions with the minister," a UNEF member commented, and their demonstrations took on the aura of a personal vendetta against whoever happened to be the current Minister of Education at the time.[51] In February 1964, for instance, the students undertook to bar entrance into the Sorbonne to the current minister, Christian Fouchet, and the visiting Italian President, Segni; the result was the arrest of more than two hundred students. But the gain for democratic values was negative. The students themselves rarely thought, in the American fashion, of getting summer jobs; and "phantom students," who enrolled solely for the benefit of obtaining financial discounts, proliferated. The students' organization, when depoliticized, was content to be an agency for generational economic elitism; when politicized, it blended its idealism with generational political elitism. The noblest of the socialist leaders, Jean Juarès, had for a few brief years at the turn of the century hoped that the French students would take the lead in guiding the working class to a cultural renaissance through *universités populaires*. Such notions proved ephemeral in the French setting.[52] Elitism, in a political or economic guise, was the underlying ideology of the French student movement. Today, two thousand students out of a total studentry of three hundred thousand are members of the Union of French Communist Students. Yet, as Keith Botsford says, "The most readily observable fact about the Communist student movement is that it is in all senses an elite movement; its most active members represent the French social and intellectual elite."[53] It has virtually no ties with the people.

REBELLION AGAINST THE SYSTEM: FOR A WORLD WITHOUT EXAMINATIONS

In May 1968 the French student movement made its most historical effort to shed its tradition of elitism and achieve a unity with the working class. It accomplished certain things: it occupied the Sorbonne for thirty-four days; it brought the General Confederation of Labor to call a general strike; it compelled the dissolution of the National Assembly, the dismissal of two ministers, and the holding of new elections. But the student activists failed in their supreme objective; they could not weld the students' and workers' movements into one. A certain sociological truth became evident; it is only in proto-industrial or pre-industrial societies, among a new, relatively unorganized working class, or among a peasantry, that student intellectuals can hope to secure the leadership. In a developed society, however, where working-class organizations have developed their own traditions, customs, and leadership, the student intellectuals cannot hope to fulfill their messianic elitism in alliance with the labor movement. Student movements will arise frequently in advanced industrial countries, but more than ever they will experience the frustration of not finding in their own societies a carrier movement or supporting class to which they can join themselves. As a consequence, the elitism in student movements will lack the countervailing populism of the past. And the idealism of student movements will partake even more of the character of a fantasy. While the workingmen accept almost unanimously the industrial society, its advantages, its organization, its inevitability, the student activists by contrast are anti-industrial, anti-organization, and voluntarist. While anarchism has virtually disappeared as an ideological trend among the working class, it has found its last outpost in the student movement, the last protest of the children's world. It was for such reasons that the unity of the student movement and the French working class against the government of President Charles de Gaulle, which for a few days seemed an irresistible political force, turned out to be more rhetorical than real.

These stirring events are recent indeed; they occurred as this volume was being prepared. All the familiar patterns of student movements were in evidence—the trivial initiating incident by a handful of students, the intervention of police, the reactive generational solidarity, the extension of issues, the confrontation of generations, the search for a class ally, the "charismatic" student leader, the withdrawal of the class ally. It began at Nanterre, a suburb of Paris, where the university maintains a liberal arts annex. A leftist student group ("groupuscule" the Communists called it) with an ill-defined anarchist ideology came into being under the leadership of Daniel Cohn-Bendit, an orphan child of German Jewish refugees, twenty-three years old, a second-year student of sociology. They called themselves the "enragés" harking back for their name to the small angry extremist doctrinaire sect which had perished at the guillotine during the French Revolution, but whose persons and principles were still extolled in such an anarchist classic as Kropotkin's *The Great French Revolution*.[54] On the morning of March 22, following an "anti-imperialist" demonstration the previous night, six student activists were arrested. The student activists were mostly drawn from the School of Arts and Letters and the School of Social Sciences which drew a goodly share of those "alienated" from the society, and their curricula were vague, disorienting, and undemanding of one's time and energy.[55] At once, several factions coalesced in protest into the "March 22nd Movement," occupied the university buildings, and disrupted the classes and examinations.[56] The movement evidently numbered about 800 out of a total student body of 11,000.[57] When the rector of Nanterre heard that a right-wing group was planning to embattle the leftist students, he closed the campus. Whereupon the students of Nanterre went to the historic courtyard of the Sorbonne in the heart of Paris to protest the closing of their campus. Then came the turning point which transformed the coalition of grouplets into a movement. The rector of the University of Paris, for the first time in the school's history, called on the police to clear the Sorbonne courtyard. Fighting began which became increasingly violent on both sides. "Students forced to choose between students and the police chose students. . . . It was not predictable. For several nights automobiles were turned on their sides . . . as the students crouched with paving stones behind their bellies, and last Friday night 188 cars ended up completely burned or badly damaged," reported a sympathetic American correspondent. "It was no longer a question of ideology, but of fraternity."[58] The police used bludgeons and tear gas; the students were "armed with chains and crowbars."[59] A tremendous sympathy for the students began to spread among the people, for their heroic undefined idealism. Nearly a million Parisian workers marched with the students on May 13 to demonstrate against the Gaullist government.

The student struggle began now to merge with larger social issues. The original student demands had been a kind of anarchist fantasy—an animus against all examinations combined with symbolic insistence that "the final examinations be held at gunpoint so that the oppressive power of the state will be clearly translated into visible action and people will see the true nature of their society."[60] The students' strike spread throughout the country into every provincial university; the demand was put forward for a radical reconstruction of the entire university and the ouster of the ministers of Education and the Interior. Student activists talked of the Paris Commune of 1871, for they had founded, they felt, something like a Student Commune of 1968: "The university and the entire Latin Quarter belonged to the students. After ten days of bloody clashes with the police, not a single policeman was in sight. Students in white helmets directed traffic. The Government had surrendered this part of the city to the students."[61] The French Communist party found itself shaken by the upsurge of sympathy for the students' attack on "Gaullism." The student activists called the Communists "Stalinist creeps;"[62] George Séguy, the Communist secretary-general of the General Confederation of Labor, asked mockingly, "Who is Cohn-Bendit?" and then went on to reject the intellectual elite: "The French workers are of age," he said. "They have no need for tutors."[63] The French Communist organ, *L'Humanité*, ridiculed the student activists as misguided "little bands of Trotskyists, Maoists, and anarchists led by papa's boys belonging to the upper middle classes."[64] The student activists, in turn, regarded the Communists as stodgy associates of the Establishment; they could idealize the guerrilla-philosopher Régis Debray but scarcely the party bureaucrat, Waldeck Rochet, general secretary of the French Communist party. But the workers were spontaneously moved by the revolutionary spectacle, by the revolutionary memories evoked at the Sorbonne, where students and professors wished to convene a States-General. The Nantes workers took the initiative; they occupied a giant aircraft factory and took hostage the managers. One worker said, "It would have happened no matter what the students did," but it was clear that the students' example had been contagious.[65] Then workingmen throughout all France began to strike; the General Confederation of Labor followed events, and declared a general strike. It was an alliance between the students and workers such as France had not seen for many years.

But the students' world and the workers' world remained distinct. The students inveighed against the Examination System, against the automated society, against the gadget economy.[66] The workers wanted shorter hours and higher wages; they wanted "nothing more than the intellectuals' scorned car, washing machine, and television set."[67] One Marxist philosophy student told his fellows: "How do we build a common view between them?" That indeed was the insuperable problem. The government capitulated to the students' demands for an amnesty, the ouster of two ministers, and the withdrawal of the police from the Sorbonne. De Gaulle dissolved the National Assembly and issued the call for a new election, demanding a vote of confidence in himself and his vague project for social and university reform. The workers slowly returned to their jobs, indifferent often to the admonitions and settlement terms negotiated by their Communist union. But when the student activists again erected barricades and embattled the police on the night of June 11, public opinion shifted decisively against the students. The national elections were two weeks away; the political parties were in their campaigns among the voters. The students, on the other hand, were visibly repudiating representative democracy in favor of their own elitist minority direct action, the so-called "participatory democracy." They gave an obvious verification to de Gaulle's declaration that they represented a totalitarian threat. There was little public protest, therefore, when on June 12, the government declared illegal the students' leftist organizations—the Movement of March 22nd, the Workers' Voice (Trotskyite), the Union of Communist Students (Communist), the Communist Revolutionary Youth (Castroite), the Revolutionary Group (anarchist), the Union of Communist Youth (Maoist), and the Liaison Committee of Revolutionary Students (Trotskyite).[68] When the elections for the National Assembly took place at the end of June 1968 the government of President de Gaulle won an overwhelming victory; the Communists lost more than half their seats, while the non-Communist Left lost even more. The nation had drawn back from the prospect of a dictatorship of the student elite.

The student revolutionary elite within a month of its greatest success found itself estranged from and rejected by the French proletariat. As Sanche de Gramont wrote:

> It was clear that workers and students did not have the same goals. The students were challenging their elders and contesting forms of authority, whether parental or governmental, which they consider bankrupt. . . .
>
> The great majority of the workers, however, showed that far from repudiating the "consumer society" decried by the students, what they really wanted was more active participation in it. They asked not for an overthrow of society, but for full membership. Ninety per cent of the students come from non-working-class families. . . . The workers are men with families, men of all ages . . . but they do not feel spiritually oppressed. They feel materially deprived.[69]

In short, in France in the spring of 1968, generational struggle could not easily coalesce with class struggle. Society had become too prosperous, and the working classes too well organized, for the student intellectuals to fulfill their longed-for role as an elite. The student activists talked of "total change"; the Trotskyites especially had their "sweetest moments of triumph" (according to an American reporter), as their students seemed to be "on every action committee and in every action," and all their charges against the embourgeoisement of the Communist leaders seemed confirmed. But what they overlooked was that the workers did not share the students' "alienation," their compulsive desire to wreck the "System." The idealistic students sought for an alternative identification with the lowly: "We are all German Jews," they chanted when Daniel Cohn-Bendit was under threats of arrest and deportation.[70] The events of 1968 suggested however that the French student movement of the future would oscillate even more between two extremes of elitism—one in which it saw itself as the chosen generation of future rulers, demanding all sorts of privileges within the system, and the other, an aimless, directionless protest against the system, an embittered last stand of the children's world, the guardians of pure values against old men. The French university studentry, which in the last ten years has grown from 175,000 to 530,000 in numbers, thus becomes a more potent source of social instability.[71] It is historically possible that stable social systems with economies of abundance may be confronted by a heightened generational disequilibrium, as aggressive energies, not challenged by external material obstacles, turn inward against the social system itself.

Meanwhile, as the astute Raymond Aron observed, the French intellectuals were "in a state of part-utopian, part-nihilist delirium." The style of the "Chinese cultural revolution," he said, permeated the Sorbonne commune. The attack on liberal democracy had been promoted by a small group which had never had the least interest in university reform. The elder academics tended to collapse in capitulation quickly. Psychoanalysis, said Aron, may possibly discover why "the young today hate both *père et maître*;" it would also have to explain why "they will have a far greater hatred for the father who surrenders and the master who abases himself."[72]

The Student Nazis of Germany

The German student movement needed no lessons in anti-Semitism, anti-liberalism, or anti-democracy from the Nazis.[73] Most of its members were doctrinal Nazis for years before they became formal Nazis. The German Student Union, recognized officially in 1920, traced its lineage to the Wartburg Festival of 1817. Now that the Kaiser was overthrown, its leaders felt that it would become the major power in the universities. That power they proposed to use on behalf of a chauvinistic German mission; all German-speaking peoples in Central Europe would be unified, and Jews, lacking German "blood," would be barred from membership. When the Prussian Minister of Education, Carl Heinrich Becker, a scholar and a nonparty man, opposed their designs, the student leaders called him a Metternich. The parliamentary republic, they said, was a disgrace to the nation, and the students should take over its leadership. "The German students," noted an observer in 1932, "are naturally quite sure that they constitute the élites. If not they, who else? . . . they ask."[74] The professors, the liberals, the pacifists became the targets of a primitive generational hatred. When the Nazis seized power, the student cry became, "With the state, against the professors!"[75]

The liberal, social-democratic state was regarded by most German students as "reactionary," as having betrayed their hopes. What these "hopes" were became embodied in the Nazi program. The so-called academic self-government which the students had demanded turned out to have been purely a slogan against liberals; under the Nazis, the students cheerfully accepted cultural coordination and regimentation. The Student Union indeed officially dissolved itself on October 18, 1935, donning the brown shirts and discarding the traditional festive caps, jackets, and banners of their century-old Burschenschaften. The promise of Wartburg and Karl Follen had found its inheritor in Adolf Hitler. Student idealism, it transpired, had a loathsome ingredient that stemmed from demonry or pathology rather than from purity of soul. Students displayed their idealism in the spring and summer of 1933 by storming into classrooms, insulting liberal professors, and physically assaulting Jewish and socialist students. Hitler praised the students' seizure of power as part of "the impulsive popular movement." In the spirit of the Wartburg Festival, the Nazi student movement too had its "burning of the books" of fifteen leading writers on the square opposite the University of Berlin. It was the younger generation which now sent the older into the fires of Moloch. The direction of generational sacrifice was reversed.

The Nazi Studentenschaft soon imposed its will on the constitution of university faculties. At Berlin they insisted in 1933 on a purge of the "non-German spirit" within the university saying, "We know the few teachers at Germany's universities who draw on and teach in the spirit in which we live and act—the spirit of the Storm Detachments. They alone have the right to criticize, because they have our confidence."[76] At Kiel they demanded the dismissal of twenty-eight professors, and largely got what they demanded. Within four years, sixteen hundred professors had been driven from the universities and *Hochschulen;* the student movement could claim considerable credit for this achievement. A few professors, previously sympathetic to the student movement and to the National Revolution, tried to reprove and moderate the students, but soon they too were banished. It was, indeed, as one of these professors, Edward Spranger, said, an uprising against the "professoriate," and he resigned from Berlin, saying he could no longer understand the new generation. This was a new phenomenon—the energies of generational revolt were being harnessed as a source of social power for the Nazi revolution, and its patterns of terrorism, amoralism, elitism, and suicidalism merged with the Nazi movement. The German students supplied Hitler with aders and heroes of his *Sturmabteilungen* (storm troopers).[77] For the zis were adept at heightening the tensions of generational conflict by sidiously de-authoritizing the elders in the eyes of the young. "With expert demagogy did Goebbels harp on the fact that the boys and girls graduated by the German schools had no outlook for the future. . . . The Youth began to feel that they were paying for the sins and crimes of the old. The Fascists, time and again, appealed to them that they should stop bearing the burdens of the old! Here was the entering wedge for the Nazi revivalist. . . ." A few months before he became Chancellor, Adolf Hitler proclaimed to the National Socialist Youth Field Day celebration, "Through our movement a new and strong generation is growing up that has new courage and does not surrender."[78]

What had occurred for nearly a century in Germany was a de-authoritization of the liberals of 1848 and a re-authoritization of the anti-democrats and militarists. In the first decades after 1848, writes a noted historian, "new forces, vital and politically successful, commanded the allegiance of a new body of students disillusioned with the ineptitude of the older liberals. German unification and control of its own politics, internal and external, had been gained through the efforts of a few men; and only an army acting on Bismarck's orders had accomplished the feat." Thus, "the generations of students attending universities in the 1880's had resumed the radical movement toward the right."[79] One student wrote that "experienced politicians are surprised by the change in the new generation; 1848 is already a mere legend."

From 1848 to 1914 the German studentry willingly acquiesced in the Bismarckian order; in exchange it had all the prerogatives of an elite-in-training. By the 1890s, "the students no longer played a prominent part in politics." They prepared for careers rather than crusades. The Social Democratic party, mistrusting their obvious elitism, was "not willing to submit to the leadership of immature bourgeois youngsters."[80] Only much later, after the war and after the Russian Revolution, the militant students returned to the fray, at a time when everything was topsy-turvy and careers no longer seemed within their reach. They played a modest part in the Communist movement; they flocked in shoals to the Nazi standards. When they became political activists, the students always moved toward the violent extremes.

A corrupting anti-Semitism came to pervade the German studentry. In fact, insofar as a German student movement existed, its principal warfare was against the Jews. An anti-Semitic petition in 1880 had, relative to the population, a great success among the students; asking the government to expel Jews from German life, it garnered four hundred signatures at Göttingen alone. The Association of German Students (Verein Deutscher Studenten—Kyffhauser Bund), organized in 1881, was dedicated to fight against materialism, liberalism, rationalism, and the Jews. The students, in elitist fashion, claimed that they looked upon the Jewish question objectively and impartially, since "jealousy of Jewish competition," they claimed, did not move them. In 1901, under pressure from students, the faculty of the University of Heidelberg prohibited the formation of a Jewish fraternity. When a famous professor of law in 1907 suggested readings in a book whose authors were Jews, he was greeted with ridicule, and when he mentioned that one of the authors had been murdered, "the students broke into thunderous applause."[81] Liberals from 1870 on were in the minority on the faculties, which "did little or nothing to discourage the growing wave of anti-Semitism." Student organizations promoted the ostracism of Jewish students, even the use of violence against them. One showed one's elite German status by refusing to duel with Jewish students, by spurning their challenge. By 1914, twenty-nine out of forty-four Austrian fraternities had actually enacted a resolution to this effect. For many of the German students, "Nazism seemed merely a logical application of the slogans which their fathers had been mouthing since their fraternity days." With the rightward movement of the German students, "bourgeois youth was lost to the Weimar Republic even before the Republic got properly started." The military debacle of 1918 produced a deep crisis within the German studentry, but they finally responded with anti-Semitism. August Bebel had said anti-Semitism was the socialism of the damned fools, the ignoramuses, but in Germany it was the socialism of the student activists. In 1922, the threat of a student riot intimidated the University of Berlin into canceling a memorial service for the assassinated Foreign Minister, Walther Rathenau, a Jew.[82]

Ninety per cent of the students came from the bourgeois class, and of course were preparing for posts in commerce, industry, government, and the civil service. The fear of defeat in the career struggle was ever present, it was the fear of sinking into the intellectual proletariat. Student anti-Semitism had an economic ingredient. "In their competition with the Jews . . . they descended to the level of using anti-Semitism to achieve their ends."[83] In 1913, there had been 78,000 university students in all Germany; in 1931, there were 124,000. "Jobs had not multiplied as fast as applicants. The spectre of unemployment frightened students."[84] The mediocre students especially were worried. "Only the Nazis offered them a really good choice." In the fall of 1932, when Hitler sustained a temporary eclipse, "Nazi students were deeply depressed." They told Professor Bonn, "Our hopes have gone—we thought the party would be in very soon. The Jewish professors would have been eliminated, exams would have been made much easier, we would have passed with flying colors and got jobs for which we have been designated."[85]

But economic causation does not suffice to explain the virulence of anti-Semitism among the German students. "Historical evidence proves that the younger generation was more vehement in its refusal to have contact with the Jews than were their elders, who remembered a previous age."[86] The German students proved altogether susceptible to the propagandist stereotypes of the corpulent Jew, the money man, the stock-exchange jobber, who in addition to money lust had a lust for Aryan women. "The resulting image used as propaganda pictured a fat Jewish banker caressing a blond woman on his knee." Was Jew hatred a displacement of the increasing generational resentment in German society? Was the fat Jewish banker a substitute symbol for the still fatter German father?

The generational conflict was persistent in German society. When Hauptmann's play *Before Dawn* was given, "the row was terrific. It was a clash between two generations. The older people were indignant that such unpleasant subjects were presented to a civilized public; the younger ones went mad with joy." The youth, noted the same observer, "distrust the ideals of an older generation, not because they have found them false, but because they want to live in a world of their own making. When their elders have been wise and have created a world offering safe careers to them, the young are bored by security; boredom has probably been a far more mighty revolutionary solvent than misery."[87]

Karl Stern, a distinguished psychiatrist, has written, "For some unknown reason, the relationship between generations, particularly that between father and son, seems much more problematic in Germany than in Anglo-Saxon countries." In schools, "the teacher was always a victim of aggression and hostility. He was attacked by means of glue on the chair, stink bombs in the stove, noises of mysterious origin. It was not always funny. In reality, to some teachers life was hell on earth." As Stern saw it, "that extraordinary significance of the struggle of generations, that most peculiar biological revolt, is nothing new in German history. It existed as 'Sturm und Drang' in the eighteenth century, it is immanent in the history of the Reformation, in other words, in the entire history of the German 'protest' of which Dostoievsky spoke." It was strong, said Stern, in ministers' sons like Nietzsche who made fun of God, "a neurosis, a revolt against the father's house."[88]

In the German Youth Movement, leather-belted, heavy-booted, long-bloused youngsters hiked, sang, played the guitar around fires, discussed philosophy. "All of them had one thing in common: a rebellious attitude against their parents' generation, or at least against the mode of living of that generation. There was a sort of ascetic protest against everything 'bourgeois'—no drinking, no smoking, no smart clothes."[89] "The Platonic idea of youth" in and for itself found expression. This was the immediate postwar period.

Violence pervaded the German student scene. In 1924, "our classmates wore daggers, revolvers and arm-ribbons." There were apparent "examples of rebellion without aim, of a cynical liking for revolution, and a love of protest and force for their own sake." "Even today, when I think of those eighteen-year-olds, I have the feeling one has while facing a man with some uncanny mental disturbance." "Protest for the sake of protest" and the "Revolution of nihilism" were descriptive phrases of the mentality of "the youngsters of Munich during the post-war years."[90] When Count Arco murdered the Premier of the Bavarian Soviet Republic, Kurt Eisner, students in meetings at the University of Munich celebrated the assassin as a hero, and demanded that his punishment be light.[91]

The short-lived Bavarian Soviet revolution of 1919, an untypical episode of socialist idealism, itself briefly had elements of a students' uprising. "There rarely ever was a rising that youth enjoyed as greatly as the Red April dream of Munich." The people's commissars were in a state of exaltation and confusion. "But the youngsters did not care. Overnight they were somebodies. They addressed meetings, invaded government offices, gave orders and enjoyed themselves as never before."[92] The Munich Soviet indeed appointed a commission of six students to work out plans for the reform of the university. Some wild speech-making ensued; the students "meant to dismiss the entire teaching body and to reappoint only those who were fellow travelers if not comrades." The student poet-soldier and cabinet minister, Ernst Toller, was imbued with generational idealism and revolt; his generational conflict merged with the workingmen's aspirations, however, in a way which was not typical of the German studentry.

As a child, Ernst Toller, had brooded, "All grown-ups are bad, but if you are cunning you can outwit them. Our gang is very cunning. . . . Grown-ups are our enemies; Julie, our old cook, is the only one who understands at all." He expressed the suicidal propulsion as he read the books banned in his high school—Ibsen, Strindberg, Hauptmann: "Standing by Hamlet's legendary grave, I waver, just as he did, between the impulse toward action and the longing for death, and when I am back again at school next term I feel fettered and imprisoned." When he returned from the war to a student's life at the University of Munich, he shared his fellows' questioning: "The war had driven them all from their study tables, they were all questioning the values of yesterday and today. But the young wanted something more than theorizing. To them the world into which they had been born seemed ripe for annihilation, and they sought for a way out of the dreadful confusion of the times; they sought to make new order out of chaos; they believed in the absolute, incorruptible mind which should recognize no master but the truth." The students listened to the prophets, to the sociologist Max Weber. They cried with Toller, "Show us the way. . . . We have waited long enough." There came the realization that the prophets could not guide them. As Toller wrote, "I died / Was reborn / Died / Was reborn / I was my own mother."[93] A handful of students looked for their answer to a liberal socialist idealism. "Our fathers had betrayed us, and the young who had known war, hard and unsentimental, would begin the business of spring-cleaning." Little university groups were formed at Heidelberg and elsewhere to protest against war; they raised a banner of generational revolt: "the youth of every country would join us in our fight against those whom we accused as the originators of the war: our fathers!" But only a few, like Toller, found an identification with the workers, with "worker personalities," as he said, "whom I had never met before; men of keen understanding, of deep insight into social problems, of profound experience of life." In November 1918, Ernst Toller was Deputy President of the Central Committee of the Workmen's, Peasants', and Soldiers' Soviets of Bavaria. Then followed defeat and prison. He brooded on the lot of the men who enter politics to "try to realize their ideals in face of the masses." Was self-destruction their fate? Was the individual intellectual at odds with the mass man? Could the intellectual lead the people to a social revolution by nonviolent means? "Was Max Weber right after all when he said that the only logical way of life for those who were determined never to overcome evil by force was the way of St. Francis? Must the man of action always be dogged by guilt? Always?"[94] Toller felt he had embodied "the youth of a whole generation." Actually, he was unrepresentative of a generation which veered very quickly to Nazism.

Why did no student movement arise in Germany after the Nazi surrender in 1945 and the end of the Second World War? One might imagine that there indeed was a situation of de-authoritization of the elder generation out of which student movements have been born. Actually, however, the precise opposite was the case. It was the student movement which was de-authoritized, because it had given itself to the Nazis lock, stock, and barrel. This was a studentry discredited by its failure of character and betrayal of intellect; it could claim no mission to redeem others. The elders of the previous generation, social democrats, liberals, conservatives, shared much less of the national guilt than the Nazi students, for the elders had been largely displaced and spiritually emasculated by the Nazis. Almost twenty years elapsed, therefore, before the signs of a restive new student movement began to appear.

The postwar German students became known as "the Skeptical Generation."[95] They were, indeed, without ideology. They had seen the holocaust the Nazis had brought, and their elder brothers, fellow-students, were tainted by the mark of fanaticism, surrenders of reason and judgment, and self-immolation to cruelty and destruction. On the other side of the border, in East Germany, they saw another type of betrayal to tyranny. Skepticism alone was the answer, and its practical consequence was the conviction that one's own private life and activity and work was the important thing. The students discarded ideology as the sign of an illness. All ideologies were false gods, and only a damned fool would run after them twice. At times, a student uprising would take place to confirm the rejection of the Nazi past. Almost twenty years after the war's end, a thousand students at Marburg, for instance, demonstrated against one of their professors, who had aroused suspicions of Nazi leanings.

By 1965, however, a new generation had come into being which had no living recollection of Nazism, and no share for its responsibility as had the immediate postwar generation. The studentry itself was not politically radical; so long as an oppressive Communist regime was its immediate neighbor, it could not be attracted to orthodox Marxism. While a poll indicated a slight majority of support for the Christian Democrats, most students remained "apolitical and apathetic."[96] Nevertheless, three thousand students in 1965 signed a petition, in the so-called "Kuby Affair," to defend the right of a critic of the Federal Republic to speak at the Free University in Berlin. A student coalition emerged which extended from the Marxist Sozialistischer Deutscher Studentenbund to the Lutheran student association. The German activists were also at odds with the past generations of alumni organized in the Burschenschaften, the fraternal dueling societies whose members, especially the prewar ones, the *alte Herren,* still constituted a reactionary phalanx. The new German student movement began to raise the typical issues of democratization of the university. The liberal *Die Welt* attacked them as "a handful of radical malcontents," and the Rightists pronounced them to be "Red students" allied to "fatherlandless intellectuals." A belated generational revolt was in the air.

In the spring of 1967, Berlin students demonstrated against Vice-President Hubert Humphrey of the United States, and made threats of assassination. A student was killed during a later demonstration against the Shah of Iran. The working class of Berlin rebuffed the student activists who went to the workers' neighborhoods for support. The working class evidently shared the opinion of Berlin's mayor that an "extremist minority" aimed at "liquidating the democratic order" through a "chain of irresponsible provocations."[97] In 1968, a new German student movement emerged; it evinced the classical traits of elitism, a hatred for liberal democracy, an attraction to violence, and the adoration of a "charismatic" leader.[98]

The Portuguese Students' Revolt against Gerontocratic Fascism

The European continent is scarcely homogeneous in its generational relationships. If the French student movement has become virtually a syndicate for self-interest, and if the German student movement was tarnished from its affiliation with the Nazis, in Portugal and Spain we see the classical pattern of self-sacrifice by students of the upper classes. The Russian Narodniki have found their successors in the Iberian Peninsula, where students—especially in Portugal—hurl themselves against an absolutist government.

The dictatorship of Premier Salazar in Portugal at first evoked only a small student protest. But when the police behaved with cruelty against the students, the familiar responses and tactics of generational protest and solidarity emerged. A decree of 1956 forbade activities by the students; it evoked demonstrations of protest in Lisbon and Coimbra. Then, in 1962, the government prohibited the celebration of the traditional Student Day, the *dia do estudiante*. The grounds of Lisbon University were invaded by police forces. Thereupon the students struck in a protest which lasted for three months, and for a time there was a general hunger strike; strikes also erupted at Coimbra and Porto. In one night as many as fifteen hundred students were imprisoned, and five thousand were involved in demonstrations. Eighty students were expelled from the university, and fifty professors as well as the rector and the Minister of Education resigned or were ousted. The students not only resented the police force which suppressed its demonstrations and violated university autonomy; they literally hated the political police (PIDE), who tortured and imprisoned their classmates. The Minister of Education held dictatorial power over the students, for he could start disciplinary trials against them in disregard of the university authorities. The government prevented a National Union of Students from being founded, while its own official fascist Portuguese Youth had little influence in the universities. The free student movement languished after 1962 as its leaders were imprisoned, tortured, or drafted into the army.[99] A participant in the 1962 protest wrote, "All these events created an air of excitement and enthusiasm. We began to feel invulnerable as night after night we met around different tables without sleeping, and set up a convoy of cars to move our mimeograph machine and tons of paper in and out of dozens of houses all over Lisbon to escape the secret police. . . . We experienced the inestimable privilege of speaking out, of making a break with the years and years of half-truths, years of humiliations both great and small."[100] March 1962 was the month in which a large number of students thrust off fear.

The authorities' use of physical force above all aroused the most primitive generational solidarity: "Their first mistake was invading the university buildings with combat troops. The sight of machine guns and two dozen wounded gave our movement its most powerful impetus."

The ranks of the activist students grew. "We were not in the majority at the outset; our members grew in direct relationship to the successive blunders of the dictatorship as it showed its true face. (Today, the following remark had become routine at political trials: 'Before 1962 I wasn't active in politics, but after . . .')." The colonial war in Angola aroused the Portuguese students as the Algerian War had the French; apart from the moral issues, there was the gloomy prospect of three and a half years of compulsory military service.

The generational patterns of violence and suicide emerged among the Portuguese activists. In January 1965, to forestall the students' celebration of the unofficial International Students Day, the Portuguese political police arrested twenty-seven secondary school and university students. A total of at least sixty students were then in jail, "some of them sons and daughters of prominent Portuguese families." The students retaliated first by assailing the rector of Lisbon University, Paulo Arsenio Cunha, former Minister of Foreign Affairs, with catcalls at a public ceremony, then by a strike which was joined by an estimated 80 to 85 per cent. Students wore black ties or gowns in "academic mourning" for their arrested fellows. Meanwhile, arrested students were tortured. One girl student had a mental breakdown; another died under suspicious circumstances—"an attack of appendicitis," said the police. Another student, Fernando Baeta Neves, twenty-three, vice-president of the Student Association of Lisbon University's law faculty, tried to commit suicide by swallowing pieces of his eyeglasses which he smashed after police threatened to inject him with a truth serum.[101]

More than five hundred students protested the cruelty of the police on January 26 by marching to the Lisbon prison and shouting "Down with the PIDE!" and "Freedom for Political Prisoners." The democratic opposition group charged the government with "driving youth to Communism." Later there were new demonstrations in which student placards bore the messages: "Freedom for the University!" and "When the State is supported by force, it reveals its weakness!"

Such was the student movement in Portugal, harried by a fascist dictatorship of old men and secret police—a dictatorship with which the students had no identification, a gerontocratic regime which enthralled the fathers but not the sons. As usual, the physical brutality of the police was the symbolic act of generational tyranny which stirred the students to a frenzy of resentment. Student terrorism made its appearance. In June 1965, nine Lisbon University students were convicted of participating in a terrorist plot. They were said to belong to the pro-Peking faction of the Portuguese Communist party, the Front for Popular Action. Their leader was a student of agronomy, twenty years of age, Artur Manuel Figueira Gouveia, the son of a wealthy lawyer. He confessed to an intention to explode a bomb "as a symbolic gesture of protest" against the Salazar regime.[102] A sixteen-year-old girl, Sara Barros Queiroz Amancio, accused of terrorist involvement, replied that she and her fellow-students "detested" state-controlled youth organizations and were resolved to continue their struggle for free associations. The Portuguese regime demanded the ouster of "Red intellectuals" in the universities. By the workings of a law of demonry, it was making every mistake that its Czarist counterparts had made years before, and was driving the student generation into despair and unreason. Yet moral factors were probably the controlling ones in the sudden emergence of the Portuguese student movement. A Portuguese student exile, Salis Cerqueira, was asked why it was that the twenty-five thousand university students of Portugal, a country of nine and a half million, had become the base for political opposition. Why did a studentry of whom almost 90 per cent came from the economically privileged classes cast their lot with rebellion?[103] His answer went beneath the manifest level of demands for student self-government, academic freedom, and university reform; it was the moral de-authoritization of the elders engaged in prosecuting several colonial wars, even as their empire visibly was disintegrating, which gave impetus to the student awakening. One student, Raimao Aires Teixeira, aged twenty-two, doubtless spoke for many when he said, "Nobody asked us students what we thought about shipping thousands of our colleagues to Angola and Mozambique."[104]

Vanguard of the Spanish Intellectual Elite

The Spanish students, unlike the Portuguese, did not require a specific crisis of de-authoritization in colonial wars to awaken them. For the Spanish intellectual class lived in the recollection that it had been crushed in the 1930s by a fascist uprising abetted by forces of Hitler and Mussolini. They bided their time, waiting to assert themselves as an intellectual elite against the military elite. And the Spanish student movement is indeed the striking force of the intellectual elite against the military. In this sense, it has been much less of a movement of generational protest, and has looked for inspiration to respected elder figures of the academic world. The Communist student organ *World Student News* noted that the Spanish student unrest began in the middle 1950s with the beginnings of a more active cultural development:

> It is this activisation of intellectual creativity, together with the inevitable critical discussion which accompanies it and the important mobilisations of the working masses in recent years that has given rise to the present situation in which outstanding personalities in Spanish cultural life, such as José L. L. Aranguren, unquestionably the most remarkable philosopher in present-day Spain and Professor of Ethics at the University of Madrid have joined with the students and even confronted the regime.[105]

Professor Aranguren was only one among a group of professors whom the Spanish regime regarded as "agitators."

A Spanish student movement arose in 1926 when university unions were organized to oppose the military dictatorship of Primo de Rivera. The student leader Sbert was exiled in 1930 to Majorca; the students stoned the dictator's house; the University of Madrid was closed, and on December 22, a student strike was an important factor in forcing the ouster of the dictator Rivera. The student leader Sbert returned in triumph.[106] During this time the students worked also for liberalizing the curriculum, for liberating it from medieval constraints, and for freedom in the classroom. "Student strikes and riots inside as well as outside of college buildings became almost commonplace for students and professors as the police and Civil Guards answered them with bullets and grenades." Jokes arose on the theme of "the Civil Guards going to school." "More than one student gave his life for academic freedom; hundreds of students now in the trenches received their baptism of fire not from the fascists of 1936 but from the police of 1923–30," wrote an American during the Spanish Civil War. The medical students of San Carlos in Madrid in a famous siege fought the cavalry with stones; that was toward the end of the monarchy. In other ways too the early Spanish student movement emulated the Russian populist spirit. The Spanish University Unions tried in 1931–1932 to found Popular Universities, to establish Educational Missions, and to send traveling theaters among the people. They were filled with a spirit which an American student leader acknowledged was "as yet unfelt by American students." These activities multiplied during the Civil War; students propagandized everywhere, presenting plays, movies, and puppet shows to the people. The student martyrology grew. Emilio de la Lona, Madrid student of law, zealous for academic freedom, member of the Executive Committee of the National Union of Spanish Students, president of "La Barraca," the traveling theater of the Spanish University Unions, joined those who rushed "to the Guadarrama mountains to block the approaching fascists with barricades built of their fallen bodies. That student leader was one whose body helped." Thus the Spanish students' heroism evoked the death-glorifying language of an American fellow-activist. Juan Lopez, general secretary of the National Union of Spanish Students, was killed in the trenches of his own University City. Rafael Carrasco, the Union's president when the war broke out, was killed in 1937 while leading a "Young Guard" battalion of the United Socialist Youth. "He is immortalized in the hearts of Spanish students as one of their greatest heroes," wrote the American student activist with moving exaggeration.[107] All this was quite forgotten thirty years later.

The new Spanish student awakening found its primary object of resentment not in any broad social issues but in a symbol of parental authoritarian control, the Sindicato Español Universitario (SEU). The Sindicato, with its one hundred thousand compulsory members, was largely controlled from above by the government through appointed student bureaucrats; on its lower levels, the various studentries could elect their own delegates. The students resented the apparatus of manipulation from above, and mocked at the notion of compulsory membership in an "autonomous" organization. More than twenty dissident illegal student groups came into existence in protest against the SEU.[108] Mostly centered at the Universities of Madrid and Barcelona, their aspirations were primarily those of a young intellectual elite; they called for "Free Student Syndicates," "The Fall of the SEU," and "Student Solidarity." They were idealistic and freedom-loving; with some exceptions, however, they did not raise demands for basic social, economic, or constitutional reconstruction. The struggle against the SEU took on, however, the familiar patterns of violence and counter-violence characteristic of student movements. There were violent conflicts at Madrid, Barcelona, Salamanca, Bilbao, Valencia, Seville, Oviedo, Valladolid, Saragossa. The students' campaign increasingly centered on one demand: the democratic reorganization of the SEU; a broad unity, which included the Catholic Student Youth, emerged from 1962 to 1965 around this issue. There was the usual provocatively stupid rector who turns up in all student uprisings, in this case the rector of Madrid, who deprived students of scholarships. The SEU itself became a kind of runaway company union. The student leaders at Bilbao, both appointed and elected, resigned in protest, and there were resignations at Barcelona and Valencia. On March 2, 1965, five thousand Madrid students celebrated in a snowstorm a Day of the Free Student with an illegal public demonstration, and elsewhere there were strikes and demonstrations.[109] The initiative moved to the socialist-minded Spanish Democratic University Federation (FUDE) and the "left-wing Falangists." At a demonstration later in March, twenty-five hundred students chanted, "Dictatorship, no! Democracy, yes!" "We demand a dialogue," they said, "and we are answered with repression."

For a brief period, the announcement of liberal concessions by the Spanish government seemed to herald victory for the growing generational revolt. The regime granted most importantly the right of students to elect their national officers democratically, though it retained the right to name a commissioner for liaison between "the institutions of the State and of the Movement." But the students' victory was scarcely a permanent one. In September 1965, the government promulgated measures which imposed a direct censorship on the publications of all Spanish students' associations. The chancellors of universities, moreover, were authorized to dismiss students guilty of agitation.[110] When 420 student delegates tried to hold a "free assembly" at a monastery near Barcelona in March 1966, they were besieged by the police, who cut off their electricity and telephones for forty-five hours. Then the police forced the monastery and captured the students. A national protest arose among the students, and again there were demonstrations: "Liberty, yes! Dictatorship, no! A free and democratic Sindicato!" During the Easter vacation nonetheless, the government imposed heavy fines on well-known intellectuals who had joined with the students at the monastery conclave.[111]

What does the chronicle of the Spanish student movement indicate? Above all, it shows that a fascist regime is not exempt from the workings of the law of generational conflict or from a revolt of the student intellectual elite. The appeal of fascism has always been to youth, its intuition, its uncorrupted ardor, its idealism, its enthusiasm. But even fascist systems grow middle-aged and old. Spanish students eagerly read contemporary world literature on the alienation and role of the intellectuals. Indeed the demonstration of February 15, 1965, in Madrid was provoked when the authorities prohibited lectures at the university on "Intellectuals and Peace" and "The Christian Vision of Alienation."[112] Student discontent also took form in demands for the modernization of the university, since the Spanish university still emphasized the humanities to the relative depreciation of the sciences; between 1941 and 1962, only 6,947 degrees in the sciences were awarded, as compared to 23,366 in law, and Spanish education, according to the philosopher José Aranguren, remained "academic, rhetorical, idealistic, mythical, unfounded and useless." Yet this demand for "modernization" was probably not sincerely meant, and was only a symbol for generational discontent. Experience shows that in the universities of Asia and Latin America even the encouragement of the governments is of little avail in persuading the students to devote themselves to the sciences rather than the humanities. But the spirit of generational revolt has always sought some expression in issues of curriculum and courses.

Above all, the Spanish student uprisings showed that in a crisis the solidarity of generational consciousness and revolt proves stronger than loyalties to the authority of the elder generation. Even the government-controlled Sindicato Español Universitario could not withstand the infectious enthusiasm of generational solidarity. In November 1964, for instance, Franco's government found itself obliged to oust the very leader whom it itself had appointed five weeks earlier to lead the Student Union—Daniel Regalado Aznar. Regalado, twenty-six years old and a graduate in chemistry, had felt the spirit of his co-generationists. His very first declaration to the students of the country had the imprint of their dissatisfaction with the status quo: "There is teaching in our country, but no education . . . and the shortcomings of our university can be traced back to our professors." Then he went on to call for a revision of the organizational structure of the SEU to permit a more "effective representation of the students for the active defense of their professional interests."[113] Regalado eschewed political issues, and confined himself to student issues. His action, however, for more effective student pressure on the state authorities opened all the possibilities of a future political uprising led by the student intellectual elite. Generational solidarity was showing itself to be a force which authoritarian organs found it hard to contain because it infiltrated not through conspiracy or secrecy but through the generosity and comradeship of student youth itself.

Basically, the Spanish student movement remained a movement of the liberal intellectual elite, with few populist overtones. There were reports that some socialist students had left the universities and, disguised as workers, were agitating among the Asturian miners. Still more students were said to be spending their summers carrying on literacy campaigns in backward areas. The student activists were also described as enjoying activity in secret organizations for the love of secrecy itself, "appealing as it does to the Latin enjoyment of secret organizations and intrigue."[114] At the same time, it was acknowledged that there were "relatively few students deeply committed to energetic radicalism" and little identification with labor. The mutual distrust and intolerance among the student factions was great. Curiously, the student activity was far weaker in Barcelona than in Madrid, a fact perhaps not unrelated to Barcelona's tradition of workers' syndicalism, anarchism, and mistrust of intellectual elitism. And women students with a middle-class background from the Faculty of Philosophy and Letters, more than half of whose students were women, were providing the chief forces of student activism, a phenomenon which reminds one of the Russian students in the nineteenth century.[115] The belief in the necessity of violence was strong among the activists. If in a time of crisis the Spanish student movement were to move from its liberal objectives to those of its minority activists, it was uncertain whether it would serve the democratic cause. It still remained historically possible, however, for the Spanish student movement to preserve a loyalty to its liberal aims and to join with other social groups to found and safeguard a constitutional social democracy.[116]

The Generational Dialectic in European Communist Systems

The Soviet and eastern European Communist countries live in the shadow of the Student Revolution which took place in Hungary in 1956. Here was indisputable evidence, if such was needed, that the "dialectical" development of a Communist society does not exclude the law of generational conflict; that the moral de-authoritization of the elder generation, even in a Communist country, would provoke an uprising of student youth.

THE HUNGARIAN STUDENT INITIATIVE OF OCTOBER 1956

The Hungarian students were the ill-fated striking force of the October revolt of 1956. In the fall of that year they began to drop out of the Communist League of Working Youth. In October, the student body of the University of Szeged founded its own independent organization; other universities then did the same. The students' action was a blow aimed at what they regarded as a morally corrupt elder generation. It was sudden, for "they had not been engaged in continuous, chronic defiance." "This organizational step was a revolutionary act; it meant that the students were shaking off the tutelage of the regime's control organs." Their first mass meetings in Budapest quickly moved not to student matters but to national problems. Their committees posed demands directed against the policies and methods of the compromised party veterans of the Old Guard; "approval or disapproval from any authority seemed to be a matter of complete indifference to them." Unlike the intellectuals of the Writers' Association, the students acted with the conviction of clear conscience; "the students' behaviour reflected no intense struggles of conscience such as the writers had gone through."

Such was the unforeseen consequence of the "thaw" which Khrushchev had promoted in the Soviet Union. A moral crisis had spread through Hungary as the intellectuals and writers who had supported the Communist regime listened to victims who had been "released and rehabilitated." "These confrontations plunged the Communist intellectuals into agonies of remorse and despair: the poems and articles they had written during the period of terror, applauding Rakosi and vilifying his victims, remained as monuments to their shame. Thereafter, remorse was a recurrent theme in the poetry of the younger generation of Communists." The Writers' Association in 1955 broke with party discipline; the Petofi Circle, a club for discussion and dissent, became a public forum against the regime. However, the students were the first to act. When they paraded on October 23, 1956, Budapest witnessed its first demonstration in years. The sight of marching students kindled people's emotions. Crowds began to join; they pressed the radio authorities to broadcast the students' demands. The radio officials declined; instead the police attacked the demonstrators, and violence broke out. The crowd wrecked the Communist party headquarters, stormed the citadel of the secret police, and lynched them. Stalin's statue was toppled.

The Hungarian students were moved by ideal, not material reasons. Youngsters threw themselves into hopeless battle. As Kecskemeti wrote, "There was in their combativeness an element of psychic compulsion, as though they were caught in a somnambulistic trance. It did not matter whether they lived or died. Only one thing counted: getting weapons and using them as much and as long as possible." Generational solidarity ("peer-group solidarity," in Kecskemeti's words) exerted its power. "When some children got weapons and went out to fight, this apparently started a teen-age epidemic: The others felt they could not remain behind." The students, with their organizations, considered themselves the elite, "the nerve center of the revolution." "They found that they could easily establish contact with any group—workers and peasants as well as government officials, professionals, and army officers. They used this easy access to all strata in order to coordinate revolutionary policies and activities." Inspired by the students' example, the first Workers' Council was organized at the Incandescent Lamp Factory in Budapest on the following day, October 24. "Within three days, a network of councils covered the entire country." A general strike was proclaimed.

It was, as Kecskemeti says, "the public discrediting of leading Party members" which served as a signal for the revolt. A "moral shock" had released forces which made for a political crisis; a "moral conflict" which in the first place was one between generations was the catalytic agent, or rather the triggering agent, of the social dynamic. "Long-suppressed moral feelings" combined with the "breakdown of previously accepted authority relationships" to make for revolt. It was not economic considerations which moved the students. The students from middle-class families with privileged careers in the bureaucracy awaiting them took the revolutionary lead—these were students who "were nurtured by the regime and could expect to rise into relatively high social brackets" but who resented dictatorial controls and repression.[117] They were weary with the spying and watching of the Party's agents in the faculty and student body, and with having their lapses from the Party's grace recorded in their "cadre" file. The Student Uprising was directed against the corrupt elders whose corruption had been made manifest to all. The uprising was crushed, but its specter continued to haunt the Communist world. Students at the universities of Moscow and Leningrad discussed it in hushed tones, and Khrushchev tried to exorcise the specter of generational conflict from Soviet society.

CIRCLES OF ALIENATION AMONG THE POLISH AND YUGOSLAV STUDENTS

What then of student movements in the post-revolutionary countries, in the Soviet Union, in Poland, in Yugoslavia? There are, formally speaking, at present no activist movements in these countries, for all organizational life is controlled by their respective Communist parties. Generational discontent exists, as dissatisfaction with the corruptions of socialist society and with the involvement of the fathers in the shame of Stalinism. The would-be student activists, however, especially in the Soviet orbit, do not know which way to go. The whole notion of "revolution" has become tarnished; the phrases of Marxism-Leninism sound hollow. The bureaucratic existence of societies, so tightly organized, provides the norms. Confronted by a society which has a ponderous stability, the critical students are devoid of any dialectical faith in the possibility of its collapse. They fall back into little circles of muted protest, into oases of free discussion among friends. In such countries, student protest takes the form of the discovery of friendship as a more significant category than comradeship. A friend is one with whom you overcome the alienation of bureaucratic society; a comrade is a bureaucratized substitute for a friend.

The Polish students, for instance, at Warsaw University and nine other university-level schools in Warsaw, were found, according to two reliable surveys in 1958 and 1961, to be unhappy with the régime of authoritarian socialism and planned economy. The word "socialism" itself still had for them "a definitely positive emotional charge," but when many concrete features of socialism were adduced they responded with negative evaluations. The great majority defined themselves as non-Marxist. "Socialism" itself had come to mean vaguely a "system one likes," and often provided little indication otherwise as to basic attitudes. The Warsaw students of 1958 were disaffected with politics; they showed a "lack of enthusiasm towards the participation in all institutionalized forms of public life, especially all such forms which might be connected with participation in political power." Thus the Warsaw students differed notably from the restive political activists in other parts of the world, as the researchers noted. To what then did they turn in their discontent? "Feeling this lack of interest for those more institutionalized forms of political activity, but at the same time experiencing the need for being useful to society, the students endeavor to satisfy these needs in different forms of activities on a limited scale, by being useful to their own small professional or social circle. . . . Others give up altogether the idea of satisfying this need."

For this was a generation of students whose hopes had soared in 1956 and then had gradually failed—a generation whose uprising had failed so that they seemed to themselves defeated and de-authoritized. What we might call a "historical pessimism" or a "socialist pessimism" came to characterize the Polish post-revolutionary student generation. They generally reacted against the "more heroic versions of socialism." They had lost the masochism of classical student movements: "The idea that the present generation should be sacrificed for the well-being and happiness of future generations was quite alien to the students of Warsaw." They wanted a society which would not restrict civil liberties, except in unusual cases for short periods, an economy in which decisions were in the hands of factory councils, and a distribution of income which would be midway between egalitarian and inegalitarian. But the Warsaw students in 1958 were not moved to political activism. Three years later, researchers found among them a slightly greater acceptance of the political status quo. At the same time, there was "a distinct increase of political indifference, along with the decreased interest in political affairs and ideology." The Warsaw student exhibited "a diminished need for involvement in the defence of any values at all, and a decreased need for involvement in anything which overpasses the narrow limits of arranging one's own private life." The students, reported the researchers, had not increased their active acceptance of socialism; rather their adaptation to it was augmented. This was an era of stabilization in which students perceived "that the possibilities for changing the world according to their values are smaller than before."[118] Such was the statistical profile of the Polish student and his historical pessimism. If a grievance of generational resentment were to offer itself, there was fuel here for a generational uprising. Meanwhile, the rule of Premier Gomulka was at least temporarily that of a man who did not bear the mark of Stalinist de-authoritization, for he had languished in Stalin's prisons. However, the generational equilibrium in Polish society was an unstable one of acquiescence to defeat. A new generation might always find the historical pessimism of its elders something not to emulate. There is a continuing unpredictable ferment in the numerous Polish students' clubs which are independent of the universities and of the Party. Their activities include jazz, poetry readings, and Hindu metaphysics, but as a Communist source reported, "in the Gothic cellars of the 'Under the Cracks' Club in Cracow, students have a passion for politics and philosophy." Nine thousand students in such clubs are the activists of generational unrest.[119] They find their generational heroes, furthermore, elsewhere than in their own society. The great majority of students in 1966 at the Cracow Metallurgy and Mining Academy chose John F. Kennedy, the assassinated President of the United States, as their "hero." Moreover, while 80 per cent of the freshman class were informed about America's political parties, only 45 per cent of the 734 students could answer correctly similar questions about Poland. Forty-two of them didn't know who was President of Poland.[120]

With a milder, more decentralized type of socialist economy, and with a government which under President Tito was the first among the Communists to declare its moral rejection of Stalinism, the Yugoslav students were less disaffected with their socialist society, less inclined to historical pessimism. Yet even among Yugoslav students a generational rejection of ideology was apparent by 1961. That year the Zagreb newspaper *Vzesnik* conducted a survey of the political attitudes of students at Zagreb University. It found that less than half of the 3,291 respondents (43.6 per cent) were prepared to accept the official view that Yugoslavia has "the best form of contemporary democracy"; almost a third (32.8 per cent) of the students had doubts as to the viability of their system; almost a fourth (23.6 per cent) were uncommitted. On the other hand, the majority of the students (63.5 per cent) still regarded Marxism as a "true revolutionary social theory."[121] There was this curious combination among the Yugoslavian students of revolutionary Marxism and political criticism of their own socialist society. The key to this phenomenon lies in the fact that among the students, especially at Zagreb University, a new Marxism was arising which was the vehicle of generational protest: the Marxism of the young Marx when he was not yet a Marxist, that which made central the "alienation" of the individual in contemporary society. The journal *Praxis*, the organ of the young dissenters for whom "alienation" was the master word, was edited by a group composed primarily of intellectuals at Zagreb. The movement of dissent was entering its circle stage, the stage of theoretical discussion which defines the new generational direction and precedes the determination of issues and points of combat.

Rather abruptly in June 1968 the students of Belgrade University engaged in a "sit-in" which lasted eight days and ended only with the personal intercession of President Tito. The immediate issues were familiar ones of student life: poor food, crowded dormitories infested with mice, poor instruction in the socialist multiversity of 30,000. More basic was the preemption of the bureaucratic posts by the old generation, so that 70,000 Yugoslav graduates had had to emigrate. By the time the sit-in ended, the students were raising the deeper generational issues, with the slogan "Down with the Red bourgeoisie" (the older generation of ill-educated partisan veterans who were said to have a monopoly on the best jobs). In the interim, there were the usual intervening issues of police brutality, the closing of the university, the punishment of guilty officials, and a student amnesty. As usual, the activists founded their own short-lived free university, the "Karl Marx Red University" they called it; and as usual the School of Philosophy was the most militant, rejecting by a vote of 567 to 11 a compromise offer by the government. But then Tito intervened; in a broadcast to the nation, he promised to resolve the students' issues or resign. Ninety per cent of the students, he said, were "honest youths of whom we did not take sufficient care"; a few Peking-oriented extremists, he acknowledged, were trying to mislead them.[122] The Belgrade sit-in thereupon came to an end. But the basic issue raised by the students of a "greater democracy, especially in the League of Communists," indicated how generational conflict could become the mainspring of social change, perhaps even liberalization, in a Communist society, provided that it could withstand the drives to irrationality.

THE RETURN OF THE REPRESSED AMONG THE SOVIET STUDENTRY

Nikita Khrushchev, in the fashion of King Canute, decreed in 1963 that there was no real conflict of generations in the Soviet Union: "In our time there is no fathers-and-sons problem in the form in which it existed in the days of Turgenev. For we live in an entirely different period of relationships. There is no contradiction between the generations in Soviet socialist society, and there is no problem of 'fathers and sons' in its old implications."[123]

There were, to be sure, even among the Soviet youth, "semi-degenerate types," said Khrushchev, "who have no love and no respect for anyone, who not only do not trust their elders, but actually despise them," who "are dissatisfied with everything, are always grumbling," and spend their days in idleness and their evenings at dubious parties. But such, he held, did not pose a politically significant problem. Yet even Khrushchev must have been well aware how in Russia's history youthful nihilism was often the prelude and postlude to revolutionary action. To talk about the generational problem was just another way of talking about the student problem. Incomprehensible and unpredictable from the Marxist standpoint, the students, with their ideal aims and literary inspiration, were unlike the world of Khrushchev and his *apparatchiki*. And there was the recollection of the anxious days of the Hungarian student initiative in the October Revolution of 1956.

The Soviet system, indeed, has always been alert to the danger of a student movement and generational conflict. As far back as December 1923, Leon Trotsky held up the specter of a rising student movement to Stalin. Stalin never forgave Trotsky's words. "The youth—the most reliable barometer of the party—reacts most sharply against party bureaucratism." For the metaphor of the student movement as the political barometer of Russian society, so often used in the nineteenth century, portended a destructive dialectic within Soviet society itself. Trotsky emerged as the restless theoretician of generational conflict extending to the Soviet order itself:

The degeneration of an "Old Guard" has been observed in history more than once. To take the freshest and clearest recent example: the leaders and parties of the Second International. . . . We ought to state—we ourselves, the "old men"—that our generation, while naturally playing the role of leadership in the party, nevertheless does not contain within itself any automatic guarantee against a gradual and unnoticeable weakening of the proletarian and revolutionary spirit, provided the party permits any further growth and hardening of the bureaucratic-apparatus method of politics, which converts the younger generation into passive material for education, and creates inevitably an alienation between the apparatus and the mass, between the old and the young.[124]

Stalin struck back against Trotsky by denying the reality of generational struggle in the Soviet party:

Where did Comrade Trotsky get this setting-against-each-other of the "Old Guard" who may degenerate and "the youth" who constitute "the most reliable barometer of the party," the "Old Guard" who may bureaucratize and the "Young Guard" who must "take the revolutionary formulas fighting"? Whence comes this opposition and for what is it needed? Haven't the young and the Old Guard gone always with a united front against the foe within and without? Doesn't the unity of the old and the young represent the fundamental strength of our revolution? Whence this attempt to uncrown the Old Guard and demagogishly tickle the youth, so as to open and widen the little rift between these fundamental troops of our party?

Always in the background there remained the possibility that young Soviet students would draw renewed inspiration from the traditions of the Russian student movement of the nineteenth century. The Soviet government had read its history, and was alert to take measures against any revival of its spirit, the readiness of its participants to risk torture, exile, death. In 1932, Stalin became fearful of "terroristic talk" among "young workers and students"; the Soviet Union was at that time in the throes of an economic crisis produced by the collectivization of the farms. Free-minded students in the universities shared Bukharin's right-wing heresy, and felt that Stalin was debasing Communism.[125] Then in 1934 the Politburo was alarmed by the report that "certain Komsomol groups—youth and students—had been discovered debating the problem of terrorism." When Sergei Kirov, next to Stalin the most powerful member of the Politburo, was assassinated in 1934 by a young man, Nikolaiev, it was found that the assassin had been deeply affected by his reading of the Russian revolutionary students of an earlier period: "He had read everything he could lay hands on of the memoirs of the terrorists—the Narodovoltsi and the Social Revolutionaries. He regarded his own act as the continuation of the terrorist activity of the Russian revolutionaries of the past." When Stalin pressed him as to his motives, Nikolaiev is said to have replied that "in the days to come my name will be coupled with those of Zheliabov and Balmashov."[126]

Naturally Soviet writers in the mid-thirties attributed any so-called generational conflict to the doings of the Opposition; frustrated oppositionist fathers, they said, were stirring up their own children to blind hatred for Soviet power. Trotsky retorted that the Stalinist arguments "sound like plagiarisms of the Czarist publicist, Katkov, who used to accuse the cowardly liberal fathers of provoking voluntarily or involuntarily the young generation to commit terrorist acts." Trotsky firmly believed that bureaucratic rule would "undermine among their own youth the confidence in and respect for the official leaders." Yet, as we have seen, no student movement arises unless there has been a crisis of de-authoritization of the elder generation. Bureaucratic rule can survive generational discontent so long as it preserves its prestige and moral authority. The annals of the underground student circles are among the most obscure in the Soviet record. Evidently around 1950 there was a protest movement of so-called "populist" students. "The 'populists' were students of the first post-war generation Moscow and Leningrad universities." They were mostly veterans who had spent time in the new Soviet satellites, "and what they saw there shook them profoundly. They found prosperity," a different way of life, different ideas. "When they got back to the capitals and became students, these people, people of the same generation who had shared the same experiences, started cautiously exchanging impressions, feeling each other out. A common attitude emerged. The questions asked were simple ones. 'Why do the people live better in the West than here? Why do they deceive us by saying that this is not so?' " The standard of judgment should be, they said, how the people live. "We are populists, said the former officers," and they thereby linked themselves with the classical tradition of the Russian revolutionary student movement of almost a century before.[127] How they all vanished into the penal camps is unknown, as likewise the degree to which they had constituted a real conspiratorial organization.

The one genuine moral crisis which the Soviet Union has experienced followed the powerful speech of Premier Nikita Khrushchev of February 1956, in which he set forth the evils done by Stalin. As *Soviet Survey* noted in 1957, "Like other recent manifestations of unrest in Soviet society, the reported wave of criticism in the universities goes back to the de-Stalinisation campaign."[128] The speech set in motion a crisis of de-authoritization of the elder generation which, however, has thus far been contained by a combination of official repression and the warning that student criticism "will be exploited by the enemy."

The official philosophers at times deny the existence of generational conflict, at other times they recognize its workings but insist that it is resolved in Soviet society. A young philosopher of history of the Leningrad faculty, Igor Kon, for instance, both acknowledged and denied the existence of generational conflict in the Soviet society of 1965:

A continuous struggle goes on within it between old and new, and everyone takes part in this struggle, willy-nilly. . . . Meanwhile, the younger generation takes shape and begins an active life in constant interaction with elders and under their guidance. This confronts us with the problem of "fathers" and "sons."

Bourgeois propagandists have done much to confuse this question. Aiming to drive a wedge between Soviet youth and the older generation of Soviet people and thus break off the revolutionary work which has been relayed from generation to generation, bourgeois propaganda repeats over and over its talk of some "conflict" between the fathers and sons in Soviet society. In reality there is no social or ideological opposition between the "fathers" and the "sons" in the U.S.S.R.

Yet in the very same article, having made his obeisance to the official denial of generational strife in the Soviet Union, the writer discusses the causes of just such conflicts! "The trouble is that youth's dissatisfaction very often has, at the beginning, anyway, a highly abstract and subjective character. Here the same negativism is frequently displayed as in personal relations with parents and with elders generally. Maximalism in youth's judgments hampers a sober understanding of social problems."

Here then precisely is a statement of the traits of the student activist—negativism (nihilism), generational revolt, tendency to extremism ("maximalism"), a misperception of reality arising from unconscious ("subjective") projections. And the student activist finds the occasion for his revolt precisely in the de-authoritization of the old. Or as Igor Kon states it in the inverted Soviet style, the style of indirect political discourse, "A sanctimonious silence about contradictions and an effort to present the wish for the reality are terrible evils in the work of upbringing." Meanwhile, he observes, the very nature of an advancing industrial society places the generations in conflict with each other: "a young engineer may be a superior of his own father and others of his father's age, he may be in charge of their work. . . . [B]ecause of the quickened pace of social and scientific and technical progress, the generations have begun to differ more sharply from one another. The tastes and habits of modern Soviet youth differ greatly from the tastes of pre-war youth." "Because of the nature of youth," continues the Leningrad sociologist, "the 'sons' are inclined to exaggerate the novelty of their own experience (for them it is indeed new; it seems to them that no one before could love so, suffer so. . . .)" Since the "fathers" in their turn are bound by their generation's tastes, pseudo-ideological issues appear: "A host of artificial conflicts arises in this way, and the question of trouser width or style of dancing is raised to the rank of an ideological issue." From Kon's description, for all its studied vagueness, one divines that underlying the pseudo-ideological, symbolic, surrogate issues are more profound, ideological and emotional ones which concern the character of the social system. He speaks of "the contradiction between ideal and reality" which impresses itself on the sons as they discover "that along with good people there are crooks, careerists and scoundrels, and that the latter often prosper." Some of the "sons" react to this traumatic discovery by giving up their ideals; others, says Kon, withdraw into solitude of their own egos. Nevertheless, he insists, a socialist society is basically unaffected by generational conflict because it retains a "community of ideological traditions and unity of goals."[129]

To measure the degree of student "alienation" in Soviet society is well-nigh impossible because of the restrictions in the Soviet Union on free student expression. After all, no students' society has access to a mimeograph machine without prior approval of the university's Communist organization. Such students' leaflets as do circulate are the clandestine products of underground typewriters. The party apparatus from time to time is reluctantly compelled to take notice of underground student restiveness. The secretary of the Central Committee of the Soviet Communist party felt obliged to report in June 1963 on one such underground student circle, while at the same time trying to divulge as little as possible:

> Some time ago a small group of young people in one district got together. They called themselves "Marxist-Futurists" ("Marfutists"). In their hand-written newspaper "The Hearse of Art" the "Marfutists" called for non-commitment in literature, for freedom of art from the Party's ideological influence. "We don't indulge in politics," they said. In reality they were up to the neck in politics, but politics alien to socialism, to the Soviet people.[130]

The student circle of Marxist-Futurists was only among the most recent of such reported groups. During 1956, according to a former Soviet student, "the Soviet press denounced by name five illegal student papers, including *New Voices* and *Heresy*. Now that the terror has begun to diminish, students apparently are ready to take chances and let their voices be heard (at least within restricted circles). Small groups of friends hammer out points of view that reject the present form of Soviet society, and they explore new systems of values."[131] Some sought for a revival of "true Marxism," others were becoming critical of Marxism itself.

The younger generation of students turned to the existentialists, to Camus and Sartre, for answers to problems which the official Marxism had long repressed. The law of the universality of ideas in the intellectual community was asserting itself, the tendency of intellectuals everywhere, regardless of differences in social systems, to read the same books and discuss the same ideas. A visiting French lecturer on literature at Moscow University in 1958 vividly characterized the generational differences among Soviet intellectuals:

> Several of my colleagues having done me the honor of attending my lectures it became easy for me, and rather natural, to distinguish three age classes among the Soviet intellectuals: first, the oldest—those who were either brought up under the old regime or had commenced their studies under Lenin; then, the victims of the twenty years in which Stalin suppressed all intellectual life; and

lastly, the young ones, quivering—as it seemed to me—with freedom to form themselves, since the death of the Personality. The oldest were talking pertinently about Charles Sorel, or about Racine or the art of the novel; the youngest were discussing Sartre or Camus, Butor or Françoise Sagan. With the victims of Stalin conversation was sometimes more uneasy, the taboos more numerous.[132]

There is a muted confrontation in the Soviet society between the existentialist student generation and those of middle age who in varying degrees bear the guilt or corruption of Stalinism. The characters in the drama of generational conflict in the Soviet Union might most accurately be described as the grandsons and the fathers. For the fathers, the Stalinist generation, destroyed the Leninist grandfathers, the Old Bolsheviks, the Makers of the Revolution. On the executed bodies of Bukharin, Zinoviev, Kamenev, and the exiled Trotsky, the Stalinist generation of bureaucrats climbed the ladder of upward mobility to power and prestige.[133] This intervening generation profited from the purges as a device which ensured it access to vacated high posts, the Soviet generational escalator.[134] The third generation, insofar as it is moved to rebellion, refuses to share the guilt of the second; the grandsons blame the fathers who murdered the grandfathers. Here were consequences of social parricide which Freud never explored.

That a crisis of de-authoritization still continues in Soviet society is evident from articles in Soviet journals which describe young people accusing their fathers of cowardice. In one such article, published in the *Nash Sovremennik* of August 1964, the writer begins, "One day a conceited young man said to his elders with all the arrogance of youth: Well, and why were you silent? Why didn't you come to his defense? . . . This controversy concerned a writer who had perished in the thirties and the conversation occurred in a writer's family." The elder tried hard to convince the young man, though not very persuasively, that well-known writers had tried to defend their innocent colleagues.[135]

This new Soviet generation finds its elders' ideology a tepid affair. They turn to the pre-revolutionary writers for spiritual sustenance. A survey of Leningrad students by the N. K. Krupskaya Institute of Culture in 1964 showed that 83.6 per cent found their favorite authors among the classical names; Chekhov, Pushkin, and Tolstoy led the list.[136] Their preferences among films likewise contravened the System's norms. The favorite movie heroes of young people, according to a questionnaire discussed in *Molodoi Kommunist* in 1965, were the individualistic, "system-free" protagonists of such foreign films as *The Count of Monte Cristo* and *The Three Musketeers,* rather than the Bolshevik personalities in such official films as *Maxim's Youth* or *Baltic Deputy*. The free-wheeling individual depicted in *The Magnificent Seven* evoked the enthusiasm of the Soviet youth despite official denunciations.[137] Probably the most significant survey of Soviet youth was made by *Komsomolskaya Pravda* in 1961 on the basis of a questionnaire addressed to its readers. The 17,446 replies accepted for study showed that as many as 16.6 per cent were what would be called "alienated" from their society; 960 young people, or 5.5 per cent of the total, were skeptics, uncertain of their society's values; while 1,931, or 11.1 per cent of the total, were outright irreconcilables. "No, my generation doesn't please me."[138] Evidently about one-third of the respondents were students; a little over eleven thousand were identified as engaged in the various occupations. The irreconcilables raised embarrassing questions, such as "Why is it that many of us drink?" Sometimes their alienation, as *Komsomolskaya Pravda* pointed out, was "the mark left by past violations of legality that occurred in the period of the cult of the individual leader. Sometimes it is hard to condemn such persons." "It is a pity," commented the Komsomol organ, "that they cannot rise above the narrow circle of personal experiences, distress and failures—these are cases in which shock beclouds judgment."[139] Yet others simply found the values of their society ("outside the films") too crass.

At times this alienation from the official values erupts with dramatic suddenness. A Princeton professor observed one incident in March 1964 at a performance for technology students in the largest theater in Leningrad of a new play, *Everything Depends on People.* The play had such unusual features as a suicide and a philosophical dialogue between a priest and scientist. Then came the open discussion between the company and the audience. An older man began an official-sounding denunciation of the play's "degenerate" aspects. The audience whistled at him and shouted him down with cries of "Go tell it to the Central Committee." The growing disaffection among the studentry with the official ideology took a variety of forms, not the least unusual of which was a "surprising revival of interest in religion."[140] "They are asking questions for which you have no answer," says the priest to the scientist in *Everything Depends on People.* A Western student of history who was at Moscow University for a year similarly reported in 1960 that some students "openly flaunt their attachment to religion" by wearing crosses, for instance, around their necks. Such gestures of social protest often brought "quite tangible deprivations—(including expulsion from the university) imposed by the Komsomol and other organizations."[141]

Two incidents impressed themselves on me during the course of my discussions with graduate students at the Soviet Institute of Philosophy in Moscow during the winter and spring of 1963. I was near the end of an interview with an able young scholar who had published a monograph on the concept of alienation. I reminded myself that I had omitted to ask his age, and did so. "Old enough to go to my Calvary," he replied. The Christian metaphor seemed a strange one in that cold room with its political iconography on the walls—Marx, Lenin. He did not answer, "Old enough to have written the Communist *Manifesto* or *What's to be done?*" but had recourse to an idiom which in those surroundings conveyed a symbolic divergence. On another occasion, when I was attending the graduate students' celebration of International Women's Day, the student next to me mentioned her interest in existentialism and the Bible. I asked her what her favorite book in the Bible was. "The Book of Job," she replied. I told her I shared her opinion and asked her why. "Because the Book of Job," she replied, "asks the questions which cannot be answered, why do good people suffer in this world, and why do evil people prosper." By our standards this was the usual view of Job, but by Soviet standards it involved a profound questioning of Soviet reality and the official optimism of dialectical materialism. Here was the suggestion of sheer tragedy in human existence which no dialectical formulas could transmute.

Under the Czars, when it was dangerous to express one's social views in an open setting, literature, and especially the novel, became the great vehicle of political criticism. Under Soviet rule during the post-Stalinist thaw, poetry has become the vehicle of political criticism. The flocking of thousands of students to the poetry readings of Yevtushenko and Vosnesensky constituted a vague aspiration toward a new independent student movement. "A part of the younger generation," wrote Yevtushenko, "naturally looked with suspicion not only on Stalin but on the past as a whole, and this doubles the distress of their parents." The tradition of public poetry readings, started by Mayakovsky but long in disuse, was revived as a vehicle for generational protest. The audiences in colleges, research institutes, and factories ranged from twenty to one thousand in numbers and reached fourteen thousand at the Sports Palace in 1963.[142] One evening at the Polytechnic Institute in Moscow, Yevtushenko for the first time recited his poem on anti-Semitism, "Babi Yar": "When I finished there was dead silence. I stood fidgeting with the paper, afraid to look up. When I did I saw that the entire audience had risen to their feet; then applause exploded and went on for 10 minutes. People leaped onto the stage and embraced me. My eyes were full of tears."

Those in generational revolt have a sense of their own International. When Yevtushenko was in New York's Washington Square, he said, "I joined American young men and girls in singing a biting song addressed to the police commissioner who had banned their gathering." Thus the message of generational revolt transmits itself from society to society, and a curious International Generational Solidarity arises. When Vosnesensky gave a poetry reading in Berkeley in the spring of 1966, the Berkeley activists were beside themselves in welcoming one who like themselves was a rebel against his Establishment.

The student activists in European communist countries are, in one respect, basically different from those in America and Western Europe. The student activist in Czechoslavakia and Poland shares with his father the oppression of the same totalitarian system. Both know the same threats of party bureaucrats, whether in the university, factory, or administrative ministry. If the student is a Jew, he experiences the same varieties of socialistic anti-Semitism as his father; indeed, in Poland, the Jewish fathers are penalized for the activism of their sons. With such a shared experience, student activists in Communist countries are not moved to agitate for "student power"; what they seek are liberties for all, not the elitist status which attracts Western European student activists. When the chief ideologist of the Berkeley Free Speech Movement, Stephen Weissman, visited Czechoslovakia during the heroic months of 1968, he therefore felt little kinship with the Czech students. The Berkeley activist told a noon rally on the Berkeley campus that the Czech students were "rebeling against the Russians, but their rebellion on the whole does not take up the same causes as liberals in the West."[143] He complained that Czech students had apologized to the American Embassy when some Vietnamese students burned an American flag and that the Czech students thought American involvement in Vietnam was justified. In short, one might say that the generational rebel of Berkeley felt vaguely the insubstantiality of his pseudo-goals as compared with those of the Czech sons who are in quest for real freedom together with their fathers. Similarly, when the West German student leader Rudi Dutschke visited Prague University and tried to convert the Czech students to his "anarcho-Maoism," "they rejected his ideas as 'absurd,' 'comic,' and not worthy of consideration by 'a fifteen-year old.' "[144]

Can a generation in revolt do more in the Soviet Union than applaud poetry readings and listen to American rock and roll? A few years ago a Western observer reported that there were many discontented students in Russia and that they were part of an "extremely large and amorphous group in Soviet society" which included "internal emigrants"—that is, those who had retreated into themselves—those disaffected by Stalinist trauma or anti-Semitism, as well as those simply resentful that they could not read what they wished. He found a multitude of "bored" students; they were bored by the drabness of Soviet life. He averred, however, that by far the greatest number of Soviet students were satisfied, complacent, and finding sufficient rewards within the context of the System. The potential for a student movement, though, cannot be evaluated by the relative percentages of discontented and satisfied. The majority of the students in China, for instance, on the eve of the formation of the May Fourth Movement would have been reckoned among the satisfied. What is most decisive is the potential for the moral de-authoritization of the ruling elite in Soviet society. And this realistic possibility is always inherent in the workings of Soviet society. In December 1965, *The New York Times* reported that two hundred students gathered in Moscow to demonstrate on behalf of the accused writers Sinyavsky and Daniel. Shortly before the demonstration, three young activists were arrested; one of them, Yulia Vishnevskaya, a sixteen-year-old poet, was expelled from her school "on the ground that she possessed a hand-written chain letter urging people to participate in the demonstration."[145] Sinyavsky, writing under the pseudonym of Abram Tertz, indeed gave voice to the views and moods of the "independent thinking section of Soviet youth. His vision of Soviet reality," as one critic said, "is their vision, his attitude is their attitude, he expresses their not entirely clear consciousness of their own situation."[146]

It is always possible that some new crisis of moral de-authoritization will ignite a student movement of massive proportions. Curiously, a recent decision on the part of the Soviet government will make for a more independent-minded studentry, for the government abrogated Khrushchev's policy of giving preference in admission to universities to persons with several years of industrial experience. This latter group, usually vouched for by Communist party factory secretaries, tended to be the most placid, conventional, and least intellectually autonomous in the studentry. Now their numbers will dwindle, to be replaced by the more activist and intellectual of the high school graduates.[147] The studentry of the Soviet Union thus remains the unknown term in the social equation, its dynamic unpredictable. Meanwhile, the conflict of generations persists.

When a student movement arises in the Soviet Union, one hopes that it will avoid the terroristic pitfalls of generational politics and link itself to democratic political means. Strangely enough, in some ways the paranoid psychology of Stalinism, like its Czarist forerunner, was stimulated by the self-destructive terrorist tactics of student activists. In 1934, as Bukharin and Nicolaevsky have indicated, Stalin was becoming "milder, more affable, more yielding," and taking pleasure in the discussions "of writers, artists, and painters."[148] Then the assassination of Kirov intervened. His assassin had imbibed his terroristic propensities from the memoirs of the old men in the Society of Former Political Exiles.[149] In July 1935, too, "a small group of Komsomol students, charged with plotting the assassination of Stalin, were tried in Moscow." Though their conspiracy never got beyond discussion, it was quite serious for "they had apparently intended to put their plans into effect." There were evidently other such cases, in which student activists had taken the initiative. From them Stalin traced his thread of suspicion and involvement to the students' professors in political science and party history, and from the latter to the former leaders of the Opposition.[150] The Nightmare of the Purges began.

One hopes that the next Russian student movement, avoiding the drama of terror and counterterror, will contrive the political means to dispel the clouds of unreason and found the bases of a democratic society.

NOTES

1. Harold J. Laski, *Faith, Reason, and Civilization* (London, 1944), p. 133.

2. Joseph P. Lash, "Awakening at Oxford," *Student Advocate*, I, No. 5 (October-November 1936), 23.

3. John Plamenatz, *The Revolutionary Movement in France: 1815–71* (London, 1952), p. 23.

4. *The Doctrine of Saint-Simon: An Exposition*, tr. and ed. George G. Iggers (Boston, 1958), pp. xxii, xxiii.

5. A recent study states, however, "Of

the 250 or more *Polytechniciens* who sympathized with the opposition to Charles X only 61 actually fought in the July Days and those only on the final day after the outcome was largely decided." The author notes, on the other hand, that law students participated in "the disorderly gatherings around the *Palais-Royal* on July 26 and 27," and that "some of them later claimed that they had excited the crowds to resistance, and one even testified that he had led a group of youths in attacks on a barracks of the *Gendarmerie,* the *Hotel de Ville,* and the Tuileries." See David H. Pinkney, "The Crowd in the French Revolution of 1830," *American Historical Review,* LXX (October 1964), 14–15.

6. Caleb Cushing, *Review, Historical and Political, of the Late Revolution in France,* I (Boston, 1833), 159–160.

7. Lucien de la Hodde, *History of Secret Societies and of the Republican Party of France from 1830 to 1848,* tr. an American (Philadelphia, 1856), p. 46.

8. *Ibid.,* pp. 28–29.

9. *Ibid.,* p. 62.

10. Louis Blanc, *1848: Historical Recollections* (London, 1858), p. 289.

11. Alvan Francis Sanborn, *Paris and the Social Revolution: A Study of the Revolutionary Elements in the Various Classes of Parisian Society* (London, 1905), p. 183.

12. La Hodde, *op. cit.,* pp. 395, 413.

13. Plamenatz, *op. cit.,* p. 63.

14. See Donald Cope McKay, *The National Workshops* (Cambridge, Mass., 1933), pp. 14, 20–22, 92, 102, 125.

15. Paul Lafargue, Marx's son-in-law, wrote in 1879, "To Blanqui belongs the honor of having made the revolutionary education of a section of the youth of our generation." See Alan B. Spitzer, *The Revolutionary Theories of Louis Auguste Blanqui* (New York, 1957), p. 12.

16. Blanqui's appeal to the intellectuals can be judged by the fact that when he founded his Société Républicaine Centrale shortly after the February Revolution of 1848, and invited thinkers and men of letters to join, Baudelaire, Charles Renouvier, Sainte-Beuve, and Leconte de Lisle were among those who enrolled. See Suzanne Wassermann, *Les Clubs de Barbès et de Blanqui* (Paris, 1913), pp. 17–18. Kautsky observed that Blanquism "found more acceptance among the intellectuals, especially students, than among the workmen." Karl Kautsky, *Terrorism and Communism: A Contribution to the Natural History of Revolution,* tr. W. H. Kerridge (London, 1920), p. 77.

17. In the history of the Paris Commune which Karl Marx edited and revised, the "students of the universities" were described as "the advanced guard of all our revolutions." Prosper Olivier Lissagaray, *History of the Commune of 1871,* tr. Eleanor Marx Aveling (2nd edn.; New York, 1898), pp. v, 91.

18. Frederick Engels, "The Program of the Blanquist Fugitives from the Paris Commune," tr. Ernst Untermann from *Der Volksstaat* (1874), No. 73, *International Socialist Review,* IX (August 1908), 99–105.

19. "Rigault and Ferré, the two most notorious Blanquists in the Commune, were both students," wrote Edward S. Mason in "Blanqui and Communism," *Political Science Quarterly,* XLIV (1929), 508. See also Lissagaray, *op. cit.,* p. 223: "The Commission of Public Safety ought to have suspended Rigault as their delegate to the Prefecture of Police"; and p. 338.

20. See especially Bertram D. Wolfe, *Marxism: One Hundred Years in the Life of a Doctrine* (New York, 1965), pp. 126 ff.

21. Almost thirty years later the Jeunesse Blanquiste in its elitism refused to intervene on behalf of the unjustly convicted Jew, Captain Alfred Dreyfus. See Sanborn, *op. cit.,* p. 167.

22. Engels, *op. cit.,* pp. 99–105.

23. Paul Lafargue, "Socialism and the Intellectuals," in Lafargue, *The Right to be Lazy, and other Studies* (Chicago, 1907), p. 93. See also Sanborn, *op. cit.,* p. 191.

24. Jean Longuet, "The Socialist Movement among the Students of French Universities," *Intercollegiate Socialist,* II, No. 3 (February-March 1914), 8.

25. *Ibid.,* p. 10. Also see Claude Willard, *Le Mouvement socialiste en France (1893–1905); Les Guesdistes* (Paris, 1965), pp. 103–104.

26. Daniel Halévy, *Péguy and Les Cahiers de la Quinzaine* (New York, 1947), p. 47. The spirit of the intellectuals in their nobility at this time was best expressed in the addresses of Anatole France to their groups: "Slowly, but surely, the human race brings the dreams of the sages to pass." See Anatole France,

The Unseen Dawn, tr. J. Lewis May (London, 1928), p. 1.

27. Longuet, *op. cit.*, pp. 10–11.

28. Sanborn, *op. cit.*, p. 203.

29. Charles Andler, *Vie de Lucien Herr, 1864–1926* (Paris, 1932), pp. 93, 96, 168, 174; Halévy, *op. cit.*, pp. 30–31. Under Herr's influence, the future first socialist Premier, Léon Blum, studied Marx and attended a collectivist students' club. See Geoffrey Fraser and Thadée Natanson, *Léon Blum* (London, 1937), p. 31; Joel Colton, *Léon Blum: Humanist in Politics* (New York, 1966), p. 17.

30. Sanborn, *op. cit.*, p. 203.

31. Edouard Herriot, *In Those Days before the First World War*, tr. Adolphe de Milly (New York, 1952), pp. 90–91, 95, 83, 143; J. Hampden Jackson, *Jean Jaurès* (London, 1943), p. 24; Herbert Luthy, "The French Intellectuals," *Encounter*, V (1955), 5; Gordon Wright, *The Reshaping of French Democracy* (New York, 1948), p. 74; Henry de Man, *The Psychology of Socialism* (New York, 1928), p. 201.

32. Leon Trotsky, *The Intelligentsia and Socialism*, tr. Brian Pearce (London, 1966), p. 7.

33. Samuel M. Osgood, *French Royalism under the Third and Fourth Republics* (The Hague, 1960), pp. 79, 83–84.

34. Colton, *op. cit.*, p. 115.

35. Eugen Weber, *Action Française: Royalism and Reaction in Twentieth-Century France* (Stanford, Calif., 1962), pp. 52, 54, 83, 84, 86, 87, 157, 162, 163, 180, 195, 302, 306, 308, 309, 311, 347, 362–363, 373, 459, 499, 547.

36. *Ibid.*, pp. 39–40.

37. See Edward R. Tannenbaum, *The Action Française: Diehard Reactionaries in Twentieth-Century France* (New York, 1962), pp. 96–97, 140–141, 155–156, 275.

38. Jean-Claude Roure, "Return to Politics," *World Student News*, XVII, No. 5 (1963), 8, 18.

39. Pierre Gaudez, *Les Etudiants* (Paris, 1961), p. 18; *Youth and Freedom*, VI, No. 6 (1964), 31.

40. Pierre Gaudez, *op. cit.*, pp. 45–51.

41. *Ibid.*, p. 47.

42. *Youth and Freedom*, III, Nos. 3–4 (1960), 22–23.

43. Charles A. Micaud, *Communism and the French Left* (New York, 1963), p. 249; *Youth and Freedom*, III, Nos. 5–6 (1961), 26.

44. Paul Leblanc, "Student Unrest in France," *New Times*, No. 51 (December 25, 1963), 17–18.

45. *Youth and Freedom*, VI, No. 5 (1964), 22–23.

46. Micaud, *op. cit.*, p. 251.

47. Keith Botsford, "Why Students in France Go Communist: Elite Proletarians All," *The New York Times Magazine*, November 13, 1966, pp. 89 ff.

48. *Youth and Freedom*, VI, No. 4 (1964), 23.

49. Raymond Aron, "Some Aspects of the Crisis in the French Universities," *Minerva*, II, No. 3 (Spring 1964), 279.

50. Aron, *op. cit.*, pp. 284–285. For the details of the increase of the French studentry from 29,000 in 1900 to 206,000 in 1960, see Gaudez, *op. cit.*, p. 23; also see Antoine Griset and Marc Kravetz, "De L'Algérie à la Réforme Fouchet: Critique du Syndicalisme Etudiant," *Les Temps Modernes*, XX (1965), 1880–1902, 2066–2089.

51. Rita Dershowitz, "Higher Education and the Student: England, Germany, France," *Youth and Freedom*, VI, No. 6 (1964), 32.

52. Harvey Goldberg, *The Life of Jean Jaurès* (Madison, Wisc., 1962), 269–270.

53. Botsford, *op. cit.*, p. 89.

54. Peter Kropotkin, *The Great French Revolution*, tr. N. F. Dryhurst (1909; New York, 1927), Vol. II, pp. 372–373.

55. *The New York Times*, May 13, 1968.

56. Martha Merrill, "To the Barricades: Paris Belongs to Us," *Village Voice*, May 30, 1968, p. 48.

57. *The New York Times*, May 6, 1968, p. 32.

58. Joseph Barry, "Something Has Cracked," *Village Voice*, May 30, 1968, p. 48.

59. Martha Merrill, *op. cit.*, p. 49.

60. *Loc. cit.*

61. *The New York Times*, May 15, 1968, p. 8.

62. *The New York Times*, May 21, 1968, p. 17.

63. *The New York Times*, May 23, 1968, p. 14; *The New York Times*, May 21, 1968, p. 17.

64. *The New York Times*, May 14, 1968.

65. *The New York Times*, May 21, 1968, p. 16.

66. *The New York Times*, May 17, 1968, p. 14.

67. Joseph Barry, "Notes on a Revolution?", *Village Voice,* June 7–13, 1968, p. 28.

68. *The New York Times,* May 17, June 13, 1968.

69. Sanche de Gramont, "The French Worker Wants to Join the Affluent Society, Not to Wreck It," *The New York Times Magazine,* June 16, 1968, p. 62.

70. Barry, "Notes on a Revolution?," p. 28.

71. *The New York Times,* May 15, 1968.

72. Raymond Aron, "After the Barricades: The Meaning of the French University Crisis," *Encounter,* XXXI, No. 2 (August 1968), 24, 26, 29. François Bourricaud, "The French Student Revolt," *Survey,* No. 68 (July 1968), pp. 29–37. Daniel Cohn-Bendit, "Notre Commune du 10 mai," *This Magazine Is about Schools,* II, No. 3 (Summer 1968), 13–22. "An Interview with 'Danny the Red,' " *Ramparts* (June 29, 1968), pp. 24–25.

73. Peter G. J. Pulzer, *The Rise of Political Anti-Semitism in Germany and Austria* (New York, 1964), pp. 252–257, 307–308.

74. Sidney Hook, "Why the German Student Is Fascist," *Student Outlook,* I, No. 5 (May 1933), 6.

75. Edward Yarnell Hartshorne, *The German Universities and National Socialism* (Cambridge, Mass., 1937), p. 45. Students with a "diseased ambition" and "inferiority complex" were most active in denouncing their liberal professors, says Julius Lips. See Julius E. Lips, *The Savage Hits Back* (New Haven, 1937), p. xxvi.

76. Hartshorne, *op. cit.,* p. 56.

77. Sidney Hook, *op. cit.,* p. 20.

78. Jay Lovestone, "The Youth Movement in the Third Reich," *Student Outlook,* II, No. 3 (February 1934), 13.

79. George L. Mosse, *The Crisis of German Ideology: Intellectual Origins of the Third Reich* (New York, 1964), pp. 191, 192.

80. M. J. Bonn, *The Wandering Scholar* (New York, 1948), p. 52.

81. Mosse, *op. cit.,* p. 197.

82. *Ibid.,* pp. 193, 195, 197; P. J. G. Pulzer, *Antisemitism in Germany and Austria, 1867–1918* (Cambridge, England, 1960), p. 285.

83. Mosse, *op. cit.,* p. 192.

84. Bonn, *op. cit.,* p. 332.

85. *Ibid.,* pp. 333, 35–36, 214.

86. Mosse, *op. cit.,* p. 135.

87. Bonn, *op. cit.,* pp. 35–36, 214.

88. Karl Stern, *The Pillar of Fire* (New York, 1951), pp. 48–49.

89. *Ibid.,* p. 47.

90. *Ibid.,* p. 63.

91. Stern, *op. cit.,* p. 166.

92. Bonn, *op. cit.,* p. 214.

93. Ernst Toller, *I Was a German: An Autobiography,* tr. Edward Crankshaw (London, 1934), pp. 14, 19, 31, 88, 91, 92.

94. *Ibid.,* pp. 95, 102, 275. For all Max Weber's "brave words," wrote Toller, "they made it clear what separated us from him. We were concerned with more than the sins of the Kaiser. . . . We wanted to create a whole new world" (p. 91).

95. Helmut Schelsky, *Die Skeptische Generation* (Düsseldorf, 1960).

96. Thomas Baylis, "Freedom and the Free University" (typescript), p. 10.

97. "A Slaying Unites German Students," *The New York Times,* June 10, 1967.

98. For later developments which occurred after the manuscript of this book was completed, see Harold Hurwitz, "Germany's Student Revolt," *Survey,* No. 67 (April 1968), pp. 90–99. Eckart Förtsch, "The New Left in the German Student Body," *Colloqiuim Tönisstein* (September 1967). Max Beloff, "Letter from Germany," *Encounter,* XXXI, No. 1 (July 1968), 28–33. Manfred Buddeberg, "The Student Movement in West Germany," *International Socialism* (Summer 1968), pp. 27–34. "Interview with Rudi Dutschke," *Young Socialist,* II, No. 8 (May 1968), 11–16. W. L. Becker, in "Upsurge of the Youth Movement in the Capitalist Countries," *World Marxist Review,* XI, No. 7 (July 1968), 18–23. "German Novelist Taunts Radicals," *The New York Times,* September 29, 1968.

99. "Portugal: Faded Hope and New Conflict," *The Student,* X, No. 4 (April 1966), 4–9.

100. Pedro Bandeita, "Letter from Lisbon," *New Leader,* XLVIII (November 22, 1965), 6.

101. *Youth and Freedom,* VII, No. 2 (1965), 19–20; "No Mood for 'Gaudeamus,' " *World Student News,* XIX, Nos. 3–4 (1965), 8–11.

102. " 'New Generation' Rises in Portugal," *The New York Times,* July 20, 1965.

103. Sherry Kelner, "Students Lack Freedom," *Toronto Varsity,* LXXXVI, No. 12 (October 17, 1966), 12.

104. " 'New Generation' Rises in Portugal," *The New York Times,* July 20, 1965.

105. "Spain: the first bastion falls," *World Student News,* XIX, Nos. 3–4 (1965), 3; "Madrid Explains Teachers' Ouster," *The New York Times,* August 29, 1965.

106. The story of these events, and the roles of the generations of 1898 and 1930 is found in David Jato, *Rebelión de los Estudiantes* (Madrid, 1953).

107. Nancy Bedford-Jones, *Students Under Arms: Education in Republican Spain* (New York, 1938), pp. 5–7, 28, 29.

108. Jake Bair, "The Spanish Student Movement," *Studies on the Left,* V, No. 3 (Summer 1965), 4; *Youth and Freedom,* VI, No. 3 (1964), 16.

109. *Youth and Freedom,* VII, No. 3 (1965), p. 21; "Madrid Unrest Seems to Be on Wane," *The New York Times,* March 4, 1965; "Madrid Students Set Public March," *The New York Times,* March 2, 1965.

110. *Youth and Freedom,* VII, Nos. 4–5 (1965), p. 28.

111. *Ibid.,* VIII, Nos. 1–2 (1966), p. 35; "Barcelona Sit-in Brings Big Fines," *The New York Times,* April 6, 1966; "Madrid to Loosen University Curbs," *The New York Times,* October 4, 1966; "University Strike is Staged in Spain," *The New York Times,* November 9, 1966.

112. "Spain: the First Bastion Falls," *World Student News,* XIX, Nos. 3–4 (1965), 5.

113. *Youth and Freedom,* VII, No. 1 (1965), 13.

114. Bair, *op. cit.,* p. 17.

115. *Ibid.,* pp. 11, 19.

116. Suicidalism has meanwhile made its appearance in the Spanish student movement. See "Spanish Student Dies During Raid," *The New York Times,* February 1, 1967.

117. Paul Kecskemeti, *The Unexpected Revolution: Social Forces in the Hungarian Uprising* (Stanford, 1961), pp. 117, 65; see also George Urban, *The Nineteen Days* (London, 1957), pp. 3–4, 12–14, 23–25, 28–32, and Leslie S. Bain, *The Reluctant Satellites* (New York, 1962), p. 92.

118. Stefan Nowak, "Social Attitudes of Warsaw Students," *Polish Sociological Bulletin,* Nos. 1–2 (3–4) (January-June 1962), pp. 91–103. Also see Zygmunt Bauman, "Values and Standards of Success of the Warsaw Youth," *Polish Sociological Bulletin,* Nos. 1–2 (3–4) (January-June 1962), p. 79; Jan Szczepanski, "The Polish Intelligentsia: Past and Present," *World Politics,* XIV (1962), 412–416; Leopold Labedz, "The Polish Intellectual Climate," *Soviet Survey,* No. 35 (January-March 1961), pp. 9–10.

119. "Boxes of Bright Ideas," *World Student News,* XIX, Nos. 3–4 (1965), 22–23.

120. "Polish Students Admire Kennedy," *The New York Times,* November 7, 1966.

121. "Zagreb Students Cool to Ideology," *The New York Times,* April 23, 1961.

122. *The New York Times,* June 7, June 10, June 12, 1968.

123. "Speech by N. S. Khrushchev, March 8, 1963," *New Times,* No. 11 (March 20, 1963), 34–35.

124. Max Eastman, *Since Lenin Died* (London, 1925), pp. 54, 57.

125. G. A. Tokaev, *Betrayal of an Ideal,* tr. Alec Brown (London, 1954), pp. 104–105, 111–112, 140–141.

126. *Letter of an Old Bolshevik,* pp. 14, 22, 29, 30. On the circumstances of the authorship of this work from Nikolai Bukharin's conversations, see Boris I. Nicolaevsky, *Power and the Soviet Elite,* ed. Janet D. Zagoria (New York, 1965), pp. 3 ff.

127. David Burg, "The Continuing Temptation," *Soviet Survey,* No. 26 (October-December 1958), pp. 59–60.

128. "The Ferment Among Soviet Youth," *Soviet Survey,* No. 12 (February 1957), pp. 2, 9.

129. Igor Kon, "Youthful Dissent: A Fresh Soviet View," *Counterpart,* I, No. 1 (January-February 1966), 5, tr. from the original article printed in *Molodoi Kommunist* (Young Communist) and *Izvestia.*

130. L. F. Ilyichov, "The Current Tasks of the Party's Ideological Work," Report to the CPSU Central Committee, June 18, 1963, *Moscow News Supplement,* June 22, 1963, pp. 11–12.

131. David Burg, "New Trends among Soviet Students," *New Leader,* August 18–25, 1958, pp. 15–16; also see "The Ferment among Soviet Youth: Part 1: Conflict between the Generations," *Soviet Survey,* No. 12 (February 1957), p. 2.

132. R. Etiemble, "The Sorbonne in Moscow," *Soviet Survey,* No. 30 (October-December 1959), p. 16.

133. Markoosha Fischer, *Reunion in Moscow: A Russian Revisits Her Country* (New York, 1962), p. 142.

134. *Letter of an Old Bolshevik* (New York, 1937), pp. 56–57; Zbigniew K. Brzezinski, *The Permanent Purge* (Cambridge, Mass., 1956), p. 89.

135. Marietta Shaginyan, "Pages from the Past," *Nash Sovremennik*, August 1964, tr. in "More about the Problem of 'Fathers' and 'Sons,'" *Research Notes on Soviet Affairs*, October 13, 1964.

136. "What is our Youth Reading?" *Leningradskaya Pravda*, September 20, 1964, tr. in "Which Books are Popular among Soviet Youth," *Research Notes on Soviet Affairs*, October 13, 1964.

137. Allen Kassof, "How Russia Samples Public Opinion," *New Leader*, June 5, 1961, pp. 8–11; *Youth and Freedom*, VII, No. 3 (1965), 19; Emila Wilder, "Opinion Polls," *Survey: A Journal of Soviet and East European Studies*, No. 48 (July 1963), p. 126.

138. "Komsomolskaya Sums up Poll on Soviet Youth," tr. from B. Grushin and V. Chikin, "Confession of a Generation," *Komsomolskaya Pravda*, July 21, 1961, pp. 1–4, in *Current Digest of the Soviet Press*, XIII, No. 34, 5.

139. *Ibid.*, p. 6.

140. James H. Billington, "Soviet Youth Is Getting out of (Party) Line," *Princeton University Quarterly* (Winter 1965–1966), p. 9.

141. Tim Callaghan, "Studying the Students," *Soviet Survey*, No. 33 (July-September 1960), p. 13.

142. Yevgeny Yevtushenko, "A Precocious Autobiography," tr. Andrew R. MacAndrew, *Saturday Evening Post* (August 10, 1963), p. 65.

143. *The Daily Californian*, August 23, 1968.

144. Vera Blackwell, "Czechoslovakia at the Crossroads," *Survey*, No. 68 (July 1968), p. 79.

145. "Izvestia Assails 2 Jailed Writers," *The New York Times*, January 13, 1966, p. 11. Callaghan, *op. cit.*, p. 17.

146. Stefan Bergholz, "On Reading Tertz," *Survey: A Journal of Soviet and East European Studies*, No. 41 (April 1962), p. 150.

147. The secretary of the Party Committee of Moscow State University has written eloquently on the prospects of the new educational reforms in improving the quality of young social scientists. But this makes it likely too that there will be a greater number of potential student activists:

> Life has shown that restricting the admission of young people straight from school to the departments of philosophy, political economy and jurisprudence led to a rise in the average age of the first-year student in those departments from 23 to 24 years. A student is 28 or 29 when he graduates from the university. After working three or four years in the national economy or in research institutions, the young specialist enters graduate school. As a result, a full-fledged specialist in the social sciences completes his training when he is 36 or 37. That is late.

Now with the admission of seventeen-year-old freshmen to the social sciences directly from high school, and without an intervening disciplining in several years of factory work, the "cadres" of a potential student movement are being readied. See B. Mochalov, "Problems of Party Work at Moscow University," *Current Digest of the Soviet Press*, XVIII, No. 36 (September 28, 1966), tr. from "Party Work in Institutions of Higher Education," *Kommunist*, No. 10 (July 1966), pp. 34–42. Harrison E. Salisbury, "'Lost Generation' Baffles Soviet; Nihilistic Youths Shun Ideology," *The New York Times*, February 9, 1962, pp. 1, 4.

148. *Letter of an Old Bolshevik*, p. 37.

149. *Ibid.*, p. 51.

150. *Ibid.*, pp. 58–59.

SEVEN Generational Equilibrium in the United States

The United States has never had a massive student movement of the national proportions of those which existed in Russia and Japan. For instance, the six hundred youngsters who participated in the Mississippi Summer Project in 1964 were a minute fraction of a total American studentry of about two million. By contrast, the back-to-the-people movement in Russia in the 1870s numbered several thousand at a time when the total studentry itself was only about five thousand. At the height of its strength in 1939, the American Student Union, claiming twenty thousand members, represented a small minority on most campuses; the American universities never knew anything like the turmoil of the Russian schools.

When the student peace movement was at its height in 1961, eight thousand students marched to the Capitol, where they were met by friendly administration officials. But even these eight thousand constituted a small fraction of the two million students in the United States.[1] Britain and America have been characterized by what we have called a "generational equilibrium," and the theoretical problem that the experience of the United States poses is why there has been almost no student movement (until recently) in its history.

What is a "generational equilibrium"? A society is said to be in generational equilibrium when no generation feels that its energies and intelligence are being frustrated by the others, when no generation feels that solely because of its years is it being deprived of its proper place in society, and when no generation feels that it is being compelled to bear an undue portion of society's burdens. Every generation believes that it deserves certain experiences; the young lad expects education, leisure, the chance for love and comradeship; the adult expects marriage, a chance to work at his vocation, and to prove himself; the older man expects the rewards of his experience and judgment in the councils of the people; the old man looks forward to the honor of work done and an example rendered. A generational disequilibrium upsets these anticipations. The young especially may feel oppressed and blocked in their ambitions; the traumas of unemployment, the humiliation of the diploma without a job nurture a sense of "generational exploitation." Why, ask the young, should they be denied their chance to work and show what they can do? The older people have had their chance. Different societies, to be sure, define their diverse modes of generational equilibrium; that of a gerontocratic society, such as the Chinese, was intrinsically unstable because it depended so much on strong paternal and ancestral counter-pressures against a restless youth. American society, by contrast, has always been characterized by a basic generational equilibrium. Only in recent years has an effort been made to depict the American student as the object of generational exploitation. In the aftermath of the Berkeley Free Speech Movement, when there was talk of a new university, one leaflet began with a paragraph by Paul Goodman:

> At present in the United States, students—middle class youth—are the major exploited class. The labor of intelligent youth *is* needed, and they are accordingly subjected to tight scheduling, speed-up, and other factory exploitative methods. Then it is not surprising if they organize their CIO. It is frivolous to tell them to go elsewhere if they don't like the rules, for they have no choice but to go to college, and one factory is like another.[2]

But this sense of generational resentment which the author, himself middle-aged, was trying to impart to students has not been a dominant theme in American history. There has been generational conflict in American colleges, yet on the whole such struggles have not been channelized in student movements. American society, in its exceptionalism, succeeded for many years in diverting the energies of generational revolt to more constructive channels than those of ideological student movements.[3]

The Absence of Generational Revolt in the Pre-Civil War Era

Generational revolt, it must be emphasized, does not necessarily accompany every social or national revolution. It is an independent factor, and may not be present to superimpose itself on events. The American Revolution was indeed a remarkable example of a political change which was accompanied by little generational unrest. A generational equilibrium prevailed in the American colonies even when the political equilibrium was disturbed. The Virginian revolutionaries, for instance, were planters' sons who had from youth been prepared for and encouraged to careers in public office: "The custom of filling offices with planters' sons made the homes of the gentry preliminary training schools for future officeholders. . . . Inasmuch as the son was often following his father into public affairs, he could profit by his father's knowledge of public questions and important men. . . . At a time when American colleges were few and small, most of the Virginians who sat in the early Congresses and who served as governor in the first years of statehood were college men." The eager-minded young Thomas Jefferson, for all his sense of political vocation, was nonetheless devoid of any trace of generational rebellion while he was a student at the College of William and Mary. He records with gratitude how his professor of philosophy, Dr. William Small, "most happily for me, became soon attached to me, and made me his daily companion when not engaged in the school; and from his conversation I got my first views of the expansion of science, and of the system of things in which we are placed." The student Jefferson was honored to break bread with Governor Francis Facquier, statesman and scientist, and his teacher of law, George Wythe, "my faithful and beloved mentor in youth, and my most affectionate friend through life."[4] He was present as a young student when Patrick Henry delivered his celebrated address of defiance in the House of Burgesses in 1765. Four years later Jefferson himself was a member of that body. No student ever sat at the feet of his teachers with more appreciation than did the revolutionary, Thomas Jefferson.

The intellectual student in colonial America knew that he would presently be called upon to help govern and administer his society. No barrier of generational hegemony was interposed against him, for all talents were needed. "In most cases the first upward step in a political career was admission to the office of justice of the peace and thus to a seat on the bench of the county court." Almost all the revolutionary Virginian statesmen and politicians began their careers in this fashion. The young justice-novice "was not secluded in a private office with reference books about him; but, like an apprentice, he was seated with several of his older and more experienced colleagues while transacting the daily routine of public business. Thus, youth learned from age, and age formed an opinion of the diligence and ability of the new members of the court."[5]

In such a social environment, revolutionists of a political kind might emerge, but no wave of generational revolt superimposed itself on the political movement. No student movement emanated from William and Mary, Princeton, King's College, Harvard, or Yale to upbraid a corrupt, deauthoritized elder generation.

Indeed America, throughout all the social convulsions it underwent during the nineteenth century, knew almost nothing of the generational unrest which made for student movements in Russia. The intense discussions and moral fervor which developed in the Northern states, and brought the Civil War closer, had a relatively small impact on the studentry. In Russia, the sons and daughters of serf owners felt themselves smitten with guilt for their fathers' sins, and threw themselves into the back-to-the-people movement. Their co-generationists in the American

South seem to have felt no such guilt, or call for self-sacrificing atonement. "The conservative atmosphere of Southern colleges," writes Clement Eaton, "was maintained and accentuated by the thoroughly conservative character of the student body."[6] Student opinion was hostile to independent thought. To be sure, the student bodies generally came from the upper classes. The University of Virginia, for instance, was regarded as a haven for aristocrats and "cotton snobs"; but when the spirit of generational revolt possesses a studentry, as it did the Russians, it overcomes economic self-interest.

Indeed, no wave of empathy or identification with the slaves' lot swept the Northern students. They remained placid, and either indifferent or hostile to the abolitionist agitation. The state of Vermont, for instance, was anti-slavery in its feelings, yet when the New England Anti-Slavery Society held its first convention at Middlebury in 1843, the college students, as Frederick Douglass recalled, "industriously and mischievously placarded the town with violent aspersions of our characters and the greatest misrepresentations of our principles, measures, and objects." Similarly, the abolitionist Stephen S. Foster, in the early 1840s met with extreme hostility from the students of Dartmouth College when he tried to move them to a sense of outrage against their elders for the foul crime of slavery: "And who perpetrates these outrages? They are the ministers, bishops . . . presidents and professors of colleges and theological seminaries. . . . We do not see them do the deeds, and so we hold them innocent. But what would you say if President Lord, of your own college, should be seen carrying home at night a stolen sheep?" At this last remark, the Dartmouth students became incensed; they would brook no insult to their president. "In answer they hissed, hooted, whistled, snickered, slapped their hands, and scraped their feet." The speaker apologized to the audience, but they would not allow him to complete his speech. At Harvard, in 1848, the year when European students were moved by revolutionary visions, Charles Sumner, a Harvard graduate and a leading Massachusetts Whig, created a furor when he dared to criticize slavery in a speech. The poet Longfellow recorded that "the shouts and hisses and the vulgar interruptions grated on my ears" so that he finally fled the hall.[7] Horace Mann was similarly received in 1851, and Ralph Waldo Emerson was "hissed and booed at by young law students" when he assailed Webster as having succumbed to Southern pressures. Although liberal, radical, and democratic elements in Massachusetts condemned Daniel Webster for his famous Seventh of March speech and for his support of the Compromise of 1850, "Harvard University, as a whole, saw eye-to-eye with Webster and the compromisers," writes Samuel Eliot Morison. In 1850, out of a hundred law students, only six were Free Soilers, and the college itself preserved a remarkably cool attitude during the Civil War. The Union was in desperate need of men in 1864; but of the twelve oarsmen in that summer's Harvard-Yale boat race, not a single one enlisted.

Only one episode in the prehistory of the American Civil War partook of the characteristics of a student movement. This occurred from 1833 to 1834 at the Lane Theological Seminary, a Presbyterian center in Cincinnati, Ohio. Here appeared the first political student leader in the United States, Theodore Weld, a powerful speaker and already a veteran of a series of causes and revivalisms ranging from temperance and coeducation to manual labor schools, in which education in the use of the plow, the hoe, shovel, and axe was combined with the discipline of Virgil, Cicero, and the Hellenic sages. A theological student in the Midwest was likely at this time to be a mature man with several careers behind him; for not infrequently young lawyers, businessmen, farmers, and teachers abandoned their occupations, in obedience to a vocation to enter the ministry. When the student abolitionist movement arose at Lane, its members were denounced in the press for not minding their own business and ridiculed as "minors" who were "dreaming themselves into full-grown patriots, and setting seriously to work, to organize a wide-spread revolution; to alter the constitution of their country." Weld, then already thirty years old, replied angrily that nine students in the theological department were between thirty and thirty-five years old, and thirty students were over twenty-six years of age. The total enrollment in the school in all its departments, literary and theological, was in 1832 only ninety. The student abolitionist movement at Lane Theological Seminary was thus composed of a group which was thoroughly atypical of the students in American colleges and universities at the time.

Theodore Weld, appointed as an agent of the newly organized American Anti-Slavery Society in December 1833, was esteemed as president of his class in 1834. "He took the lead of the whole institution," recalled the seminary's head, "they thought he was a god." Weld organized a series of eighteen meetings on the slavery question, which turned into anti-slavery revivals, characterized by a highly charged atmosphere and the narration of "experience." "Nearly half of the seventeen speakers," recalled a fellow-student, "were the sons of slave-holders: one had been a slave-holder himself; one had till recently been a slave; and the residue were residents of, or had recently traveled or lived in slave states." They told of the gruesome character of the institution of slavery. In short, this was a collective experience of guilt in which the sons tried to thrust from themselves the evil of their fathers. The students after nine evenings voted overwhelmingly in favor of the immediate abolition of slavery. They next sought to move from creed to deed, from theory to practice, by establishing an anti-slavery society to work for the immediate emancipation of the slaves through nonviolent, Christian persuasion. The board of trustees, mostly made up of solid businessmen of Cincinnati, would not brook this outright abolitionism, and ordered that the anti-slavery society be dissolved. The young, they held, must first complete their education before they were "fitted to engage in the collisions of active life." The board was prepared to allow only such associations as were devoted to the improvement of studies; it proposed, it said, to discourage "such discussions and conduct among the students as are calculated to divert their attention from their studies, excite party animosities, stir up evil passions amongst themselves, or in the community, or involve themselves with the political concerns of the country." Though the trustees considered expelling Weld, they contented themselves with empowering the executive committee to expel any student it felt necessary. The faculty supported the trustees' rules as consistent with common law in all well-regulated institutions, while reiterating their support of free inquiry "in subordination to the great ends of the Institution." The students replied this was all "words, Words, WORDS"; and on October 15, twenty-eight of them asked for their collective dismissal. The next day they were joined by eleven more; Weld himself resigned on the seventeenth. The majority of the students withdrew to a neighboring village, where they denounced the Lane authorities for their infraction of the right of free speech:

> Free discussion being a duty is consequently a right, and as such, is inherent and unalienable. It is *our* right. It *was* before we entered Lane Seminary. . . . Theological institutions must of course recognize this immutable principle. Proscription of free discussion is sacrilege! It is boring out the eyes of the soul. . . . Better, infinitely better, that the mob demolish every building . . . than that our theological seminaries should become Bastiles [*sic*], our theological students, thinkers by *permission*. . . .

The Rebels (as they then became known) subsequently seceded to Oberlin. At that institution a majority of students had by a vote of thirty-two to twenty-six just declared themselves against admitting a Negro, but the Lane Rebels brought their own temper of mind, and above all secured a guarantee that Oberlin's trustees would not meddle in the "internal affairs" of the college.[8]

The student uprising at Lane Theological Seminary thus arose, like so many others around the world, over the question of rules of freedom of speech and action. In their desire to go forth to work at "elevating the colored people in Cincinnati," and in their founding of a lyceum for Negroes, the Lane students evinced that missionary, self-sacrificing quality, the back-to-the-people spirit, which is the high calling of student movements. On the part of the Southern group in the Lane studentry, the uprising had all the traits of rejection of the old generation by the younger one. Almost all these "students," however, were persons who had experienced defeat in their occupations and felt a certain "alienation" from society. They were akin to the eternal, middle-aged "students" who have hovered around educational institutions to enact and re-enact in a compulsive way their unsuccessful generational revolt. But the Lane Rebels were truly exceptional among the American studentry.

Oberlin, indeed, was the only college where abolitionist radicals found a home.[9] Fifty students left the Phillips-Andover Academy in 1835 because they were not allowed to organize an anti-slavery society, and some students quit Marietta College for a similar reason. At Amherst and Hamilton, however, the anti-slavery societies were disbanded without difficulty by order of the authorities; while at Harvard, no abolitionist student movement ever developed. Such was the situation generally in American colleges.

At Harvard, indeed, the Northern students remained on the warmest personal terms with their Southern classmates. William Francis Bartlett, the most distinguished soldier to emerge from the Harvard undergraduates, recorded in his diary the grief with which he had said good-bye to his Southern classmates who left college when their states seceded from the Union. "One of the most painful aspects of the Civil War," writes Mark De Wolfe Howe, "was the fact that classmates and companions whose friendships before 1861 had been intimate, after Sumter became enemies."[10] Gallantry and chivalry there was a plenty, "the normal impulses of youth to participate in great and exciting events," but there was none of that ideological elitism which characterizes student movements. The studentry had never agitated for war or organized any students' abolitionist crusade. There were occasional individual abolitionists at Harvard such as Wendell Phillips Garrison who, with the reformer's zeal, also sought to have his fellows give up smoking, drinking, and frivolity. Oliver Wendell Holmes, Jr., was moved by the abolitionist cause on ethical grounds, "The morality of Pickwick seemed to me painfully blunt," he recalled, and he was shocked by the way Southern whites used slave women: "I have heard a most humane and tender-hearted Southerner use language that made me shudder." In later years, Holmes was rather ashamed, as Mark Howe writes, of his early abolitionist faith; few of his classmates, however, shared his abolitionist convictions, and Holmes was among those one evening who stood guard at an anti-slavery meeting against ruffians. No wave of generational resentment surged through the studentry to create a student movement. At the Free Academy of New York, later the City College, and center of many storms in the 1930s, the life of the classroom continued in its placid way, untroubled by any sign of a student abolitionist movement. During the winter of 1860–1861, with war on the horizon, the literary society, Phrenocosmia, finally debated the issues of secession. The two speakers who upheld it later joined the Confederate Army, while their two opponents served in the Union Army.[11] But the pre-Civil War Phrenocosmians were not touched with the psychology of student movements. The students of the Free Academy were typically sons of the middle and upper classes who under other circumstances have been the mainstay of student movements. In 1864, of the 351 members of its "introductory" class, only twenty-four were the sons of mechanics or artisans.[12] The prevailing generational equilibrium, however, dispersed any moods of political unrest.

During this period, generational struggle in American universities took organizational form in the founding of fraternities. Although unrelated to any socio-political movement, and devoid of ideological significance, the fraternities were nonetheless at first generational secret societies. Their origin was marked by strife on American campuses. The University of Michigan, in 1849, with the outbreak of its so-called "Society War," was one such principal case. The university consisted that year of a faculty of seven professors, several assistants, and an undergraduate body of eighty-nine. There was no president or other administrative officer. The regents, who exercised authority directly, promulgated a "Rule 20" aimed against fraternities and all other secret societies. Several of the regents had been members of the Anti-Masonic party, and had shared in the revulsion against secret societies. The students balked at Rule 20, and began to counter-organize.

Meanwhile, the professor of intellectual and moral philosophy, Andrew Ten Brook, became aware of secret goings-on among the students. Then townspeople reported that students were burning rail fences and "committing acts of depredation." Asked to investigate, the professor of moral philosophy found that Michigan students had built a cabin deep in the forest off the campus, where, in flagrant violation of Rule 20, they were holding secret fraternity meetings. Such was the subversive origin in 1845 of the first fraternity house ever built in American history, Chi Psi. When the students refused to admit a raiding professor-chancellor, agitation, threats, and punishment followed. Chi Psi was banned. The regents were inclined to compromise, but the faculty, largely composed of ministers, called the fraternities "a detail of obliquities" whose existence posed "a great irresponsible authority; a monster power, which lays its hand upon every college faculty in our country." They accused them of "debauchery, drunkenness, pugilism, and duelling" and of wielding "the despotic power of disorder and rowdyism, rife among their German prototypes."

> There are young men whom we might name, of the most dangerous character, who coil an influence through these organizations at which many a parent has reason to weep and tremble. There are artful seducers whom we could name who are this day through these societies standing not only between faculty and student, but between the parent and the deluded victim.

The regents finally upheld the faculty and suspended a third of the students —all the members of Chi Psi, Alpha Delta Phi, and Beta Theta Pi. Seven suspended students appealed to the legislature; their families turned lobbyists for an investigation; the citizens of Ann Arbor stood firm for the abolition of fraternities. The legislature, however, was of a more pliant mind. The fraternities were allowed to return; the most anti-fraternal professors resigned. But the studentry in 1850 had declined by 50 per cent.[13] Gradually the fraternities changed. Professors were initiated as members. By 1885 most colleges accepted them as useful agencies for education, and aids to the maintenance of order.

Cycles of Generational Conflict in the American Colleges: The Case of Harvard

During the nineteenth century in America, generational conflict in the colleges expressed itself in a kind of perpetual warfare between students and professors, but not in any student political movement. Whereas today students call for a personalized university, with much informal contact with one's teachers, this was not the case in the nineteenth century. At that time, a student who seemed friendly with professors was regarded by his fellow-students as something of a traitor. "Within very recent decades and often now," wrote G. Stanley Hall, "student censure is meted out to those who call upon an instructor socially, or seek information about reading or studies from one who if he made a friendly call on a student would be suspected to be a spy, and the familiar terms—bootlicks, blues, curriers, piscatores—indicate the ostracism experienced by those who seek the good-will of instructors." Even lying to the faculty was justified, and a common unspoken bond of secrecy united students. Open and covert hostility to professors sometimes issued in personal assaults upon professors, more often concerted rebellion:

> College revolts of old were based more often upon complaints regarding commons' food, but suspicions of favoritism, any increase of the wonted stint of study or augmented vigor of examination, suffice. The latter caused the famous Harvard outbreak of 1790 which was not settled for seven years. The Harvard rebellion of 1766 interrupted work for about a month. Still more serious rebellions occurred there in 1807 and 1830. In the Southern colleges riots have not been infrequent. In 1808 about one-half the students were expelled from Princeton; in 1845 all the students but two freshmen were expelled from another institution; a State university not many years ago expelled the entire senior class . . . and in many faculties there is still a fear that the whole student-body is capable of being unified and arrayed in organization against their authority.[14]

This was at a time when most American colleges kept students in "a state of pupilage," with watchmen in the dormitories, regulations for hours of sleep, chapel, punctuality, and deportment.

American students in the nineteenth century were often mischievous and boisterous; their annals are replete with anecdotes of anti-professorial pranks. But they never felt the kind of de-authoritization of the older generation which is essential for an ideological, political student movement to arise. Harvard students in the 1820s used to torment tutors by throwing cups, knives, and biscuits at them during breakfast, and hurling pennies at the feet of professors leading them in prayer.[15] When John Dewey was a student at the staid University of Vermont in the late 1870s, the students imprisoned their professors by tying the classroom doors; they set fire to the campus green, and staged small riots in the dormitories. Twenty-one of them, including John Dewey, absented themselves in concert from military drill at one roll call in 1878, and received five demerits each.[16] Lincoln Steffens, as a freshman at the University of California in 1885, "found already formed at Berkeley the typical undergraduate customs, rights, and privileged vices which we had to respect ourselves and defend against the faculty, regents, and the State government." One evening he was taken out by some upperclassmen to help teach the president a lesson. That personage was blamed for trying "to govern the private lives and public morals of university 'men.'" The student raiding party swung a long ladder back and forth against a window of the president's house, meanwhile chanting obscene songs and breaking everything within that was breakable. The president soon resigned, and young Steffens reports he "noticed that not only the students but many of the faculty and regents rejoiced in his downfall."[17] Such episodes were frequent among the American studentry, but there was never that upsurge of revolt against the older generation in the name of a new ethic and a new philosophy which characterizes a student movement. The young and the old in America lived by the same dreams and shared the same values.

Generational unrest, when it did exist, spent itself in campus outbreaks; it never merged with politico-ideological issues to constitute a student movement.

Almost every generation at Harvard College saw some uprising, a normal cycle of student unrest; but it was not until 1910, with the advent of the Harvard Socialist Club, that (though on a small scale) the unique conjunction of generational unrest with a broad socio-political and moral issue which is characteristic of student movements took place. "The earliest recorded College rebellion occurred in the spring of 1766 over bad butter at commons." The slogan of the ringleader, Asa Dunbar, was "Behold our Butter stinketh!" His fellow-students demonstrated in his support, whereupon Dunbar was condemned by the faculty to confess to the sin of insubordination. Thereupon the students the next morning had, not a sit-in, but an eat-out; they breakfasted in town. A faculty committee made some concessions but adjudged the student behavior as treasonable. The corporation, overseers, and governor of Massachusetts insisted that the students apologize or leave. The students protested this unconstitutional oppression; finally, however, 155 of them did sign a confession of "irregular and unconstitutional proceedings," with a "Promise of future good Conduct." Asa Dunbar, the first American student leader, was a grandfather of Henry David Thoreau.[18]

A generation later, the ratification of the Federal Constitution was accompanied by a series of student disorders, inspired perhaps by an enthusiasm for liberty. The most serious occurred when a new rule for the public examination of the three upper classes was announced. The students argued this was an ex post facto rule, therefore unconstitutional. On the morning of the examination, some students poured a large dose of emetic into the water used by the college at breakfast; the examination took place under conditions of extreme physiological discomfort. The undergraduates at this time looked upon their tutors as their natural enemies, though the tutors were generally very young and fresh out of college. "A lad who treated his tutor as a friend was looked down upon as a 'fisherman,' and the tutors regarded the undergraduates as inmates in a reformatory."[19]

The students, however, never became political radicals; the older generation was never de-authoritized in its eyes; rather its authority was high. "The typical student of the early seventeen-nineties," writes Morison, "was an atheist in religion, an experimentalist in morals, a rebel to authority."[20] The authority, however, against which he rebelled was only collegiate. When trouble arose with revolutionary France, every member of the college, with one exception, wore the black cockade, not the tricolor. Almost the entire student body of 170 signed an address in support of President John Adams, while the Hasty Pudding Club toasted Washington on his birthday: "May the government of *our own choice* never be assailed by Jacobinism."[21] The town of Cambridge was Jeffersonian, but Harvard was Federalist. The students tried to crowd into the town meeting to jeer the local "Jacobins." Here was no back-to-the-people spirit, though plenty of generational ebullience.

During the Jeffersonian era, however, another "Bread and Butter Rebellion" took place when students in 1805 walked out in protest against "bad commons." Half the college was suspended, as in 1766. The students refused to submit, and the overseers divided on party lines over the question of students' rights. Twenty-nine Federalists supported authority, as against twenty-six Republicans. The students themselves, however, do not seem to have been moved by the Jeffersonian ideology. Then, in 1818, still a third "bread and butter" insurrection took place, during which the sophomore class, Ralph Emerson among them, gathered around Rebellion Tree to swear loyalty to four rusticated classmates and undying opposition to tyranny. Old John Adams wanted flogging to be revived, but "a new crop of rustications and suspensions followed," sending Emerson home for a few weeks, until "this burlesque of patriots struggling with tyrants gradually played itself out, and came to an end."[22]

Harvard was not alone as a stage for generational conflict. Every American college records its "great rebellion." At Princeton, as often elsewhere, generational protest in the late eighteenth and early nineteenth centuries took the form of adherence to atheist and deist philosophy, opposition to Christianity, and physical assaults on the university. "It is hard for the undergraduate of to-day, when the tone of the College is so distinctively Christian," wrote George Wallace in 1893, "to realize the moral atmosphere of seventy-five years ago. French philosophy was still fashionable, and French skepticism was carefully cherished by young men as the badge of polite learning and freedom. The gay and reckless spirit which always accompanied this philosophy of life was not wanting. It was necessary to ride hard, drink deep, and fear nothing." Even as late as 1841 there were only twelve Christians at Princeton. The students, somewhat older at this time, perpetuated a tradition of rebellion against discipline. In March 1802, they completely gutted Nassau Hall, with its library and apparatus. Nothing remained but the bare, brown walls! Then in 1807 came the "Great Rebellion." For some reasons not definitely known, a spirit of discontent which had been growing culminated in open revolt. The students barricaded, fortified, and stocked Old North, and elected two consuls who "held sway over an elaborately organized state." A citizens' guard was mobilized in town to defend the college. Students were expelled. At a judicial assembly, "when this business was about to begin, one of the leaders of the association rose and gave a signal to the rest, and they rushed out of the hall with shouting and yelling."[23] Out of two hundred students, one hundred and twenty-five were suspended. Subsequently, nearly half were readmitted. Seven years later, in 1814, the college outbuildings were set on fire, and the Prayer Hall seriously damaged by a large bomb, an "infernal machine."

The rebellion of 1823 at Harvard was the most serious in its annals. Forty-three students out of a senior class of seventy were expelled almost on commencement eve. There had long been discontent with the uninspiring system of rote recitations, but the class of 1823 was unusually restive. Tutors' voices were drowned out in classroom and chapel, cannonballs were dropped from windows, there were explosions in the yard, and tutors were soaked with buckets of inked water. The studentry was divided between "high fellows" and obedient "blacks." One black turned informer. Thereupon the rebels swore under the Rebellion Tree that unless the informer was expelled, and his victim reinstated, they would leave college. Their own expulsions followed. George Ripley, later leader of the communistic Brook Farm, curiously was among the law-abiding "blacks."[24] Some reform of education, however, in the interests of special classes for the better students, soon followed, though the disciplinary rules became even more severe.

Then in 1834 another major rebellion took place which led to the suspension on May 29 of the entire sophomore class for the remainder of the academic year. A dispute in which, according to one version, the lowerclassmen struck against a pedantic Latin professor was followed by an assault on their tutors' windows and furniture, and the ringing of the college bell in the middle of the night. Unable to discover the window breakers, the president appealed to the grand jury of Middlesex. Thereupon the students were incensed that public authorities had been brought inside the university, in violation of academic tradition. "The 'black flag of rebellion' was hung from the roof of Holworthy. Furniture and glass in the recitation rooms of University were smashed." The juniors voted to wear crepe on their arms, issued a leaflet impugning the president's character, and hung him in effigy on the Rebellion Tree. A committee of seniors published a circular and lost their degrees. But their document was so cogent that it prompted the overseers to issue a forty-seven-page pamphlet by the president in reply.[25] Expulsions helped make the class of 1836 the smallest since 1809, except for the rebellion class of 1823.

Such, then, were the periodic rebellions at Harvard of 1766, 1805, 1818, 1823, and 1834. Although there were bread and butter episodes in later years, the pattern of escalation failed to operate, and they never developed into major rebellions. The elective system introduced by Charles W. Eliot after the Civil War removed the principal educational grievance. According to Morison, "as athletics increased, riots and disorders faded out."[26] In any case, the pre-Civil War rebellions never involved any social-ideological factor. These were pure generational uprisings, but they were never student movements seeking to transform the political universe. In the post-Civil War period, the relatively friendly relations that developed between teachers and students made obsolete the insurrections of previous generations. "By 1900 caste feelings in the Faculty had completely vanished."[27] Harvard was united in defense of the social order. During the great railroad strike of 1877, Charles W. Eliot could answer on Harvard's behalf to the workingmen's agitation; he promoted the rifle club among the students, drilling them himself so that they would be ready to suppress the mobs.[28] There was a flurry of discussion at the time of the Spanish-American War when William James warned his class: "Don't yelp with the pack!" but no real student protest.[29] Settlement work in Boston, and two Cambridge evening schools, conducted by student volunteers on the example of London's Toynbee Hall, were the closest approximation at Harvard to a back-to-the-people spirit.

The advent of a student socialist club brought to Harvard the flavor of a student movement, and the class of 1910 briefly led the way. "There was talk of the world, and daring thought, and intellectual insurgency," reminisced John Reed:

> Students themselves criticized the faculty for not educating them, attacked the sacred institution of collegiate athletics, sneered at undergraduate clubs so holy that no one dared mention their names. . . . Some men, notably Walter Lippmann, had been reading and thinking and talking about politics and economics, not as dry theoretical studies, but as live forces acting on the world, on the University even. They formed the Socialist Club, to study and discuss all modern social and economic theories, and began to experiment with the community in which they lived.

Under their stimulus, the college political clubs which had been mostly beer societies took on a new significance. The Club worked for the Socialist party in the city elections, and introduced social legislation into the Massachusetts Legislature. Its members charged the university with not paying its servants a living wage. They agitated for women's suffrage, and petitioned the faculty for a course in socialism. "The Club encouraged all sorts of radicalism in the undergraduate world in music, painting, poetry, the theater. . . . The more serious college papers took a socialistic, or at least progressive, tinge." Students turned from dilettantism to earnest social purpose.[30] But only a small percentage of them were touched by the spirit of a student movement.

Generational Conflict in the American Colleges: the Post-Civil War Era

The American colleges in the post-Civil War era were generally benevolent theocratic paternalisms ruled by their presidents. Evidently, however, beneath the surface, tensions and resentments smoldered. Under Mark Hopkins at Williams, for instance, things seemed to go smoothly. Then suddenly while the benevolent Hopkins was away making a speech, the "rebellion of 1868" erupted. The faculty, in a show of independence and severity, enacted a strict rule for giving students zeros when they missed recitations. The senior class assembled, denounced the rule, and threatened to resign from the college en masse. A boycott of classes was almost universally successful; only two students attended recitations. The students' journal came out against the whole idea of a marking system. An article, "Right to Revolt," ridiculed the absurdity of grades based on a point evaluation of scholarship, orderly behavior, regularity, moral conduct, general deportment. "What we would like to see," it concluded, "is the abolishment of marks and prizes." Every American student movement has echoed this demand. The rebellion, lasting almost a week, ended with personal visits by Mark Hopkins to each of the rebels. The faculty, in retreat, revised the controversial rule to make it agreeably ambiguous. The idea of the college as akin to a family ruled by the president was preserved, and the students seemed satisfied. In 1872, their journal, *The Vidette,* declared: "We would have Williams remain a conservative college."[31] The Williams uprising nonetheless was a harbinger of what was to come.

It is largely forgotten that American colleges in the latter part of the nineteenth century went through a crisis of generational conflict. At the same time that Russian students were plotting to murder their Czar, American students were plotting how to oust their college presidents. Therein is the measure of difference and similarity in the student unrest of the two countries. The American students never felt themselves in basic alienation from a de-authoritized elder generation. The American generational equilibrium was stable.

In part, the student revolt of the late nineteenth century was directed against the doctrine of *in loco parentis.* Probably the revolt was not unrelated to the fact that the students were getting older. According to Julius Seelye, president of Amherst, the average student in 1882 was two years older than he had been a generation earlier. At Harvard in 1856, the average age of entering freshmen had been seventeen years and seven months; by 1866, it had risen to eighteen years and two months; and in 1875, it stood at eighteen years and six months. In 1894, the *Williams Weekly* reported that the average age of students at Harvard (at graduation) was twenty-two and seven-tenths years. Earlier in the century, in 1828, the Yale Report had indicated that the expected ages of college students were from fourteen to eighteen.[32]

The student journals carried on a campaign against the doctrine of *in loco parentis*. The college, they said, should adjust itself to changes in the structure of the American family. "Few parents would attempt any such government of 20 year olds as do colleges of their students," wrote the *Williams Argo*. It attacked the rule compelling students to attend religious services every day and twice on Sunday.[33]

This parochial version of the generational crisis was endemic among Eastern colleges between the years 1881 and 1887. "As a shared experience, the crises which reached their peaks at Dartmouth, Union, Bowdoin, Wesleyan, and Williams within the six years, 1881 to 1887, and at Amherst in 1894, were without precedent. Student newspapers continually called attention to the incidence of undergraduate uprisings."[34] The *Wesleyan Argus* reported, "Two years ago it was at Dartmouth; a little over a year ago Hamilton was the scene of such a rebellion. Later still, it is Princeton that we see embroiled in general conflict between faculty and students." At Union College, the entire student body, late on a March day in 1888, marched in a driving snowstorm behind a drum corps down the main street of Schenectady to present a petition to the trustees threatening to resign unless a president were elected that semester.[35] They had indicated who their candidate was, a Professor H. G. Webster, who had led them in their fight against the previous President Potter. The students got their candidate. This was a period in which college communities held public "trials" of their presidents on the initiative of faculty and students; there were such proceedings at Dartmouth, Union, and Hamilton.[36]

At Bowdoin, an outbreak of riots took place against its military president, Major General Joshua Chamberlain. As a result of what has been called "the greatest student rebellion in Bowdoin's history," the general resigned in 1883.[37] The provocative incident was the expulsion of eleven out of twenty-seven sophomores for involvement in a hazing incident; thereupon the rest of the student body almost seceded, and had to be begged to come back to classes. Student direct action was becoming the crucial factor in determining the removal of presidents. The whole of Middlebury College went on strike in the fall of 1879, and desisted only when the trustees came up from New York, conducted an investigation, and installed a new president. Ambitious faculty men who allied themselves with student uprisings found a new avenue for upward mobility.

Discontent with the curriculum was only a marginal factor in the student unrest. Whether the curriculum was elective or prescribed, outbreaks against presidential rule were likely to occur. Not the content of courses but the sheer autocratic power of elder-generational rule was the target of student revolt. At Dartmouth, for example, the president favored a rigid curriculum; at Union, on the other hand, the president had put through a free elective and liberal disciplinary system, against the faculty's opposition; at Hamilton, however, the president stood for free electives and strict discipline.[38] But outbreaks occurred in all these colleges during the 1880s. For the student revolt defined itself as being in opposition to the system of intellectual patriarchalism, or "intellectual fiefdoms." The college president of the nineteenth century was, indeed, an intellectual patriarch; often in fact the presidency descended within one family.[39]

The crises in the short run tended almost to destroy the colleges. At Union College, from 1884 to 1888, attendance fell more than 50 per cent. In 1887, only twenty-four students enrolled in all its departments.[40]

Rebellion in a most celebrated case came to Amherst College in 1894. Its student leader was Harlan Fiske Stone, later Chief Justice of the United States Supreme Court, but in 1894 the master-mind and organizer of the so-called "Gates Rebellion" at Amherst College. Ostensibly it began when its President Gates, in January 1894, summarily dismissed a student who had intercepted a letter from the college to the student's father telling him of the son's unexcused absences from classes. The students felt this summary action violated the established principle of Amherst self-government. Stone was chairman of the Senior Class Committee which presented the student's case. But the quarrel over the handling of a student's dishonesty was only the occasion, the provocative incident, for an outbreak of long-standing bitterness on the part of the student body. The rebellion aimed to destroy "an egotistical and narrow-minded fundamentalist," President Gates. Many years later, in 1939, Stone still recalled with anger that the college president had "deliberately turned his back on the president of the senior class [Stone] at his [Gates'] reception, after reproaching him, in the presence of a large number of guests, with having done the college a 'very serious injury.' " Stone recalled that at "the root of the trouble lay the fact that President Gates did not know how to deal with young men, and especially how to appeal to the manly and generous instinct of young men. It was inevitable that a clash would occur." This presumably was a revolt against a man the students didn't like. "The truth is beneath President Gates' rather showy exterior were only a shallow intellect and shallow character. When this opinion became widespread, Gates was doomed." Thus spoke Stone in 1935. Gates, with his swagger, his name-dropping, and his "Chesterfieldian" manner, offended the students; also they disliked his course in political ethics.

The rebellious students, however, were in no sense political radicals. The great majority of them were Republicans—only twenty were Democrats among 145 student voters. In October 1892, when eighteen Amherst professors published an appeal for Grover Cleveland, the Democratic candidate for the presidency, the students vehemently protested in a college parade with a placard: "18 Profs can't fool us—Tammany Faculty—Christian College." A year later, Harlan Stone himself, age twenty-one, became chairman of the Amherst Republican Town Committee. Generational tension did not beget a political student movement. There was no merging of generational revolt with political and economic discontent, no projection of generational revolt into political terms. When Stone gave his commencement speech, "Two Epochs of Socialism," he did not even remotely suggest a student revolutionary. He talked of the "first epoch," the violent excesses of the French Revolution, the failure of its republicanism in the rule of the "ignorant" and "vicious." The "second epoch," in his view, was that of socialism in America, the horrible spectacle of Coxey's Army and the "waves of Populism." The "extremist" demands of inland American farmers, said the young Harlan, were like the "unrestrained socialism" of the Terror. Would America withstand the "peasant onslaught"? queried the student orator. This student leader felt no back-to-the-people kinship with the Pullman strikers or the Populists. He concluded, "As the earlier epoch of socialism failed, so will its American prototype, not because of its own frenzied bloodshed and violence, but because of an insurmountable obstacle—patriotic Americanism."[41] Two students of the next class, '95, who participated in some of these Amherst events were Dwight Morrow and Calvin Coolidge, the former as chairman of the editorial board of the *Amherst Literary Monthly*, the latter marching in 1892 with the torchlight procession of the college Republican club.[42]

The Amherst students led by Harlan Stone were involved in a generational revolt against theocratic paternalism. They won support from a faculty which had its own causes for resentment. As George E. Peterson writes:

> The truth was that many students and faculty alike were determined to discredit Gates. It is hard to comprehend today how virulent an issue had developed over the place of Christianity in the college purpose. As one student of the time later wrote, "It is difficult to explain how thoroughly the undergraduate body, quietly backed up by a number of the faculty, were rebelling against the old religious outlook which placed so much emphasis on evangelism." The most influential professor of the period, Charles Garman, openly spoke against the President in his classes. When Gates brought the evangelist, B. Fay Mills, to spread his emotional piety at Amherst, one can be sure that the historians, philosophers, and scientists on the faculty made clear their disgust.[43]

The students had grown up in homes with conventional evangelical parents. Gates was the convenient target for an anti-evangelical generational protest, a substitute for the battle which would have been too painful to fight at home.

The students' leader, Harlan Fiske Stone, was a veteran of generational warfare against collegiate clericalism; he had been dismissed from the

Massachusetts Agricultural College for his activism in a chapel riot.[44] Young Harlan, a perpetual rebel, had been found guilty by the latter's faculty "of five different violations of college discipline," whose occurrence Stone admitted. The faculty minutes tell the story of a student's revolt against his father's religion; "May 4, 1889 . . . A Petition from Stone was read asking to be excused from prayers. It was voted that his petition be not granted."

Then one March day in 1890, Harlan Stone took matters into his own hands. When the hymn singing and the Scripture reading were over, all the students, at a signal, "arose en masse and made for the single exit." The stairway was jammed, and the banister swayed perilously. The chaplain seized student Harlan Stone by the collar. "Take your damn hands off me!" shouted the embattled sophomore. One week later Stone was expelled by a vote of the faculty. Denied an honorable dismissal, Stone had difficulty getting admitted to Amherst. A half-century later, he sheepishly narrated the incident: "I turned and grabbed him and shook him until the teeth rattled. I continued shaking him till I suddenly discovered who he was!"[45] He was seventeen and a half years old at the time. Amherst's evangelical religion and its chaplain stood for all that young Harlan Stone had suffered under the stern discipline at home. His father's "Puritanism . . . sanctioned corporal punishment, stern and inexorable." The father reinforced the Calvinist terror not only by his great strength but by delaying execution of the punishment until his temper was cool. The horsewhip was used. Stone in later years "insisted that his father's harshness had been wholly salutary. It had made 'a man' of him."[46] Every Saturday evening was spent at a Bible lesson, Sunday at church, with supplemental temperance teaching by the father. But young Harlan at Amherst no doubt had a version of his father's harshness less sentimentalized by the passage of years.

Yet it would be wrong to characterize the student revolts in the American colleges of the 1880s as examples of a student movement. For they lacked, as we have mentioned, several ingredients of student movements. They did not merge with political objectives for the social and economic reconstruction of society. They were not accompanied by the elitist spirit of the mission of the intellectual class to redeem society. They accepted the society as it was, and looked forward in the course of time to becoming its leaders. They proposed no frontal attack to supplant the existing leadership with their own. They did, indeed, call for a "new system" of student government, but "once student government was a reality, the undergraduates lost much of their enthusiasm." "To the *fin de siècle* undergraduate, independence meant freedom from faculty interference in his extracurricular organizations, freedom to devote himself to football and crew, and freedom from excessive study or chapel attendance."[47]

It is noteworthy that small enrollments were no bar to intense student unrest. Union College, for instance, in the time of its troubles in 1881–1882 had an enrollment which had fallen as low as 187 students. Moreover, although it canceled tuition for two-thirds of its students, it had a high rate of "drop-outs." Eighty-four students left its three upper classes in 1879.[48]

The student revolts on the New England campuses for the most part achieved their aims:

> None of the presidents following after the campus disruptions ever endorsed the controversial slogan (*in loco parentis*). The change in actual practices, if not so dramatic, were also very real. When President Gates left, the last Amherst student had had to kneel with the president in spoken prayer, while both asked God to lay bare any rebellious secrets that lay hidden in the student's heart.[49]

The era of student uprisings was shortly followed by an unprecedented expansion of the New England colleges, and a rise in both their prosperity and self-discipline. They grew in the next period at the fastest rate in their history and under harmonious administrations. During the twenty years from 1860 to 1880, the total enrollment at six colleges—Amherst, Bowdoin, Dartmouth, Union, Wesleyan, and Williams—had grown by only forty-three students (2.8 per cent); but during the ten years from 1890 to 1900 it grew by 557 (35.1 per cent).[50]

It is said that out of these battles emerged a "New Dartmouth" and a "New Williams," that gains were achieved so that these battles never had to be fought again. The old type of "rigid," "ascetic," and "evangelical" president was replaced by the "urban," "generous," and "statesmanlike" man of affairs, "endowed with a sense of humor." Where ministers continued to be chosen as presidents, they were less autocratic, less evangelical. "It was the matter of religion that irremediably divided the old presidents from the new."[51] This change of presidential temperament heralded, too, an altered primacy in fields of study; no longer was the small college essentially a training center for the ministry and the devout. The college was adapting to the emerging modern business civilization. The college president, the father figure, began to vanish from the scene. Students would no longer bear the stamp on their characters of such men as Mark Hopkins or Julius Seelye. "The ideal of the old-time college had been to have a personable, fatherly president as the obvious head of the campus community."[52] The new president was a business executive with a flair for administration; he no longer took time to give the culminating course of philosophy in the senior year.

In the new institution, the faculties enjoyed a greater degree of academic freedom; students won the right to have student juries, liberalized rules, and self-government. Especially was the question of self-government a critical one at the end of the nineteenth century; it opened the door to autonomous decisions for baseball and social life. The fear that the creation of student senates would mean the passage of the real governing power to the students proved unfounded. The students finally didn't wish to be bothered. A disillusionment with student self-government set in. The

Bowdoin Orient editorialized, "The students do not desire to govern themselves nor is there any logical reason why they should be expected to do so."[53]

During their uprisings of the eighties and nineties there were no real political, economic, or ideological differences between the students and their teachers and trustees.[54] All had the same class background and hopes; all shared the American faith and optimism, and usually, too, loyalty to the Republican party. The student revolt, directed against the transcendentalist survival of ministerial leadership, was one which faculty and trustees could ultimately endorse. No students assailed the trustees as captains of industry or the professors as servitors of capitalism.[55] The students themselves looked forward to becoming captains or even colonels of industry.

For such reasons, Thorstein Veblen, the sardonic critic of the universities, showed no interest in the student unrest; from his standpoint, the student activists remained junior henchmen of the pecuniary culture. The elective system in curricula, he noted, would be governed by the students' pecuniary interest. Students were going to choose courses primarily for their contribution to material success. Young nonscholars were going to shape the colleges and universities: "A decisive voice in the ordering of the affairs of higher learning has so been given to the novices, or rather to the untutored probationers of the undergraduate schools, whose entrance on a career of scholarship is yet a matter of speculative probability at the best."[56] The primacy among pragmatic interests, noted Veblen, had passed from religion to business; the school of commerce had replaced the divinity school.[57] The social scientists, he felt, shared "the prevailing opinions of the conservative middle class," and their leaders were large and aggressive mediocrities.[58] The undergraduate college, from his standpoint, was still a "school for preliminary training," preparatory to the university, hence its "boarding-school circumstance" was an "unavoidable" evil.[59] What Veblen wished to do was to keep the university free from this undergraduate incubus. The university revolved around "personal contact and cooperation between teacher and student."[60] Thus the significance of the student uprisings was nil for Veblen. In *The Higher Learning in America*, there are chapters on the governing boards, the academic administration, material equipment, the academic personnel, the scientist, and vocational training, but none on the students, though Veblen recognized that no good scientific work could be carried on through a course of years "by any scientist without students, without loss or blunting of that intellectual initiative that makes the creative scientist."[61] Veblen felt estranged from an American studentry which had no basic quarrel with its society.

Americans in the latter part of the nineteenth century found it hard to understand the Russian student world, with its savage passions. American society, where the conflict of generations was in equilibrium, seemed far removed from the searing oppositions of *Fathers and Sons*. The surviving abolitionists were the sole group which felt a kinship of spirit with the Russian nihilist students. Delivering the Phi Beta Kappa address at Harvard in 1881, soon after the assassination of Alexander II, the abolitionist Wendell Phillips joined the nihilists with the fathers of the American Revolution. Some contemporaries regarded his discourse as epoch-making in the way in which Emerson's celebrated "American Scholar" oration had been; Phillips assailed the timidity of scholars in failing to lead in such "great social questions" as the emancipation of women, temperance, and the revolutionary causes in Russia. The Russian nihilists, he declared, were the living representatives of Sam Adams, John Brown, and George Washington; for every single reason that our fathers had for rebellion, Phillips said, Russians count a hundred: "The cant of Americans bewailing Russian Nihilism is the most disgusting." Russia, without a free press or free debate, had no basis for peaceful change: "In such a land dynamite and the dagger are the necessary and proper substitutes for Faneuil Hall and *The Daily Advertiser*. . . . Nihilism is the righteous and honorable resistance of a people crushed under an iron rule. Nihilism is evidence of life. . . ." Thomas Wentworth Higginson, his fellow-abolitionist, reported that Phillips held the audience spellbound, but that the next day many a respectable lawyer and divine felt his blood run cold when he realized that he had applauded to an echo a fascinating orator who "had really made the assassination of an emperor seem as trivial as the doom of a mosquito."[62] Indeed, the aged abolitionist sensed a kinship between the nihilists and the comrades of his own youth—the death-longing which could pervade the highest flights of political idealism. When the old abolitionist Higginson met Turgenev, he told him that the theme of *Virgin Soil* was universal, that he had known many Americans whose emotions were those of their Russian counterparts.

Though Tolstoy and Turgenev met with an earnest, admiring reception in America, and a genuine Tolstoyan cast of mind influenced such persons as Jane Addams and Clarence Darrow, and George Kennan's *The Siberian Exile System* was widely read,[63] there was no generational unrest in America that compared with that in Russia. Henry James, writing on Turgenev, could find nothing to say about generational conflict, and found Turgenev "wantonly melancholy," while the reviewer, T. S. Perry, found a certain sickness in Russian society, based on an "outward show of civilization, thinly covering the fury of untamed half-savage natures." The madness of the sons' revolt, the parricide, which rose so readily from the Russian unconscious to consciousness in its literature, marked a disequilibrated, half-insane world, a world of the abnormal and disorderly, from which America, in its generational equilibrium, was happily spared.

Insofar as the students of this period were moved by a back-to-the-people spirit, it took the form of an adherence to the settlement movement. Its pioneers were stirred by the spirit of a "new Franciscanism," by "stories of Russian college girls who had gone to live with the people," and by the example of Toynbee Hall in London. Graduates of Amherst and Smith College took rooms in New York's Lower East Side to work among its people. The expressman who moved Stanton Coit's goods "was inclined to question his sanity."[64] Settlements in the United States "were just such protests by students against a learning that was never put to use. All the first settlement founders were young men and women freshly out of college, most still in their twenties. All had experienced during their undergraduate years the 'sense of futility, of misdirected energy,'" that dismayed Jane Addams, and believed, with her, "that the pursuit of cultivation would not in the end bring either solace or belief." The settlement movement offered the college students a chance to prove their ideals in the new slums. "Settlements caught up an entire college generation in their enthusiasm." It began with the founding in New York of the Neighborhood Guild (later the University Settlement) in 1886 by Stanton Coit; and by 1911, it is estimated, 2,500 residents and up to 15,000 volunteers were involved in 413 settlements—the majority of them young college graduates. The percentage of the involved American studentry was far higher in the settlement movement than in the Peace Corps a half-century later. "To the early settlement leaders it seemed inevitable that students should predominate in the movement." "Our so-called educated young people," said Jane Addams, "who bear the brunt of being cultivated into unnourished, oversensitive lives," were the ones who felt most sharply the contradiction between the existence of a cultured leisure class and an uncultured, working class; this was the estrangement they felt.[65]

The great state universities which were then emerging were surprisingly free from the rebellions which characterized the colleges. The University of Michigan, for instance, had from the seventies to the nineties trebled its enrollment to three thousand students, but there were no student movements or rebellions. The students were rambunctious and "organized impromptu processions at the slightest provocation merely to demonstrate the vaunted 'Michigan spirit.'" "It was the era of the great beginnings of Michigan football," and students identified themselves with the "rough, tough, fighting band of Wolverines."[66] It was a world wholly unlike that of the Russian terrorist students; their dimensions were incommensurable. The Panic of 1893 did not seriously affect the spirit of what became known as the "McKinley Prosperity." Most of the university's students celebrated at the World's Exposition at Chicago that year, wearing exhibitionist clothes—"enormous four-in-hand cravats with knots more than two inches long . . . stiff, stand-up collars, horseshoe stickpins, starched shirt fronts, suede gloves, bamboo canes," white spats, and skin-tight trousers.[67] Townspeople were annoyed. But coeducation was flourishing, and there were no ideological movements. There was one major riot in May 1892 when about three hundred students tried to rush the circus that was playing in town. The circus crew fought the students, while Ann Arbor's two policemen were in absentia. Finally the militia was summoned, a fire began, the animals roared, and the fire department moved into action. Many students were arrested.[68] The episode, however, was hardly ideological.

At the University of Illinois, a "military rebellion" broke out in 1880 when the faculty tried to raise the requirements for military commissions. The aged President Gregory ten years before had pioneered a comprehensive plan for student self-government. "Student life at the struggling institution had the natural breadth of democracy. The undergraduates were almost without exception poor."[69] In 1880, the upperclassmen refused to fill their posts in the battalion. The military mutiny lasted for the winter semester; the president subsequently resigned. But there was no political student movement. Even under the progressive governorship of John P. Altgeld who, as Allan Nevins says, had "read too much German Socialism," and who worked hard to open the university to the most impoverished students and to liberalize its curriculum, there was no stirring of political student activity.[70]

These large state universities were the homes of the burgeoning fraternities, which were also agencies for the maintenance of generational equilibrium. The fraternity, as Allan Nevins noted, "is much more than a club; for it is a home which takes the place of the dreary small-town boarding house, and offers many comforts and a picked companionship at low cost. The University would be a crowded and more cheerless place without it."[71] In those days, poor students would bring their potatoes and cornmeal in order to "bach it." There was a natural, homespun democracy in the state university, where at least 35 per cent of the students would be earning part of their expenses. "Bricklayers, barbers, carpenters, all attend the University. A few years ago several farmers' sons borrowed the family cows, drove them to the University, and lived comfortably and independently during their college course by selling milk morning and evening."[72] The sons of middle- and upper-class and personalistic Amherst and Dartmouth were rebels; not so the sons of proletarian, impersonal Illinois. There was a time during the 1890s when the struggle between freshmen and sophomore classes grew too violent, and a wild post-football outbreak took place in 1908, but these patterns of violence gradually receded.[73]

In Missouri, in 1887, a student protest with a political aspect did arise, but it was, interestingly enough, of a "reactionary" character. That year the president, Samuel Spahr Laws, was denounced by unreconstructed Confederate politicians as a "damn Yankee," and his ouster was demanded by forty-four students. A few months later, students demanded that the regulations against students' crimes be deleted from the university catalogue. The president finally resigned.[74]

The student uprisings of the eighties and nineties occurred not in the large state universities but in the small colleges, not in the universities where students were from the lower classes but in the colleges of the more well-to-do, not in the universities where the sciences and the practical arts were pursued but in the colleges of the liberal arts. Generational uprising, indeed, found its home, not in the impersonal universities but in the small personal colleges. Seventy-five years later the students at Berkeley complained that theirs was a revolt against the "alienation" of the impersonal "knowledge factory." Quite the opposite was the case earlier. The students of 1900 were stirred to no protest by the bigness of Michigan or Illinois. The class origin of the students, indeed, was a decisive factor in their unrest, but in a way precisely opposite to what a Marxist might have expected. The Michigan or Illinois student had no energy to spare for surrogate generational struggles. He came from a home where life's struggle was real and keen; he came to a state university because it was virtually free; often he worked his way through college; he chose his courses with an eye to his livelihood; he found his companionship in his self-organized fraternities, which in those days were less aristocratic enclaves than cooperatives for housing and dining. When the obstacles of life are genuine and concrete, when the struggle for survival is real, with its concern for tomorrow's breakfast and tomorrow's lunch, then there are no surplus energies available for generational revolt. The university is not then a theater, a stage, in which one acts out against the president one's resentments against one's father. The university is a place where one already has the problem of standing on one's feet, and getting the maximum skills for doing so further.

To this extent, the revolts in universities have been the expression of the motivations of the children of the more well-to-do. Those whose fathers are supporting them financially will be more likely to be among the activists. Energies which might otherwise go into a job, and to earning one's living against real obstacles, into the ordinary demonstration of one's manhood, seek out surrogate ways for demonstrating one's manhood in generational conflict.

But none of these revolts became a political movement. That came in the thirties, when students in New York found themselves faced with joblessness, something the earlier generation had not known, and above all, when the threat of Nazism became a never-ending menace and concentration camps loomed in the students' universe.

1900–1930: Generational Equilibrium and the Intercollegiate Socialist Society

The remarkable fact in the history of the American generations is the unusual equilibrium which prevailed for the first thirty years of the twentieth century.[75] Adult revolutionary intellectuals worked hard to found a revolutionary student movement, but their achievement was meager. The widespread labor unrest in the years before 1914 had small impact on the American student. A few were stirred by a back-to-the-people spirit, but no more. As late as 1927, when leading American intellectuals were aroused by the pending execution of Sacco and Vanzetti in Massachusetts, there was small concern on the part of students on campuses. Some petitions were signed and gathered, but there is no record of any massive student demonstration. The protest on behalf of Sacco and Vanzetti was an adult one: Felix Frankfurter, John Dewey, Edna St. Vincent Millay, Heywood Broun, Walter Lippmann were typical names. The adult liberal intellectuals fought hard and unsuccessfully, but no students marched from Harvard, Yale, or City College to do battle by the elders' side.

A handful of young American students were indeed moved by the combination of elitism and populism characteristic of student movements. They sought out the lowliest of the people with whom to identify themselves, and they felt a kinship with the Russian student revolutionaries. Ernest Poole, for instance, went in 1902 from Princeton to the University Settlement on New York's Lower East Side. He had read Tolstoy and Turgenev, and had then been moved by a book on tenement-house life in the Lower East Side—*How the Other Half Lives*. At the settlement house were a group of young men like himself—Walter Weyl, William English Walling, Leroy Scott. Weyl told him, "Make friends with these tenement people and listen, listen all the time. They've got a lot to teach us boys, so for the love of Jesus Christ don't let's be uplifters here."[76] Henry Moskowitz guided them

> to countless cafes, large and small, Russian, Polish, and German cafes, Socialist, Anarchist, free love, freethinker and actor and poet cafes, where coming from the oppression of Europe into the sudden freedom here to argue and shout and write as they pleased, young Jews were burning up their lives in this great furnace of ideas. Over black coffee and cigarettes they would talk fervently half the night and then, after three or four hours' sleep, go to the sweatshops where they worked from dawn till late evening, when again they'd rush for those midnight cafes to plunge into the ferment of new dreams![77]

Another student generation, sixty years later, was to idealize and identify with the Negro, with his speech and ways. This earlier generation felt the same about the Jew: "I watched their faces, scowls and smiles, the flashes in their quick black eyes. I heard their bursts of laughter or loud excited argument. I was learning Yiddish now and caught fragments of their talk. . . ."

Then that first year, Poole met Abraham Cahan, "the first real revolutionist and writer from Russia I'd ever seen. Quickly he became my friend and opened up a Russian world of revolution, books and plays, that stirred me deep. . . ."[78]

It was this settlement group that was especially active in helping found and promote the Intercollegiate Socialist Society. "Quickly we formed group after group in a score or more of colleges," tells Ernest Poole.[79] The Intercollegiate Socialist Society was indeed the first political student movement in American history.

The American student movement, paradoxically enough, was founded by a group of nonstudent adults. This in itself bore witness to the weakness of its roots. Under the leadership of Upton Sinclair, then writing *The Jungle,* ten persons, including the celebrated writer Jack London, the labor lawyer Clarence Darrow, the octogenarian abolitionist Thomas W. Higginson, and the wealthy William English Walling, signed a call to found an Intercollegiate Socialist Society "for the purpose of promoting an intelligent interest in Socialism among college men and women, graduate and undergraduate, through the formation of study clubs in the colleges and universities. . . ."[80] Their first organizational meeting took place on September 1, 1905. An executive committee was elected which had exactly one undergraduate member, Harry W. Laidler of Wesleyan, who was included because another student felt there ought to be at least one student member in the leadership of a student movement. Jack London was unanimously elected president.

The year 1905 was a watershed in the history of the early American student movement, "a propitious time," as Harry Laidler said, for its formation.[81] The reports of the Russian Revolution of 1905 were stirring young people. This was the time when socialism in America was making rapid strides. The Socialist presidential candidate in 1904 had received four hundred thousand votes, four times the number received in 1900. Upton Sinclair within a year was at the pinnacle of fame which *The Jungle* brought, while Jack London was the most picturesque, magnetic, and individualistic character who ever embarked on a proselytizing tour for the student movement. The excitement of the Russian Revolution of 1905 was in the air, and Jack London thrilled to its drama. He felt a brotherhood with the Russian student martyr-assassins. He wrote:

> I am a revolutionist. I speak and I *think,* of these assassins in Russia as "my comrades." So do all the comrades in America, and all the 7,000,000 comrades in the world. Of what worth an organized international, revolutionary movement if our comrades are not backed up the world over! The worth is shown by the fact that we do back up the assassinations by our comrades in Russia. . . . Our comrades in Russia have formed what they call "The Fighting Organization." This Fighting Organization accused, tried, found guilty, and condemned to death, one Sipiaguin, Minister of Interior.[82]

The founder of the Intercollegiate Socialist Society, Upton Sinclair, was still smarting with resentment against his classics professors at City College, who had made Latin and Greek meaningless for him, and against the professor of English, a Tammany appointee, who had taught his subject from the Catholic standpoint; Sinclair was contemptuous of an educational system which had taught him nothing of Kropotkin and Kautsky.[83] He became convinced, as he still wrote in 1922, that "Our educational system today is in the hands of its last organized enemy, which is class greed and selfishness based upon economic privilege. To slay that monster is to set free all the future."

Proud in later years that he was the one man in the class of '97 "who had come to be known throughout the civilized world in less than ten years" though his teachers never would have predicted it, Upton Sinclair knew why the others had failed—"the machine had rolled them flat!"[84] The familiar themes of student leaders resounded in the calls of London and Sinclair, the summons to fight the disabling machine, the system, the monster. The heroes in Jack London's stories were always haunted by a need to prove their masculinity. Now, as the president of the society, London undertook a spectacular speaking tour through the larger universities, from California to Harvard and Yale. Striking in appearance, handsomely dressed in "white flowing silk tie," he addressed the Yale students crowded in Woolsey Hall on the "Present Crisis":

I went to the university. I found the university in the main, practically wholly so, clean and noble, but I did not find the university alive. . . . And the reflection of this university ideal I find—the conservatism and unconcern of the American people toward those who are suffering, who are in want. And so I became interested in an attempt to arouse in the minds of the young men of our universities an interest in the study of Socialism. . . . If collegians cannot fight for us, we want them to fight against us. . . . Raise your voices one way or the other; be alive.

During 1906, socialist groups sprang up at Columbia, Wesleyan, Yale, Harvard, and other colleges.[85] For the next twenty-five years, the Intercollegiate Socialist Society (renamed, after the war, the League for Industrial Democracy) sent out its organizers on nation-wide propagandist missions. But it never succeeded in founding a genuine student movement. The clubs which were organized remained arrested in (what we have called) the "circle" stage of student movements, rarely moving on to issues and back-to-the-people action. Paul Blanshard, able field secretary of the society from 1922 into the depression years, "the world's greatest college trotter" as Harry Laidler called him, explained in 1925 the recalcitrance of American students to participating in student movements:

The twin evils of the modern college world and the chief obstacles to interesting college students in labor conditions are football—which is symbolical of the over-organized life of our college youth—and the diluted culture of salesmanship. College students are more conservative than their professors because they too often regard college as a backdoor to big business. The average college professor in this country is one hundred per cent more revolutionary in his views about industrial democracy than the average laborer, and the professors are not parlor bolshevists either, but genuine scientists.[86]

In short, the American student, far from regarding American business leaders as a de-authoritized group, admired and looked forward to joining them; he regarded the intellectuals as ineffectual, effeminate failures, and his professors as men who had withdrawn from the world. Owen Wister's immensely popular story, *Philosophy 4: A Story of Harvard University*, first published in 1901, probably captured the dominant values of the studentry. Its chief characters, two zestful, unstudious students hold on to their vigor of intellect and originality; twenty years later one has become the treasurer of the New Amsterdam Trust Company and the other the superintendent of passenger traffic of the New York and Chicago Air Lines; the bookish intellectual, on the other hand, the son of the poor immigrant parents, evolves in sorry fashion into a book reviewer for the *Evening Post.*[87]

Though Jack London's lectures were a personal success, insofar as they drew immense audiences, the actual results for the student movement were small. In apocalyptic words, he spoke for the inexorable mandate of history: "Seven million men of the working class say that they are going to get the rest of the working class to join with them. . . . The revolution is here, now. Stop it who can!" When he lectured in January 1906 at the Grand Central Palace in New York, every socialist on the East Coast tried to be there, four to ten thousand of them, but "there were probably not a hundred college students scattered among the thousands of working people."[88] Jack London dreamed and wrote of the young Ph.D. in sociology at Berkeley who went to the San Francisco masses "South of the Slot" and was transformed from a professor into the militant labor leader of the "notorious Cooks' and Waiters' Strike."[89] But almost nothing of the sort happened in real life. The back-to-the-people spirit was relatively feeble among American students. When Anna Strunsky, London's close friend, tried to found a chapter of the I.S.S. at Stanford, she failed: "Ten students were required to make a 'Chapter,' and I could find only two who were willing to study socialism."[90] Thanks to the indefatigable organizers, however, some slow progress was made. By 1907, the national movement had seventy-five members. Six years later, in 1913, the society had sixty-four undergraduate chapters; and by the following year, 1914, the organization as a whole numbered approximately one thousand students, of whom half were not socialists. During a five-month period, reported the organizing secretary in May 1915, he had spoken to more than ten thousand college men and women in more than fifty universities, and given over fifty lectures to economics and sociology classes. The new Vassar chapter, one of the strongest, boasted a paid-up membership of eighty-six. Yet the secretary recognized, in January 1916, that with over 1,300 colleges and universities in the country, and a student population of over 250,000 they had after a decade's work still "a well-nigh unlimited field" before them.[91] The glaring truth was that the student radical movement, after ten years of hard work and with a corps of the ablest young speakers and writers who have ever been enlisted in an American movement, had succeeded in enrolling in its membership one fourth of one per cent of the American studentry. Such was the fruit of the numerous lecture tours and seminars by Walter Lippmann, Jack London, John Spargo, William English Walling, Harry W. Laidler, Florence Kelley.

Though scarcely of basic political significance, the accomplishment of this small student movement was nonetheless real. They helped open the intellectual doors of colleges and universities to new ideas. The Harvard chapter in 1910, led by its president and founder, Walter Lippmann, organized a petition by three hundred students for a course on socialism, which the college then provided.[92] John Reed in 1917 recalled the achievements of the Harvard Socialist Club:

The Club drew up a platform for the Socialist Party in city elections. It had social legislation introduced into the Massachusetts Legislature. Its members wrote articles in the college papers challenging undergraduate ideals, and muckraked the University for not paying its servants living wages, and so forth. Out of the agitation sprang the Harvard Men's League for Women's Suffrage, the Single Tax Club, an Anarchist group. . . . Prominent radicals were invited to Cambridge to lecture. . . . An open forum was started. The result of this movement upon the undergraduate world was potent. All over the place radicals sprang up, in music, painting, poetry, the theatre. The more serious college papers took a socialistic, or at least progressive tinge. Of course all this made no ostensible difference in the look of Harvard society. . . . But it made me, and many others, realize that there was something going on in the dull outside world more thrilling than college activities, and turned our attention to the writings of men like H. G. Wells and Graham Wallas, wrenching us away from the Oscar Wildean dilettantism that had possessed undergraduate littérateurs for generations.[93]

A member of the Williams chapter wrote in 1913, "Two years ago Socialism was tabooed at Williams. It was not to be mentioned; now it is a theme of common talk and discussion. . . . In May we had a debate on Socialism in the economics class and it was with difficulty that the professor could find anyone to uphold the negative."[94]

The student activists of 1910 hoped, however, for much more than a freed classroom and curriculum. Walter Lippmann, Harvard 1910, addressing the fifth convention of the Intercollegiate Socialist Society in December 1913, chose as his theme "Obligations of I.S.S. Members after Graduation."[95] Socialist students after their graduation, he urged, should then work to realize the socialist philosophy in the economic and political life of America. Lippmann's youthful hopes were soon nullified by realities, though a distinguished minority did cling for varying periods to their socialist faith.

And here we are confronted once again by the basic question: Was the influence of the student socialist movement from 1900 to 1930 a healthy one on the political lives of its members? The evidence strongly suggests that the intense activity of the student circle tended to alienate its members from American life and realities. The most distinguished figures, in order to make their most significant adult contribution, had not only to outgrow but to overcome their fixation in the ideology of generational revolt. Paul H. Douglas, for instance, of Bowdoin 1913, chairman in 1914 of the Columbia chapter of the I.S.S., later chairman of its New England

Committee, as a young instructor in economics at the University of Illinois urged students to get their faculty to join,[96] and to beware of the "Washington Square attitude"; he began a long association with third-party sects which persisted for many years while he was professor of economics at Chicago. It was in this spirit that he longed to see, and persuaded himself in 1928 that he saw, something of a socialistic millennium in the Soviet Union.[97] With the passage of years, he became one of the most distinguished United States senators, contributing to notable legislative reforms, and was for a while in the 1950s the favorite presidential candidate of his colleagues. Probably his contribution to American life was diminished by his earlier activism. Another example was Walter Lippmann, who was president in 1910 of the Harvard Socialist Club, and in 1917 still looked to socialism as the solution to the problem of war.[98] His friends used to toast him as the future president of the United States, and indeed he was generally recognized by a variety of persons, from Theodore Roosevelt to Graham Wallas, as the most acute political analytical intelligence of his generation in the United States. One gathers that his student socialist loyalties separated him for some crucial years from the main current of American existence; he was then cast in the role of sideline coach, adviser, and commentator, critical intellectual rather than man of creative leadership, for which he evidently had all the powers.

That the mood of the I.S.S. was largely one of generational uprising is brought home in the vivid narrative that its founder, Upton Sinclair, wrote in *The Goose-Step* of the travails of American students and professors. Seventeen years after the founding, Sinclair still retained the psychology of the student activist. As a nonstudent agitator among students, he embodied the culture of generational revolt. It was a struggle, he wrote, between the League of Youth and the League of the Old Men:

> I have shown you the League of the Old Men, suppressing thought and wrecking the world; and now here is the answer—the League of Youth! The Old Men were raised in the old order, their thinking is bound by its limitations. But we, the youth of the world, live in a new age, and have new problems to deal with. We cannot well do worse than our elders have done; we may very well easily do better. Since we have longer to live in this world than our elders, we have surely the right to save it, if we can![99]

Like the Berkeley students several generations later, Sinclair denounced the American college as a "factory" run on the principles of business: "I have compared Columbia and Minnesota to department stores and Clark and Johns Hopkins to Ford factories; and in so doing I was not merely calling names, but making a diagnosis."[100] These were typical themes of the generational struggle as it sought to merge itself with the class struggle.

There were Americans during this time who wished that American students were more like the Russians. Albert Edwards recalled nostalgically how, when he was in Russia in 1906 and 1907, "politics were certainly the principal preoccupation of the student body. In fact most of them were on strike. And it was a strike with 'sabotage.' . . . They had decided to get a constitution for their country rather than degrees for themselves. . . . A dream that ended blindfolded before the firing squad or . . . in some forgotten prison."[101] In Russia, Edwards had known intimately a circle of twelve such students; now in 1913 only two were alive and free, five had been "shot at sunrise. All at different times—alone," two had died in prison, and "the rest are waiting for death." The author concluded admiringly, "Russian students are a serious lot. They can't understand our interest in athletics." The same complaint was voiced by the president of the Chicago student chapter, who contrasted his fellow-students unfavorably with those of Warsaw. While the Chicago students, he said, were interested in no social or spiritual question, "outside of matters relating to baseball and football," the Warsaw studentry not only participated in the social and intellectual life but, he wrote, "moulds and partially leads it." "The majority of the Chicago students take the American business man's viewpoint of life and learning," he said.[102] Until they graduate, they are happy to regard themselves as "mere school boys and school girls." In short, the ideological generational struggle was singularly absent from the American campus. Can we imagine, wrote the author, people calling the police to investigate the University of Chicago for alleged radicalism? The Russian government was honoring its universities in this way all the time.

The complaint about the contentedness of the American student was taken up again and again by would-be leaders of radical student movements—that is, of generational revolt. Jessica Smith observed the tragic phenomenon that students, far from seeking to identify with labor, were actually ready to act as strikebreakers:

> But American students have the opinions of old men—the old men who control the distribution alike of wealth and ideas. They remain aloof in their narrow academic universe, and are only occasionally roused to action through hysterical propaganda. Thus we have the shameful phenomenon of American students breaking strikes. This very year, for example, students earned nine dollars a day pin money, thereby preventing trained railroad workers from securing an increase to a much lower wage.[103]

The emotional dynamic of the would-be American student leaders was in essential respects similar to that of the Russian student leaders. But in America their mood was exceptional among the studentry, among whom they encountered a basic generational equilibrium. American students did not worship assassins, nor were they often moved by inner guilt to dedicate themselves to the lowliest. Consequently, the small American student movement remained fixated in its "circle stage"; it was always nascent, but rarely crescive. Selig Perlman, later the author of *Theory of the Labor Movement*, and one of the few alumni of both the American and Russian student circles, observed their identity of spirit: "When I first came to

Wisconsin, sixteen years ago, I immediately joined the socialist club and I found that the intellectual intercourse in that club was a direct continuation of my experience with similar socialist study circles, to which I belonged when a student in Russia."[104] But there the similarity ended. In America the circle remained generally a "Social Problems Club," reaching ordinarily "a small fraction of the college body."[105] Even at the City College of New York, the center for the sons of immigrant, working-class, Russian and Polish Jews, this was the usual extent of the "student movement" for many years. A "fine year's work" for the year 1920 meant "an imposing array of speakers": Fiorello La Guardia, Judge Parker, editors Don Seitz and Oswald Garrison Villard, with audiences of six hundred.[106]

The outbreak of the First World War practically terminated all the activities of socialist student circles.[107] Organizing efforts of the Intercollegiate Socialist Society resumed, however, after the war. The climate of discussion remained free despite the strains of the postwar years, with only rare interference from College authorities. In response to a questionnaire of the society among students and professors in November 1919, thirteen out of fifteen colleges in the Middle Atlantic States "declared emphatically that students were free to organize."[108] Much the same was true in the other regions of the United States; freedom to speak and discuss in one's own organizations was generally recognized. The outstanding exceptions were the City College of New York, where some speakers such as John Reed were forbidden, and the University of California, which denied the chance to speak, among others, to Upton Sinclair.

One personality emerged out of the decade 1910–1920 who during the thirties became a symbol for the Communist student movement; that was John Reed. When his old friend, Walter Lippmann, having become an editor of the newly founded *New Republic* in 1914, was trying to disengage himself from the mentality of the politics of generational revolt, he wrote a powerful essay which was also a self-analysis, called "Legendary John Reed." Both men were still in their mid-twenties. Lippmann in effect probed all the themes of generational politics: the self-destructive element, the romantic quest, the identification with the lowliest, the attraction to the foreign, the anti-American, the sordid, the propensity for violence. By contrast, Lippmann was summoning his generation, just four years out of Harvard, to responsibility and the long haul. Lippmann had already written Reed that when the latter would have burned himself out in the radical movement, he, Lippmann, would still be doing useful work.[109] "Legendary John Reed" tried to get at the fatal flaws in the political behavior of generational revolt: "Though he is only in his middle twenties and but five years out of Harvard, there is a legend of John Reed." He had been the "most inspired song and cheer leader that the football crowd had had for many days." He had been something of an exhibitionist, and the "club men" didn't like him. "Even as an undergraduate, he betrayed what many people believe to be the central passion of his life, an inordinate desire to be arrested." He had been jailed in England, France, Spain, and New Jersey. The magazine *Masses* advertised him as its "jail editor." He rejected altogether what later was called the Establishment; he regarded all capitalists as "fat, bald, and unctuous," all reformers as "cowardly," all newspapers as "corrupt," and all moderate socialists and union leaders as a "fraud on labor." He idealized the workingman as "a fine, statuesque giant who stands on a high hill facing the sun. . . . He talked with intelligent tolerance about dynamite." He became wildly enthusiastic about Pancho Villa and the Mexicans as "real people" (as a later generation was to become about Fidel Castro and the Cubans). He wrote back to us, said Lippmann, "that if the United States intervened to stop the revolution he would fight on Villa's side." "He did not judge, he identified himself with the struggle. . . . Revolution, literature, poetry, they are only things which hold him at times, incidents merely of his living. . . . He is the only fellow I know who gets himself pursued by men with revolvers. . . . Reed is one of the intractables, to whom the organized monotony and virtue of our civilization are unbearable." He rejected the rational arguments of a Lippmann

> Who wants the human race and me
> March to a geometric Q. E. D.[110]

This was the portrait of the eternal rebel, the man fixated in generational rebellion, and it was a direction which Lippmann carefully defined in his friend so as not to take it himself.

Walter Lippmann was not wrong in his perception of his friend.

In 1917, Jack Reed, approaching the age of thirty—the watershed of youth—wrote a private confession, which with rare candor illuminated the motifs of the person who chooses to express his generational revolt in political action. "Almost Thirty" confirmed all that his friend Walter had said. Reed described the guilt and the search which followed his Harvard days: "All I know is that my happiness is built on the misery of other people, that I eat because others go hungry, that I am clothed when other people go almost naked through the frozen cities in winter; and that fact poisons me, disturbs my serenity, makes me write propaganda when I would rather play." He went looking for an identification. He immersed himself in the emotions of the Paterson strike. Such men as Bill Haywood attracted him by the way in which they embodied violence and revolt. Disillusionment with the people, however, haunted him: "I am not sure any more that the working class is capable of revolution, peaceful or otherwise." The search continued; he was always ready to regain his illusions with a new identification; Pancho Villa in Mexico was next. John Reed needed the proximity of death. "When I first crossed the border deadliest fear gripped me. I was afraid of death, of mutilation. . . . But a terrible curiosity urged me on; I felt I *had to know* how I would act under fire, how I would get along with these primitive folks at war. . . . I made good with these wild fighting men." And yet, he confessed, "In thinking it over, I find little in my thirty years that I can hold to."[111] At this point the document ends. A few months later Reed found a new identification and locus for revolt in the Bolshevik Revolution. Russia gave him a new illusion, then disillusionment, and death. He had indeed burned himself out. The politics of generational revolt partake of the ephemeral quality of the youthful athlete. Of John Reed, buried with honor in the Kremlin, one might recite the lines of A. E. Housman's "To an Athlete Dying Young":

Smart lad, to slip betimes away
From fields where glory does not stay,
And early though the laurel grows
It withers quicker than the rose.*

Lenin with cold realism didn't want to give Jack Reed more than five minutes of his time.

The twenties too were an era of generational equilibrium which saw almost no political unrest on the campuses. No student movement, as we have seen, took up the cause of Sacco and Vanzetti in 1927. There were poorly attended meetings of protest called by socialist, liberal, and social problems clubs; some signatures on petitions were collected; but there was no single incident of massive protest by students. In May 1927, when tension over the Sacco-Vanzetti case had been mounting for several months, the *News-Bulletin* of the League for Industrial Democracy reviewed the activities that Spring of its chapter and affiliates in twenty-three colleges and universities, including Columbia, Chicago, Cornell, Michigan, Illinois, Minnesota, and Haverford. Out of at least ninety-one meetings which had been held, only three had been devoted to the Sacco-Vanzetti case. A small discussion group at Oberlin, a meeting at the University of Chicago and one at Yale—this was the sum total of reported involvement of the American student movement in the issues of the Sacco-Vanzetti case. The favorite subjects at meetings were the British Labour party, the situation in China, and Norman Thomas's "Why I Am a Socialist."[112] Activity was all in the discussion circle stage, not the stage for involvement and action. Generational revolt was not in the air.

Students everywhere went about their usual work. They were not the "striking force" of the intellectual class at the time of the Sacco-Vanzetti case. The quiescence of the students at this time is indeed evidence for the hypothesis that unless a generational resentment has been intensified by some de-authoritization of the older generation, unless generational struggle is thus brought to a level of stress and strain, a massive student movement will not arise. This was still a time, as the head of the Swarthmore

* A. E. Housman, "To an Athlete Dying Young," from " A Shrophire Lad," authorised edition, from *The Collected Works of A. E. Housman*. By permission of The Society of Authors, London, and Holt, Rinehart and Winston, Inc., New York. Copyright © 1939, 1940, © 1959 by Holt, Rinehart and Winston, Inc. Copyright © 1967, 1968 by Robert E. Symons.

chapter reported in 1927, when "the faculty is incomparably more interested in public questions than the student body."

There was some sporadic action on college campuses in the mid-twenties against compulsory Reserve Officers' Training Corps (R.O.T.C.) courses, but it never reached the proportions of involvement of a student movement. The mid-twenties were a time of a pacifist reaction against the First World War; such motion pictures as *The Big Parade* were attracting large, appreciative audiences. At the City College of New York in the fall of 1925, the editor-in-chief of *The Campus,* Felix S. Cohen, chose Armistice Day for the beginning of a campaign against compulsory R.O.T.C. The appeal was strictly on pacifist grounds. Cohen reprinted in the editorial columns several excerpts from the *Manual of Military Training* which appealed to the savagery of soldiers: "The inherent desire to fight and kill must be carefully watched for and encouraged by the instructor." The editorial attracted much attention, and soon the training manual was withdrawn from use. Then the City College students declared themselves in a referendum by a vote of 2,092 to 345, as opposed to compulsory military training.[113] The president of the college ordered *The Campus* to desist from further editorials on the subject; Cohen responded by publishing three blank columns, draped in black, as his muted editorial protest. Within a year, the faculty voted to make the course in military science optional. This episode awoke a great deal of interest in the United States. It represented the first entry of City College students, who were largely Jewish and children of immigrants, into the national political arena. A national movement as such, however, never emerged. This episode was a portent of the bitter student angers which arose in the thirties. The *New York World* observed with some exaggeration at the end of 1926 that a "student revolt" was taking place against stupid courses, abridgement of free speech, the cheap commercialism of endowment drives, the official interpretations of American history, and against the R.O.T.C.[114] Against the background of the prosperity and expansion of the Coolidge era, one could detect some slight signals of generational discontent. Basically, however, the elder generation was in full moral confidence and control. The City College episode was primarily a revolt of Jewish students, ambivalent concerning their own parental traditions and rebelling against college authorities who often regarded them as undesirable aliens.

The Communist *New Masses* scanned the student scene in its very first issue, in May 1926, for some signs of a student uprising.[115] It perceived the American colleges, as had Upton Sinclair and Jack London twenty years before, as dominated by the War Department, Babbitt, the Church, and the dry-as-dust Ph.D. It took heart, however, from rallying forces which were in the making; students were criticizing courses and curricula, and rebelling against compulsory chapel and compulsory drill. "Overwhelming evidence of a new adventurousness is creeping into the college press," it said; "a revolt of learners" was in the offing. Much more typical, however, was the situation which Dwight Macdonald has described: "At Yale I looked with bored amusement on the earnest handful who struggled to keep alive the Liberal Club—there were no campus Marxists in those pre-depression days, at least I never heard of any."[116] Macdonald's generational revolt was limited to nonideological objectives: a letter against compulsory chapel, a demand by the lower classmen that they share the seniors' privilege of not wearing a hat on the campus, and criticism of the professor in the new Shakespeare course. It was an era not unlike the America of 1885. The basic generational equilibrium was marred only in the later twenties by peripheral episodes. The early thirties, however, brought Nazism, the growing threat of war, and the depression. New anxieties, new resentments, new forces affected American students, arousing some nation-wide student actions.

The Movement of the Thirties

GENESIS OF THE MOVEMENT: TO THE HARLAN MINERS

Despite its varied activities and the immense publicity it aroused, the American student movement in the thirties was relatively small in numbers. At the height of its strength in 1939, the American Student Union claimed twenty thousand members; of these, says Robert W. Iversen, "perhaps 12,000 were paid up and the remainder were delinquent or simply sympathizers."[117] Actually, the figure was much smaller. Student officers at this time were notoriously evasive, even with their friends, when asked about the size of the actual membership.

The onset of the depression gave to the small circles of radical students the opportunity for evolving into a movement of populist enthusiasm and action. In the spring of 1932, a group of students, mostly from New York, engaged in a back-to-the-people gesture which dramatized their desire to found a new student movement. About eighty students left in chartered buses for Harlan County, Kentucky, to bring aid and sustenance to striking miners. Compared to the several thousands of Russian students who went back to the people in 1874, at a time when the total Russian studentry was about five thousand, the American bus contingent was a minuscule gesture.[118] It attracted wide attention, however, for its drama of youthful idealism and concern.

The students were coming forth as the conscience of the country, superseding the old, as they proclaimed their pilgrimage to Harlan, Kentucky. On March 23, 1932, the students' bus, with its New York activists and a handful from Harvard, Smith, Cincinnati, and Tennessee, departed from the campus of Columbia University. Self-consciously in revolt against older generation liberals, the group anticipated bloodshed and the possible sacrifice of their own lives. As one participant wrote a friend shortly before the bus departed, "Next Friday has meaning to me now, though in the light of X's romanticism, I may not be alive next Friday."[119] The Harlan action was the first of a newly formed organization, the National Student League, expressing the new radicalism of the new generation. Its members differentiated themselves from the tired veterans of the twenties in the League for Industrial Democracy. As a leading participant described it:

The Columbia Social Problems Club has started a rebellion against the L.I.D. because of the latter's pink-ribbon tactics. They have succeeded in forming a strong nucleus of college clubs, called the National Students League, which graduation may destroy, but which at present is very active. Easter 150 of us are going down to Harlan: the original purposes were: 1) to bring in food and clothing, 2) to focus publicity, 3) to diffuse publicity throughout the country since this will be an intercollegiate caravan. . . . I suspect we'll find our caravan of cars and trucks blocked on some narrow Kentucky road, but I don't think we'll return looking sheepish. Y and I are going in the Columbia delegation. The expenses will be $20 a person, but at Columbia it seems to be easy to raise funds for that sort of thing. They're allowed to canvas the classes and dormitories.

Even the older generation liberals could not forbear financing idealistic youth; they couldn't say no, and perhaps envied the apparent moral call of the youth:

I went up to Professor Edman and told him I wanted him to contribute to sending me down. He disapproves completely, thinks it a foolhardy expedition, but says he: "X, if you wanted to hear Mozart I'd give you five dollars to do so; since you want to do this I'll give you five dollars, but I do not approve of your adventure." . . . His greatest worry in this business is that one of us shouldn't get killed. He really has a lot of feeling for his students.

The students went in expectation of violent conflict:

I don't want to prophesy about the trip. One hundred and fifty students will not be as easily cowed as eight or ten writers; and I don't think we'll sublimate abrogations of our constitutional privileges, so unless the faculty men keep us well under control I see no reason why there shouldn't be a fight. We're not going down to provoke the sheriff but most of us are impressed with the seriousness of the venture from a historical point of view. Mr. Tyndall of the English Dept. thinks I shall return with a broken head. Should the same happen to Y, you can be my executor and have my books.[120]

On the jolting bus ride to Kentucky, there was the usual youthful singing and comradeship—for students in a student movement always sing. The generational comradeship cut across sectarian divisions. From the bus in Tennessee came another letter: "I have never seen a finer or more intelligent set of Communists than those with whom we traveled. Not only our songs harmonized, but they even listened sympathetically to X's plea for a united proletarian movement that would utilize socialist tactics where the class struggle was not sharp enough or effective to stress."[121]

The sense of being a historical elite, bringing victory to the otherwise defeated miners, was joined with the back-to-the-people spirit, the need for self-sacrifice, and a confident belief in the moral superiority of the younger generation, all experienced as unique to itself. This emotional amalgam accompanied the birth of this American student movement.

REVOLT AGAINST THE LIBERALS OF THE ELDER GENERATION

It was characteristic of the small American student movement, as of others, that its participants felt resentment toward the liberal leaders of the older generation and tried to discredit them as far as possible. Walter Lippmann, for instance, was portrayed as a fallen idol, a thinker whose career "revealed the subtle influences that remold the vigorous, radical thinker into a dangerous defender of the established order."[122] The movement tried to depict the Old Liberals as fools, knaves, or morally corrupt. Every incident in which an older person refused to come forward to defend the deeds of a young militant was officially interpreted by the student movement as casting doubt on the older man's integrity. When Reed Harris, editor of the *Columbia Spectator*, was expelled in April 1932 for a long series of "discourtesies, innuendoes, and misrepresentations" toward the university, a large student protest took place. But the faculty, wrote James Wechsler, was reticent in a way in "which the strike participants will never forget." Only one of them, shortly to lose his post, supported the "walkout." "When John Dewey was approached for aid, he said that he 'knew nothing about it'—a rebuff which some of his disciples bitterly remembered." The professors kept "an almost hushed silence," deplored "hasty action," and cited "loyalty to the dean," according to the indignant young Wechsler.[123]

When a Columbia professor of history in 1933 described to his class how the United States had entered the First World War, "the class hissed with a beautiful spontaneity. It was a remarkable and inspiring demonstration," wrote young student Wechsler to his elder brother.[124] At the City College, when twenty-one students were expelled after the so-called "umbrella" clash with the president, the older generation of liberal professors, Morris R. Cohen, Harry A. Overstreet, William Bradley Otis, were denounced for their capitulation to authority:

> The City College faculty had always enjoyed a reputation for liberalism. . . . Yet when the College was precipitated into the seething cauldron of administrative despotism, all the liberals executed a complete about-face. Men who had but recently proclaimed their independence, men who had but recently walked in the pure atmosphere of freedom and personal integrity, now refused to lift a hand in protest while the fetters of a reactionary administration were being fastened upon them. They could not pass the test, these liberals. A critical moment demanded their decision. And placing their jobs above their intellectual honesty, they capitulated. The liberal tradition was utterly obliterated

and displaced by the sycophancy and lackeyism manifested by the faculty. . . . Men like Professor Morris R. Cohen began to invoke the time-honored criticism of student uprisings. Young men should be polite, should behave like gentlemen. Boys, you should not break the rules even if they are designed to prevent you from registering your protest. Liberalism had lacked the courage to withstand the wave of reaction instigated by an administration which had sacrificed justice and ordinary decency at the shrine of Tammany saber-rattling patriotism.[125]

Socialist sentiment became widespread in the colleges in the early 1930s. New York's colleges led the way in the renaissance of unrest. At Columbia in 1932, with two-thirds of the student body voting, Norman Thomas was a decisive victor, receiving 421 votes to 307 for Herbert Hoover, while Franklin D. Roosevelt trailed with only 221. William Z. Foster, the Communist candidate, received only twenty-one votes. In the poll for the university as a whole, Thomas had 1,033, Hoover 833, Roosevelt 547, and Foster eighty-one.[126] The same was true at the more lower-class, "proletarian" City College where Norman Thomas was the overwhelming choice of the students in 1932, receiving twice as many votes as Roosevelt.[127] Franklin D. Roosevelt was regarded as the candidate of the party whose last president, Woodrow Wilson, had betrayed his idealism and his nation by going to war. The "betrayal" of 1917 was seized upon as the issue for generational resentment, even as Nazi student youth at the same time was assailing liberals and social democrats for their alleged "stab in the back," the "betrayal" of 1918 ending the war.

The *Student Review,* the organ of the Communist National Student League, made the liberals a chief target for ridicule and denunciation. A conference on students in politics was reported by Joseph Starobin: "The afternoon was devoted to a monologue by the philosopher M. R. Cohen on 'the Good life,' and a riproaring militant speech by Reinhold Niebuhr, largely an attack upon the Communist Party."[128]

The figure of Morris R. Cohen attracted the special bitterness of the New York student movement. For Cohen above all symbolized their fathers; he, like them, was a Russian Jewish immigrant, speaking English with a Yiddish accent and a Talmudic intonation, and his idiom was of the East Side. He was the first of the fathers to have won recognition in the American academic and liberal world. In an atmosphere of generational conflict, he tended therefore to become the surrogate object for vehement attack.

The student leaders during the formative years of their movement in the thirties looked with a supercilious, even contemptuous regard upon the Roosevelt administration and its liberal tinkerings with capitalism. How ridiculous or corrupt it seemed to them not to acknowledge that the old order was dying, and that a new world was being born! They imposed on their perception and analysis of social events a generational a priori—they projected their own revolt as the inner mechanism and striving in society. A well-known nonstudent leader in the American Student Union was filled with this mood as he described his first meeting with Eleanor Roosevelt:

I was in Washington last week for the national council meeting of the American Youth Congress. Was one of the five chosen to have tea with Mrs. Roosevelt. She's a good woman utterly lacking in knowledge of social forces and systems and why good men are helpless without organizations. She thinks she can reform capitalists by inviting them to the White House for dinner and a good talking-to. I'm convinced she's opposed to fascism, and that she as well as her husband would go much further if they felt they'd have support. But every time they take an even mildly progressive stand they antagonize some group or other within the Democratic party which in their view it is important to hold together at all costs in order to insure re-election and other legislation which is not progressive. It was a pleasant tea. We stayed for two hours. We had little cream puffs and were waited upon by butlers. I lectured her for about twenty minutes about the sharecropper situation and her answer was ghastly. She claimed to know all about it, but was helpless because the senators from Arkansas were "medieval" in their outlook. She said that perhaps the only remedy for the situation was bloodshed, but as Thomas said when I repeated the tale to him, "the planters have all the modern shooting weapons." She was always sympathetic but helpless or sure that education alone would provide the solution.[129]

Unlike its predecessors from 1905 to 1930, the student movement of the thirties was from its inception drawn to orthodox Marxism as its ideology. For this there were three principal reasons. First, the unparalleled intensity of the depression, which affected many of the students' families and made the increasing misery of the proletariat an observable everyday fact rather than a doubtful economic thesis; class struggles were erupting everywhere, among seamen, miners, automobile workers, steel workers. Second, the menace of Nazism, and the collapse of liberal socialist governments in the face of it, betokened a collapse of a soft elder generation, and a historical warning that a tougher, more uncompromising doctrine and psychology would be required to withstand and conquer the Nazis. Third, the Soviet Union, by contrast to the capitalist world, seemed to be going from one economic success to another; here was a land too where all the ethnic peoples lived in harmony; the October Revolution had shown the way.

The leaders of the student movement tried therefore to analyze their own generational revolt in terms of a Marxist economic primacy. Years later, James Wechsler still warned against the pitfalls of what he called a "psychological determinism" in the study of student movements: "If we are to say that American radicalism can invariably be traced to the dropping of some babies on their heads by careless handlers, we are on the road to a psychological determinism as rigid as the Marxist 'inevitabilities.' By this dogma, ideas and ethics are deprived of any independent validity," he wrote.[130] Yet his reminiscences were testimony to the degree to which the emotions of generational revolt, rather than realistic perception and rational analysis, shaped the responses of the radical student movement. The movement of the thirties having begun with a de-authoritization of the liberals, Wechsler recalls:

The liberals had had their chance, from the time of Teddy Roosevelt through Wilson's New Freedom and the lost-cause adventure of Bob LaFollette, Sr., and the feverish efforts of all the reformers in cities scattered from coast to coast. And where were we now? The trust-busters had had their day but they had never dared to go far enough; the reformers had had a few big innings but invariably lost the ball game; the idealists had merchandised a war to enthrone freedom on earth and Versailles had ended all that. All the noblest strivings of the best spirits had come to naught because they couldn't beat the "system." . . . We inherited a wasteland crowded with hollow men.

A liberal like Franklin D. Roosevelt aroused no enthusiasm in 1932 among activist students:

Franklin D. Roosevelt was the candidate of the party whose last President was held responsible for the betrayal of idealism. There were few among us, faculty or students, who doubted that the war had symbolized the treachery and failure of our civilization. It is one of the extraordinary aspects of that time that Wilson's name meant little more to us than that. The "New Freedom" had a hollow sound; it was the primer of liberal failure. We were reading Dos Passos, Hemingway and Remarque. Wilson was the real villain in all the horror stories that bared the cruelty and waste of war.

The favorite terms of the generational a priori, the categories of its perception of liberals, were "betrayal," "hollow men," "insincere"; the liberals were the impotent, unmasculine fathers, who for all the good intentions they once had, had proved to lack manliness. The "system" had to be fought; the whole heritage of the elder generation had to be uprooted.

At Columbia University, Nicholas Murray Butler was turned into the symbol of the elder generation under attack. Twenty years later the former student leader on the Morningside Heights campus pondered the generational skirmishes and forays of that time:

The scenes he [N. M. B.] encountered on the campus in the first years of the thirties must have been baffling and painful to him. The hubbub was incessant; he was forever being picketed, whether it was because of the inadequacy of wages paid employees in the Teachers' College dining halls or the expulsion of a dissident. He in turn lamented the bad manners of modern youth and was promptly rebuked for suggesting that we who were about to die should lower our voices.

There were good men around, far better than I had humility or perception to recognize at the time.[131]

A few years later, the *Student Advocate*, the organ of the American Student Union, devoted a whole series of articles to "Academic Napoleons," appropriate symbols of the imperial tyranny of the older generation, Ruthven of Michigan, Moore of U.C.L.A., Butler of Columbia, Bowman of Pittsburgh, Colligan of Hunter, Marvin of George Washington.[132] Directing missiles at stuffed shirts, unravelling their stodginess, timidities, equivocations, was a favorite sport of the student movement; it was all in the tradition of generational satire of authorities, though in 1936 and 1937 it had an ideological theme.

The need to picket perpetually was the hallmark of generational protest. New issues were always found to provide the *causa belli* of generational guerrilla action. Old issues were revived, as the archives showed that Butler had evidently ousted faculty members during the World War, had denied that child labor existed in America, and regarded "capitalism" as a "debating term invented by Karl Marx."

In the very early thirties, the de-authoritization of Wilsonian liberal idealism was a significant theme. As the thirties went on, this was replaced by a new de-authoritization of the liberals, owing to their failure to stand up to the Nazis. The American student movement, for the most part, felt that only the Communists would really fight the Nazis; the liberal fathers were too weak.

Twenty years later, many former radicals reexamined their youthful motives in testimony to congressional committees. Again and again one finds in their autobiographical accounts that it was this sense of the Nazi threat and the liberal weakness which, far more than the depression, moved young activists. The leading member of the National Student League at Harvard in 1933, a graduate student who had witnessed the rise of Hitlerism in Germany, returned home "considerably distressed," resolved to work against fascism. He did not even mention the economic impact of the terrible depression years as he told a congressional committee of his motivations.[133] A young physicist recalled that "in the late 1930's it appeared to many people that it was the Communists who were putting up the strongest and perhaps the only successful fight against the growing fascism in Europe."[134] Another young instructor in chemistry in 1938 joined the Communist cell at the Massachusetts Institute of Technology because, he said, of "a feeling of inner rage at the situation in Europe in which nazism was rampant—I am of Jewish extraction—I felt that personally somewhat deeply."[135] The economic depression was not the primary formative experience, although those who referred to the unemployment of the thirties did so in the context of a belief that liberal government would fail to solve the problem.[136] They were prepared to overlook, belittle, or repress the political facts concerning the linkage of the Communist party to Soviet totalitarianism. The attraction to communism was not confined to students of the humanities and social sciences. Young instructors and students of science also felt a strong inclination to embrace Marxism and communism, and to join student movements. A professor of physical chemistry at M.I.T. tried to explain it in intellectual terms as an extension of the scientific attitude:

> A relatively large number of scientists joined the Communist Party partly because their training and activity make it natural for them to do so. A scientist, by nature, is a radical person. He is inclined to question everything, to revolt against that which he thinks the present facts are . . . and it is my belief that the most radical of the natural scientists or of scientists are probably the mathematicians. . . . I believe the physicists are a close second, and the chemists and biologists and so forth would bring up the rear.[137]

But the fact of the matter is that the overwhelming majority of American scientists remained conventional in their political and economic views.[138] The unconventional ones were meek and unquestioning in the face of party authorities. Only where a spirit of emotional revolt, derived from other sources, supervened, was there the tendency to link oneself to student and radical movements; and then authoritarian dictatorship was accepted, since it satisfied aggressive needs. Such scientists, as the M.I.T. professor described them, were then "more prone to go into an unpopular organization such as the Communist Party in an attempt to find out what it is all about." This motivation to join an unpopular organization for its own sake, and to describe it as a matter of scientific curiosity, was precisely part of a spirit of generational revolt in displaced form. An unpopular organization may be defined as one which one's father wouldn't have joined.

ECONOMIC MISERY, THE WAR MACHINE, AND GENERATIONAL CONFLICT

At the outset, the National Student League, as a Marxist-Communist organization, thought that it should begin with the economic basis of student existence, and campaign to better students' welfare. The *Student Review*, in March 1933, at the height of the depression, declared:

> Students are starving! Every day we receive numerous reports from campuses located in various parts of the country relating the same tale.[139] "Students here subsist on one meal a day. . . . Students destitute . . . live on crackers and milk for weeks." . . . On the whole the reaction of the student body has been one of passive acquiescence to their "fate."

With the Soviet model as its alleged guide, and Marxism as its ideology, the *Student Review* called for free board and stipends for students, on the order of those which it said the Soviet Union provided. "The working class has shown the way!" it declared, and it called on its members to "organize mass struggles around concrete specific demands for immediate cash relief through governmental and academic channels for needy students." But leaders, membership, and students at large never became deeply concerned with activities to improve students' economic conditions. Instead, it was the attack on the "war machine" which mostly absorbed their energies. The student movement, for all its Marxism, thus parted company with the labor movement. Labor, especially with the formation of the Committee for Industrial Organization in 1934, was aiming especially to organize the unorganized mass industries and to secure higher wages and shorter hours. It was in a political alliance with the Roosevelt administration, and relatively indifferent to questions of foreign policy. The student movement, both Communist and socialist, for all the economic hardship of the period, turned to warring against university administrators and the R.O.T.C.[140]

At the City College in New York economic misery was especially acute, but the student movement followed the typical channel of generational protest. A City College Communist student leader in 1933 described the extent of his fellows' misery:

> None of the students come from wealthy homes. Now things are getting worse. I have known students in my classes who ran up enormous absence records because they couldn't get carfare to come to school. There are many who go to classes hungry. The extent of unemployment among parents must be startling. Most of the students either work or look for work. Many of them are forced to see that the future holds no promise of revolutionary comfort.

He observed, however, that the "group of radicalized students is only a minority."[141] The minority, however, was shortly galvanized by an incident which became a curious symbol of generational conflict.

The president of the City College was Frederick B. Robinson, a successful man, calculating rather than generous, with an administrative cast of mind, and a confirmed advocate of capitalism. He became for the City College student movement the embodiment of all they warred against. He encountered the activist students on May 29, 1933. On that day they acted with aplomb to interfere with the college's annual Charter Day observance. A review of the cadets' corps by the president and invited guests was scheduled to take place at Lewisohn Stadium. When classes were dismissed at noon, "anti-war protesters and sympathizers" tried to hold protest meetings and stage picket lines one block away from the stadium entrance, but were dispersed by the police. Then they began to use force. "The picketers attempted to enter the Stadium at the Amsterdam Avenue entrance but were not successful until about fifteen minutes later when the gate was forced and about 200 entered." Detectives, however, pursued them and forced them out. The students next convened near an adjoining building, Townsend Harris Hall, where more speeches were made. Then the president, several army officers, including a general and colonel, and several Daughters of the American Revolution were espied approaching the stadium. The account of the students' defense committee continues:

> At the sight of the group, the students raised derisive shouts, and jeered and booed the party. Highly indignant and enraged, Dr. Robinson took four paces to the middle of the street, and layed about him with his umbrella, handle protruding. At first the students were astonished, but soon the president was seized and held.[142]

Detectives rushed to the rescue. Thirty-one students were subsequently expelled or suspended by the unanimous action of a faculty committee.

An atmosphere of repression and generational mistrust settled over the campus. "After the 'Umbrella Attack,' City College became an armed camp. Police cars patrolled it at all times. Stool pigeons were all around. Riot cars came racing down the avenues. Students in groups were in danger of having their names taken down by detectives."[143]

The president of the City College was, of course, caricatured throughout the country by activist students and radicals for his use of an umbrella against the students. Versions of the affair varied. One newspaper account had it that the president "was set upon by a milling crowd of pacifist students rioting in protest of the drill and review of the College's R.O.T.C. Dr. Robinson laid about himself valiantly, using his umbrella as a weapon, but was powerless to withstand the yelling crowd of students." This version was substantively accepted by Professor Iversen in his comprehensive *The Communists and the Schools:* "The N.S.L. surged forward to block his path, whereupon he proceeded to hack his way through the jeering throng with his umbrella."[144] The Communist students' version, however, was that the president had left the sidewalk to attack the students. All agree, in any event, that students pinioned his hands and wrenched the umbrella away.[145] The account of the student defense committee, according to which the president encountered the crowd after only four steps, indicates that they had certainly pressed forward close to the party.

More significant are the exaggerated interpretations which the student activists attached to this miserable occurrence. Adam Lapin, secretary-elect of the student council, later Washington correspondent of the *Daily Worker,* wrote shortly afterward:

> There is no describing the anger and resentment of the students. In that brief moment their relation to the administration became clear. For years the radicals had maintained that the administration and the war department worked hand in hand. But when Dr. Robinson hit the students over the head with an umbrella, he betrayed his solidarity with the war-makers. That was unmistakable language.[146]

Significantly, the single most famous student article written during this period was from its first words a document of utter generational revolt. "My Father Is a Liar!" was the title of an essay published by Nancy Bedford-Jones in *New Masses* in 1935.[147] It was in reply to an article written by her father, a well-known novelist, under a pseudonym in *Liberty* magazine, "Will the Communists Get Our Girls in College?" Nancy's father purported to describe his daughter's activities with the student movement in the S.L.I.D. and N.S.L., for which she spent, he said, "half her nights away from college in squalid roosts in the lowest sections of town." He told how a nationally known student leader had misled her into communism and free love; in the background also there had loomed a Russian agent. Nancy said her father's article was a "vicious attempt to fill American fathers with a deathly fear of their daughters." As Robert W. Iversen says,

"The episode revealed the depths of family disintegration that could accompany the activities of the 'rebel generation.'" But the facts of the case made it clear that generational revolt was an active precondition of student activism. *New Masses* was confirming many student activists in their unconscious uprising against the fathers.

THE OXFORD PLEDGE

What was the net effect of the American student movement in the 1930s? Did it contribute to the strengthening of American democracy and the development of clear thinking? Or was its action warped too by patterns which derived from generational revolt, and which superimposed irrationality on the political process? Here the evidence, for all the idealism and self-sacrifice of the students, points to a negative verdict.

During the first six years of their existence, from 1931 to 1937, the principal issue which the student organizations raised was involvement in war, and their principal target was the R.O.T.C. on the campus. When in 1933 the Oxford Union in Britain voted by 275 to 133 that "this House refuses to fight for King and country in any war," it found an already sympathetic ally in the American student movement.[148] Precisely at a time when the shadow of Hitlerism was rising, precisely during those early years when collective action could have halted the rearmament of Germany, the militarization of the Rhineland, precisely during those years was the American student movement enacting its rebellion against a previous generation which had followed Woodrow Wilson into war, and disarming itself intellectually and physically before the Nazi advance.

Despite the economic hardship students suffered during those first years of the 1930s, especially in New York, the remarkable thing, as we have seen, about the so-called student movement is that it made such little effort to remedy these basic problems. It gave itself with ardor to a generational struggle against university presidents; it tried to misperceive the R.O.T.C.'s as the legions of an American fascism; it saw college athletes as vigilantes and storm troopers; it erupted in campus riots and disturbances, and ridiculed the naïveté of the Roosevelt administration and the weakness of the liberals. Meanwhile it was weakening the resistance which should have been made to Hitler. Generational struggle, its slogans and antics, carried the day.

The Oxford Pledge for a number of critical years continued to blind the American student movement. On April 24, 1936, with Hitler engaged in full rearmament, *The Campus* at City College, center of the Jewish students, proclaimed, "Again the resounding roar of 'We refuse to support any war which the United States government may undertake' shows the will of the great majority of the student body for the Oxford Pledge."[149] It called on the students to "join the ASU and make the College chapter the stronghold of the student movement."

During the next years, the principal actions of the student movement were the so-called annual strikes against war which took place on a given day and hour at the colleges and universities.

The so-called student strikes of 1934, 1935, and 1936 fit the pattern of generational rebellion—with their critique of the "war machine" of the older generation. The use of the word "strike" for these one-hour demonstrations was symbolic; although they were not strikes, the word was retained because it smacked of warfare, generational warfare against the "system." When the first strike was proposed to the Harvard Liberal Club, the majority were opposed; a small minority of six, moved largely by generational solidarity, circulated the strike calls. As one participant wrote, "The strike was important, not from the standpoint of Harvard locally, but in its status as part of a national move. . . . We, at least, would have done our duty."[150] Above all, it was stressed that "strikes" were a "dress rehearsal" to prepare the students for war if it actually came. Then, in accordance with Lenin's teaching, the student movement would work to transform the imperialist war into a civil war. The City College newspaper, for instance, described the response at its campus to the third student strike, which took place on April 22, 1936: "A 'dress rehearsal' for action in time of war was staged by thirty-five hundred students at the College Wednesday who walked out of classes at 11 A.M. to jam the Great Hall in a mass strike meeting." The editor, Lawrence Knobel, acted as chairman and sounded the keynote: "The warlords of Europe are no longer rattling their sabers. They have drawn their swords and are brandishing them close to our throats. . . . Roosevelt will no more keep us out of war than Wilson did."[151]

Many troubled students still wondered why the student movement was insisting on calling its action a "strike." The term, they said, was a misnomer, suggesting that the action was directed against the authorities. In reply, the student leaders said that any other term, such as "peace mobilization," would lack the "drama and effectiveness of the strike." "Strike" carried with it in the collegiate context the note of a generational uprising which no other term had. It was totally unlike a workers' strike, for it stated no specific demands or grievances. But it connoted a diminution in stature of the authorities; also the term carried a populist flavor of unity with workers; above all, it smacked of the Leninist warning of civil war. As two student leaders wrote: "What we are staging is our most dramatic 'dress rehearsal' for a future emergency. . . . It is also an essential part of our strategy for disrupting mobilization plans should they be imposed upon the universities. To the extent that administrators are preparing to accept those plans, the strike is directed 'against' them."[152] A large-scale meeting held after school hours, said the leaders, would not have suited their needs. "This challenging character would be lost," "its values as a dress-rehearsal would be seriously diminished," the "emotional content" would be sacrificed. If one asks what was this "challenging" and "emotional" function which had to be subserved, it was something over and above what political analysis indicated; it was a tactic of generational revolt, the common cause against the elders. Above all, the student leaders felt the "strike" action made them mature; it was a rite of sociological coming of age, and it enhanced generational solidarity. As the leader of the Student League for Industrial Democracy wrote in 1934:

It was the most challenging and politically mature gesture ever undertaken by the students of this nation. But it has a much greater significance for us. . . . The strike had a cohesive force weaving a bond of solidarity from campus to campus. When news was received at Columbia University that police were attempting to disrupt the strike meeting at the City College, the Columbia men wanted to march up to St. Nicholas Heights. This feeling of solidarity marked the crystallization of the student movement in America.[153]

By the time of the third student strike, the nonstudent leaders were growing in confidence and militancy. "Five hundred thousand strike for peace" was their claim in 1936; "there was much greater support than ever before for the Oxford Pledge." A warning was sounded to the System: "The student movement may be compelled to call a strike against the R.O.T.C., refusing to return to classes until Congress heeds our demands."[154] The warning was served—"forceful, explosive methods" would be used for "letting governments know our intention not to be drafted into another holocaust of destruction. This is the chief purpose of the Oxford pledge."[155]

Thus, the American students were misled by generational fervor into the sorry path the Oxford Union had taken in 1933. "Ever shameful" was the way Winston Churchill later characterized the Oxford vote:

It was easy to laugh off such an episode in England, but in Germany, in Russia, in Italy, in Japan, the idea of a decadent, degenerate Britain took deep root and swayed many calculations. Little did the foolish boys who passed the resolution dream that they were destined quite soon to conquer or fall gloriously in the ensuing war, and prove themselves the finest generation ever bred in Britain. Less excuse can be found for their elders. . . .[156]

Meanwhile, however, Mussolini was much impressed by the resolution as evidence of the moral weakness of Western democracy. The passage of the Oxford Pledge was indeed in large part due to the considerable influence which Communist students were then enjoying at Oxford.[157] Generational errors, however, recur; for passions are reborn with each generation, generational revolt runs amok; generational wisdom is hard to come by. In May 1965, the Oxford Union was again debating a resolution: "That this house would not fight for Queen and country." Two of its four trustees resigned in protest. One of them, Sir Roy Harrod, the distinguished economist, recalled the fruits of the flurry of the Oxford student movement in 1933, the familiar fruits of self-destruction: "The motion [in 1933] did make a recognized contribution in building up the idea around the world—which was present even in the mind of the father of the late President Kennedy, who was United States Ambassador here—that the British were played out and could not be depended upon."[158]

In reply the current president of the Oxford Union, a twenty-one-year-old Pakistani, declared that every generation should review its commitments. "War should be constantly reviewed as an institution lest we become complacent and fatalistic." Yet one cannot help noting that there is little cumulative wisdom in the succession of generations. The physical sciences can transmit their past experiences in formulae for the next generation. But in social matters, each generation seems destined to repeat the same mistakes. In science, the presumption of truth lies with the received equation. In social matters, however, generational revolt attaches a presumption of falsehood to all wisdom, for wisdom is cross-generational, what the old tell the young.

THE SPANISH CIVIL WAR AND THE WILL TO IDENTIFICATION AND MARTYRDOM

The Spanish war provided the most dedicated student activists with a rare occasion for self-sacrifice and ultimate identification. Eugene Bronstein, a City College student who had been suspended for involvement in the umbrella fracas in 1933, later a graduate student in philosophy at Harvard, was typical of this group. "I know I'm going to get killed," he said, before an aerial bomb killed him.[159] The *Harvard Communist* printed a long commemorative article on Eugene and a letter from him on the theory of monopoly capitalism. This young man had experienced all the back-to-the-people longings and the compulsion to self-negation characteristic of student activists. A student in philosophy for two years, he finally was unhappy with his studies; he became a founder of the *Harvard Communist*. Then he left the university to do "unionization work at the Woven House factory" in Cambridgc. Hc changed his attire, hair style, and speech to be as one of the workers. He became a militant in the United Rubber Workers Union, and served as a workers' delegate in the Cambridge Central Labor Union. But this self-submergence into the "proletariat," this self-destruction of himself as an intellectual, failed to still Eugene Bronstein's unrest. Twenty-three years old, he went to Spain as political commissar of the second section of the George Washington Battalion. A few weeks before his death he wrote a letter to a friend in which Marxian eschatology enveloped his feelings. He looked back to a dispute in his "buro class" to find the meaning of his imminent self-immolation:

June 4, 1937

Dear ———,

All the barracks are in commotion. We have orders to stand by, ready on 15 min. call, with full equipment. Maybe we'll leave for the front tomorrow morning. . . .

Rereading your letter, mention of ——— reminded me of something he said at a buro class before I left. . . . "That capitalist production grew up inside the womb of feudalism. . . . But that socialist production does not grow up inside capitalism." This is correct, I believe, in a general way, but is not sufficiently refined. Because monopoly capitalism is the dialectical opposite of free competition, the cornerstone of capitalism; and the fact that it is the highest form of socialist production under capitalism, shows the growth of socialist production in contradiction to private ownership.

I don't know why it occurred to me, except the recollection of ——— . . .

Best comradely wishes,
Gene

The *Harvard Communist* said, "It is impossible to grieve for one who has done all that he could to further the welfare of the people, the masses for whom he felt it his duty to work. . . . The death of Eugene Bronstein made complete the integrity of his life."[160] Yet as one read the last letter of this student, with its unreal incantation of dialectical phrases, one's grief grew, for here was death in obedience to a drive that was so ill-understood that it set a young man on its quest in a back-to-the-people heroism; death was the highest act in this political-mystical philosophy in which one merged oneself presumably with history.

If seamen and longshoremen were the largest single group among the Americans who fought in Spain, the second largest of about four hundred came from the colleges, according to Robert W. Iversen.[161] "To the American student Communist, Spain was a test of the depth of his commitment." Don Henry, sophomore president at the University of Kansas of the local American Student Union, enlisted through the office of the campus Communist official. When he was killed in September 1937, recruiting speeches to Kansas students sounded the theme: "Avenge Don Henry."[162] Alvah Bessie, historian of the Lincoln Battalion, brooded over the reasons which brought his comrades to Spain:

Men went to Spain for various reasons, but behind almost every man I met there was a common restlessness, a loneliness. . . . I knew, about myself, that the historical event of Spain had coincided with a long-felt compulsion to complete the destruction of the training I had received all through my youth. There were two major reasons for my being there; to achieve self-integration, and to lend my individual strength (such as it was) to the fight against our eternal enemy-oppression; and the validity of the second reason was not impaired by the fact that it was a shade weaker than the first, for they were both part of the same thing. It was necessary for me, at that stage of my development as a man, to work (for the first time) in a large body of men; to submerge myself in that mass, seeking neither distinction nor preferment (the reverse of my activities for the past several years) and in this way to achieve self-discipline, patience and unselfishness—the opposite of a long middle-class training. . . . There is much truth in the old saws—for a desperate disease, a desperate cure.[163]

Here in this passage we have a description which well applied to so many student activists, the "restlessness," the "loneliness," the compulsion to undo one's "long middle-class training," to complete its "destruction," and this desire to achieve a new "self-integration" as the primary factor: by a curious process of projection and misperception, "our eternal enemy-oppression" was somehow identified with the source of their middle-class training. To undo the latter, to confound their middle-class origin and training, they must "submerge" themselves in the mass, seeking nothing for themselves. This was the classical self-punishment theme which runs through so much apparent idealism; you must annihilate your identity in the masses, obliterate yourself, mortify your ambitions and desires. Behind this self-punishment always lies some gnawing guilt—like that which ate at the conscience of Joseph Conrad's Lord Jim, and made him long to forget himself in the environs of a distant people of a different color and culture, whom he could serve as a suffering servant. It was a "desperate disease," wrote Alvah Bessie, and it required a "desperate cure." And, in truth, it was a disease, this hatred for one's origins which one would destroy, this longing to rend the elder generation in all its ways. This hatred brought with it guilt, the guilt which in the midst of all its revolt afflicts the sons for their destructive intent against their fathers, and from this guilt there followed a drive to punish oneself, to prove to one's conscience one's essential goodness despite one's murderous impulses. Always, however, the generational ideology asserted itself. The young had an insight into the truth denied to the old. "The young Americans who went to Spain to fight," wrote their historian, "and to die as so many did in their effort to preserve the Republic, were clearer sighted from the very beginning than most men are in the quiet deathbeds of old age. . . . They anticipated their contemporaries and their elders. Their betrayal was too mocking and cynical, their deaths—for lack of arms, not courage—too bitter."[164]

THE TRAGEDY OF JULIUS ROSENBERG, STUDENT ACTIVIST

The student movement of the thirties found its most tragic, ambiguous martyrs belatedly a decade and a half afterward in the persons of Julius and Ethel Rosenberg, found guilty of atomic espionage, and executed in 1953.[165] While he was in the death-house, Julius reviewed the formative events in his life. He recalled a demonstration at City College, and he wrote his wife Ethel several paragraphs about it:

> There is another incident still fresh in my mind. It happened during my first year at City College in 1934. . . . The president of the college, Frederick B. Robinson . . . invited a delegation of foreign students from fascist Italy. . . . When the president got up to speak he was greeted by a chorus of boos. He was forced to sit down without being able to speak, though he managed to state that our "conduct was befitting guttersnipes." To re-establish order they allowed Eddie Alexander, president of the council, to take the rostrum. The hall was

perfectly quiet when he began: "I was given permission to speak if I don't say anything derogatory against fascism, but I want to convey a message to our enslaved and tricked brothers under Italian fascism." The truth cut too deep and the fascist students dragged him away from the microphone and a free-for-all began. Three thousand voices thundered in the Great Hall: "Abbasso il fascismo!" [Down with fascism!] At this point the prexy called in New York City's finest and the college student body was treated to a lesson in night-stick civics. Within a week almost the entire student body was wearing buttons that read: "I am a guttersnipe. I hate fascism!" Subsequent events such as Il Duce's bringing "civilization" to Ethiopia, *via* bombs, flames and death, proved we were correct. But 21 students were expelled.[166]

Julius became active in 1936 in the American Student Union and Young Communist League; he and Ethel went to anti-Nazi meetings and to rallies for the Spanish Loyalists, and sang "Solidarity Forever." In April 1936, Julius and Ethel marched in the City College students' strike for peace. Julius wrote leaflets and operated the mimeograph machine, and graduated in February 1939. A fellow-student who had once planned with him to go to Spain to fight the Fascists recalled that after the capitulation at Munich, "some of us got together and sought out Julie; we turned to him because he was so politically mature. . . . Julie had that sense of history which never left him and which allowed him to be cheerful when others were full of gloom."[167] During his last two years at college, "Julie never missed a leaflet distribution, no matter how early in the morning," his friend added. Against the searing background of the poverty and unemployment on the East Side, with the stark threat of fascism and anti-Semitism documented in every day's newspaper, "Julius' primary obsession was Fascism." To this was added the estrangement from father, the conflict of generations. Julius had graduated with honor at the Downtown Talmud Torah, and was so devoted to the study of Hebrew and the prophets that his father, a poor tailor and an orthodox Jew, expected he would become a rabbi. Then Julius began to change; his father could not understand it. A few years later, the father berated his son for his intolerance to Trotskyites and for forgetting that America was a "free country." By 1945, the old man refused to see his son. Ethel hated her devout, illiterate mother, and modeled herself, in every way, to be her opposite.[168] The reason-blinding passion of generational hatred begot a corrupted idealism which led to treason, to what Josiah Royce called "the hell of the irrevocable." Idealism deserved a nobler cause. It is a pseudo-idealism which issues from generational hatred.

THE COMMUNIZATION OF THE STUDENT MOVEMENT AND ITS COLLAPSE, 1935–1941

By the mid-thirties the student movement had come under virtually the complete control of the Communist party. The process began in 1935 when the socialist-led Student League for Industrial Democracy united with the Communist-led and Communist-controlled National Student League to form the American Student Union. The "apparatus" of the latter was composed of stalwarts from the Young Communist League who nullified the presence of their executive secretary, a socialist. The American Student Union achieved an influence far beyond its meager numbers. At Vassar College, for instance, high in the social hierarchy, the *Miscellany News*, the college's newspaper, was edited by a series of Young Communists and Student Unionists who shaped its policy in the required political direction. In a basic sense, however, the American Student Union was no longer a student movement but the youth auxiliary of the Communist party, an association predominantly of fellow-travelers officered by young Communists. The emphasis was on disciplined action for the Party's objectives. The Communist elders controlled student policy. The A.S.U. in colleges acted as a pro-Communist party. Generational protest, therefore, was channelized in highly controlled ways. Not student elitism but student proletarian populism and subservience and self-abnegation in a masochistic spirit before the Party were stressed.

In New York City, at the City College, the "student movement" succeeded in getting control of the student government and acquired enough power to prevent the dismissal of a Communist instructor. For the first time in the history of the student movement the "sit-down" tactic was used, and with evident success. To be sure, it was in a slightly longer run a Pyrrhic victory. For the next three years, however, it gave the Communist instructors and students a tremendous self-confidence in their recruiting activities. Many joined the Communist party in self-dedication during the next year, making a commitment to its tactics and secret-society ethic. In 1936, in its heyday, the pride and confidence of the student movement under Communist leadership rode high. The story of its victory that year deserves retelling.

Late in April 1936, the City College newspaper, *The Campus*, announced, "Morris U. Schappes Fired"; its editorial, "Schappes Must Stay," linked this demand with the students' endorsement of the Oxford Pledge.[169] A Defense Committee was organized on behalf of the dismissed instructor of English, the president of the student council availed himself of Charter Day exercises to urge his reappointment. Hatred for the college's president became obsessive. An editorial, "The President Grins," said, "Is it a grin of pride or of shame and embarrassment? . . . The students of the College have seen that grin. They do not like it. They intend to get rid of it as soon as possible." A mock trial of the president was held, an editorial urged a student strike for Schappes, and three thousand students signed petitions on his behalf. Then on Thursday, April 30, a "sit-down" demonstration started. One thousand students waited for four hours in Lincoln Corridor in front of the president's office in a spontaneous demonstration. It was repeated again on the following Monday, May 2, but on Tuesday efforts to stage another demonstration failed. Student militancy during the next three weeks moved to picket lines in a seamen's strike; then, on May 20, the slate of candidates nominated by the American Student Union ran virtually unopposed in the elections for the student council. The editorial on the front page of *The Campus* said, "Vote Student Union! This year there is but one party running, the A.S.U. ticket." "Every vote for the A.S.U. ticket is a vote to oust President Robinson and reappoint Morris Schappes." The college paper ridiculed the students who marched in the Charter Day "Jingo Day Parade" as "eight hundred students who have succumbed to the war-mongering propaganda." In the usual generational terminology the paper attacked the emasculating war machine: the language was virtually identical with the language Berkeley student leaders used almost thirty years later: "We at the college can strip the teeth from only one cog in the war-machine; but the work we do here is being carried on by thousands of students throughout the country—stripping the teeth from thousands of cogs to demolish the war-machine." A Counter-Jingo Day rally was joined by a thousand students who picketed the Charter Day parade; several students in the R.O.T.C. band goose-stepped to show they regarded the army as fascist. At Hunter College, the women's city college, the entire American Student Union slate was also elected on a platform advocating support of the student peace strike and formal recognition of the A.S.U.[170] "A.S.U. slates in five colleges," announced the *Student Advocate*, "have swept the Student Council elections and we have sizeable minorities on the other councils. The majority of college papers are edited by A.S.U. people and utilize the A.S.U. programs as the basis for editorial policy. . . . This is not just a New York phenomenon."[171]

The fight for Schappes was won. At that time the whole problem of the secret society in politics and its deleterious effects on democracy was ill-understood. The noted democratic Marxist philosopher, Sidney Hook, was, for instance, a strong supporter of the reappointment of the Communist instructor. This was an election year, moreover; support of the newly organized American Labor party was important in the coalition for President Roosevelt, and the Communist party was entering its phase of advocacy of a People's Front. More than a fifth of the City College studentry in a straw vote that fall supported the Communist presidential candidate, while many fellow-travelers were among those who supported Roosevelt:

Straw Vote—October 26–27, 1936[172]

CANDIDATE	PERCENTAGE	NUMBER OF VOTES
Roosevelt (Democrat)	63%	914 (Dem.) 449 (A.L.P.)
Browder (Communist)	23%	504
Thomas (Socialist)	11.8%	261
Landon (Republican)	3.5%	78
		Total 2,206

The growth of Communist influence at the City College had thus within three years been considerable. In 1933, the National Student League had numbered about 150 members. In 1936, the successor American Student Union controlled the entire student body, its organizations, its newspaper. The students' political preferences, under the influence of the student movement, moved from social democracy to communism. In 1932, Norman Thomas was the presidential choice of the college studentry; Franklin Roosevelt got only half the votes Norman Thomas received. Four years later the Communist candidate received twice as many votes as the socialist Thomas. The Communist student movement from the outset indoctrinated the students with the concepts of illegality and the secret society. Their gifted spokesman in 1933, Adam Lapin, explained the superiority of the National Student League to the democratic Student League for Industrial Democracy: "The only organization capable of effective and, if necessary, illegal organization is the N.S.L. Such is the problem at City College."[173]

The Communist influence in the colleges began to subside only with the signing of the Stalin-Hitler pact in August 1939. Doubts appeared where there had been certainties. The most ardent student activists suppressed their doubts, and gave themselves even more self-sacrificially to the movement. But the studentry as a whole began to move away from the Communist-controlled "student movement." The saddest day for the American student movement was February 10, 1940, when several thousands of students gathered at the White House for an address by President Franklin D. Roosevelt. It was a rainy afternoon. The students of the American Youth Congress were a large silent crowd, a few of whom occasionally booed as the President spoke truthful words concerning the Soviet Union. He had, he said, "with many of you hoped that Russia would work out its own problems. . . . That hope is today either shattered or is put away in storage against some better day. The Soviet Union, as a matter of practical fact, as everybody knows, who has got the courage to face the fact, . . . is run by a dictatorship, a dictatorship as absolute as any other dictatorship in the world."[174] These were realities the American student movement could not honestly confront; they held on to the generational illusion. Finally, the movement collapsed in moral confusion. In March 1941, former Communists began identifying more than thirty instructors of the City College faculty as members of the Communist party.[175] All of the latter were brought under subpoena before the state investigating committee; all of them concealed their party membership and were subsequently dismissed from their posts. Students held meetings, where they listened to speeches and sympathized with those losing their jobs. But the sympathy was for the calamity that had overtaken them; it was hard to feel a spontaneous sincere moral admiration for a perjurer. Why hadn't they stood up for what they believed? Reasons were given, and many students tried hard to persuade themselves to feel a more righteous indignation on behalf of their professors. The student movement, committed to the tactic of deceit, became itself de-authoritized in the spring of 1941. The American Student Union dragged on a shadowy existence till the end of 1941. In June of that year, Hitler's legions attacked the Soviet Union. The Communist-controlled students were happy to drop their attack on the war as one "to perpetuate imperialist rule over colonial areas." No longer did they have to ridicule the "aid to Britain nonsense"; instead, they called for more aid and intervention. The organization voted in December 1941 to discontinue itself as a national entity. Its legacy to its members, it transpired, was a burden of moral entrapment; it imposed on them a guilt and consequent "depoliticization" which were the major causes for the weak rebuttal to Senator Joseph McCarthy and his allies a decade later.

The Silent and Conservative Generations

Sociological generations have their own law of time. In critical times of repeated ordeals, there is a more rapid succession of generations; each generation then becomes shorter, and short age groups become still more differentiated within themselves into generations. A generation is a group which in adolescent years is shaped by a critical historical experience; a generation defines its character by its response to that critical situation. And if the critical situations alter drastically within a few years, persons who biologically are only a few years apart may yet be sharply differentiated as "generations." Thus, from 1949 to 1963, there was a rapid succession of "generations"—the silent, the conservative, the beat, the New Left. The silence of the "silent generation" in the United States from about 1949 to 1953 was in part a rebuke of shame to an elder generation of radicals who were now revealed as having been involved in deceit, apology for Stalin's crimes, and espionage.

The elder liberals, to save their own faces, blamed the students' silence on the fears induced by McCarthyism. The *New Republic* editorialized in 1951:

> Most campuses are close enough to the outside world to share its current obsession for political orthodoxy. Why take a chance on being called a "Red" later on? Little things like signing a petition or joining a staunchly anti-Communist liberal group may come to the attention of a conservative-minded future employer. Besides, what can a student do politically? These are the considerations that have recently cut down political activity in the universities.[176]

Student political groups had indeed almost vanished, or were reduced to a few hardy political souls. "It is common knowledge that the student socialist movement is moribund," the fellow-traveling *Monthly Review* reported in 1951.[177] The Student League for Industrial Democracy was said to be down to about 150 members in six colleges, although its secretary claimed six hundred members in twenty chapters. In any case, its numbers were minuscule. The largest national group, the Students for Democratic Action, claiming 2,500 members, proposed to launch an "Operation Free Thought" against McCarthyism, but it reported "a difficult time combating student apathy and, on a number of campuses, overt Administration hostility."

The real source of student apathy and silence, however, was neither economic sanctions nor fears; other student generations have taken risks under far more fearful and trying conditions. Rather it was that the radicalism of the older generation was hopelessly de-authoritized. The silence of the successor "silent generation" was largely an outcome of generational conflict; the sons rejected the fathers' political gods as broken idols. They saw the fathers as naïve, effeminate do-gooders whom Stalin had used. The late forties and early fifties saw the depressing spectacle of a shattered generation of Old Leftists. They trooped before congressional committees and invoked the Fifth Amendment. It was a new precedent in American radicalism. The early radicals and socialists such as Eugene V. Debs used to welcome every subpoena to court and committee as an opportunity conferred by the System to defend with pride and honor their political words, deeds, and membership. Now the procession of Old Leftists, instead of defending what presumably had been noble in their youth, and rejecting straightforwardly the ignoble, committed their last acts of political blindness and, marching head downward, pleaded the Fifth Amendment. Professors were ousted in several colleges and universities, but in no case did any significant student movement arise in protest. A studentry, though always sympathetic to the underdog, cannot be moved by lying and evasion. There was such a lack of candor and of manliness in honest defense of what one was that it was hard to engender a genuine respect for the Old Left. The latter tried hard, and with some success, to create a stereotype of "McCarthyism" as solely a persecution of innocent people. But what could not be obliterated was the fact that McCarthyism was the projected creation in large part of the bad conscience and cowardice of the radicals—Communists, former Communists, and fellow-travelers themselves. The shadow of Lenin's demand that every Communist party must have its underground apparatus had darkened their consciences with the deceit of a secret society.[178] So the tired procession of radicals of the elder generation pleaded the Fifth Amendment, making their final pathetic bow to the history they had planned to make. There were others involved in tawdry espionage: Alger Hiss of the Harvard Law School, Remington of Dartmouth, Judy Coplon of Barnard. This was, as Alistair Cooke said, "a generation on trial," and it failed in its time of crisis.[179]

The conservative students of the 1950s strongly supported Dwight Eisenhower as President of the United States. General Eisenhower indeed became a father figure for them: a man of action, character, and judgment whom they preferred to the liberal, doubt-tormented intellectual, Adlai Stevenson.

A representative poll of forty-five editors of college and university newspapers in the spring of 1956 showed that 62 per cent supported Eisenhower for President; only 28 per cent were for Stevenson. Twenty-five editors agreed that the Republicans had done well in basing themselves on the potent issue of "peace and prosperity." The majority supported the President's refusal to recognize Communist China. The collegiate editors were emphatic in their belief that the student bodies of their respective institutions were indifferent to politics; by a margin of six to one they testified to this view, although they themselves, almost 95 per cent of them, asserted that college papers should promote political interests. One New Yorker said, "Most college students simply do not connect themselves with political affairs. . . . Education has failed so far." The editors themselves were mostly moderate in tone, even on the most emotional issues; "sophistication rather than provincialism," reported the *Nation*, "appeared to be the only noticeable trend in this poll of college editors." A few months later, at the height of the presidential campaign, the college editors by a vote of thirty to twenty-three still agreed that "college students are generally apathetic to politics." Again a New York editor opined, "Either the educational job is an inadequate one . . . or this generation of new and potential voters is a selfish and self-satisfied one."[180]

It was during these years of the silent and conservative generations that something like a return to religion on the campuses was observed. It reached a dramatic crescendo in a night of confessions in February 1950 at Wheaton College, a nondenominational school near Chicago, where more than half of a student body of 1,500 was swept into a mass revival. They trooped into the chapel and mounted the pulpit to unburden their consciences; they spoke in self-criticism of their cheating, pride, meanness toward others, violations of college rules, impure thoughts. They were still confessing thirty-eight hours later when the college's president thought it time to stop.[181] Thus one group of students of the silent generation tried to overcome its alienation. Eight years later the president of Union Theological Seminary, Henry Van Dusen, could still report, "Nowhere do the tides of religious awakening flow more powerfully than among the younger generation, especially on college and university campuses. Visiting preachers never have known such large, eager and responsive student congregations. Chaplains and teachers of religion are in short supply."[182] At Cornell University, a new course in Christian theology attracted more than three hundred students. "Religious Emphasis Week" drew the spontaneous interest of undergraduates from Middlebury to the Redlands. The number of full-time religious workers on campuses rose from fewer than five hundred in 1947 to more than 1,500 in 1958. The "religious revolution" was the emotional-intellectual expression of the conservative generation, its own generational rebellion against the radical ideology of its forerunner, the depression generation, whose principles had turned into an amorality which sanctified Stalin's crimes. Very quickly, however, the conservative generation disappeared. Sons were soon entering the colleges and universities whose own fathers had known little or none of the political experience of the thirties. Religion in the fifties had supplanted ideology, but now the cycle completed itself as the longing for ideology revived and replaced religion. Veterans of the thirties, such as Daniel Bell, had heralded the "end of ideology." The decade of the sixties, however, became that of the ideological counterrevolution. The quest for ideology permeated the campus intellectuals and made them activists of the student movement.

By the early sixties, according to a survey conducted from 1961 to 1963, the force of the religious revival among the American studentry was spent, as far as the overwhelming majority were concerned. The responses of undergraduates sampled at Yale, Marquette, Boston University, Indiana, Harvard, Reed, Davidson, Brandeis, and Stanford indicated that a majority of the students at every college, with the exception of Marquette, had experienced a significant reaction against their religious tradition, and that in nearly half these cases the anti-religious rebellion was first experienced after the student had gone to college.[183]

Conservatism as an ideology remained a persistent current among a large sector of the American studentry. Senator Barry Goldwater was a much-sought-after campus speaker. A dean at Cornell University spoke of the "apparent resurgence of conservatism" on American college campuses, and said it was part of the dissipation of the "apparent apathy of the college students in the 1950s." A dean at Stanford said that " 'conservatism' has suddenly gained respectability." Dean Roger W. Heyns of the University of Michigan (later a Berkeley Chancellor), as usual on both sides, found "a resurgence of both liberalism and conservatism."[184] Whatever the revival of conservative philosophy may have been, however, no student movement based on conservatism could possibly emerge. For a student movement has its roots in an emotional revolt against the older generation. It can be radical, revolutionary, or reactionary, but its driving force is always an assault on the status quo. The conservative, the person not dominantly motivated by generational revolt, will experience no emotional need to participate in a student movement. Consequently, as the revival of the student movement gained momentum, the voice of conservative student opinion was virtually drowned in the agitated oratory of radical student revolt. The closest approximation to a reactionary student movement was to be found in those circles devoted to the objectivism of the novelist Ayn Rand, which was a mixture of atheism, elitism, laissez-faire, and social Darwinism; such sympathies flourished somewhat at Stanford and Boston universities, where 7 and 5 per cent of the studentries respectively were drawn to objectivism in 1962, but these were small proportions compared to the liberal and radical percentages. What was striking was the high percentage of students with socialistic convictions, even among the wealthiest.[185] At Williams College, where 75 per cent of the students' fathers were Republicans, and actually richer than Yale fathers, nearly a third (31 per cent) of the students favored the government ownership of basic industries; at Yale this figure reached 18 per cent; while at Reed, 26 per cent were inclined toward socialism. At Reed, while not a single student had moved from "conservative to more conservative," two-fifths had moved to the left of an originally liberal position. Brandeis was the outstanding exception as one of two cases where a trend from liberal to more conservative had been discerned; there 16 per cent had moved in a conservative direction, while 13 per cent had evolved to the liberal side. Eighty-six per cent of Brandeis parents were registered Democrats to begin with, the sons with the conservative drift evidently included many whose ideas had moved from the far left to the moderate left; only 7 per cent of the students actually regarded themselves as conservatives.

The intellectual culture of the colleges and universities without doubt made for a radical tendency. Three-fourths of all Yale students substantially changed their political views at college; and of these, two-thirds regarded their lectures and readings as primary reasons for this change. In nearly three-fifths of the cases, the change was in a more liberal direction. Though about one-third of the national sample still described themselves as "conservatives," the initiative was passing into the hands of the leftist-minded student movement.

The Old Readers of the Old Left

By the end of the 1950s, the readership of the leftist journals was almost entirely middle-aged; Old Leftists felt themselves to be the last of the Marxist Mohicans. A journal of fellow-travelers, the *Monthly Review*, in 1957, its ninth year, reported on the basis of the responses of 25 per cent of its subscribers that its average reader "is a professional man, probably a college teacher, 31 to 50. . . . He has done graduate work, and belongs to several professional societies . . . he subscribes also to magazines like *The New Yorker, The Saturday Review, Consumer Reports,* and *Scientific American.*" Only 15.4 per cent of the *Monthly Review*'s readership was below thirty years of age. From their data the editors calculated the size of the middle-aged, Intellectual Left in 1958: "The figures indicate that this sturdy band of citizens (bless them all) numbers no more than 60,000. In a nation with a population of 170 million the Left-press reaches just about 1/30th of 1 per cent of the people. This tells the story of radical weakness as perhaps nothing else does."[186]

Even the magazine *Liberation*, founded in 1955 as the organ for an absolute ethic and for nonviolent direct action for racial rights and peace, was in 1959 also a journal of the Old Left. Of the two hundred and twenty persons who responded to a readers' poll in May 1959, only sixty-two were under the age of twenty-nine. The largest single group were teachers, while students numbered only about 11 per cent of the readers.[187] Within a year or two, however, the cycle of generational revolt was to create the periodical literature of a Young Left.

The "Great Awakening" of the American student movement, we might say, began in 1960. By 1962 it had brought into existence a whole new group of student magazines; a partial inventory of them that year enumerated twenty-eight new student political journals.[188]

What then were the social and psychological sources of the New Student Movement? What were its aims and hopes?

NOTES

1. Philip Altbach, "The Quiet Campus," *New Leader*, XLVI (August 5, 1963), 12. This article, written by an analyst of student movements, showed the pitfalls of misperception and misprediction. In 1963, the author reported that student political activity had "quietly melted away" and was "a shadow of its former self."

2. *We Want a University: Dedicated to the 800*, p. 1. The quotation was from Paul Goodman, "Thoughts on Berkeley," *New York Review of Books*, III (January 14, 1965), 5.

3. "In the midst of the continual movement that agitates a democratic community, the tie that unites one generation to another is relaxed or broken; every man there readily loses all trace of the ideas of his forefathers or takes no care about them." Alexis de Tocqueville, *Democracy in America*, ed. Phillips Bradley, tr. Henry Reeve (New York, 1945), II, 4.

4. Thomas Jefferson, "The Autobiography of Thomas Jefferson," in Adrienne Koch and William Peden (eds.), *The Life and Selected Writings of Thomas Jefferson* (New York, 1944), pp. 4–5; Charles S. Sydnor, *American Revolutionaries in the Making: Political Practices in Washington's Virginia* (New York, 1962), pp. 14–15; Gilbert Chinard, *Thomas Jefferson: The Apostle of Americanism* (Boston, 1929), pp. 8–26.

5. Sydnor, *op. cit.*, pp. 100–101.

6. Clement Eaton, *The Freedom of Thought Struggle in the Old South* (Harper Torchbook ed.; New York, 1964), p. 236.

7. Frederick Douglass, *Life and Times of Frederick Douglass* (rev. ed., 1892; New York, 1962), p. 227; Hazel Catherine Wolf, *On Freedom's Altar: The Martyr Complex in the Abolition Movement* (Madison, Wisc., 1952), p. 70; Edward L. Pierce, *Memoir and Letters of Charles Sumner* (London, 1893), III, 173–175.

8. Samuel Eliot Morison, *Three Centuries of Harvard, 1636–1936* (Cambridge, Mass., 1936), pp. 290, 303.

9. Robert Samuel Fletcher, *A History of Oberlin College from the Foundation Through the Civil War* (Oberlin, Ohio, 1943), I, 34, 37, 151, 156–157, 158–159, 160, 162, 163, 171, 178, 184.

10. Mark De Wolfe Howe, *Justice Oliver Wendell Holmes: The Shaping Years, 1841–1870*, I (Cambridge, Mass., 1957), 48–49, 70–72.

11. S. Willis Rudy, *The College of the City of New York: A History, 1847–1947* (New York, 1949), p. 85; Henry Edward Tremain and Charles F. Horne, "The College in the Civil War," in Philip J. Mosenthal and Charles F. Horne (eds.), *The City College: Memories of Sixty Years* (New York, 1907), p. 371.

12. Samuel Middlebrook, "A Foreigner Looks at the Free Academy," *City College Alumnus*, LXI, No. 3 (December 1965), 8.

13. Kent Sagendorph, *Michigan: The Story of the University* (New York, 1948), pp. 72–75. Also see Charles W. Ferguson,

Fifty Million Brothers: A Panorama of American Lodges and Clubs (New York, 1937), p. 38; Wayne M. Musgrave, *College Fraternities* (New York, 1923), pp. 18–19; Albert P. Jacobs, *The Greek-Letter Societies* (Detroit, 1879), p. 7.

14. G. Stanley Hall, *Adolescence: Its Psychology* (New York, 1914), II, 413.

15. Robert Elton Berry, *Yankee Stargazer: The Life of Nathaniel Bowditch* (New York, 1941), p. 205.

16. Lewis S. Feuer, "H. A. P. Torrey and John Dewey: Teacher and Pupil," *American Quarterly*, X (1958), 49.

17. Lincoln Steffens, *The Autobiography of Lincoln Steffens* (New York, 1931), pp. 117–118.

18. Morison, *op. cit.*, p. 118.

19. *Ibid.*, pp. 177–179.

20. *Ibid.*, p. 185.

21. *Ibid.*, p. 186.

22. *Ibid.*, p. 210.

23. George R. Wallace, *Princeton Sketches: The Story of Nassau Hall* (New York, 1894), pp. 77–86.

24. Morison, *op. cit.*, p. 231. Ripley wrote his mother on May 2, 1823, "The class—that is to say, of course, all the friends of order—are in a state of infuriated excitement and rebellion." Then, the next day, "In consequence of the expulsion of four who were distinguished in the attack, the class, or a considerable portion rather, rebelled, and they are all gone. Those who remain are sober men of both parties. As regards myself, I am so fortunate as to have escaped any censure from the government of the class. True to my old principles, of course, I did not join the mob, and have endeavored to keep myself quiet." See O. B. Frothingham, *George Ripley* (Boston, 1888), p. 16. Charles Crowe, *George Ripley: Transcendentalist and Utopian Socialist* (Athens, Georgia, 1967), p. 28.

25. Morison, *op. cit.*, p. 253.

26. *Ibid.*, p. 401.

27. *Ibid.*, p. 404.

28. Charles E. Norton, *Letters of Charles Eliot Norton*, eds. Sara Norton and M. A. De Wolfe Howe (Boston, 1913), II, 81.

29. Morison, *op. cit.*, p. 413.

30. John Reed, "Almost Thirty," *New Republic*, LXXXVI (April 29, 1936), 332–333; Granville Hicks, *John Reed: The Making of a Revolutionary* (New York, 1936), pp. 33, 73–74.

31. George E. Peterson, *The New England College in the Age of the University* (Amherst, Mass., 1964), pp. 62–64.

32. Peterson, *op. cit.*, p. 232.

33. *Ibid.*, p. 146.

34. *Ibid.*, p. 137.

35. *Ibid.*, p. 107.

36. *Ibid.*, p. 109.

37. *Ibid.*, p. 137.

38. *Ibid.*, p. 110.

39. *Ibid.*, p. 101.

40. *Ibid.*, p. 107.

41. Alpheus T. Mason, *Harlan Fiske Stone: Pillar of the Law* (New York, 1956), pp. 38, 62–63.

42. William Allen White, *A Puritan in Babylon: The Story of Calvin Coolidge* (New York, 1938), p. 35; Harold Nicolson, *Dwight Morrow* (New York, 1935), p. 30.

43. Peterson, *op. cit.*, p. 132.

44. *Ibid.*, p. 132. Also see Charles Edward Garman, *Letters, Lectures, and Address*, ed. Eliza Miner Garman (Boston, 1909).

45. Mason, *op. cit.*, pp. 37–39.

46. *Ibid.*, pp. 28–29.

47. Peterson, *op. cit.*, p. 145.

48. *Ibid.*, pp. 103–104.

49. *Ibid.*, p. 147.

50. *Ibid.*, p. 147.

51. *Ibid.*, p. 138.

52. *Ibid.*, p. 139.

53. *Ibid.*, p. 145.

54. The Canadian student revolt at the University of Toronto in 1895, though similar to its New England counterparts, curiously had a much greater ideological bearing. The future Prime Minister of Canada, the student William Lyon Mackenzie King, led in 1895 what was the longest strike that had ever taken place in an English-speaking North American university. The students were not only groping toward a concept of the "secular university," but were also expressing resentment toward a European faculty which regarded them as colonials. Mackenzie King himself was experiencing a severe religious crisis of guilt; it filled him with a back-to-the-people zeal which sent him into projects varying from reforming prostitutes to volunteer hospital work and founding a newsboys' association. Then, moved by Arnold Toynbee's personality, he went to Chicago to work at Hull House with Jane Addams; he also studied sociology and economics at the university, where he found the sardonic Thorstein Veblen "the best lecturer I have as yet

listened to." Students at Toronto were beginning to read Shaw and Bellamy, and their inquiries into socialism and their invitations to labor speakers aroused opposition on the part of the faculty. See W. Stewart Wallace, "Background," in Claude T. Bissell (ed.), *University College: A Portrait, 1853–1953* (Toronto, 1953), p. 14; B. K. Sandwell, "Student '97," in Bissell, *op. cit.*, pp. 116–118; R. MacGregor Dawson, *William Lyon Mackenzie King: A Political Biography, 1874–1923* (Toronto, 1959), pp. 34–39, 58–61, 81; Hector Charlesworth, *More Candid Chronicles: Further Leaves from the Note Book of a Canadian Journalist* (Toronto, 1928), pp. 57–92.

55. Alvin Johnson, student at the University of Nebraska in the early 1890s, was a Populist in his sympathies, and spent a back-to-the-people vacation with migratory hobo workers. He found no support for these emotions, however, at his university: "Politically I felt alien to the institution and rarely discussed politics at all." See Alvin Johnson, *Pioneer's Progress: an Autobiography* (New York, 1952), p. 87.

56. Thorstein Veblen, *The Higher Learning in America* (New York, 1918), p. 195.

57. *Ibid.*, pp. 204–205.

58. *Ibid.*, p. 186.

59. *Ibid.*, pp. 24–25.

60. *Ibid.*, p. 26.

61. *Ibid.*, p. 273.

62. Dorothy Brewster, *East-West Passage: A Study in Literary Relationships* (London, 1954), pp. 105–106; Thomas W. Higginson, *Cheerful Yesterdays* (Boston, 1889), p. 314.

63. Brewster, *op. cit.*, p. 131. See also Jane Addams, *Twenty Years at Hull-House* (1910; reprinted, New York, 1961), pp. 187–188, 196–197.

64. Robert A. Woods and Albert J. Kennedy, *The Settlement Horizon: A National Estimate* (New York, 1922), pp. 42–45.

65. Peterson, *op. cit.*, pp. 182–184. See also Jane Addams, "The Subjective Necessity for Social Settlements," in Jane Addams *et al.*, *Philanthropy and Social Progress* (New York, 1893), p. 6; "A Function of the Social Settlement," *Annals of the American Academy of Political and Social Science*, XIII (1899), 339–340; *Twenty Years at Hull-House*, pp. 91 ff.

66. Sagendorph, *op. cit.*, p. 173.

67. *Ibid.*, p. 194.

68. *Ibid.*, pp. 182–185.

69. Allan Nevins, *Illinois* (New York, 1917), p. 90.

70. *Ibid.*, p. 158. See also Harry Barnard, *Eagle Forgotten: The Life of John Peter Altgeld* (New York, 1938), pp. 401–402.

71. Nevins, *op. cit.*, p. 305.

72. *Ibid.*, p. 307.

73. *Ibid.*, pp. 311–313.

74. Frank F. Stephens, *A History of the University of Missouri* (Columbia, Mo., 1962), pp. 312–317.

75. At Williams College, for instance, such a rebellious spirit as Max Eastman, entering in 1900, found that his "rebel opinions" were regarded as a "lively firework varying the monotony" rather than as a "serious attack upon its frame and foundation of decorum." See Max Eastman, *Enjoyment of Living* (New York, 1948), p. 199.

76. Ernest Poole, *The Bridge: My Own Story* (New York, 1940), pp. 70–71, 65. See also the essays of Ernest Poole and Howard Brubaker in Anne Strunsky Walling (ed.), *William English Walling: A Symposium* (New York, 1938), pp. 25, 35; J. Salwyn Schapiro, "Henry Moskowitz: A Social Reformer in Politics," *The Outlook*, CII (October 26, 1912), 446–449.

77. Poole, *The Bridge*, p. 73.

78. *Ibid.*, p. 74.

79. *Ibid.*, p. 196.

80. *Twenty Years of Social Pioneering: The League for Industrial Democracy Celebrates its Twentieth Anniversary December 30, 1925* (New York, 1926), pp. 7–8. Also see Morris Hillquit, *Loose Leaves from a Busy Life* (New York, 1934), pp. 60–62.

81. Harry W. Laidler, "Forty Years of L.I.D.," in *The League for Industrial Democracy: Forty Years of Education, A Symposium* (New York, 1945), p. 17.

82. Jack London, *Revolution and Other Essays* (New York, 1910), pp. 9–10.

83. See Upton Sinclair, *Love's Pilgrimage* (New York, 1911), pp. 35, 529, 535.

84. Upton Sinclair, *The Goose-Step* (rev. edn., Pasadena, Calif., 1923), pp. 9, 478.

85. Heywood Broun, a charter member of the Harvard Socialist Club, and later America's greatest columnist, wrote at the age of thirty, "The most prolific period of

pessimism comes when the first attempt is made to translate dreams into reality. . . . Often it is made at college." See Dale Kramer, *Heywood Broun* (New York, 1949), p. 26.

86. *Twenty Years of Social Pioneering,* p. 23. The unconventional Vincent Sheean, a student at the University of Chicago in 1919, described "the social system of the undergraduate world" as composed of "a couple of thousand young nincompoops, whose ambition in life was to get into the right fraternity or club, go to the right parties, and get elected to something or other." See Vincent Sheean, *Personal History* (New York, 1935), p. 9.

87. Owen Wister, *Philosophy 4: A Story of Harvard University* (New York, 1903), pp. 94–95.

88. Irving Stone, *Sailor on Horseback: The Biography of Jack London* (Boston, 1938), p. 222.

89. Jack London, "South of the Slot," in *The Strength of the Strong* (New York, 1914), pp. 34 ff.

90. *Twenty Years of Social Pioneering,* p. 39.

91. "I.S.S. Progress," *Intercollegiate Socialist,* II, No. 1 (October-November 1913), 15; "I.S.S. Convention," *Intercollegiate Socialist,* II, No. 3 (February-March 1914), 25; "Ten Years Old," *Intercollegiate Socialist,* III, No. 4 (April-May 1915), 4; Harry W. Laidler, "Ten Years of I.S.S. Progress," *Intercollegiate Socialist,* IV, No. 2 (December-January 1915–1916), 21.

92. Mira Weisenberg, *The L.I.D.: Fifty Years of Democratic Education, 1905–1955* (New York, 1955), p. 9.

93. John Reed, "Almost Thirty," p. 333. According to Harry W. Laidler, Reed joined the Harvard Socialist Club shortly after it was founded in 1906 by Walter Lippmann and his friends. See Laidler, "Forty Years of L.I.D.," *League for Industrial Democracy: Symposium,* p. 19.

94. *Intercollegiate Socialist,* II, No. 1 (October-November 1913), 25.

95. *Ibid.,* II, No. 3 (February-March 1914), 25.

96. *Ibid.,* IV, No. 1 (October-November 1915), 29; *Ibid.,* V, No. 3 (February-March 1917), 17.

97. Lewis S. Feuer, "American Travelers to the Soviet Union, 1917–32: The Formation of a Component of New Deal Ideology," *American Quarterly,* XIV (1962), 124.

98. "Socialists and the Problems of War: A Symposium," *Intercollegiate Socialist,* V, No. 4 (April-May 1917), 19.

99. Sinclair, *The Goose-Step,* p. 473.

100. *Ibid.,* p. 460.

101. Albert Edwards, "The Spirit of the Russian Student," *Intercollegiate Socialist,* II, No. 1 (October-November 1913), 14, 25.

102. Samuel P. Gurman, "The Collegian in Warsaw and Chicago," *Intercollegiate Socialist,* VI, No. 4 (April-May 1918), 21–23. Also see William English Walling, *Russia's Message* (New York, 1908), pp. 182–183, 100. Walling spent almost two years in Russia in 1905 and 1906 and came into contact with the student movement there.

103. J. S. (Jessica Smith), "To College Students," *Socialist Review,* IX, No. 5 (October 1920), 174.

104. *Twenty Years of Social Pioneering,* p. 51. Selig Perlman was "discovered" at the age of eighteen in Europe by William English Walling, through whose help in 1907 he was then enabled to enroll at the University of Wisconsin. See essay by Selig Perlman in Anne Strunsky Walling (ed.), *William English Walling: A Symposium,* pp. 89–90.

105. *Twenty Years of Social Pioneering,* p. 16. Walter Lippmann, A *Preface to Politics* (New York, 1917), p. 191.

106. "College Notes," *Socialist Review,* IX, No. 1 (June 1920), 47. See also "College Notes," *Socialist Review,* VIII, No. 5 (April 1920), 320; and "The Collegian in the Social Movement," *Socialist Review,* VIII, No. 3 (February 1920), 188.

107. *Twenty Years of Social Pioneering,* p. 14.

108. "Freedom of Discussion in American Colleges," *Socialist Review,* VIII, No. 4 (March 1920), 253.

109. Heinz Eulau, "Mover and Shaker: Walter Lippmann as a Young Man," *Antioch Review,* XI (1951), 307.

110. Walter Lippmann, "Legendary John Reed," *New Republic,* I (December 26, 1914), 15–16. Lippmann in his maturity criticized the generational segregation promoted by "youth movements" as "reactionary." See James R. Kearney, *Anna Eleanor Roosevelt: The Evolution of a Reformer* (Boston, 1968), p. 44.

111. John Reed, "Almost Thirty," pp. 267–270, 332–336.

112. *News-Bulletin, League for Industrial Democracy*, V, No. 3 (May 1927), 8. See also David Felix, *Protest: Sacco-Vanzetti and the Intellectuals* (Bloomington, Ind., 1965), p. 181.

113. James A. Wechsler, *Revolt on the Campus* (New York, 1935), pp. 379–380. S. Willis Rudy, *The College of the City of New York: A History, 1847–1947* (New York, 1949), p. 405.

114. *Students in Revolt: The Story of the Intercollegiate League for Industrial Democracy* (New York, 1933), p. 7.

115. Norman Studer, "Revolt in the American Colleges," *New Masses*, I, No. 1 (May 1926), 16, 23.

116. Dwight Macdonald, *Memoirs of a Revolutionist: Essays in Political Criticism* (New York, 1957), p. 7.

117. Robert W. Iversen, *The Communists and the Schools* (New York, 1959), p. 139.

118. The total number of Russian students in 1875 was 5,151. See Nicholas Hans, *History of Russian Educational Policy (1701–1917)* (London, 1931), p. 238.

119. Letter to a friend, March 18, 1932.

120. *Idem.*

121. Letter to a friend, March 27, 1932.

122. Lewis S. Feuer, "The Strange Career of Walter Lippmann," *Revolt*, I, No. 2 (December 1932), p. 9. See also "Philosophy Follows the Flag," *Student Outlook*, II, No. 3 (February 1934), 5 ff; "Upton Sinclair, Socialist?" *Student Outlook*, III, No. 1 (October 1934), 7–8.

123. Wechsler, *op. cit.*, p. 119.

124. James A. Wechsler, *The Age of Suspicion* (New York, 1953), p. 48.

125. Pamphlet, *City College and War: Why Were Twenty-One Students Expelled?* October 1933, pp. 13–14.

126. Wechsler, *The Age of Suspicion*, pp. 40–41.

127. Adam Lapin, "The Crisis in City College," *Student Review*, III, No. 1 (December 1933), 9, 21.

128. Joseph Starobin, "The National Student League," *Student Review*, III, No. 3 (February 1934), 18.

129. Letter to a friend, January 29, 1936.

130. Wechsler, *The Age of Suspicion*, p. 36.

131. *Ibid.*, p. 45.

132. Clifford McVeagh, "Academic Napoleons No. 1: Ruthven of Michigan," *Student Advocate*, I, No. 1 (February 1936), 13–15; Nancy Bedford-Jones, "Academic Napoleons No. II: Provost Moore of U.C.L.A.," *Student Advocate*, I, No. 2 (March 1936), 19 ff.; Roger Chase, "Academic Napoleons No. III: Nicholas Murray Butler," *Student Advocate*, I, No. 3 (April 1936), 20–21; Arthur Wilson, "Academic Napoleon No. IV: Chancellor Bowman of Pittsburgh," *Student Advocate*, I, No. 7 (February 1937), 21–23; Theresa Levin, "Academic Napoleon No. 5: Dr. Colligan. Tammany's Aloysius," *Student Advocate*, II, No. 2 (October 1937), 9 ff.; Alberta Reid, "Academic Napoleon No. 6: Marvin of George Washington U.," *Student Advocate*, II, No. 3 (December 1937), 13 ff.

133. Testimony of Harry J. Marks, *Hearings before the Committee on Un-American Activities, House of Representatives, Eighty-Third Congress, First Session* (Washington, D.C., 1953), pp. 1846–1847.

134. Testimony of Paul Rudolph Zilsel, *Hearings . . . on Un-American Activities* (Washington, D.C., 1953), p. 1044.

135. Testimony of Isadore Amdur, *Hearings . . . on Un-American Activities* (Washington, D.C., 1953), p. 1047.

136. Testimony of Dr. William T. Martin, *Hearings . . . on Un-American Activities* (Washington, D.C., 1953), pp. 1015, 1019; Testimony of Dr. Norman Levinson, *Hearings . . . on Un-American Activities* (Washington, D.C., 1953), pp. 1100, 1083.

137. Testimony of Isadore Amdur, *Hearings . . . on Un-American Activities*, p. 1054.

138. Anne Roe, *The Making of a Scientist* (New York, 1933), pp. 60, 225.

139. Editorial, unsigned, *Student Review*, II, No. 5 (March 1933), 3.

140. Richard M. Scammon and Lester Breslow, "Booting out the R.O.T.C.," *Student Outlook*, III, No. 1 (October 1934), 13–14; Edwin Johnson, "An American Hitler's 2nd Lieutenants," *Student Outlook*, II, No. 3 (February 1934), 7–8; "Students Against War," *Student Outlook*, III, Nos. 2–3 (November-December 1934), 15, 28–29.

141. Lapin, *op. cit.*, p. 8.

142. *Student*, Alumni Issue, III, No. 3 (June 21, 1933), 1.

143. George Fenner, "Umbrella over City College," *Student Outlook*, II, No. 1 (November 1933), 22.

144. Iversen, *op. cit.*, p. 129.

145. *City College and War*, pamphlet issued by the Committee of Expelled and Suspended City College Students, October 1933, p. 10; Wechsler, *Revolt on the Campus*, p. 386.

146. Lapin, *op. cit.*, p. 7.

147. Nancy Bedford-Jones, "My Father Is a Liar!" *New Masses* (September 3, 1935), pp. 9–11.

148. "Refuse to Fight! an Editorial," *Student Outlook*, I, No. 5 (May 1933), 3; Wechsler, *Revolt on the Campus*, p. 140.

149. *The Campus*, LVIII, No. 21 (April 24, 1936).

150. Democritus, "Harvard," in "Students Strike Against War," *Student Outlook*, II, No. 5 (May 1934), 12.

151. "Mass Strike Meeting Endorses Oxford Oath," *The Campus*, LVIII, No. 21 (April 24, 1936). "If the World War was a catastrophe to the college generation of that period, think how much more so another would be to ours. It would wipe us out. It would be the end of civilization. . . . Drastic action is demanded. We must utilize forceful explosive methods of letting governments know our intentions not to be drafted into another holocaust of destruction. This is the chief purpose of the Oxford Pledge." See Joseph P. Lash, "Are Liberals Immune?" *Student Advocate*, I, No. 1 (February 1936), 26–27. After the Second World War, Lawrence Knobel reappeared as leader of the Communist faction of the American Veterans Committee. See Robert L. Tyler, "The American Veterans Committee: Out of a Hot War and Into the Cold," *American Quarterly*, XVIII (Fall 1966), 425.

152. Joseph P. Lash and James A. Wechsler, *War Our Heritage* (New York, 1936), pp. 98–99.

153. Joseph P. Lash, *The Campus Strikes Against War* (pamphlet; New York, 1934), p. 11.

154. Joseph P. Lash, "500,000 Strike for Peace: an Appraisal" *Student Advocate*, I, No. 4 (May 1936), 3–5.

155. Joseph P. Lash, "Are Liberals Immune?" *Student Advocate*, I, No. 1 (February 1936), 26–27.

156. Winston S. Churchill, *The Gathering Storm* (Boston, 1948), p. 85.

157. *John Cornford: A Memoir*, ed. Pat Sloan (London, 1938), p. 159.

158. "Oxford Debaters Revive War Issue," *The New York Times*, May 17, 1965.

159. Edwin Rolfe, *The Lincoln Battalion* (New York, 1939), p. 102. See also *Hearings before the Committee on Un-American Activities, Eighty-Third Congress, First Session (Education—Part 6), June 22, 1953*, p. 1851.

160. "Eugene Bronstein: A Tribute," *Harvard Communist*, IV, No. 1 (November 1937), 3–4.

161. Iversen, *op. cit.*, pp. 142–144.

162. Sam Levinger, chairman of the American Student Union Labor Committee at Ohio State University, was also killed. He had wandered from college to strike-torn Gastonia, in North Carolina, to the "American Lower Depths," in his quest, and then to his death in Spain. With him among the dead were Joseph Seligman of Swarthmore, and Leo Torgoff of Brooklyn College. Sixty "A.S.U.'ers" were reported to be fighting in Spain. See Clara Distel, "Modern Odyssey of a Young American," *Student Advocate*, II, No. 3 (December 1937), 6 ff.

163. Alvah Bessie, *Men in Battle: A Story of Americans in Spain* (New York, 1939), pp. 181–182.

164. Rolfe, *op. cit.*, p. 16.

165. Recently accounts have appeared which depict the City College radicals as student leaders who then evolved into the middle-aged leaders of American sociology. This latter group, however, were all anti-Communists as students. They were burdened by neither the degree of alienation nor generational revolt characteristic of activists in student movements. Most of them had a positive interest in Jewish culture; they were not rejecting their fathers. The student anti-Communists, a small intellectual group, really were apart from the City College student movement; it confuses matters to think of them as student leaders or activists. See David Boroff, "A Kind of Proletarian Harvard," *The New York Times Magazine*, March 28, 1965.

166. *The Testament of Julius and Ethel Rosenberg* (2nd edn.; New York, 1954), p. 114.

167. Virginia Gardner, *The Rosenberg Story* (New York, 1954), pp. 53–54.

168. Jonathan Root, *The Betrayers: The Rosenberg Case—A Reappraisal of an American Crisis* (New York, 1963), pp. 31–33, 54, 59, 79.

169. *The Campus,* LVIII, No. 21 (April 24, 1936).

170. *The Campus,* LVIII, No. 29 (May 26, 1936); No. 28 (May 22, 1936); No. 27 (May 20, 1936); No. 26 (May 19, 1936).

171. Joseph P. Lash, "Action Notes," *Student Advocate,* I, No. 5 (October-November 1936), 28.

172. *The Campus,* LIX, No. 13 (October 30, 1936). I have not tried to correct discrepancies in the published figures.

173. Lapin, *op. cit.*, pp. 9, 21.

174. *The New York Times,* February 11, 1940. See also Joseph P. Lash, *Eleanor Roosevelt: A Friend's Memoir* (New York, 1964), pp. 55–58.

175. Iversen, *op. cit.*, p. 213.

176. "Are Students Afraid of Politics?" *New Republic* (October 29, 1951), pp. 16–17; Paula Goldberg, "League for Industrial Democracy," *New Republic* (December 10, 1951), pp. 2, 4.

177. James Webster, "A New Road for Student Socialism," *Monthly Review,* III, No. 6 (October 1951), 175.

178. The third of the twenty-one conditions which the Communist International required, in July 1920, of its affiliated parties was as follows: "In nearly all countries in Europe and America the class struggle is entering the stage of civil war. Under these circumstances the Communists can have no confidence in bourgeois legality. They must *everywhere* create a duplicate illegal apparatus, which, at the decisive moment, could help the Party to perform its duty to the revolution." See V. I. Lenin, *Selected Works,* X: *The Communist International* (New York, 1938), 202.

179. Alistair Cooke, *A Generation on Trial: U.S.A. v. Alger Hiss* (New York, 1950).

180. Lawrence Barrett, "What the Campus Thinks: Polling College Editors," *The Nation,* CLXXXII (May 12, 1956), 402–403; "College Press for Ike," *The Nation,* CLXXXIII (October 27, 1956), 336.

181. "College Revival Becomes Confession Marathon," *Life,* XXVIII (February 20, 1950), 40–41.

182. Jones B. Shannon, "Religious Revolution on the Campus," *Saturday Evening Post,* CCXXX, No. 39 (March 29, 1958), 20.

183. "A Survey of the Political and Religious Attitudes of American College Students," *National Review,* XV, No. 14 (October 8, 1963), 291.

184. "Conservatives on the Campus," *Newsweek,* LVII, No. 15 (April 10, 1961), 35.

185. "A Survey of the Political and Religious Attitudes of American College Students," *National Review,* XV, No. 14 (October 8, 1963), 279–302.

186. The Editors, "Who You Are," *Monthly Review,* IX, No. 12 (April 1958), 426–431.

187. Roy Finch, "The Liberation Poll," *Liberation,* IV, No. 8 (November 1959), 14.

188. Robert Martinson, "State of the Campus: 1962," *The Nation,* CXCIV, No. 20 (May 19, 1962), 434. The inventory of students' political journals was as follows:

NAME OF JOURNAL	PLACE
Cambridge 38	Harvard
Alternatives	University of Illinois
Albatross	Swarthmore
Awareness	University of Chicago
Nightshade	University of Connecticut
A Liberal Light	Miami
The Activist	Oberlin
New University Thought	Chicago
New University News	Chicago
Reed	Tulane
The Phoenix	Chicago
Our Generation against War	Montreal
Comment	Harvard
Studies on the Left	Wisconsin
The Fat Abbott	Boston
Advance	Harvard
New Freedom	Cornell
Warbaby Review	Harvard
Mosaic	Harvard
The Lion Rampant	Harvard
Adams House Journal of the Social Sciences	Harvard
Yale Political	Yale
The Root and Branch	Berkeley
The Second Coming	Columbia
Tocsin News Forum	Harvard
Venture	New York
Audit	Buffalo

EIGHT *The New Student Left of the Sixties*

1960: The Issue-Searching Stage

The student movement in America as it revived in 1960 was very much in its issue-searching stage. The numbers involved were small. At the University of California, according to two activists in 1960, "out of a student body of nearly 20,000, the student movement has a fluctuating core of about twenty-five to fifty students and several faculty members. Another few hundred students regularly offer their support on specific causes. When a real controversy arises, probably no more than five thousand people, or a quarter of the student population, are even aware of any unusual activity. But this is a real increase over previous times."[1] The student movement had not yet perceived the strategic significance of the merger of its own generational struggle with the civil rights movement. The first book to emanate from the student movement in a generation, *Student,* published in 1962 and written by David Horowitz, a leading Berkeley activist, in its headings of seventeen chapters dealing with various student causes never mentioned the civil rights movement. It gave primacy rather to criticizing the university as "an assembly line for high-grade technicians"; "the most powerful force defeating us in our lives as students," it said, "is the irrelevance of knowledge in America today." The book treated such matters as the hunger strike of a student against compulsory R.O.T.C. in October 1959, the university directives of 1959 which forbade the student government to speak for the student body on off-campus political issues, the student campaign against capital punishment, their vigil the night a prisoner was executed in San Quentin, the controversy over an English examination question which cast slurs upon the F.B.I., the students' demonstration in the San Francisco City Hall on May 12, 1960, against the House Un-American Activities Committee, the arrests and trials that followed, the campaign against the film *Operation Abolition,* the report by J. Edgar Hoover on Communist activities among the youth, the resignation of the *Daily Californian* editors when they were forbidden by the student government to support one particular student political party, the shooting of an activist professor and the killing of an assistant by a demented former graduate student, an extravagant charge that "the administration in Berkeley played the same role in the [latter] Parkinson case that officials have played for years in the South," the protest inspired when one student was failed in military science for wearing his uniform on a picket line against the R.O.T.C., the Easter Peace Walk, the address on campus of a speaker who had recently been convicted of contempt of Congress, the trial of a student accused of hitting a policeman with a club at the San Francisco City Hall riot, the university rules and the student protests against the Cuban invasion in April 1961, and the prospect for a new politics. In its search for a strategic issue, *Student* was characterized by all the themes of generational mission, generational conflict, and student elitism: "The campus is the last refuge of true democracy in America. Only on the campuses was there widespread support of the right of self-determination for the Cuban people; only on the campuses has there been large-scale community action in the defense of free speech."[2] These students, "as yet out of power, still at work in the universities, represent a new and dynamic group who will one day take the reins of this great nation." Strangely the civil rights struggle was only in passing mentioned in this book. A few sentences told how a student chapter of CORE had picketed the local Woolworth and Kress stores that year, and how the student government had enacted a resolution in support of the Southern sit-ins. But the campaign against capital punishment was given far more space, and still many more pages were devoted to the House Un-American Activities Committee. The final political statement by a graduate student in economics, Robert Scheer, was primarily a document on cultural alienation; it assailed "the humanly debasing mediocrity of T.V.," criticized society's manipulation of man for profit, defended the takers of pot or Plato, and warned that "inside every socialist lurks a puritan."[3] But throughout this program-manifesto, there was no mention of the struggle for the Negro's civil rights.

Traits of the New Student Movement: Rejection of Labor

The new student movement, unlike the old, made no pretense of being rooted in economic issues. Early in its issue-searching stage, an article in one of its organs observed:

> Little, if any, concern has been evidenced over economic issues—certainly only a very few students have shed tears over the strike defeats of unions, massive

unemployment, right-to-work laws, urban re-development, etc. The dramatic, clear-cut, and relatively easy-to-comprehend yet appalling conditions of the farm laborers have aroused some sympathy—but mostly in the highly politicized California area. Affluent society or not, these issues are strange to primarily middle-class students, and are far too complex to arouse a moral or emotional reaction, except for a few from pro-labor backgrounds.[4]

No longer could the American student activist satisfy his back-to-the-people impulse by identifying with the labor movement. Labor had ceased to be a movement; it had its everyday material interests but no apocalyptic goals; it was smug, self-satisfied, suspicious of idealistic intellectuals. A former president of the newly organized Students for a Democratic Society a year later described the students' disenchantment with labor: Labor, he said, had once been an "opposition group," championing the causes of the people against the starkest oppression, and putting forward a set of values and a social image of industrial democracy:

> No longer does labor have this image. It appears not as an opposition group but as a reform club within the "establishment." It does not call for militant rank and file action, it does not basically challenge the structure of the Democratic Party, it doesn't challenge the economic privilege of corporate elites. Even more disheartening to students, its failure to banish discrimination from within its own house makes it a party to the racism that pervades almost every institution of American life.[5]

Labor had "acceded to Johnson as Kennedy's second man. . . ."

The New Left was one which rose predominantly out of an "affluent society" and moreover out of a relatively stable system; it therefore tended, when it thought critically, to do so in moralistic rather than economic terms. The New Left also was an indicator of the pattern which generational revolt takes in a prosperous society. The young activist, filled with aggressive emotion, found no objective, economic institution against which to direct his feeling. "Free-floating" aggression is much more likely to take a moralistic form; the very values of the System as a whole are rejected, precisely because the System is so economically stable that it provides jobs and opportunities for the willing and capable. The values of Vocation, Work, and Success are made the targets of generational revolt; hence the New Left has a propensity toward the beatnik and the hippie. A Communist writer noted this contrast between the present generation's radicalism and his own:

> The revolt is generally expressed in the idiom of modern sociology and psychology rather than in the terms of political economy that were in vogue a generation ago. There is much talk about values, but a radical Rip Van Winkle who might mutter, "Ah, yes, exchange value and surplus value . . ." would soon be puzzled—the common current usage refers to moral and not economic categories.
>
> Frequently this difference between the generations is enveloped in mystery, or it is made to appear that the moral concerns of this one are somehow

superior to the materialistic emphasis of its predecessor. It is really not so mysterious and spiritual—the generation that came of age in the 1930's experienced a shattering economic crisis, while the college radicals of today are children of the "affluent society." . . .

Among some student leaders there is a powerful sense of mission. One said, "If this student generation does not bring about meaningful social change I am afraid it will never come."[6]

What the new student radicalism resented most, however, was probably not the Affluent Society or the Organized System but the Stable System. It would have welcomed a chance to make a society affluent or to organize a system if it could do the organizing. But a Stable System defeats the possibilities of change which only an unstable society provides. The metaphysical value of the young is change; and the restless desire to direct and dominate change, and to see one's energies actualized, made the Stable System an alienating, impersonal object.

Rejection of the Old Liberals

If the New Student Left, disenchanted with labor, was at odds with the Old Marxists, the Old Left, it also utterly rejected the Old Liberals. The latter had committed the unpardonable sin—they had joined the Establishment. The new student movement refused utterly to identify with any part of the System or Establishment. It scorned the Old Liberals as Establishment Intellectuals. A vice-president of the National Student Association said in June 1963, "Involvement has meant to the post-war intellectual service in the Establishment . . . So that, in the late fifties, there was a good deal of celebration of the fact that intellectuals were to be found in all power structures of the society. . . ." Now, however, new alternatives existed for the intellectual—it was no longer a choice of either the Establishment or Isolation. "For the first time there is a base of power outside the university to which the intellectual can turn." The Young Left sought a new road to power. "The intellectual can obtain power by involving himself in the emerging centers of power in society: the civil rights movement, the peace movement, the discussion of economic issues."[7] The will to political power of an intellectual elite was never more clearly stated.

The New Left in the sixties was as contemptuous of the Old Liberals as the young activists of the thirties had been of the liberals of the twenties. As one New Leftist wrote:

> The symbol of the "old order," of the intellectuals of the fifties, is Arthur Schlesinger, and the reaction to Arthur Schlesinger underlines the healthy reaction of the intellectual to the trap that they were (and Schlesinger is) in. And the more articles that Arthur Schlesinger writes, lecturing intellectuals, telling them that they are out of their minds not to be serving the Establishment, the better off we'll be.[8]

Such a middle-aged radical as James Wechsler was dismissed as essentially well-meaning but ineffectual because he was too involved with the System. His *Reflections of an Angry Middle-Aged Editor* was treated in much the same terms in which Wechsler himself had described the Columbia liberals thirty years before: "For all Wechsler's amiable arguments, this is a depressing book. He says so many of the right things, more or less as they have been said for so many years, and it is not enough. In his way he is as devoted to *realpolitik* as are Nixon and Johnson."[9] The trend of the New Left was to work "outside the framework of party politics." It was attracted to the tactic of direct action, to emulating the examples of the Montgomery bus strike, the sit-downs in the South, the pacifist demonstrations against atomic installations and bomb testing. One could pass directly from moral principle to direct action without the distortion of an intervening refractory political machine. One could pit one's will against the System, and it would yield. One could make history instead of being made by it.

Emergence of an Elitist Ideology: Intellectuals, Especially Students, as the Primary Agents of Social Change

An elitist trend in the American student movement emerged early in the sixties, finding its most explicit spokesman in C. Wright Mills. Disillusioned with labor, and at odds with the middle class and what he called the "power elite," Mills, by a process of elimination, had only the intellectuals to turn to as agents of social change. He was recapitulating the same processes of disillusionment with the people and apotheosizing of the intellectuals which the Russian populists had undergone. As the Russian students became disillusioned with the Bakuninist metaphysic which exalted the revolutionary potential of the masses, so now Mills threw aside the outmoded "labor metaphysic":

> What I do not quite understand about some new left writers is why they cling so mightily to "the working class" of the advanced capitalist societies as *the* historic agency, or even as the most important agency, in the face of the really impressive historical evidence that now stands against this expectation.
>
> Such a labor metaphysic, I think, is a legacy from Victorian Marxism that is now quite unrealistic.[10]

Mills made the intellectual class into the historical elite, the makers of history. "Who is it that is thinking and acting in radical ways? All over the world—in the bloc, outside the bloc and in between—the answer is the same: it is the young intelligentsia":

> In the Soviet bloc, who is it that has been breaking out of apathy? It has been students and young professors and writers. . . . That is why we have got to study these new generations of intellectuals around the world as real live agencies of

historic change. . . . "But it is just some kind of moral upsurge, isn't it?" Correct. But under it: no apathy. Much of it is direct non-violent action, and it seems to be working, here and there. Now we must learn from the practice of these young intellectuals and with them work out new forms of action.

Some student activists had misgivings about Mills' espousal of intellectual elitism, though he had clearly caught an undercurrent of the student movement. "The books of C. Wright Mills are well-thumbed by us, and it is his sort of radicalism with which many of us identify. Yet Mills is not our intellectual leader, nor are we blind to his faults. We criticize him for his elitism and a certain callousness toward fact," wrote a Stanford student leader, the head of the Palo Alto Fair Play for Cuba Committee.[11] Some student idealists were reluctant to look at themselves as candidates for power in their own right rather than as trustees for the masses. They argued that Mills' elitism could lead to the support of undemocratic regimes such as Castro's.[12] They held on to the hope of a "pacifist-liberal-labor-Negro coalition." Others argued that where the students and young intellectuals had been able to make their contribution, it was by merging themselves with the revolutionary masses: "The social value of the Cuban intellectual has stood in direct proportion to his willingness to fuse his own identity with that of the Cuban worker and peasant."[13]

The neo-elitist ideology often expressed itself in an adulation of identification with such figures as Fidel Castro. Castro, an intellectual, a student leader, had galvanized the masses. Castro was anti-American, and the new student movement was emotionally attracted to whoever was anti-American. Anti-Americanism was the ideology of rejecting all that the fathers stood for. History was going to be made by the anti-Americans of the world, the "uncommitted" peoples of the world, the colored races of Asia, Africa, and Latin America, the Negro in the United States. The fathers were defined by the unconscious of the students in the student movement as without virtues, the oppressors "of all that was living in the world."

Search for a Foreign Identification: The Appeal of Castro

To the new student activists casting about for some personality with whom they might identify, Fidel Castro was what we might call a "generational hero"; he had destroyed the order of the fathers. The young bearded Cuban doctor of law, leading his band of student revolutionaries to victory over the System, and to the founding of a New Humanistic Society, was quickly exalted in the new revolutionary mythology. Fidel Castro synthesized the ingredients of the New Ideology, anti-Americanism, intellectual elitism, revolutionary activism, and a sense of generational mission. One student leader in 1961 explained this identification in astonishingly naïve terms: "To a remarkable degree there are ideological similarities between the Cuban and Campus revolutions. Both Cuban and Campus rebels are *strong* dissenters, firm in their convictions and willing to speak out and act militantly in spite of the mighty coercive powers of the American state." Castro had not yet declared himself a Marxist-Leninist or his regime Communist. Therefore young student activists could the more easily project their own free-wheeling rebellion on him:

> Both Cuban and Campus revolutions are inexperienced, groping movements, sometimes stumbling. . . . Most important, their motivating ideologies are neither socialism—Marxian or otherwise—nor liberalism, although they combine elements of both. Rather, the ideology of both the *Barbudos* of Cuba and the Campus revolutionaries is a refreshing combination of humanism and rationalism. . . . In at least one sense the Fidelista is very fortunate. He is confronted with the opportunity to steer Cuba's, and perhaps Latin America's destiny upon the path which he chooses. . . . Many students at U. of C., Stanford, San Francisco and San Jose State College, at Wisconsin, and Chicago and N.Y.U. grasp and appreciate this attempt to direct human history.[14]

The emotional appeal of Castro to American students was founded on precisely its amalgam of elitism and populism. American activists longed to share such an experience as the Cuban students' back-to-the-people movement:

> They had all volunteered to leave their homes and promising careers for three years to go to the mountains to teach the children there the simple elements of a basic education. . . . Fidel Castro was speaking. He warned them of the difficulties they would face there, their isolation from all to which they had become accustomed in their lives, and the natural resistance they would find among the peasants to the new venture. He urged patience upon them and then thanked them for their sacrifice.[15]

To lead the people, to be its pure, youthful guides, to sacrifice oneself for them, to live by an ideal higher than the ordinary goods of careers, and by a faith nobler than the objectivities of science, such was the creed of which Castro seemed the prophet. When the missile crisis of 1962 took place, and the United States insisted on the withdrawal of the Soviet missile installations, the student activists were ready to believe it was all an invention of the Central Intelligence Agency. As the Cuban crisis receded, as Castro became embroiled with Communist China over her attempts to dominate his policy, and as Cuba itself became less stridently anti-American, the student activists became perceptibly less enthusiastic over Castro. Then the Vietcong's guerrilla warfare and the grandiose anti-American onslaughts of Mao Tse-tung became more suitable objects for generational admiration.

But a foreign identification was never a sufficient channel for the back-to-the-people longings of the emerging American student movement. If there was no proletariat, no peasantry, no downtrodden people with whom to merge oneself, there was a challenge of identification with the lowliest of Americans, who stood outside the ordinary boundaries of the class system—the Negro. In 1960 the sudden rise of the Negro student movement gave a fresh stimulus to the American student movement.

The Negro Student Movement for Civil Rights

The Negro student movement came spontaneously into existence on February 1, 1960.[16] Its immediate objective was to desegregate lunch counters; its ultimate aim was to destroy the entire "Jim Crow" system of discrimination in transportation, rest rooms, restaurants, and recreational facilities. On February 1, 1960, four Negro students sat down at a dime store counter in Greensboro, North Carolina, and asked for cups of coffee; they set off a chain of reactions on the campuses of Negro colleges throughout the country, and had the deepest subsequent effect on the American student movement generally. The students were bullied and beaten, but they could not be browbeaten. Their sit-ins were truly spontaneous, for no organization such as NAACP, CORE, or the Southern Christian Leadership Conference planned or organized them.[17] The initiative during this period was that of Negro students, though they had the example before them of the Montgomery bus boycott of 1955. A Negro seamstress, Mrs. Rosa Parks, had boarded a bus in Montgomery after her day's work on December 1; when the bus driver ordered her to yield her seat to a white passenger, she refused. Her arrest aroused the Negro community, which organized a nonviolent boycott of the bus line. Hardships, arrests, imprisonment, and terrorism followed; almost a full year later, on November 13, 1956, the United States Supreme Court declared unconstitutional Alabama's laws on segregation in buses, and a few weeks later integration on the buses was realized. The name of the young leader of the boycott, a twenty-seven-year-old Baptist minister, Martin Luther King, Jr., was written down among those of the outstanding Americans of his time. It was the Negro middle class which had conceived and inspired the Montgomery boycott;[18] it was their sons who less than three years later proceeded to the even more direct "confrontation" of sit-ins. The fathers had abstained from using a public utility; the sons demanded the use of one.

The wave of sit-ins which took place was unprecedented in the history of the American student movement. "The Greensboro sit-ins struck a special chord of repressed emotion," writes Howard Zinn, "and excitement raced across the Negro college campuses of the South."[19] This was the direct action of a Negro student movement. The chronological list for the month of February 1960 alone indicates the readiness to spontaneous action among the Negro studentry:[20]

DATE	CITY AND STATE	SCHOOL	ACTION	NO. ARRESTED AND CHARGES
Feb. 1	Greensboro, N.C.	N.C. Agricultural and Technical College Dudley H.S. Bennett College	Sit-ins Picket and Boycott	4: Trespass
Feb. 8	Durham, N.C.	N.C. College	Sit-in	
	Winston-Salem, N.C.	Winston-Salem Teachers' College	Sit-in	25: Trespass
	Fayetteville, N.C.	Fayetteville Teachers' College	Sit-in	
Feb. 9	Charlotte, N.C.	Johnson C-Smith Univ.	Sit-in Picket and Boycott	3: Assault and violating fire law
	High Point, N.C.	William Penn H.S.	Sit-in	1: Blocking sidewalk
	Concord, N.C.	Barber-Scotia College	Sit-in and religious service on court-house lawn	
	Elizabeth, N.C.	Elizabeth City Teachers' College	Sit-in	
	Henderson, N.C.	Kittrell College	Sit-in	
Feb. 10	Raleigh, N.C.	Shaw Univ., St. Augustine College	Sit-in	43: Trespass
Feb. 11	Hampton, Va.	Hampton Institute	Sit-ins and Picket	
	Portsmouth, Va.	Norcom H.S.	Sit-ins	28: Disorderly conduct
Feb. 12	Rock Hill, S.C.	Friendship Jr. College Clinton Jr. College		

DATE	CITY AND STATE	SCHOOL	ACTION	NO. ARRESTED AND CHARGES
Feb. 13	Nashville, Tenn.	Fisk Univ. Tenn. State College	Sit-ins Boycott	76: Conspiracy to violate commerce laws; disorderly conduct
Feb. 19	Chattanooga, Tenn.	High School	Sit-ins	59: Loitering
Feb. 20	Richmond, Va.	Va. State Univ.	Sit-in Picket Boycott	63: Trespass
Feb. 22	Petersburg, Va.	Va. State College	Library Sit-in	14: Trespass
Feb. 25	Montgomery, Ala.	Alabama State College	Sit-in March to state capital	34: Disorderly conduct
	Tuskegee, Ala.	Tuskegee Institute	Boycott of classes March	
Feb. 29	Tallahassee, Fla.	Florida A. & M. Univ.	Sit-in Boycott	6
	Nashville, Tenn.	Fisk Univ., Tenn. Agri.	March to court	

Thus, within the first month of sit-ins, February 1960, the students of at least twenty-six Negro institutions were involved in direct action to secure the abrogation of racial restrictions. The following month of March, twenty-seven more Negro institutions of learning were drawn into spontaneous sit-in movements. Then, as Tom Kahn writes, "as the novelty of the demonstrations wore off, newspaper reporting became increasingly meagre."

Generational Revolt in the Negro Student Movement

Underlying the Negro student movement, the spontaneous uprising of the sit-ins, was a profound de-authoritization of Negro students' own fathers, their older generation. The Negro student movement was thus directed, not only against white oppression, but also against the students' fathers; it was a generational conflict at the same time. "The sit-ins," writes Louis Lomax, "were a revolt against both segregation and the entrenched Negro leadership." To the students' minds, their own fathers seemed too often cowed and emasculated by centuries of white oppression and humiliation. The fathers failed as moral guides in the struggle for emancipation.[21] Often professors were cast in the role of de-authoritized fathers by their students. As one Negro student leader, Glenford Mitchell, editor of the student newspaper at Shaw University and member of the Intelligence Committee which led the sit-in demonstrations in Raleigh, North Carolina, described this generational division:

The Intelligence Committee at Shaw University and St. Augustine's College asked the students not to elicit advice or opinions from their instructors. "This," we asserted, "is a student movement, manned by students, planned by students, and controlled by students. We do not need faculty advisors on this venture. . . ." We are always very cautious not to allow Uncle Toms to share our plans and decisions. Heaven knows how far such plans would get before we were ready to execute them. We have reason to regard some of our faculty members as such, and there are even some among our ranks. . . . Our indifference to administration and faculty on this issue is well understood by both sides . . .[22]

At the largest Negro university of the United States, Southern University in Baton Rouge, the administration and parents made common cause against the students. The president of the university, Dr. Felton G. Clark, felt himself obliged to invoke disciplinary action against participants in sit-ins. When the students protested, seventeen of them were expelled. "Their schoolmates decided to boycott all classes until they were reinstated. In retaliation the administration called the parents of students and told them the student leaders were inciting to riot. Upset parents summoned their children home." When many students proposed to withdraw in protest, the university required that they secure the approval of their parents for such a step. For a brief period after student demonstrations the university was closed, and at the request of the authorities, police cars patrolled the campus to maintain order and rebuff demonstrations on behalf of the expelled students. Subsequently, the student leaders advised their almost five thousand fellow-students to return to classes.[23] Southern University thus became the unique battle ground of two generational standpoints. Dr. Felton Grandison Clark, president of Southern University, was a noted educator who had done much to advance Negro rights and opportunities. His father before him had been president of the institution too, and both believed in the efficacy of quiet, persistent pressure and education. Dr. Clark had proved effective, for example, in persuading a Southern chemical plant to hire its first Negro chemists; but when his students were arrested for off-campus sit-in demonstrations, he found himself bound to comply with the mandates of the State Board of Education. The students charged him with "knuckling under." The president replied that a state regulation provided for the suspension of arrested students until their cases were decided by the courts.[24] To the embattled students this constituted an evasive, cowardly, hypocritical administrative legalism.

The Negro student movement, whose participants yearned for inclusion in the rights and privileges of middle-class America, was relatively free of the beatnik, nihilist elements which characterized the white student movement. Students in the Negro colleges were content with the everyday culture of American life. One observer reported, "They are more likely to quote you Harry Golden than Gandhi or Thoreau. In a meeting with a group of leaders from Virginia State, one proclaimed: 'We have no intellectuals, we read no books. I'll be blunt with you, man: We're conservatives.' "[25] A Berkeley activist felt himself out of place at the leading Negro institution, Howard University.[26] The sit-ins contrasted strangely with the "tameness" of Negro campus life.

> Absolutely no forms of rebellion exist: no bohemianism, no orgies, no riots, no radical discussion groups—not even walking on the grass! Everyone dresses like the pictures in Sunday magazines—pressed pants, shined shoes, ivy shirts and flouncy dresses. Girls, as a rule, must be safe in their dormitories by 10:30 PM—even on weekends—and to be caught drinking is cause for expulsion. Fraternities are rife and claim fanatic loyalty.

The virtues of the "Protestant Ethic," of hard work, conscientiousness, and thrift, for the Negro student often constituted goals sought in his generational protest. Often he knew only too well that at one generation's remove his own forebears had lived the life of the lowliest, with their disorganized families, absent fathers, and sexual promiscuity. This was a heritage which the young Negro student wanted to overcome by his self-discipline.

Moreover, the students were no longer content "to thrive on handouts from the white community." "Since the professors and administrators have lived in just this way, they come in for a good deal of contempt." This was the de-authoritization of the old out of which every student movement is born. "For, when asked why they rebel actively where their parents did not, the students reply, 'You can't keep an educated man down.' Half a loaf is ashes in the mouths of the new generation."[27]

The Impact of the Negro Student Uprising on the White Student Movement

The wave of sit-ins in 1960 by Negro students had a tremendous effect on Northern white students. It prepared the emotional basis for a new back-to-the-people identification on the part of white students, for the old identification with the labor movement had vanished and left a vacuum. Organized labor was now regarded as one of the comfortable, narrowly oriented, and relatively culture-less interest groups of American society; furthermore, the workers had made it plain that they could do without the intellectuals.[28] But if the Marxist notion of the proletarian mission to reconstruct society seemed to the students an antiquated myth, it had expressed their emotional longing to merge themselves with the lowly and the exploited. Now the Negro students' heroism set an example for white students; an interracial unity in a common struggle for the voiceless Negro masses—here was an ideal perhaps even nobler than that of the workingmen's internationals. Southern Negro student emissaries toured the Northern campuses. On April 1, 1960, for instance, Berkeley students crowded into their largest auditorium to hear Thomas Gaither from Claffin College in South Carolina.[29] His grammar was poor, his words eloquent, when he told how his four hundred fellow-students had been soaked with fire hoses and tried for breach of the peace. The Negro students' example was evidently a powerful one, for the following month more than sixty Californian students behaved similarly in protest against the House Un-American Activities Committee in San Francisco, and were also hosed with water and arrested.[30]

Civil rights now rapidly became the dominant issue in the new student unrest. It allowed the coalescence of all the emotional sources of student movements. It provided a back-to-the-people identification in a way in which no campaign for the abolition of capital punishment could; it offered a chance for utter self-sacrifice far more than any pacifist campaign against bomb testing or military installations could, for it brought one face to face with the most violent and vindictive elements of society. This, moreover, was the one issue in which moral right and wrong stood out most clearly. The ethic of racial justice had a simplicity which was absent from the complex considerations and counter-considerations of such issues as capital punishment or war. And finally, the civil rights issue was the one which embarrassed the elder generation most. How seriously had the liberal elder generation meant its liberalism to be taken with respect to racial relations? How sincere were the elders?

The Negro and white student movements now started to merge in one back-to-the-people movement. Negro students, veterans of the sit-ins, and several white students, resolved to form a protest organization of their own distinct from the three existing adult organizations, NAACP, CORE, and the SCLC. Thus the generational division and generational revolt manifested itself in the organizational structure of the civil rights movement itself, and in the spring of 1960, SNCC came into existence, the Student Nonviolent Coordinating Committee. Sixteen staff people worked at its headquarters in Atlanta at only subsistence wages.[31] The adult organizations took its existence as a rebuke, but it was indeed the students' own. Its organizers were college youngsters, who "decided to drop everything—school and family and approved ambition—and move into the Deep South to become the first guerrilla fighters of the Student Nonviolent Coordinating Committee," wrote Howard Zinn.[32] By the middle of 1964, there were about 150 of them working full time, of whom approximately 80 per cent were Negro. Moreover, this Negro student movement was unusual in the history of student movements inasmuch as its members came predominantly from poor and working-class families. A census late in 1963 of the forty-one field workers in Mississippi showed that of the thirty-five Negroes, the twenty-five who were from the Deep South "came from homes where the mothers were maids or domestics, the fathers factory workers, truck drivers, farmers, bricklayers, carpenters."[33] The sons were usually college graduates. They went about in Mississippi conducting Freedom Schools, teaching the theory and practice of democracy, cajoling the passive, the timid, and the indifferent to register to vote. In the summer of 1964, there were 650 of them, "the volunteers," mostly Northern white students, drawn by the spirit of idealism and self-sacrifice to the calling of missionaries of democracy. These several hundreds of idealistic college students were statistically a minute fraction of their two million fellow-students in the United States. Yet their moral influence was immense.

Fortunately, however, the civil rights movement never became altogether a student movement. A measure of generational equilibrium remained, with the influence of Martin Luther King, the NAACP, and the Kennedy administration itself strong. Left to itself, the student movement, in the form of the SNCC, would have mounted a series of actions which might well have led to massive outbursts of directionless violence; personal disillusionment and the alienation of the white liberal community would have resulted. At this critical juncture, the influence of the Kennedy administration kept the student movement along constructive channels. As Tom Hayden wrote:

The Kennedy Administration made clear that it believed and was willing to support the idea that the vote, not the lunch counter, must be the ultimate focus of the integration movement. . . . Prominent individuals and foundations met with student representatives from SNCC and promised financial help for massive voter registration efforts. Coupled with the virtual promise of full Justice Department support, the promise of financial help considerably enhanced the possibility of a fruitful voter campaign.[34]

This, then, was a back-to-the-people movement conducted in part with the blessing and advice of the government. Many in SNCC were restive about the role of the government, accusing it of passivity and betrayal, and many caviled at the continuing advice and participation of the adult liberals of NAACP and SCLC. Nevertheless, the fact that this student movement could pursue a path which led to constructive legislation and extension of the democratic process, that it did not terminate as so many of its forebears in disillusionment with the people and individual terrorism, was probably due to the cross-generational cooperation which was maintained. Perhaps the administration's helpfulness arose in part, as some students charged, from its desire for Southern Negro votes in 1962 and 1964, but as Tom Hayden conceded, this was "not to gainsay the validity of the administration's viewpoint."

The Will to Martyrdom Ingredient in the New Student Movement

The students who converged on Mississippi were not altogether representative of the growing American student movement. They were subject to adult controls. "The screening process for volunteers had been rigorous. From Stanford University, only 45 of an original 300 applicants eventually got to Mississippi, and at Wesleyan University half of the students who wished to participate were not admitted." Professor John Maguire of Wesleyan indicated that they aimed to exclude "two types: those who are looking for a new kind of 'kick,' sexual or otherwise; and those evangelical souls" who, with no understanding of the concrete situation, will "turn their eyes skyward and say, 'Lord, here I am.' "[35]

Elitism, populism, and the tragic ingredient of suicidalism, however, were all present in this new back-to-the-people movement. One student noted, "Some of these people think that they are going to reform our entire civilization and that the Negro will be the spearhead of this new age."[36] There was suicidalism. The columnist, Joseph Alsop, wrote, "It is a dreadful thing to say, but it needs saying. The organizers who sent these young people into Mississippi must have wanted, even hoped for, martyrs."[37] It was an "undeclared guerrilla war," wrote William McCord. In seminars they learned how, if caught in a violent mob, to crouch with knees up to protect the belly, and to wrap one's arms around one's head.

The letters, for instance, of the young martyred Episcopal seminarian, Jonathan Myrick Daniels, murdered by a white racist sadist in August 1965, expressed this high note of self-sacrifice and the self-destructive desire to become immersed in the life of the lowliest. An essay of his, printed in the *Episcopal Theological School Journal*, a mimeographed student publication at his seminary in Cambridge, told how in Selma a "redneck turned and stared at my seminarian's collar, at my ESCRU (Episcopal Society for Cultural and Racial Unity) button, at my face":

> He turned to a friend: "Know what he is?" The friend shouted: "No." Resuming, the speaker whinnied, "Why, he's a white niggah." I was not happy thus to become the object of every gaze. And yet deep within me rose an affirmation and a tenderness and a joy that wanted to shout, yes! . . . I should be unspeakably proud of my title. For it is the highest honor, the most precious distinction I have ever received. It is one that I do not deserve—and cannot ever earn. As I type now, my hands are hopelessly white. "But my heart is black. . . ."

When a Negro child of four said she did not love him, Jonathan was smitten with guilt. "A part of me seemed to die inside, and I fought back tears." There was the student's alienation from the world: "We are beginning to see as we never saw before that we are truly in the world and yet ultimately not of it."[38]

To merge himself with the Negroes, to be "black in heart," here we have the typical mechanism of identification with the lowliest which characterizes student movements. It fused itself with an extinction of both one's selfhood and selfishness through a death-seeking for the movement's sake. The students became death-seekers.

The strange suicidal trait manifested itself with unprecedented strength in the new American student movement. As the volunteers gathered to prepare for their civil rights campaign in Mississippi during the summer of 1964, the awareness that they were embarking on an encounter with death cast its enthrallment upon them. "I may be killed and you may be killed," said James Forman, executive secretary of the Student Nonviolent Coordinating Committee, to two hundred of the college students. "If you recognize that, the question of whether we're put in jail will become very, very minute."[39] The students, noted the reporter, had "an unmistakable middle-class stamp," and many were from the best schools in the East and West, Harvard, Smith, Stanford. Their common interest, apart from civil rights, seemed to be folk singing. Yet in their search for community, meaningfulness, for overcoming alienation, the death-motif was dominant. Some could offer the reporter "only the vaguest of explanations for deciding to join the project," but in their letters the Mississippi volunteers documented once again the death-wish which has hovered over all student movements:

"I've thought about death a lot and what death means about life, and I know that right now I don't want to live any way but the way I am. . . ."

"To us it was something new, something unbelievable, that we were putting our lives on the line, that some of our team-mates had been killed. . . ."

"He said what I knew all along, but it has made this place seem like a funeral parlor. People just walk around and sing, or are silent."

"If we realize that safety is a myth, aren't we in a sense 'saved' by that knowledge and acceptance of death?"

The students recognized that their ideological dedication had its unconscious sources:

"There's a lot of truth about all of us—y'all too—in Eric Hoffer's *The True Believer*."

"*Look* magazine is searching for the ideal naive northern middle-class white girl. For national press, that's the big story. And when one of us gets killed, the story will be even bigger."

Though "most of the staff and volunteers were agnostic nonviolent technicians," masochistic imagery of crucifixion and Jesus came into evidence:

"We must also learn to take the worst. Some of the Staff members walk around carrying sections of hose. This strangely terrible training in brutality may well save lives. (I must confess, I have not been able to take part in even the screaming of a mob scene. . . . Wherever possible, I am among the victims.)"

"[Bob Moses] is more or less the Jesus of the whole project."

"Furthermore, did Jesus Christ say, 'Let the experts preach the gospel'? No! He commanded everyone who loves Him to 'take up thy cross and follow me.' "[40]

The Mississippi volunteers were usually acting against their parents' wishes, asserting their generational independence. As the editor of their letters writes, "Some parents were sympathetic. But many were uncomprehending, others were simply afraid for their children. Thus a number of volunteers had gone to Oxford secretly. Or against the wishes of their families. They tried to explain." For instance:

"By now you know what I told you about my plans for the summer was in part a deliberate lie."

"I want to fulfill myself. . . . I do not want to spend my life in the pursuit and enjoyment of comfort and security. . . . I 'save' myself by committing myself to the concerns of other men. . . . I sense somehow that I am at a crucial moment in my life and that to return home where everything is secure and made for me would be to choose a kind of death."

The Mississippi student leaders were aware of the suicidalism which characterized many of the participants in the project, but they resented the suggestion made by some Northern writers that the summer volunteers were being "used as unwitting martyrs to provoke federal intervention." This suggestion especially infuriated young Robert Moses, graduate of Hamilton and Harvard, who for three years had been working in Mississippi as a SNCC field secretary, often virtually alone and ignored. "He was," said an interviewer, "understandably irritated at the implication that he is a Machiavellian who sits in an office somewhere coldly sending innocents to the slaughter." The movement's leaders emphasized that "the Summer Project volunteers were repeatedly warned ahead of time of the dangers they would be facing." Yet it was conceded that the presence of death-minded students was helpful to the movement: "They acknowledge that protection for Negroes in Mississippi is likely to be provided only when whites are involved." A local girl in the Holly Springs Freedom School wrote in its mimeographed newspaper that she and her friends were hurt but not shocked by the disappearance of the three freedom workers: "Many of our people have come up missing and nothing was said or done about it. . . . But never have I heard it said on the news or over T.V. or radio."[41] The death-seekers, it was surmised, perhaps were the needed martyrs of social advancement. Suicidalism, in the language of sociology, was said to have an essential functional role in a social movement.

The self-destructive theme in the student movement was at its height in Mississippi. In a lesser guise, it reappeared from time to time in the Berkeley student movement two years later. The prosaic, organization-minded Communist student leader in Berkeley was so much disturbed by this tendency in the "peace movement" to choose the most self-destructive tactics that she characterized this trend in un-Marxian terms as "self-immolation": "We are witnessing the self-immolation of a very important section of the movement. We must stop it."[42]

Rejection of the Peace Corps

The new student activists, especially the revolutionary ones, had little interest, however, in the Peace Corps. The Peace Corps was recognized as an imaginative effort by the administration of President John F. Kennedy to channelize constructively the populist, back-to-the-people impulses of young idealists. It was first proposed to students on October 14, 1960, on the steps of the Student Union Building of the University of Michigan at Ann Arbor. Greeted by a large, enthusiastic crowd of ten thousand students, candidate John F. Kennedy, speaking extemporaneously, challenged the students' idealism: "How many of you are willing to spend 10 years in Africa or Latin America or Asia working for the U.S. and working for freedom? How many of you [who] are going to be doctors are willing to spend your days in Ghana? . . . On your willingness to do that . . . I think, will depend the answer whether we as a free society can compete." But this challenge to idealism lacked one ingredient vital to the student activist; it lacked the anti-elder generation, anti-System element. It offered the possibility for an identification but not for aggression. And a revolutionary student movement above all seeks a channel for aggression. A movement sponsored by the government, by the oldsters, is simply too tame for the activists.

From its inception the student activists criticized the Peace Corps as pro-Establishment and nonrevolutionary, and when the war in Vietnam broke out they cited more specific rationalizations for their animus against the Peace Corps. Thus, students of a Committee on the Peace Corps and the Vietnam War circulated a statement in November 1965 which said in part, "I cannot serve in good conscience while the same government which would employ me to help people in one part of the world is killing, maiming, and leaving homeless men, women, and children in Vietnam," and they applauded a young associate professor who denounced the Peace Corps as a plot of the older generation. "The administration is using the Peace Corps as a playpen to keep unruly students out of the kitchen where adults are cooking up a war." The Peace Corps, he said, "is in fact the sugar coating to our war pill."[43]

Thus, the Peace Corps was perceived as a "playpen" for children to make it all the easier for the evil-minded adults to go about their nefarious work. The slogan-metaphors of an emotive generational revolt permeated the rationalization for spurning the Peace Corps. When the newly appointed director of the Peace Corps appealed for volunteers on the campus of the University of California, the questions from a hostile audience of activists aimed at the involvements of the United States in Vietnam and Santo Domingo. The older generation was presumably unmasked and exposed.[44]

Thus, the student movement generally stood opposed to the 10,200 volunteers who in 1966 were at work in forty-six countries on a variety of projects. The Peace Corps represented an isolation in pure form of the back-to-the-people component of traditional students' movements; it was the idealism, the altruism, in its pure state. In six African countries, more than one half of all high school teachers with college degrees were Peace Corps volunteers; in Nigeria, one-third of its students, more than fifty thousand of them, were being taught by Peace Corpsmen.[45] But the student activist regarded them with something of the bemusement which activists fifty years ago reserved for settlement house workers. The Peace Corps volunteer was still part of the System; the activist wished to secede from it, and destroy it. The volunteers were not generational revolutionists.

Failure of a Quest: Rejection by the Poor

Activists and student leaders, rejecting the Peace Corps and governmental projects, sought to contrive new forms of populism dissociated from the Establishment and expressive of their generational revolt. They tried to go back to the people directly in the slums, without benefit of mediation by the government or the labor movement.

Tom Hayden, a founder of the Students for a Democratic Society, and later a participant in the three-man mission of self-appointed diplomats who went to North Vietnam in December 1965, was one such ideal-typical activist filled with a missionary, back-to-the-people spirit. An admiring article in the *Village Voice*, organ of the young intellectuals of Greenwich Village, held him up as a model.

> For the last year-and-a-half Tom Hayden, 26, has been invisible to the mass media as he worked to build a community union in Newark's Negro ghetto. He led an exhausting, spartan life there. He ate and slept irregularly, worked hard, lived with frustration and failure.
>
> But NCUP (Newark Community Union Project) persevered. . . . Eventually, there were small triumphs: better garbage collection, repairs of rundown tenements, the de-activation of the city's urban renewal scheme that would have uprooted thousands of low-income families.
>
> Hayden, a former graduate student at the University of Michigan . . . was there—in Newark—because he chose to live his theory that social change comes from the disinherited of society. He disagreed with the wisest—and often the best—of the older radicals. . . . Hayden could have had his choice of juicy jobs. . . . Instead, he chose to live on $10 a week and remain invisible in Newark where he sometimes seemed a religious prophet fasting outside the gates of Sodom.[46]

Here, in Newark, said the writer, the root ideas of the New Left were being tested. "Could a lasting alliance be forged between university intellectuals bred on Mills and Camus and the excluded of the ghetto with their lack of education and enormous despair?"

Very quickly, however, American student activists began undergoing an experience very much like that of their Russian forebears. They found themselves rejected, in a sense, by the poor whom they came to save. In 1963, for instance, the Students for a Democratic Society had resolved to make the organization of the white poor its main objective. "The young people who joined SDS after Kennedy and the mass media discovered the poor saw the organization as one which would organize the poor." Michael Harrington, author of *The Other America*, prophet of poverty, was received on many campuses by enthusiastic audiences. Two years later, however, this back-to-the-people spirit had ebbed and was being replaced by a more unadorned elitism of the intellectual class. *Viewpoints*, a journal by members of New York Students for a Democratic Society, tried to explain the reasons for this intellectual and emotional change. The projects, it said, "have disappointed many others who had higher hopes. . . . The fact that the poor as a 'class' do not have the power to change society by themselves is coming to be understood by more and more members." Meanwhile, the intellectuals were on the march; "The anti-war movement and the Berkeley events have brought into visible protest middle-class intellectuals, faculty members, political figures, and a few trade unionists." The emphasis was increasingly strong on middle-class intellectuals as the chosen disinherited. "Middle-class groups such as teachers, welfare workers, and other white collar elements are coming to be seen along with the working poor and unionized workers as groups which have problems, suffer alienation, are organizable and, in fact are organizing already." Lastly, the students were getting tired of giving their emotions so fully to the poor. As the author put it more circumspectly, "perhaps most important, is simply that this generation of students is far too flexible and fluid to stay with any perspective once it begins to be dogmatic and limiting."[47]

The failure of the masses to respond, and the plain fact that the "initiative" was that of the "students and professors" began to affect student ideologists. They began to recognize and accept their apparent role as the primary makers of history. They began to conceive the role of intellectuals exactly as Lavrov had when he told the Russian students, disillusioned with the people's passivity, that the historical mission belonged to the "critically thinking individuals." The chief ideologist of the Free Speech Movement in Berkeley in the fall of 1965 was metamorphosing into such an ideologist of intellectual elitism. "Extreme action on their [the students'] part," wrote Steve Weissman, "might move whole other sectors of the population. If not, we should perhaps find out now so that we can plan our futures differently."[48]

The ebullient chief writer of the Berkeley Student Movement, laureate-expellee from both Brandeis University and the Trotskyists, and promoter with petit-bourgeois zest of the sales and production of *MacBird,* became utterly disillusioned with the American working class when it failed to heed the New Leftist summons to oppose the war in Vietnam. He wrote bitterly of the pro-war workers' demonstration in New York:

It was the day of the great workers' march, a marvelous day. . . . A hundred thousand workers marched down Fifth Avenue. . . . Seamen, Teamsters, Longshoremen, Auto Workers, Carpenters, Bricklayers, and many others. . . .

It was last Saturday, May 13, the day of the March to Support Our Boys in Vietnam, and the most popular chant was: "What do you want?" "Victory!" "When do you want it?" "Now!"

You will forgive me for seeing everything in class terms, but you see I Was a Teenage Trotskyist (at 19 I joined the Young Socialist Alliance) and that experience taught me to believe that my place was with the workers, however backward and lacking in true consciousness they might be. . . .

Anyway, the next time some \$3.90 an hour AFL type workers go on strike for a 50¢ raise, I'll remember the day they chanted "Burn Hanoi, Not Our Flag," and so help me I'll cross their ——— picket line. . . . They are grownups responsible for their own acts . . . evil, ugly people in their own right, every bit as bad as the Madison Avenue hipster. . . .

So what if the peace march on April 15 had a "middle-class" tone and the war march on May 13 had a "working-class" tone? Does that mean the middle-class types should be embarrassed and apologetic that they're not the "real" people? Of course not. . . .

As for the occupations themselves, schoolteaching and computer programming are ways of making a living every bit as honorable as carpentry or plumbing, and much more honorable than loading ships bound for Vietnam.[49]

The New Left thus differed in one basic respect from the Old; more elitist, disenchanted with the working class, looking elsewhere to satisfy its needs for a populist identification, it was prepared, if need be, to look finally to the intellectuals themselves.

The so-called New Left which came into existence between 1960 and 1965 was under an emotional resolve to differentiate itself from the Old Left. The dividing line, however, remained primarily generational rather than ideological; the new emotions of revolt sought their own distinctive "style," vocabulary, and tactics. But when it came to the formulation of an explicit ideology, the New Left found itself, to its embarrassment, repeating the lines of the Old Left. The Old Left demanded to know precisely how the New Left differed in what they were saying from what socialists had always said. The New Left found it hard to define its ideological break with the Old Left.[50] Their generational rejection was clear; the Old Left in their eyes was de-authoritized, defeated. In Berkeley, they ignored the plea of the fifty-year-old socialist and Trotskyist, Harold Draper, that they recognize their socialist identity with the Old Left; the New Left, feeling that they were making mass history, talked disparagingly and mockingly of the aged "grouplets." The new student activists, wishing to maintain a generational autonomy, searched for a corresponding ideological demarcation. Clark Kissinger, the former national secretary of Students for a Democratic Society, for instance, tried to portray the New Left as less dogmatic: "The old Marxist Left was intensely ideological. They could rattle off the cause of any war as capitalism, imperialism, fight for markets: one, two, three. We are characterized primarily by skepticism." Actually, however, the New Left was equally hostile to the skeptics who proclaimed the concept of the "end of ideology." They "denounce that whole concept as part of the previous generation's sellout. (Says Kissinger, 'When they proclaim the end of ideology, it's like an old man proclaiming the end of sex. Because he doesn't feel it any more, he thinks it has disappeared.')"[51] The real cleavage still remains generational. The New Left rejects whatever smacks of the older generation, whether it is ideology or the end of ideology. "Virtually the entire established Left, from Norman Thomas to the Communist party, is viewed as having 'copped out' to 'the power structure' or 'the Establishment.' "[52] The LID, its parent organization, was described by a New Leftist as "a kind of camp for itinerant old Leftist intellectuals—or those who think old."[53]

The New Left is the most Traditional Left in its repetition of the classical themes of student movements. We have witnessed these recurrent themes—the desire to identify with the lowliest combined with elitism and an anti-democratic impulse. Both rejected by and rejecting labor as too "prosperous" to be a reliable ally, and finding their home middle class, their own, as clearly no force for radical social change, the New Left looks temporarily to the poor for its allies, the voiceless, unorganized poor, who have no union bureaucracy, no defensive organizations. At its extreme, the New Left, we might say, is the first movement to seek for an identification with the lumpenproletariat (in Marx's idiom) or the lower-lower class (in Lloyd Warner's usage). The chief spokesman for this neo-populism within the New Left was at the outset Paul Goodman, in whose writings it found a mélange of advocacy of criminal vandalism, homosexuality, and (what we might call) the "anti-virtues" of an un-Protestant ethic.[54] The Enemy, from this standpoint, is not the bourgeois system, not the socialist system, but the "Organized System" which necessarily maims and crushes man. The New Left, the *New Generation,* thus merges in part with the ethic of the Beat Generation, and with their successors three years removed, the hippies. It rejects *in toto* vocations and career jobs, refusing to capitulate to the System, refusing to become organization men. At its Goodmanian extreme, it claims to seek, in protest, the most menial jobs, thereby boycotting the "Rat Race." "Among some of the Beats, such a principle of integrity is clearly operating in the choice of job. . . . Farm labor, hauling boxes, janitoring, serving and dish-washing, messenger—these jobs resist the imputation of uselessness (or exploitation). . . . These *are* preferred Beat jobs."[55] The Beat Generation was said to have contrived a "pattern of culture that, turning against the standard culture, costs very little and gives livelier satisfaction."

Yet in one respect the New Left has absorbed and gone beyond the Beat Generation. For the beats remained bound to their fathers, defying their values, but living on their allowances as remittance-men.[56] The beats wrote Abomunist Manifestoes but were essentially apolitical. They sought to found a subculture of their own within the interstices of the System, but they were not interested in proselytizing or building a mass movement.[57] The New Left endorses the moral critique of the Beat Generation, but adds to it the all-powerful strain of activism. The beatnik immersed himself in Zen, the ideology of secession and masochism; the New Leftist goes on to aggression, participatory democracy, and the young Marx. The political cycle, however, then continues. When he is rejected by his hoped-for lowly class allies, the New Leftist turns either to individual violence or individual withdrawal; the terrorist and the hippie are the commingling alternatives within the next stage of the New Left.

The New Leftist meanwhile tries to organize the poor to wage their own war against poverty and urban renewal. The poor themselves are urged to call their own strikes against slumlords—"No Rent for Rats"—and to exert pressure for improved garbage collections. The poor, the lower-lower, the permanently alienated, are seen as recruits in training for the guerrilla warfare against the Establishment.

"Participatory Democracy": Lenin Updated

"Participatory democracy" is the contribution of the New Student Left to political theory. It was born of their meetings, small and large, minute and mass, where the speaker, heckler or chairman, would feel that he had articulated in words what was trying to emerge from a long, often inchoate discussion. Suddenly the mass seemed inspired; words passed to action; the spontaneity of the mass broke through the formal paraphernalia of formal democracy with its parliamentary rules. "Participatory democracy" was "democratic anarchy" fulfilled. The phrase appeared in the Port Huron statement of the founding convention of Students for a Democratic Society in 1962: "In a participatory democracy, the political life would be based . . . (on the principle that) decision-making of basic social consequence be carried on by public groupings." An issue of the pacifist Bulletin of the Committee for Nonviolent Action undertook to explain how it had operated in the Assembly of Unrepresented People (AOUP), a group of two thousand, mostly composed of students, drawn from all segments of the "New Left," which convened for four days in Washington in August 1965 to press for peace in Vietnam, and which led to the arrest of more than 350 demonstrators:

AOUP had no organizational structure nor established discipline because its decision-making process was by "participatory democracy." This meant that not a single policy was predetermined and imposed; all policies could be established or modified by the participants in the Assembly. Because participatory democracy is likely to be around the radical movements for some time and may eventually be accepted almost universally, it is important that this mode of organization be studied and understood.

Participatory democracy has no initial organization or policies for a demonstration. . . . Decision is by neither voting nor consensus. In fact, decisions in the usual sense don't occur. Policies are set and action determined by those who in the maelstrom of discussion and debate, exert the most influence through courage, articulateness, reasonableness and sensitivity to the feelings of the group. Influence is enhanced by image characteristics such as reputation, looks and style of living that appeal to young people. . . .

Participatory democracy is unsuited for steady activities in which careful reason dominates, clear policy statements are important, and dissonant minorities would become conspicuous. The method is best suited to an action movement, mobilizing and focusing the moral energies of young people in brief, one-event actions. In such a milieu a leader's declaration of intent is a policy, his actions a decision; all currents move toward a crescendo, overwhelming discordant notes.[58]

The advocates of the new "participatory democracy" explained that what they were advocating was a democracy of direct action in which the concerned activists could intervene directly in political processes, and affect their outcome without the intervention of an electorate and the machinery of representative democracy. The direct actions of a "participatory democracy" would be set up parallel to the institutions of representative democracy which they would then supersede. Staughton Lynd, an active civil rights worker and an assistant professor at Yale, saw "participatory democracy" as an American version of the Russian Soviet, with admixtures of Gandhi's pro-village ideology and of the back-to-the-people spirit of the Russian student movement of the nineteenth century. Staughton Lynd wrote:

In form, parallelism suggests a kinship between participatory democracy and Trotsky's conception of the Soviets as a "dual power," or Gandhi's concern to preserve the Indian village analogy. . . . Let the teacher leave the university and teach in Freedom Schools; let the reporter quit his job on a metropolitan daily and start a community newspaper; generally, let the intellectual make insurgency a full-time rather than a part-time occupation. As the Russian radical movement grew from Tolstoyism and the Narodniks' concern to dress simply, speak truth, and "go to the people," so participatory democracy at this point speaks most clearly to the middle-class man, daring him to forsake powerlessness and act.[59]

The participatory democrat saw the people bestirring themselves spontaneously from the fetters of the System, throwing off its rigidities, its formalistic elections and bureaucracies, and acting directly, humanly. A spontaneous protest might suddenly grow into a direct action against the government itself. Lynd wrote, with apocalyptic emotion, of a demonstration in Washington against the war in Vietnam:

Still more poignant was the perception—and I checked my reaction with many others who felt as I did—that as the crowd moved down the Mall toward the seat of government . . . so that there was nowhere to go but forward toward the waiting policemen, it seemed that the great mass of people would simply flow on through and over the marble building, that our forward movement was irresistibly strong, that had some been shot or arrested nothing could have stopped that crowd from taking possession of its Government. Perhaps next time we should keep going. . . .[60]

The kinship between "participatory democracy" and "Soviet democracy," which Lynd acknowledges, takes us to the heart of the political theory of the New Left. In essence, it is Lenin's theory of revolutionary action by a small, dictatorial elite translated into the language of the "nonviolent" movement. Where Lenin wrote that the people would dispense with parliamentary procedure and substitute for it the direct action of "the simple organisation of the armed masses (such as the Soviets of Workers' and Soldiers' Deputies . . .),"[61] Staughton Lynd has the nonviolent student mass surging forward to take possession of the government. The Senate and House of Representatives would be closed permanently, as the Constituent Assembly was in St. Petersburg in 1918. The "complex machinery" (as Lenin called it) of people's formal elections in representative democracy would be replaced by "participatory democracy." Just as Lenin promised that in the soviets within twenty-four hours of the revolution, there would be a "universal participation of the people" to replace all the machinery of the bourgeois state and economic administration, so the New Leftist envisages the direct action-participation of the moving mass as supplanting the Establishment, the organs of the System. As Lynd writes:

One can now begin to envision a series of nonviolent protests which would from the beginning question the legitimacy of the Administration's authority where it has gone beyond constitutional and moral limits, and might, if its insane foreign policy continues, culminate in the decision of hundreds of thousands of people to recognize the authority of alternative institutions of their own making.[62]

The crux of a revolution, says Lynd, learning from Trotsky, occurs when the troops desert to the side of the rioters. This he envisages as a "scenario" for America. "A constitutional crisis" exists in America, he declares, "we have moved into a twilight zone between democratically elected authority and something accurately called 'fascism.' " He envisages the denouement of the next major demonstration: "Perhaps next time we should keep going, occupying for a time the rooms from which orders issue . . . until those who make policy for us . . . consent to enter into dialogue with us and with mankind."

Behind all the phraseology of dialogue there is the simple fact that the ideology of the New Left is one of imposing the will of a small elite, a band of activists, on national policy. The students are summoned to be the shock troops of the elite: "If students chained themselves to the Capitol this summer in wave after wave of massive civil disobedience, even the Johnson Administration would be constrained in its choice of means." What begins as talk of a higher form of democracy, of people directly participating in decisions, turns out to be the defensive formula for action by a student elite which would contravene the will of the majority as expressed in the institutions of representative democracy. "The Movement," like "the Party," seizes power; the one invokes the myth of "participatory democracy," the other invoked the myth of the soviets.

As the civil rights leader, Bayard Rustin, trenchantly declared, "Under whose mandate are the 20,000 Washington marchers entitled to occupy 'their government' for even ten minutes? Does Lynd believe that they represent the views of anything approaching the majority of the people on the question of Vietnam? . . . What gives the disaffected sons and daughters of the middle class the right even symbolically to become the government?"[63]

The tactical means of "participatory democracy" was identical (though translated into ostensibly "nonviolent" terms), with the principle of political tactics which Lenin enunciated in justifying the seizure of power, and in defending his dissolution of the democratically elected Constituent Assembly: "Have an overwhelming superiority of forces at the decisive moment at the decisive point—this 'law' of military success is also the law of political success, especially in that fierce, seething class war which is called revolution."[64] It was simply not possible, said Lenin, for the working class to acquire a sufficient firmness of character, perception, and wide political outlook to enable them to vote intelligently;[65] therefore, he argued, a minority must seize the state power; then, holding power, it would in "a long and fierce struggle" "'convince'" the majority of the workers to accept its policies. The "participatory democrat" likewise has no use for elections, votes, parliamentary procedures; his basic argument is that since the masses are nonparticipant, the elite activists must act on their behalf. The votes of the electorate and of Congress are simply dismissed; somehow the "power structure" has purloined or befuddled the masses and their political expression. The "participatory democrats" will surge forward, take hold of the state, and establish new organs of rule, of their own hegemony. Thus, the line of reasoning which began with the intellectual elitism of C. Wright Mills, with his ridicule of the "labor metaphysics," culminated in Staughton Lynd's conception of the dictatorship of a student elite in the guise of "participatory democracy."

The notion of "participatory democracy" involved a basic alteration in the concept of civil disobedience. Originally, as conceived by such persons as Martin Luther King, it was basically an appeal to the conscience of the community; the civilly disobedient undertook to violate some unjust or unconstitutional ordinance in order to draw the attention of the electorate and the government to ignored wrongs. The civil disobedient still retained a faith in the workings of representative democracy. The student movement, on the other hand, rapidly losing faith in representative democracy, began to conceive of civil disobedience as a first step in a "confrontation" with the "power structure" which would lead in some vague, undefined way to a seizure of power by the student movement. The two conceptions of civil disobedience clashed basically in Selma, Alabama, in the spring of 1965. As Staughton Lynd writes:

> The old politics and the new confronted each other once again in Selma. SNCC was the first civil rights group on the ground there. . . . Then, by agreement with SNCC but nonetheless traumatically for the SNCC workers in Selma, Dr. King's Southern Christian Leadership Conference moved in. SCLC's focus was the passage of national legislation, not the political maturing of persons in the Alabama Black Belt. . . . SNCC could only experience Selma with mixed feelings and considerable frustration. The "march" of March 9, when Dr. King led people to a confrontation he knew would not occur and then accused the police of bad faith for exposing his hypocrisy, must have seemed to those in SNCC a symbolic summation of much that had gone before.[66]

"SNCC," wrote James W. Silver, "is seldom amenable to compromise. . . . These activists were unimpressed with legalism and constitutionalism; they were the 'new abolitionists.' "[67]

What SNCC had wanted was the kind of movement Staughton Lynd had dreamed of, the confrontation, the unpredictable occurrence, the elite and their allies surging forward, the seizure of power, the creation of the New Society, the release of the creative energies of all activists in the student movement and their allies, and finally, though it was only slowly avowed, violence.[68]

The fate of the notion of "participatory democracy" is instructive. It began as the apparent expression of a strong populist identification, with the "unstated assumption," in Lynd's words, "that the poor, when they find voice, will produce a truer, sounder radicalism than any which alienated intellectuals might prescribe."[69] As the doctrine evolved, however, it became the ideological bearer of elitism. It began ostensibly by seeking a political participation by the American citizen which would be more than "the annual act of pulling a lever in a little curtained room."[70] But as the citizenry proved quiescent, or failed to follow the students' lead, the doctrine, with its "insistence that decisions should come about through a process of personal confrontation and encounter," metamorphosed into an apologetic for the "putschist" action of a small student elite, abetted by the violence of the alienated "guerrillas," to impose its will on the recalcitrant majority of the people. Thus, "participatory democracy" was recapitulating in large measure the career of "proletarian democracy." Between the intellectual elitism of C. Wright Mills and the "participatory democracy" of Tom Hayden and Staughton Lynd there was a clear line of continuity; the last fulfilled the first. All were intellectual authoritarians, the only difference being that Hayden and Lynd used an existentialist vocabulary whereas Mills spoke in neo-Marxist terms.

The Teach-In: The Authoritarianism of the Student Intellectuals

The spring of 1965 saw the elitism of the student movement being expressed in the form of a new political institution, the "teach-in." It began at the University of Michigan, where a group of thirteen professors had originally announced that they planned to cancel their classes on March 24 as a protest against the policy of the United States in Vietnam. When their plan was condemned by both the governor and the legislature of Michigan, they were induced to alter their plan to an all-night protest on March 24; this was attended by about two thousand students and supported by about two hundred professors.[71] The idea soon spread to other universities, including Columbia and California.[72] Student movements took it up, and a new political claim was advanced: that the national administration was under an obligation to be confronted by the academic community, that it was especially incumbent upon the administration to defend its policies before the academic community, and that this was an obligation especially mandatory for those administration officials who had an academic background. A national teach-in in Washington which was broadcast on television took place on May 15, 1965. When the administration spokesman, McGeorge Bundy, failed to arrive (because, as it later transpired, he had had to go to the Dominican Republic for important negotiations), the organizers of the teach-in rebuked him strongly for having failed to fulfill his duty to the academic community. As the *Times* correspondent reported, "Few were willing to await the explanation for Mr. Bundy's withdrawal before imputing dishonorable motives to him."[73]

On the face of it, the "confrontation" of the teach-in seemed to be altogether consistent with the workings of the democratic process. Actually, however, it constituted a demand for special status and privilege. The radical activists of the academic community were in effect organizing themselves into a renovated Second Estate, a clerisy to replace the church, and demanding that the government especially justify its policies with them in debate. However, we have in the United States a representative democracy, a Congress and a Senate, to which we elect representatives whose debate presumably becomes a sifted mirroring of our views. Now the radical intellectual elite demanded a special priority in the debate. It demanded a privileged recognition as the most qualified constituency to which the government must submit its decisions and policies. If this had been a debate among professors of differing views, it would have been a straightforward "teach-in." Certainly there was no lack of able professors and students who shared the government's position and were prepared to argue for it with fellow academicians. But what the radical elite wanted was to compel a "confrontation" with the government, to place it under a special obligation to defend itself before an activist minority, itself already rejected by the people in accordance with the workings of representative democracy. In short, the rejected elite was looking for some elitist, nondemocratic basis for influence. The subtle anti-democratic bias, the perverse elitism hidden behind the phrase "participatory democracy" thus emerged again. Once more it was the formula according to which a radical intellectual elitist minority, backed primarily by a student movement, tried to impose its will on the government directly in a face-to-face challenge. Those overtones were apparent to the observer. Abetted by audiences which it usually controlled, the elitists, unconsciously following Lenin's tactical principle, brought to bear a maximum of force on the government in the strategic setting of their choice. The *Times* correspondent wrote:

> To observers here, most of the organizers and audiences appeared to be motivated by much more than the subtleties of Vietnam policy. In many remarks and questions there lurked distrust and hostility toward the Government itself. Mr. Bundy was the preferred official spokesman because others from the campus seemed really to want to ask, "Et tu, Brute?" . . . There was evidence of a still wider gulf between the capital and the campus. . . . And there may have appeared a gulf between generations.[74]

The new student generation could not recall the experience with American appeasement and inaction before the Second World War; they had not known the cost of rethinking which had been involved in stopping Stalin and Soviet imperialism after the war. They were a generation which knew not Joseph because it knew not Pharaoh. For the terrible fact about sociological experience is that, difficult as it is to impart from generation to generation in normal times, it is abruptly dismissed when generational struggle grows intense. "[M]any of the younger critics could not or would not remember or accept the analogies of the nineteen-thirties and nineteen-fifties for the nineteen-sixties." A generational equilibrium allows for a cumulative principle of sociological experience and wisdom. The conflict of generations negates it.

Thus, the teach-in enabled students and teachers to thrust themselves upon a national audience "with the blessing of the Administration they condemn for secrecy" . . . and all for an investment of less than thirty thousand dollars. Never before in American history had a "group of intellectuals been hurtled so swiftly into the political arena."[75] In this manner, an intellectual elite, with its student infantry, reached for an authoritarian hegemony in the national councils; "participatory democracy" meant the authoritarianism of the young intellectuals and their allies of the moment.

The overwhelming majority of the American studentry, however, unlike their classmates in the "student movement," continued to support American involvement in the Vietnam War. The Survey Research Laboratory of the University of Wisconsin in 1966, for instance, found that 72 per cent of the students favored American participation in the war, while only 16 per cent were opposed. Only 12 per cent, moreover, felt that this state university was "highly depersonalized." It was evident that the "student movement" did not democratically represent the American studentry, but only its "alienated" segment.[76]

The Generational Selection of Political Issues: Emergence of Anti-Americanism as a Student Ideology

In the first months of 1965, the student movement began to turn rapidly from the civil rights issue to that of Vietnam. It was not that the problems of civil rights had suddenly ceased to exist; rather the issue no longer offered as good an emotional opportunity for conducting a generational struggle. The Free Speech Movement at Berkeley, for instance, when it was at its height in 1964, proclaimed its primary concern with civil rights and the welfare of the Negro community. For a brief while subsequent to its success, there was a flurry of concern over establishing volunteer tutorial classes for Negro children which would enable them to compensate for deprivations in their backgrounds. Within a few weeks most such efforts and concerns had strangely vanished. The passage of the Voter Registration Act made it harder to draw a strict generational line on the question of civil rights; with every act and intervention of the government, the student movement's enthusiasm for organizing classes for Negro children dwindled. An issue was most attractive to the degree that it could readily channelize generational resentment; involvement in an issue subsided when the issue failed to provide the occasion for a clear generational struggle. It is this motivation which primarily explains the curious movement from issue to issue on the part of the student movement. Thus, there arose the Vietnam Day Committee in Berkeley to supersede the dominant concern with civil rights. Its chief spokesman wrote:

> The VDC began as an idea in the heads of four people over supper one day last April, an idea to organize a large community teach-in at a time when the civil rights and free speech movements were waning. . . .
>
> The same individuals involved in free speech and democracy on the campus, and civil rights, became involved in the struggle against USA policy in Vietnam.[77]

Thus, the emotion of generational struggle defined the direction of transition from issue to issue. The young student, who just a few weeks earlier had thrilled to the thought of teaching Negro children, lost interest in the project. To parade, protest, to "confront" the local police were more of an adventure, and more satisfying to one's aggressive impulses. "Confrontation" always had the generational overtone of the son standing up to the father; and if an issue, or a cause, lacked this element of "confrontation," it was not emotionally satisfying. Pure "do-gooding" would never satisfy the student activist, because it lacked this element of confrontation, of conflict, of the occasion for aggression. The VDC spokesman, by contrast, was able to redefine themes for generational conflict. When the older generation in its anti-poverty program tried to reduce the number of school drop-outs, the *VDC News* proclaimed the meaninglessness of schools, and called for a revolt against them: "We should ask people to quit school and forget middle-class futures and join a movement to change America."

The theme of identification with the lowliest, that theme recurrent in all student movements, reached a new stage. Identification with the people, peasantry, proletariat, the Negro and poor of one's own country was now supplanted altogether by an identification with the backward peoples and races of other continents.

> On the back of the VDC membership card is written the words: "We must build a New America and join with those peoples in Asia, Africa, and Latin America building a New World. . . ."
>
> The USA is for the status quo. But I as an American want to be with those making history, not with those freezing it.[78]

Anti-Americanism thus became a recognized article of faith in the ideology of generational revolt. Naturally, it was cast in the current idiom of "alienation": "We are the country's alienated—alienated by America's values, alienated by America's mass culture, alienated by America's image of the Good Society. We are repelled by the idea of exporting Americanism overseas."[79]

In the thirties, the student activists had been able in the time of the economic depression to forecast the breakdown of American capitalism and the future hegemony of the working class. In the mid-sixties, the American capitalist system was impressively stable and prosperous, and its workers largely contented. The rebellious activists, feeling a diffused resentment, called it "alienation," but their rejection of America sometimes tended to be total, as they felt themselves bereft of class allies in America and frustrated by the society's stability. Therefore, they began to turn abroad for their identifications. They were rather anti-American than anti-capitalist. When they criticized the capitalist order, it was because it partook of American, Western civilization.

As the new student movement found itself "alienated" in American society, its most activist element began to move toward an exaltation of violence. The May Second Movement, a group attracted to Mao and Castro, were among the first to voice this trend. They welcomed the Watts riots as a "people's uprising" against "imperialist" America, as part of the same "guerrilla warfare" which was being carried on from Vietnam to Los Angeles against the United States:

> Vietnam, of course, is the most organized and coherent of the self-determination movements, but the seemingly structureless riots in Watts heralded the beginnings of the organized build-up of Negro militance and even violence in this country. . . . Watts was a "people's uprising," as the *Liberator* said. There were no illusions about who the enemy was—the Los Angeles police and "imperialist" merchants of the Watts shopping areas . . . the sniping and guerrilla action had become tightly organized. . . . The Chinese Communist Party maintains that at this time the Negro struggle, like the Vietnamese, is a national struggle, and Mao Tse-tung has said, "In the final analysis, a national struggle is a question of class struggle. . . ." Revolutionary action by the black citizens of the U.S. is neither foolhardy nor an adventurist fantasy—in truth there is no other choice.[80]

The student as a "guerrilla fighter" came to be the image which most appealed to young student activists. The beatnik metamorphosed into a "guerrilla" fighting in the fastnesses of the city. In 1962, for example, the San Francisco Mime Troupe had called themselves disciples of the "theater of the absurd." They went to the people in parks with their pornopolitical plays. Five years later they said they were a "guerrilla theater," attacking the System, making money, withdrawing, attacking. The absurd had evolved into a guerrilla; the unconscious generational violence became conscious.[81]

Ethic of the Student Movement: From Absolutism to Amoralism

The activists of the student movement feel a need to define their virtues as unique to their generation, as distinct from those of the middle-aged and middle-class generation. Student leaders enumerate the virtues of their generation—authenticity, courage, truthfulness. One might say that every virtue they could name had been expounded and argued for by some philosopher of the older or past generations. One might even say that all virtues are "bourgeois" virtues, in the sense that they have been defined and advocated by "bourgeois" philosophers. "Authenticity," apart from the word, received its magisterial advocacy from John Stuart Mill in *On Liberty*, in which he argued for individuality and character. Immanuel Kant carried truth-telling to its last consequence. Spinoza, Russell, Tillich have written philosophies of courage.

Nevertheless, the students' underlying emotion is undeniable—their will to define themselves as different, as uncorrupted (unlike the elders), as determined to change the world the elders transmit to them. Each successive generation has a tendency to want to blame its elders for the kind of world it inherits, forgetting the element of truth in Marx's statement that men, at any given social stage, "enter into definite relations that are indispensable and independent of their will."

To overcome alienation, to achieve a new mystical community, the striving of the new student movement is for an all-embracing generational consciousness. At the National Coordinating Committee Convention to End the War in Vietnam, in Washington in November 1965, for instance, Delmar Scudder, described as "the new traveling salesman of 'soul,'" said, "First people have to touch one another. That's where program comes from." His words were said to have been the "most penetrating" spoken at the meeting. The theme of "touching one another" was dearest to the new activists, so that soon they felt discomfited by hardened organizational operators who were less interested in tactual mysticism. The theoretician of the Free Speech Movement lamented, "Unfortunately once the convention had started it was perhaps too late to have a convention in which people could touch one another."[82] The old-fashioned Trotskyist Young Socialist Alliance was described as having "fueled the fires of mistrust by its failure to practice the candor which we have the right to ask of those who believe in democratic centralism." Staughton Lynd has said that the New Left must regard itself as a "blessed community, a new society." "The left must not lose all the beautiful elements of spontaneity and comradeship."[83]

Civil disobedience itself was a tactic which emphasized the community of the young as well as the defiance of the old. It carried with it an unusual emotional satisfaction. The leading ideologist of the Free Speech Movement told of the joy which the practice of civil disobedience brought, the momentary euphoria of the Blessed Community:

Dear Co-conspirators,

. . . Civil disobedience is good when it feels good—not only at the point of disruption, but also as one looks back after the euphoria and the crowd have dispersed. . . . But, dearies, we can't let that moment of apparent pleasure arising out of frustration ruin a life of happiness and community service. For my own part, I find a correlation between the political effectiveness of C.D. and its long-lasting pleasurability.

How then to sustain this Generational Community, this Conquest of Alienation? The father, we might say, could only be destroyed once, and "depoliticalization" rather than "politicalization" easily followed in its wake—"the disillusionment and depoliticalization that often follow those grueling days in court."[84]

But even before a stage of disillusionment was reached, too often the Ethic of Community was transmuted into an Ethic of Destruction.

Such observers as Michael Harrington have written eloquently of the high ethical vocation of the student movement. The young radicals of today, he says, are without cynicism; they believe in freedom, equality, justice, world peace; "they became activists in order to affirm these traditional values with regard to some ethical cause."[85] They have a painful consciousness, he writes, of American hypocrisy. Yet this interpretation, with its segment of truth, leaves unexplained the amoral cynicism of student activists; Berkeley, for instance, became the famed center of thievery by student activists. Documents were stolen from administrators, goods were stolen from both merchants and the student cooperative. Moral standards in various ways declined within the student movement. Harrington recognizes the generational animus in the New Left: "It is, I suspect, this unique Fifties-Sixties experience which gives the New Left its distinctive flavor: a sense of outrage, of having been betrayed by all the father-figures, which derives from an original innocence." By the same token, however, it was true that the most unethical means and conduct of life too were adopted whenever they led to the discomfiture of the elder generation. The theft of documents, for instance, was not the behavior of irresponsible exceptions; it was approved by the chiefs of the Berkeley student movement. Photostatic copies of confidential letters were purloined from the office of the president of the university.[86] A year later, confidential documents were stolen from the file of the chancellor's assistant: "Two weeks ago, certain delegates to the Constitutional Convention secretly removed letters and memoranda from a file that belonged to me. Last Thursday, those delegates mimeographed one of the confidential papers and distributed it to hundreds of people on the campus." Far from being embarrassed by the accusation of theft, the leaders of the student left-wing political party (Slate) defended their right to thievery: "In fact, the file and papers were public, although secret. They concerned matters which students have a right to know about."[87] The student leaders argued that they had rendered a service to their electorate by stealing and publishing the documents. This had been the classical ethic of student movements from Karl Follen to Gavrilo Princip: the end justifies any means. If there is a hypocrisy of the old, there is a hypocrisy of the young as well.

The decline of moral standards, the confusion of good and evil which Vera Figner long ago observed in the Russian student movement emerged very early in the new American student movement. This decline was dramatized vividly in Berkeley in 1963. In January of that year, the left-wing student leader on the campus was arrested for stealing a book from a local bookstore. Subsequently, he pleaded guilty to a charge of malicious mischief. Under pressure from conservative students, he resigned from his seat in the student senate. What was noteworthy, however, was that he refused to take full responsibility for his individual act of dishonesty, but instead tried to give his deed a social justification. "I would like to say a few words about 'morality' and 'public virtue,' " he declared in his statement of resignation:

Probably as many as 90 per cent of the people in the U.S. could be put behind bars this moment for criminal conduct. . . . Our laws are outdated, our penal system prejudicial to the wealthy and white, and our police forces brutal and grossly unfair. Ordinarily students who take books are not even arrested, but are simply referred to the District Attorney or the Dean of Students. My major mistake was being a controversial figure. This is not to say that theft is not wrong. . . .[88]

Never did the student leader simply say his theft was wrong; the most he conceded was an ambiguous double negative.

By 1965, the "Campus Left" was notorious on the Berkeley campus for its petty larcenies; the most militant, the students of the Progressive Labor Movement, the so-called Maoists, boasted especially of their accomplishments in thievery.[89]

The New Student Movement began early to voice its sympathies with the abnormal, the extreme, the unreal. The beatniks early affiliated themselves as associate members with life standing of the New Student Movement. The editor of the *Berkeley Barb* (described as "the most successful of the left-wing papers which have sprung up in Berkeley since the free speech movement") documented this evolution. The New Left, he claimed, was much more an outgrowth of the "beatnikism" of the 1950s than of such phenomena as the civil rights movement. "A look at the personnel will show," he says, "that the same people who outraged the establishment culturally with their seemingly selfish 'art for my sake' crusade have turned altruistic and taken to outraging the establishment on the political level."[90] The beatnik influence made itself felt especially in the elevation of drugs, marijuana, and hallucinogens as an adjunct of the New Student Movement. In 1965, for instance, a student leader at Berkeley wrote for the movement a vigorous pamphlet exposing the economic holdings of the regents of the university; the next year that same student leader was writing sympathetically of the growing number who "are experimenting with such extraordinary hallucinogens as LSD, DMT, and mescalin; it has taken on the proportions of a social movement." One didn't wish to be left aside: "Something is happening, something new, something big, something with great dangers but also possible benefits."[91]

These "consciousness-expanding" drugs had their appeal for student activists. Rebellious against the affluent society, the life of prosperity, the bourgeois existence, their fathers' condition, the students hearkened to the call of the hallucinogens, their new world of fantasy and new perceptions. Here was a generational consciousness which was radically new. One could be swept into a half hour's euphoria by Joan Baez singing of freedom; the movement itself was a hallucinogen. Why not seek its effects directly? Such was the decision at Berkeley of the 40 per cent of the student body who (according to a university criminologist) used drugs intermittently, and the 20 per cent (according to the chief psychiatrist) who were smoking marijuana. "They are vaguely leftist, disenchanted with

American policies in Vietnam, agitated because there are Negro ghettos and bored with conventional politics. They do not join the Peace Corps, which, a student at Penn State said, 'is for Boy Scouts.'" And most of them were in the humanities or social sciences, with fewer in the sciences.[92] Their profile indeed was that of the typical rank-and-filer of the New Student Movement.

The hallucinogenic phase of the New Student Movement was rooted in the self-destructive ingredient characteristic of such movements. Here was an assault upon one's personality, one's reason, upon the categories of everyday existence. The rebellion against the father, the generational revolt, in this extreme manifestation took the form of a rebellion against the qualities of ordinary consciousness itself; one was destroying one's psychological bond of continuity, severing the psychological umbilical cord itself that united one to one's father, the elder generation. This was the most eloquent symbolic rejection of the virtues of the Protestant or Jewish ethic.

Every student movement, furthermore, has tended to produce new forms of sexual behavior; the ascetic unions of free love in the Russian student movement, the homosexual loyalties of the Burschenschaft, the choices of romantic love by Chinese students rebelling against the family system, were all instances of student generational revolt in sexuality. The New Student Left in the United States has shown certain embryonic developments in this regard whose significance and extent at the present time it is hard to evaluate.

Among a segment of activists of the Berkeley student movement, three forms of sexual behavior appeared which had the significance of a revolt against the elder liberals. Sexual behavior began to take on an ideological function: one had "ideological sex." The elder liberals had long ago evidently won the right for love's choice in premarital intercourse. The new activists felt impelled to go far beyond that to, first, a positive advocacy of interracial sexuality, second, a positive advocacy of promiscuity, taking form in, third, a positive advocacy of "sheer, undiluted orgy-ism."

The pattern of interracial sexuality especially characterized the chapter of Berkeley CORE in 1962–1964 during the period of its highest activity in pickets and sit-ins. Two of its officers at that time remarked that a sociogram of the group would show that almost all of its members were involved at that time in interracial sexual liaisons. Sexuality tended to become an avenue for the expression of guilt feelings. At discussions in cafeterias and in their apartments, white middle-class undergraduate girls heard of their participatory guilt in fostering American racial inequality. Interracial sexual relations became a form of atonement for this participatory guilt. The trend toward orgyism on the fringes of the New Left was exuberantly narrated in its press. Certainly it went far beyond Bertrand Russell's *Marriage and Morals* of a previous generation. The chief Leftist, student-directed newspaper in Berkeley described it enthusiastically:

It seems, in fact, that Berkeley is fast becoming the great experimental "freedom lab" for the whole country and the world! In Berkeley, amidst all the other forms of rebellion afoot, there is very much a sexual rebellion in the making also. The rebellion here spoken of is not mere "shacking." . . . What is here referred to as betokening a greater rebellion in Berkeley is the incidental rise of sheer, undiluted orgy-ism. Consistent with our point here, this would seem good and desirable, the first positive step in unrepressing our repressions. Indeed, Freud's description of "repressed" sexual desires is certainly a description of orgiastic impulses. The mood that is arising in Berkeley seems to state implicitly that there is nothing wrong with orgies if entered into uncoerced and for mutual pleasure. . . . Evidences that such an orgiastic rebellion is taking place in Berkeley can be glimpsed in such things as anonymous ads appearing with increasing frequency on Student-Union bulletin boards, in the *Barb*, and elsewhere. The content of all these ads all but unabashedly advertised for other couples interested in "sexual-communal" living, "coterie" living, "get-togethers" and other less sensational, but unmistakable, wordings.[93]

The teaching of the new sexual ethic provided the content of one of the courses in the so-called Free University of Berkeley, which came into existence in February 1966 as part of the rejection, in its words, of "an Educational Establishment which produces proud cynicism but sustains neither enthusiasm nor integrity." Its twenty-eight courses, ranging in subject matter from Vietnam to Beethoven to Soviet thought to Afro-American music to black nationalism, were mainly taught by graduate students. But one special course was added, to be given by the president of the Sexual Freedom League, "The History of Western Anti-Sensualism." The overcoming of alienation, of isolation, of separation, was sought in the most direct way by communitarian sexuality. A newspaperman who ventured into one of these orgies, principally composed of "students in their twenties," reported:

By 1 o'clock, with the music still playing and the wine still flowing, the floor, couches and two bedrooms of the apartment had become the frenetic scene of what Richard Thorne, the 29-year-old head of the Sexual Freedom League, likes to call a "sheer, undiluted orgy." "Actually, we think there's nothing wrong with orgies," explains Thorne casually. "The Greeks had them, and to be able to fully participate in an orgy without feeling ashamed or guilty is a sign of a truly healthy attitude toward sex.[94]

A segment of the New Student Left thus experimented in sexuality without alienation, the Sexual Community. As one spokesman (whom we have previously cited) wrote, "The radical political fraternity . . . believes strongly that movement that screws together glues together. Or, to be specific, that Socialists who sleep together creep together."[95]

The rational student, with liberal political and economic ideas, found himself under great pressure to conform to the "generational line." Generationalism thus made for irrationalism. Student movements have always had their own insistence on generational conformity, on following the "generational line." They have been radical in their demands, but never authentically liberal in their philosophy. They have never accepted fully the notion of a free competition of ideas. Although they have defended radical professors from ouster, they have usually been just as ready to force the ouster of reactionary or conservative professors. At other places and times, the pattern has been the reverse. Student movements are not exponents of freedom of thought. Student demonstrations against individual professors have thus been part of the movement from its Russian beginnings to the Latin American present; the City College in the thirties and Berkeley in the sixties saw similar attempts to defame and "ostracize" certain professors. The student movement at the City College in 1940 was reluctant to defend the right of Bertrand Russell to teach (when a judicial decision denied him an appointment), because they were at that time partisans of the Stalin-Hitler Pact and disapproved of his advocacy of the Allied cause.

Thus, there was the pressure on the student to accept too, even against his better judgment, the "generational line" on questions of sexual morality. This generational pressure was pointedly described by Jed Rakoff, '64, of Swarthmore College, president of its student council, editor of the *Phoenix*, the student newspaper, and "a radical rules reformer." While he was president of the student council in 1963, Rakoff had supported the use of "civil disobedience" to express student opposition to the rule requiring that a young man's door be open when he was receiving women guests. Little more than a year later, meditating at Oxford University on his Swarthmorean activities, wondering what their rationale had been, whether the students had fought for a "freedom" in which they didn't believe, Rakoff wrote about how generational conformity is produced:

> I can still remember, sophomore year, when some *Phoenix* pollsters asked a random sample of fifty Swarthmore men "Would you care if the girl you married wasn't a virgin?" To our shock all but two of the respondees answered "yes." We decided not to publish the results.
>
> . . . I think that when you frankly examine Swarthmore men's sexual attitudes (mine included) you find that they are too often selfish and materialistic—and ought to be discouraged.
>
> . . . Of course, some people will say that the Swarthmore sex rules represent an infringement on individual freedom of choice, that by the superb age of seventeen and over each individual ought to be left free to make his or her own moral decisions.
>
> *Such humdrum ignores the obvious fact that a Swarthmore student's opinions are framed in the context of a considerable social pressure in favor of premarital intercourse,* and thus the sex rules serve merely to restore a partial balance. Quite irrespective of the rules of the Administration, *Swarthmore students enjoy very little freedom of thought on sexual matters. I doubt, for instance, that I could have written this article while at Swarthmore.*[96]

Jewish Students as the Bearers of Generational Conflict in the United States

Jewish students have been the mainstay of such an American student movement as has existed. "This is indisputable," wrote James Wechsler in 1935, "a large number of those who inaugurated the left-wing student movement, for example, were Jews. That, remember, was late in 1931."[97] When the Berkeley Free Speech Movement burgeoned thirty-three years later, in 1964, a majority of its steering committee of eleven were Jewish.[98] A survey of the student body at the University of California by Kathleen E. Gales, of the London School of Economics, showed that the "strongest level of approval" of the Free Speech Movement was found among Jewish students.[99] Andrew Goodman and Michael Schwerner were the names of the two white boys among the three martyred in Meridian, Mississippi, in June 1964. Two-thirds of the first Freedom Riders who went to Jackson, Mississippi, were Jewish.[100] The phenomenon aroused the deepest interest and concern of Jewish organizations. When it was discussed, in June 1965, by the National Community Relations Advisory Council, the delegates agreed that "Jewish youth were disproportionately numerous in the student movement."[101] When the leftist students occupied five buildings in Columbia University and caused the suspension of classes in May 1968 it was noted that "the activists are typically very bright and predominantly Jewish. . . ."[102]

Various explanations have been proposed at different times for the preeminence of successive generations of Jews in the student movement. In 1965, the explanation proposed by Jewish officials was that Jewish students especially were in revolt against middle-class values and liberalism. Jewish parents, it was said, were overwhelmingly among the middle-class, self-described liberals "against which the whole [student] movement was essentially in revolt." "The middle-class establishment is the enemy" in the students' eyes, it was said, and "the Jewish community is an integral part of this establishment in the minds of these students." The Director of Social Action of the Union of American Hebrew Congregations, Albert Vorspan, declared that the Jewish students rejected "the middle-class values of self-indulgence and country-club materialism which they see as a corruption of the American way of life—values to which, in their view, Jews have acquiesced."[103] Jewish students themselves, on the other hand, said they did not feel that the spirit of revolt on the campus was a rebellion against the older generation. In September 1965, 215 Jewish students, leaders of Hillel Foundations on 123 college campuses, convened and discussed this question. Their dominant view was that the Jewish students involved in political activist movements were not acting in any way as Jews but as Americans; Jewish values did not seem consciously involved.

And they felt indeed that the 325,000 Jewish students in American universities were akin to them in this latter respect.[104]

Why then have Jewish students been for the last sixty years foremost in the recurrent, small American student movements? The answer in my view lies in the recurrent de-authoritization of the older Jewish generation in each recent historical era. The Jewish student shared experiences of de-authoritization of their elders similar to those which called forth student movements in Russia, Bosnia, and Japan, but with a peculiar poignancy derived from their situation as an ethnic minority.

This was already evident in the earliest Jewish student movement in the United States at the turn of the century, when a group of City College students led by the young Morris R. Cohen, and jointly inspired by Karl Marx and a wandering "chaplain," Thomas Davidson, dreamed that by founding workingmen's colleges, "breadwinners' colleges," they could plant the roots of socialist emancipation among the workers. One of them, Joseph Gollomb (later a mystery story writer), recalled how Morris Cohen, a product of the literary clubs and the socialist platform at the Suffolk Streeters' hangout, "now a Doctor of Philosophy and tutor in the subject at City College, and a score of other East Siders had organized a group with the objective of emancipating the working class of the whole world, not directly through revolution but by the route of education. It would be different from the Educational Institute, which was primarily a helping hand from 'uptown'; Breadwinners' College was to be an enterprise in self-help. Workers, and sons and daughters of workers, would-be teachers, pupils, and often both." A score volunteered to teach. "Enthusiasm mounted, and Moey Cohen, for once the rhapsodist, wound up the meeting with the prophecy that workers throughout the world would emulate Breadwinners' College and effect a social revolution by the sheer power of enlightenment." When Gollomb left the fold, Cohen told him with all self-righteousness, "You'd rather see some dinky little piece of yours in a yellow sheet than stick by a social good in the throes of its birth. We'll survive your loss, but some day we'll remind you of what King Henry said, 'Go hang yourself, brave Crillon, we won at Arques, and you were not there!' "[105]

It was Morris R. Cohen himself who perceived that generational conflict was the deepest psychological problem of the Jewish students. As a young student, at the age of twenty-one, he wrote:

> The most important practical question on the East Side is undoubtedly the strained, I might say the tragic, relation between the older and the younger generations. The younger generation has, as a rule, been brought up under entirely different circumstances from those of its elders, and therefore naturally entertains radically different aims and ideals. The older generation does not sympathize with these new ideals, and in the ensuing discord much of the proverbial strength of the Jewish family is lost. This is fraught with heart-

rending consequences. When the home ceases to be the center of interest the unity of life is broken, and the dreariest pessimism and cynicism may follow. . . . You cannot and must not expect the younger people to become false to their own best insight at the very entrance of life![106]

The young students inhabited a cultural universe which their parents could not comprehend. Often their mothers and fathers were illiterate; and if they could read Yiddish, they were still alien to the American culture and language of Emerson, Bryant, Whitman. With their lack of dignity and their seeming acquiescence to persecution and poverty, with their lack of manliness and resistance, they were depreciated by the standards of the new literary-philosophical culture which the sons imbibed in school. They were at the lowest rung of society, defeated, always fleeing, and their lips could not form the words that schoolteachers spoke. The sons were ashamed of their parents and prone to accept a redemptive philosophy which would acknowledge the claim of intellect to leadership and which would usher in social justice.[107]

But these early Jewish student groups revered the authority of the academy. Uprisings against the latter began to appear only with the First World War and the introduction of R.O.T.C. training into the college. And it became more acute with the depression. The Marxist student leaders explained the greater radicalism of the Jewish students in historical materialist terms:

Jewish students reacted to the economic crisis in greater numbers than did others because the burden of that decline, in its inception, fell most heavily upon them. Even in times of comparative prosperity, they did not enjoy many of the benefits which accrued to their Christian colleagues; they were barred from jobs because of their religion, professional schools systematically rejected their applications, advertisements concluded with the age-old warning: "Christians only need apply."[108]

The Jewish students who became activists in the student movements, however, were notable for rejecting the moderate socialistic views of their workingmen fathers as passive, lacking in energy, quiescent, unaggressive, purely sentimental. The story of Herbert Zam, "the energetic and aggressive leader of the Young Communist League in the 20's," became typical in the early thirties:

I was born and raised on the Lower East Side of New York. My father was a garment worker, a passive Socialist and a reader of the *Forward*. . . . While in high school I joined the YPSL's, bringing a whole gang with me. The League did not seem to be sufficiently active politically. They appeared to us more like a marriage club. . . . I entered City College in June, 1920, at the age of 17. There, for the first time, I heard of Communism. There was a Social Problems Club on the campus. Sidney Hook was a member. All the club did was to have an occasional lecture. . . . The limited scope of the club looked ridiculous to me. I secured a list of twenty Communist students. . . . At the next elections we ran Sidney Hook, a Left-Winger but not a party man, against Emil Schlesinger, a senior and a Socialist. The club grew, numbering several hundred. The Communists controlled the club for a long time. . . .[109]

The passive socialistic fathers were being put aside. If the host culture had welcomed them, the sons would not have gone to a more radical stage of radicalism. Rejected themselves in part by the dominant American culture, and themselves rejecting their fathers' ways, the activist students inclined toward a Marxism which was a higher rejection in turn. The experience of John Gates, editor of the *Daily Worker*, veteran of the International Brigade, prisoner in the Atlanta penitentiary, was similarly, as Earl Browder wrote, "representative of what happened to a generation of young Americans who approached maturity during the shattering days of 1929 to 1934." Gates insists he had a "happy childhood" and led a "normal, typical life," and that his politics was not touched with neurosis. His actual autobiography depicts a transition of generational creeds and practices and a desperate search for a new religion, born of an acute psychological rejection of his father and what he stood for. Gates was born Sol Regenstreif—the son of a Jewish immigrant candy storekeeper, "rigorously orthodox in his faith," stern, with a strong sense of right and wrong. The depression reduced the family further in poverty, as the father lost in his stock speculations. "We students in the first years of the Hoover depression were the Aimless Generation. But our very uncertainty drove many of us to search for answers and for a cause to live by."[110] He joined the Social Problems Club at City College, and when a young Communist leader was suspended for an infraction of college rules, was moved to take a vigorous part in the campaign for his reinstatement; as a consequence of this incident, he joined the Young Communist League. His search for a religion to replace his father's was over. "Only the Communists were able to infuse youth with idealism, missionary zeal and a crusading spirit. And with these, they invoked a willingness to undergo any hardship, to sacrifice life itself if need be, for the cause of the socialist revolution." All the motifs of generational revolt were here—the idealism, elitism as missionaries, populistic zeal, the death-longing. The professors at college became the surrogates for a rejected elder generation: "As I became filled with the superiority of my new-found faith, I was sure there was nothing that college could teach me. I wrangled with my teachers and developed a contempt for them."[111] Gates and a friend took three months off "unofficially" from college to study Marx's *Capital;* then, embarking on their own back-to-the-people crusade, they "formed a club to stop evictions, called the Young Hunger Fighters."[112]

The generational rejection of their fathers by the Jewish students had one curious consequence which cannot otherwise be explained. The Jewish activists never raised squarely the issue of anti-Semitism in the academic world. Rejecting their fathers' Jewish culture, they repressed any forthright mention in their demands of anything which stemmed from their own situation. Jewish premedical students at the City College knew, for instance, that they were virtually excluded from the medical schools of Columbia and Cornell universities. One might have expected a student union to undertake picketing on their behalf or to raise the issue in some public way. Yet one searches through the magazines and reports of their activities in vain to find a single case in which a protest was made. One might have expected the student unions to have lobbied the legislature and political parties to found state medical schools. When such suggestions were made, however, the student leaders were singularly uninterested. The full-scale report delivered by the secretary to the biggest convention of the American Student Union on December 27, 1938, dealt extensively with educational reform, the reform of the curriculum, and the reform of the national Administration; it congratulated the Supreme Court for its favorable ruling on behalf of a Negro student in the Gaines case. But it would have gone against the grain of the student leaders, Jews though most of them were, to raise the issue of abolishing discrimination against Jews in universities and professional schools.[113]

If the unusual economic hardship and deprivation suffered by Jews had been the all-explaining factor that sent a disproportionate number of Jewish students into the student movement, one would have expected them to raise precisely those issues where as Jews they were made to bear additional burdens of economic and educational discrimination. But the Jewish activists of the student movement, largely moved by the psychology of generational revolt, repressed these issues. They went on instead to attack the R.O.T.C. and to support of the general line of Soviet foreign policy.

When the revival of the American student movement commenced in 1960, the head of the National Hillel Summer Institute, a man with considerable experience among university students, noted that the activism of Jewish students was founded in some obscure way on their rejection of their traditional religion. He wrote in 1961:

> Despite the close link between the ethical and religious elements in Jewish tradition, and despite the reform emphasis on prophetic Judaism, few if any Jewish students considered their radical views an expression of a Jewish religious conviction or commitment. Jews were among the leaders of the social action projects and radical movements on campus. But their radicalism, whatever its source, was a form of rejection, and substitution for, Judaism.[114]

The Jewish students who participated in the Mississippi Summer Project of 1964 likewise found in this activity satisfaction of their generational rejection of their Jewish identity and of their de-authoritized fathers and at the same time an expression of their own inner resentment against what Jews have had to experience in recent history. At a public dialogue under Leftist auspices, seven students who had been in Mississippi clearly exhibited this rejection of their Jewish identification.[115] They disclaimed any connection between their involvement and awareness of Jewish values. One, a Bank Street School student, spoke of her "own lack of Jewish consciousness," and justified the Negroes who told Jews they were "tired of hearing about the six million." Another, a Radcliffe student, complained that Jews, having experienced war and the Nazi holocaust "sit back and feel, well, we have suffered, therefore we don't need to help anyone else because we have enough of our own problems." She complained that her home Jewish community in Harrison, New York, was addicted to "a very shallow type of success," the "sickness" of the Jewish community. "I didn't see really anything to be proud of in this kind of Judaism." A third, a Columbia Law School student, spoke of the Jewish community in Jackson, Mississippi, and tried to explain Southern white anti-Semitism much as Russian student activists justified Russian pogroms seventy-five years before: "There are 100 Jewish families, close to a quarter of whom are millionaires. . . . You get the 'Shylock' kind of thing." Northern Negro anti-Semitism was given a similar sufficient explanation; the existence of Jewish slumlords and discriminators was cited by the young activist. This student, a Brandeis graduate, spoke plainly about the element of generational revolt. His participation, he said, "was a kind of revulsion to the reaction of most first generation American Jews, who were born here and feel this strong kinship for Israel. My strongest drive and motivation was to my nation, which I consider to be America." Although "large numbers of the participants in the struggle were Jewish . . . they don't go into the Jewish community and see how the Jewish community feels." This Jewish student believed he was the only one who had made an effort to seek out the Jewish community. According to another participant, the Gentile wife of a Jewish student, "one-third to one-half of the white participants in the struggle today were Jewish," but evidently this startling fact was glossed over by participants, rather than analyzed.

The Communist speaker at the symposium was more aware of the heart of the problem: "It's one thing to turn away from the rabbi. It's another thing even to turn away from your parents. But, to turn away from a people, that's another thing." As one student, also a Mississippi participant, plainly put it, "There is a tremendous desire on the part of many Mississippi Jewish freedom workers to deny their identity with Judaism." The Communist speaker dwelled on the psychological rejection of generational heritage which persisted among the Jewish students. It was no longer directed against orthodox immigrant parents in a proletarian East Side, for the new student was born into affluence, literacy, culture, and progressivism. He tried to explain the suppression of and hatred for their Jewish roots as the fault of the elders: "They probably all come from liberal-progressive parents," from "homes where progressive ideals were uppermost, but were presented in such a way as to disguise and therefore keep from these younger people the Jewish element in the struggle."

The young Jewish student activist is eager to become an expert on Negro history. He hates to know about Jewish history. There is an ugly component of self-hatred in the Jewish student which has impressed the Negro observer:

A Negro student once came to me in a class with an odd kind of complaint. He said to me, "Mr. Schappes, you know I have a great number of Jewish friends who are very active in the civil rights struggle. I find that they know more about Negro history than I do. But when I ask them a simple question about Jewish history, or Jewish affairs, they don't know the answer." And he added: "I'm beginning to get suspicious of them. What are they up to? Are they missionaries? Are they in this for some kind of ulterior purpose?"[116]

Indeed, the Negro student had grasped the nub of the problem. There was an "ulterior purpose"—a repressed, often unconscious search for identification with another people's suffering, an identification which would go hand in hand with a refusal to dwell on the experience of one's own people. The contemporary Jewish student of liberal parents was in strange revolt against them and their heritage, even as the liberal fathers had revolted against their immigrant grandfathers. In the case of Jews in the student movement, there was no return of the third generation to the heritage of the first; Marcus Hansen's law of the immigrant generations did not hold. For the Jewish generations, it was always a negation of the negation. The basis of the revolt was always oddly much the same, and had little to do with economics. In previous generations Jewish students felt ashamed that their often cultureless parents were a persecuted people, always passive, always suffering, telling horrid stories of the indignities of pogroms. Their fathers seemed lacking in manliness. Their misfortunes lacked the heroic cast, and were therefore devoid of the nobility of tragedy. When a new generation after the Second World War heard of Jews, it was as victims, again almost always passive, of the Nazi holocaust, of those who had had torn from them the last shreds of human dignity as they were led in queues to abattoirs. The Jewish students of successive generations felt that their parents—orthodox, liberal, religious, agnostic—somehow shared in the psychology of passive acquiescence, that as the persecuted, they had been virtually deprived of their manhood, emasculated. Books, plays, films such as the *Diary of Anne Frank* or *The Deputy* probably made the Jewish would-be student activist wish all the more to repress his Jewish origins. The elder generation, for all its anti-Nazism, somehow shared in the collective guilt; it had not acted forthrightly, dramatically, to prevent such things from taking place. Thus the Jewish activist student tried to obliterate his Jewish derivation. Nevertheless, he felt he had been conceived in a world which enveloped him with injustice. The Jews were a chosen people, in that the world had chosen them for genocide and pogroms. And the Jewish student activist felt called upon to protest, without, however, drawing attention to the fact that he was a Jew—to protest against racial hatred, genocide, culturocide, while repressing at the same time the fact that he came from a people which had experienced all these demonic forces. Hence the young Jewish student was especially prone to finding in the Negro people a surrogate for his own. He could thus reject his father, even as he projected his protest against the indignities his father had experienced, in the guise of protesting on behalf of another, even more despised race, whose members, unlike himself, could never escape visibility and identification with their people. Thus, the basic reason for the continued high involvement of Jewish students in the small American student movement has been the successive de-authoritization of the older generation by successive waves and forms of historical anti-Semitism. It was not in their case a revolt against middle-class values, any more than the earlier movement of City College men had been a revolt against their fathers' proletarian situation. What was involved was the peculiar de-authoritization of a generation associated with the passive recipience of persecution.

Conclusion

What, then, have been the achievements and failures of student movements in the history of the United States? The movements were always a source of intellectual ferment on the campuses; they had a sense of the drama of ideas. They made the average undergraduate and professor more aware of the emerging problems and realities of the world. They were a channel for the noblest idealistic aspirations of adolescence. At the same time, they were also a channel for emotions of generational revolt. They tended, therefore, to extremes of doctrine, the rejection of the elders' liberal values and a choice of self-destructive means in political action. The student movements from 1905 to 1940 could point to no single accomplishment of legislation, no statute, no New Deal measure, for which they could truly claim credit. The thirties saw the blind alley of the Oxford Oath and the corruption of Communist hegemony during the time of the Hitler-Stalin Pact. The most notable achievement of the sixties was the Mississippi Project of 1964; but the student civil rights movement came repeatedly into conflict with the leadership of the older generation, a conflict which reached its climax in 1965 at Selma, Alabama, in the clash with Martin Luther King. Legislative victories followed, but the success of the movement depended on the maintenance of a generational equilibrium within it. Persons of all ages and classes were summoned to the movement; it was not allowed to become a student movement. The distinctive student vector has emerged in its advocacy of violence, guerilla warfare, and its hostility to the liberal democratic process.

The student movements are presumed to have been a remarkable training ground for political action and initiative. Too often, however, they burned out their participants. The activist lived at a level of excitement which he could not long maintain. Activist at twenty-one, de-activated at twenty-two became a familiar pattern. Political action born of generational revolt tended to be self-terminating; it ended when some measure of generational independence was achieved. Meanwhile, the leading political student leaders were often disabled by extreme commitments from assuming the role of leadership they might otherwise normally have filled.

Compare the histories of the labor and student movements. The labor movement went through the bitter school of poverty, fought to keep its organizations alive and to give its members a philosophy. It too had its lapses into illusion, violence, and self-destruction. But it has written its achievements into volumes of legislation while at the same time rejecting the elitist myth that it was the Elect of History. By contrast, student movements have always been laden with emotion and doctrine concerning themselves as the elitist makers of history. Unlike the labor movement, they have often tended to represent not the reason of the studentry but its unreason. If students in the United States have generally held aloof from student movements, it was not always because of smugness or selfishness but because they felt that social idealism too readily went hand in hand with social irrationality.[117] Student movements as agencies of generational revolt have distorted and thwarted the generous emotions which were also their partial inspiration.

NOTES

1. Marshall Kaplan and Richard Weddington White, "Birth of a Student Movement," *Liberation,* V (June 1960), 13.
2. David Horowitz, *Student* (New York, 1962), p. 151.
3. *Ibid.,* pp. 154–157.
4. Otto Feinstein, "Is There a Student Movement?" *New University Thought,* I, No. 4 (Summer 1961), 24.
5. R. Alan Haber, *Students and Labor,* leaflet, Students for a Democratic Society (New York, September 1962), pp. 5–8.
6. Al Richmond, *Campus Rebels,* (pamphlet; San Francisco, 1960), pp. 20–21.
7. Paul Potter, *The Intellectual as an Agent of Social Change,* leaflet, Students for a Democratic Society (New York, June 1963), pp. 2–5.
8. *Ibid.,* p. 3.
9. Charles Chadwick, "Angry Liberals," *Liberation,* V, Nos. 5–6 (July-August 1960), 29.
10. C. Wright Mills, "On the New Left," *Studies on the Left,* II, No. 1 (1961), 70–71. See also Saul Landau, "C. Wright Mills—The Last Six Months," *Root and Branch,* No. 2 (1962), p. 7; Hans H. Gerth, "C. Wright Mills, 1916–1962," *Studies on the Left,* II, No. 3 (1962), 11.
11. Dale L. Johnson, "On the Ideology of the Campus Revolution," *Studies on the Left,* II, No. 1 (1961), 75.
12. Wayne Price, "Letter to the Editor," *Viewpoint,* I, No. 10 (1965), 11.
13. Robert Wolfe, "Intellectuals and Social Change," *Studies on the Left,* II, No. 3 (1962), 65.
14. Johnson, *op. cit.,* p. 74.
15. Horowitz, *op. cit.,* p. 11.
16. Howard Zinn, *SNCC: the New Abolitionists* (Boston, 1964), p. 19.
17. Louis E. Lomax, *The Negro Revolt* (Signet edn.; New York, 1963), pp. 96, 134; Tom Kahn, *Unfinished Revolution* (New York, 1960), p. 12; *Sit-Ins: The Students' Report,* accounts by Patricia Stephens, Edward Rodman, Paul Laprad, Thomas Gaither, Major Johns, Martin Smolin (New York, May 1960); James Peck, *Freedom Ride* (New York, 1962), pp. 56 ff.
18. Martin Luther King, Jr., *Stride toward Freedom: The Montgomery Story* (New York, 1958), pp. 131, 36.

19. Zinn, *op. cit.*, p. 18.

20. See Kahn, *op. cit.*, pp. 32–33; also Glenford E. Mitchell and William H. Peace III (eds.), *The Angry Black South* (New York, 1962), p. 103.

21. Lomax, *op. cit.*, p. 133; Abram Kardiner and Lionel Ovesy, *The Mark of Oppression* (New York, 1951), pp. 46, 59–60, 366, 381.

22. Glenford E. Mitchell, "College Students Take Over," in Mitchell and Peace, *op. cit.*, pp. 92–93.

23. *Ibid.*, p. 94; see also Major Johns, "Baton Rouge: Higher Education—Southern Style," in Peck, *op. cit.*, p. 70.

24. "Educator in Quandary: Felton Grandison Clark," *The New York Times*, January 22, 1962. See also Adolph L. Reed, "Crisis on the Negro Campus," *The Nation*, CXCIV, No. 6 (February 10, 1962), 111–113.

25. Jeremy Larner, "The Negro in the South: 'Half a Loaf Is Ashes,'" *New Leader*, XLIII, No. 35 (September 12, 1960), 11.

26. Art Goldberg, expelled from Berkeley for his obscenitarian leadership in 1965, enrolled at Howard University the next year. He sent back a pathetic complaint about the middle-class values of the Negro students to the *Daily Californian*: "The first day I came to register at Howard I was wearing Bermudas. . . . So I went into the Law School. . . . Everyone else had on a suit. . . . I later found out that the students couldn't figure out what this nasty, funky white boy was doing sitting on the floor in the lobby. . . . I would constantly get into political fights about Vietnam. . . . The Greeks control the school and they are even worse than the white fraternities and sororities. They adopt the worst patterns of middle-class white people." See Art Goldberg, "On Negro Universities," *Daily Californian*, June 29, 1966, p. 12.

27. Larner, *op. cit.*, p. 11.

28. Kermit Eby, "Expert in the Labor Movement," *American Journal of Sociology*, LVII (1951), 27–32; "Young Idealists in Labor Unions," *Christian Century*, LXVI (1949), 1009–1010; "Organization, Bureaucracy, Loyalty," *Antioch Review*, XV (1955), 195–203.

29. Peck, *op. cit.*, pp. 73 ff.

30. Lewis S. Feuer, "Youth in the '60's," *New Leader*, XLIV, No. 10 (March 6, 1961), 18–22; reprinted in Albert T. Anderson and Bernice P. Biggs (eds.), *Focus on Rebellion* (San Francisco, 1962), pp. 142–151.

31. Lomax, *op. cit.*, p. 139; Larner, *op. cit.*, p. 11; Zinn, *op. cit.*, p. 13.

32. Zinn, *op. cit.*, p. 3.

33. *Ibid.*, pp. 3, 9–10.

34. Tom Hayden, *Revolution in Mississippi* (New York, 1962), p. 7.

35. William McCord, *Mississippi: The Long, Hot Summer* (New York, 1965), p. 53.

36. *Ibid.*, p. 64.

37. *Ibid.*, p. 65.

38. "Excerpts from the Slain Seminarian's Essay," *The New York Times*, August 21, 1965.

39. Claude Sitton, "Students Briefed on Peril in South: Rights Campaigners Warned of Death in Mississippi," *The New York Times*, June 17, 1964.

40. Elizabeth Sutherland (ed.), *Letters from Mississippi* (New York, 1965), pp. 24, 27, 28, 17, 18, 136, 13, 15, 20.

41. Calvin Trillin, "Letter from Jackson," *New Yorker*, XL, No. 28 (August 29, 1964), 101–102.

42. "Bettina: The Movement's 'Self-Immolation,'" *Daily Californian*, March 24, 1966, p. 8.

43. "Boycott Peace Corps' Rally," *Daily Californian*, November 5, 1965; "Hypocritical, Peace Corps Boycott Urged to Protest War in Vietnam," *Daily Californian*, November 2, 1965.

44. "Corps Director: Peace Corps—'Outside Politics,'" *Daily Californian*, March 9, 1966.

45. *Peace Corps World: 1966* (Washington, D.C.), p. 1.

46. Jack Newfield, "Tom Hayden: Prophet Comes to Sodom," *Village Voice*, January 20, 1966, p. 1. Newfield is a leading practitioner of the New Leftist style in political journalism. He wrote, for instance, of Senators Robert F. Kennedy and Eugene McCarthy: "They are both politicians, both whores working in the same Democratic Party whorehouse." Jack Newfield, "The Arrogance of Class: Humphrey is the Enemy," *Village Voice*, May 2, 1968, p. 6.

47. Steve Max, "The 1965 SDS Convention: From Port Huron to Maplehurst," *Viewpoint*, I, No. 10 (Summer 1965), 7–10.

48. Steve Weissman, "Civil Disobedience in Action," *Students for Democratic Society Bulletin*, IV, No. 1 (1965), 7. A similar evolution from activist confron-

tationism to populism to disillusionment with the poor marked the Canadian student movement. When the Student Union for Peace Action voted to disband in September 1967, the student newspaper of the University of Toronto summarized its career: "SUPA decided to stimulate Berkeley-type confrontations on campuses across the country. It was tried in a few places, but although administrations were terrified, there was little to fear. . . . Other SUPA members went off into community organizing binges—to Saskatchewan among Indians and Metis; to Kingston with slum dwellers and so on. Most of the young radicals came back from those experiments disillusioned. They found they couldn't so easily leave their affluent backgrounds and live among poverty cultures." See editorial, "Supa: what is accomplished," *The Varsity*, October 2, 1967, p. 4.

49. Marvin Garson, "The Ombilical: When the Workers Start to Move," *Berkeley Barb*, May 19, 1967, p. 12.

50. One New Leftist, Andrew Kopkind, resigned from the *New Republic* on the ground that it was too closely tied to the "Establishment." At a "counter-convention" to the National Student Association which he helped organize, he was asked what the alternative institutions he stood for were. He was at quite a loss for an answer, and fell back on saying that what was needed was to make an "attitudinal leap, to drop out of the Establishment, to put the radical idea first"—in short, an "attitudinal leap" of generational revolt, with the program to come later. Kopkind added that it was hard to propose alternatives "in a world of large institutions." See Steven V. Roberts, "The Voices of the Campus," *The New York Times*, August 20, 1967.

51. Steven Kelman, "SDS: Troubled Voice of the New Left," *New Leader*, XLVIII, No. 19 (September 27, 1965), 12.

52. *Loc. cit.*

53. The "new radicalism," or the "student left," wrote Andrew Kopkind, "is closer to Mario Savio than to Marx." See Kopkind, "New Radicals in Dixie," *New Republic*, CLII, No. 15 (April 10, 1965), 13; also his "Of, By and For the Poor: The New Generation of Student Organizers," *New Republic*, CLII, No. 25 (June 19, 1965), 15.

54. Paul Goodman, *Growing up Absurd* (New York, 1960), p. 202.

55. *Ibid.*, p. 68.

56. *Ibid.*, p. 123. See also Lewis S. Feuer, "Cult of the Rebel," *New Leader*, XLIV, No. 25 (June 19, 1961), 21–23.

57. The "hipster," noted Eugene Burdick, " 'disaffiliates.' This means that he withdraws from the senseless organizations of orthodox society, whether these be political parties or corporations. . . . No figure of speech is used as often as 'Christ-like' in the beat vocabulary." Yet he sounded too "like the younger Bakunin." Eugene Burdick, "The Politics of the Beat Generation," *Western Political Quarterly*, XII (1959), 553–555.

58. Bradford Lytle, "After Washington?—Three Views," *Committee for Nonviolent Action Bulletin*, V, No. 5 (August 27, 1965), 1–2.

59. Staughton Lynd, "The New Radicals and 'Participatory Democracy,' " *Dissent*, XII (1965), 328–329.

60. Staughton Lynd, "Coalition Politics or Nonviolent Revolution?" *Liberation*, X, No. 4 (June-July 1965), 21.

61. V. I. Lenin, *The State and Revolution* (New York, 1932), p. 75.

62. Lynd, "Coalition Politics or Nonviolent Revolution?" pp. 19–21.

63. Bayard Rustin, "The New Radicalism: Round III," *Partisan Review*, XXXII, No. 4 (1965), p. 537.

64. V. I. Lenin, *The Constituent Assembly Elections and the Dictatorship of the Proletariat* (Moscow, 1954), p. 14.

65. *Ibid.*, pp. 27, 31.

66. Lynd, "The New Radicals and 'Participatory Democracy,' " pp. 326–327.

67. James W. Silver, *Mississippi: The Closed Society* (New York, 1966), pp. 342–343.

68. In 1967, the Student Nonviolent Coordinating Committee dropped its tactical fiction of "nonviolence" and advocated violence, especially "guerrilla warfare." Curiously, in its espousal of "guerrilla warfare," it was following in Lenin's footsteps. William English Walling, activist at the turn of the century, reported from Russia how Lenin favored "guerrilla warfare," and how the lesson of the Revolution of 1905 was "the possible success of guerrilla tactics in a modern city"; guns could be passed, house owners could be terrorized, and the chance of detection

was small. See William English Walling, *Russia's Message* (New York, 1909), pp. 358, 370.

69. Lynd, "The New Radicals and 'Participatory Democracy,'" p. 328.

70. Lynd, "Socialism, the Forbidden Word," *Studies on the Left*, III, No. 3 (1963), 19.

71. "Michigan Faculty Created Teach-In," *The New York Times*, May 9, 1965.

72. "Now the Teach-In: U.S. Policy in Vietnam Criticized All Night," *The New York Times*, March 27, 1965.

73. Max Frankel, "Future of the Teach-In," *The New York Times*, May 17, 1965.

74. *Idem.*

75. *Idem.*

76. "Poll Contradicts Students' Image," *The New York Times*, January 16, 1966.

77. Jerry Rubin, "October 15–16 and the VDC," *VDC News*, published by the Berkeley VDC, I, No. 4 (October 11, 1965), 1.

78. *Idem.*

79. *Idem.*

80. Dave Slavin, "The Watts Ghetto: A People's Uprising," *Free Student*, No. 5 (n.d.), p. 12.

81. Robert Hurwitt, "Mime Troupe Always Set to Shuffle," *Berkeley Barb*, July 28-August 3, 1967, 9.

82. Steve Weissman, "The National Coordinating Committee Convention," *Liberation*, X (January 1966), 48–49.

83. John Corry, "'We Must Say Yes to Our Souls'—Staughton Lynd: Spokesman for the New Left," *The New York Times Magazine*, January 23, 1966, p. 12.

84. Steve Weissman, "Civil Disobedience in Action," *Students for a Democratic Society Bulletin*, IV, No. 1, 6.

85. Michael Harrington, "The Mystical Militants," *New Republic*, CLIV, No. 8 (February 19, 1966), 20. See also Lucille Birnbaum, "The Unkempt Prophets of Berkeley," *Issue: Those Who Make the Waves*, III, No. 1 (Spring 1965), 23–27.

86. *Daily Californian*, November 5, 1964, p. 1.

87. *Daily Californian*, February 28, 1966, p. 1.

88. "Cloke's Statement of Resignation," *Daily Californian*, March 6, 1963, p. 1.

89. Morris E. Hurley, "Minority of One," *Daily Californian*, July 23, 1965, p. 9.

90. Davis Allen, "The Barber of Berkeley: Interview with Max Scherr," *Daily Californian*, March 8, 1966, pp. 9–10.

91. Marvin Garson, "Cal Goes on a Bad Trip," *Daily Californian*, February 15, 1966, p. 12. See also Garson, *The Regents* (Berkeley, 1965).

92. John Corry, "The Use of Drugs on College Campuses Is a Growing Problem," *The New York Times*, March 21, 1966. There is some evidence too that suicidalism increased at this time among American students. The United States Public Health Service estimated that adolescents of college age constituted the nation's highest potential suicide risk group. See "College Suicides Put at 1,000 in '66," *The New York Times*, October 4, 1966; also see "Pressure—and Suicides—Rising on Campus," *The New York Times*, October 9, 1966.

93. Richard Thorne, "A Step toward Sexual Freedom in Berkeley," *Berkeley Barb*, February 4, 1965, 5.

94. Adam Hochschild, "The Way-Out Set: Reporter Visits a Nude Party," *San Francisco Chronicle*, March 1, 1966, pp. 1, 10.

95. David Kamen, "The New Left—the New Fraternity," *Daily Californian*, August 10, 1966, p. 10.

96. Jed Rakoff, "Social Rules Are 'Good Thing,'" *Swarthmore College Phoenix*, LXXXVI, No. 24 (December 12, 1965), p. 2.

97. Wechsler, *Revolt on the Campus*, p. 359.

98. Jack Weinberg, Art Goldberg, Suzanne Goldberg, Stephen Weissman, Michael Rossman, Bettina Aptheker served on the Steering Committee. Information of Marilyn Noble, secretarial manager, Free Speech Movement, September 1, 1965.

99. Summary of lecture by Kathleen Gales, *Berkeley Daily Gazette*, July 28, 1965.

100. See *Jewish Currents*, XIX, No. 7 (July-August 1965), 14.

101. Irving Spiegel, "Jewish Officials Vexed by Youths: Students Said to Regard Agencies as 'Banal,'" *The New York Times*, June 26, 1965.

102. *The New York Times*, June 10, 1968, p. 53.

103. *The New York Times*, June 26, 1965.

104. Irving Spiegel, "Students Ponder Role of Judaism: Moral and Social Issues are Weighed by Hillel Group," *The New York Times*, September 5, 1965.

105. Joseph Gollomb, *Unquiet* (New York, 1935), pp. 366, 400–401, 436.

106. William Knight (ed.), *Memorials of Thomas Davidson: The Wandering Scholar* (Boston, 1907), p. 87. See also Leonard Prager, "Of Parents and Children: Jacob Gordin's The Jewish King Lear," *American Quarterly*, XVIII (Fall 1966), 506–516. "Hundreds and thousands," wrote David Philipson in 1905, "are leaving the old paths; the religion of their fathers is repugnant to them. In many instances, it is hated because it is synonymous with the old life of the ghetto and oppression." See "Strangers in a New Land," *American Jewish Archives*, XVIII (November 1966), 130; see also Hutchins Hapgood, *The Spirit of the Ghetto: Studies of the Jewish Quarter in New York* (rev. edn.; New York, 1909), 32–38.

107. See Melech Epstein, *Jewish Labor in U.S.A.: An industrial, political and cultural history of the Jewish Labor Movement, 1882–1914* (New York, 1950), pp. 355–356. Even "many radical parents also saw their children becoming alienated from them and things Jewish."

108. Wechsler, *Revolt on the Campus*, p. 359.

109. Melech Epstein, *The Jew and Communism: The Story of Early Communist Victories and Ultimate Defeats in the Jewish Community, U.S.A., 1919–1941* (New York, 1959), pp. 201–202.

110. John Gates, *The Story of an American Communist* (New York, 1958), p. 16. See also Nathan Glazer, *The Social Basis of American Communism* (New York, 1961), p. 137.

111. Gates, *op. cit.*, p. 19.

112. *Ibid.*, p. 23.

113. Joseph P. Lash, *The Student Movement Comes of Age* (pamphlet; New York, 1938).

114. Alfred Jospe (ed.), *The Legacy of Maurice Pekarsky* (Chicago, 1965), p. 144.

115. Eight who were in Mississippi [and] James A. Jones, Morris U. Schappes, "Jewish Young Freedom Fighters and the Role of the Jewish Community: An Evaluation," *Jewish Currents*, XIX, No. 7 (July-August 1965), 4–33.

116. *Ibid.*, p. 25.

117. According to the Playboy College Opinion Survey, a large majority of the American studentry, 82 per cent, felt that the United States was obligated to provide active military aid to South Vietnam. Only 6 per cent opposed any American involvement. One thousand students on two hundred campuses provided the sample. An overwhelming majority of 90 per cent felt that an American was obligated to accept military service even if he disagreed with his government. "Playboy's Poll Says Students Favor 'Bomb Hanoi' Policy," *Daily Californian*, November 23, 1965, p. 11.

NINE The Berkeley Student Uprising: 1964–1966

Berkeley in 1964: The Freest University Campus in the United States

No other student uprising in the United States has ever impressed the public imagination as much as that which took place at the University of California in Berkeley in the fall of 1964. Its story is one of the usual dualities which have characterized student movements: selfless idealism matched with ugly hatreds of generational revolt, high moral ends and low immoral means, a vision of Utopian community and a reality of destruction, a populist yearning joined with an elitist self-assertion. Within two years the student movement, which began with an avowal of nonviolence and a higher ethic, was becoming the apologist for violence and political amorality. The classical patterns of student movements, familiar enough in nineteenth-century Russia, began to appear, of all places, in the most advanced university and the most modern state of the United States. Theoreticians who for fifteen years had been telling themselves that such movements were incidents of "developing countries," "emerging new nations," and "underdeveloped areas" found themselves confuted by a movement which had grown, unperceived and uncomprehended, a few yards from their studies. Why did it happen at Berkeley?

The student body at Berkeley was not a radical one. Indeed, in the national election of 1956, it was more conservative than the population at large; a sample poll indicated that 71 per cent of the Berkeley students had supported President Eisenhower as the candidate for election to a second term.[1] During the years from 1960, however, to 1964, a tension spread among a section of the studentry. It linked itself successively with a series of issues, especially with the growing civil rights movement in the

United States; these youth experienced a sympathy, sometimes an identification, with the struggles and sufferings of the Negro people. For a year or two, in little circles organized by such groups as the Congress of Racial Equality (CORE), they picketed retail stores, department stores, restaurants, and apartment houses to protest against practices of racial discrimination in these establishments.[2] They organized boycotts, which often were successful; and they experimented with sit-in tactics, which proved effective enough to put one large store out of business completely. In the spring of 1964, several hundreds of students were arrested in San Francisco when they staged massive sit-ins in Automobile Row and the Sheraton Palace Hotel. Nevertheless, agreements were secured which evidently raised the ratios of Negroes employed in these enterprises, and the student activists felt that at long last they had found a tactical weapon through which they could directly compel social change: civil disobedience in the form of the massive sit-in.[3] A back-to-the-people spirit together with a messianic feeling surged among the student activists. "A weekend of songs, sit-ins, and sleep-ins," rejoiced the *Daily Californian,* as it announced the victory: "Demonstrators 1—Sheraton Palace O." They, the students, became confident in noble exaltation that by their sheer heroism and resourcefulness they would lead the Negro masses; the downtrodden would lift their heads. Several Berkeley students had been Freedom Riders in Alabama and Mississippi two years earlier; now in 1964 their successors went as volunteers to the Summer Freedom Project in Mississippi, volunteers to lead voter registration drives and Freedom Schools. That summer, the first "long, hot summer," three civil rights volunteers were murdered in Mississippi; the missing bodies of Andrew Goodman, Michael Schwerner, and James Chaney haunted the summer's weeks until they were discovered buried in a ditch on August 3. The first two boys were college students from New York, the third was a Negro co-worker from the neighborhood. They had been tortured and shot. Their murderers were citizens whose identity was known but who seemed to have an immunity before the law. Meridian, Mississippi, became the symbol of the martyrdom of the American student volunteer.[4] The nation was aghast over the brutality, cruelty, and indifference which were meted out upon the young idealists.[5] Older people began to experience a sense of guilt in the sacrifice of the young as well as of their de-authoritization as they saw the young prove their martyrdom; this new generation was ready to put its convictions to the test of individual direct action; the student activists by the fall of 1964 had assumed the role of conscience of their society.

Moreover, in 1964, a "generational complex" had become strong in Berkeley. Its chief symptom was a readiness on the part of student activists to demonstrate at the slightest real or imagined provocation. A demonstration became a compulsive gesture; the will to demonstrate was experienced apart from and prior to any specific issues. It was a readiness to serve notice on the elders, to "confront" them. As one young assistant professor told his fellow "peace" advocates, they were minded for civil disobedience and then looked around for a cause to justify the means. The means were the real end; the apparent "end" was an occasion for their use. The will to demonstrate, to be disobedient, to "bring the system to a grinding halt," to "lay one's body on the line" became like an obsessive Kantian a priori category. As the poet Kenneth Rexroth noted, a group had arisen of "compulsively addicted demonstrators. One week they are Youth, next week they are Negroes, next week they are Free Speechers, or for Peace or against the Atom. The beards, duffle coats, bare feet, jeans, dirty hair, remain the same." And Rexroth, trying to define the compulsion, wrote, "They are voluntary outcasts who identify their own personal alienation with the actions of others protesting to achieve definite goals within society." He once asked a compulsive demonstrator in the sit-ins whether she knew how many Negroes had been employed since the sit-ins. "She gave me a look of withering contempt," wrote Rexroth, "and said, 'I couldn't care less.' "[6]

The University of California at Berkeley was probably the freest campus in the country. Its administration in April 1964 had been awarded the Alexander Meiklejohn Prize by the American Association of University Professors for its advances and steadfast adherence to academic freedom.[7] Communist speakers and organizations had the freedom of its campus rooms; an outdoor free speech area was available to all.[8] The university had refused to consider disciplinary action against students convicted of violating the law during civil rights disturbances. Student pickets on the campus grounds had agitated against compulsory Reserve Officers' Training Corps (R.O.T.C.) courses unmolested, and student petitioners set up their tables on the steps of the administration building; the university nonetheless pursued its liberal policy, and terminated compulsory military training. When, during the Cuban Bay of Pigs crisis, a graduate student spoke for eight hours at an unauthorized meeting at an out-of-bounds center of the campus, he received only a gentle reprimand. When Mme. Nhu of South Vietnam came to Berkeley, she was greeted by student pickets. The organizations of the New Left flourished at Berkeley meetings as they did on no other campus in the United States. Yet it was precisely here that the activists raised the cry that they were being persecuted and deprived of freedom.

Then, too, Berkeley had become a center for nonstudents, a relatively new phenomenon in American social history but one which was familiar in Europe wherever a student movement flourished. Every classical student movement, beginning with the German and Russian movements in the nineteenth century, has attracted to itself nonstudents, many of whom find their life's calling in a prolonged adolescence and repetitive re-enactment from year to year of the rebellion against their fathers. A few thousand such nonstudents lived in proximity to the University of California at Berkeley, attracted there by the salubrious climate, the gentle sunny surroundings, the relaxed mode of life, the record shops, bookstores, restaurants, and students' apartments, the reputation of the Berkeley police force for its tolerance toward deviants, nonconformists, and militants, and the university's free offering of immense cultural riches in lectures, plays, concerts, books. When the beatnik community came to feel that San Francisco was becoming too bourgeois and tourist-ridden, it largely migrated to Berkeley. The "hidden community," as the students' newspaper called the nonstudents, was significant in the Berkeley student uprising among other reasons because it provided members who were available for full-time activity in any action against the Establishment or the System, and who in any situation were inclined to choose the most provocative speech and action.[9] When the *Spartacist*, an organ of a Berkeley Trotskyist sect, published a long article explaining why the student uprising had erupted at Berkeley, it proudly claimed a primary causal role for the nonstudent corps:

> Berkeley has accumulated over the years a sizable fringe of disaffected semi-bohemian elements who, while they have no formal connection with the University, cluster around it and form a supportive element for student radicals. . . . They find in Berkeley an atmosphere conducive to living on their political light-duty slips. In short, the student radical does not face a harshly hostile environment once he steps beyond Sather Gate.[10]

Moreover, Berkeley and its environs during the years had become the last sanctuary for the defeated activists of the thirties. In Berkeley they found a liberality of spirit which revived their flagging revolutionary ardor; they even found jobs in the university institutions, institutes, and adjacent operations, and such part-time employment gave them a base for commencing a new agitational career among the students. An able former editor of a New York Trotskyist magazine, *Labor Action*, after the demise of his magazine and movement, turned from labor action to student action; he secured part-time employment in the university library, and in 1964 conducted a notable University Socialist School with a course entitled "Ten Revolutions that Shook the World." There were five evenings, with two revolutions an evening and ten lecturers; for a total tuition fee of one dollar, the student was offered a chance to re-experience the high emotions of the Paris Commune, the Revolution of 1848, the Russian and Chinese Revolutions, the Spanish Civil War.[11] The hundred or so activists who attended the school heard lectures on the value of the revolutionary experience; revolution seemed the culmination of one's life, the moment of heroism, the moment of meaning. A few months later the same activists were seeking their own revolutionary experience on the Sproul steps and the plaza. As the French revolutionists had stormed the Bastille and occupied the Tuileries and Versailles Palace, as the Bolshevik-led masses had occupied the Winter Palace, the students would surge forward to occupy the open administration building, Sproul Hall.

Former Trotskyists, socialists, and Communists were drawn to Berkeley as a new political fountain of youth. A former Communist, presenting himself regularly to student groups as a Soviet expert, martyred during the so-called McCarthyist era, complained to the students that the university refused to appoint him to its faculty; the student activists, always quick to sympathize with a presumed underdog and to empathize with his criticism of authority, were left ignorant of the fact that the self-styled Soviet expert had testified before a congressional committee in 1952 that Stalin never killed his political opponents and that there were no slave-labor camps in the Soviet Union. A former Trotskyist organizer and later labor journalist now graced by an institute retainer gave his ardent blessing at rallies to student activists. And when the moment of action came, the activists marched under banners to occupy Sproul Hall to the singing of the beautiful and famed folk singer, Joan Baez. No spontaneous student action was ever staged with such a remarkable directorial flair, before so many television cameras, and with such an entranced audience.

What Is a Nonstudent?

What is a nonstudent? This new American sociological type, which emerged at Berkeley, often defines himself as a "guerrilla fighter" against society. He admires the "guerrilla fighter" who at any given time most challenges the System. Castro, Mao, Che Guevara, the Vietcong have all been guerrilla superegos for the nonstudents. Oldsters who associated themselves with the students pictured themselves too in this guise; when the actor Sterling Hayden was arrested in the San Francisco sit-ins in the spring of 1964, he described himself to reporters as being engaged in a sort of "guerrilla warfare" against the System. The nonstudent was in part a nihilist, though from 1963 on he was tending to move from pure nihilism to life as a full-time (if possible) guerrilla fighter against the System. As a nonstudent, he was the first in the history of American society to define himself negatively. He indeed lives in negation; he has no job, no calling, no vocation. If the System has had its yes-men, he will be a total no-man. He denounces the Impersonal Society, the Organized System, and the Bureaucracy. Yet he is strangely parasitic on the System. He lives in its interstices, needs its systematic conveniences, and above all requires the student environment. Himself permanently fixated or arrested in the stage of adolescent revolt against authority, and having failed to acquire the habits of work and discipline, the virtues of the "Protestant ethic," he requires the emotional reassurance of the youthful audience, their naïveté, ready sympathy, and shared rebelliousness. The nonstudent, in short, is under a compulsion to live in perpetual generational revolt. To every virtue which his father upheld he counterposes an anti-virtue. A job, responsibility to one's family, the value of work, the insistence on ethical means in political action—all are rejected as Establishment tainted. Living on his father's donations, or the government's unemployment insurance, or student hospitality, the nonstudent is a luxurious excrescence of the affluent society. The leading nonstudent of the Berkeley Free Speech Movement, Jack Weinberg, once described his political and private history in the characteristic idiom of the nonstudent; it was an autobiographical document representative of several hundreds, and later thousands, like him. He explained:

> I became an activist before the FSM. I worked with CORE in the South in 1963 so the FSM didn't screw up my private life. It was already screwed up and I loved it.
>
> The FSM, though, has been the most complete experience of my life, the most all-encompassing. Very complex, a tremendous amount of responsibility, working 16 hours a day.
>
> It gave me a sense of comradeship we had not known existed.
>
> It gave me insights into myself that I will need years to define.[12]

Once people used to define themselves by what they did, by their function. Living in permanent generational revolt, this new group defined itself negatively, by what it didn't do; its adherents even contrived an ideology for their existence as nonexistence. One nonstudent said:

> It is invariably the radicals, not the conservatives, who drop out of school and become activist nonstudents. . . .
>
> "We don't play a big role politically," says one. "But philosophically we're a hell of a threat to the establishment. Just the fact that we exist proves that dropping out of school isn't the end of the world. . . . We're respectable. A lot of students I know are thinking of becoming nonstudents."[13]

Berkeley, of all places in America, was the promised land for the nonstudents. "The climate is easy, the people are congenial, and the action never dies." For instance, Jim Prickett, nonstudent, became an editor of *Spider*, dedicated to "sex, politics, international communism, drugs, extremism and rock 'n roll." He had "quit the University of Oklahoma" and been dropped for poor grades from San Francisco State College. He came to Berkeley because "things are happening here." A fellow-editor of his lived with three other nonstudents and two students in a comfortable house. They clung to their post-student prolongation of the student existence. For the psychological essence of the nonstudent is that he cannot give up being a student. He is fixated in its psychology, and from this standpoint the term "nonstudent" is a misnomer. The nonstudent views with horror having to give up student existence, with its privilege of intellectual and emotional freebooting. He lacks the intellectual self-mastery or love for a subject or science which would lead him on to complete his studies, but he loves the externalities or pseudo-externalities of student life. Instead of having completed his adolescent rebellion by defining his own vocation, he actually remains emotionally dependent on his father, on the elder generation; he has to remain in proximity to students because he has to re-enact the pattern of opposition, of revolt. He remains a rebel because he has never fulfilled his emotional revolution, and he is trapped in a compulsive repetitive pattern. Hence at Berkeley the nonstudent projected his illness on society: "What this country needs is a revolution; the society is so sick, so reactionary, that it just doesn't make sense to be part of it." Here in their communal apartment, there was not Permanent Revolution but Permanent Rebellion:

> Papers litter the floor, the phone rings continually, and people stop by to borrow things: a pretty blonde wants a Soviet army chorus record, a Tony Perkins type from the Oakland Du Bois Club wants a film projector; Art Goldberg—the arch-activist who also lives here—comes storming in, shouting for help on the "Vietnam Day" teach-in arrangements. It is all very friendly and collegiate. People wear plaid shirts and khaki pants, white socks and moccasins. There are books on the shelves, cans of beer and Cokes in the refrigerator, and a manually operated light bulb in the bathroom. In the midst of all this it is weird to hear people talking about "bringing the ruling class to their knees. . . ."[14]

The nonstudents' choice of metaphor was revealing. Not the positive vision of betterment but the image of humiliating the enemy, making him cringe, the fantasy of a sick adolescent everlastingly plotting to reduce his father and reverse social relations. Another nonstudent, an editor of *Spider*, said he became a radical after the 1962 civil rights demonstrations in San Francisco: "That's when I saw the power structure and understood the hopelessness of trying to be a liberal. After I got arrested I dropped the pre-med course I'd started at San Francisco State. The worst of it, though, was being screwed time and again in the courts. I'm out on appeal now with four and a half months of jail hanging over me." Above all, the nonstudent was estranged from America and in quest of another loyalty. The chairman of the Vietnam Day Committee wrote, "In most of the world people are eager and optimistic, making a new history, trying out new forms, experimenting. . . . The U.S.A. is for the status quo. But I as an American want to be with those making history, not with those freezing it. This is my own personal view. It is why I quit a newspaper job after five years to become involved in politics. It is why I left graduate studies to become involved in politics. It is why I choose to spend my time with the VDC."[15]

The Berkeley nonstudent, fixated in the student condition and consciousness, came to think of himself by a curious twist of logic as the "true student" on the university campus. When the chancellor of the university in November 1965 expressed his concern with the fact that organizations "nominally registered" as student organizations were "in fact controlled and run by nonstudents," he was bitterly criticized by the leading nonstudent organizer of the Vietnam Day Committee. The nonstudent declared, "I am a nonstudent and I consider myself an integral part of the

University." He was "thoroughly disturbed" by the official "definition of a student." "The University should be a community of ideas open to all who wish to use it." Because of the "cash register, grocery store-style of education offered here," said Jerry Rubin, "many nonstudents are more serious about education than the students."[16] Becoming a nonstudent was often the consequence of a conversion-like experience; one believed oneself to have seen the Evil of the System, and would have no part of it. "I consider myself a full-time political activist," said Jerry Rubin. "I've dedicated my life to changing the country. . . . I voluntarily became a nonstudent because I was totally disheartened by the reality I saw as a student. . . . I took seriously the idea that the university was a place for education and meaningful social action."[17]

The Berkeley student movement was not unique for the presence within it of "nonstudents." Every student movement has been conspicuous for the sheltering environment it gave to these extreme exemplars of its own motivations to generational revolt. The nonstudents hailed Berkeley for what it meant in their lives:

> There is a thing characteristic of Berkeley, and that is a fantasy, a thing in the mind. In these United States, Berkeley is unusual, for it is a continuing, never-concluded experiment, with people as voluntary self-subjects. No city has quite such a transient group as Berkeley people, yet they cohere into a community like any other. These people have filtered out of The New Deal, The New Frontier, The Great Society, and landed here. One large vehicle of the filtration process is the great learning machine in our midst (or are we in its midst?). . . . Almost anyone with a moderate amount of aspiration to personal humanity has got to try it, even if it can't last for some and they must finally describe the Berkeley experience as simply an experience, something which they had to try. But it is that fantasy, that radical thing in the mind, which, though perhaps never to be totally realized in a larger context, is the Berkeley constant.[18]

Thus the fantasy world of the nonstudent—generational revolt permanent and continuously consummated, the tired revolutionists rejuvenated, the Berkeley experience, the Berkeley constant.

There can be little doubt, however, that without the individual leadership of the sophomore, Mario Savio, the Berkeley student uprising would never have reached the proportions that it did. Savio not only articulated latent sources of student unrest; he partially created them by the oratorical fervor of his moral indignation. He was himself in the throes of a personal generational rebellion. Born December 8, 1942, in New York on the Day of the Immaculate Conception, named Mario for St. Mark, he had spent his first collegiate year at Manhattan College, an institution run by the Christian Brothers; Mario had found it "too parochial."[19] Then he went to Queens College, where he was president of the Fraternity of Christian Doctrine.[20] He experienced an inner turmoil concerning Catholic theology. The next year at Berkeley, Mario once interrupted his philosophy class, vehemently declaring, "But the most important thing we must first do is to decide whether Thomas Aquinas is right." His father, a sheet-metal worker, was evidently unaware of his son's emotional-intellectual travail. He said that when Mario was at home he attended church with his family, and he spoke with pride of Mario's presidency of the Fraternity of Christian Doctrine. As with so many student activists, the university constituted a surrogate father against whom all the emotions of generational revolt could be channelized. Apparent family equilibrium was often maintained because the university provided a substitute target, psychologically *in loco parentis*. Mario's father took pride in the awards his son had won, even from the Veterans of Foreign Wars. They were part of America, though the grandfather in Italy had been a Fascist.

Mario, as he departed from Catholic doctrine, sought a philosophy by which to live. He therefore "majored" in philosophy; within a few months, however, he found its "analytic" linguistic emphasis of little interest. He was briefly associated with the Young People's Socialist League, but more important, read Marx and Marxist literature. Marx's concept of alienation impressed him as a master key for dealing with human problems. He sought for causes to which to give himself, in the typical pattern of the unhappy youth who seeks to assuage his unhappiness by working among those living under greater, starker misery. The summer of 1963 he spent in the Taxco area in Mexico, helping to build a laundry for its people to prevent cholera infection. The next summer, in 1964, he was among the teachers in a Mississippi Freedom School. He recalled how two men armed with clubs had assaulted and pursued him and two others. He was filled not only with a back-to-the-people zeal but also with an elitist sense of historic mission. He wrote that spring to a friend of his, "I'm tired of reading history. I want to make it."[21] Before an audience, his personal doubts and hesitations vanished. The larger the crowd, the more liberated did he seem from his own inner conflict. In private conversation "a marked stutterer,"[22] he all but lost his impediment when he felt the support of a sympathetic mass. He talked of how on October 2 he had held the great crowd in the Plaza "in my hand," and how they would have obeyed him in anything he might have asked. He looked back on the December sit-in as his high moment of encounter with history:

> Whenever I go into Sproul Hall and see all the footprints on the lower part of the wall where we sat through the night awaiting arrest, I feel a bit sad. You know, it has a kind of macabre quality. To remember what was going on there once. For a moment all the hypocrisy was cleared away and we all saw the world with a much greater clarity than before. It seems in some ways frightening now that the old shell of hypocrisy that we exposed is beginning to repair itself. It seems frightening that there is such a difference between the way things are and what people actually say—people like Clark Kerr—and then the things they actually do when they are put under pressure. I feel a wistfulness that the time is gone. But also I feel pride.[23]

He felt that the students should not be punished but should receive "the kind of public apology that Socrates suggested . . ."

Like all the student leaders of history, with Karl Follen, Sergei Nechayev, and Gavrilo Princip, Mario Savio felt moved to indicate the "hypocrisy" of his society; like all of them, he was scarcely sensitive to the "hypocrisy" which might infect his own project for the making of history.

The Student Uprising of 1964: Chronicle of Events

An incident of small proportions in September 1964 became the center for the accretion of generational resentment during what became the Berkeley Student Uprising. By itself, the original dispute could have been easily resolved. But the student activists and their nonstudent auxiliaries felt themselves enveloped in the mantle of the civil rights movement, and were heady with the urge to civil disobedience. Every violation of a university rule was represented as allied with the dramatic legal violations of the civil rights movement; every generational rebel had found a banner to unfurl over whatever action his spirit drove him to. A puzzled university administration bungled and fumbled, fearful of being accused of hurting the civil rights movement if it disciplined disobedient students engaged in crude insults and floutings of rules. And when it did try to act, the administration was defined in the activists' eyes as the Cruel, Heartless, Impersonal Father who aimed to destroy his sons. At the height of the student uprising in November and December 1964, the issue of civil rights disappeared almost completely from the students' speeches and leaflets.

Every student movement, as we have seen, has tried to attach itself to a more enduring pervasive and massive carrier movement, whether it be a labor, peasants', nationalistic, or even fascist movement. The generational struggle during the summer of 1964 had merged itself with the civil rights struggle; the older generation was relatively de-authoritized on this issue. This gave to the Berkeley activists their moral hegemony over their elders in the fall of 1964; the administration was consequently timid about reacting to the most flagrant disregard for college order. But as the weeks passed, and conflicts with the elders multiplied, the issue became almost blatantly one of sheer generational solidarity and revolt, with the multiversity cast in the role of an I.B.M. machine which was mutilating (castrating) its children.

During the summer of 1964, when the Republican National Convention took place in San Francisco, there were evidently some complaints from supporters of Senator Goldwater, a presidential nominee, that the university grounds were being used to organize disorderly forays on behalf of another Republican nominee, Governor Scranton. At any rate, in September, the university administration undertook to enforce the existing regulations concerning the university's political neutrality. For several months it had allowed such groups as the Student Nonviolent Coordinating Committee (SNCC) and the Congress of Racial Equality (CORE) to place their tables across the street side of Sproul Plaza and to solicit funds and volunteers for sit-ins. The university's regulations actually forbade both the soliciting of funds on university grounds as well as their use for organizing outside political drives. In all likelihood, it would shortly have relaxed back into connivance in the violation of these regulations by civil rights groups; furthermore, given the trend in the liberalization of its rules during the previous years, and the extent of faculty involvement in the civil rights movement, a more formal amendment of the rules probably would have followed a period of discussion. The chancellor of the Berkeley campus, Edward W. Strong, was, according to the "official" history published by the Free Speech Movement itself, "a genial if austere liberal who seemed to mirror the principles of freedom and enlightenment the President [Clark Kerr] frequently espoused."[24] But the student activists, veterans of civil disobedience actions from San Francisco to Mississippi, resolved precipitously, after some provocative challenging ("Will you dare use civil disobedience?"), to employ their well-practiced tactic on the university itself. First, they invaded the university's convocation with protest signs, parading and exhibiting them in the aisles. Then, a few days later, a group of students, after exhortation by several nonstudents ("What will they think of you if you submit?"), invaded the administration building for their first, rather short sit-in.

The mood for direct action, for civil disobedience, was growing among the small group of activists who sensed that they had fallen upon a weapon which unnerved the administration; in the fall of 1964, administrators and officials in the United States lived in fear of civil disobedience, for any arrests by them of participants in it were promptly used to link them with all the repressive racists of Mississippi and Alabama. The Berkeley activists were small in numbers. The combined membership of SNCC, CORE, Slate (a student political party embracing all varieties of protest—Stalinism, Maoism, beatnikism, anarchism, and sheer orneriness), and the YSA (Trotskyist Young Socialist Alliance), was no more than 170 students out of a total student population of more than twenty-seven thousand. It was these four organizations which on Tuesday, September 29, set up their tables in front of Sather Gate in contravention of the rules. The dean's representatives persuaded a few of the students to identify themselves but allowed the tables to remain. The fervor of civil disobedience now began to spread, all the more so as it became clear that the authorities were embarrassed and reluctant to act. The next day, about four hundred students signed petitions to the dean declaring that they too were guilty of having manned the political tables in conscious violation of the university's rules. A sit-in then began which lasted into the early morning of October 1. That day the university finally suspended eight students. Meanwhile, a continuing demonstration was maintained on the steps of the administration building.

Then came the first clash with the police. The dramatic universal patterns in the history of student movements repeated themselves in a familiar succession of scenes. Always in the past, in nineteenth-century Russia, in China, in Burma, the appearance of the police to enforce a university rule had produced an immediate "escalation" of minor incidents into major events; the appearance of policemen seemed to recall childhood traumas of harsh authority. The amiable campus guards at Berkeley were viewed as "fascist cops," as "Mississippi sheriffs and deputies." All the unconscious sources of generational solidarity began to feed energies of revolt.

The specific occurrence which then sparked the actual clash was unpredictable, but that something like it would take place was highly predictable from the whole history of student movements. The *Newsletter* of the Free Speech Movement, which shortly came into existence as a Soviet-style coalition of fourteen student groups ranging from Khrushchevites to Goldwaterites (for a brief period), tells the story vividly.[25]

Then came the unpredictable. At noon the following day a rally was held to protest the suspensions and the freedom limitations. Tables were set up in opposition to the ban. Among this[?], campus police arrested Jack Weinberg, who was manning a table for CORE. He went limp and was carried into a police car. When the police tried to drive the car off campus, someone sat down in front of it and a moment later the car was completely surrounded. Speakers addressed the crowds from the top of the car, and so the vehicle, now Jack Weinberg's cell, became the focal point of the rapidly accelerating movement.[26]

We have already met the police car "limpnik" (the word is mine), the nonstudent Jack Weinberg. Twenty-four years old, a former graduate student in mathematics, an activist in CORE, Weinberg said, "I decided I'd rather work for civil rights than study math." But another remark of his became celebrated because it revealed plainly the generational animus underlying the Berkeley Student Uprising: "We have a saying in the movement that you can't trust anybody over 30."[27] The "someone" who placed himself obstructively in front of the police car was likewise a nonstudent—chiefly famed for his tireless advocacy of the use of drugs, and at the time of these occurrences on parole from a jail sentence.[28]

From noon Thursday until 7:30 P.M. Friday, the student activists held the police car with its prisoner hostage. The policemen behaved good-naturedly and worked out arrangements to provide for the physical needs of their prisoner. It was their first encounter with moralistic civil disobedience, and they feared to incur the wrath of the community on any issue even remotely related to "civil rights"; they restrained their impulse to arrest those who were hindering the enforcement of the law.

The vigil around the car was maintained through the night by about seventy students on blankets; some trying to read by lamplight and searchlight, others with guitars singing ballads of themselves and creating the legend which they will embroider in later years; all of them weary, fighting vaguely for a cause they could hardly explain, but moved to this declaration of generational independence. When daylight came, it brought a mercilessly hot sun. The acrid smell of the crowded, sweating, unbathed students reminded one observer of long since forgotten smells among soldiers in the Pacific twenty years before. The overheated oratory vied with the sun, never ending, always strident, a ceaseless flow of "manifestese." One student declaimed, "Clark Kerr has written that the university is a factory. He deals with us as numbers. Well, that's the language he understands, so we are here as numbers—hundreds and thousands. . . ."[29]

The numbers fluctuated from several hundred to close to six thousand Friday evening. Always there was the oratory, the invective against the bureaucrats, the demand for freedom. There were signs and slogans, a medley of the heroic and scurrilous; a former CORE officer bore aloft a quotation from a book signed by "Clark Cur." Shamefacedly she admitted that she had not even read the sign she was carrying, but she was demonstrating, protesting, rebelling. Generational solidarity carried the day as undergraduate neophytes and graduate political sectarians somehow defined a common enemy in Paternalism (a word endlessly repeated) and the System. There were no stepsons; all the activists were sons against the father.

The United States had never seen the like. The official report of the Berkeley police transcribed the scene and its ending:

> On Friday, October 2, the university announced the intention to take police action and again requested mutual aid assistance. Six hundred and forty-three officers from the Berkeley and Oakland Police Departments, the Alameda County Sheriff's Office and the California Highway Patrol were assembled on the campus, briefed and prepared for action within a period of three hours. At 6.00 P.M., the time selected for police action, the police command group was notified that representatives of the university and the demonstrators were negotiating and that the operation should be delayed. At 7.10 P.M., the dispute was compromised and the police force dismissed.
>
> The riot potential was extreme on Thursday and Friday.[30]

The several hundred sitting demonstrators dispersed when Mario Savio, the chief student leader, told them from the police car of the agreement with the administration. The several thousand spectators, sympathizers, and opponents of all degrees quit the Plaza. But that evening hysterical and emotionally wrought students were still standing on the abandoned battlefield which groundsmen were trying to clean. They could not leave the scene where they had embattled the administration; the battered police car was the enemies' pillbox which they had taken. Angry, sleepless voices charged that their leaders had sold them out. The editor of the *FSM Newsletter* met one of her former teachers. She was carrying a beautifully wrapped gift box. She explained that in it was an air valve of the tire from the police car. It would be cherished in later years as a sacred relic, a pathetic reminder of how a new generation of student activists sought its Guadalcanal and Iwo Jima and believed itself to perceive the enemies' visage in the chiefs of the "multiversity."

After the October days there were weeks of negotiation, followed by the university's proposal of broad provisions for freedom of speech, organization, solicitation of funds and members, and actions in the community—everything short of explicit permission to use the university's facilities to organize illegal actions in the community at large.[31] But the student activists, conforming to the strange workings of the psychology of generational rebellion, demanded that the university promulgate their right to engage in illegal action; it was as if the children wanted their fathers to formally acknowledge the moral sovereignty of their offspring; the old superego was to formally abdicate in favor of the moral authority of the young, to acknowledge its own de-authoritization in the right of the sons to be illegal—that is, to destroy the old. Therefore, the student activists persisted in their demonstrations. On November 20, they attracted thousands to the Plaza to hear Joan Baez sing of freedom and love. As she sang "We Shall Overcome," they marched in solemn procession to University Hall, where the regents were convening. For several hours there was more singing, then anger and tears when the regents would not concede the students the strange new "right"—the right to be illegal.

Nonetheless, during the last week of November, it seemed as if the university might at last know some respite from the troubles which had plagued it. Generational struggle is the preoccupation of student activists, but not of the majority of students who find in their everyday studies and advance to independence a more normal path to emotional autonomy. The daily demonstrations and noon orations were dwindling in numbers to some two hundred or so of the faithful; another sit-in came to an end after three hours when the graduate students withdrew their support.

Then, a week later, all the unconscious forces of generational struggle and generational solidarity were once more ignited. Four student leaders were summoned, in accordance with the regents' decision, to appear before the Faculty Committee on Student Affairs to discuss charges that they had committed acts of violence in early October against the campus police. Mario Savio in particular was accused of having bitten a policeman in the left thigh while the officer was trying to close the door to Sproul Hall. The administration's action was like a challenge of the older generation to the young. The student activists were no longer compelled to invent scholastic arguments for an alleged right to organize illegal actions on the campus. Now they could rely on the elemental reaction of their fellow-generationists against the Cruel Heartless Administration which wanted to punish Mario Savio for biting a policeman's thigh, an incredible charge. The administration, said the organ of the Free Speech Movement, "never dreamed that the threat to expel four FSM leaders would provoke such a massive reaction of solidarity."[32] What is more, the student orators intimated, the charges were frame-ups; why, they said, one of the accused had been nowhere near Sproul Hall. In any case, almost everyone had put the October events aside, and had taken it for granted that the cases would not be pressed by the administration. Instead, said the student activists, their trusted leaders were going to be picked off one by one and penalized; the elders were described as engaged in a crafty conspiracy to undo the young.

Thereupon, on December 1, the activist leaders submitted an ultimatum saying that unless the charges were dropped within twenty-four hours, the students would resort to massive tactics of civil disobedience. The Graduate Co-ordinating Committee, the "soviet" of delegates from the graduate students of the various departments, authorized its Strike Committee to call a general strike of teaching assistants if necessary.

The next day there took place with solemn ceremony the students' occupation of Sproul Hall. At noon Mario Savio addressed a crowd of several thousand. He attacked Clark Kerr as a manager, responsible to a board of directors, one who treated the students as "raw material": "It becomes odious so we must put our bodies against the gears, against the wheels and machines, and make the machine stop until we're free." Once more Joan Baez sang the Lord's Prayer and "We Shall Overcome" and about one thousand students marched in holy procession to occupy the administration fortress. In Sproul Hall they quickly set up a "Free University of California" and announced a course on music by Joan Baez as well as courses on the nature of God and the logarithmic spiral, wild Spanish, and arts and crafts, with a special section for making strikes and signs. The halls were like an indoor bivouac of boys and girls enjoying a rare all-night party; since the doors were closed, food was hoisted through the windows. At 3:00 A.M. the chancellor, Edward Strong, pleaded with the students unavailingly to leave. His words were rational and sincere, but the students were now in the full mood of generational uprising and Socrates himself would have got no hearing from them. Thereupon the police, acting under the orders of the governor of the state, began to arrest and remove 814 sit-down occupants, of whom 590 were students.

The police action took twelve hours and was generally without violence. In several cases, the students' tactic of going limp resulted in some forcing and pushing. The inevitable cry of "police brutality" was later acknowledged by many of those arrested to have been a reflex exaggeration. But exaggeration or not, the spectacle of 635 police on the campus acting against students had the effect hoped for by the student leaders. They had intended their move (as they said) to provoke the calling of the police, counting on generational solidarity to succeed where their argument had failed.

The next day, Thursday, December 3, saw the students' strike of Berkeley. Picket lines paraded in front of the classroom buildings. At the gates, strike leaflets were issued. They put their appeal in the primitive terms of generational solidarity:

Our fellow students are being dragged off to jail. You must not stand by and do nothing. It does not matter whether you support a particular tactic. The matter is that the police are on our campus sending students to prison farms in an attempt to crush the free speech movement. . . . There are only two sides—you must choose yours. . . . Defend your fellow students. Join them in a massive university-wide strike. Do not attend classes today. Strike.

That day and the next there were feverish meetings on the campus: a huge one of several thousands, an improvised one of a thousand faculty members, students, and onlookers, and in every department small ones of anxious professors and graduate assistants. In the social sciences, the departments generally allowed or advised the assistants not to meet their classes temporarily. In the departments of engineering and chemistry, the strike was unsuccessful. Probably half the classes in the university did not meet in those days.

Finally on Monday, December 7, President Clark Kerr addressed the students directly for the first time since the eruption of the three-month-old crisis. Eighteen thousand students and professors in the Greek Theater heard him accept a proposal that the university should press no prosecutions; furthermore, he guaranteed that no regulations would be imposed which involved either prior censorship or double jeopardy in connection with student political activities; he expressed his willingness to test in court difficult issues which might arise. These proposals, which were indeed radical ones, the most advanced which any American state university administrator had ever proposed, did not still the turbulent fever of rebellion among the Berkeley students.

As the meeting was being adjourned by the chairman, Professor Robert Scalapino, the student leader, Mario Savio, stalked across the platform and tried to seize the microphone. The police removed him bodily, but he was later allowed to go back to announce his own daily meeting. His followers were at first shocked by what he had done, yet by the afternoon they were busy inventing rationalizations for the tactics of the coup. The "Free Speech" Movement was showing quite clearly that, like so many student movements, it had within it an anti-democratic potential, with a conception of "free speech" compatible with taking over other people's meetings. According to its rationale, at every inaugural of a President of the United States the defeated Communist candidate would, at the ceremony's conclusion, be entitled to seize the microphone to demand a "confrontation." The orations of the student leaders about "alienation," their diatribes against "pluralistic democracy," even Mario Savio's citing of Plato for a new concept of "organic democracy" reminded one unpleasantly of young German students talking in a similar vein in the early thirties.[33] Insofar as this would become the shape of an American student movement, it was clearly no safeguard for democracy.

The following day the faculty of the University of California capitulated emotionally and intellectually to the student activists. One was reminded of scenes during the nineteenth century when in many American colleges professors together with their students were swept from time to time by an emotional revivalism. Two years later *The New York Times* observed in an editorial that the Berkeley faculty had "wavered badly in its dedication to principles of responsibility in the initial uprising of two years ago."[34] During the intervening two years the Berkeley Student Movement provided a kind of laboratory test tube in which the American people could observe the psychology of generational political revolt. A noted political sociologist recalled the circumstances under which on December 8, 1964, a de-authoritized elder generation abdicated in fear and confusion: "The Academic Senate meeting of that day occurred under conditions never before witnessed on an American campus. The campus had been tied up by a student strike, backed by a faculty minority. The debate at the meeting was piped outside to loudspeakers, and over 5,000 students stood outside cheering or booing the speeches made by their professors inside."[35] Moved by fear of the students, but very largely too by anger against the administration for the intrusion of the police, desirous of the good opinion of the activists, bewildered in its reasoning by eager doctrinaires, exalted by its new role as the university's emancipators, and with a vacuum of leadership caused by the absence of an administration spokesman, the Berkeley faculty resolved by an overwhelming vote "that the content of speech or advocacy should not be restricted by the university." It renounced any limitation whatsoever on the content of speech; it pointedly rejected an amendment which would have affirmed to the student body the American constitutional principle that freedom of speech does not extend to the advocating and organizing of immediate acts of force and violence. One Noble Laureate explicitly defended the students' use of "force"; a professor of philosophy warned his colleagues this was no time to think, that a mob of students was at the doors; the chairman of the department of sociology declared eloquently that the Berkeley Community should dispense with the reminder of American constitutional restraints on violence. The faculty promulgated a charter which could be used to safeguard the advocacy and planning of direct acts of violence, illegal demonstrations, interferences with troop trains, terrorist operations, and obscene speech and action. By the very generality of its resolution, added to its rejection of the constitutional limitation, it indicated that as far as it was concerned, university facilities were available for the extremes of speech, including the unconstitutional. Let the civic authorities exercise their powers in this realm, it said; the university washed its hands.

Thus the Berkeley faculty in effect created a moral and political vacuum in the heart of the university. It founded an enclave which canceled the limits of any previously defined freedom of speech. This university enclave was unique in the United States, for it was the only one in which for all practical purposes political authority was excluded, since both university and civic powers renounced their responsibilities. On the one hand, the administration was bound by its faculty to refrain from all restraint of speech; on the other, the civic powers by long custom and usage were reluctant to enter the student terrain: they did not understand it, they feared it, and they felt it to be the university's business. The Generational Revolt had won a marked victory in Berkeley. There were other fruits, like the ouster of the chancellor, which perhaps was its most symbolic achievement in generational triumph. But the faculty resolution of December 8 was what it later boasted of most. An unusual experiment in unrestrained advocacy by the student generation thus began. Its consequence during the next two years was an accelerated deterioration of student ethics and of freedom of speech in Berkeley.[36]

TRAITS OF THE BERKELEY STUDENT MOVEMENT: DECLINE OF THE STUDENT ETHIC, MISPERCEPTION OF SOCIAL REALITY

The patterns of action, emotion, and experience of the Berkeley Student Movement were indeed those of the classical student movements of the nineteenth century.

In the first place, like its predecessors, the Berkeley movement exhibited very rapidly the phenomenon of moral decline; it quickly came to believe that its high vocation entitled it to practice deceit and thievery whenever they advanced its situation in generational struggle. The student leaders, for instance, misled the student body concerning the truth of the charge that Mario Savio had bitten a policeman in the left thigh. To secure immunity for their leader's act of individual violence, they were prepared to cloak themselves in the protective mantle of the nonviolence movement. Joan Baez was enlisted to sing of love and freedom, and several hundred students marched in heroic illusion to occupy Sproul Hall. Only several months later did Mario Savio acknowledge publicly in a debate before the Berkeley High School students that he had bitten the policeman; the high school students were stunned by this admission.[37] Yet on December 2 the student leaders had been prepared to involve several hundred students in arrests rather than have their chief take the responsibility for his own individual act of violence.[38] Then the seizure of the microphone at a meeting organized and conducted by a faculty group was a reversion to the tactics of Nazi and fascist students in Europe thirty years before; it showed an instinctive preference for a procedure of mass generational intimidation to one of liberal democracy.

During the weeks that followed the students' victory, incidents of dishonesty on the part of student leaders multiplied. The student Leftist political party, Slate, published a review of professors and courses in the university, their Counter-Catalogue. On its bright pink cover it bore a quotation which it falsely attributed to Professor Robert Scalapino: "No one wants this university to become an arena for controversy and debate." Professor Scalapino wrote publicly on February 4, "Far more serious, however, is the fact that the error was known to the Editor and to a large group of Slate workers prior to publication." The editors promised to remove the cover, but instead scratched his name out though it remained "clearly visible beneath the erroneous statement." More important than this personal matter, observed Professor Scalapino, "is a question that goes to the very heart of all crises in our times. I cannot explain how individuals who want (and deserve) freedom and respect for their own views choose not to grant that to others."[39] A few days later the director of the Student Health Service accused a Slate representative publicly of having sent out a deceitful letter to fifty colleges and universities misrepresenting his stand with respect to contraceptive advice for students; the action of the student leader, he said, was "unethical, irresponsible, and immature," "deceitful behavior," which added "an unwelcome element of distrust and suspicion to constructive efforts and discussions."[40] The Slate representative then apologized.

The moral level of the University of California became the lowest in the history of American education among both the students and the faculty. Professor Seymour Martin Lipset the next year recalled, "A number of letters were stolen, telephones were tapped—the whole thing was a mess!"[41]

The so-called students' Counter-Catalogue published by Slate became a weapon both for the political intimidation of professors and for the lowering of academic standards. The chairman of the department of classics, a socialist who had earnestly supported the student activists, reported sadly, "When in September I asked to see the questionnaires on one of my courses, I found that they had conveniently been lost. If not dishonest, the course reports are incompetent; but worst of all is the anti-intellectual attitude and the slant toward the non-serious student."[42] In its next September issue the Counter-Catalogue renewed its efforts to intimidate recalcitrant professors. It characterized the chief campus mediator, a professor of industrial relations whom it disliked, as "a terribly dull, insincere professor who should be avoided at all costs"; it described a liberal economist, who became vice-chancellor, as one who "presents a liberal apology for capitalism"; it conceded that the chairman of the political science department was "an excellent teacher of constitutional law," but said that because he had failed students who had missed their examinations to go picketing, their "rating of him as a human being would be much lower."[43]

The decline of student ethics was elevated into a principle of generational revolt during March 1965 in the curious episode of the student movement's obscenitarian phase. It began on March 3, when a nonstudent began to walk up and down the University Plaza carrying an obscene placard. When he was arrested, several of the original "Free Speech leaders" raised a sign urging students to contribute to the "——— Defense Fund." The principal theoretician of the Free Speech Movement, Stephen Weissman, delivered a speech whose argument was the following: obscene speech is the language of the masses; correct speech is the language of the middle-class pluralistic liberals; therefore, to make contact with the masses, the students must use obscene speech and fight for their freedom to do so. The student body generally, however, failed to respond to the obscenitarian issue. A student movement is moved as a whole only when a highly moralistic-political issue is invoked in terms in which the elder generation can be judged as de-authoritized. In this sense, the obscenitarian issue misfired. The students sensed that the flaunting of obscene words had more to do with shocking the elders the way children do than with establishing contact with the masses; the obscenitarians seemed more intent on outraging the university's officers than achieving social goals. In short, when the obscenitarian rationale was seen to be a pretext for generational revolt, and nothing more, it collapsed at once as a political cause. In the meanwhile, the president and chancellor of the university submitted their resignations in protest; faculty radicals gave bold speeches which had obscene innuendoes; a corps of administrators and committees were baffled; and the authority of the elder generation was suitably flouted. Mario Savio came back from Selma, Alabama, to discourse on obscenity and violence. If he hadn't been in jail at the time, he said, he probably would have taken part in the obscene speech movement. For "sound tactical reasons," however, he now advised against it: "We have a professor here, Lewis Feuer. Lewis Feuer was falling over himself to prove in *The New Leader* that the FSM was based on a corporate Oedipal complex, yes, a corporate Oedipal complex. Therefore, there should have been no free sexual intercourse movement."[44] Thus, the student leader warned his activist followers to suppress their obscenitarian impulse lest they provide the observer with overt evidence for what they covertly felt. The generational revolt had to present itself in terms of an issue which was more moralistic, less blatantly one to shock the elders.

This address of Mario Savio's to an estimated 1,500 persons was remarkable as a new landmark in the decline of the ethics of the student movement; for the first time, nonviolence was ridiculed and violence extolled. It was the first and familiar step, oft-repeated in the history of student movements, a veering toward the doctrine of elitist violence. First, the student leader launched into a bitter denunciation of Martin Luther King, ridiculing him for his religious affirmation at Selma: "We'll put our bodies on the altar, and God is with us." Selma, said the student leader, had been a "demoralizing experience," a "Children's Crusade" led by Dr. King; but, he added, "the movement isn't Dr. King." Then Savio went on to mock nonviolence and to indicate a new attachment to violence. He now doubted, he said, whether he had done the right thing on October 2 when he had told the thousands of students to go home to avoid an encounter with the police. Thus violence began to emerge as an attractive means for student action, as the political method of those who felt that they would not survive the more rational judgment of the community acting through institutions of representative democracy.

The decline of student ethics was evident not only in their political actions; it affected their personal lives.

To be a guerrilla fighter against the system began to mean for the students a warrant for theft and dishonesty. The more guerrilla-like one's ideology and model, the more thievery was authorized. Bookstores, supermarkets, small grocers, entrepreneurs, and cooperatives could all be directly expropriated. The student Maoists were evidently pre-eminent on the Berkeley campus for their exploits in thievery. "The PLM (Progressive Labor Movement)," wrote the *Daily Californian*, "is a hard-core coterie of Peking-oriented agitators. Notorious even among the campus Left for their petty larceny (no honor among thieves?), these ideologues despise the Communist Party for its moderation."[45]

The Berkeley Student Movement thus scarcely proved to be the harbinger, as so many persons had hoped, of a higher student ethic. The aftermath of the student uprising of 1964 brought to the city of Berkeley a period of unprecedented crime. According to the annual police report, almost half of the persons arrested in Berkeley during 1965 (the year which followed after the student uprising of 1964) were "students" of various kinds. Close to three thousand students of all sorts and schools were arrested during that year. In a five-year period, which coincided with the rise of the student movement, burglaries had increased from 147 to 1,164 and thefts from 305 to 664. While the city as a whole during 1965 sustained an 11 per cent increase in crime, the increase in the campus area was 39 per cent. The chief of police reported that the most striking upsurge in crime took place at the end of 1964—that is, at the height of the student uprising.[46]

The aftermath of the student movement brought to Berkeley also an astonishing increase in rape. Twenty-one instances of rape were reported in 1965; by 1966, the figure had increased by more than 100 per cent to fifty-five reported cases. Most of the assaults, moreover, took place in the south-side area adjoining the campus.[47]

The Berkeley Student Movement tended also to search for its distinctive form of protest in sexual behavior. Every student movement in history has tried to define the counterpart of its political revolt in sexual terms. The German student movement always had a touch of homosexuality in the *Burschenherrlichkeit* which was its romantic stand against the paternalistic bourgeois society. The Russian students sought to carry the sincerities of free love to their last consequence, living in passionate austerity like the hero and heroine of Chernyshevsky's *What's to be Done?* The American student activists of the thirties found their manuals for sexual activity in Bertrand Russell's *Marriage and Morals* and Leon Blum's *Marriage*. The Berkeley Student Movement had on its fringes bold new practitioners of ideological sexuality, an "undiluted orgyism" in which alienation presumably was totally overcome. Again it was the nonstudents who tried to create this new trend

There were various evidences of "orgiastic rebellion" in Berkeley—advertisements, for instance, on student union bulletin boards for "sexual-communal" practice.[48] Within two years, the chief student nonstudent organ was publishing news reports of public sexual intercourse to the "applause for the stars" from the spectators. The United Sexual Rights Committee was quoted: "Watching someone else screw can be very enlightening."[49] It was argued that the pleasure principle was thus made fully operative in people's lives, and that public sexual communism would diminish anxieties. Thus, an almost ultimate stage in generational revolt in the realm of sexuality was being pioneered in Berkeley. All the child's repressed sexual questions would be answered publicly; the whole code of sexual behavior transmitted by the fathers would be flouted. It seemed indeed as if only the advocacy of incest were left.

As the movement continued during 1965–1966 and 1966–1967 with largely the same cast of leading characters, it exhibited repetitively the compulsive traits which have characterized generational revolt in politics. Faculty enthusiasts for the student movement (who had enjoyed vicariously a delayed foray into the Making of History, especially when others took the risks) were sometimes perturbed by these traits; they tried to comfort themselves with the notion that the movement was entering a decadent stage. One such professor complained that "there has been a serious degeneration within the Berkeley student movement recently, that the standards of last year's movement are not being upheld, and that some students have vastly exaggerated certain deficiencies which exist in our campus rules governing activity." He objected to the students' comparing their situation on campus with that "of oppressed Negroes in Mississippi"; their doing so, he wrote, was "an insult to the intelligence of our student body . . . and a cheap attempt to exploit anti-racist sentiment by turning it into a situation where it is totally irrelevant."[50] Actually the tactics and amorality of the student leaders were remarkably the same from one year to the next. In the first year, they secured stolen files from the president's office and published them; the next year, they rifled the files of the chancellor's assistant and photographed them. No student leader or faculty activist condemned the thievery in the first year, and the chancellor's assistant, a former activist, was in no position to complain in the second.[51] If student leaders insisted in the first year that the Berkeley streets were like those of Montgomery, Alabama, and the University Hall like the Mississippi capitol, then during the second year they maintained that the streets of Berkeley were like those of Saigon, and the Berkeley police were to be fought with "guerrilla" tactics. If the activists said in the first year that the university was plotting to destroy the civil rights movement, then in the next year they said it was plotting to destroy the Vietnam protest movement. If the chancellor's assistant was called a "liar" in the second year, his erstwhile student confederates had so denominated the president during the first year. If there were legal avenues of protest and reform available in the second year, they had also been available during the first year but were disregarded in the haste for civil disobedience. The speeches which called the second student strike in December 1966 were almost verbally identical with those of December 1964.[52]

Such were the continuous traits of the Berkeley Student Movement: a misperception of social reality guided by the wish to discredit that reality as the product of a corrupt elder generation, a belief that their own elite status and Messianic calling exempted them from the laws of morality, a readiness to identify in quick succession with whatever lowly group they could accuse the elder generation of suppressing, a tendency to regard the university as "plotting" to destroy their movement, an utter disregard of the fact that existing institutions allowed for discussion and reform, because their own desire to use tactics of generational insurrection and direct action led them to regard every issue as an occasion for "confrontation." "Confrontation" was the latent goal of the student movement; the changing issues became so many occasions, so many pegs on which to post confrontations.

"Confrontation" could be simply defined: it was an occasion for a pitched battle of generational struggle.[53] It suggested generational violence against individuals. The language of warfare came naturally to the confrontationist engaged in successive re-enactments of generational uprising. When Mario Savio addressed the Independent Socialists Club after the end of the second student strike of December 1966, it was natural that the leaflet announcing the meeting was emblazoned "The Second Battle of Berkeley."[54] Its slogan, "No More Cops," echoed the familiar childhood trauma of the frightening policeman. And curiously, with the second strike, the inner destructive tendency in the student movement emerged more clearly through the various ideological guises. The Strike Committee threatened to destroy the university if its wishes were not heeded. The regents, it said, "recognize that if they took direct action against us the University would be destroyed . . . in the future they are ready to force this destruction rather than accede to our just demands."[55] Destruction, self-destruction, the haunting nemesis of student movements, was clearly in evidence among the Berkeley student leaders. They were brethren to the Russian student leaders who thought they triumphed over the older generation when they brought the universities to close their doors.

Berkeley activists were always ready to make common cause with any foreign antagonist of the System or Establishment. The System of their fathers defined a Common Enemy. In a series of international crises, the

Berkeley Student Movement was always predictably aligned with the anti-American power. When Khrushchev precipitated the Berlin crisis, and said the situation was intolerable, the Berkeley student activists echoed his words and charged the United States with endangering world peace. They provided a variety of arguments to prove America simply had to abandon Berlin. Then Khrushchev altered his stand, and the "intolerable situation" was forgotten. When Khrushchev placed missiles in Cuba, Berkeley student leaders first charged the story was a C.I.A. fabrication; later they defended the emplacement of missiles and stormed against President Kennedy for insisting that they be removed. When Khrushchev broke the moratorium on the testing of nuclear weapons, Berkeley student activists staged an all-night vigil on Sproul steps, not in criticism of the Soviet decision, but to protest any American retaliatory testing. The emotional a priori of student revolt defined their fathers' enemies as the sons' friends. It was part of the misperception of social reality inherent in generational revolt.

The Anti-Democratic Bias of the Berkeley Student Movement: Attraction to Violence and Suppression of Free Discussion

Above all, the Berkeley Student Movement tended, like its forebears in the nineteenth century, finally to destroy the confidence of its followers in the processes of representative democracy. It became an elitist, direct action group; it saw no democratic decision in the votes of the two American political parties. If in one breath it assailed the Republican candidate for governor, Ronald Reagan as a right-winger, it asserted with the next that Governor Pat Brown, the Democratic liberal, was just as bad; and anyhow, it reasoned, if the Democratic liberals were destroyed, the New Left might take over the Democratic party. Like the Communists of the early thirties, the New Left reserved its greatest hatred for the liberals. When the New Left movement held its conference in California on October 1, 1966, participants listened to discourses by such senior gentlemen as Bishop James A. Pike; but its activist rank and file was the student movement, and the "new politics" was described in terms which the Berkeley Student Movement had made familiar. The manifesto of the New Left spoke of the "new politics" as "pressure-point politics," "guerrilla politics," "like jazz." The generational revolt was stressed: "Anybody who can take leadership is free to do so without waiting in line to acquire seniority in the old politics."[56] When Bishop Pike tried to speak on behalf of those who opposed the "boycott Brown" resolution, he was hooted down. Two hundred delegates, mostly relative oldsters, walked out after the "anti-Brown resolution" was passed. The

New Left activists were untroubled by the split. One of their leaders, a young college teacher, put it all in generational terms: "This meeting helped separate out the old liberals from the New Left radicals."[57] The Conference of the New Left aptly enough was held on a college campus in Los Angeles, and its leading figure was Robert Scheer, a product of the Berkeley Student Movement.

Robert Scheer only a few months before, in June 1966, had tried to capture the Democratic nomination for Congress in the Berkeley district. He ran against the incumbent, a liberal trade unionist who supported President Johnson. Scheer was above all the candidate of the Alienated New Left. His candidacy was, according to *The Activist*, "first suggested by Vietnam Day Committee activists last year after the death of the Free Speech Movement, when a new radical project was being sought."[58] "Scheer's organization developed autonomously, but with exaggerated dependence on the campus community."[59] Almost all student-faculty activism converged on behalf of his candidacy; Scheer carried Berkeley by a decisive majority, 14,625 votes to 12,165, though he lagged elsewhere in the county and lost by 25,270 votes to the victor's 28,751. As a product of the Berkeley Student Movement, he had all its taste for violent language and direct action. While a graduate student in economics in 1961, he was an editor and founder of a magazine of the New Left, *Root and Branch*. "The college left," he wrote at that time in an ugly vocabulary, "consists of a few thousand cultural freaks. Its membership is weighted heavily to New York Jews, children of older generation radicals, and Bohemians. For reasons of culture, personality, or choice, they are generally impervious to the normal rewards and concerns of American society."[60] He articulated the underlying emotion of the nonstudent: because the intellectuals were alienated from society, he wrote, they clung to the university—"the University is 'home'; this is the world we understand, and the other one frightens the hell out of us." He was aware of the roots of the New Left in student generational revolt: "Anybody who protests today is a reasonably sharp, overeducated egghead who has extracted himself from the clutches of neighbors, parents, and T.V." Scheer defended Fidel Castro, jibed at John F. Kennedy, and was mildly pornopolitical. Five years later the New Left tried to associate itself with the youthful glamor of President Kennedy's name, but in 1962 Scheer wrote denigratingly of the liberal, "We cannot expect a Jack Kennedy to feel the necessity of political freedom—he has never been threatened by the state, never questioned by the secret police (F.B.I.), never seen his parents arrested as political prisoners, never been carried limp into a southern jail or in a police instigated riot."[61] Drawn by the calling of nonstudent, Scheer grew a shaggy, Castro-like beard, and went to work as a salesman for the famed literary center in San Francisco's beatnik quarter, the City Lights Bookshop. Subsequently, the System, through the beneficent Center for the Study of Democratic Institutions, published a paper by him on Vietnam. He spoke at "teach-ins" and, according to Vietnam Day Committee spokesmen, was one of those who favored militant action in their parade of October 15, 1965, against the Oakland police formation. For some time he had been using the rhetoric of a seizure of power by the Oakland poor, and during one speech left some listeners gasping with his extremism: "If the Viet Cong are the only alternative in Vietnam, then I'm for the Viet Cong."[62] Then the student leader became a candidate for Congress. He trimmed his beard so that he looked like a New England whaling captain and began to wear a bourgeois jacket such as befitted a well-groomed candidate.[63] He even began to dissociate himself from the hyper-extremist tactics of the over-alienated section of the New Left. Student and faculty activists gave time and money to the Scheer campaign, which cost seventy thousand dollars, "the largest ever for a House congressional election in the State of California," they claimed. They availed themselves of old and new political technique, from hard precinct work to demagoguery and sexagogy. One day the New Left brought a leading San Francisco go-go dancer to the Lower Plaza of Berkeley's university to lure the students into politics. She danced for the multitude but embarrassed her sponsors by telling a reporter that she didn't know who Robert Scheer was. Here and there a puritanical Old Leftist would look disapprovingly on this swinging campaign, but the New Leftist could gleefully cite a text from the Marxian Dead Sea Scrolls: the young Karl Marx himself had written eloquently on the potency of can-can dancing as a way of overcoming alienation, "the boldness, the frankness, the graceful petulance and the music of that most sensual movement."[64] Several months after his campaign was over, Scheer took the next step and called for a coalition with the "LSDers and the swingers."[65] This marked the emergence of psychedelic politics under the auspices of the Berkeley Student Movement.

Meanwhile, under the hegemony of the New Left, freedom of discussion seriously declined on the Berkeley campus. The New Leftist student activists, though a minority, felt themselves privileged to disrupt and threaten other people's meetings, to insist on "confrontations" on their terms. It was a pattern which Berkeley student leaders hoped to diffuse through the nation. Indeed, when the Secretary of Defense, Robert S. McNamara, visited Harvard University, he was met by a disorderly demonstration of members of the Students for a Democratic Society "designed to force a direct confrontation" (in their words) with their spokesman, the Berkeley activist, Robert Scheer. It was of small moment to the Harvard imitators of Berkeley that their spokesman had recently been confronted by the voters in a democratic election; theirs was the new concept of "participatory democracy," invented by the student movement, in which a minority used the threat of disruption to impose its will on the majority.[66] The majority of the Harvard undergraduates apologized to the Secretary of Defense; as one of them said, "The crux of the matter was that the crowd physically took away the rights of a human being, and . . . this sort of thing could stifle free exchange . . ."[67]

Free discussion indeed vanished on the Berkeley Plaza under the dictatorship of the New Left. As a professor of history described it:

> Sproul Steps have long since degenerated into a demagogic and anti-intellectual institution, inimical to rational discourse and geared essentially to the shock-effects of vituperation and vilification—of the administration, of the faculty, of the larger society, of almost everything in sight. This degeneration of free speech has affected not only the Plaza but the whole of the campus as well. The tone of the Steps has undermined the community's respect for the ethics of controversy and the canons of evidence appropriate to political debate in a university. . . . Worse still, the power of the Steps constitutes a kind of censorship over who can speak on campus . . . Cases in point are Senator Clark, who refused to come at all even though he had ample free time while in the Bay Area, and the expert on foreign affairs, Prof. Henry Kissinger of Harvard, who spoke almost surreptitiously in a classroom, without publicity, since he did not wish it to be known that he had been here.[68]

The faculty and administration were indeed intimidated by the Berkeley New Left. The most militant young faculty supporter of the Free Speech Movement, who as a result of the turmoil was made chancellor's assistant as a way of conciliating the student movement, more than a year later made a revealing confession of the deterioration of a university's ethic. The university, he said, had for eighteen months submitted to a "peculiar brand of blackmail"; there had been numerous "sordid incidents" in which the Berkeley administration had looked the other way to "avoid trouble." "That's the pattern of blackmail we've been under," said Professor John Searle, and the newspaper reporter noted that "Searle finds himself in a position 180 degrees from two years ago when he was one of the F.S.M.'s most ardent and articulate backers."[69] Thus, under the impact of the Berkeley Student Movement, the values of liberal democracy declined at the University of California. The patterns of generational struggle, the emotional drive toward "confrontation" with the elders, toward the demonstration of "student power," imposed themselves on the discussion of underlying issues. In short, the student movement imposed its patterns of irrationality on the social processes of the university.

The Berkeley Faculty Capitulates: An Elder Generation De-Authoritized

Every student movement owes much of its influence to the fact that the surrounding society regards it as its pure, idealistic children. Thus the Russian students were regarded, thus the Japanese activists of Zengakuren. The Berkeley Student Movement was remarkable for the psychological changes it wrought in the university's professors. Something of the confessional spirit and the campus revivalism of a century and a half before returned in modern ideological guise as professors rose in self-criticism before their students. During the first Berkeley strike, for instance, in December 1964, at a large faculty-student meeting, the director of the Chinese Center, a researcher on communist self-criticism, confessed that he had been guilty in the past for neglecting his students; one could almost imagine the scene transplanted from Communist China. The next month the chairman of the department of sociology told a large student meeting how he and the faculty were grateful to the students for having reminded them of the significance of freedom. For a while the elders of the faculty subscribed to a New Cult of Youth, according to which the student activist was the Community's Prophetic Conscience. A professor of English poetry departing on a leave of absence delivered a farewell address in which he spoke of the "beautiful and strong Mario Savio." A chairman of a department of science, who happened to be a member of a religious sect, became convinced that Mario Savio was a reincarnation of Jesus; even his militant colleagues were discomfited by this unusual theology. The philosophers were not far behind the scientists; their chairman told an excited student assemblage after the Greek Theater microphone seizure that they had all the power. Professors of biochemistry included such questions as the definition of "civil disobedience" on their examinations.[70]

What were the sources of the psychological capitulation of a large section of the Berkeley faculty? Many were simply shocked by the sight of police contingents on the campus, and by way of protest, voted for leftist resolutions. But other factors were at work too. A professor of history, observing his colleagues during the second Berkeley strike, wrote that his fellow-historians "in some small way want a taste of making history as well as writing it."[71] This remark actually went to the heart of a great deal of the psychology of the Berkeley Intellectual Class, as indeed of that section of the American Intellectual Class which is spiritually affiliated to the so-called New Left. From the time of the Pythagorean sect, intellectuals have felt a vocation to rule. The Utopias which they have envisaged, from Plato to Edward Bellamy and H. G. Wells, have usually involved a rule of society by the intellectuals. If the intellectual today feels "alienated," his alienation is that which Plato knew and described: the frustration of lack of power, the sense that his participation in events is always vicarious, through books, commentaries, and footnotes. Suddenly in Berkeley the dream world of books seemed to intersect with the real world of action. The men of books, who had rarely known the responsibilities of action, were lifted by the student activists into a new realm. The author of a Ph.D. thesis on German socialism, who had always admired Rosa Luxemburg's faith in the spontaneous action of the masses, found himself talking dithyrambically of the creative spontaneity of the students; the historian-admirer of the abolitionists saw himself in the resurrected company of William Lloyd

Garrison and the Underground Railway. There were physicists who reacted as if they were fighting anew for J. Robert Oppenheimer and the *esprit de corps* of the scientific elite. A sizable group of vaguely pro-Soviet sympathizers, who felt inwardly ashamed for their timid silence during the previous decade, relished a personally nondangerous ideological foray. Scholars who had repressed their resentment against the bureaucratic machinery of universities enjoyed seeing the latter discomfited by student guerrillas. Then there was the guilt which the successful academic felt; he had knowledge but it had often been rendered impotent by his fears and ambitions. He enjoyed substantial salaries and comforts, but felt the guilt of being part of a new leisure class. Noted faculty leaders, moreover, were having difficulties with their own adolescent children; adopting a radical stance at the university helped secure generational peace at home. A new post-Marxist historicism arose in which the student youth replaced the proletariat as the historical elite. A young author of several sociological treatises on social change was quoted for his remark that the student movement would inevitably achieve its objectives. Many professors were reluctant to condemn the students' actions which had been consciously calculated to provoke the intervention of the police. They succumbed either to the fashion set by the Nobel Laureate in Physics who extolled the students' "force and violence" or to the professor of philosophy, who invoked the several thousands of threatening students at the door.[72] A noted sociologist two years later pleaded that there were extenuating circumstances for the Berkeley faculty—"a thousand academics of all varieties and disciplines, most of whom had little contact with the dispute until the Sproul Hall sit-in."[73] Actually, however, the Berkeley faculty was widely regarded as among the most politically sophisticated in America. Many of its members had lived through the years of the Loyalty Oath controversy and the Oppenheimer-Teller debate; for more than two months they had been arguing about the Free Speech Movement. Above all, one must remember that two years later the majority of the Berkeley faculty, experiencing a second student strike, did not respond too differently from the way it had earlier. And those differences which did emerge were regarded by the students as the outcome primarily of the election of Republican Governor Ronald Reagan and the outspoken, widespread criticism of the university among the people at large.

But why was it precisely the Berkeley faculty which was prone to such militance and sympathy for the New Left? It was a faculty which had expanded very rapidly within a few years. The university's liberal president sought to build both a large and an outstanding staff. To Berkeley's faculty came, for instance, former Trotskyist and socialist student leaders as well as the former national chief of the Communist youth. But they were not a significant factor in the growth of the Berkeley New Left. Of high importance was the character of the Berkeley faculty, most ideal-typical of the science and scholarship of the modern American university. A corps of ambitious middle-aged and younger scholars had been recruited throughout the entire country for this burgeoning corporate center. Their vocation as teachers was sometimes vestigial; they regarded Berkeley as an institution to be exploited for its grants and allowances. The Scholar-Bureaucrat, beset by guilt, felt a curious attraction to the Student Activist, the symbol of what he in his careerism had rejected. A strange symbiosis arose between the bureaucratic faculty and beatnik activists; indeed, the New Left is a coalition of the two psychological types. The activists could externalize every grievance and guilt which the bureaucratic professors nourished; they could badger the administration, and occasionally opened new avenues for "upward mobility" as new assistant chancellorships and boards were created. Those departments of the more traditional kind which had not shared in the affluence of the departments of physical and social science nourished their own grievances of diminished status. Classicists, historians, philosophers, professors of English and American literature, felt a kinship with the student activists who assailed the modern impersonal university, that is, the one in which their status was declining. To some, moreover, the student movement seemed to have overcome alienation and to have founded a new university political constituency. It was a remarkable sociological phenomenon to watch a Vietnam Day Committee Parade and see a Nobel Laureate in Physics marching in new-found community with the nonstudent "drop-out" activist.

Faculty activism at Berkeley often extorted a spiritual toll. Take, for instance, the case of the most militant faculty activist who, for a few feverish months, was indeed the paradigm of the faculty rebel; he had brought back from Oxford the mien of the Angry Young Man. In November 1964, he stood before the students on the Plaza, and said, "The University is out to destroy the civil rights movement." And though he neither sat-down with the students nor shared their jail sentences, he encouraged them with spirited words and admiration. Appointed the new chancellor's special assistant on student affairs in 1965, he expected the student activists to learn conformity, emulating his own collaboration with the new chancellor, Roger Heyns, author of *The Anatomy of Conformity* and *The Psychology of Personal Adjustment*. Evidently fancying himself like his fellow-Oxonian, T. E. Lawrence, an uncrowned king of student guerrillas, he assured skeptics that he would be able to control the student activists. He imagined that he had helped to lead a successful revolution, which the student activists would now obediently bring to a close: "What really happened in Berkeley last year? In the 1964–65 year something very like a revolution took place on this campus." The leaders of "successful revolutions," he wrote, must then take measures to control extremists who do not accept the historic decision. He wrote and spoke sometimes like a Girondin proposing to control the Jacobins, at other times like a disciple of Stalin invoking discipline against

Trotskyists and Maoists. He assured the American intellectual community that now that he was running things, "every attempt to attack the university in 1965–66 was completely unsuccessful."[74] Several of his leading fellow-faculty activists joined in depicting a university which through the Student Revolution had emerged as a Great Community of Scholars; they seemed ready to excommunicate anyone who dared question their achievement.[75]

Within two months of the time the faculty activists published their pronouncements, the outbreak of the "Second Battle of Berkeley," the second student strike in December 1966, harshly refuted their words. At that time (as we have seen) the chancellor's assistant resentfully revealed that the university had been "blackmailed" by student activists during the past eighteen months in a series of "sordid incidents." He acknowledged that the so-called university community was a fiction: "The mistrust is going to last for a long time; in fact, it's spreading. The students now mistrust the faculty."[76] Thus, the practitioners of generational revolt broke ranks, devouring each other, in accordance with the law of revolutions, whereby parricide initiates a series of fratricides—after the father is killed, the brothers rend each other. In reality, however, the Berkeley Student Uprising was not a "successful revolution." This was the language of the misperception common to generational rebels. There were several hundred students awaiting jail sentences two years after the occupation of Sproul Hall. Those who stormed the Winter Palace or the Tuileries never had to go to court and jail for their "successful revolution."

The Berkeley Student Movement as a Generational Uprising

How can one test the hypothesis of generational struggle as the prime underlying factor in the Berkeley Student Movement? The most crucial test is the character of the emotions which prevailed at the moments of decision, the moments of action. The essential question is: to what emotions did the basic speeches and leaflets which moved large masses of students appeal? Under the impetus of the movement, emotions which otherwise were recessive, and scarcely played a part in the students' consciousness or behavior, emerged into the forefront. The movement became the matrix in which "collective representations" (as Durkheim would have called them) were created.[77] The movement shaped the dominant emotions of the activists and participants to a degree which they never would have known or exhibited in the isolated environment of an interview or questionnaire. The activists were certainly predisposed to such action to a greater degree than the nonactivists, and had more elements of "alienation" and "community longing." Yet even that degree would often have been a small one, and perhaps even undetectable in many cases by the customary methods of interrogation. It is all the more important, therefore, to ask what were the dominant slogans, symbol-words, which caught the emotional allegiance of students, and which expressed, shaped, and constituted the moving quality in the movement.

The most striking fact is that after the first September weeks of 1964, during which the references to the civil rights struggle were frequent, the speeches and leaflets increasingly defined the Enemy as the Impersonal University, the Machine, the Administration. There were continuous attacks on Paternalism, the System, Bureaucracy, IBM Machines. The pamphlet, *The Mind of Clark Kerr,* which many student activists took as their official manifesto, was an attack on bureaucracy that never mentioned the racial problem. The most invoked metaphor was that of the IBM card: "I am a UC student. Please don't bend, fold, spindle or mutilate me," and "Are you a student or an IBM card?" Others were similar: "Nobody knows my name."[78] In upwards of one hundred student speeches, not more than five made any reference to civil rights goals. And when Mario Savio called on his followers to occupy Sproul Hall, it was (as we have seen) in terms of an attack on a university administration which treated the students the way an impersonal corporation would treat "raw material." The civil rights movement was only vaguely in the background; the First Battle of Berkeley, as the students later called it, was a battle of generations.

Like every student movement, this one suffered from the misperception of social reality characteristic of the "alienated." The "alienated" never looked closely into themselves to find the subjective cause of their "alienation." Instead, they projected upon the Impersonal Knowledge Factory and the Administration all the traits which would justify their revolt; their fruitless rebellion never reached to the unconscious cause within themselves, the inner, inaccessible Being who tyrannized over and emasculated them. Many of the student leaders had come to Berkeley precisely because they wanted to have the experience of generational revolt. The will to revolt, the "alienation," was present long before a *causa belli* had been defined. Such students came to the university in quest of a bill of particulars to justify their "alienation." Such was the author, for instance, of the principal activist pamphlets, including one on the regents. Expelled from Brandeis University for an episode of blasphemy, he became alternately a student and nonstudent at Berkeley. Such too was the student who became in 1966 leader of the Strike Committee; his career at Harvard had been terminated.[79] One day he told me that I was quite right, that as far as he and his friends were concerned, they had been "alienated" long before they ever got to Berkeley, and that they had come there because it was the vantage point in the United States for expressing such alienation. They chose to come to the "multiversity" rather than go to any one of the many excellent smaller campuses in California or other states because they were looking for a generational battlefield.

The generational misperception of social reality expressed itself in numerous ways. Placards were held aloft, "Two Chancellors, Hitler—1934, Strong—1964," equating the Nazi Führer, the exterminator of the Jews, with the Berkeley chancellor who had once testified on behalf of Communist professors and was too gentle to enforce campus rules against civil rights activists. The campus policemen, who were always worrying lest they infringe upon any student's rights, became "fascist cops," and the University Hall was a replica of the Mississippi Capitol. One non-student irreconcilable, a Maoist, presenting himself to a protest rally as an epileptic maltreated by the police, kept intoning in a strange whine, "Cops are cops; they are the same everywhere. Let's escalate now."

"Bureaucracy" became the slogan-word for all the harsh impersonal paternalism against which the Berkeley students believed themselves in revolt, the Projected Father Image in the Era of the Computer Machines. Yet it was the selective nonstudent environment and selective migration of "alienated" students to Berkeley which brought to the fore the usually contained ingredients of generational revolt. There was scarcely any unrest in other major state universities in the United States, scarcely any at such campuses as Los Angeles, Minnesota, Washington, or the many other Californian universities. At many campuses there were discussions as to why they had not experienced a Berkeley-type movement. The discussion at Pennsylvania State University, which had upward of twenty thousand students, was typical. "Why is there no general revolt at Pennsylvania State?" queried the students. One official answered, "We have no city. The non-college population is not full of semi-professional agitators. . . . Our dropouts give up and leave town. They don't become a parasitic 'hidden population' agitating for revolt. That's the curse at Berkeley." Another administrator said that fortunately Pennsylvania State was "not a subway campus." Still another pointed out that Pennsylvania State had a smaller graduate population. "The graduate students are where the impetus is coming from. They appear to be among the propagators of revolt and it filters down." There was a student movement, an Ad Hoc Committee on Student Freedom, led by a Jewish graduate student of philosophy, but he acknowledged that "the tactics of Berkeley are not appropriate here." The student activists, it was noted, "are, for the most part, clean-shaven, well-dressed and exceptionally articulate."[80]

Bigness, impersonality, bureaucracy, by themselves failed to arouse revolt on the greater number of American campuses. Los Angeles saw no revolt although it was big, urban, and had a nonresident studentry. The City College of New York, a big, impersonal "subway campus" experienced virtually no agitation in 1964–1965. Certainly Berkeley had become the nation's primary gathering place for the "alienated" nonstudents and students of America. Just as Marxists once emphasized that the workers by themselves would not rise to a socialist consciousness, and often not even to a clear class consciousness, without the help of "intellectuals," so likewise, the kindling of generational consciousness to an insurrectionary degree required a group fixated in the emotions and mentality of permanent generational rebellion. This was not a sufficient condition for the Berkeley Student Uprising, but it was a necessary one.

As with every student movement, there was the singing, the brotherhood, the comradeship. As the St. Petersburg students had known their happiest days of unity and love in the comradeship of prison, so the Berkeley students violating the law found a new comradeship. For if, on the one hand, a student movement is a generational struggle, it is also the last cry of the children, in despair at leaving the child's world, beholding with horror the competitive world of the adult, in which each man is every man's enemy, in which hierarchy will emerge, in which one's friends will be transmuted into strangers. It was noteworthy that so many of the student leaders—Mario Savio, Suzanne Goldberg, Michael Lerner, Robert Atkins—were philosophy students, unable to adapt to a prosaic vocation, seeking the meaning of things in a life which seemed to be rising up harshly against them. When the second Berkeley strike ended, the Strike Committee, in its terminal leaflet, even as it spoke of the "destruction" of the university, talked in children's language of the hoped-for community of love:

> A community which had seemed submerged has revealed itself again, discoverable and developing. . . . The Yellow Submarine was first proposed by the Beatles, who taught us a new style of song. It was launched by hip pacifists in a New York harbor, and then led a peace parade of 10,000 down a New York street. Last night we celebrated the growing fusion of head, heart and hands; of hippies and activists; and our joy and confidence in our ability to care for and take care of ourselves and what is ours. And so we made a resolution which broke into song; and we adopt for today this unexpected symbol of our trust in our future, and of our longing for a place fit for us all to live in. Please post, especially where prohibited. We love you.[81]

The most unusual leaflet of a strike committee probably in all the history of strikes, it echoed the trauma of adolescents. This was a movement which sought for a "counter-community" in which something of the children's world, snug and secure, could be preserved. When the second Berkeley strike was suddenly called in 1966, a student leader wrote that "the latest revolt was a lightning bolt which shot furiously through our routines. It left activist students disoriented within themselves but with a sense of community lacking since the 1964 uprising." A girl added, "When the strike started, for the first time since I came here, I had a tremendous feeling of accomplishment, of getting somewhere."[82] This concept of the counter-community had been circulating for some time among student activists; it was in the nature of a generational secession, a withdrawal from the adult world; only in the counter-community, it was said, would "the values of honesty, concern, and commitment permit the clarity and moral indignation necessary to meet the dangers of atomization by H-bombs, bureaucracy, and race hate. And it is only in this counter-community that these virtues can survive, for the other community is designed to further conformity, apathy, and 'shaping up' as virtues." The activists rejected any prolongation among themselves of the disputes of the Old Leftists, the "distrust and prejudice based on the experiences of their 'fathers.' . . ."[83] They sought to preserve their generational unity, and believed firmly that the bond of youthful idealism would surmount ideological differences.

Thus, this new generational politics seemed indeed to overcome all alienation, all estrangement, for its participants. It was, as one of its advocates wrote, a substitute for psychotherapy:

> What enlivened the Free Speech Movement was the exhilaration of feeling that you were, for once, really acting, that you were dealing directly with the things that affect your life, and with each other. You were for once free of the whole sticky cobweb that kept you apart from each other and from the roots of your existence, and you knew you were alive and what your life was all about. ("For a moment all the hypocrisy was swept away and we saw the world with a greater clarity than we had before." Savio). . . . The F.S.M. was a swinging movement. The F.S.M., with its open mass meetings, its guitars and songs, its beards, and its long-haired chicks, made the aloofness and reserve of the administrators, the turgid style of the pronouncements emanating from the University Information Office, the formality of the coat and tie world, seem lifeless and dull in comparison.[84]

It was a singing, swinging movement, yet they could march self-destructively to beautiful song; but there was always the memory of their beautiful Pied Piper, Joan Baez, her long black hair waving in the wind, her olive face lit by the sun, as she sang with proud head thrown back and her guitar more summoning than any bugle call—singing of love, as the children marched into Sproul Hall in defense of the right of Mario Savio to bite a policeman in the left thigh.

Resistances to the Theory of Generational Struggle: The Aftermath of Berkeley's Symbolic Parricide

When the first analysis of the Berkeley Student Uprising in terms of the theory of generational struggle was published, there was a tremendous cry of outrage. To study the impact of the emotions of generational revolt on the tactics and goals of the student movement was regarded as the height of calumny. Student leaders, nonstudents, and their professorial allies had reveled in analyzing the alleged moral corruption of their elders;

but when their own motivations and behavior were exposed to scientific scrutiny, they gave way to anger and fury. Their indignation had all the earmarks of the "resistance" phenomenon. In truth, the student activists had long been conducting their agitations under the cover of a privileged exemption from analysis; they claimed the right to analyze others, to dissect the System, to expose the Establishment, but they claimed unconsciously the privilege of immunity to such a study of themselves. And in this respect they were typical of student movements; they regarded themselves as an elite, as the conscience of the community, as its valued children, and they expected the privileges at once of irresponsibility as children as well as the obeisance due to society's conscience. Activists of all varieties, pacifists, anarchists, Communists, Trotskyists, socialists, existentialists, hangers-on, all joined in a universal chorus of denunciation of the effort to examine their underlying motivation of generational struggle. The motives of all those actually and symbolically under thirty were claimed to be sacrosanct, and he who studied them was sacrilegious; the student movement presumed so much precisely because indeed it was the bearer of all the resistance mechanisms of the generational unconscious.[85]

Gradually, however, the outcry and resistance to the theory of generational struggle subsided. Instead theoreticians of the student movement, as they adapted themselves to its truth, advanced a new standpoint; they acknowledged that generational struggle was at the heart of the Berkeley Student Movement, but tried to use this very concept to justify and validate the movement. As one such writer said:

> Although none of the other liberal critics of the F.S.M. have articulated the cry of "generational revolt" as Feuer has, I think that an examination of this concept provides a key to understanding not only what the Free Speech Movement was all about, but also why it has been attacked with such enmity by many academy liberals. . . .
>
> I agree with Feuer that "generational revolt" was a critical underlying force moving the Free Speech Movement, without which the events of Berkeley could never have taken place in the way that they did. I do not believe that this discredits the F.S.M., however; I believe that this is precisely what validates it and makes the Free Speech Movement of major political and social significance. . . .

"The revolt of the generation coming into being against the generation in power, the revolt of the sons against the fathers, is a sign of, and a measure of, the failure of the older generation," continued this writer. "Specific events have specific causes," and the specific cause in the present instance was society's failure "to provide for its children a society compatible with the fulfillment of their needs. . . ."[86]

Now it is certainly true that the impulse to generational revolt always attaches itself to some underlying carrier wave of discontent; a student movement always seeks to find a wider justifying cause in a labor movement, peasants' movement, civil rights movement, anti-colonialist movement. What the writer failed to grasp, however, is that the superimposition of the generational struggle on the carrier movement of class, national, or racial struggle involves a superimposition as well of means, which tend to be irrational and self-destructive. The unconscious drives of generational struggle project themselves on the materials provided by the other underlying social struggles, deflecting them into irrational channels. Even the writer of the above article, a participant in the San Francisco sit-ins, thus confessed in an aside that the avowed, overt, manifest goal of jobs for Negroes was only a "pretext" for something else he was seeking, the community of the young, and that the political means by which they chose to achieve the latter were finally "demoralizing" and self-defeating for the civil rights movement as a whole:

> So when the press pointed out the following day that eighty per cent of the demonstrators at the Palace were white students, and questioned what they were really there for, whether they were agitating for jobs for Negroes or only using that as a pretext for something else, they were essentially right. We were concerned about those jobs, but there was much more at stake that night.
>
> What this experience gave us, and what their experience in the civil-rights movement gave the students who committed themselves to it, was the knowledge that a community is possible. . . . The group which sponsored that demonstration, a coalition of youth and student groups . . . was never able to muster that kind of strength again; partly because of the demoralizing effect of the arrests and trials that ensued . . . but even more importantly for another reason.
>
> The demands of the civil-rights movement were demands made on behalf of the Negro, and most of us were not Negroes. As we in the North attempted to get more Negro working people involved in the struggle . . . a growing sense of frustration set in; for we were outsiders . . . and there was a gap between us that all our good intentions could not breach. . . . Finally, we were haunted by the knowledge that we had returned, in our own lives, after the Sheraton-Palace, to the same jobs and the same neighborhoods. . . .[87]

It was the familiar story of the frustration of the back-to-the-people mood of the students; as they had felt rejected by the Russian peasants in the nineteenth century, so they felt rejected by the American Negro in the twentieth. And with that sense of frustration, the search for an occasion for desperate acts of their own direct intervention against the System grew. There was, too, the poignant search for a counter-community of the young against the old, the invariant emotion which ran through a succession of causes and "pretexts," the pervasive emotion of revolt. This invariant emotion imposed its "passionate style," its compulsion for irrational means and self-destruction, on a succession of causes. This was most clearly perceived by a student leader, a member of the Executive Committee of the Free Speech Movement at Berkeley, who accepted the thesis of generational revolt but was troubled by the self-insight which it brought. It is wrong, he wrote, "to deny the interrelation between political radicalism and generational revolt, and to assert that our politics rests solely on rational judgment." While acknowledging an "intense personal projection" in the student activist, he argued nonetheless that "precisely the underlying revolt against the sins of the fathers vindicates that radicalism." At the same time, the student leader agreed that a "political short-sightedness," a "passionate black-and-white morality" went hand in hand with the rejection of the fathers' political order. When students rebelled against the university, it was a "revolt against the values and mores with which our parents had constructed their own self-images and life styles." The administration symbolized that judicious, moderate life style. By contrast, FSM signified "the passionate style in Berkeley politics." Inherent in generational revolt, that "passionate style," he wrote, "becomes a barrier to effective political action when it clouds our perceptions. Revolutions devour their children, for many reasons, among them the fact that revolutionaries, bound as they are to the passionate style, have a disturbing tendency to devour each other." Thus, the student leader conceded, as he observed the "passionate style" among his fellow-members of the Executive Committee, that they had a compulsion to devour each other; the sons, guilt-smitten with having killed their father, killed each other; some were devoured because they seemed to take on their fathers' ways, others for the opposite reason. Once the FSM Executive Committee debated the question whether or not to request that its demonstrators wear neat dress at one of their rallies. At once one faction was ready to destroy the other for a generational betrayal: "The intensity of those who held that to ask our supporters to dress neatly was to 'sell out' was disturbing . . . many fought for the no-dress position not so much like men arguing for a particular tactic as like cornered wild animals fighting for their existences. The no-dress request position won. . . ."[88]

Such were the consequences of the superimposition of generational struggle on political struggle as they manifested themselves in the Berkeley Student Movement. After its activists had forced the ouster of the chancellor, many were numbed by feelings of guilt. Two years later a prominent Berkeley student leader accounted for a certain passivity on the part of veteran activists by reference to "tremendous guilt feelings on the part of those still around from 1964 who have never gotten over their previous parricide."[89]

Meanwhile, there had been all the distinctive traits—the readiness for self-sacrificial tactics (in the arrest and trials of several hundreds for the occupation of Sproul Hall in generational solidarity), the longing to see the overthrow of some father figure (in this case the chancellor, Edward Strong), the fitful movement from issue to issue (the civil rights movement on the campus virtually collapsed a few weeks after the uprising, for its strategic potential as a generational issue was exhausted, and the promises which had been made to tutor Negro children were promptly forgotten except by a few dedicated "do-gooding" but nonactivist students; for a while, the activists tried to exploit the potentialities of obscene speech, but this failed; shortly thereafter they transferred all their energies to the issue of the war in Vietnam), and last, the idealization of a student leader who was a model of readiness to challenge the collective father.[90]

The debilitating effect of generational politics and its destructive impact in the long run not only on the students' personalities but on their presumed goals of civil rights work was nowhere stated as eloquently as by a student leader, a former member of the Free Speech Movement's Executive Committee, as he appraised the fruits of the first "Year of Our Victory."

From the high point of our Solidarity, 800 indignant students who so violently and decisively threw themselves into the machinery of our insensitive educational "factory" have been transmogrified into: 5,000 days of suspended sentences, $400,000 in appeal bail tied up for about two years, approximately 1,000 man-years of appeal to higher courts, 1,200 years of court probation, $75,000 in fines, and individual jail terms ranging up to 125 [days] for each of the defendants. The "eight hundred" students, the "two hundred" faculty, the community of a year ago were all lost somewhere in the shadow "between the motion and the act."

We fought for political freedom. We skipped classes. We flouted rules. Petitioned. Sat. Bit. Spent sleepless days and nights. Finally, after the faculty resolutions of December 8, and the revised University-wide rules, we thought we had won. . . .

And now that we have our rights basically secured to wage the Revolution in peace, we have been seized by a peculiar immobility. The two civil rights organizations that formed the backbone of the FSM leadership have run into trouble finding things to do, and have considered holding joint meetings. . . .

Instead of undergoing an evolution of thought, we have been sucked into a helpless goal-less evolution turning constantly in on itself.

Political stagnation is followed by political incest, and that soon by widespread political cretinism. . . .

Back in the old bad days, before the administration provided us with loudspeakers and assured us that almost anything we did was A-OK, Berkeley students fought for and got: the abolition of compulsory ROTC, the elimination of the controversial speakers ban, a highly satisfactory settlement on minority living from the San Francisco hotels. . . .

And if we try to discover the sources of our political sickness, even now we can find no answers. . . . Has enervation permanently captured our minds? It seems that we have reached the end of politics. . . . We ask only to be allowed to "forget about today until tomorrow."[91]

The chief ideologist of the Free Speech Movement, Stephen Weissman, was writing only a year later of the "myths" which had moved them, and the self-destruction of idealism which it had brought in its wake:

Radicals increasingly feel themselves operating in a vacuum. There is no apparent perspective, agency, or hope for radical structural change in America. The Delano grape strike, for example, or the prospect of unionizing the working poor, no longer create the myths or hold forth the promises that many of us saw in Civil Rights on campus movements a year or two back.

From the "history of radical politics," the student ideologist reflected, one learns "about the destruction of ideals—and idealism—that occurs when people are used. . . ." He now found it unreal to equate the Berkeley police with the Saigon police, though such equations had been the rule the year before.[92] As the generational revolt ebbed, it left a hollowness in the "idealism" which it had inspired.

And the Berkeley faculty? Slowly recovering from their euphoristic revivalist mood of 1964–1965, they were well characterized in 1967 by Mario Savio and his friends as "wishing us all back into the pre-1964, anti-bellum period."[93]

A *bellum* it had been, and it left the generations two years later more estranged than ever. The second strike played all over again, though longer, for several days in December 1966 the themes of generational betrayal and the impersonal corporation. In June 1967, Mario Savio entered prison to serve his four-month sentence for the events of two and a half years before, together with many of his fellow-students.[94] Faculty activists who had spurred him on with admiring words now held various administrative posts. They wished he would leave Berkeley.

With the election of the Republican candidate, Ronald Reagan, as governor of California, the university administration was impelled to take a firmer stand on the enforcement of existing rules and laws with respect to nonstudents making the campus their agitational base; many rank-and-file student activists began to see how the basic animosity of the movement to the democratic process provoked a counter-intellectualism.[95] In the summer of 1967, the war between Israel and the Arab countries estranged many liberal students, especially Jewish ones, from the New Left; the latter suddenly externalized so much masochism, self-hatred, and anti-Semitism that the effect was therapeutic. Above all, the inner mainspring of the student movement during 1965 to 1967 in generational revolt became painfully clear. The movement tended toward a bifurcation—on the one hand, to the secession of the hippies, in nihilistic rejection of all received values, to utter irrationalism and the fantasy of drugs; and, on the other, to the violence of "guerrilla warfare" against American society. The moderate students and activists began to feel they had been misled and misused. When Clark Kerr was dismissed from the presidency of the university in January 1967 by Governor Reagan, Mario Savio and other student leaders rejoiced, "Good riddance to bad rubbish." Many former activists emerged from psychological enthrallment to "charisma" and generational solidarity. The "collective consciousness" of the student movement could, like an unstable compound, disintegrate under the power of light. A next generation of students might, however, re-enact the same drama.

The dream of an idyllic university community as a generational counter-community was lost as the dialectic of generational revolt fulfilled its course. The self-congratulation of student activists, their faculty allies, and their nonstudent auxiliaries, proved to be hollow. The upshot of two years of generational revolt by the Berkeley Student Movement was summed up by the students' president when he addressed the faculty of a strike-torn campus in December 1966: "We protest the general state of non-community on campus; we protest the hostility, distrust and rampant disrespect which pollutes the university atmosphere; we protest the sickness pervading the university."[96]

> Three years ago almost to the day we sat in to defend our right of free speech. Today, the gains of that sit-in have all but been eradicated. . . .
>
> Last month . . . the Regents re-adopted their prohibition against on-campus organization of off-campus illegal activity. . . .
>
> And instead of educational reform we got the quarter system; instead of channels of communication we got the ineffectual, dormant rules committee; and Tuesday night the Chancellor, in effect, castrated the ASUC.
>
> All the while espousing liberal attitudes the administration has successfully maneuvered the students back into their position of impotency before the FSM sit-in and strike.[97]

When Vice-Chancellor William Boyd arose to address the graduating class of 1968, he could not indulge in self-congratulation. This class in its four years had seen the beginnings of the student uprising and its consequences. The vice-chancellor said: "Now our very name is shorthand for trouble, our budgets are inadequate, our lagging salary schedules make faculty recruitment ever more difficult, and the public holds us in varying degrees of disgust. To the extent that the objectives of student activism for the past four years were to produce a better university, they have failed miserably."[98]

Such was the story of the Berkeley Student Movement in its first chapters. It repeated the themes of generational conflict; it was driven, despite all its idealism and democratic aspiration, to trying to project the irrational patterns of generational struggle on American life. "Berkeley" became a byword throughout North America for a generational running-amok.

The Consequences of the Berkeley Student Movement for the American People

What were the consequences of the Berkeley Student Movement for the United States as a whole?

It is undeniable that "Berkeley" became a symbol for student generational militancy. Every campus newspaper in the United States pondered the meaning of "Berkeley," and university administrators took mutual counsel as to how to avoid a "Berkeley" on their campuses.[99] "Berkeley" entered the idiom; whether it was student unrest in Berlin or London, the question as it tended to formulate itself for Americans was whether another "Berkeley" was going to occur.[100] What, however, were Berkeley's deeper consequences for good or evil?

In the first place, there can be little doubt that the Berkeley Movement contributed to the atmosphere of violence and lawlessness which began to develop in the United States in 1965. The worst of these episodes took place in the summer of 1965 in the Watts region of Los Angeles, California. One might question whether any connection between Berkeley and Watts might be more than tenuous. The average Californian, however, perceived a relationship in spirit between the two outbreaks. He sensed the effect of the televised broadcasts over several months of the Berkeley studentry "mobilizing" and violating laws and rules, the scenes of angry speakers, the students defying policemen and claiming the warrant of a higher ethic, the massive meetings, the arousing singers. No ordinary lawbreakers these, but students at California's highest university. Disobedience, violation, the flouting of the democratic process, resistance to law, were given the sanction of the community's intellectual elite. If the educated, the learned, the intelligent, approved of violating the law in a democratic society, then this path was so much the more indicated for those less fortunate and less endowed. Berkeley was the intellectual precursor for Watts. The student leader Mario Savio denounced Martin Luther King for failing to lead his people to violence at Selma, Alabama. And when violence came to Watts, Berkeley student leaders predictably welcomed it. The cult of violence in Berkeley even allowed the founding of a "guerrilla training school." "A group of Berkeley students," reported the university newspaper, "convinced that the political situation in the United States has degenerated to a point beyond remedy by peaceful means, has taken, so to speak, to the hills. This committee, meeting at 5:30 A.M. every weekday morning in Strawberry Canyon, above the football stadium, is the Berkeley Guerrilla Training School."[101] This represented a handful, no doubt, but it imparted to the atmosphere of violence in the community at large.

At its inception, leading activists of the Berkeley Student Movement said they were disciples of Camus. Two years later, a survey reported that Camus was "losing ground on campuses to Che Guevara and to Frantz Fanon," exponents of guerrilla warfare. Within those two years the Student Nonviolent Coordinating Committee had evolved to the full advocacy of violence and guerrilla warfare. The Berkeley Student Movement had indoctrinated students with the notion of bringing the System to a grinding halt by direct physical action; it had been vague, ambiguous, open-ended as to the employment of violence. When the System failed to yield to nonviolent direct action, by a gradation of rapid steps the transition was made to the apotheosis of direct violence.[102] Berkeley activists, employed in "poverty programs," regarded their federal employment as an opportunity for agitation to arouse the Negroes to direct action; they said they were emulating Lenin, who had used German imperial funds to make the Bolshevik Revolution. But the name that above all "cropped up in talks in college cafeterias whenever the New Left's current infatuation with direct action was mentioned," according to *The New York Times,* was Che Guevara's. His "bearded likeness was encountered on the walls of the littered offices of radical newspapers and left-wing groups." One young woman student activist, twenty-one years of age, "at that citadel of the New Left, the University of California campus at Berkeley" (in the correspondent's words), said, "I recognize that violence may be necessary. . . . I'm a white middle-class girl, but I understand why Negroes, Puerto Ricans, or Okies riot. I feel the same frustrations in myself, the same urge to violence."[103]

This urge to violence, reported so honestly by Lena Zeiger, was becoming characteristic of the American student movement, as it had been of its European predecessors. Berkeley led the way. The national secretary of Students for a Democratic Society declared himself in 1967 a disciple of Che Guevara:

"Che's message is applicable to urban America as far as the psychology of guerrilla action goes. . . . Che sure lives in our hearts." "Black power," he added, "is absolutely necessary." White student activists warmly noted that "black nationalists are stacking Molotov cocktails and studying how they can hold a few city blocks in an uprising, how to keep off the fire brigade and the police so that the National Guard must be called out. . . ."

The New Left has an apocalyptic sense that it defines the dividing point in history, the "historical moment which will divide that which went before from that which follows." California, it says, first defined the pattern of the future—"the rocking and the rolling that many now feel may be the beginning of the new social earthquake. The war triggered it, but there were obviously deeper causes. It is not inappropriate that in California, which gave the world Watts and the hippies and Ronald Reagan, the major cracks are appearing."[104] Berkeley led the way in applauding the advocates of racial war. In the fall of 1964, the Berkeley activists welcomed the playwright LeRoi Jones with masochistic fervor as he told them how he advocated a civil war of the Negroes against the whites. Two years later they were similarly applauding Stokely Carmichael, the advocate of "guerrilla warfare" for "black power." In the Berkeley area in 1968, violence became a political norm. The lives of the officers of the student body at Oakland's Merritt College were threatened; they were a group of moderate Negroes which had defeated a more militant faction. The entire group of moderate officers resigned. That spring too the whole University of California campus was plunged into darkness when its transmission tower was dynamited and its guard struck unconscious.[105] Of all American universities, Berkeley and its student movement did the most to prepare the capitulation of young American intellectuals to "guerrilla warfare."

The pamphleteer of the "Free Speech" Movement, Marvin Garson, enumerated with pride (in *The Village Voice*, July 11, 1968) the bombings which had become a standard procedure in the political life of Berkeley and its environs:

> The series of successful and highly popular bombings which have occurred here recently: the steady bombing of the electric power system from mid-March when the lines leading to the Lawrence Radiation Lab were knocked down, to June 4, when on the morning of the California primary 300,000 homes in Oakland were cut off; the dynamiting of a bulldozer engaged in urban renewal destruction of Berkeley's funkiest block; three separate bombings of the Berkeley draft board; and finally, last Tuesday night, the dynamiting of the checkpoint kiosk at the western entrance to the University campus, a symbol of the Board of Regents's property rights in the community of scholars.

On September 3, 1968, *The New York Times* reported that the city of Berkeley was declared to be in a state of civil disaster; the city authorities invoked emergency police powers, and the campus of the university was placed under curfew rules.

Curiously, one aspect of the student movement's abdication from reason was the frequency with which the word "charismatic" appeared in their writings and conversations. America hitherto has had little use for this word; it pertains to the hero-worshiping and hero-strutting characteristic of societies with totalitarian tendencies. Invariably, however, the new generation of student leaders in America have been seen as "charismatic." Mario Savio was pre-eminently the "charismatic." And although "Snick" (Student Nonviolent Coordinating Committee) embarked on a campaign against "charisma," as it turned toward violence, it elected Stokely Carmichael, "its most charismatic remaining member" (*The New York Times* called him) as chairman.[106] The "charismatic" sickness came to the American student movement with Berkeley, a sickness both of the "hero" and the group which emotionally needs one—as from Karl Follen to Nechayev to Savio.

With the student movement's attraction to violence, direct action, and generational elitism, it was natural that devotion to academic freedom and liberal discussion should decline at Berkeley. The chief ideologist of the Berkeley activists boasted that the departure from Berkeley of Professor Seymour Martin Lipset was "one of the 'Movement's' major contributions to intellectual integrity." There is no record that a single Berkeley professor had the courage to protest this statement. No student movement in the world has ever shown itself in the long run to be attached to the values of academic freedom. Berkeley was the first in the United States ever to break openly with the hard-earned tradition of academic freedom.[107]

The Berkeley Student Movement contributed to the psychological disorientation in the United States; there had been a confrontation of generations, and the elder generation had capitulated abjectly. This mood of the elders bowing before an allegedly "higher morality" of the young spread rapidly through the country. An eminent critic, for instance, found himself swept into the current of moral abdication; he wrote of "my own ambivalence, my own fear, my own hopes and misgivings before a generation more generous and desperate and religious than my own," and found himself trying to make sense of himself before them.[108] From this moral surrender of the elder generation, and the moral vacuum that came with the "dethronement of the super-ego," there sprang the movement known as the "hippies."

The "hippies" appeared in San Francisco and Berkeley in the wake of the Berkeley Student Movement.[109] Hunter S. Thompson reported:

> In 1965, Berkeley was the axis of what was just beginning to be called the "New Left" . . . and many professors approved. Now, in 1967 . . . the end result is not exactly what the original leaders had in mind. Many one-time activists have forsaken politics entirely and turned to drugs. Others have even forsaken Berkeley. . . . The "Hashbury" is the new capital of what is rapidly becoming a drug culture . . . perhaps as many as half are refugees from Berkeley and the old North Beach scene. . . .[110]

A psychological parricide had taken place on a massive social scale; the fathers were in debacle, defeat, de-authoritized, floundering; the fathers confessed that their values were wrong, but only under the physical compulsion of the sons. Freud once described the guilt which followed a primal parricide. Here the parricide was psychological, and compounded by the elders' own abdication. What were the consequences? Not guilt (at least for a while), but a loss of all standards, a collapse of all conceptions of right and wrong. Was there anything valuable which the elder generation could transmit? Every student movement evokes moral nihilism; the hippies, in a prosperous society, carried to a last conclusion the nihilization of all the values which bourgeois society had labored to achieve—honesty, self-reliance, self-respect, work, cleanliness. Moreover, in accordance with the example of the Berkeley Student Movement, it was proposed to attain the New Non-Society by direct action, simply by living it, without the bother and distortion of an intervening political movement. Drugs became the mark of the expanding consciousness of the ex-student activist, along with promiscuous sexuality, with a special leaning toward homosexuality and interraciality. Bourgeois sexuality, the sexuality of the fathers, was accused of being slave to bourgeois privacy; the hippie wrote in praise of public sexuality. A visiting sociologist from Oxford University wrote:

Hippies merge with the new radicals, who, in Berkeley student co-operatives, have old roots. But this is a radicalism that has replaced self-denying puritanism with self-indulgence. For hippies, if not for their activist New Left allies, the millennium of socialist society is too remote for their enthusiasm: in the psychedelic age, pleasure may be got now, where drugs and sex, and the scene are all available. One local, far-Left Democratic candidate, urging hippies to political action, concedes that drugs and nude parties are great before talking about nationalizing public utilities.[111]

The Berkeley Student Movement lowered the whole level of the country's political ethics. In its own activities it had quickly adopted the maxim that the end justifies the means. It imparted this doctrine to the discussions of political issues in avant-garde circles. From Berkeley came the play *MacBird,* written by a student who had served as press officer for the Movement. Originally published by Berkeley's Independent Socialist Club, it was soon winning accolades from youth-adoring New York critics, some of whom rejoiced that the Berkeley studentry had given the country not only its new political leader but its playwright as well.[112] The political content of the play was clear: it insinuated that President John F. Kennedy had been assassinated at the behest of Lyndon B. Johnson. The author's husband, another student and nonstudent activist, whom we have already encountered, also served as a "secret agent" of one of the groups trying to discredit the Warren Commission's report on the assassination of President Kennedy.[113] *MacBird* enjoyed a considerable success in New York as the dramatic achievement of the New Left. Its message spread to other continents. In Caracas, Venezuela, the play was advertised as "an extremely informative" account of the "assassination of J. F. Kennedy." London could not go quite that far, but its New Leftist justified the fantasy by saying that American society was so grotesque and fantastic that such a fantasy had poetic truth.[114] Thus, the political amorality of the New Left was guided by Berkeley activists to a new theory of twofold truth: the objectively false was politically "true"; the illusion was the reality.

Third, the Berkeley Student Movement evoked a strong reaction among the people of California especially, and America generally, of anti-intellectualism. The fissure between the people and the intellectuals became deeper than it probably has ever been in American life. The Berkeley student activists generally professed contempt for the American political process; there was no basic difference, they said, between a right-wing Republican and a liberal Democrat—both were part of the "System." The lawless actions of the Berkeley Student Movement were a principal issue in California's election of 1966. The elected Republican, Governor Ronald Reagan, took a moderate course with respect to the university, his principal proposal being to call for small increases in fees by the students. The student activists demonstrated against him at the state's capital, Sacramento, a Berkeley campus Communist leader boasting how several thousand students had driven in their cars to the demonstration.[115] Many Californian workingmen no doubt thought that students who could afford cars could afford to pay small increases in fees. The governor's popularity rose steadily with his every act of resistance to the intellectuals' economic demands—the students' for lower fees, their professors' for higher salaries. By June 1967, after a half-year in office, his popularity was at its highest, with 74 per cent of the people, according to a public opinion poll, indicating their approval of his administration.[116] It was the community now which felt "alienated" from its intellectuals, and which regarded the universities as a special-interest group, with professors ready to exploit the rest of the community economically and students regarding themselves as a privileged elite immune to the law.

The Students' Seizure of Columbia University: The Battle of Morningside Heights

"Berkeley started it, Columbia will finish it!" shouted a student orator on Morningside Heights. The events of April and May 1968 at Columbia University were in some ways even more significant for America than those at Berkeley. Violence became much more the norm; the themes of generational rebellion were reiterated—the destroying of the system, the apotheosis of guerrilla warfare, amorality, the misperception of reality, the search for the strategic, vulnerable issue in terms of which the older generation could be de-authoritized, generational solidarity aroused by police intervention. Let us without trying to write a chronicle of the events at Columbia observe the recurrent themes and patterns of generational conflict.

STUDENTS FOR DEMOCRATIC SOCIETY'S SEARCH FOR A STRATEGIC ISSUE

In October 1967 the chairman of the Columbia S.D.S. drew up a "Position Paper for Rest of Year—University Complicity." It envisaged the achievement of two goals, the "radicalization" of the students, "showing them how our lives really are unfree in this society (and at Columbia)," and "striking a blow at the Federal Government's war effort ('resistance')." The student leader planned to secure a referendum on university complicity in the war by March 10, a final ultimatum on March 15, and then by April 5, "a sit-in at Low Library which, after one day, turns into a general student strike. University capitulates."[117] This was the master-plan for student activist tactics. Its intent governed subsequent events, but in one important respect it was modified through improvisation. It transpired that America's involvement in the war in Vietnam simply did not de-authoritize the older generation to the extent that a large-scale student uprising required. A new issue came to the fore in April with which the students could move with greater confidence against the university, knowing that when this issue was raised, the university would be hesitant; naturally, as in Berkeley, it was the racial issue.

Columbia University had begun to build a gymnasium on a rocky slope of Morningside Park, the upper stories to be used by its students, the lower stories by the community of Negro Harlem. Several years of discussion with the city's authorities, the state legislature, and the community's organizations had preceded the approval of the project. As Arnold Beichman wrote:

The Harlem community, when the idea was first broached . . . *wanted* the gymnasium because part of its facilities would have been given to Harlem youngsters. It was a way of rehabilitating a park rendered unusable because of the dangers of criminal attack against passersby, black or white. Most of the land taken by the university for the gym was a sheer cliff, an escarpment functionally useful to flies.[118]

Young Negro extremists organized in the Students' Afro-American Society first voiced the complaint that Columbia was encroaching on the Negro community, and that the rear of the gymnasium would look down symbolically on Harlem. The leftist white student organization now seized on this issue as its strategic one. As two participants wrote:

The gym was made an issue because it would coalesce the black radicals behind the protest. . . . But the three issues [the gymnasium, the university's affiliation with the Institute for Defense Analysis, and the demand for an amnesty for those who seized and barricaded the university's buildings] were pretexts. The point of the game was power. . . . It was revolution. . . . Everywhere the purpose was to destroy institutions of the American Establishment. . . .[119]

The student leader, Mark Rudd, had little emotional interest in the racial question. He stated: "I was never really attracted to civil rights. There was too much idealization of Negroes, and they didn't seem too effective. I've always felt a tremendous barrier between me and blacks."[120] The issue at any rate was one around which a generational battle could be most readily pitched. For several years the young Mark Rudd had been seeking an occasion to express his "will to revolution." He said:

I had always had a humanist bent, but when I got to Columbia I started reading people like Marcuse and Lenin. Marcuse was very important to me. He made it clear that revolutions come from the will to revolution. . . . Then I met these guys who were in S.D.S. They were people I could respect. . . . You trust people first and then accept their opinions.

In short, Rudd's experience was a typically conversionary one, searching for a comradeship linked by the "will to revolution," that is, generational revolt translated into an emotive a priori through which all social events would be perceived. He made his pilgrimage in March 1968 to Cuba, the

Mecca of the New Leftist creed, and "came back more enthusiastic than ever about the Castro regime and Ernesto Che Guevara," the slain guerrilla fighter who has become the ego-ideal of the student activists. If Mark Rudd thought himself the prophet of a higher society, the vice-president of the university, David B. Truman, characterized him as "totally unscrupulous and morally very dangerous," as an "extremely capable, ruthless, cold-blooded guy, . . . a combination of a revolutionary and an adolescent having a temper tantrum. No one has ever made him or his friends look over the abyss. It makes me uncomfortable to sit in the same room with him." Born of Jewish parents, the son of a middle-class realtor, young Rudd used to urge his father to pay his Negro employees higher wages. The father observed that the son never had to worry about making a living: "We're glad he has time to spend on activities like politics."[121] With no challenge of the material environment to call upon his efforts, the aggressive energies in this rebellious Jewish youngster sought their channel. Fortunately, the university was at hand, the surrogate father, on whom the will to revolution could be vented.

On April 23, 1968, three hundred students occupied Hamilton Hall, the building for undergraduate instruction, barricaded its doors, and held the dean of students as hostage. Mark Rudd announced they were prepared to stay there until the university agreed to discontinue the construction of the gymnasium as well as its involvement with the Institute of Defense Analysis. "We're going to take a hostage to make them let go of I.D.A. and let go of the gym," he said.[122] David Truman offered to meet immediately with the students, but they refused. They demanded later a prior written guarante of amnesty for all their actions. Again this curious trait of student revolutionists appeared—the demand to be regarded as adult citizens and the demand for special privileges as students, for exemption from the civil and criminal law. It was the recurrent elitism of revolutionary student movements.

The occupation of Hamilton Hall was itself the culmination of several preceding episodes in the course of which the student activists found that an association with the racial problem provided them with the most strategic base for operations against the university. A campus memorial service for the Reverend Martin Luther King, Jr., two weeks earlier had been interrupted by these same student activists who had always ridiculed his non-violent philosophy. Now, however, the full momentum of student uprising was released. As at Berkeley and almost every center of student movements for a hundred years past, the instinctive strategy of the student movement was to act in such a way as to provoke the intervention of police force; then it could hope to see the emotions of generational solidarity transform its minority uprising into a majority revolt.

Meanwhile, however, the Negro Black Power students broke with the white leftists. The Negro students were uninterested in the white students' talk of university reform; they said frankly that they simply wanted a victory over the white university. A Negro student leader said: "Black university students have barricaded themselves here to protest a white racist university that encroaches on the Negro community."[123] The white leftists decided to appease the Black Power faction. They left Hamilton Hall to the Negro students on the night of April 24; the whites seized the office of President Grayson Kirk and its environs in the Low Memorial Library. At this juncture, only 150 students of a total studentry of 27,500 were involved in the occupations. Signs and posters in the new language of generational revolt went up on the walls of the buildings, inside and outside. The activist unconscious with its fantasies of guerrilla uprisings and guerrilla heroes enveloped the reality of Columbia University.

SYMBOLS AND EMOTIONS OF GENERATIONAL REVOLT

Student activists proclaimed the "liberation" of the Low Memorial Library. Posters announced: "Liberated Areas, Be Free to Join Us." On Hamilton Hall the posters were icons of the students' faith—posters of Che Guevara and Malcolm X. One sign announced: "Malcolm X University, established 1968 A.D." Slogans were scratched on the walls: "Lenin won. Fidel won. We'll win." The white student activists in Low Library vandalized President Kirk's office. A warm sympathizer of theirs in the *Village Voice*, telling how the student activists felt, gave the best picture of their underlying seething irrational motivation, of the emotional unconscious beneath their surface political consciousness:

> Don't underestimate the relationship between litter and liberty at Columbia. Until last Tuesday, April 23, the university was a clean dorm, where students paid rent, kept the house rules, and took exams. Then the rebels arrived, in an uneasy coalition of hip, black, and leftist militants. They wanted to make Columbia more like home. So they ransacked files, shoved furniture around, plastered walls with paint and placards. They scrawled on blackboards and doodled on desks. They raided the administration's offices (the psychological equivalent of robbing your mother's purse) and they claim to have found cigars, sherry, and a dirty book (the psychological equivalent of finding condoms in your father's wallet).[124]

Moved by the compulsions of generational struggle, the student activists tried to destroy the university fathers by whatever means they could. As at Berkeley, they stole letters from the files of their university president, made photocopies, and published them.[125] The student leader, Rudd, said they were being distributed to "educate" his fellow-students. They dealt with administrative relations between Columbia University and such agencies as the Asia Foundation and the Institute for Defense Analysis. It was only too apparent how the rights of individual freedom and personal inviolability were scrapped by student activists. One sensed that their emotions would condone their own dictatorship and their own police terrorism far beyond anything which the much denounced "system" and its investigative agencies would allow. "Participatory democracy" rapidly metamorphosed into exclusive dictatorship. As one participant described it, at Hamilton Hall where the nonstudent activist Tom Hayden was in charge, "participatory democracy" signified that "a highly organized minority . . . is able to cow the unorganized, apolitical majority into acting against its better judgment." "Self-appointed censors" supervised all efforts at writing: "Later, when the intimidation went beyond verbal admonishments, I saw them as part of a kind of Stalinist approach to the truth that many of the radicals observed. Nothing was to be written that did not conform with the immediate demands of the 'revolution.' Every word had to follow the SDS line. . . . I was told by members of the Steering Committee that I had to clear anything written about the commune with them."[126]

Then too the seizure of the university buildings had the aspect of a mass generational celebration, a triumphal festival of the young. The *Village Voice* reporter wrote enthusiastically:

> You entered Fayerweather Hall through a ground floor window. Inside, you saw blackboards filled with "strike bulletins," a kitchen stocked with sandwiches and cauldrons of spaghetti, and a lounge filled with squatters. There was some pot and a little petting in the corridors. But on Friday, the rebellion had the air of a college bar at 2 a.m. . . . On the other side of the campus, the mathematics building was seized. . . . The rebels set about festooning walls and making sandwiches. Jimi Hendrix blared from a phonograph. Mao mixed with Montesquieu, "The Wretched of the Earth" mingled with *Valley of the Dolls*.[127]

Still, however, only about a fifth of the daytime studentry were not attending classes; the great majority were still meeting. The student activists held fast to their determination to provoke the intervention of the police. They seized three more buildings. They ignored the trustees' approval of the decision to suspend construction of the gymnasium. They rejected all offers to mediation by a faculty group on the ground that they were not assured of amnesty for every violation of rule and law they had committed. Among moderate students, sentiment was strong against the activists; two hundred of them, organized as a "Majority Coalition," and dressed in conventional jackets and ties, "held the line" successfully against an activist contingent bringing food to the Low Library occupiers. But university authorities and faculty prevailed on student moderates not to act to regain the buildings from which they were violently barred. The initiative was allowed to remain in the hands of a violent minority.

GENERATIONAL SOLIDARITY AND POLICE INTERVENTION

Then on the night of April 30 one thousand policemen, in accordance with a request from the university authorities, intervened to remove the occupying students. The Negro students evacuated Hamilton Hall peacefully; but at Fayerweather, a line of faculty activists tried to interpose itself between the students and police. A kind of hysteria of generational ferocity overcame student activists. One shouted at three middle-aged men near Hamilton Hall: "I hope you old . . . die! I hope all you old . . . die. Go ahead and watch us and die!" Another shouted as he was arrested: "I'm going to rape your daughter." A girl student screamed: "First they arrest the workers and now they arrest the intellectuals!" The neo-Marxist symbolism substituted for reality: What workers were being arrested? Had a single New York workers' organization or trade union indicated any solidarity with the Columbia activists? The student activists taunted the police with obscenities and epithets, seeking to provoke the longed-for "police brutality." Violence and counter-violence, at times indiscriminate in the hysterical atmosphere, became general. Seven hundred and twenty persons were arrested, one hundred and nine were injured, including seventeen policemen. *The New York Times* correspondent described this night of higher education: "Somehow the whole night seemed unbelievable, a mixture of moods that seemed to have no relationship to each other: violence and compassion, talk of hatred and death and talk of gentle philosophers, ugliness of action and of speech, and moments of tenderness, a place of learning become a place of destruction."[128] It was the familiar combination of emotions that generational revolts have, as we have seen, always engendered.

The next day saw the oft-repeated pattern of the coalescence of generational solidarity. Indignation was high with the intervention and "brutality" of the police. The student activists called a university-wide strike while the university itself closed the campus; the faculty called for a day of reflection and discussion upon the aims of the university. On May 5, the faculty of Columbia College ended all formal classes, provided for grades of pass or fail on the basis of work already done, and asked for university reforms. The university on its side announced the appointment of an eminent commission of inquiry headed by a Harvard Professor of Law and former Solicitor General, Archibald Cox. As was to be expected, the student activists declared they would boycott the commission's inquiry as a device of the System for diverting the militancy of the students. It was the familiar pattern of student activism—that of avoiding the use of available legal channels for the expression of discontent in favor of "participatory democracy" and "confrontation," that is, the force of a small elitist minority. A Columbia Strike Coordinating Committee came into existence to organize picket lines and courses in a fantasy "Free University"; the schools of Engineering, Law, and Business Administration were scarcely affected. The evening students of General Studies, usually working for their living, and the graduate students in the natural sciences, with their concrete goals and curricula, evinced little interest in the strike; but Hamilton Hall, the undergraduate humanities building, was void of both pupils and professors. The student activists in their fantasy felt they were making their own "cultural revolution"; they spoke the Maoist language of communes, their own "great leap forward" into liberated classes. Signs announced: "The Math Commune meets at 3"; "The Law Commune meets at 5."[129]

Thus the academic year wound to its end. The president of the university, confronted with threats of student disruption, announced he would not address Columbia's commencement assembly. Another occupation of Hamilton Hall took place on May 21 to protest the suspension of four student leaders who refused to appear in the associate dean's office. Again there was violence; fifty-one students and seventeen policemen were injured. The students' amorality reached new proportions when they broke into the office of an assistant professor of modern European history, who had dared to criticize them, and burnt his private research papers.[130] One had a preview of what liberty would mean under the rule of the New Left. The "creative vandalism" which their publications and prophets extolled could now be seen in practice.

A vandalism of the spirit, moreover, one more corroding than the physical kind, had made its appearance among professors as well as students. There was, for instance, the professorial expert on African politics who predicted and threatened "that if the police came—the university would be burned down."[131] As at Berkeley, academic demagogues made their appearance, seeking and needing the emotional responses of crowds. A well-known professor of drama stood before a "teach-in" at Teachers' College in early May at last finding a drama of which he was not the mere critic but in which he could cast himself as a hero among the characters. These are "days," he said, "in which everything is possible." He described how he had gone forth to confront President Kirk, looking for him in the men's rooms of the Low Library. He defended the activists' thievery of the president's files. "Violence was not committed; the files were only violated," he said in a shrill voice, and finding a curious satisfaction in his sexual imagery and pun. But when much of the audience, composed of adult teachers, failed to respond to the professorial daring, he apologized for his levity, and became more argumentative: "If you approve of our aims," he said, "you must approve of our means. . . . This country exists on the basis of armed revolt. . . . We have gotten glimpses of a new type of education. . . . You must strike."[132] It was the typical middle-aged seeker of student rebellions, seeking to appease his inner irrationality by helping to realize an external one among the pliable, susceptible adolescents.

Why was Columbia University so vulnerable to the tactics of a small activist student minority? Why did similar tactics that same month of May 1968 fail to provoke for instance a rebellion and stoppage at Brooklyn College? Both institutions were large, both were urban, and in both cases, large percentages of the student bodies, especially of the activists, were Jewish, though, of course, the total Jewish percentage at Brooklyn

College was estimated to be as high as 85 per cent. The tradition of activism has been much greater at such free, "proletarian" colleges as Brooklyn and the City College reaching back through years when middle-class Columbia had been relatively quiescent. Over the years, however, the class differential between Columbia and the municipal colleges had declined; at Brooklyn College, for instance, a survey in 1962 showed that a majority of the freshmen had fathers who were either in small businesses, sales, or the professions.[133] Yet two differences remained which were important. Brooklyn College was a "subway college," composed entirely of commuters; therefore generational struggle was apt to express itself directly in the family environment rather than on the campus where the student spent a few brief, instrumental hours. Second, Brooklyn College was composed of urbanites, predominantly lower middle class, as compared to suburbanite, upper middle class Columbia. As persons struggling themselves for a foothold in society, with parents of whom at least one was in many cases an immigrant, the Brooklyn undergraduate was far less susceptible to feelings of guilt concerning the racial problem. Usually he had gone to public elementary and high schools with Negro students; often he estimated their abilities and characters as realistically as he did his own. If his parents had worked their way up from East Side and Brownsville slums, he felt others could too with hard work; he had no consciousness whatsoever that he had ever imposed a burden on the Negro. This relative absence of guilt over the racial issue was probably the chief factor in the failure of would-be student uprisings at Brooklyn and at City College, though the latter was situated even closer to the heart of Harlem and had expanded relatively far more than Columbia. Of course, as a private institution, Columbia could be depicted as an "encroacher" far more than the public City University; Columbia's guilt-consciousness could be the more easily aroused. Yet after all these factors are weighed, one must still recognize that a majority of the students at Columbia probably would have opposed the "occupiers" and dislodged them, if they had not been restrained by professors and administrators.[134] The Columbia studentry was moderate; only the preceding year, in a referendum of undergraduates as to whether the college should permit all governmental and business agencies, regardless of their involvement in the Vietnam War, to recruit staff on the campus, a decisive majority of 67 per cent had voted in favor of so doing, and had rejected the standpoint of the student activists. If the violent occupiers had been expelled the first day, the majority of the students no doubt would have approved. Clearly, the effects of a psychology of deauthoritization had deprived the Columbia authorities of their powers of response.

The immediate consequences of the Columbia student uprising were clear. For one, it brought an atmosphere of anti-intellectualism into New York which that city had never known before. A poll conducted by Public Opinion Surveys of Princeton indicated how feeling against the students had grown. To a random sample of residents of the New York metropolitan area, the question was put concerning the "extensive student protest" in the past week: "Who do you think is more to blame for this situation—the people running Columbia University or the students involved?" Fifty-five per cent, a decisive majority, blamed the students more, while only 11 per cent blamed the "people running Columbia."[135] As many as 83 per cent felt the university was right in calling the police to remove the protesting students from university buildings; and 58 per cent approved of the degree of force that had been used against the student activists. Among the working classes the resentment against the Columbia students was especially great. Of those respondents without college education (of whom the working class constitutes the largest group), the overwhelming number, 86 per cent, approved of the calling of the police, while 63 per cent endorsed the degree of force they had used. Far from promoting a bond between the people and intellect, the student activists had promoted a rift which could have serious consequences. The average citizen of New York tended to identify more with the policemen, as men without educational advantages, coming to blows with academic upper-class, indeed, leisure-class youth.

Second, the faculty itself, the senior intellectuals, tended to discredit themselves in the eyes of the American people. The Columbia professors generally responded with more critical acumen than their Berkeley colleagues had three and a half years before. Perhaps no other university in the United States includes among its scholars so many well-known critics of and commentators on American society as does Columbia. Nevertheless, when the student uprising came, not a few such distinguished writers found themselves indecisive and inclined to yield in varying degree to the "confrontation" of the activist minority.[136] According to the Cox Commission, the group of faculty which interposed itself between the students and the police "increased the likelihood of violence and magnified the reaction by lending an air of legitimacy to use of the tactics of disruption. . . ." There was a pressure on professors to sacrifice convictions for the sake of classroom popularity; professors knew that the moderates, liberals, and conservatives would never disrupt their classrooms; only the activists would. Therefore, professors tended to respond to the crisis with a touch of the classroom demagogue, yielding to a kind of pressure or threat from the extreme left.[137]

Third, the Columbia episode was a pilot project in New York for the use of violence for political aims. Here, the intellectual elite itself, the educated class, the favored sons of the well-to-do, were acting lawlessly, violently, moving in mobs, shrieking obscenities. They gave the sanction of similar action to the uneducated and the poor. The university was superseded as a moral force in the community—to be replaced by the New Left and its amoral force. The university ceased to be the conscience of the community; it became an enclave for the rule of the id. The Columbia episode added to the difficulties of the community of New York City trying to solve its racial problems in a rational way. The student movement had once more acted self-destructively because such destruction was part of its unconscious aim.

Lastly, the revolt of Negro student extremist activists against their own more moderate elders made the probable path of relations between white and black even more difficult for the future. The head of their organization at Columbia told the white students: "Remember that in a few years when you get off at the 116th Street subway station and head for your classrooms, you'll be the minority and we'll be the majority."[138] The Negro students asserted that Columbia was encroaching on the black community when it bought properties in the neighborhood. By the same token, white persons could argue that Negroes should be kept from encroaching on white communities. The kind of polarization which divides societies, and makes it hard to achieve rational reforms, was abetted by the Columbia student uprising.

When the whole story, however, of the American student movement is reviewed, it becomes clear that it remained peripheral to the philosophies and lives of the vast number of American students. Unlike the Russian activists of the nineteenth century, the American activists were still estranged from the mass of American students. Although at least 221 demonstrations occurred at 101 colleges and universities (apart from Columbia) during the interval from January 1 to June 15, 1968, only 38,911 students were involved, that is, 2.6 per cent of the American studentry. As compared with the more than 80 per cent involvement of Russian students at critical times, the American figure was minute; by the barometer of student activism, one might say that the generational equilibrium of American society was not basically impaired. It was rather the secondary consequences of student activism which brought dangers to the United States—their example of violence and contempt for American democratic procedure, their disruption of traditionally peaceful electoral debates and speeches, their intimidation of the majority, their disregard of political ethics, and the ensuing polarization of American society and the reactive growth of anti-intellectualism. Of the 221 demonstrations, 97 were evoked by aims of black power, 50 were directed toward student power, while only 45 were related to the Vietnam War or military factors. A small number of students were suspended, 60 throughout the nation, and 124 expelled, without reinstatement.[139] The percentage of American students incurring such penalties was infinitesimal compared to what the Russian students sustained. Evidently, the elder generation in the United States was not morally de-authoritized in the eyes of the younger in anything like the proportions which had obtained in prerevolutionary Russia.

NOTES

1. Hanan C. Selvin and Warren O. Hagstrom, "Determinants of Support for Civil Liberties," *British Journal of Sociology,* XI (1960), 56; "Student Attitude Survey Revealed," *Daily Californian,* May 12, 1959.

2. "CORE in the Negro Uprising," *American Liberal,* III, No. 10 (November 1962), 8.

3. Sara Shumer, "The Demonstrations: A Moral Defense," *Liberal Democrat,* IV (1964), 10–12; Jim Willwerth, "A Weekend of Songs, Sit-ins and Sleep-ins," *Daily Californian,* March 9, 1964; Nancy Tolbert, "Demonstrators 1—Sheraton Palace O," *Daily Californian,* March 9, 1964.

4. Three years later the father of Michael Schwerner, Nathan Schwerner, was booed at a meeting of the Student "Nonviolent" Coordinating Committee. His son's martyrdom was scorned by the student activists, who were now shouting, "Keep it violent!" See "That New Black Magic: 'Keep it Violent'," *Village Voice,* September 7, 1967.

5. "Nation Mourns Slain Workers," *Student Voice,* V, No. 21 (August 19, 1964), issued by the Student Nonviolent Coordinating Committee.

6. Kenneth Rexroth, "Compulsive Demonstrators," *San Francisco Examiner,* October 14, 1964.

7. "Educator and Libertarian," *Daily Californian,* April 29, 1964. See also E. W. Strong, "Shared Responsibility," *Bulletin of the American Association of University Professors,* XLIX (June 1963), 109–113.

8. The Communists found the Berkeley campus so free that "its organizational profusion might seem excessive. . . ." See Al Richmond, *Campus Rebels* (San Francisco, 1960), p. 11.

9. Steve Phipps, "The Invisible University Community: A Report on the Underground Student," *Daily Californian,* March 13, 1964. At that time, a few months before the Berkeley Uprising, the writer estimated the "hidden community" as several thousands in number.

10. Geoffrey White, "The Student Revolt at Berkeley," *Spartacist,* No. 4 (May-June 1965), p. 14. Stephen Weissman, the chief ideologist of the Free Speech Movement, in an interchange in the *New Leader,* denied that nonstudents played an important part in the Berkeley student movement. A year later, however, he acknowledged: "But let's face it . . . we cannot do without nonstudents." Not to have them, he said, would impose an intolerable handicap on the Berkeley student movement. *Daily Californian,* March 24, 1966, p. 11.

11. See *2nd University Socialist School, An Unofficial Supplement to the Curriculum, Ten Revolutions that Shook the World: Sponsored by the University Democratic Socialist Club,* a brochure, February 18, 1964.

12. "Leader of FSM Sums up Battle," *Open City Press,* I, No. 8 (January 27, 1965), p. 2.

13. Hunter S. Thompson, "The Nonstudent Left," *The Nation,* CCI, No. 9, (September 27, 1965), 156.

14. Thompson, *op. cit.,* p. 157.

15. Jerry Rubin, "Oct. 15–16 and the VDC," *VDC News,* No. 4 (October 11, 1965), 1.

16. Jerry Rubin, *Daily Californian,* November 12, 1965, p. 1.

17. "Jerry Rubin: the Regents are Nonstudents too," *Berkeley Citizen,* I, No. 37 (December 9, 1966), 4.

18. Shea Weré, "The Berkeley Constant," *Berkeley Barb,* February 11, 1966, p. 4.

19. Paul Weissman, "Close-up of Mario Savio," *San Francisco Examiner,* December 9, 1964, p. 1.

20. "Mario's Father Approves," *San Francisco Examiner,* December 9, 1964, p. 75.

21. "A Rebel on Campus: Mario Savio," *The New York Times,* December 9, 1967.

22. Weissman, *loc. cit.*

23. "Mario Savio: The World Was Clear But a Moment," *Open City Press* (San Francisco), February 10-16, 1965,

pp. 1–2. Also see Mario Savio, "An End to History," *Humanity: An arena of critique and commitment* (Berkeley), No. 2 (December 1964), pp. 1, 4.

24. A *Brief History of the Free Speech Controversy: University of California, September-January, 1964–5*, a publication circulated by the Free Speech Movement.

25. Several critics took umbrage at the description of the Free Speech Movement as a "Soviet-style coalition" of student groups. With some disingenuousness they suggested this was a charge that the Free Speech Movement was a Communist organization. To any student of political science it was clear that I was referring to the mode of organization which sprang up spontaneously during the Revolutions of 1905 and 1917 in Russia in which workingmen's, peasants', students', and soldiers' groups sent their representatives to councils and contrived a form of organization outside the usual legal channels, the so-called "dual power." The Free Speech Movement was such a "dual power" of representatives alongside the official Associated Students Union, which it ridiculed as an agency for "sandbox politics." See Hal Draper, "FSM: Freedom Fighters or Misguided Rebels?" *New Politics*, IV, No. 1 (Winter 1965), 25; J. B. Neilands, "The Rise of Freedom at Berkeley," *Frontier*, XVII (October 1966), 5. For my original statement, see Lewis S. Feuer, "Rebellion at Berkeley," *New Leader*, XLVII, No. 26 (December 21, 1964), 5.

26. *FSM: Free Speech Newsletter*, undated, circulated October 12, 1964, p. 4.

27. James Benet, "Growing Pains at UC," *San Francisco Chronicle*, November 15, 1964, p. 6.

28. A graduate student in sociology, Ursula Cadalbert, chanced to take a film of the episode and kindly allowed me to study it in several showings.

29. *FSM: Free Speech Newsletter*, October 12, 1964, p. 4.

30. *Berkeley Daily Gazette*, October 30, 1964.

31. "It seems very likely now," wrote Barbara Garson plaintively, "that the University will liberalize its regulations on free speech and political activity. . . . But must we always make this massive effort in order to effect a minor change? The answer is yes." See Barbara Garson, "Freedom Is a Big Deal," *FSM Newsletter*, No. 4 (November 17, 1964), p. 3.

32. *FSM Newsletter*, No. 5 (December 10, 1964), p. 2.

33. See Lewis S. Feuer, "Rebellion at Berkeley," *New Leader*, XLVII (December 21, 1964), 8.

34. *The New York Times*, December 8, 1966.

35. Seymour Martin Lipset, in "Berkeley and Freedom. Comments and Criticisms," *Atlantic Monthly*, CCXVIII, No. 4 (October 1966), 105.

The atmosphere of the collective irrationalism in this meeting of the Berkeley faculty is well described in a letter circulated by David Shwayder, later chairman of the department of philosophy: "I attended the meeting in company of four of my departmental colleagues, all of whom, during the previous weeks, had expressed against the students indignation of a kind I could never muster. Only one of them (besides myself) voted for the Feuer Amendment, and all of them voted twice for the unamended resolution. . . . It was all very sheeplike, a kind of cowardice of conformity, very depressing to observe, especially since no one had anything palpable to lose by standing their ground. I must laugh at the repeated compliment members of the Senate have paid themselves for the orderly manner in which the meeting was conducted: most of us were simply cowed into silence. But academics are just that way, I guess, as was shown over and over again in Germany from 1815, and as was even confirmed by the behavior of the '200' at Berkeley. They knew what they wanted and they knew what was happening. I asked one of the most conspicuous of them—also a departmental colleague—why none of them had sat-in, and received the bland reply that the question had been considered but that they had decided that it would be foolish for they might go to jail! . . . They depended upon the students and non-students to make the case and to carry it along, and also to pay the price, while they conspired with their sense of responsibility, exuded words, and had the time of their lives. . . ." (Letter of March 6, 1966.) Professor Denzel Carr, formerly chairman of the department of Oriental languages, wrote of the "mass hysteria" of the meeting of the Academic Senate and its "incredible feature." See the *Atlantic Monthly*, CCXVIII (October 1966), 43. The former chairman of the department of Near Eastern languages wrote that "in the crucial weeks of November and December of 1964 I felt that the campus in fact had fallen victim to totalitarian tactics and totalitarian mentality. As chairman of my department at the time I can testify that some of my colleagues had their classes disrupted or dismissed not by their own actions or by the decision of the students . . . but by well-planned tactics organized by students (or even 'non-students') who had nothing to do with the classes in question. Similar occurrences were reported at the time by members of other departments on the campus and by chairmen. I could not then, and cannot now, conceive of a grosser invasion of the academic freedom of the faculty than those events." See Jacob J. Finkelstein, in "Report of the Committee on Academic Freedom," *Meeting of the Berkeley Division of the Academic Senate*, October 17, 1966, p. 5. Professor Seymour M. Lipset, in a generous defense of the Berkeley faculty, advanced the novel idea that cowardice and confusion are virtues of the tragic hero. See Lipset, "Berkeley and Freedom," p. 106.

36. The overwhelming majority of the Berkeley studentry, nonetheless, in 1964, disapproved of the tactics of the Free Speech Movement; a gulf existed between the student body as a whole and the activists, the "student movement." The students generally were working at their studies in libraries and laboratories; they were not on the Plaza except when Joan Baez was singing, and they found the whole affair unpleasant and turned aside. A poll of student opinion taken in the Social Science Integrated Course toward the close of the semester of uprising revealed the separation in spirit between the student body and the student movement. The course was composed of freshmen and sophomores, with about 54 per cent in the liberal arts and 46 per cent studying engineering. The poll was conducted by assistants predominantly supporting the FSM; their lenity in assigning grades was later shown to be proportionate to their political involvement in the FSM; the professor in charge, Nathan Glazer, was known to have been a warm partisan of the FSM during its formative phases. Yet the students decisively expressed their disapproval of the Free Speech Movement. Of the 390 respondents, the percentage of opinions were distributed as follows:

OPINION	PERCENTAGE
(a) Agreed with FSM on issues and methods	19%
(b) Agreed with FSM on issues, but questioned methods	39%
(c) Agreed with FSM on issues, but disliked methods	24%
(d) Disagreed with FSM on issues, and disliked methods	17%
(e) Other	1%

Eighty per cent of the students thus either questioned or disliked the methods of the Free Speech Movement; only 19 per cent endorsed them. And since the "student movement" was one which insisted above all on the tactics of civil disobedience and sit-ins against the university, it is clear that it possessed the support of a minority of students. However, that minority could muster and mobilize far more activists than could the majority of the student body. The engineering students "were somewhat more likely to dislike the FSM," though "results did not vary greatly by major." It was the "student movement," the "alienated," who imparted, however, the dominant tone to the Berkeley campus, and the decline in ethical sense which followed. See posted document, *Some Results of the Social Science Integrated Poll on Class-members' Involvement in the FSM Controversy and Reactions to it*, January 1965.

37. The debate between Mario Savio and myself at the Berkeley High School on February 5, 1965, was reported the next day in the local newspapers.

38. A Trotskyist organ held, "The students were most grateful for the support of folk-singer Joan Baez, for example, but when she called on them to enter Sproul Hall with love in their hearts this plea was received with considerable cynicism." See Geoffrey White, "The Student Revolt at Berkeley," *Spartacist*, No. 4 (May-June 1965), p. 14.

39. *Daily Californian*, February 4, 1965.

40. *Daily Californian*, February 16, 1965.

41. *Berkeley Barb*, June 3, 1966, p. 3.

42. *Daily Californian*, February 12, 1965.

43. Lewis S. Feuer, "Should College Students Grade Their Teachers?: The

Risk is 'Juvenocracy,'" *The New York Times Magazine*, September 18, 1966.

44. Lewis S. Feuer, "Pornopolitics and the University," *New Leader*, XLVIII (April 12, 1965), 14–19.

45. Morris E. Hurley, "Minority of One," *Daily Californian*, July 23, 1965, p. 9.

46. The facts of the case did not prevent Paul Goodman, fifty-four years old, from declaring that crime and delinquency were lessened by the Berkeley Student Uprising. He called instead for more "creative disorder" and "anarchic incidents"; "the community spirit of Berkeley this year is better than ordinary," he wrote. See Paul Goodman, "Civil Disobedience Decreases Lawlessness," *Daily Californian*, April 13, 1966, p. 13.

47. Judy Zimring, "Mostly on Southside: Sudden Increase in Berkeley Rape Cases," *Daily Californian*, February 1, 1967, p. 1.

48. "A Step Toward Sexual Freedom in Berkeley," *Berkeley Barb*, February 4, 1965, p. 5.

49. *Berkeley Barb*, III, No. 22 (December 2, 1966), 9. See also a series of news stories devoted to Berkeley sexual group communism, *Berkeley Barb*, May 6, 1966, pp. 1–2; February 18, 1966, pp. 1–7; February 25, 1966, pp. 2, 7; April 15, 1966, pp. 1, 10.

50. Professor Reginald Zelnik, in the *Daily Californian*, March 7, 1966; March 15, 1966.

51. The Berkeley student ethic was a revival of Nechayevism. Their thievery was like Nechayev's. As Bakunin wrote in 1870, "When you are out, he will open your drawers and boxes and read your letters; if he finds anything that could embarrass you and your friends, he will steal it and hide it in order to use it later against you and your friends." See Michael Prawdin, *The Unmentionable Nechayev: A Key to Bolshevism* (London, 1961), p. 53.

52. Thus, in 1966, Mario Savio "decried a situation in which the only way the students could get the administration to listen was to use their power of coercion. . . . Hal Draper, a nonstudent and writer on students and the radical left, called vehemently for a strike, although he insisted he was 'just speaking historically'" [a weather-beaten device of Marxist agitators], *Daily Californian*, December 1, 1966, p. 2. The correspondent for the "underground" Michigan State newspaper reported, "Also there re-appeared a cast of Mario Savio, Bettina Aptheker, Jerry Weisberg, Jerry Rubin and other legendary characters." See Mike Price, "Son of FSM: Berkeley Report," *The Paper* (December 8, 1966), p. 9.

53. "Confrontationist students," observed three student writers, "seize every opportunity to block meaningful dialogue on the subject." See the *Daily Californian*, November 21, 1966, p. 12.

54. Circular of Independent Socialist Club Forum, December 8, 1966.

55. Circular, The Strike Committee, *Masskoercion: Resolution of the Strikers' Meeting in 2000 LSB, December 6, 1966.*

56. "Election Divides Coast Liberals," *The New York Times*, October 2, 1966.

57. "New Left Parley on Coast Denounces Brown and Backs Black Power," *The New York Times*, October 3, 1966.

58. Robert Kuttner, "Robert Scheer Trims His Beard: The Birth of Wishy-Washy Radicalism," *The Activist*, VI, No. 3 (May 1966), 8.

59. *Ibid.*, p. 9.

60. Robert Scheer, "Notes on the New Left," *Root and Branch*, No. 2 (1962), pp. 17, 19, 22.

61. Scheer, "Notes on the New Left," p. 26; "Poet is Priest," *Root and Branch* (Winter 1962), p. 71.

62. "Some people gasped" when Scheer advocated the poor should seize Oakland. "Watts rather than Ghetto—Scheer Says," *Berkeley Barb*, February 4, 1965, pp. 2, 7. Scheer subsequently became the spokesman for the "Egyptian position," anti-Israel and pro-Nasser, at the grotesque National Conference for New Politics in Chicago in September 1967 at which time, according to one writer, he also evinced "considerable talents as a trimmer." Martin Peretz, "The American Left and Israel," *Commentary*, XLIV, No. 5 (1967), 34. The Jewish Communist organ wrote that Scheer "did not help matters" by his calling for support of the Arab guerillas, the "Palestine Liberation Front," against Israel. Jack W. Weinman, "New Politics is Born," *Jewish Currents*, XXI, No. 11 (December 1967), 8.

63. Kuttner, "Robert Scheer Trims His Beard," pp. 7–10.

64. Karl Marx and Frederick Engels, *The Holy Family, or Critique of Critical Critique*, tr. R. Dixon (Moscow, 1956), pp. 91–92.

65. *Berkeley Barb*, January 13, 1967, p. 5; "The Community for Old Politics," *Berkeley Barb*, January 13, 1967, p. 7.

66. Robert E. Wood, Roger A. Rosenblatt, Joseph J. Persky, "Harvard War Protest," *The New York Times*, November 20, 1966.

67. *The New York Times*, November 11, 1966.

68. Martin E. Malia, in the *Daily Californian*, May 19, 1966, p. 12.

69. Alan Cline, "Faculty View: 'Eighteen Months of Blackmail,'" *San Francisco Examiner*, December 2, 1966. There had been "18 months of activist blackmail," said Don Wegars, "UC Rebuffs Strikers," *San Francisco Chronicle*, December 3, 1966. The student leaders denounced their quondam faculty ally as a "fink." See Hal Draper, "The Confessions of John Searle," *Berkeley Barb*, December 5, 1966, Strike Committee Special Issue, p. 3. "Another head that will have to roll is John Searle's. In the recent disturbances, he was reduced to the level of a nametaker. Nobody really takes John seriously anymore." See Stewart Albert, "Guru, or Gorilla?" *Berkeley Barb*, January 13, 1967, p. 7; Michael Lerner, "On Mourning Clark Kerr," *Daily Californian*, January 24, 1967, p. 12; Michael Lerner, "The Times They Are A-Changing," *Daily Californian*, January 9, 1967, p. 12. The Communist party (East Bay Section Committee) said, "Searle now speaks with the voice of the administration. . . . That he is roundly despised by militant students for the traitorous act is right and proper. And the demagogic way he often tries to justify the repression of student activity by invoking the very principles of FSM is beneath contempt." See "C. P. Answers Dewgood," *Berkeley Barb*, July 28-August 3, 1967, p. 10.

70. See the *Daily Californian*, March 8, 1965; *Berkeley Daily Gazette*, February 5, 1965. The chairman of the sociology department reverted curiously to his standpoint as a student activist twenty years earlier. "We should work as political missionaries, from within, sharing inevitably what is culpable . . ." Philip Selznick, "Revolution Sacred and Profane," *Enquiry*, II, No. 2 (1944), 18.

71. Letter to the author, December 6, 1966.

72. Daniel Arnon, professor of cell physiology, replied: "We are told a mob is waiting outside and unless we vote 'right,' we'll never solve the problem." See *San Francisco Examiner*, December 9, 1964, p. 75.

73. Lipset, "Berkeley and Freedom," p. 105.

74. John Searle, in "Berkeley and Freedom," *Atlantic Monthly*, CCXVIII, No. 4 (October 1966), 111.

75. See Mark Schorer, "Final Thoughts on Berkeley," *Atlantic Monthly*, CCXVIII, No. 5 (November 1966), 38; Herbert McClosky, "Berkeley and Freedom," *Atlantic Monthly*, CCXVIII, No. 4 (October 1966), 108. See also the *Daily Californian*, August 24, 1966, in which several faculty activists joined with the editor, John F. Oppedahl, in writing a series of articles which provide unusual documents for the study of the psychological consequences of generational animus in an academic community.

76. Roger B. Henkle, "The Pattern of Confrontation," *Bay Guardian*, I, No. 4 (December 20, 1966), 1.

77. The chief ideologist of the movement almost personified it in totemistic fashion: "The 'Movement' is a strange beast. It is neither a formal organization nor a fixed doctrine, but rather a loose community of people, activities, and ideas held together by loyalty and mutual self-identification." Stephen Weissman, original copy of letter in "Berkeley and Freedom," *Atlantic Monthly*, CCXVIII (October 1966), 109.

78. Even the account in the Communist W. E. B. Du Bois Club journal conceded that the object of hostility and cause of alienation is summed up in the symbol of the IBM card which was prevalent on the posters, placards, and lips of the FSM. See Robert Kaufman and Michael Folsom, "FSM: An Interpretive Essay," in *FSM: The Free Speech Movement in Berkeley* (San Francisco, 1965), p. 29. See also S. E. Stern, "A Deeper Disenchantment: The Anti-Bureaucratic Revolt at Berkeley," *Liberation*, XI, No. 11 (February 1965), 19; "Do Not Fold, Bend, Mutilate, or Spindle," *FSM Newsletter*, No. 5 (December 10, 1964), p. 2.

79. *The New York Times*, December 8, 1966; James Wilson, "The Rebel Behind 'MacBird,'" *World Journal Tribune Magazine*, January 22, 1967, p. 11.

80. Donna S. Clemson, "There's Activism but No Revolt," and Bill Welch, "Students Seek 'Bill of Rights,'" *Centre Daily Times* (State College and Belle-

fonte, Pennsylvania), June 30, 1965, pp. 17–18.

81. Leaflet, The Strike Committee, *Masskoercion: Resolution of the Strikers' Meeting in 2000 LSB on December 6, 1966.* Shortly after the strike the student activist leaders announced a new coalition with the "hippies." It was an all-embracing coalition of generational revolutionists. The word was spread: "It's happening. Berkeley's political activists are going to join San Francisco's hippies in a love feast that will, hopefully, wipe out the last remnants of mutual skepticism and suspicion. The Thing is called A Gathering of the Tribe, a Pow Wow and Peace Dance, a Human Be-in. . . . The two radical scenes are for the first time beginning to look at each other more closely. What both see is that both are under a big impersonal stick called the Establishment. So they're going to stand up together. . . ." See "The Beginning is the Human Be-In," *Berkeley Barb*, January 6, 1967, p. 1. This was the prelude, they said, to revolution. "The Human Be-in is the message, it will say, 'We're here, together, free, alive, creative, and this is the way the whole world will be when it's ours.' "

82. Peter Benjaminson, "Jottings on a revolution . . ." *Bay Guardian*, I, No. 4 (December 20, 1966), 2.

83. Otto Feinstein, "Is there a student movement?" *New University Thought*, I, No. 4 (Summer 1961), 27.

84. Gerald Rosenfield, "Generational Revolt and the Free Speech Movement (Part 2)," *Liberation*, X, No. 10 (January 1966), 18–19.

85. "The punditry race is on to fathom the significance of the Free Speech Movement. At this moment the front-runner is Lewis S. Feuer. . . ." See Jack Weinberg, "The Free Speech Movement and Civil Rights," *The Campus Core-Lator*, January 1965, p. 6. The student Communist organ wrote of my "vituperative article in that old Cold War follower, the New Leader" (December 21, 1964) as abolishing "political meaning from the FSM by explaining its motivations as mere 'generational conflict.' . . ." "No bumptious 'adolescents,' " it replied, "would waste so much energy, sacrifice, and dedication simply to exercise hostility towards another generation." See Robert Kaufman and Michael Folsom, "FSM: an Interpretive Essay," *FSM*, W. E. B. Du Bois Clubs of America, San Francisco, 1965. See also Geoff White, "The Student Revolt at Berkeley," *Spartacist* (organ of "the Revolutionary Tendency expelled from the Socialist Workers Party"), No. 4 (May-June 1965), pp. 12–14. "Thus they (the New Conservatives) find it necessary to attribute the cause of anti-authoritarian protest to pathology (Feuer) . . ." See James Petras and Michael Shute, "Berkeley 1965," *Partisan Review*, XXXII (Spring 1965), 315–317, 322. Also, Jane Burnett, "Multiversity Bends to Protests," *New America*, IV, No. 20 (February 8, 1965), 8. James Petras, "Berkeley and the New Conservative Backlash," *New Left Review*, No. 31 (May-June 1965), p. 62. "A professor at the university, Lewis Feuer, in an article which otherwise showed understanding of the terrible effects of the 'multiversity,' also had to explain much of the student revolt as being instigated by a collection of Maoist-beatnik-sexual libertine pseudo-students who were all looking for some synthetic revolution to make up for the emptiness which they felt in their lives." Sol Stern, "The Anti-Bureaucratic Revolt at Berkeley: A Deeper Disenchantment," *Liberation*, IX, No. 11 (February 1965), 20. An article by two academics in the throes of vicarious revolt said it was "almost delusional" to regard such a movement as a "generational uprising." "There is, for example, Professor Lewis Feuer's denial that there were any genuine issues at stake and his claim that very few genuine students were involved in the controversy. He attributes the uprising to the powers of a handful of crackpots, political extremists, drug addicts, and sexual libertines, most of them, thank God, not students at all, but spoiled personalities, tormented members of that underground Berkeley community of lumpen-intellectuals who managed to dupe thousands of innocent and true students into believing that there were real issues, thereby capturing the ever present hostility of the young against their elders and mobilizing it into a 'generational uprising.' " See Sheldon S. Wolin and John H. Schaar, "The Abuses of the University," *The New York Review of Books*, IV, No. 3 (March 11, 1965), p. 17. Similarly, the novelist Ayn Rand complained of my "Marxist-Freudian appraisal, ascribing the rebellion primarily to 'alienation' . . . and to 'generational revolt.' " See Ayn Rand, *The Cashing-in: The Student "Rebellion"* (New York, 1965), p. 10, reprinted from *The Objec-*

tivist Newsletter, July, August, September, 1965. "And (so to speak) along came Feuerysides and explained. . . . 'This is just a Generational Conflict.' " "Professor Feuer, in his article, which is perhaps the most violent, vitriolic and virulent attack on the FSM, called the FSM a 'Soviet-style coalition.' " See Draper, "FSM: Freedom Fighters or Misguided Rebels?" pp. 25, 33. A professor of sociology complained that my articles in the *New Leader* were "the most public and malicious maligning of the acts and motives of the students, which was part of the vital context of events and a part of the events themselves. . . ." See John R. Seeley, review of *The Berkeley Student Revolt*, in the *American Sociological Review*, XXXI (February 1966), 108.

86. Rosenfield, *op. cit.*, p. 13.

87. Rosenfield, *op. cit.*, p. 17.

88. Michael Golden, "The Passionate Style in the New Student Politics," *The Activist*, VI, No. 3 (May 1966), 33–36. The article began by observing that my articles had begun a new phase in the analysis of the psychology of the new politics, but then argued that I had used the notion of "generational revolt" to discredit the student movement. "Rosenfield," it said, "arrives at a different conclusion after having agreed with Feuer that 'generational revolt' is the underlying avenue of the New Radicalism."

89. Michael Lerner, *Daily Californian*, October 17, 1966.

90. When asked at one student meeting what he had required most psychologically to fight the administration, Mario Savio replied, "Balls." This simple psychology also characterized faculty supporters who were urging the student activists on. One of them, a professor of biochemistry, agitating a large student assemblage to militancy, said, for instance, "Then you (the students) will have the faculty by the testicles and I hope you squeeze." See Professor John B. Neilands, *Daily Californian*, December 6, 1966, p. 8.

91. Brian Turner, "Nine Thermidor: Thoughts of a Dry Brain in a Dry Season," *Daily Californian*, February 18, 1966.

92. Steve Weissman, "The Movement," *Daily Californian*, April 19, 1966, p. 12.

93. *Daily Californian*, January 26, 1967, p. 3.

94. "Savio Goes to Jail for '64 Sit-in-Role," *The New York Times*, July 1, 1967.

95. The chief faculty agitator of 1964–1965, John D. Searle, said in May 1967, "The student movement isn't dead —it's just asleep and not very healthy." See the *Daily Californian*, May 15, 1967. Robert H. Cole, who helped draft the faculty resolution in 1964, said three years later: "I was a revolutionary in 1964—a faculty Young Turk. Now I'm an administrator, and I'm tired, very, very tired. We all are." Nan Robertson, "The Student Scene: Militant Anger," *The New York Times*, November 20, 1967, p. 30.

96. Benjaminson, *op. cit.*, p. 2.

97. *Daily Californian*, November 30, 1967, p. 8.

98. *Berkeley Daily Gazette*, June 15, 1968.

99. Two and a half years after the Berkeley events, the chairman of a meeting of the Canadian Association of University Student Personnel, Erik Hansen of Acadia University, said that student agitation in Canada probably had its origin "in the Berkeley confusion." See the *Toronto Globe and Mail*, June 14, 1967, p. 3. The student newspaper at the University of Toronto, for instance, referred to "Berkeley" symbolically in issue after issue. See, during a two-week period when Berkeley itself was not making news, *The Varsity*, October 26, 1966, pp. 5, 8; October 28, 1966, pp. 1, 5, 21; November 7, 1966, pp. 3, 5. "Berkeley, where it all began," noted Katherine O'Keefe, in "Accident, etc." *The Varsity*, October 6, 1967, p. 11. During a series of visits to American campuses in 1966–1967, the writer found "Berkeley" always used as a symbol of generational disorder. At the City College of New York: "At 11:30 President Gallagher appeared before the students at the sit-in, where he was . . . asked to identify who he thought 'interned at Berkeley.' " See "Sitting-In Made Simple," *Main Events*, November 14, 1966. At Michigan State University: "All the while I was at MSU, people worried about its becoming another Berkeley," said R. A. Ogar in "Nothing Serious—Just a Case of Déjà-Vu," *The Paper*, November 3, 1966. Also see Glenn Becker, "Berkeley Now," *Collegiate Press Service*, November 11, 1966. When a wave of antiwar protests took place in October 1967 *Time* magazine wrote, "The antiwar sentiment ignited the San Francisco Bay Area, tinder-

box of every antimovement of recent years. Boiling out from the University of California campus at Berkeley, aggressively nonviolent protesters—many of them non-students—descended 10,000 strong upon Oakland. . . ." See *Time* (Canadian ed.; October 27, 1967), p. 20.

100. See, for instance, *Time*, June 30, 1967, p. 32. When leftist students in Berlin threatened to "assassinate" the visiting Vice President of the United States, Hubert H. Humphrey, then a few weeks later cursed their country's President to his face, and when students in June exploded smoke bombs in the path of the Shah of Iran, *Time* magazine wrote, "The scenario sounded like a rerun from Berkeley, but the setting was a long-way from California. . . ." When the London School of Economics was beset by unprecedented student strikes, sit-ins, and demonstrations in March 1967, its leader was Marshall Bloom, a Berkeley alumnus of 22; "parallels with the student disturbances that periodically shake the Berkeley campus students of the University of California have been widely drawn," reported the press, as London students "turned to direct action, Berkeley style." See "U.S.-style student protests rock London School of Economics," *Toronto Globe and Mail*, March 16, 1967.

101. Paul Glusman, "The Guerrilla Training School," *Daily Californian*, April 17, 1967, p. 12.

102. "The fresh-faced new leftists on the Berkeley campus who a few years ago were so devoted to non-violence have grown increasingly grim . . . left-wing political activists—some college drop-outs and some Ph.D. candidates—inquire of their friends with forced casualness about rifle clubs and karate courses . . . it is not the easy joke it would have been a year or two ago when sensible radicals all scorned the 'guerrilla complex.' " See Marvin Garson, "Vietnam Summer No. 4: By the San Francisco Bay," *Village Voice*, August 24, 1967, p. 5.

103. Paul Hofmann, "Today's New Left, Amid Frustration and Factionalism, Turns Toward Radicalism and Direct Action," *The New York Times*, May 7, 1967.

104. Andrew Kopkind, "America's 'Blue Fascism,' " *New Statesman*, July 7, 1967, p. 4.

105. "Berkeley Stirred by 'Black Power,' " *The New York Times*, October 30, 1966. Pamela McCorduck, "Protest Rolls Off the Assembly Line," *Village Voice*, May 16, 1968, p. 7. *Berkeley Daily Gazette*, March 21, 1968.

106. Gene Roberts, "The Story of Snick: From 'Freedom High' to 'Black Power,' " *The New York Times Magazine*, September 25, 1966, p. 124.

107. Stephen Weissman, "Berkeley and Freedom," *Atlantic Monthly*, XXVIII (October 1966), p. 108; Arthur O. Lovejoy, "Academic Freedom," *Encyclopaedia of the Social Sciences* (New York, 1930), I, 387.

108. Leslie A. Fiedler, "On Being Busted at Fifty," *New York Review of Books*, IX, No. 1 (July 13, 1967) 10.

109. "Organized Hippies Emerge on Coast," *The New York Times*, May 5, 1967; *Time* (July 7, 1967), p. 27. Telegraph Avenue, adjacent to the Berkeley campus, was the birthplace of the "hippie sub-culture." While recognizing its idealistic potential, a Berkeley professor of sociology acknowledged that it also had the seeds of "a potential youth fascism (such as in Hitler's Germany)." See Carol Matzkin, " 'The Hippies': A Permanent Subculture?" *Daily Californian*, May 25, 1967, pp. 1, 10.

110. Hunter S. Thompson, "The 'Hashbury' is the Capital of the Hippies," *The New York Times Magazine*, May 14, 1967, p. 29.

111. Bryan Wilson, "The Here and Now of Hippy Escapism," reprinted in *The Toronto Globe and Mail*, March 31, 1967.

112. See the discussion which followed the publication by Dwight MacDonald, "MacBird," *New York Review of Books*, VII (December 1, 1966), 12 ff. Herbert Gold notes, "The Free Speech Movement in Berkeley . . . inspired this play." See Herbert Gold, "Where the Action Is," *The New York Times Magazine*, February 19, 1967, p. 51.

113. Richard Warren Lewis, "The Scavengers," *World Journal Tribune Magazine*, January 22, 1967, p. 4.

114. "The beauty of that play is not its text but its innuendo. It had all the fascination of a wicked rumor in the midst of partial knowledge and confused information. No one in his right mind could take its premise seriously. But, as in the case of rumors, sometimes one entertains an idea simply because it *is* grotesque and incredible. In regard to the Kennedy-

Oswald-Warren trinity, 'MacBird' is consistent with the extravagance of contemporary history. That is why I think it is popular in America. Not as a 'new play' by a 'new author' but as another notorious development in the mind-boggling saga which the Kennedy assassination unleashed. . . . Questions of 'responsibility' are utterly irrelevant." See Charles Marowitz, "Theatre Abroad: 'MacBird' Gets the Bird," *Village Voice*, April 27, 1967, p. 24. The ethics and logic of this defense of *MacBird* were precisely those used by apologists for the *Protocols of the Elders of Zion*.

115. "We had six bus loads and an inestimable number of private cars going," he said. "There were probably about 2,500 to 3,000 from Berkeley," said Brian O'Brien, a member of the Teaching Assistants' Union, and a charter organizer of the Campus Chapter of the American Communist party. See the *Daily Californian*, February 3, 1967, p. 2; February 14, 1967, p. 1.

116. *The New York Times*, July 23, 1967.

117. *The New York Times*, May 13, 1968.

118. Arnold Beichman, "Where Does Columbia Go From Here?" *New York Magazine* (May 27, 1968), p. 20.

119. Dotson Rader and Craig Anderson, "Rebellion at Columbia," *The New Republic*, CLVIII, No. 19 (May 11, 1968), 10.

120. *The New York Times*, May 19, 1968.

121. *The New York Times*, May 19, 1968.

122. *The New York Times*, April 24, 1968; Graduate Sociology Students Union, Columbia University, *Conflict at Columbia* (mimeographed; August 14, 1968), p. 2; "The Siege of Columbia," *Ramparts*, VI, No. 11 (June 15, 1968), 35.

123. *The New York Times*, April 25, 1968.

124. Richard Goldstein, "Insurrection at Columbia: The Groovy Revolution: Fold, Spindle, Mutilate," *Village Voice*, May 2, 1968, p. 1.

125. "Liberated Documents," *Rat Subterranean News*, May 3, 1968, pp. 8 ff. *The New York Times*, May 5, 1968. Graduate Sociology Students Union, *op. cit.*, pp. 2–3.

126. Dotson Rader, "More about Columbia," *The New Republic*, CLVIII, No. 23 (June 8, 1968), 23.

127. Goldstein, *op. cit.*, p. 18.

128. *The New York Times*, May 1, 1968.

129. Bernard Bard, "Rebels on the Campus," *The New York Post*, May 4, 1968. Graduate Sociology Students Union, *op. cit.*, p. 5.

130. *The New York Times*, May 23, 1968.

131. Max Lerner, "Agony at Columbia," *The New York Post*, May 3, 1968, p. 54.

132. Personal observation, Teachers' College, Columbia University, May 2, 1968.

133. M. A. Farber, "Brooklyn vs. Columbia," *The New York Times*, May 24, 1968, p. 33.

134. Beichman, *op. cit.*, p. 22.

135. *The New York Times*, May 9, 1968. A survey of the opinions of the student body at Columbia University showed that an overwhelming majority disapproved of the tactics of the seizure of buildings. Sixty-eight per cent of a responding sample of 1,726 students said they were against such tactics, while only 19 per cent favored them; 13 per cent were undecided. *The New York Times*, June 6, 1968. Also see Graduate Sociology Students Union, *op. cit.*, p. 5.

136. It transpired, as Arnold Beichman wrote, that the faculty and administrators "are not as well informed or politically intelligent as they thought they were." Beichman, *op. cit.*, p. 22.

137. *The New York Times*, May 12, 1968.

138. Beichman, *op. cit.*, p. 21.

139. The statistics were collected by the National Student Association. See "Student Survey Shows 38,911 Staged 221 Protests," *The New York Times*, August 27, 1968. Also see "Campus Protests Find Many Issues," *The New York Times*, January 21, 1968.

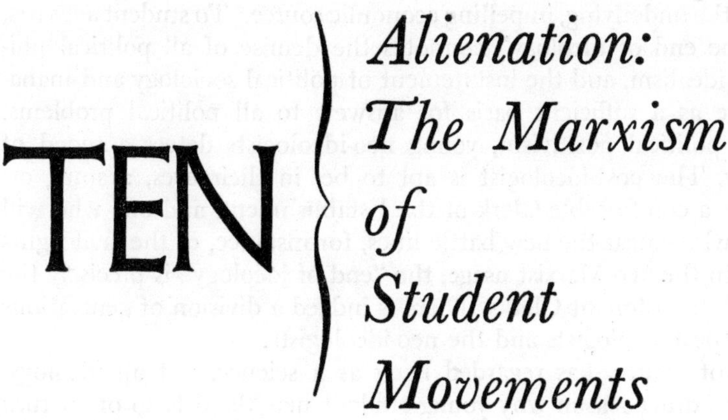

TEN Alienation: The Marxism of Student Movements

The Revival of Ideology

When Marx and Engels were young men in 1844 and 1845, they dreamed of communities which would overcome all human alienation—alienation from other human beings, alienation from one's work. They dreamed of the moral redemption and realization of man's essence. They even began to take steps toward founding an ideal community on the pattern of the American communitarian settlements.[1] Community was the answer to alienation. Marx and Engels at this time, as young disciples of Ludwig Feuerbach's philosophy, sharing his conception of "alienation," sought to realize its vision in Utopian communist enclaves. Three years later they had already shed their youthful idealism in favor of class struggle; revolutionary violence superseded communal love as the mechanism for social change. "Alienation" vanished from their vocabulary, and, in the *Communist Manifesto,* they ridiculed its use. They wanted now to abolish exploitation, not to overcome alienation, and they postponed their total hopes of the immediate regeneration of man's nature. But concepts have their own laws of recurrence and revival. Today the concept of alienation has the same appeal for circles of student activists as it once had for the young Feuerbachians. Those who feel a comradeship in direct action for personal rights, peace, and civil rights find its language congenial, and often share the same encompassing hopes for overcoming all alienation.

"Alienation" is the answer the student activists make to the "end of ideology" standpoint which they reject as the tenet of middle-aged and middle-class post-Marxists. The latter phrase itself comes from Engels, who used it to signify the end of all forms of thinking in which the thinker is unconscious of the underlying, impelling economic source.[2] To student activists, however, "the end of ideology" connotes the demise of all political philosophy and idealism, and the instatement of political sociology and managerial science as a sufficient basis for answers to all political problems. Behind this political positivism, young neo-ideologists detect a mood of complacency. The post-ideologist is apt to be, in their eyes, a smug ex-Marxist, now a comfortable Clerk of the Establishment, and one who will be found nowhere near the new battle lines, for instance, of the civil rights movement. In the neo-Marxist usage, the "end of ideology" is precisely the ideology of Establishment Clerks. There is indeed a division of generations between the post-ideologists and the neo-ideologists.

Marxism, of course, has regarded itself as a science, not an ideology. And here is another reason why young student neo-Marxists so often turn to alienationism; for what they find lacking in classical Marxism is precisely a philosophy. The mature thought of Marx consists of social science and a political summons, but the ethical-philosophical basis of his individual choice is repressed; indeed, the grounds of individual decision are a kind of "unproblem" for Marxism, and *Capital* regards persons solely as personifications of economic categories.[3] In contrast, the notion of the recovery of one's essence from the alienated self corresponds to the ethical sense of striving for one's freedom in the liberated community. The student movement as a movement founded on a higher ethic and morality, not on economics, spontaneously seeks for a moral concept to articulate its thought. Its adherents are, we might say, the first truly philosophical Marxists.

Marx's ethical prophetism, his condemnation of the existing bourgeois order, his Promethean spirit of revolt, his confidence in the triumph of the ethical, provided a standpoint and a vision which could inspire young student activists far more than any theory of Weber or Pareto or Parsons. The students' spirit was exactly that of the young student Marx who at the age of eighteen wrote:

Not for me a life untroubled,
Not for my tempestuous soul.
Let my life be full of struggle
For a great and lofty goal. . . .

Let us march into the distance
On a journey hard and far.
Not for us a drab existence
With no aim or guiding star.

Not for us a life of languor
In a miserable pen.
Let us feel desire and anger,
Passion, pride—as should real men![4]

Weber may have seen himself in the role of a modern Jeremiah, but his forecast of a bureaucratic world does not stir human energies; likewise, Pareto's immutable cycle of the circulation of elites imparts a lesson of historical futility, while Parsons has everyone subservient to the controls and equilibrating mechanisms of the social system. Marx's vision, by contrast, seems at the minimum a possible form of social development, a dream which may become reality if one has but the will and resolution. And as a possible form of social development, it seems to each new generation an unrefuted hope.

Are we confronted finally by an antimony of human progress? Does the advancement of the human race require social movements founded on a self-dedication which only irrational, ideological men possess? Do scientific, non-ideological men lack the irrationality essential for commitment to social movements?[5] Is there a "contradiction" between social wisdom and social progress? In any case, the new "ideological man" is emerging in the student movements of the world; there is where the revival of ideology is taking place. As the notion of exploitation was the ground for the theory of class struggle and the ideology of the workers' movement, so the notion of alienation, derived from the youthful Marx, provides the basis for student movements and the theory of struggle between generations.

Alienation: The Key Notion in Student Ideology

The concept of alienation is the central meaning of Marxism for the student movements of the world today—whether they be those of the United States, Japan, the Soviet Union, or Africa. This remarkable convergence in ideology obtains in the discussions of student activists all over the world; the language and metaphor of alienation capture most poignantly the underlying spirit of younger-generation revolt. The history of Marxism has once more taken a turn which nobody foresaw. "Alienation" has been the chief slogan-word in the students' protest in the United States, Japan, and the Soviet Union.

During the autumn of 1964, at the University of California in Berkeley, when demonstrations on the campus were taking place almost daily, the word which was always on speakers' lips was "alienation." The student crowd, fluctuating from several hundred to several thousand, sensed in this word the symbol of their basic discontent. Their spokesman, Mario Savio, formulated one evening the ideology of the student movement as he conceived it:

> A lot of Hegel got mixed in with Marx's notion of history. Max Eastman pointed this out. The dialectic was a way in which Marx made the course of world history coincide with his unconscious desires. Nevertheless, the most important concept for understanding the student movement is Marx's notion

of alienation. Its basic meaning is that the worker is alienated from his product, but the concept is applicable to students too, many of whom don't come from the working class. Somehow people are being separated off from something. We have too many bureaucracies; their mechanical functioning makes for splits in people's personalities. Marx's concept of alienation was worked out for a two-class society. But it applies equally to our bureaucratic society where there are several centers of economic power. The labor movement has taken on the same impersonal quality as management. The students are frustrated; they can find no place in society where alienation doesn't exist, where they can do meaningful work. Despair sets in, a volatile political agent. The students revolt against the apparatus of the university.

This is the motive power of the student movement. I thought about it and my own involvement when I went to Mississippi where I could be killed. My reasons were selfish. I wasn't really alive. My life, my middle-class life, had no place in society, nor it in me. It was not really a matter of fighting for constitutional rights. I needed some way to pinch myself, to assure myself that I was alive. Now we will have to break down the fiction of the separation of student and citizen. We are breaking down the fiction of roles. We are breaking down barriers set up in a lot of people's personalities. That is what drives the student movement on.[6]

Across the Pacific Ocean, leaders of the Japanese student movement had found likewise, especially from 1960 on, that the concept of alienation articulated the consciousness of their movement. Satoshi Kitakoji, president of Zengakuren in 1960–1961, and his close friend, Toru Kurokawa, reiterated to me, "How to overcome alienation? That is our problem. We will not allow alienation. Men are now alienated from their labor. We must analyze it and overcome it."[7] Neither of these students came from workingmen's families. Kitakoji was the son of a Communist teacher, Kurokawa of a doctor. The one was studying political economy at Kyoto University, the other literature at Tokyo. Both of them admired exceedingly the writings of a young Marxist philosopher, Kanichi Kuroda, who was teaching that the concept of alienation would provide the basis for criticizing all bureaucracies, whether Japanese or Soviet. These young activists traced the degradation of Stalinism to its suppressing of this essential idea of Marx. Shigeo Shima, secretary-general of the Communist League (also called the Bund) from 1958 to 1961, and a member as well of the Central Executive Committee of Zengakuren from 1956 to 1958, spoke of the motive power of alienation in 1960 in the student movement. Even Marxist organizations as they declined, becoming mechanized and stereotyped, gave rise, he said, to their own species of alienation:

At the time of Ampo (the struggle against the Security Treaty with the United States) in 1960, the world was bright, but we felt ourselves alienated. Out of the sense of alienation, we were driven to do anything. Bund was sympathetic with the early Marxian concept of alienation, which enchanted the minds of the seriously thinking students. The concept of alienation was tied up with the abolition of capitalism. . . . The original spirit of the Bund was a protest against that type of Marxism characterized by the absence of man, and against capitalism that alienated man. But when the initial spirit was translated into stereotyped expressions such as "making the vanguard party," "revolution cannot be achieved by students alone," etc., it lost its original inspiration, and that was a major reason why the Bund was bankrupt. There is a parallelism between the Bund and the prewar orthodox Rightist movements. They are both revolutionary movements starting from the sense of alienation in man.[8]

To Shigeo Shima's mind, the primacy of the concept of alienation in the student movement was comparatively recent. In fact, its rise would correspond to that phase of the student movement which began in 1956 when Japan seemed to have emerged from its postwar crisis and to have entered the era (as Shima put it) of the "mass society." Before 1956, he said, "economic life was very bitter. It was hard for students to eat."[9] The various student actions against the so-called "Red purge," increases in tuition fees, visiting American lecturers, and involvement in the Korean war were all primarily inspired, though indirectly, by the misery of their material existence. "To eat, however, was no longer the main problem after 1956." The students began to enjoy unprecedented material prosperity as part of a Japanese "mass society." The Japanese "bureaucracy" itself became the primary enemy for the student movement; and it was after 1956, said Shima, that the theme of the Japanese student movement was the overcoming of alienation.

In those years Soviet students also began to discover the concept of alienation. It first appeared in Soviet philosophical literature, according to Father Joseph M. Bochenski, in 1958 by way of a review of a book by Jean Calvez on Marx, but its use in the official philosophical literature was "still slight."[10] In the spring of 1963, however, I found it to be the concept most provocative and illuminating to young Soviet graduate students and philosophers. One professor of philosophy at Moscow State University remarked to me, "They are interested in Marx when he was not yet a Marxist." Their critique of bourgeois society and philosophy was less in terms of the economic contradictions of capitalism than of its alienation of the spirit of man. To their readers was left the unspoken task of testing the achievement of Soviet society in the light of this universal concept, powerful because of its very vagueness.

Pyata P. Gaidenko, a gifted young philosopher at Moscow State University, for instance, contrasted Marx with the Western existentialists:

> This is the crux of Marxian criticism of capitalist society. Marx rebelled against capitalism because capitalism crushed the personality and converted it into a thing. . . . In contrast to Marx the existentialists believe that the alienated mode of being is rooted in the very nature of man. . . . In the world of commonplaces the individual lives conformingly; responsibility for his actions lies not with himself but with "one" (i.e., with them), for while living in such an environment man the individual is not free in his actions, but obeys certain laws, precepts, dicta of public opinion, etc. . . . But to be free, to be a person,

is far more difficult than to withdraw into a humdrum world where there is no need for the individual to make his own decisions, to be responsible to himself.[11]

Existentialism, says the writer, developed when the individual in the capitalist world became "aware of himself as something alien to this whole and even inimical to it."

How does the young Soviet student read such a passage? He recognizes in its description of the pressure of bureaucracy, public opinion, and impersonal institutions the analogue of what he has experienced in his life. The circumpressures of Komsomol, Party, and faculty committee, pervading the lecture halls and seminars where they make a tedium of the curricula in literature, philosophy, and history, imposing a party line on every essay he submits in every course, and requiring that he see things falsely and purvey hollow words that are not his own—of all this the young Soviet student is aware. Perforce he finds himself, therefore, a Soviet existentialist, a protestant against bureaucratic society with its estrangements.

The young Soviet students, to be sure, always criticize the bourgeois existentialist thinkers for failing to perceive the social sources of alienation in the bourgeois society. But the domain of applicability for concepts cannot be thus contained. The young Soviet readers value these writings, not for their routine refutations of the bourgeois existentialists, but for their portrayal of the experience of alienation itself. They have been given a word with which to convey their own discontent with the Bureaucratic Society. Fortunately, Marx himself used the word, a youthful Marx, unpublished and unread in the Stalinist era, but now exhumed by a later generation of youth speaking in indirect discourse of its own alienation from the bureaucratized Stalinist generation.[12]

The Emotive Appeal of "Alienation"

Thus the student movements today in the advanced countries confront a world which is both bureaucratic and stable. Whether in the United States, Japan, or the Soviet Union, they perceive a society dominated by large, impersonal institutions which impose the elders' norms of conformity. Hierarchy and impersonality loom as hostile, alien forces against the students whose way of life is still one of comradeship and personalism. The most cited student leaflet at the University of California, for instance, echoed in its title the protest against impersonal, mechanized institutions, "Are You a Student or an IBM Card?"[13] It told of the student depersonalized by institutions which determined his sleeping quarters, his studies, his life, and rendered him impotent. But the System, though hateful, is stable. Marx assailed the bourgeois society because of its "anarchy" of production. There is no anarchy, however, in the System.

Its equilibrating mechanisms, on the whole, work well; there are inefficiencies but evidently no "contradictions." The System achieves an equilibrium, even if not at a maximum level. The economic foundation of society seems relatively invulnerable to criticism; the students have as yet no basic changes to propose in the economic substructure. Theirs tended to be the "politics of the superstructure," the politics of the quality of life, of human relations, of civil rights, peace, and humanism.[14] The concept of alienation is the key to the critique of the superstructure, as the concept of exploitation was to the critique of the foundation. But the activists longed to convert their superstructural criticism into a foundation one.

It is the very ambiguity of the concept of alienation which lends itself to the Marxism of the student movement. In the thirties, when the depression was at its height, the students identified themselves with the protest of the workers against exploitation. "Exploitation" was a definable economic process, and measures were proposed to eliminate it. The exploiting persons and the devices of exploitation could be located; the bourgeois society seemed visibly founded on the exploitation of the lower classes. An alternative society was envisaged which would be classless, in which no men would exploit others. Surplus value would cease to be an economic category in a socialist society.

The new student movements, however, are utterly vague as to the society they propose. They are against the bureaucrats, but they scarcely know what to say when asked for the lineaments of the nonbureaucratic society. They find it more congenial to concentrate on specific issues, such as civil rights, peace and disarmament, or compulsory courses in military science. Indeed, at its revival in America, the student movement claimed to be "issue-oriented" and without an ideology.[15] Yet students soon felt that the "end of ideology" was precisely the ideology of the Establishment, of the Bureaucracy, of the Consensus, in which all basic issues of political philosophy were settled. Left and right for such people had merged into an all-inclusive center; such differences as remained for them were differences as to means, not as to ends. All shared a common vision or absence of one. The Bureaucratic Establishment was scientific and elitist; those who rose to the places of power were required to be competent in the administration of an advanced technological society. The Establishment could hardly be expected to show reverence for the people, proletariat or peasantry. As a scientific elite, the Bureaucratic Establishment was convinced that the techniques of applied sociology would suffice to resolve conflicts. Sociological science, not ideology, held the intellectual allegiance of the Academic Establishment.

"Scientific socialism" therefore lost its appeal for student activists precisely insofar as it was scientific. The new "socialism" such students professed would now be ethical and voluntaristic; the motive power of history, if they but chose, was not impersonal forces but their own personal will, not the indirect pervasive effect of economic pressures but their own direct action, their individual intervention. Every revolutionary generation reselects its Marxist passages and texts for its purposes. The new student generation found the forgotten texts of "alienation."

Above all, the notion of "alienation" is suited to express the varied moods of resentment of youth. For this resentment is not founded upon the students' place in the mode of production. The students of today are the most well-to-do in history—with a richness of scholarships, fellowships, and assistantships before them that no previous generation ever enjoyed. They often linger for many years in the status of graduate students because their lives are so comfortable. They marry and remarry and have families on their stipends, salaries, and subventions. Undergraduates often drive their own cars and are free from economic concern. This revolt, therefore, cannot be ascribed to economic goals. Students in the thirties who experienced generational resentment sublimated and translated it into concern with theirs and their fathers' economic problems. There was a kind of healing therapy in dealing with the economic problems of themselves and their society. But the new resentment is unable to attach itself to any central exploitation which it experiences. The aggressive energies of youth are frustrated in a well-ordered, well-to-do society. When an energy of discontent floats about aimlessly, unable to find an appropriate object, it requires an equally ambiguous word, equally devoid of any directional definition, to describe it; such a word is "alienation." Thus the early Marx provided the emotive symbol for idealistic students in generational revolt against the System. In effect, the new student movement is standing the mature Marx on his head, and the alternation of ideological generations persists, each trying to turn the Ideological Father topsy-turvy. The very vagueness of the concept of alienation thus makes it the most appropriate verbal vehicle for the younger-generational unconscious. Since the unconscious source of discontent is usually repressed, the young student activist feels a kind of nameless malaise. He is unable to focus or localize or define it clearly. The sense of alienation seems to diffuse through everything he does; it feels like a universal ether in which every act of his social existence takes place. And the word "alienation" is endlessly multi-potential with meanings corresponding to virtually every situation and relationship in which he may find himself.[16] Yet the motive energy for its every twist and turn is the underlying, unanalyzed sense of thwarted generational uprising. The son cannot describe the world in which he will lose the sense of alienation, but he knows he feels alienated from his father's world.

The use of the concept of alienation, furthermore, appeals to the sense of intellectual elitism in student movements. It therefore marks in this respect a regression in the history of Marxism, a reversion to the stage of "philosophical socialism"—when Marx looked to the intellectuals, not the workers, as the bearers of the great socialist renovation. When Marx and Engels began to view the workers as the historical class, they shifted the emphasis to "exploitation," not "alienation." The new student movements, however, as we have mentioned, have been arising at a time when societies are enjoying relatively full employment and affluence. The working-class movement is no longer a movement but an interest group which accepts the System; the trade union leaders are part of the Establishment. The concept of alienation expresses also the feeling of separation which the students insofar as they are intellectuals experience with regard to the society around them. They are rejected not only by the upper bureaucratic echelon and middle class but also by the workers. Hence, there arises a new vocabulary to express the lines of division in society; every bureaucrat has his beatnik, and the enemy is no class enemy but the "square."[17] One is embattled, not with the Ruling Class, but with the Establishment, which embraces the bureaucrats of all classes and strata, from financiers to union leaders. A historian of the beatniks writes in the language of the early Marx: "This is not the politically oriented alienation of the thirties. The present generation has . . . passed on beyond them to a total rejection of the whole society, and that, in present-day America, means the business civilization. The alienation of the hipsters from the squares is now complete. . . . [T]his is not just another alienation. It is a deepgoing change, a revolution under the ribs."[18]

A revolt against the bureaucrats of all classes, including those of labor, means that the traditional slogans of classical and Leninist Marxism can no longer stand muster. For Lenin was pre-eminently an admirer of Bureaucracy, Organization, System. The new student movement finds itself at odds with itself as it looks for an organizational form. It finds itself drawn to spontaneous, quickly mounted, guerrilla actions against the System, and it feels an admiration for guerrilla tactics, whether by Fidel Castro or Vietcong. Yet it has to seek a permanent form of organization, and the devil bureaucracy begins to intrude. Both in Tokyo and Berkeley, the student movements have been described as Blanquist in spirit and tactics.[19] The era of the Automatized Social System is curiously vulnerable to human assault at its weakest links of dehumanized control.

The alienation of the generations, the mainspring of student movements, involves an immense social tragedy. It brings a resurgence in action of hitherto unconscious impulses of destruction, of oneself and others. Student movements, as we have noted, have a propensity to veer from terrorism to suicidalism. We have seen that student movements tend to arise only in countries which have a youth-weighted suicide rate. Japan, with its recent influential student movement, as well as Tsarist Russia, exhibited this characteristic, whereas in "normal" countries such as Switzerland the older people have the higher suicide rates.[20] In Japan, the suicide rate from 1952 to 1954 for the ages from twenty to twenty-four years was 60 per 100,000, as compared to 27.4 in Austria and 25.4 in Denmark. "Suicide had become for youth in Japan the number one cause of death in individuals under 30." It was during the efflorescence of the Japanese student movement that the suicide rate for Japanese youth reached its highest proportions, "with the period between 1955 and 1960 showing the highest rates reported then for youth than at any other time in Japanese history."[21] Krupskaya, Lenin's wife, writing her article on suicide among the Russian studentry, had spoken of the alienation of the generations and the terrible psychological state of loneliness which afflicted the student.[22]

These phenomena of the alienation of generations stand remarkably outside the purview and concerns of historical materialism. The emphasis on "alienation" rather than "exploitation" involves, indeed, a vague feeling on the part of its users that a new conception of history must replace the materialist. The primacy of the mode of production and economic factors is displaced; historical materialism is put aside, and with it as well the notion of workingmen as the progressive, history-making class. The mature Marx wrote, "It is not the consciousness of men that determines their existence, but, on the contrary, their social existence determines their consciousness." The young Marx, however, could write, in Hegelian paraphrase, that history was constituted by man's consciousness transcending his existence; "as an act of coming-to-be it is a conscious self-transcending act of coming-to-be. History is the true natural history of man."[23] The emphasis on alienation, on man's trying to recover his essence, involves a notion of man's consciousness determining his existence. For if the materialistic conception of history were true, if men's psychologies were shaped as superstructural elements to conform to the requirements of the economic foundation, then no revolutionary social movements could arise. Of course, the very fact that a class becomes revolutionary, rejecting the presuppositions of the social system, constitutes evidence that the material base does not determine consciousness, that the ruling ideas of each age are not necessarily the ideas of its ruling class. Man, striving to realize his essence, regards the mode of production as an alienating agent insofar as it frustrates his inner aims; hence, in critical junctures he transcends the constraints of the mode of production.

The strivings of youth's generational struggle are, however, the chief example of the consciousness trying to overcome the constraints of the social system; thus, the consciousness of generational "alienation" seeks to determine its existence. The materialistic conception of history, in short, applies to those periods of human history in which man acquiesces to his alienations; but it breaks down precisely in the revolutionary eras when his consciousness transcends his material existence, and he becomes truly Promethean, more truly man. Thus, the standpoint of alienation leads to a conception of history which, if not idealistic, involves the primacy of emotional striving; as the driving force in social processes the repressed unconscious, seeking a conscious determining role, emerges as the primary activator of historical change. The modes of emotion, of consciousness, are the substance of history rather than the modes of technical production.

The Classical Marxists and Romantic Students

We can well understand, then, why mature Marxism was always suspicious of student movements. We have seen that Marx and Engels regarded students with suspicion and dislike. After a brief period of hope for the student movement, Lenin decided it offered no revolutionary possibilities. Marx, Engels, and Lenin all seemed to have sensed that the materialistic conception of history was belied by the younger-generation uprisings of idealistic students. Generational solidarity was a phenomenon which, unlike class solidarity, obviously required psychological categories. The philosophical-idealistic aims which aroused the self-sacrificial enthusiasm of students were far removed from the motives of economic self-interest expressed in class struggle. Student movements for Marx and Engels were an irrational intrusion in the historical movement toward a classless society. On the one hand, the students seemed to nurture their own ambitions as an elite in the socialist society, as emancipators of the proletariat who would be its new rulers; or, on the other hand, they were given to extremes of self-destruction and terrorism, to a politics of the absurd. Either alternative did violence to the materialistic conception of history.

The later socialist student movement too, such as it was, in Germany in 1890 aroused little enthusiasm in Engels. The students, he said, were arrogant young declassed bourgeois "arriving just in time to occupy most of the editorial positions on the new journals which pullulate and, as usual, they regard the bourgeois universities as a Socialist Staff College which gives them the right to enter the ranks of the Party with an officer's, if not a general's brevet." Engels ridiculed the "literati and the student revolt" with their "convulsively distorted 'Marxism.' " He had the same low opinion of them as he had had of the students of 1848, those "representatives of intellect" who "were the first to quit their standards, unless they were retained by the bestowal of officer's rank."[24] Most of the students who professed themselves revolutionary socialists impressed Marx and Engels as either careerist or corrupt. As for Lenin, we have seen how he began with hope in the student intelligentsia, but as time went on he lost both faith and interest in the student movement as a vehicle of social change and turned exclusively to the workers.[25]

For not only did the student movement fail to subordinate itself to the Bolshevik party as Lenin had hoped, but its very existence contravened historical materialism. Even at the height of his enthusiam for the student movement, Lenin objected to any analysis which emphasized the "unselfishness and purity of aims" of the student consciousness; this was a misleading idealistic interpretation of history, since "the students cannot be an exception to society as a whole, however unselfish, pure, idealistic, etc., they maye be."[26] Lenin, having made his own ultimate commitment when his youthful circle merged itself with the Social Democratic party, was tired of the perpetual drama of each student generation's experiencing its alienation, and he had no intention of seeing generational conflict imported into the Bolshevik faction. He could recall that, when he himself had been only twenty-five years old, he had already been regarded by a rival circle composed of Social Democratic students in St. Petersburg as one of the *stariki* (elders); the enemy faction called themselves *molodye* (young ones). To be an old man at twenty-five! Generational struggle could not be brooked in a Bolshevik party. Hence, Lenin became disenchanted with the "circle spirit" of the student movement. By 1908, he no longer professed to see in the student movement the replica of the class struggle in the nonstudent world.[27]

The Generational Division in Marxism: The Middle-Aged and the Young

The will to revolt, the Promethean impulse, is largely founded on generational protest. Modern revolutionary movements characteristically derive from a union of class and generational struggles. The conflict of generations, a universal theme, imparts to the class struggle aims which transcend those of economic class interest. When the Promethean impulse dies, it can bring a tremendous gloom to the young, who then veer further to self-destruction. Even Marx in his last years became downhearted as the dialectic of history seemed to enclose a fatality of decline to which he had hitherto been insensitive. In 1881 he was attracted to an essay by his friend and adviser, the eminent scientist, Edwin Ray Lankester, on "Degeneration," which questioned the "tacit assumption of universal progress—an unreasoning optimism," and reminded Victorian England "that we are subject to the general law of evolution, and are as likely to degenerate as to progress."[28] "Does the reason of the average man of civilised Europe," asked Lankster, "stand out clearly as an evidence of progress when compared with that of men of bygone ages? Are all the inventions and figments of human superstition and folly, the self-inflicted torturing of mind, the reiterated substitution of wrong for right, and of falsehood for truth, which disfigure our modern civilisation—are these evidences of progress? In such respects we have at least reason to fear that we may be degenerate." "With regard to ourselves, the white races of Europe," said Lankester, "the possibility of degeneration seems to be worth some consideration."[29] Such were the melancholy passages in Marx's mind toward the end of his life; they represented a complete reversal in spirit from the young student Marx enthralled with the vision of man's conquest of alienation. The aged Marx beheld rather an alien universe which would conquer man. The dialectical philosophy, with its eternal rebirth, had proved to be largely a generational projection, the ideology of student intellectuals projecting their eternal creative synthesis, the young destroying the old, and the world forever young. This was not a proletarian metaphysics, but a generational one, a restless, ever-questing romanticism, quite unlike proletarian modes of thought. The eternal student rebel expressed his generational alienation in a philosophical sense by portraying for himself a world which was in similar eternal revolt. Li Ta-chao, the librarian at the University of Peking who organized a small group of students in 1921 to found the Chinese Communist party, thus spoke in the metaphysical accents of the youth movement: "The Universe is eternal, hence youth is eternal, hence I am eternal."[30] The contemporary student activist has a similar metaphysics.

What has happened to Western Marxism today is a bifurcation into two ideologies—managerial middle-age and alienationist youth. Social theory, we might say, oscillates for the moment between the two extreme standpoints of the bureaucrat as against the beatnik, hippie, or guerrilla warrior. Managerial Marxism accepts the historical inevitability of a bureaucratized society; it perceives the hierarchy of new administrative skills as the basis for a new class structure, and refuses to be deceived by what it regards as myths and illusions about the creative capacity of the lower classes. It accepts economic planning, and believes it can reconcile liberal democracy with the leadership of an intellectual elite. It regards the residual anomie of people in our society as the necessary social cost for the unprecedented rise in our standard of living, and would even assert that this anomie or alienation has declined from its level in past societies. Alienational Marxism, on the other hand, refuses to be reconciled to bureaucratic society; it is voluntarist rather than determinist; it affirms the power of the individual will as against historical inevitability; it identifies itself with the lowliest in society in gesture, speech, clothes, and song; it finds a higher virtue in the Negro, or the Cuban, or the Chinese, than in the white American. It believes in its own direct action rather than in the processes of representative democracy. It is against the System, against the Establishment. It seeks a new mutuality in which there is no elite, for every elite involves a corresponding *rejeté*. When the "Free Speech" Movement won its "victory" at the University of California, its young activist participants could not bring themselves to disband. For several weeks in demonstrations, sit-ins, strikes, and vigils they had found a new political communion, and communion alone conquers the separateness and isolation of alienation. How then to perpetuate this communion? They circulated a leaflet, in the first week of January 1965, expressing this exhilaration and longing: "Happiness Is a Thing Called People . . . We've Discovered Each Other. We Don't Want to Lose Each Other. We're Having a People to People Rally."

This bifurcation in Marxism is something which was never anticipated. The analysts of industrial and managerial society inherit the scientific content and method of Marxism; the alienationists have exhumed its repressed ethical protest and revolutionary metaphysics. Here is a novel stage in the history of Marxism more profound in its significance than any of the revisionist heresies, and perhaps even the Leninist modifications; for it portends the duality in conflict of that next era of managerial, industrial society to which we are tending, the conflict between managers and managed, between the alienators and the alienated, finally founded on that between the fathers and sons. Here is an emerging schism in Marxism which is as universal as the dualities in human nature itself. The new student Marxism seems destined to remain restless and anarchic. The old Marxists knew what they meant when they proposed to expropriate the expropriators. But the new Marxists find themselves at a loss to explain how to achieve the alienation of the alienators. As the Primal Sons destroyed their Father, one of them took on the role anew. And soon one was middle-aged and part of the System himself.

Nihilism as Total Alienation

When alienation is total, it takes the form of nihilism, so that at times the ideology of student movements tends to reduce itself to nihilism. In the formative stages of student movements especially, before organizational patterns and slogans have been superimposed, the "nihilistic" motivation may characterize many activists. What is nihilism? We can define it most simply in generational terms: it asserts that whatever our fathers taught us is wrong. Nihilism is thus the pure form of the aggressive component in younger-generational revolutionary ideology: it states that the values, philosophies, attitudes transmitted to us, foundations of our cultural heritage, are basically at fault. In this sense, nihilism is anti-cultural, for if culture as Edward B. Tylor defined it is that "complex whole which includes knowledge, belief, art, morals, law, custom, and any other capabilities acquired by man as a member of society," the purport of nihilism is to negate this whole heritage in fundamental ways.[31] Nihilism shares no common ground with the spirit of scientific doubt, for it does not challenge specific items of the cultural heritage on the basis of new evidence. Rather, nihilism is characterized by a psychology of compulsive negation; it is a generational "No," the cultural equivalent of the primal parricide.

The merger of nihilism and idealism in student movements is never a real one, for they arise from contradictory emotions of hatred and love. "Beware the Nihilists!" was the title of a student article in November 1965 at Berkeley. It reported the recrudescence of nihilism in the deceptive guise of a higher ethical idealism:

In many ways this student generation is healthy and is free from many of the racial, sexual, class and cultural straitjackets of middle-class America. . . .

Yet intermingled with these healthy trends is a strong strain of sheer Nihilism. The Campus Left is crawling with Nihilists—who discharge their personal hostilities and frustrations beneath the mask of radical politics.

Haven't you seen the people who talk of "peace" and "non-violence" with hatred glowing in their eyes? Haven't you noticed that many who shout of "human brotherhood" are cool and calculating in their personal relations?

Haven't you seen the people who wear "free speech" buttons while they heckle, jeer and laugh at speakers with whom they disagree?

Haven't you noticed the people who talk of "civil rights" but hound any Negro as an "Uncle Tom" if he doesn't agree with their "militant" politics?

And haven't you seen people who scream insults and epithets at police, accusing the police of "police brutality" while they deliberately attempt to provoke the police into committing brutality?

You haven't seen them? Where have you been in the past few years?

These Nihilists pervert radicalism. Genuine radicals have aspirations, hopes and dreams. . . .

But the Nihilists are destructive for the sake of destruction . . . they are anti-American, anti-government, anti-liberal, anti-moderate, anti-Peace Corps, anti-University.

They attack the "Establishment," whether L.B.J. or the University—simply because it is an establishment, simply because it is authority. American institutions are attacked as tyrannical and University rules on speech as "atrocities" but the Nihilists never mention the slaughter of Hungarians by the Soviet Union or the "thought control" in Communist China.[32]

What runs through the nihilistic attitudes and gives them a pervasive continuity which they otherwise would lack is precisely their expression of total generational revolt. The fathers favor a policy of war in Vietnam; therefore, the rebellious sons are for peace. The fathers criticize the Communists; therefore, the sons refuse to criticize the Communists. The "brotherhood" the nihilist seeks is one against the father, and the "hatred" which the student writer perceived glowing in their eyes was in its primal source father-hatred. The ideological language was that of idealism and love; the underlying, impelling unconscious reality was a longing to destroy the father and all associated with him.

The Manifesto: The Literary Form of Student Alienation and Protest

The typical form of student protest literature is the *manifesto,* and its typical language is *manifestese.* Ivan Maisky, the former Soviet Ambassador to Britain, tells of an incident which has since repeated itself thousands of times in student circles. One day a friend of his said, "We must issue a manifesto!" "All right," replied Ivan, "let's issue one." Then Maisky adds,

"I did not know what a manifesto meant, but thought it better not to show my ignorance."[33] What, then, is a manifesto? It is a bill of grievances of the younger generation against the older. Its tone is always one of righteous indignation. It depicts the pure and ethical persons being crushed by a cruel, sadistic authority. It is filled with a sense of history, but only in its futuristic aspect; we the uncorrupted, it says, represent the future. There is even the sense that with us history only begins, that all which has preceded is only prehistory, or the sense that a new claim for the making of history has emerged. The making of history is a curious obsessive goal for student movements; not the pursuit of happiness but the pursuit of a role in history is their aim. Thus, the Berkeley student leader wrote in 1964, "The bureaucrats hold history as ended. As a result, significant parts of the population both on campus and off are dispossessed, and these dispossessed are not about to accept this a-historical point of view." "As bureaucrat, an administrator believes that nothing new happens. He occupies an a-historical point of view."

It is characteristic of the manifesto that it pictures the society as dehumanizing (even castrating) the suffering young; all society, from Mississippi to California, is seen as sharing in this plot against youth:

> In our free speech fight at the University of California, we have come up against what may emerge as the greatest problem of our nation—depersonalized, unresponsive bureaucracy. We have encountered the organized status quo in Mississippi, but it is the same in Berkeley.
>
> The two battlefields may seem quite different to some observers, but this is not the case. . . . In California, the privileged minority manipulates the University bureaucracy to suppress the students' political expression. That respectable "bureaucracy" masks the financial plutocrats; that impersonal bureaucracy is the efficient enemy in a "Brave New World."

Always the manifesto attacks those who find it possible to pursue their life's work in the system. It is the mark of generational purity that it must reject the System.[34] All manifestoes attack the "careerist"; he is the son who is relatively exempt from generational resentment, or who has known how to sublimate his generational drives along constructive lines of scientific or objective achievement:

> The "futures" and "careers" for which American students now prepare are for the most part intellectual and moral wastelands. This chrome-plated consumers paradise would have us grow up to be well-behaved children. But an important minority of men and women coming to the front today have shown that they will die rather than be standardized, replaceable and irrelevant.
>
> They are people who have not learned to compromise. . . . And they find at one point or other that for them to become part of society, to become lawyers, ministers, business men, people in government, that very often they must compromise those principles which were most dear to them. They must suppress the most creative impulses that they have; this is a prior condition for being part of the system.[35]

The language of manifestoes is always apocalyptic. The young are rising up to destroy the old. Each manifesto believes its emotion and aspiration to be new. Actually, it is a repetitive form of literature, as repetitive in its themes and metaphors as the cycles of generational revolt.

The Berkeley manifesto, with its depiction of the university, alma mater, betrayed by an impersonal administration, and to be rescued by the young son, was interchangeable in spirit and metaphor with the manifestoes of the St. Petersburg students in 1899:

> We know now what our universities are and what they should be. The university is not the temple of learning, nor is it served by its professors; the students are not citizens but schoolboys. The University is a Government Department, the professors its officials, and the chiefs of the university Sonin and Co. [like Kerr and Co.]. How can one go further? Comrades! And they have cut off more of us recently. From our ranks they are tearing away even the illusion of free learning with which the Russian studentry has lived up to now, hoping to see the dawn of true learning. But as they take away the illusion, they intend to give us not free learning which ennobles, teaches, and prepares for critical thinking, but only as much as will enable us to produce petty "serious minds." . . .
>
> Brothers, let us clasp each other's hands, and conclude that union of friendship of all young and old citizens who are oppressed by the eternal burden of despotism . . .[36]

A manifesto is something more than a statement of principles, program, or policy. It aims to make manifest an emotion which has hitherto been held in abeyance. It is a generational document because it announces the young emerging to dethrone the old. It is this stylistic quality of generational uprising which is the common property of all manifestoes, of literary movements, artistic ones, and political. The old are wrong, the young are right; the old are corrupt, the young are pure; the old have done a bad job with history, the young will succeed; tradition's chains must be unbound, a new society must be forged; the lifeless and obsolete will be replaced by the fresh and living. Such is the language of the generational dialectic, the vision of history in which the young rule because they are the noblest in heart.

Thus, a remarkable uniformity prevails in the anonymous leaflets and manifestoes of all student movements. Because they are all documents of generational struggle, they have a common quality, common emotion, and common metaphors. No matter whether they were composed in Russia in 1900, Germany in 1818, or America in 1965, they are oddly interchangeable. Take the additional following leaflets, for instance, of the year 1899 in the Russian student movement.

> From the Students of the Kiev Union
>
> Comrades! Since the time when we rushed forward into the struggle for freedom and for the inviolability of one's person, we have received countless proofs

of the same savage arbitrariness against which we rose like one man on that memorable February 17th.

Now we have again a lot of facts which are no less important than those of February 8th; from these we shall quote briefly.

1.—The shocking punishment of our comrades by our university heads in their most corrupt union with the police, a punishment the more shocking because their coarse hands were laid chiefly on that element without rights on which accusations are showered in order to hide the true significance and meaning of facts.

2.—The Bartholomew night perpetrated by the glorious General Novitsky (150 comrades are in prison).

3.—The savage violence of the police towards our Riga comrades.

4.—The revolting handling in prison which led our Moscow comrade to burn himself.

5.—Exile and the mass arrests in all universities.

6.—The whole series of suicides and poisonings caused by the wild bacchanalia of the heads, etc.

Comrades! Don't these facts tell us clearly enough that we must act now, or still better, what we should do now? Do those few careerists confuse us, those few careerists who could not resist the temptation of passing their exams easily, and who stifled the voice of their conscience. Let us forget for a time at least our own personal matters and petty interests! For the last time we call on you comrades to stand up to the end for our holy cause like all our other comrades.[37]

Then again the Proclamation of March 23, 1899, signed by "The Second Replacement of the Organizational Committee."

The Second Replacement of the Organizational Committee believes that now, at the critical moment of the struggle, at a moment when all petty egoistic feelings have to give way to the feeling of duty and solidarity,—the studentry unites even more closely and in friendship, and will strive unanimously to attain the designated goal,—seeing the assurance for its successful achievement in the fact that all fellow students without exception have returned.

And, lastly, from the leaflet "About Solidarity," published by a grouping of St. Petersburg students, the General Union of Sponsors:

During all the time of the movement the word "solidarity" has been pronounced quite often.

Notwithstanding the fact that our movement did not have the character of a military solidarity . . . everybody will act together, not waiting for anyone else, and each university will carry through the movement.

Through these leaflets of the Russian student movement run certain characteristic themes—the cruel violence of the police, the treachery of the university administration, the mass punishment of students, the immorality or moral inferiority of the older generation, the self-immolation of students, the humiliations and callous brutality in prison, the holiness of the student cause, the contempt for student careerists concerned solely with their studies, the overcoming of egoism, the achievement of student solidarity.

At Berkeley, California, the hundreds of leaflets published in 1964–1965 all had the same themes. A Russian student of 1899 could have used the Berkeleyan leaflets with only the most minor changes, yet the one student movement was embattled with Czarist absolutism, and the second was assailing a liberal university administration. That the latter would use language as desperate and vitriolic as the first shows how the inner emotional demands of generational revolt impose common categories and a common intensity on situations which differ so enormously in objective fact. The emotion of generational revolt does its own defining of the situation so categorically that it perceives a liberal American university president as its predecessors did the Russian Czar.

A few extracts from the Berkeleyan leaflets will indicate the community of emotional themes in generational revolt. A leaflet of December 3, 1965:

It Is Happening Now

In the middle of the night, the police began dragging 800 of your fellow students from Sproul Hall. Sproul Hall was turned into a booking station; the University has become an armed camp—armed against its own students.

Why did the students have to protest? And why is the Administration using Police force to break a protest that could have been peacefully settled? The Administration brought about this confrontation. The initiation of disciplinary action against FSM leaders directly attacked and challenged the FSM; it flagrantly violated the spirit of the specially delegated faculty voice. Now the police have taken over. Instead of recognizing the legitimacy of the students' demands, the administration is attempting to destroy the FSM. Five police forces are being used; exorbitant bail ($800–$1400) has been set. The administration position is clear. It is saying "We decide what is acceptable freedom of speech on this campus. Those who disagree will be ignored; when they can no longer be ignored, they will be destroyed."

We have not been defeated by the University's troops. Our protest will continue until the justice of our cause is acknowledged. You must take a stand now! No longer can the faculty attempt to mediate from the outskirts of the crowd. No longer can students on this campus afford to accept humbly administrative fiat. Raise your voice now!

WE SHALL OVERCOME

On December 2 the Strike Committee of the Graduate Coordinating Committee had published a leaflet:

Why Strike?

Because we must strike back in self-defense—in defense of our leaders, of our various organizations, of our constitutional rights.

Chancellor Strong has started disciplinary proceedings, against 3 FSM leaders: Mario Savio, Art Goldberg and Jackie Goldberg. . . .

The move against the leaders is based solely upon their role in helping direct the defense of free speech on this campus. It is a vengeful act of political persecution. Otherwise, why have not the scores of other students who engaged in acts identical to those for which the three have been nominally cited also been threatened with disciplinary action? . . .

Its intent is thus crystal clear: to expel the leaders, cripple the organizations and thus destroy through administrative force the movement whose defense of students' constitutional liberties could not be overcome in debate or in the arena of public opinion. The Chancellor has struck a new and more antagonistic posture. . . .

We cannot cooperate in the illusion that the educational process can proceed unscathed and blithely unaware as students rights are being infringed and student leaders and organizations persecuted right outside the classroom. . . .

We are a large and potentially powerful student body. If we act together we CAN defend ourselves and our rights, and end the tradition of administrative autocracy which has become a major impediment to serious education in this university.

The Berkeley leaflets assailing a liberal university administration strangely echo those of the Russians attacking Czarist absolutism more than sixty years earlier. The police have been brutal to your fellow-students. The university heads are corrupt and in active collusion with the police. An atrocity toward the students has been committed in the middle of the night. The student cause is a sacred, righteous one on behalf of constitutional liberties. The university is an autocracy which makes education impossible. The students' leaders and organizations are being arbitrarily persecuted. Students must all stand together in solidarity.

Thus, refracted through lenses of generational revolt, through categories imposed on reality, two different historical situations, so wholly unlike, were perceived and reported in words and images largely identical. Indeed, one would think from reading the students' leaflets that the Berkeley campus was an American version of the Russian universities of Czarist times, that students' socialist and Communist clubs had been denied the freedom of assembly and speech and choice of speakers. Quite the opposite was the case, so much so that the preceding year (as we have seen) the university had received the Alexander Meiklejohn award for its achievement in civil liberties from the American Association of University Professors.

The Mythological Ingredient in Student Ideology

The ideology of the student movement has always combined mythology with social science. The theme of alienation is the latest form of this amalgam of myth and science. In its mythological aspect it is the last successor to the myths of the birth of the hero. There has been a whole cycle of such myths, as Otto Rank noted, with heroes such as Sargon, Moses, Karna, Oedipus, Gilgamesh, Cyrus, Hercules, Jesus, Siegfried.

These myths have invariant traits. They justify the hero for his rebellion, for his revolt against the father. Moses as a hero, for instance, was alienated from the bureaucratic Egyptian society against which he led the direct action of the slaves' secession. In myth, the father tyrant tries to destroy the son by exposing him to danger; the son, however, is rescued by some intervener. The murderous attempt by the tyrant excuses the revolt of the son. "In the original psychological setting, the father is still identical with the king, the tyrannical persecutor." Finally, the son's revolt is successful. The myth, according to Rank, has an egotistical, paranoid structure. It culminates in the son's exaltation when he can say, "I am the emperor." "All he accomplishes thereby is to put himself in the place of the father. . . ." The first heroic act in history was thus the revolt against the father, and the various myths celebrated the trials and triumph of the son.[38] Indeed, wrote Rank, "every revolutionary is originally a disobedient son, a rebel against the father." To this latter generalization we cannot agree. Class struggles, nationalist struggles, ethnic struggles, are not reducible to generational struggle. But in student movements, where the theme of generational struggle is paramount, where strong unconscious forces are at work, the mythopoeic urge creates the myth of the heroic rebellion of the son against the Cruel, Sadistic, Impersonal Father who would have castrated, killed, or depersonalized him.

This mythopoeic urge, common to all movements of generational revolt, was repeatedly and spontaneously in evidence in the speeches and writings of the Berkeley activists of 1964–1965. The cruel administration was cast in the role of the heartless tyrant aiming to "castrate" his son. We may cite some examples. A leaflet of April 23, 1965:

> The continuing crisis on campus is due to gross and vindictive misadministration. The rights of students have continually been abused. We can no longer tolerate such treatment. *The Regents Have Gone Too Far!*
>
> The University obscenity hearings were obscene in their vulgar parody of due process. . . .
>
> This series of attempts to *castrate* [italic mine] the legitimate efforts of students to obtain control over their own lives has made it clear who our enemies are. . . .
>
> Rally Today * Sproul Steps * Freedom Singers * Noon

The cruel administration as aiming to mutilate, to depersonalize the student was the theme of the leading article in the *FSM Newsletter*, No. 5, of December 10, 1964, written directly after the students had achieved what they regarded as victory. The exposure of the students by the administration to the cruel police became in the new myth the equivalent of the "exposure" theme in classical hero myths. But the students with their secret source of power triumphed, as Hercules did, over the father's evil agencies. This leaflet compared the source of the administration's power with that of the student activists:

The source of their power is clear enough: the guns and clubs of the Highway Patrol, the banks and corporations of the Regents. But what is the source of our power?

It is something we see everywhere on campus but find hard to define. Perhaps it was best expressed by the sign one boy pinned to his chest: "I am a U.C. student. Please don't bend, fold, spindle, or mutilate me." The source of our strength is, very simply, the fact that we are human beings and so cannot forever be treated as raw materials—to be processed. Clark Kerr has declared, in his writings and by his conduct, that a university must be like any other factory—a place where workers who handle raw material are themselves handled like raw material by the administrators above them. Kerr is confident that in his utopia "there will not be any revolt, anyway, except little bureaucratic revolts that can be handled piecemeal."

As President of one of the greatest Universities in the world, one which is considered to lie on the "cutting edge of progress," Kerr hopes to be able to make U.C. a model to be proudly presented for the consideration of even higher authorities.

By our action, we have proved Kerr wrong in his claim that human beings can be handled like raw material without provoking revolt. We have smashed to bits his pretty little doll house. The next task will be to build in its stead a real house for real people.

The students, collective sons of alma mater, experienced a new sense of brotherhood when the chancellor of the university, the father figure of the campus, was forced to leave as a consequence of the student uprising. They sang of the revolt explicitly as a conflict of generations. In one song, the chancellor was an old man resentful of the growing strength of the children:

I WALKED OUT IN BERKELEY
(Tune: *Streets of Laredo*)

As I was out walking one morning in Berkeley,
As I walked out in Berkeley one day
I spied an old man all sad and dejected
His hands they were shaking, his hair it was gray.

"I see by your books, boy, that you are a student
Come sit down beside me and hear my sad story."
He then shook his head and he gave a deep sigh.

"It is here on the campus that I am the Chancellor
I push the buttons and run the whole show,
These are my children but now they're ungrateful
They think they are adults, they think they are grown.

"Can you hear them shouting and screaming and singing?
They think they're so smart and they think they're so strong
They want to make speeches but never say nice things,
But they're only students so they're in the wrong."[39]

In another song, the mythopoeic urge reached to the proto-myth of the student destroying the president-father so that he could have the mother. The university in fantasy became the "womb" which the students were capturing from the father, and the university president was the father who still wished to diaper the student and keep him sexually immature:

WOMB WITH A VIEW

I said to my mama, I'm going down town
She said looky here son, Why do you put me down?
I'll send you to a place where they love you like me
Gonna send you to Berkeley, to the University.
Chorus: Where it's warm (pretty pretty, and oh so warm)
People there love you like a mama would do
And it's oooo, pretty pretty, it's a womb with a view.

So I packed up my clothes, put on my hat,
I asked a policeman where is Berkeley at,
He said, "That's in California where the livin' is fine,
With lots of pretty women you can ball all the time."

I walked up to Mr. Kerr with my hat in my hand,
I says, "Sir, won't you let me be a college man?"
He looked me in the eye, he patted my head,
He changed my diaper and here's what he said. . . .

What is a hero in the regard of the youthful unconscious? "A hero is a man who stands up manfully against his father and in the end victoriously overcomes him," wrote Freud.[40] The heroism of miners, pioneers, seamen, railwaymen, builders is of a different order; the struggle with the material environment, with a hostile nature, for the sake of one's survival, livelihood, or the advancement of human knowledge, calls on all one's resources, and makes obsolete and irrelevant one's conflicts with one's father. Perhaps in the normal rhythm of life, the struggle for existence is the therapy for generational conflict. If all one's aggressive energies are needed in the struggle for existence, one is not going to waste valuable energy in fighting one's father, in his real or surrogate form. But a student movement arises in what is biologically an abnormal setting. Large numbers of vigorous youth, often enjoying the securities of bourgeois existence, with all their "free-floating" aggressive energies seeking an outlet, a cause, congregate in the universities. Once there was no need for "causes" because the struggle for life, for physical survival, was the task assigned by existence itself. A "cause" is needed partially as a substitute for the struggle for existence. In prolonged adolescence, childhood and adolescent conflicts continue to hold the stage. So the Berkeley student activists sang of their revolt against "paternalism," the institutionalized rule of the father:

WE DON'T WANT
YOUR KIND PROTECTION

We don't want your kind protection
Of our young and tender brains,
All we want is a chance to think freely
Give us back our rights again.

As sons revolting against their fathers' middle-class ways, they rejected their fathers' cleanliness and physical neatness. They wore the garments of the generational hero:

HEY, MR. NEWSMAN

Yes, my hair is long, and I haven't shaved in days,
But fighting for my freedom
While clean-cut kids just look the other way.

Hey, Mr. Newsman, Abe Lincoln, he had long hair too
Or did you want Abe Lincoln
Would have a crewcut just like you?

In classical myths, when the tyrant father "exposes" the child to its death, as the Pharaoh did when he commanded the death of the newborn Moses, there generally appears an adopting father, usually of the lower classes, a shepherd, or a slave, who succors the abandoned child and raises it as his own, with his philosophy and religion. Thus it was too that the mythopoeic urge set the Berkeley students to finding for themselves loving adopting fathers who would replace the cruel administrative ones. It was after the events of December 1964 that the student activists sought to find themselves a new father to fill in their minds the now empty place of intellectual and moral authority. They had listened in the preceding months to some middle-aged figures, an array of defeated revolutionists and campus mountebanks, but their messages were the stale ones of a previous generation. They began to invite fresh voices to the campus, to listen to their messages. One such, for instance, in the aftermath of the December events, was writer Paul Goodman, fifty-four years old, but not a radical of the thirties, whose authority was invoked in a leaflet of the Free Speech Movement entitled *We Want a University: Dedicated to the 800.* ("The 800" alluded to those arrested in the "sit-in" in Sproul Hall on December 2, 1964): "At present in the United States, students—middle class youth—are the major exploited class. . . . Then it is not surprising if they organize their CIO."

Student activists were pleased and flattered to read that they were the most exploited class in America. No matter that the statement flew in the face of social reality; it fulfilled the function of a neo-parental blessing. For the mythopoeic urge in generational revolt is strong, confusing its illusion with reality, and then drawing the consequences in action of its will to illusion.

Middle-Aged Seekers of Student Movements: From Plato to Paul Goodman

To student movements there have always been attracted middle-aged "alienated" persons seeking in youth the redeemers from their own tragic alienation. The elderly would-be leaders of student youth are a melancholy recurrent type in the history of mankind. Plato was the greatest of them. Plato's yearning for power on behalf of the intellectuals, and his conception of the academy as a base for exercising political power, was indeed the outcome of a conjunction of "alienations." As the distinguished legal scholar, Hans Kelsen, states, "Because he [Plato] could not attain leadership in the state, he founded a school; and thus the school became for him a substitute for the state."[41] There was, moreover, as Kelsen emphasizes, in Plato's case a direct relationship between his political ideology and his homosexuality, "an inner connection between the Platonic Eros and his will to power over men, between his erotic and his pedagogic-political passion."[42] A sense of guilt and estrangement from Athenian society was a consequence of his homosexuality; it limited his availability for political life, for public opinion was largely hostile to the deviant sexuality of Plato's circle.[43] Plato wondered in the *Gorgias* whether it would be his fate to "creep into a corner for the rest of my life, and talk in a whisper with three or four admiring youths." His whole political philosophy exalted the right of the philosopher-teacher to rule, for the latter alone possessed knowledge, virtue. And his conception of the teacher had its homosexual vector; the Platonic teacher, we might say, is a "psychological imperialist"; he needs disciples; he must be a student leader, for, in Kelsen's words, "the urge to dominate is already in Socrates' manner of loving youth, most deeply hidden away." "The wise lover," says Socrates, "seeks to win his beloved youth, and then to praise him." The Platonic search for political power through the action of philosopher-disciples was in this curious way a political ideology of homosexuality.

Strangely enough, this motivation on the part of middle-aged would-be student leaders reappeared in the American student movement of the mid-sixties. On many campuses, the most sought-after spokesman of discontent was indeed Paul Goodman, who had become well known after the publication of *Growing Up Absurd.* Goodman had taken no part thirty years earlier in the student politics of his class of 1931 at the City College of New York; his aestheticism and homosexuality were alien to the working-class students of that college, who found him unreal and irrelevant. As with Plato, the tragedy of the aging homosexual became acute, and this was indeed Goodman's meaning of "absurd": "My social existence is absurd. In God's creation I'm a kind of juvenile delinquent, a kind of Manfred." The symbolic use of Manfred, beset by guilt and torment, we have seen before in the annals of the student movement (as in Ivan Maisky's recollections). Goodman, quoting rabbinical sources, felt the guilt of his homosexual status, and its sordidness, as he grew older: "My disadvantages are so many—I am not young, not atrractive." He felt exploited: "A 'minority' exists because of a psychic boundary. . . ."[44] Seeking desperately for recognition, he projected his bitterness as an "absurd" homosexual into a presumed "absurdity" of the American student, the American youth. His classification of American society, the Organized System as against the Independents, was indeed a perspective of America from a homosexual's standpoint. The System, from workers to managers, had alienated him so that he stood outside it; not class or status or racial struggle, but his own psychic struggle constituted the substance of his social reality, so that the other groupings coalesced into the persecuting Organized System. From time to time the projection's source became overt. In a televised discussion with Stokely Carmichael and others on violence in July 1967, for instance, when the whole question of racial violence was on America's mind, Goodman could find nothing to contribute except to dwell on the humiliations and resentments of the homosexual. He had made something of a cult of violence himself by admiring the juvenile delinquent: "A band of kids decide it would be bully to remove the blocks and set a huge truck in motion downhill, resulting in $10,000 worth of damage. But of course it *is* bully (I think so)."[45] Thus he struggled to be "manly" (his favorite adjective). And American activists were taken by his attack on the System, and his flattery of them as "the major exploited class" in America.[46] Goodman in turn went from campus to campus, seeking disciples as a "psychological imperialist," a curious symbiosis with the pathological element in the student movement. His existentialist philosophy made much of not treating the human subject as an object. But the whole situation of the aging homosexual, as Hans Kelsen indicated of Plato, was the pathetic one, of his alternately seeking dominance over youth, and then humbling himself abjectly before them, treating the subject as object sadistically and then asking masochistically to be treated as object himself; such was the tragic vocation of the middle-aged student leader. In no one was it more poignantly exemplified than in the life of the greatest nineteenth-century Russian revolutionist, Michael Bakunin.

Probably the most revered of names in the Russian student movement of the nineteenth century was that of the anarchist Michael Bakunin. Unlike Marx, Bakunin cultivated the revolutionary students, looking to them to lead the "uncivilized" peasant to triumph. He became a legendary figure among the students. When toward the end of his life, in his midfifties, he visited the Russian student circle in Zurich, "All at once fell silent. The eyes of all were involuntarily riveted on Bakunin. . . . The attention of all present was fixed on him. . . . Not only at his table was there a solemn, rather obsequious, silence. . . ."[47]

The middle-aged Bakunin was susceptible to the emotional contagion of student movements; it brought him political and personal tragedy, and contributed to the collapse of the International Workingmen's Association. Bakunin was utterly deceived (as we have seen) and misled into grotesque and grandiose schemes by the most unscrupulous student leader of all time, Sergei Nechayev. As Avrahm Yarmolinsky says, the young man "exercised a strange ascendancy over the shaggy giant." This famed revolutionist, whose sexual impotence was the subject of gossip among his comrades, gave to Nechayev, as presumable representative of a putative Russian Revolutionary Committee, a token of his "complete submission" which he signed "Matryona" (a woman's name, derivative from the word for mother).[48] Bakunin, as E. H. Carr writes, was "infatuated at first sight" with Nechayev. The infamous *Catechism of the Revolutionist*, which he wrote while under this emotional enthrallment, is the classical document of the professional revolutionist, of the man who from student days on experiences the need for re-enactment of his revolt against the elders. The revolutionist is fixated in the neurosis and guilt of the permanent student activist, but he dares not probe the unconscious source of this guilt: "The revolutionist is a doomed man. He has no personal interests, no affairs, sentiments, attachments, property, not even a name of his own. Everything in him is absorbed by one exclusive interest, one thought, one passion—the revolution. . . . Day and night he must have one thought, one aim—inexorable destruction."[49] Student circles thrilled to the psychology of the "doomed man." They empathized with a guilt so isomorphic with their own, and with the drive to "destruction" of themselves as well as others. "At fifty," wrote Bakunin's friend Herzen, "he [Bakunin] was still the same wandering student,—the same homeless Bohemian, craving nothing for the morrow . . . borrowing indiscriminately . . . with the same simplicity with which children take from their parents and never think of repayment. . . ." This fifty-year-old "wandering student"—that is, nonstudent—was a prototype for a whole species. At any rate, in the homosexual-power needs of this human variety from Plato to Bakunin and Paul Goodman, one discerns the unconscious source of the fixated "nonstudent" activist.[49]

Conclusion

What, then, is the upshot of our discussion?

The conflict of generations is a universal theme in history; it is founded on the most primordial facts of human nature, and it is a driving force of history, perhaps even more ultimate than that of class struggle. Yet its intensity fluctuates. Under fortunate circumstances, it may be resolved within a generational equilibrium. Under less happy circumstances, it becomes bitter, unyielding, angry, violent; this is what takes place when the elder generation, through some presumable historical failure, has become de-authoritized in the eyes of the young.

Every student movement is the outcome of a de-authoritization of the elder generation. This process can take place in small colleges as well as impersonal universities, in industrialized countries as well as underdeveloped ones, in socialist as well as capitalist ones.

Thus student movements have emerged in small, provincial German universities, in urban Russian institutions, and in Chinese schools of all varieties. They have flourished alike among the children of arisocrats and the middle classes, but less so among the sons of the working class. Student activists in different historical circumstances have tended to come from the most diverse fields of study: they were young theologians in the Germany of 1817, they were enthusiasts for natural science in Russia in 1874, they were social scientists in Asia and Africa in our time. Certain subjects in different historical circumstances were the ones in which generational conflict could define itself most clearly. Thomas Hobbes in the middle of the seventeenth century felt that the study of the classics in the universities was undermining the political order because students were "furnished with arguments for liberty out of the works of Aristotle, Plato, Cicero, Seneca, and out of the histories of Rome and Greece, for their disputation against the necessary power of their sovereigns."[50] Therefore he despaired "of any lasting peace among ourselves" until the universities desisted from teaching subversive subjects or ideas, and presumably occupied themselves with natural science and materialistic philosophy such as his own.

Student movements have been the chief expression of generational conflict in modern history. As intellectual elites of the younger generation, they have had their special ethic of redemption, self-sacrifice, and identification. They have attained the greatest heights of idealistic emotion even as they have been enthralled by compulsions to destruction.

These student movements are more than an episode in the "modernization" of developing nations, for they can affect advanced industrial societies as well as traditional or transitional ones. They arise wherever social and historical circumstances combine to cause a crisis in loss of generational confidence, which impels the young to resentment and uprising. Student movements have arisen in recent years in "underdeveloped countries" because generational disequilibrium is likely to arise in traditional societies which are sustaining the impact of advanced ideas. At the same time, student movements are likely to arise in advanced industrial, prosperous societies precisely because such societies do not afford environments with real, objective tasks, material challenges to youthful, aggressive energies. America in the nineteenth century was changing rapidly; it was neither in a class nor an economic equilibrium; it was, however, in a generational equilibrium. Rapid social change in and of itself does not necessarily involve student unrest.

We have tried to unravel the nature of political idealism, the complex of emotions of love, destruction, self-sacrifice, and nihilism on which it is founded. The unconscious ingredient of generational revolt in the students' idealism has tended to shape decisively their political expression. We have tried to bring to consciousness what otherwise are unconscious processes of history. That has been the whole purpose in our use of the psycho-historical method—to help defeat the cunning of history which has so often misused the idealistic emotions. With a melancholy uniformity, the historical record shows plainly how time and again the students' most idealistic movement has converted itself into a blind, irrational power hostile to liberal democratic values. Yet we refuse to accept a sociological determinism which would make this pattern into the fatality of all student idealism. Our working hypothesis is that knowledge can contribute to wisdom. When students perceive the historical defeat which has dogged their youthful hubris, they may perhaps be the more enabled to cope with irrational demonry; they may then make their political idealism into an even nobler historical force.

For student movements have thus far been too largely an example of what we might call *projective politics,* in the sense that they have been largely dominated by unconscious drives; the will to revolt against the de-authoritized father has evolved into a variety of patterns of political action. This hegemony of the unconscious has differentiated student movements from the more familiar ones of class and interest groups. The latter are usually conscious of their psychological sources and aims, whether they be material economic interests or enhanced prestige and power. Student movements, on the other hand, manifest a deep resistance to the psychological analysis of their emotional mainspring; they wish to keep unconscious the origins of their generational revolt. A politics of the unconscious carries with it untold dangers for the future of civilization. We have seen the students Karl Sand and Gavrilo Princip adding their irrational vector to deflect the peaceful evolution of a liberal Europe; we have seen the Russian students helping to stifle the first possibilities of a liberal constitution; we have seen the American student movement in its blind alley of the Oxford Pledge and its later pro-Soviet immolation. All these were fruits of the politics of the unconscious. It is only by persisting in the understanding of these unconscious determinants that we can hope to see a higher wisdom in human affairs.

Guilt feelings fused with altruistic emotions have led students to seek a "back to the people" identification. In Joseph Conrad's novel, the guilt-tormented Lord Jim could conquer his guilt only by merging his self in the most romantic dedication to an alien, impoverished, exploited people. The aged ex-revolutionist Stein saw Jim's salvation rendered possible only by his immersing himself in the "destructive element"; thereby, guilt was assuaged. And since it is guilt which assails the sense of one's existence with the reproaches of one's conscience, it is by the conquest of guilt in a higher self-sacrifice that one recovers the conviction of one's existence. In a sense, every student seeking to merge himself with peasant, proletarian, the Negro, the poor, the alien race has had something of the Lord Jim psychology. His guilt is that of his generational revolt, his would-be parricide. He can conquer this guilt only with the demonstration that he is selfless and by winning the comforting maternal love of the oppressed; they bring him the assurance of his needed place in the universe. To reduce this determinism of unconscious guilt has been one purpose of this study. For only thus can we isolate and counteract the ingredient of self-destruction.

When generational struggle grows most intense, it gives rise to generational theories of truth. Protagorean relativism is translated into generational terms; only youth, uncorrupted, is held to perceive the truth, and the generation becomes the measure of all things. This generational relativism in the sixties is the counterpart of the class relativism which flourished in the thirties; where once it was said that only the proletariat had an instinctive grasp of sociological truth, now it is said that only those under thirty, or twenty-five, or twenty, are thus privileged. It would be pointless to repeat the philosophical criticisms of relativist ideology. This generational doctrine is an ideology insofar as it expresses a "false consciousness"; it issues from unconscious motives of generational uprising, projects its youthful longings onto the nature of the cosmos, sociological reality, and sociological knowledge, but represses precisely those facts of self-destruction and self-defeat which we have documented. Moreover, the majority of studentries have usually been at odds with the student activists, whose emotional compulsions to generational revolt they do not share. The engineering and working-class students, who so often have been immune to the revolt-ardor of middle-class humanistic students, stand as dissenters to the doctrine of generational privilege. They have held more fast their sense of reality, whereas the literary-minded have seen reality through a mist of fantasy and wish-fulfillment.

The reactionary is also a generational relativist, for he believes that the old have a privileged perspective upon reality, that only the old have learned in experience the recalcitrance of facts to human desire. But the philosophical truth is that no generation has a privileged access to reality; each has its projective unconscious, its inner resentments, its repressions and exaggerations. Each generation will have to learn to look at itself with the same sincerity it demands of the other. The alternative is generational conflict, with its searing, sick emotions, and an unconscious which is a subterranean house of hatred.

The substance of history is psychological—the way human beings have felt, thought, and acted in varying circumstances—and the concept of generational struggle which we have used is a psychological one. There are those who see the dangers of "reductionism" in our psycho-historical method; they feel that the genesis of student movements in generational conflict has no bearing on the validity of their programs, goals, objectives. Of what import, they ask, is the psychology of student movements so long as they work for freedom, for liberating workers and peasants and colored races, for university reform, and the end of alienation? To such critics we reply that the psychological origin of student movements puts its impress on both their choice of political means and underlying ends. Wherever a set of alternative possible routes toward achieving a given end presents itself, a student movement will usually tend to choose the one which involves a higher measure of violence or humiliation directed against the older generation. The latent aim of generational revolt never surrenders its paramountcy to the avowed patent aims. The assassination of an archduke, for instance, may be justified by an appeal to nationalistic ideals which are said to have a sanctity overriding all other consequences; actually the sacred cause, the nationalistic ideal, becomes too easily a pseudo-end, a rationalization, a "cause" which affords the chance to express in a more socially admired way one's desire to murder an authority figure.

When all our analysis is done, however, what endures is the promise and hope of a purified idealism. I recall one evening in 1963 when I met with a secret circle of Russian students at Moscow University. There were twelve or thirteen of them drawn from various fields but moved by a common aspiration toward freedom. Among them were young physicists, philosophers, economists, students of languages. Their teachers had been apologists for the Stalinist repression, and the students were groping for truthful ideas, for an honest philosophy rather than an official ideology. Clandestine papers and books circulated among them—a copy of Boris Pasternak's *Dr. Zhivago,* of George Orwell's *1984*—reprints of Western articles on Soviet literature, a revelation of the fate of the poet Osip Mandelstamm. The social system had failed to "socialize" them, had failed to stifle their longing for freedom. The elder generation was de-authoritized in their eyes for its pusillanimous involvement in the "cult of personality." Here on a cold March night in a Moscow academic office I was encountering what gave hope to the future of the Soviet Union. The conflict of generations, disenthralled of its demonry, becomes a drama of sustenance and renewal which remains the historical bearer of humanity's highest hopes.

NOTES

1. Lewis S. Feuer, "The Influence of the American Communist Colonies on Engels and Marx," *Western Political Quarterly,* XIX (September 1966), 456–474.

2. Karl Marx and Frederick Engels, *Basic Writings on Politics and Philosophy,* Lewis S. Feuer (ed.) (New York, 1959), p. 238. Daniel Bell made the phrase "end of ideology" well known in his *The End of Ideology* (New York, 1960). It later acquired the connotations of a slogan-

word. The notion, however, was a common one among sociological writers. See Raymond Aron, *The Opium of the Intellectuals,* tr. Terence Kilmartin (London, 1957), p. 305. Lewis S. Feuer, *Psychoanalysis and Ethics* (Springfield, Ill., 1955), p. 126.

3. For the usage of "unproblem," see Lewis S. Feuer, "Problems and Unproblems in Soviet Social Theory," *Slavic Review,* XXIII (1964), 60–74.

4. Karl Marx *et al., Communist Morality* (Moscow, n.d.), p. 19.

5. Georg Lukacs believed quite frankly that Marxism was the ideology of irrational men who nonetheless were elected to make history: "We Marxists do not only believe therefore that social progress is led by the frequently disturbed 'mentality' but we also know that it is only in Marx's teachings where this 'mentality' has come to self-awareness and is destined for leadership." See Victor Zitta, *Georg Lukacs' Marxism, Alienation, Dialectics, Revolution: A Study in Utopia and Ideology* (The Hague, 1964), p. 181.

6. Mario Savio, "The Future of the Student Movement," speech at Symposium of Young Socialist Alliance, Westminster Hall, Berkeley, November 20, 1964. See also T. Walter Herbert, Jr., "To Whom it May Concern," *Daily Californian,* November 19, 1964, p. 9.

7. Interview with Satoshi Kitakoji and Toru Kurokawa, August 3, 1962, Tokyo, Japan.

8. Interview with Shigeo Shima, July 29, 1962, Tokyo.

9. Interview with Shigeo Shima, Hiroko Shima, Mitsuo Nakamura, August 17, 1962, Tokyo. See also Lewis S. Feuer, "Currents in Japanese Socialist Thought," *New Politics,* I, No. 2 (1962), 119; "A Talk with the Zengakuren," *New Leader,* XLIV, No. 18 (May 1, 1961), 20.

10. See Milorad M. Drachkovitch (ed.), *Marxist Ideology in the Contemporary World—Its Appeals and Paradoxes* (Stanford, Calif., 1966), p. 71; also the original mimeographed version of Father Bochenski's essay, Stanford, October 1964.

11. Pyata P. Gaidenko, "Existentialism and the Individual," *Soviet Review,* III (1962), 18. Translated from *Vestnik Istorii Mirovoi Kultury,* No. 5 (1961).

12. Yuri Davydov, *Trud y Svoboda* (Moscow, 1962), pp. 55, 58.

13. Leaflet of the Independent Student Association, December 1, 1964.

14. See Lewis S. Feuer, "Youth in the '60's," *New Leader,* XLIV, No. 10 (March 6, 1961), 18.

15. A student publication in 1961 said, "We call the basis upon which we work together the 'lowest significant common denominator' and we link this concept to the idea of 'issues orientation.' It is not our purpose to develop an ideology." *About Slate,* pamphlet, Berkeley, 1961–1962, p. 7.

16. Lewis S. Feuer, "What is Alienation? The Career of a Concept," *New Politics,* I (1962), 116–134.

17. "Square-Conformist, Organization Man, solid citizen, anyone who doesn't swing and isn't with it. Also called Creep and Cornball. Man, if you still don't dig me, you'll never be anything but—." See Lawrence Lipton, *The Holy Barbarians* (New York, 1962), p. 318.

18. Lipton, *op. cit.,* Preface.

19. *International Correspondence of RMF-JRCL* (Revolutionary Marxist Faction of Japan Revolutionary Communist League), Tokyo, No. 1 (December 1, 1964), p. 5.

20. Louis I. Dublin and Bessie Bunzel, *To Be or Not to Be: A Study of Suicide* (New York, 1933), pp. 409–410.

21. George DeVos, *Role Narcissism and the Etiology of Japanese Suicide,* mimeographed (Berkeley, Calif., 1964), pp. 6–7. The impact of suicidalism was felt too in the Burmese student movement. See U Ba U, *My Burma: The Autobiography of a President* (New York, 1959), p. 42.

22. N. K. Krupskaya, *Pedagogicheskie Sochineniya,* I (Moscow, 1957), 139.

23. Karl Marx, *Economic and Philosophic Manuscripts of 1844,* tr. Martin Milligan (Moscow, 1961), p. 158.

24. Frederick Engels, *Germany: Revolution and Counter-Revolution* (New York, 1933), p. 103. Frederick Engels, Paul and Laura Lafargue, *Correspondence* (Moscow, 1960), II, 386. Lewis S. Feuer, "Marx and the Intellectuals," *Survey,* No. 49 (1963), p. 103. Vernon L. Lidtke, *The Outlawed Party: Social Democracy in Germany, 1878–1890* (Princeton, 1966), p. 311.

25. V. I. Lenin, "The Tasks of the Revolutionary Youth," a mimeographed pamphlet printed in 1903, in Lenin, *Collected Works* (Moscow, 1961), VII, 44; see also Lenin, "The Signs of Bank-

ruptcy," *Iskra,* February 15, 1902, in *Collected Works,* VI, 81.

26. Lenin, "The Tasks of the Revolutionary Youth," *Collected Works,* VII, 53.

27. Lenin, "The Student Movement and the Present Political Situation" (October 1908), reprinted in *The Young Generation* (New York, 1940), pp. 14, 19, 20.

28. Karl Marx and Frederick Engels, *Selected Correspondence* (Moscow, 1953), pp. 409, 435. See also Boris Nicolaievsky and Otto Maenchen-Helfen, *Karl Marx: Man and Fighter,* tr. G. David and E. Mosbacher (New York, 1956), p. 370.

29. E. Ray Lankester, "Degeneration: A Chapter in Darwinism," in *The Advancement of Science* (London, 1890), pp. 47–48.

30. Benjamin I. Schwartz, *Chinese Communism and the Rise of Mao* (Cambridge, Mass., 1952), pp. 10–11.

31. Edward B. Tylor, *Primitive Culture* (7th edn.; New York, 1924), p. 1.

32. The Eyrie, "Beware the Nihilists!" *Daily Californian,* November 5, 1965, p. 12.

33. Ivan Maisky, *Before the Storm: Recollections,* tr. Gerard Shelley (London, 1944), p. 115.

34. Mario Savio, "An End to History," *Humanity,* No. 2 (December 1964), p. 4.

35. Debbie Meier, "Careerism on Campus," *Anvil and Student Partisan,* VIII, No. 3 (1956), 9–12.

36. G. Engel and V. Gorohov, *Iz Istorii Studencheskago Dvizheniya, 1899–1906,* pp. 25, 21.

37. A. and V. Chertkoff (eds.), *Studencheskoe Dvizhenie 1899 Goda* (Essex, England), p. 46.

38. Otto Rank, *The Myth of the Birth of the Hero and Other Writings,* ed. Philip Freund, tr. F. Robbins and S. E. Jelliffe (New York, 1964), pp. 69–96.

39. *Free Speech Songbooks, Songs Of, By, and For the F.S.M.* (Berkeley, Calif., 1965).

40. Sigmund Freud, *Moses and Monotheism,* tr. Katherine Jones (New York, 1955), p. 9.

41. Hans Kelsen, "Platonic Love," *The American Imago,* III (April 1942), 85. For the Pythagorean clubs as an even earlier agency of generational revolt, see Alban Dewes Winspear, *The Genesis of Plato's Thought* (New York, 1940), p. 81.

42. *Ibid.,* p. 77.

43. *Ibid.,* p. 44.

44. Paul Goodman, *Five Years* (New York, 1966), pp. 152, 181, 192, 164, 67; "We Won't Go," *New York Review of Books,* VIII (May 18, 1967), 17 ff. An admirer wrote that "one of Goodman's most distinctive and refreshing traits as a social critic is his impish habit of arguing issues *ad hominem.*" Theodore Roszak, "The Future as Community," *The Nation,* CCVI, No. 16 (April 15, 1968), p. 500. Goodman had analyzed John F. Kennedy's sense of duty as that of a "little boy who disciplines himself from masturbating."

45. Paul Goodman, *Growing Up Absurd* (New York, 1960), p. 202.

46. Paul Goodman, "Thoughts on Berkeley," *New York Review of Books,* III, No. 11 (January 14, 1965), p. 5.

47. E. H. Carr, *Michael Bakunin* (1937, Vintage edn., New York, 1961), p. 465.

48. Avrahm Yarmolinsky, *Road to Revolution: A Century of Russian Radicalism* (New York, 1959), p. 152. Yarmolinsky finds the evidence for this incident "reliable," but Carr does not. Carr likewise belittles the significance of Bakunin's use of "Matryona," saying it "was probably an example of Michael's predilection for the childish mystification of code names, and was not invested with the significance which rumor attached to it." The very fact, however, that Bakunin took pleasure in the childish paraphernalia of a secret society is important for a psychological understanding of the revolutionist, and the particular code name he chose is invested with unconscious signification. See E. H. Carr, *op. cit.,* pp. 392, 239, 266. Curiously the one Englishman who tried in the nineteenth century to found something like a student movement, John Ruskin, suffered tragically, like Bakunin, from sexual impotence. As Professor of Art at Oxford, Ruskin led his pupils to mend a bit of neglected road nearby. Their road, from the constructional standpoint, was a failure, but from this back-to-the-people gesture issued the spirit which led to the University Settlement movement. Like other would-be student leaders, Ruskin envisaged a hierarchical society modeled on the medieval and on Plato's Republic. He tried to found such a guiding model, the Guild of St. George; he himself was to be "Master" of the Companions. Work would merge with enjoyment. All these themes, the need for disciples, the medieval model, reappear in Goodman's *Grow-*

ing Up Absurd. See Peter Quennell, *John Ruskin: The Portrait of a Prophet* (London, 1949), pp. 222, 262; Frederic Harrison, *John Ruskin* (London, 1902), p. 141; J. A. Hobson, *John Ruskin: Social Reformer* (2nd edn.; London, 1909), p. 305. Mary Lutyens, *Effie in Venice* (London, 1965), pp. 20–21. Bernard Shaw, *Ruskin's Politics* (London, 1921), pp. 25–32.

49. The English magazine *Anarchy* in 1966 devoted a whole issue to an apology for "creative vandalism." It began with a quotation from Bakunin and ended with an essay by Goodman. See *Anarchy*, VI, No. 3 (March 1966).

50. Thomas Hobbes, *Behemoth: The History of the Causes of the Civil Wars in England*, in Hobbes, *The English Works of Thomas Hobbes*, ed. Sir William Molesworth (London, 1840), VI, 233. See also Thomas Hobbes, *Leviathan*, ed. Michael Oakeshott (Oxford, 1960), p. 214.

Index